THE
GREAT BOOK
OF THE SEA

THE
GREAT BOOK
OF THE SEA

A COMPLETE GUIDE TO MARINE LIFE

COURAGE
BOOKS

an imprint of
Running Press Book Publishers
Philadelphia, Pennsylvania

This edition first published in the United States in 1993 by Courage Books, an imprint of Running Press Book Publishers.

Copyright © 1988 Arnoldo Mondadori Editore S.p.A., Milan
Photographs and text copyright © 1980, 1981, 1982 Kodansha – Europa Verlag
English translation copyright © 1993 Arnoldo Mondadori Editore S.p.A., Milan

Canadian representatives: General Publishing Co., Ltd., 30 Lesmill Road, Don Mills, Ontario M3B 2TS.

Library of Congress Cataloging in Publication Number 92-54935

ISBN 1-56138-270-1

Printed and bound in Spain by Artes Graficas, Toledo
D.L.TO:1898-1992

Published by Courage Books, an imprint of Running Press Book Publishers, 125 South Twenty-second Street, Philadelphia, Pennsylvania 19103

CONTENTS

PREFACE

Since the dawn of time man has attempted to portray the animal kingdom for himself and for generations to come through illustrations. From the Altamira cave drawings of the Stone Age, to the seventeenth-century naturalist paintings of Merian, to the beautiful natural history books of the nineteenth century, the study of nature has always relied on pictures for immediacy.

There was a time when art and science were part of one discipline which sought to classify the natural world, for it was thought that only with the use of illustration could full knowledge be achieved. Later, the study of natural history evolved, becoming wider and more accurate with the advent of the microscope and photography. However, even today, illustrations will often improve much on the stark images of photographs, particularly when a certain detail or effect is desired.

It was for these reasons that the Great Book of the Sea *was designed to allow maximum space to illustrations. It draws on a magnificent collection of pictures by talented artists who adopted this traditional form of illustration. Accompanying the full-color pictorial content is an informative text that presents a comprehensive study of the life and habits of the most interesting species colonizing our seas.*

Beautiful pictures introduce the amazing animal life of the oceans with a clarity and immediacy that invites the reader to a fuller understanding through the text – two forms of comprehension, vital to do justice to the fascinating world of the deep.

INTRODUCTION

THE MARINE ENVIRONMENT

The marine environment is sometimes known as the "halobios," from the Greek word for salt. Together with the freshwater environment or "limnobios," it makes up the total aquatic environment or "hydrobios," in which the fundamental medium of life for plants and animals is water. In the seas of the world water contains mineral salts in varying ratios. In the oceans the ratio generally varies between 34 and 36 parts per thousand; this ratio is used as an indicator of salinity. The scale of the marine environment is very large; the oceans altogether occupy 70.8% of the surface of our planet; they amount to 140 million square miles (360 million square km), compared with 58 million square miles (149 million square km) of dry land. In the ocean trenches depths of over 36,000 feet (11,000 m) have been recorded, while the average depth is about 12,000 feet (3,700 m). It should also be noted that the oceans form a single, continuous body of water, whereas the terrestrial and freshwater environments are broken up into many discontinuous units.

There is no part of the marine environment that does not contain living organisms, even at extremes of depth or latitude. It is generally held that life originated in the sea. This view is supported by the most ancient fossils of living creatures and by the fact that the saline composition of the blood and lymph of most animals is similar to that of the sea. This helps to explain the fact that nearly all the phyla of the animal kingdom are represented in the sea and that some phyla (such as the echinoderms) are found only in the sea. Forms of adaptation of marine animals to their environment are numerous and are regulated by complex genetic and physiological mechanisms that have developed in the course of the long evolution of the biosphere. For a better understanding of these adaptations it is useful to begin with a review of the principal ecological characteristics of the marine environment.

A fundamental distinction arises from the fact that with some organisms the relationship they have with their surroundings is confined to the waters immediately about them, while with others there is also an important relationship with the sea floor. The first of these two groups comprises the plankton (divided into zooplankton for the animals and phytoplankton for the plants); the second group comprises the benthos (similarly divided into zoobenthos and phytobenthos). Some marine animals, such as pelagic fish, squids, and whales, are not limited to floating with the current or small horizontal movements like the zooplankton, but are capable of extensive and rapid movement and can make headway against the currents of the ocean if necessary. These animals make up the nekton.

It must be stressed that, whereas plant life is directly dependent on sunlight and therefore comes to an end at a depth of about 650 feet (200 m), animal life extends right down to the greatest depths of the oceans. Animals living at great depths are either predators, killing and eating other animals, or scavengers, living on the organic detritus that rains down on them from higher levels. (The adjective "saprophagous" is sometimes applied to scavengers.)

Certain physical and chemical properties of sea water have a vital influence on marine animals. Temperature is of course an important factor in any environment, but it presents some special features in the seas. Water has a high specific heat; this means that masses of water absorb heat or yield it up only very slowly. There are consequently no very abrupt changes of temperature, except in the uppermost layers. Between the surface layer, which follows the changing temperature of the atmosphere, and the deep waters, whose temperature remains constant, we find a mixed layer known as the "thermocline," in which the temperature falls rapidly with increasing depth to a level of between $32 - 37°F$ ($0 - 2.5°C$). This is the constant temperature of oceanic waters below a depth of $1,650 - 3,300$ feet ($500 - 1,000$ m). In land-locked seas, however, where the total mass of water is much smaller, the temperature may remain above this level, even at great depths. In the Mediterranean, for example, the temperature does not sink below $55°F$ ($13°C$) even at depths of more than 13,000 feet (4,000 m). The resistance of marine animals to changes of temperature is very variable. Certain species – mainly those living well out to sea and at considerable depths – are "stenothermic," which means that they can only resist small changes of temperature; they consequently have very restricted areas of distribution. Other species, living mainly on the bottom in coastal waters are "eurythermic," which means that they can adapt to great changes of temperature; these species have very large areas of distribution. Especially eurythermic are marine mammals and marine birds, thanks to their warm-bloodedness, which enables them to maintain a constant body temperature.

The geographical distribution of marine animals shows a marked tendency to follow lines of latitude, so that we find quite different faunas in the arctic zone, the temperate zone, and the tropical zone. The variation in temperature according to depth has an important influence on marine fauna, and depth also determines other important factors, such as the progressive increase in water pressure and the progressive decrease in penetration of sunlight. It is the thermocline, however, that often marks a boundary between species adapted to life in warm water (above) and species adapted to life in cold water (below).

An important characteristic of the marine environment is the hydrodynamics, or water movement. Constant movements such as currents, periodical movements such as tides, and irregular movements such as waves, all affect the conditions of life for marine animals.

Currents can have various indirect effects. They change the distribution of nutrients and affect local values of water temperature and salinity. Rising currents sometimes bring the nitrates and phosphates necessary for plant life to the surface, indirectly enriching the life of marine animals. Sinking currents transfer oxygen and food from the upper layers of water to the animals living on the sea floor and help to wash away their waste products. Ocean currents also play a more direct role when they transport plankton from place to place; it must be remembered that plankton includes many of the larvae of animals forming part of the nekton and the benthos. Currents also influence the movements – and still more the orientation – of nektonic creatures such as fish. The geographical distribution of marine animals is thus largely dependent on the currents.

Tides have a great effect on the benthonic flora and fauna of the upper zone of the shore – the so-called intertidal zone. The organisms living in this area are subject to alternate submersion and exposure. The plants and animals that live there are consequently adapted to a variable set of conditions, including changes in moisture, temperature, and salinity, over and above the direct effects of the movements of the water. The influence of tides is at its greatest where the rise and fall of the water is at its highest. This can vary remarkably, for

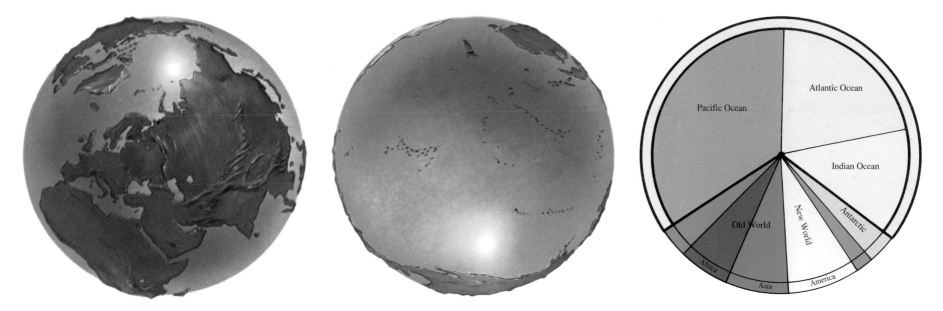

example vertical difference between high and low tides is very marked in the seas of northern Europe but very small in the Mediterranean.

The action of the waves has significant effects on all the coastal fauna, but especially for members of the sessile benthos which are exposed to pounding by masses of water and also by stones and other extraneous bodies that the waves bring with them. The inhabitants of the benthonic region accordingly develop special defensive adaptations, such as clinging organs and equipment for burrowing into the substratum, and supportive or protective structures, such as shock-proof shells or skeletons. Waves also have an indirect effect of great importance – they facilitate exchanges between the sea and the atmosphere, favoring the circulation of oxygen, heat, and nutritive salts in the upper layers of water. In relation to the turbulence of the water, we may distinguish two types of benthonic region: exposed areas, typical of rocky coasts, and protected areas, typical of gently sloping coasts. Each has very different types of fauna. Rocky bottoms generally present cracks, caves, and other cavities of various shapes and sizes, which create numerous microhabitats differing from each other in their degree of exposure to the violence of the sea and also to sunlight. This has a marked effect – and often a favorable one – on the opportunities for settlement offered to various benthonic animals.

Variations in the density of sea water are very important to the zooplankton. The density increases with each rise in salinity but decreases with each rise in temperature; such variations in density are utilized by floating planktonic organisms for purposes of their vertical migration.

The mean salinity of the oceans is about 35 parts per thousand, but its variations are

Above: These diagrams give an idea of the ratio on the earth's surface of land to sea. It is indeed the oceans that take up most of the world's surface area.
Below top: A number of different marine environments can be distinguished, in terms of their depth below the surface and their distance from the coast. Each environment shown in the diagram is inhabited by a different fauna, corresponding to variations in physical conditions and the availability of energy.

Below bottom: The map shows variations in the surface temperature of the oceans of the world. Local temperatures are governed by latitude, by distance from the coast, and by ocean currents.
Opposite above: Fish make up the largest group of vertebrates. They live in a wide variety of habitats and can be found in nearly all water environments. Their vertical distribution is also extensive – from Lake Titicaca (16,500 ft [5,000 m] above sea level) to the deepest reaches of the oceans (over 36,200 ft [11,000 m]).

considerable. Landlocked seas into which many rivers flow, such as the Baltic and the Black Sea, have very low salinity – only 18 parts per thousand in the Black Sea, and only 5 parts per thousand in the Gulf of Bothnia. The fauna of such seas, especially at the mouths of the rivers, may contain many freshwater species. Tropical waters such as the Red Sea may have a salinity of above 40 parts per thousand. Very high salinities, up to 100 parts per thousand, are found in rock pools situated in certain reefs. The crustacean *Artemia salina* forms part of another very specialized fauna that is found in highly saline surroundings. Sea water is similar in its saline composition to the internal bodily fluids of sea-dwelling animals, which are consequently in osmotic equilibrium with their environment. This does not apply to teleostean fish, to reptiles, to birds or to mammals.

Reactions to variations in salinity are varied. Some animals, especially pelagic species, have a low resistance to such variations and are described as "stenohaline"; others can survive violent changes in salinity and are described as "euryhaline." Among the latter are the various species of fish that migrate from the rivers to the oceans or vice versa for purposes of reproduction.

Whereas the proportion of the principal types of ion remains constant, other dissolved substances may vary to a considerable extent. Among these other substances are some of great biological significance, even if they are only found in trace quantities. Examples are iron and copper, which enter into the composition of the respiratory pigments of vertebrates and mollusks respectively. Others are silicon, which forms the skeletons of Radiolaria and many Porifera, and calcium, which enters into the structure of the shells and skeletons of

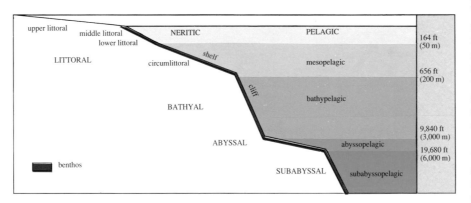

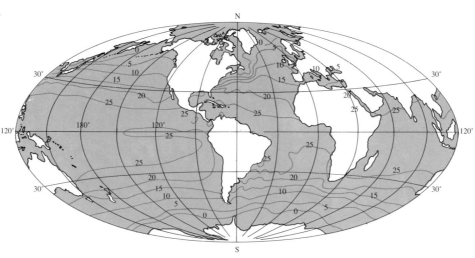

many marine animals. There are also certain chemical elements that are generally rare in the marine environment, but can accumulate in very high concentrations in the tissues of animals. A famous case is that of the mercury scandal in Japan. Mercury – in the form of methyl mercury chloride – was present in Japanese waters as a result of the discharge of industrial waste. The original concentration of the chemical in the sea water was very low, but as it passed through the food chain of the marine fauna it became so concentrated it caused fatal poisoning among the fishermen of Minamata Bay ("Minamata disease"). In a similar way, vanadium, found in the blood of Tunicata, occurs in a concentration 50,000 times stronger than that normally present in sea water.

Land animals, living in the atmosphere, seldom suffer from a lack of oxygen, whereas shortages of this indispensable gas can occur in the sea, especially in deep water. Sea water gets its oxygen from the atmosphere and the largest proportion that can enter into solution is about 8.5 parts per thousand. The actual quantity present is variable and may sink to zero – as it does for example below 660 feet (200 m) in the Black Sea, where there is no trace of animal life.

Light is one the most important factors in the marine environment. It is mainly derived from solar radiation, but there is also another kind of light, of biological origin, that is found in the depths of the ocean and is produced by various animals, including certain fish, squids, and crustaceans that are equipped with the capacity for luminescence. As solar radiation passes through the successive layers of water, both its intensity and its color composition are modified. Down to a depth of 330 feet (100 m), blue light undergoes the smallest amount of absorption and consequently provides the dominant color. We may distinguish three zones: the euphotic zone, which extends from the surface to a depth of 165 or 330 feet (50 or 100 m) according to the transparency of the water, and is well lit; a dysphotic zone, which goes on down to 660 feet (200 m) and is badly lit; and finally an aphotic zone, below 660 feet (200 m), which receives absolutely no light from the sun. In the euphotic zone plant life is possible and there is consequently a primary production of living matter that can be utilized directly by plant-eating animals and indirectly by the larger animals that prey on them. Animal life is accordingly both abundant and varied in this zone; it is also represented at lower levels, in the form of predators and scavengers. All of these species are however indirectly dependent on the organic material produced at the surface.

Animal life is strongly influenced by variations in the available light. The daily cycle of light and darkness, for example, regulates the vertical migrations of the plankton, which rises towards the surface in the evening and descends to greater depths in the morning. Similar light-dependent migrations are carried out by nektonic forms, such as certain fish that live on plankton. The coloration of marine animals, which varies according to the depth, is also in the final analysis controlled by light. There are many cases of protective coloring, designed to harmonize with the background. In surface waters animals need to protect themselves from excessive absorption of sunlight and consequently develop heavy pigmentation of the skin, find shelter by burrowing in the substratum, or descend to greater depths during the most brilliantly lit hours of the day or seasons of the year. Animal members of the plankton are often protected from excessive absorption of solar radiation by their transparency.

In addition to daily rhythms, such as the vertical daily migrations of the plankton described above, there are also monthly rhythms, such as those exhibited by the reproductive behavior of the palolo worm *Eunice viridis*, which is a member of the Polychaeta. These monthly rhythms occur in time with phases of the moon and seem to be controlled directly by the variations in its light rather than indirectly through its influence on the tides. Seasonal rhythms

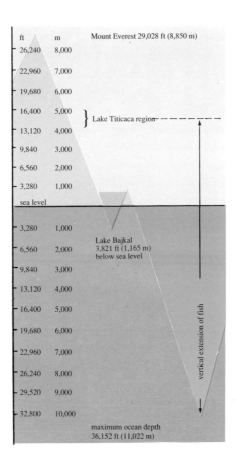

Below: The distribution of marine organisms is directly associated to the penetration of light into the water : plant life is restricted to the upper levels, while only carnivores live in the deep reaches.

can also be detected in the reproduction of many marine animals and are controlled not only by temperature but by the amount of daylight, too.

Another physical factor of considerable importance in the marine environment is water pressure. This increases at the rate of about one atmosphere for every 33 feet (10 m), and consequently exceeds 1,000 atmospheres in the deepest parts of the oceans. Even these pressures do not exclude the possibility of animal life and species belonging to various zoological groups are found in the oceanic trenches. Most animals, however, are adapted to specific levels of pressure. We may distinguish eurybathic species that are more tolerant of variations in pressure from stenobathic species that are less so. Surface species generally cannot survive submersion to great depths and the inhabitants of very deep waters generally die if they are brought up to the surface. Sperm whales, which breathe atmospheric air, can dive to a depth of 3,300 feet (1,000 m) without coming to any harm. The special capacity of these creatures to withstand high pressure – so much greater than that of man – is explained by their ability to absorb pressurized air during submersion and by their possession of special physiological mechanisms affecting respiration and circulation.

The adaptations of marine animals

Marine animals have a large range of adaptations to their environment and these affect their morphology, physiology, and biology. Some of the most important adaptations are discussed below.

Osmoregulation. This term covers adaptations to variations in salinity. Among invertebrates the animal's skin does not generally provide it with an effective barrier against the environment. The animal's internal saline concentration is therefore similar to that of its surroundings and varies with it. Such animals are known as "poecilosmotic." Fish (including both selachians and teleosteans) and certain mollusks and crustaceans keep their internal saline concentration at a constant level, even when the external concentration varies, and are described as "isosmotic." The blood of selachian fish contains a high quantity of urea, which makes it almost isosmotic with sea water. The urea that these fish excrete is in fact absorbed back into the blood stream through the kidneys. Teleosteans, or bony fish, on the other hand, have less concentrated blood, which is hypotonic in comparison with sea water. They avoid dehydration by ingesting large quantities of water through the digestive tract and eliminating excess salt through the gills.

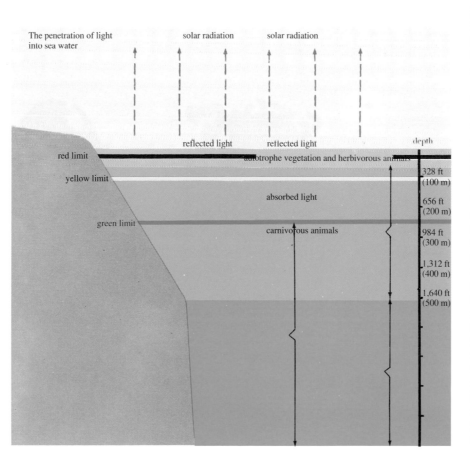

The penetration of light into sea water

Feeding habits. The feeding habits of marine animals are highly characteristic and extremely varied. Many species, belonging to the most disparate zoological groups, are microphagous – in other words, they live on minute organisms such as bacteria, protista, etc., or on particles of detritus suspended in the water. These species catch their food either by means of tentacles, like the Coelenterata, or by means of vibratory, mucus-associated cilia. The animals often have special filtratory equipment with which they strain the finely separated particles of food out of the water before ingesting them, either individually or in bulk. Filtratory species include both benthonic animals (such as sponges, Bryozoa, Lamellibranchia, and Tunicata) and also planktonic species (such as copepods and the larvae of many benthonic species). The feeding mechanisms of the filtratory species vary greatly from group to group. The food of sponges consists largely of bacteria which are absorbed by cells known as choanocytes, situated in the animal's internal cavities. In many of the Anellidae (Polychaeta), which live on plankton and detritus in suspension, the cephalic region is equipped with thread-shaped gills covered with cilia and mucous glands, whose sticky secretion traps the food particles. Filtratory crustaceans, such as the copepods, strain out their food by means of the dense covering of bristles on their locomotory and buccal appendages and on their antennae. These cilia create a constant flow of water by their continual movement.

The Lamellibranchia (Mollusca) have large branchial plates in the pallial cavity, which are covered with cilia and mucous material. These plates trap the food particles contained in the water that passes over them and these particles are conveyed by the vibrating cilia towards the animal's mouth. Large quantities of organic material are captured in this way. In polluted waters this material may include pathogenic bacteria and viruses (such as the microorganisms of typhoid, cholera, poliomyelitis, and viral hepatitis) and also various poisonous substances. A real health risk is consequently presented by edible Lamellibranchia, such as oysters and the various kinds of mussel, if they are consumed without proper care. Many pelagic fish, including the herring, also use their gills as filters. Filtration is also practiced by some large marine mammals, such as baleen whales which filter out plankton with special plate-like structures suspended from the palate.

Among benthonic animals living on soft bottoms we find examples of limivorous feeding. This means that food particles are ingested together with sand or mud. In certain other species, the food particles are ingested separately, after being agglutinated

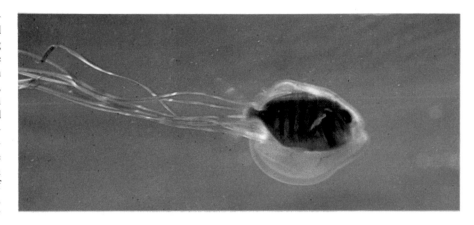

into globules or filaments by means of a mucus produced by the animal itself. Tunnels are dug for this purpose by numerous species belonging to different groups, including Polychaeta, Holothuria, and Spatangidae (Echinoidea); the tunnel may be temporary or permanent and a flow of water is maintained through it to bring in a supply of food particles in suspension. These particles are captured and accumulated with the help of the animal's mucus and are then transferred to its mouth.

Above: Among the animal inhabitants of the sea, there are many strange examples of symbiosis between creatures belonging to different zoological groups. The photograph shows a fish of the *Nucrates* genus in association with a jellyfish.
Below: The diagram shows a marine food chain. Sunlight penetrates into the upper layers of water and is used for photosynthesis by macroscopic algae and by phytoplankton. The living material produced by these organisms is then utilized by the primary consumers, which in turn provide larger animals with nourishment.
Opposite: An example of colonial organization in which several individuals form a sort of superindividual (in the illustration a *Physalia*).

Among the crustaceans many Amphipoda dig tunnels in the soft substratum and sort through the particles of mud or sand with their gnathopods, retaining the food particles which are subsequently ingested.

Other Amphipoda, such as the Caprellidae, find their food by scraping the substratum; they rasp an alga or a colony of hydroids and scrape up the minute organisms that were sticking to it. Some fish, such as mullets, constantly patrol the bottom, sucking up the top layer of mud into their mouths, together with a certain amount of water. The mixture is passed out through their gills, where special attachments filter out the organic material. In addition to microphagous feeding habits, macrophagous eating patterns are also common among marine animals. Some species follow a vegetarian diet, eating the algae and the phanerogamous plants that live in the sea.

Among the mollusks, the Amphineura and the Gasteropoda are equipped with a special rasp-like organ, the radula, which is covered with tiny teeth. This enables them to rasp off the layer of encrusting algae that covers the surface of the rocks. Among the

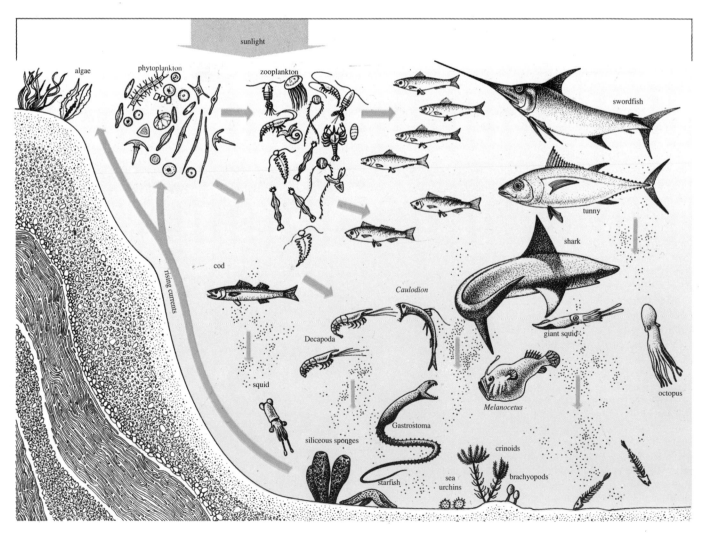

crustaceans, the isopod *Limnoria* tunnels into wood and feeds on the cellulose. The lamellibranch *Teredo navalis* also burrows into wood, sometimes damaging the hulls of ships (although this was a more serious matter in the old days of sailing vessels), but it lives on the food particles that are liberated during the burrowing process.

Most macrophagous animals, however, are predatory and feed on other animals. Methods of predation vary greatly. The Coelenterata are equipped with tentacles that grasp their prey and paralyze it with the aid of specialized stinging cells, or cnidoblasts. These form nematocysts, which are capsules filled with poison and provided with an extensible stinging filament. Medusae are famous for their stinging propensities, and so are certain hydropolyps of the coral reefs, such as the fire coral. The Cubomedusae of the Indian Ocean and the Australian coasts possess stings that can be fatal to man. The Turbellaria and the Polychaeta possess an extroflexible muscular pharynx with which they can capture small prey animals. The Nemertea have developed a long proboscis that can be instantly darted out to catch prey. Some gasteropods (such as *Nassa*, *Natica*, and *Murex*) possess a proboscis at the base of which is a radula and a gland that produces an acid secretion. With this they can perforate the shells of other mollusks. The predator then thrusts its proboscis through the hole to the soft parts of its victim. *Natica* does much damage to oyster beds in this way. Gasteropods of the *Conus* genus paralyze their prey with the secretion of their poison glands, which in certain species can be fatal to man. Crabs seize their prey first with their claws and then with their mandibles and then break it up with their other buccal appendages. Cephalopods, such as the octopus, have tentacles equipped with suckers, with which they grasp their prey before biting it with their powerful mandibles and paralyzing it with the poisonous secretion of their salivary glands. Many fish, including both pelagic and benthonic species, are predatory. Notable is the shark, which is dangerous to man and whose powerful teeth are continually renewed by fresh growth. Other large marine predators include the toothed whales, such as the cachalot and the killer whale.

Parasitism is widespread in the sea as well as on dry land. It may be defined as a system whereby one animal feeds on the blood or the tissues of another without rapidly causing its death. *Sacculina carcini* is an endoparasitic crustacean that provides an extreme example of this system. It spreads and ramifies among the tissues of the crab which acts as its host, absorbing nourishment by osmosis; only the sac containing its reproductive organs projects out-

side the body of the host. Ectoparasites generally have clinging organs that enable them to hang on to the host and suck its blood. The Cymothoidea (a family of Crustacea), on the other hand, are ectoparasites that attack fish and devour their tissues slowly until they die. Many species of tapeworm are found as endoparasites in the alimentary canal of fish, the contents of which they absorb by osmosis. The tapeworm thus does not need any alimentary canal of its own. (It should be noted, however, that the alimentary canal may be lacking in animals that are not endoparasites, one example being the Pogonophora, a group of thin, worm-like animals that live in the muddy floor of the ocean depths and absorb organic material by osmosis through minute external appendages known as pinnules.)

Visual organs and luminescence. A special adaptation of the visual organs to the marine environment is exemplified by the telescopic eyes of many bathypelagic crus-

taceans and fish. The optical axis is greatly lengthened so that the lens can concentrate the feeble radiation produced by the luminescence of other creatures onto a narrow area of light-sensitive cells, thus producing an improved visual image. Abyss-dwelling fish react to their special surroundings in different ways: while some, as we have seen, develop telescopic eyes, or increase the size of their eyes in order to make them more sensitive to light, other species have eyes of reduced size or even no eyes at all. The luminescence characteristic of the inhabitants of the bathypelagic or abyssal environment depends on the reaction of two substances, luciferine and luciferase, in the presence of oxygen. The light may be produced in the cytoplasm of a fish, in extracellular secretions, or by symbiotic bacteria. In the Ctenophora, the light is produced by glandular structures situated in the eight meridian channels below the longitudinal series of paddles. The vibration of the cilia on the paddles gives an effect of iridescent

and changeable luminous stripes. Luminescence of a glandular character is also found in Polychaeta (Anellida) such as *Chaetopterus*, which lives buried in the sand, and in certain crustaceans and mollusks.

A more specialized form of luminescence occurs in the Euphausiacea among the crustaceans, in the Cephalopoda among the mollusks, and in various bathypelagic and abyssal fish. It involves complicated organs known as photophores. These are roughly spherical structures, the external hemisphere of which is made up of a crystalline substance, while the internal hemisphere is composed of concentric, cup-shaped strata of light-producing cells, reflecting cells, and pigmented cells which have a shielding function. (The light-producing cells often contain symbiotic luminous bacteria.) The animal's surroundings can thus be illuminated by a sort of lamp, in a manner that helps both the search for food and the search for mates. Luminescence is in fact used for this last purpose by certain surface-dwelling marine animals, such as the Syllidae (Polychaeta), and on dry land by fireflies. Abyssal species of Cephalopoda emit clouds of luminous particles that disorient predators and thus perform the same protective function as the ink clouds of the cuttlefish.

Reception and production of sounds. Sound waves travel faster in water than in air. In fish the main organ for the reception of sound is the inner ear, which is connected with the swim bladder in certain teleostean fish. The lateral line of fish also contains auditory organs that are sensitive to low frequency vibrations, such as the pressure waves caused by the movements of other animals. Certain blind fish living at great depths have a highly developed lateral line that helps them to detect possible prey. Some marine animals are also capable of emitting sounds. Fish of the Sciaenidae family produce sounds with the aid of their swim bladder which seem to be mating calls. Other fish make noises by scraping the rays of their fins or chattering their teeth. Some crustaceans, such as *Crangon*, produce a strident noise by knocking their claws together; others, like *Squilla*, knock their uropods against the lower surface of their telson; while yet others rub various parts of their exoskeleton together. Crustaceans hear these and other noises through their statocysts, which are organs of hearing as well as of balance. The ability of whales to emit and receive an astonishing variety of acoustic signals is well known. Experiments with dolphins have shown that they have an extraordinary sensitivity to sound, far greater than that possessed by man.

Introduction

Balancing organs. Efficient balancing organs are very important to marine animals. They generally take the form of statocysts. A statocyst is a sac, which may be completely enclosed or may communicate with the exterior. It contains one or more statoliths, which are small, heavy bodies that may be produced by the animal itself or may be introduced from outside. When the animal moves, the statoliths shift within their sac and stimulate various sensitive points on its lining. This provides the animal with the necessary information to enable it to maintain a suitable orientation in space. Among the more complex statocysts are those of the Ctenophora (also known as "apical organs") and those on the edge of the bell of the Medusae known as *Scyphozoa* (where they occur in association with ocelli and are known as "rhopala"). Simpler types of statocysts are found in Hydromedusae, Polychaeta, Platelmintha, and Crustacea. Among vertebrates, the semicircular canals and certain other structures of the inner ear are statoreceptors, or organs of balance associated with organs of hearing.

Coloration and mimicry. Marine animals present a huge range of colors and patterns. There is an obvious tendancy to adapt to surroundings, so that the most lively and brilliant coloration is found in coastal regions, especially in the tropics, whereas the inhabitants of deep waters are generally neutral in appearance and dark or reddish in hue. The zooplankton consists largely of transparent animals, whose coloration is correspondingly weak and delicate. Little is known about the nature of the pigments exhibited by animals, especially invertebrates. We can however say that they include carotenoids, pyrrholic pigments, purins, indoles, and quinones. Some colorations are not caused by pigments but by physical phenomena of diffraction or by the presence of symbiotic bacteria or algae. Coloration may be influenced by diet and still more by light. If the light is too intense, the cutaneous surface protects itself by producing melanin and so becoming darker in color. Changing color to match the background is a clear case of adaptation to the environment and is as common in the sea as it is on land.

Crustaceans such as the Decapoda, cephalopods such as the octopus and the cuttlefish, and benthonic fish such as the sole, can all modify their coloration rapidly to match different backgrounds. This is achieved by rapid expansion or contraction of specialized cutaneous cells of ramified appearance; these are the chromatophores, each of which contains grains of pigment. This mechanism enables the octopus to change to a grayish, reddish or yellowish

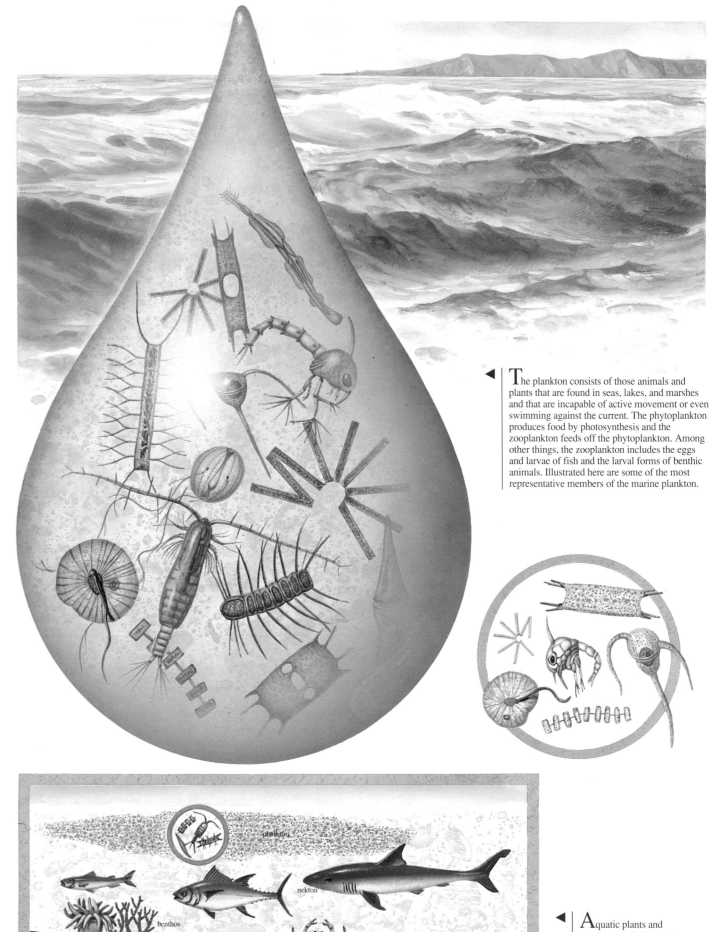

The plankton consists of those animals and plants that are found in seas, lakes, and marshes and that are incapable of active movement or even swimming against the current. The phytoplankton produces food by photosynthesis and the zooplankton feeds off the phytoplankton. Among other things, the zooplankton includes the eggs and larvae of fish and the larval forms of benthic animals. Illustrated here are some of the most representative members of the marine plankton.

Aquatic plants and animals are divided into three categories on the basis of where they occur in the water.

14

hue. The sole imitates the bottom on which it rests, changing its general coloration and the arrangement and appearance of its spots, according to whether it is lying on sand, detritus or mud. In some cases the chromatophores may operate without the message passing through the central nervous system, in response to direct external stimuli. Examples are the shrimp *Palaemon,* the crab *Uca,* and certain fish. These creatures modify their coloration to suit surrounding conditions of darkness or light even when they have been blinded. Coloration to match the background is very common among marine animals with most diverse habitats. Those that live on sandy bottoms have a gray–brown back with white spots; animals belonging to the plankton are often bluish in color; pelagic fish have steel blue backs and silvery white bellies; the shrimp *Hyppolite varians* takes on a green color when it lives among Posidonias or Chlorophycea, but changes to other colors in other surroundings.

In some cases, including many of the fish that inhabit coral reefs, coloration is not imitative but contrasting and so fulfils a warning or threatening function. These fish are generally poisonous or dangerous in some way to possible predators, which are warned off in this manner. They also often have an eye mark near the tail, while the real eye is masked by strips of dark color. This confuses the aggressor regarding the direction in which the fish is likely to move, thus improving its chances of escape.

Colony formation and polymorphism.
The formation of colonies occurs only among aquatic animals and is common in the seas of the world. Colonies in this sense are formed when an organism produces a substantial number of offspring by asexual reproduction and those offspring remain organically linked to each other. The formation of colonies is especially common among the animals of the benthos, such as Anthozoa, Bryozoa, and Ascidiacea; but it is also to be found among the animals of the zooplankton, such as the Siphonophora, a group of Hydrozoa, and the Thaliacea (Tunicata). Colonies differ greatly in shape; they may be ramified, encrusting or globose, with many variations. The shape is determined partly by a specific hereditary factor and partly by the effects of the environment on the conditions of growth. Polymorphism among the individuals is a further adaptation presented by some colonies. In the case of the Siphonophora, for example, we find a whole series of medusae modified in various ways. One, known as the pneumatophore, acts as a float, others, known as nectocalices, help to propel the colony as a whole by expanding and contracting; others again, known as bracts,

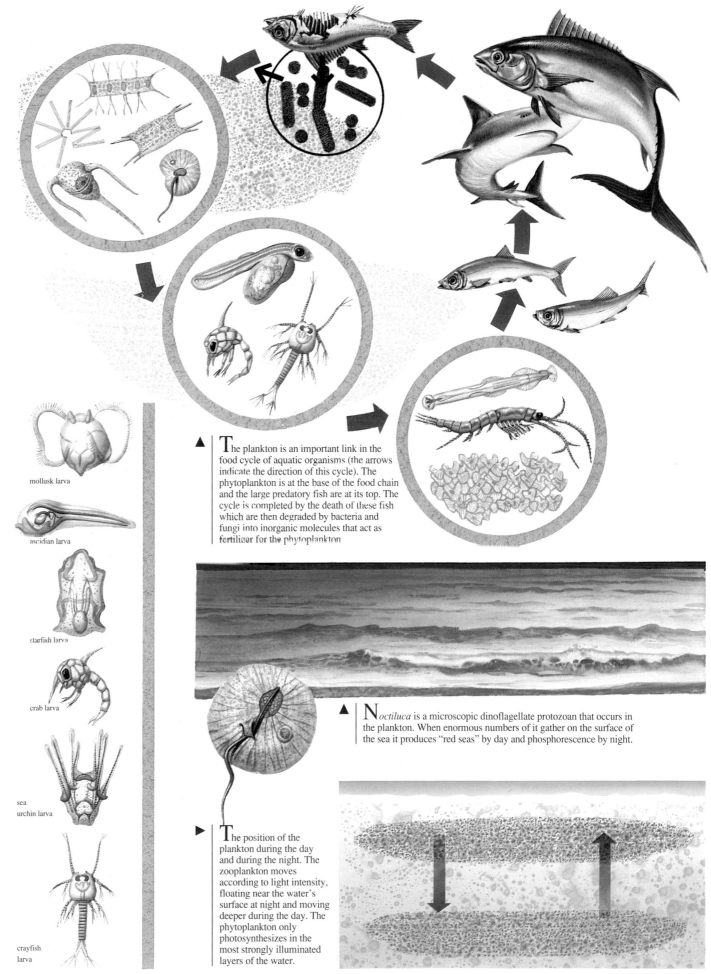

mollusk larva

ascidian larva

starfish larva

crab larva

sea urchin larva

crayfish larva

▲ The plankton is an important link in the food cycle of aquatic organisms (the arrows indicate the direction of this cycle). The phytoplankton is at the base of the food chain and the large predatory fish are at its top. The cycle is completed by the death of these fish which are then degraded by bacteria and fungi into inorganic molecules that act as fertilizer for the phytoplankton

▲ *Noctiluca* is a microscopic dinoflagellate protozoan that occurs in the plankton. When enormous numbers of it gather on the surface of the sea it produces "red seas" by day and phosphorescence by night.

▶ The position of the plankton during the day and during the night. The zooplankton moves according to light intensity, floating near the water's surface at night and moving deeper during the day. The phytoplankton only photosynthesizes in the most strongly illuminated layers of the water.

have developed into protective scales.

Polyps have also been modified to a greater or lesser extent into three classes: gastrozoids, which are concerned with nutrition; gonozoids, which are concerned with reproduction; and dactylozoids, which are shaped like tentacles for purposes of defense.

In colonies of Bryozoa we also find two classes of modified zooids. One class are known as Aviculariae and are shaped like the beaks of birds; they capture small organisms and discourage the settlement of larvae of their own species within the colony, thus avoiding overcrowding. The other class of modified zooid are known as Vibraculariae; they are shaped like tentacles and help to keep the colony free of detritus and larvae that might otherwise accumulate there.

Epibiosis, commensalism, and symbiosis

The marine environment, and especially that of the benthos, is particularly well adapted to the formation of associations between animals and plants, or between one species of animal and another, over a range that extends from the simple case of epibiosis to the most specialized types of symbiosis. The creatures involved in epibiosis are generally sessile and live either literally on top of one another or in very close contact. On the sea floor there is intense competition for the conquest of the substratum between algae, sponges, Coelenterata, Bryozoa, tube-dwelling Polychaeta, lamellibranch mollusks, cirriped crustaceans, Ascidiacea, etc.

The surfaces or body cavities of sessile organisms may be settled by mobile creatures of the benthos, such as crustaceans, Polychaeta, mollusks, fish, sea urchins, etc. For example, the internal channels of the large tropical sponges belonging to the *Spheciospongia* genus harbor a multitude of different creatures, belonging to very different zoological groups and running to thousands of individuals. In some cases the guest animal makes use of the cavities of the host purely as somewhere to live; this relationship is known as "tenancy." In other cases the guest animal may enjoy an improved supply of food in the cavities or in the neighborhood of the host; and this relationship is known as "commensalism." Endoecia is a special type of commensalism, practiced by animals that live in burrows excavated by other animals or in tubes produced by other animals. An example of this is provided by the sipunculid *Urechis*

Above: A sea urchin of the genus *Echinometra*. The sea urchin's mouth possesses a characteristic part that regulates the movement of five teeth. These teeth converge towards the center of the oral opening and protrude in order to eat (often large quantities of food, albeit very slowly) and even to dig a nest in the rocky bed.

Opposite: Sponges on the sea bed of the Caribbean. The size and shape of sponges vary tremendously, from tiny spheres a few millimeters across to tall cylindrical or branched shapes up to six feet tall and to wide irregular tubular masses often three feet across.

caupo, which digs tunnels in the mud within which it spins a network of mucous material. It then pumps water through the tunnels by peristaltic movements of its body, so that suspended particles of food are trapped in the mucus. The tunnels are inhabited by numerous tenants and commensals. Small fish of the goby group use the tunnels mainly as a refuge from danger; polynoid members of the Polychaeta move in alongside the body of the host and ingest pieces of the mucous network; other guests found in the same tunnels include small crabs and Lamellibranchia.

Attachment to the body of another ani-

mal is highly advantageous to various creatures, which eat the leavings and derive oxygen from the respiratory currents of their host. Various hydroids and poriferans attach themselves to the shells of crabs for these reasons. These associations may become indispensable to certain species, in which case they must be classified as cases of symbiosis in the strict sense. Certain pagurid crabs, which live in the empty shells of gasteropods, have a relationship of this kind with the sea anemones and sponges also living on the shells. In European waters two species of crab live in close association with two species of sea anemone – *Eupagurus bernhardus* with the sea anemone *Calliactis parasitica* and *Eupagurus prideauxi* with the sea anemone *Adamsia palliata*. When one of these crabs has to change shells, it transfers its sea anemone to the new one. It has been proved that there is a reciprocal advantage in this association. The crab is defended from predators by the poison stings of the sea anemone, while the sea anemone gains mobility and improved access to food from its association with the crab.

Mutually beneficial symbiosis also occurs in the Indian and Pacific Oceans between small fish of the *Amphiprion* genus and the huge sea anemones of the *Stoichactis* genus. These particular fish are able to swim among the tentacles of the sea anemone without coming to any harm because they are immunized against its poison. At the same time they also receive protection against the predators. The sea anemone benefits from access to the leavings of its guests.

There are many other cases of commensalism. *Fierasfer*, a very small species, frequents the cloacal cavity of various Holothuria, apparently in response to a chemical stimulus provided by the host. The Carangidae accompany sharks, swimming in small groups just in front of them or just below them – hence their common name of "pilot fish." Certain small fish, and also certain species of shrimp, act as cleaners to large fish, removing parasites and detritus; for this purpose they swim right into their mouths and gill slits. Remoras have dorsal suckers, with which they attach themselves to sharks, whales, and turtles. Some of these associations between different species are essential to the existence of at least one partner. They involve some definite means of recognition, which makes it possible for the guest species to find its host and enter into partnership with it. In cases where the association is a very intimate one, the means of recognition often takes the form of specific chemical messages.

There are many cases of important symbiotic associations in the marine environ-

ment that involve partnership between bacteria or unicellular algae on the one hand and more highly developed creatures on the other. Bacteria often live in symbiosis with sponges, sometimes accumulating in such numbers that their weight exceeds that of their host. Symbiosis with bacteria provides a basis for the functioning of the luminescent organs of teleostean fish and of cephalopods. Symbiosis with Cyanobacteria (cyanophytes) is also common among sponges. The commonest type of symbiosis with unicellular algae are those involving Chlorophyceae or Zooxanthella. One example is provided by the large lamellibranch mollusks of the *Tridacna* genus, which live in coral reefs. The Zooxanthellae are found in great numbers on the edges of the mollusk's mantle, alongside the siphon. The edges of the mantle are fitted with bodies resembling lenses through which the sunlight penetrates deeply into its tissues. The Zooxanthellae gather below these lenses in great numbers, turning the mantle a characteristic dark green or blue–green color. The mollusk exposes the edge of its mantle to the sunlight as much as possible. It can thus be said to cultivate the microorganisms in its own tissues, and indeed to harvest them, for they are continually conveyed into the animal's digestive tract, while their place on the mantle is soon taken by a fresh crop.

Zooxanthellae are also very commonly found inside Coelenterata. These algae are indirectly responsible for the building up of the great coral reefs, shoals, and atolls of the tropics. The algae play an essential role in the metabolic processes that lead to the formation of the calcareous skeleton of the coral animal though they do not contribute to its nourishment, corals being carnivorous. The distribution of reef-building corals is consequently strictly dependent on the presence of favorable ecological conditions for this particular alga. Living coral reefs are found only in the tropics, in water not more than 100 feet (30 m) in depth where the temperature never goes below 68°F (20°C); they avoid turbid waters, such as those near the mouths of rivers, and prefer the eastern coasts of continents (which are generally washed by cold currents in the tropical zone) to the western shores.

Other unicellular algae that are found in symbiosis are the Zoochlorellae, which generally occur in association with freshwater animals, but are also found in a few marine invertebrates, such as *Convoluta* (Turbellaria). In these associations between algae and animals, the alga benefits from the shelter afforded by its host, and also by substances such as CO_2, phosphates, and nitrates, which are produced by the metabolism of the host and are therefore much more abundant inside its body than in the open sea. The sea water of the tropics is in fact very poor in nutritive salts and consequently also poor in plankton; the unicellular algae living in association with corals may therefore be regarded as a sort of captive phytoplankton. The animal receives oxygen and nutritive substances from the algae, and finds them helpful in the elimination of various catabolic by-products. The algae may also act as a shield against excessively intense light and (as we have already seen) they may aid in the chemical process of constructing a calcareous skeleton.

The benthos

The animal life of the marine benthos is extremely rich and includes representatives of every animal phylum except for the Onychophora. In the euphotic zone, especially where the bottom is hard, there is also very rich plant life, which makes up the phytobenthos. In the dysphotic and aphotic zones, on the other hand, animals are the only living things to be found on the sea floor (except for bacteria). The nature of the substratum is a very important factor. We can divide benthonic animals into two main classes: those that live in the substratum, which are known by the name of "endofauna"; and those that live on the surface of the substratum, surrounded by water, which are known as the "epifauna." There are of course many intermediate forms, such as the Mollusca and Polychaeta which live in burrows in the substratum, but protrude siphons or tentacles into the water; there are also some crustaceans that spend alternate periods burrowed in the sediment and swimming in the water above. The endofauna is more highly developed where the bottom is soft, in sandy or muddy regions, whereas the epifauna is characteristic of places where the bottom is hard, such as rocky shoals. Hard bottoms are quite common down to the edge of the continental shelf (approximately 650 feet [250 m]), but at greater depths the bottom is nearly always soft. The two kinds of bottom have very different fauna. The soft substratum provides a home for many marine invertebrates of burrowing habit, such as Polychaeta, Echinoderma, Lamellibranchia, and Gasteropoda; hard bottoms harbor most kinds of algae and sessile invertebrates such as sponges, Anthozoa, Bryozoa, Ascidiacea, etc. Another difference is that the fauna of soft bottoms is uniform over huge areas, the nature of the endofauna being dependent more on the composition of the sediment in which they live than on climatic conditions, whereas the fauna of rocky bottoms is very variable, because of the presence of numerous separate microhabitats, each of which has its own microclimate. For these reasons communities of soft bottoms are uniform and stable, with relatively small numbers

of species and large numbers of individuals, whereas those of hard bottoms are unstable, with many species and relatively few individuals.

The animals of the benthos are influenced, not only by the substratum, but also by considerations of latitude and depth. The latitude – and hence the influence of the climate – has an effect mainly on the coastal epifauna and epiflora. Among the coastal species most clearly affected by the latitude are those associated with mangroves and coral reefs, both of which are confined to the tropics.

The benthonic fauna is even more sharply differentiated by considerations of depth, on which many other ecological factors depend, such as the penetration of sunlight, the water pressure, the amount of physical disturbance to which the water is subject, the temperature, and the availability of oxygen and nutritive substances. The ecosystem above the continental shelf is based on the existence of a flourishing flora. Beyond the edge of the shelf, however, there is no plant life at all on the sea bed and the ecosystem at that level has to derive its energy from material that floats down from the upper layers of the sea. Even in the euphotic zone there is a significant difference in the availability of sunlight at different depths. We can distinguish two types of fauna on this basis: the first is characteristic of brightly lit habitats, and is known as "photophilic"; the second is characteristic of relatively shady regions, and is known as "sciaphilic." This distinction is not entirely determined by depth, but also by the physical conformation of the coast and the presence of features such as cliffs and caves.

In terms of size, the zoobenthos can be divided into macrobenthos (animals measuring more than 0.08 in [2 mm]), meiobenthos (0.04 to 0.08 in [1 to 2 mm]), and microbenthos (less than 0.04 in [1 mm]).

Another criterion that can be used to subdivide the benthos is that of its capacity for movement. Among the epifauna, we may distinguish a sessile benthos (the members of which remain fixed to the substratum for the whole of their adult life, examples being sponges, Anthozoa, Bryozoa, Ascidiacea, and Cirrhipedia) from a sedentary benthos (the members of which generally cling to the substratum but are capable of moving over short distances, examples being limpets and various species of sea urchin and starfish). There is also a herpetic epifauna (which can move by crawling, examples being Platelminthea, Polychaeta, and Mollusca) and an ambulant epifauna (the members of which move about on articulated limbs, examples being certain decapod crustaceans of the *Reptantes* group); finally, there is a swimming epifauna (the members of which swim just above the sea floor from time to time, examples being fish, decapod crustaceans of the *Natantes* group, and nudibranch Gasteropoda). The epifauna is not confined to hard surfaces, but extends also onto soft bottoms, where it is represented by the epipsammon, the members of which live on the surface of the sand and may occasionally burrow into it.

The endofauna may also be divided into various ecological categories. There are, for example, animals that make holes in various types of hard substratum and live in the resulting cavities. Sponges of the Clionidae family make holes in rocks and in the calcareous shells of various animals. Among the Lamellibranchia, we find *Lithodomus* and other *Lithophaga* that make holes in calcareous rocks with the help of an acid secretion, the Pholadidae that make holes in clay, and the Teredinidae that tunnel into submerged wood, such as the hulls of sailing vessels, piers, etc. Isopods of the *Limnoria* genus also tunnel into wood. The greater part of the endofauna, however, lives in mud and sand. The more highly specialized forms maintain contact with the

Above: A typical community of a soft area of sea bed. 1) the gasteropod *Nassarius*; 2) the lamellibranch *Mya*; 3) the lamellibranch *Cardium*; 4) the lamellibranch *Macoma*; 5) the polychaete *Pygospio*; 6) the polychaete *Arenicola*; 7) the shrimp *Crangon*.
Below: A marine annelid.
Opposite: *Asterias rubens*, the starfish common to European waters. It feeds mainly on bivalves and is found particularly in mussel beds. To open a shell, the starfish climbs on top with its mouth opening over the point where the bivalve would open, were its valves not held tightly closed. Then with all five arms on either one or other of the valves, it exercises all the pressure its muscles can produce. In this way it makes a gap large enough to insinuate its body.

surface of the substratum and with the water above it by means of tubes or channels, one example being the Polychaeta *Arenicola*. Lamellibranchia live buried in the sand or mud, with only a pair of siphons emerging from the substratum. The mesopsammon is a particular subcategory of the endofauna of soft bottoms and consists of animals living in the interstices between the grains of sand, feeding on minutely separated organic detritus and on microorganisms. This is a very specialized subfauna, comprising members of various zoological groups, such as Protozoa, Ciliata, Turbellaria, Nematoda, Polychaeta, Tardigrada, Nemertina, etc. There is a certain similarity of general appearance between all these creatures that is dictated by the highly specialized nature of their environment: their bodies are generally long and flat, their pigmentation is slight, their eyes are reduced in size, and they often have clinging organs such as papillae.

Most of the animals of the marine benthos produce planktonic larvae. This is a valuable adaptation and (together with a high level of general fertility) enables sedentary creatures, firmly moored to the substratum, to achieve the diffusion necessary for the survival of their species. Some zoological groups, such as the sponges and the Coelenterata, produce larvae that live only for a few days – in some cases only for a few hours – before settling on the substratum to change into the adult form. These larvae are "lecitotrophic" – that is they do not eat during their brief larval period but live on their bodily reserves. Other zoological groups, such as Polychaeta, gasteropods, Lamellibranchia, and echinoderms, produce larvae with a relatively long life span, measurable in weeks or months. These larvae can make long journeys, crossing large expanses of sea – even whole oceans – with the aid of marine currents; they feed on other plankton and are therefore described as "planktotrophic." When the time comes for these larvae to metamorphose, their previous positive orientation towards sunlight is replaced by a negative one, which makes them leave the surface and swim down to the bottom. They explore the sea floor carefully to find a suitable site where they can settle permanently. This is believed to be the basis for the gregarious behavior of barnacles, mussels, oysters, etc., which live in closely packed communities. It seems that the larvae of these creatures settle only where they find organic substances produced by other members of their own species who have settled there at some time in the past. An area marked in this way, having been colonized in the past, is likely to be favorable to the development of these new arrivals.

Introduction

The levels of benthonic domain

The benthonic domain can be divided into two main regions: the littoral region (shoreline), which is characterized by the presence of autotrophic plants, and the region of the deeps, where plants of this kind cannot live. The littoral region comprises the following levels: upper littoral, middle littoral, lower littoral, and circumlittoral. The region of the deeps comprises the following levels: bathyal, abyssal, and subabyssal. These levels can be further divided, in the vertical direction, into horizons. In the horizontal direction, they can be topographically divided into facies, each with its own characteristic fauna and flora.

The upper littoral level marks the transition between the terrestrial and marine environment. The water of the sea reaches it only during storms or spring tides. The sea creatures that live there have to be able to endure long periods of life out of the water and exhibit various adaptations that enable them to do so. Characteristic of the fauna at this level in temperate latitudes are alga-eating gasteropods such as winkles (*Littorina*), isopods of the *Ligia* genus and the Chthamala – barnacles found in dense colonies on the upper littoral rocks that are capable of storing water inside their shells for a considerable period. The mobile members of the fauna carry out significant vertical migrations in response to calm or rough weather. A special biotope is that of rock pools situated on reefs; the fauna consists of creatures adapted to wide variations of salinity and temperature. Another characteristic fauna is found on the masses of detritus that the waves wash up on the shore; jumping amphipods of the *Talitrus* and *Orchestia* genera and other crustaceans (including crabs) mingle with terrestrial animals such as flies and beetles. On tropical shores we find land crabs such as *Uca*, which dig their burrows well above the high-tide line.

The middle littoral level extends from the high-tide line to the low-tide line. It is therefore more significant in regions where the rise and fall of the tide is considerable. In the seas of northern Europe there may be a vertical difference of many feet, while in the Mediterranean it does not exceed one foot. The fauna of this level is alternately submerged and exposed by the tides. Cirripeds such as barnacles, gasteropods such as limpets, and Lamellibranchia such as mussels are all common. Cracks and other small cavities may harbor a rich shade-loving fauna, including sponges, Cnidaria, Bryozoa, Polychaeta, hole-boring Lamellibranchia, and isopods. On soft bottoms we may find various Polychaeta, including the characteristic *Arenicola*. At the middle littoral level of tropical shores, mangroves

are often found; these are trees with aerial roots and partially submerged trunks. The water is muddy, rich in organic material and poor in oxygen; it harbors a fauna with wide toleration of different degrees of temperature and salinity, living mainly on detritus, and including many groups of invertebrates. A typical fish of the mangroves is the pop-eyed, amphibious teleostean *Periophthalmus* that clambers about at the foot of the mangrove roots with its modified pectoral fins.

The lower littoral level extends out to a depth of 66 feet (22 m) in turbid waters, but may go out to a depth of 150 feet (45 m) in clear conditions. This zone has a wealth of light-loving algae and underwater meadows of marine phanerogamous plants such as *Posidonia* and *Zostera*, thanks to the abundance of sunlight. The water is often agitated, principally by the movement of the waves. In temperate seas most communities on hard bottoms are dominated by plants, in the shape of various kinds of algae, among which live many sessile animals, such as hydroids, Bryozoa, sponges, ascidians, and barnacles, together with mobile gasteropods and plant-eating Polyplacophora, hermit crabs wearing the shells of gasteropods, Polychaeta, Asteroidea, Ophiurida, and various species of fish, mostly teleosteans of the wrasse, goby, and blenny families.

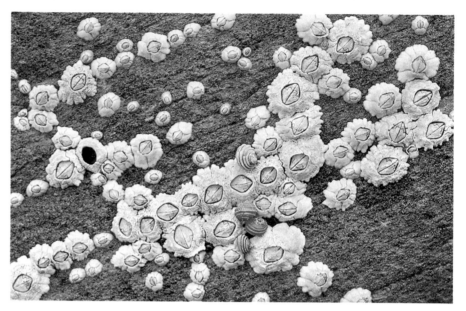

There are, however, also communities in which the animal element is predominant, the most significant example being provided by the coral reefs of the tropics. These formations are extremely important, by virtue of their sheer size, the extraordinary richness of their fauna, and the large number of different species that live in them. The result is an enormous biomass, with very high productivity and a complex

network of ecological relationships. The calcareous mass of coral structures is formed not only from the skeletons of the coral animals themselves, but also from the skeletons of other organisms such as the Millepora (also known as fire corals because of their stinging propensities), various other Anthozoa, mollusks such as the huge *Tridacna*, etc. A rich sessile fauna lives on and inside the coral formations; it includes Alcyonacea, Gorgonacea, sponges, etc. There is also a mobile population of Polychaeta, crustaceans, mollusks, and Echinoderma. Around the reefs, we find a rich, rainbow -colored multitude of fish of all sizes. Many of these fish are totally dependent on the substratum which provides them with both shelter and food; some of them, such as the parrot fish, live on the coral polyps themselves. Certain larger fish, such as the sharks, visit the reefs to eat the fish that live there. The richness and complexity of the fauna has the effect of making coral reefs extremely stable; they are in fact among the oldest types of varied habitats on our planet. Recent years, however, have seen considerable destruction of coral reefs in the Pacific and Indian Oceans by *Acanthaster planci*, a large, predatory species of starfish, otherwise known as the "crown of thorns." This is thought to be due to an ecological imbalance in the sea, perhaps caused by pollution.

Below: Plankton consists of organisms of many kinds, both animal and vegetable, all of which are incapable of sustained horizontal movement. The plankton includes some quite large animals, such as certain of the jellyfish, but the majority of its members are not more than a few millimeters in length, and often much smaller. From top to bottom: a lobster larva (*Phyllosoma*); a *Sagitta;* a medusa or jellyfish; a copepod (*Calocalanus*); a siphonophore (*Abylopsis*).

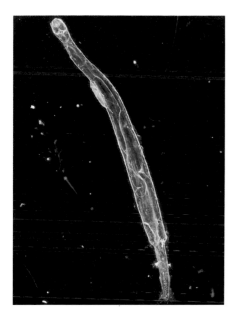

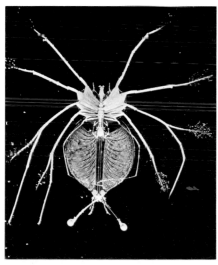

Another interesting habitat is that of the sponge beds – areas of sea floor rich in detritus and covered with a multitude of commercially valuable sponges. Also important are the pearl-bearing oyster beds of the tropics. A special fauna develops in the undersea meadows of *Zosteracea*, which occupy enormous areas of the lower littoral level. *Posidonia* and *Zostera* are the most important species in temperate seas, while *Thalassia* is the dominant species in tropical waters. Some animals pass their lives clinging to the leaves of these plants, while others live on their roots in the sea bed.

The sandy or muddy soft areas of sea bed in the lower littoral level are occupied by a series of living communities, each of which is characterized by different species of Lamellibranchia, gasteropods, Polychaeta, and crustaceans. The precise nature of the local fauna depends on the type of bottom, so we can actually find pairs of similar communities at quite separate geographical points. They are "parallel" communities, not identical to each other, but formed of different species from the same genera. These are known as "vicarious" species. One of the commonest of the communities found on sandy bottoms at the lower littoral level in the Mediterranean is the one characterized by the edible lamellibranch *Venus gallina.* In temperate waters cephalopods such as cuttlefish are common on sandy bottoms, whereas the octopus is found principally in rocky areas with plenty of detritus. Also common on sandy bottoms are fish such as *Rhombus*, the sole, and the weever with its poisonous sting.

The circumlittoral level extends from the bottom of the lower littoral level down to the bottom of the continental shelf – that is to say, from about 115 feet (35 m) to about 580 feet (175 m). The circumlittoral area is, however, taken to include cave-dwelling communities, even if they are situated at lesser depths, because they too consist of shade-loving species.

The vegetation on the sea bed becomes progressively thinner as the light reaching it becomes weaker with increasing depth.

Macrophytes – the larger algae – disappear almost completely at about 330 feet (100 m). This depth is consequently taken as the boundary between the circumlittoral zone above it and the lower littoral zone below. Coralligenous communities are characteristic of hard bottoms; here we find organic concretions laid down principally by so-called "coralline" algae, which have calcareous thalli, and are accompanied by sponges, Bryozoa, serpulid Polychaeta, Anthozoa, etc. Above these formations, we find a rich epifauna of sponges, Coelenterata (especially Alcyonacea), Gorgonacea, Madreporaria, Echinoderma (especially Ophiura), Polychaeta, and Lamellibranchia. Inside the calcareous blocks are many cracks and microcavities inhabited by a rich endofauna of Polychaeta, crustaceans, Ophiuroida, Lamellibranchia, Nematoda, and also hole-boring sponges.

There is an interesting resemblance between the coralligenous formations of temperate waters and the true coral formations of tropical seas; in both cases calcareous structures formed by one set of organisms provide a home or a place of refuge for others. The actual organisms involved are, however, quite different in the two cases. Like the two corals of tropical waters, the coralligenous formations of temperate seas have a rich fauna and an irregular physical structure that attract many mobile animals from outside. These include many benthonic fish from the surrounding sandy, muddy or rocky areas.

In underwater caves living organisms congregate mainly on the walls, forming a rich, stratified epifauna comprising sponges, Coelenterata, mollusks, and members of other zoological groups, together with coralline algae. These creatures give an extremely colorful and striking appearance to the walls of many underwater caves. It must be remembered, however, that the fauna of these caves varies according to the depth below the surface, their topography, and their size. In some particularly extensive caves we can distinguish three zones. First there is the entrance to the cave, which has a rich flora of shade-loving algae. Next

comes a slightly darker region, where shade-loving animals predominate and the largest number of animal species is to be found. Finally there is a dimly lit or completely dark zone, where the fauna becomes much less abundant, and is limited to a small number of specialized forms.

The soft bottoms of the circumlittoral level are generally composed of mud or detritus. The fauna of muddy bottoms includes several categories of animal: those that live buried in the mud, such as various bivalve mollusks and *Holothuria*; those that take root in the mud but emerge from it, like some of the Pennatulacea; sessile forms, such as certain Alcyonacea and Ascidia; and forms that live on top of the sediment, such as various Polychaeta, crustaceans, and gasteropods. Facies of various very different types occur on bottoms rich in detritus, according to the percentage of mud, the type of detritus involved, the nature of ground currents, etc. Among the most characteristic invertebrates to be found here we may mention the sea pen *Pennatula rubra* (which is phosphorescent), various Lamellibranchia such as *Arca* and the scallops, gasteropods such as *Turritella*, Echinoida, and Ophiuroida. Bottoms of this kind are also inhabited by many species of benthonic fish, including the sea scorpion.

The aphytal or deep water region comprises about 92% of the total sea floor. But although its area is so vast compared with that of the phytal or littoral region, it has a much less rich and varied fauna and no flora at all. The sea floor of the ocean deeps is almost invariably soft with a small number of sessile animals equipped with a peduncle to anchor them to the bottom. Burrowing and fully mobile animals are much more numerous. The bathyal level lies along the continental slope from a depth of 660 feet (200 m) to 10,000 feet (3,000 m). The bottom is almost always muddy and is populated by both sessile and mobile epibiotic animals such as Echinoderma, sponges (especially Tetractinellida and Hexactanellida), Coelenterata, decapod crustaceans, and various kinds of fish. There are also endobiotic species,

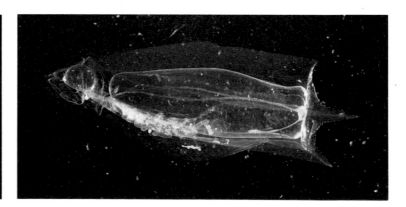

21

especially mollusks. Hard bottomed areas constitute a different habitat, characterized by the large, colonial white corals, which often destroy the nets of fishermen. The abyssal level, which is situated between 10,000 feet (3,000 m) and 20,000 feet (6,000 m), has a specialized fauna, including characteristic groups such as the Molpadiidae and other Holothurioidea, as well as Ophiuroidea and Polychaeta.

The subabyssal level, comprising the great oceanic trenches, begins at about 21,000 feet (6,500 m) and goes on down to the greatest depths recorded – something over 36,000 feet (11,000 m) in the Challenger trench near the Marianas. Research so far carried out indicates that the muddy bottoms of the Aleutian and Kurile trenches harbor a fauna consisting basically of

Holothuria, Pogonophora, Echinoidea, and a few species of Polychaeta. In the Philippines trench, at depths exceeding 33,000 feet (10,000 meters), the following animals have been discovered: Amphipoda, Isopoda, bivalves, Holothurioidea, Echiuroidea, and endemic species of Actinia.

The plankton

The term "plankton" comprises all floating organisms that cannot swim strongly enough to resist the natural movements of the water and must therefore allow themselves to be passively transported by the currents and the waves. We can distinguish a plankton composed of animals or "zooplankton," from a plankton composed of plants or "phytoplankton." The name

Above: The most conspicuous section of the plankton comprises creatures measuring more than $\frac{1}{2}$ in (1 cm) – and sometimes more than 4 in (10 cm) – and is known as "megaloplankton." Its members include many Medusae (see photograph), Siphonophora, Salpidae (Tunicata), Ctenophora, various crustaceans (especially of the Euphausicea group), and a number of other forms. The megaloplankton is the main source of food for the largest of all marine animals, the whale.

Opposite: Sea anemone. Despite its appearance, this creature has much in common with the jellyfish. Small fish of the genus *Amphiprion* swim among its tentacles. These fish, known as anemone fish, live in symbiosis with the sea anemone.

"pleuston" is given to planktonic animals whose body floats partly out of the water, so that they are driven along by the wind. Examples are provided by some of the Hydrozoa, such as *Velella* that has a float bladder with a projecting ridge to catch the wind. The term "holoplankton" comprises creatures that pass their entire life cycle in the pelagic environment; the name "meroplankton" is given to animals whose eggs or larvae form part of the plankton but whose adult forms live on the sea bed.

Planktonic organisms vary greatly in size. The megaloplankton comprises creatures measuring more than 0.4 inches (1 cm), and includes some species measuring more than 4 inches (10 cm); examples are certain Medusae, Siphonophora, Salpidae, Ctenophora, Euphausicea crustaceans, etc. The macroplankton includes species measuring between 0.04 and 0.4 inches (1 and 10 mm), such as Chaetognatha, Polychaeta, and various larvae of fish and crustaceans. The mesoplankton comprises animals measuring between 0.02 and 0.04 inches (0.5 and 1 mm) such as Copepoda, Ostracoda, and various types of larvae. The microplankton, whose measurements go from 60 microns to 0.02 inches (0.5 mm) consists mainly of minute plants but also contains some Protozoa. The nanoplankton, with measurements between 5 and 60 microns, comprises the greater part of the phytoplankton – mainly single-celled algae such as diatoms. The ultraplankton, the members of which measure less than 5 microns, comprises bacteria and viruses.

In terms of its relationship with the coast, plankton is divided into two categories. Neritic plankton is found over the continental shelf and is mainly meroplanktonic; pelagic plankton is found beyond the edge of the continental shelf and is essentially holoplanktonic.

The creatures making up the plankton have adapted themselves to their special environment in many ways. Among these we may note various devices to increase buoyancy. Many species of zooplankton have developed plates or thread-like excrescences, or long tentacles. Other planktonic species have improved their buoyancy by means of floats full of air or other gases, or by building up reserves of oil or fat – one example being the pelagic eggs of various fish and Radiolaria. The necessary gases and oils are often produced by the animal's own metabolism. The locomotion of members of the plankton is generally limited to the vertical plane, although short horizontal movements are also sometimes possible. Movements may be achieved either by expanding and contracting the body, or with the aid of special organs of movement, like the *velum* of the Medusae, the vibrating paddles of the Ctenophora, the cilia and

flagella of Protozoa and various types of larvae, the tentacles possessed by various other creatures, etc. The principal journeys carried out by the plankton are, however, passive in character and are effected by the movements of the water. The development of these creatures follows a seasonal cycle, particularly well marked in temperate seas. During the winter the surface waters of those seas are enriched with the phosphates and nitrates essential to marine life. The storms of winter stir up the waters and bring up these substances from the sea bed, where the dead bodies of marine organisms accumulate and decompose during the rest of the year. As spring advances and the daily sunlight increases in duration and intensity, the enriched surface waters nourish an abundant growth of phytoplankton, and the zooplankton that feeds on the phytoplankton multiplies accordingly. The zooplankton then becomes the first link in a food chain composed of fish and other nektonic predators. The dead bodies of many planktonic and nektonic organisms fall to the sea floor, where they are consumed by scavenging benthonic animals. The meroplankton may also be captured while still alive by filter-feeding benthonic animals. The phytoplankton, together with the zooplankton, thus provides a basis for the general productivity of the sea and for its production of fish in particular. It is responsible for the biological equilibrium of the marine environment.

The exact timing and the intensity of the annual resurgence of the plankton varies from year to year and from region to region according to the temperature of the water and the availability of nutritive material. Plankton is extremely abundant in the arctic seas, where the phytoplankton can multiply unceasingly throughout the period of continual sunlight, which may last for weeks or even for months. A further factor is that the life span of the individual creatures making up the plankton is longer in the cold waters of the arctic, because their metabolism is slower. In tropical seas, the presence of a thermocline impedes the mingling of the surface waters with the waters of the deep. This causes a shortage of phosphates and nitrates at the surface level, with a reduction in the growth of phytoplankton, which in turn restricts the growth of zooplankton. In certain parts of the tropical seas – especially off the western coasts of the continents, where there is a characteristic circulation of cold currents – we find areas of upwelling, where the nutritive salts contained in the deeper waters are brought up to the surface and nourish an abundant growth of plankton. These areas are particularly rich in fish; the coastal waters of Peru are an example. Sometimes an excess of nutritive salts may be brought up, or some other imbalance

23

may be introduced into the marine environment causing an excessive production of phytoplankton. The so-called "red tides" are a result of this phenomenon (known as "eutrophication"). They do considerable harm, since the decomposition of the excess phytoplankton fills the sea with toxic substances that may kill large numbers of fish and other marine animals.

Phytoplankton is found only to a depth of 660 feet (200 m) but zooplankton is found at every level from the surface to the maximum depth, although its composition varies accordingly. When we consider the vertical distribution of zooplankton, we can distinguish the following zones: epipelagic, from the surface to 165 feet (50 m); mesopelagic, from 165 to 660 feet (50 to 200 m); infrapelagic, from 660 to 2,000 feet (200 to 600 m); bathypelagic, from 2,000 to 8,250 feet (600 to 2,500 m); and abyssopelagic from 8,250 to 23,000 feet (2,500 to 7,000 m). Many planktonic animals carry out daily migrations in the vertical plane, coming up to the surface at night and passing the day in the deeper layers. The object of these movements seems to be to avoid diurnal predators. The availability of food also plays a part in these vertical migrations: the copepod *Calanus*, for example, lives on phytoplankton which itself spends the nights on the surface but migrates to deeper waters during the day. Dense shoals of planktonic animals, such as Euphausiacea (Crustacea), sometimes form at a considerable depth; they show up on the screens of ultrasonic sounding equipment and account for the phenomenon known as the "deep scattering layer" or "DSL."

Planktonic organisms also travel considerable distances horizontally, generally following the movement of the currents, but sometimes making use of their limited swimming powers to move into currents that will transport them over longer distances. Each current carries a particular range of planktonic organisms, determined by the physical and chemical nature of its waters. It is thus sometimes possible to identify currents by the characteristic species they contain. One well known example is provided by the Chaetognatha of the *Sagitta* genus. *Sagitta setosa* lives in the North Sea, in water the salinity of which is reduced by the presence of estuaries; it cannot survive either in more saline waters such as those of the oceans, or in less saline waters such as those of the Baltic. *Sagitta serratodentata*, on the other hand, prefers water of very high salinity, and *Sagitta lyra* prefers warm and shallow waters.

The nekton

The nekton consists of strongly swimming pelagic animals, capable of making head-

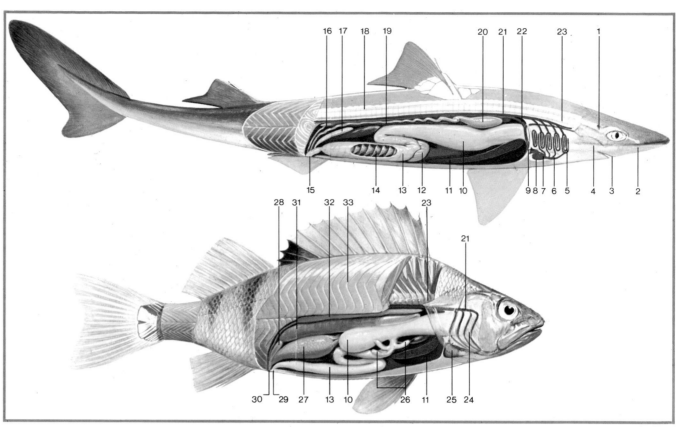

Above: Fish are the largest group of vertebrates and make up a superclass including the two living classes of cartilaginous fish (or Chondrichthyes) and bony fish (or Osteichthyes). Top: diagram of the organization of a cartilaginous fish; bottom: that of a bony fish. In both diagrams: 1) spiracle; 2) nostril; 3) mouth; 4) pharynx; 5) gill slits; 6) ventral aorta; 7) atrium; 8) ventricle; 9) sinus venosus; 10) stomach; 11) liver; 12) pancreas; 13) intestine; 14) spiral valve; 15) cloacal aperture; 16) kidney (non genital); 17) rectal gland; 18) spiral medulla; 19) deferent duct; 20) testicle; 21) dorsal aorta; 22) posterior cardinal vein; 23) vertebrae; 24) gills; 25) heart; 26) pyloric caeca; 27) gonad; 28) urinary vesicle; 29) anus; 30) genital aperture; 31) swim bladder; 32) kidney; 33) myomeres.
Below: An octopus (*Octopus vulgaris*).
Opposite: A ferocious predator of our seas, the killer whale. This is the biggest and best known of the cetaceans. It has a very distinctive appearance so is hard to mistake for any other species. It occurs in all the seas of the world and is most frequent in the waters of the Arctic and Antarctica, especially around colonies of Pinnipedia, its favorite prey. The killer whale is also present in tropical and equatorial waters and even, though rarely, in the Mediterranean.

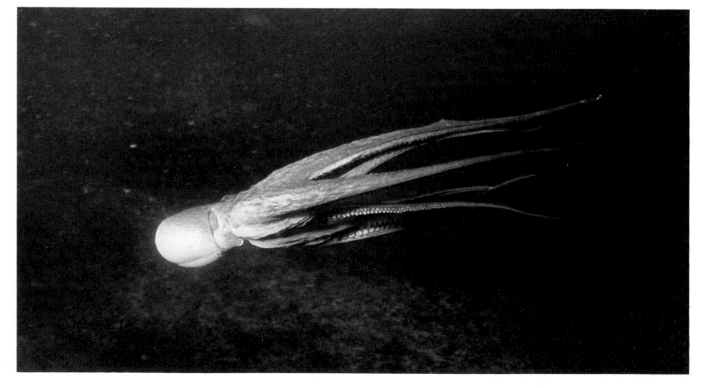

way against the waves and currents of the sea. Most nektonic animals are structurally and functionally organized for the business of swimming and exhibit various adaptations of an appropriate kind for this object. We may, for example, contrast the streamlined shape and well developed fins of the squids, which are pelagic cephalopods, with the bulky body and lack of fins exhibited by the octopus, which is a benthonic cephalopod. Among fish, too, pelagic species generally have a more elongated shape and better developed fins than benthonic species. A process of convergent adaptation has given the whales, which are the principal nektonic marine mammals, the external appearance of fish, with limbs closely resembling fins.

Although nektonic animals can move from place to place very easily, the individual species are confined to more or less well defined geographical areas, the boundaries of which are determined by invisible barriers of a very effective type. These are based on the physical and chemical conditions of the water, including temperature, salinity, and oxygen content, as well as on the availability of food. In some groups, such as the herrings, we may find that various local races have developed in response to different ecological conditions.

The nekton includes species belonging to three great zoological groups: cephalopods, such as the squids; teleostean and selachian fish; and cetaceans. Many species live in the open sea, but approach the coasts in the course of their seasonal migrations. Other species live in the neritic waters of the coasts and may consequently form associations with the creatures of the sea floor; these make up an intermediate category between the nekton and the benthos. There is also a bathypelagic and abyssal nekton with special characteristics of its own. Pelagic fish seldom have conspicuous coloration; in most cases they are dark blue or silvery in color; their body is long and tapered to facilitate their passage through the water. Teleostean fish are generally gregarious and a number of species carry out extensive migrations, sometimes taking them from fresh to salt water or vice versa. These migrations are known as "genetic" in cases where they are carried out for the purposes of breeding and "trophic" if they are made in search of food.

Many species, such as cod, herring, and tunny, undertake long migrations entirely within the marine environment. Herrings, which are common in northern seas, lay their eggs on the sea floor. A week or so later, the eggs hatch and the fry swims up to the surface and begins to feed on plankton. The herring now passes through three stages of existence: in the first it is passively transported by the currents; in the second it increases in size and follows the movement of the plankton; and in the third it swims against the currents to return to its breeding grounds, usually after an absence of about four years. Cod, which are common in the Atlantic and its adjoining seas, gather into huge shoals as winter approaches and make their way to their breeding grounds off the coasts of Iceland and Newfoundland. Cods' eggs are of the floating or pelagic type, and a single female may lay as many as 9 million, thus ensuring the continuation of the species in spite of the very high mortality experienced at the various stages of development.

In the Mediterranean seasonal migrations for breeding purposes are carried out by tunny and swordfish. Salmon and sturgeons migrate from the sea into fresh water in order to breed, and are described as "anadromous." As the breeding season comes on, large shoals of salmon approach the mouths of rivers and swim up them, fighting their way against the current and overcoming various obstacles such as rapids, waterfalls, etc. Having arrived at the calmer upper reaches of the river, the females lay their eggs and the males fertilize them. Although weakened by their efforts, a minority of salmon succeed in returning to the sea, where they live in the depths for three or four years before running up the rivers again for a second breeding season, depositing their eggs or milt in the same place as the first time. The new generation of salmon stays in the river for about two years, feeding on plankton; then it makes its way out to the depths of the sea and stays there for another two years before returning to the river to breed.

Eels, on the other hand, are "catadromous" – they reach sexual maturity in fresh water and run down the rivers to breed out in the depths of the oceans. The baby eels, or elvers, lead a pelagic existence and allow the currents to take them back towards the coasts from which they came. At this stage they lose their sight and undergo certain other physical changes, after which they run up the rivers to complete their growth, attaining sexual maturity at about twelve years of age. They become silvery in color and are visited by an irresistible urge to leave the places where they have lived for so long and make their way down to the sea again. It seems that all the eels from the rivers and lakes of Europe congregate in a well defined region of the Atlantic Ocean

known as the Sargasso Sea to breed and lay their eggs at a depth of 660–1,000 feet (200–300 m).

Among the inhabitants of the open sea are *Exocoetus* and other flying fish, which can glide through the air for considerable distances with the aid of their enlarged pectoral fins, remaining aloft for as much as 30 seconds. The Elasmobranchii or selachans include the sharks, some of which are among the most terrible predators in the sea, such as the white shark, which may exceed 40 feet (12 m) in length and is common in warm seas, and smaller species, such as the blue shark, found in the Mediterranean. There are also some nonpredatory sharks, like the huge *Cetorhinus* or basking shark, which may be as much as 50 feet (15 m) in length, but is completely inoffensive, living entirely on plankton.

Cetaceans exhibit a large number of adaptations to life in the sea – a most unusual environment for mammals. There are other cases of land animals that have returned to the sea, such as seals and turtles; but these creatures have to come ashore for purposes of reproduction, whereas whales spend their whole lives in the sea, mating, giving birth, and suckling their young in the water. They have a long, tapered body and a broad powerful tail. They have no hindlimbs, and the forelimbs are represented by horizontally mounted flippers. The lungs are very capacious to enable them to spend long periods under water and the nostrils are situated at the top of the head to enable the animal to breathe with most of its body submerged. The nostrils emit jets of water vapor; if the air tempera-

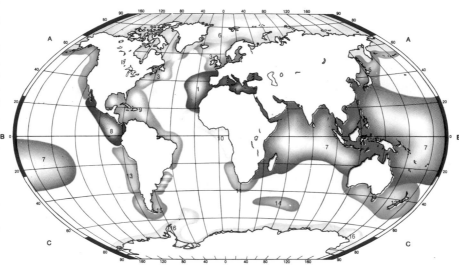

ture is low, the vapor immediately condenses, giving the impression that jets of liquid water are being exhaled.

Cetaceans may be divided into two groups, with different environmental adaptations. The Odontoceti, including dolphins, narwhals, killer whales, and sperm whales, are all predators and consequently equipped with teeth. The Mystacoceti (subdivided into Balaenidae and Balaenopteridae) live on plankton; instead of teeth they have a series of flattened horny plates mounted on the palate that act as a filter for the plankton. These plates are known as "whalebone."

There are many other marine vertebrates, all with specific adaptations to life in the sea. Among the reptiles, there are sea turtles and sea snakes; among the birds are many

Above: The map shows the marine zoogeographical regions of the continental shelf. 1) Mediterraneoatlantic region; 2) Sarmatic region; 3) Boreoatlantic region; 4) Baltic region; 5) Boreopacific region; 6) Arctic region; 7) western Indo-Pacific region; 8) eastern Pacific region; 9) western Atlantic region; 10) eastern Atlantic region; 11) southern African region; 12) southern Australian region; 13) Peruvian region; 14) Kerguelan region; 15) American Antiboreal region; 16) Antartic region.

Below: An abyssal fish, *Chauliodus danae*. Its horrific teeth are clear evidence of its predatory nature. In the ocean depths the lack of algae means most species are predators, whose food in turn depends on the phytoplankton in the illuminated zone.

Opposite: A group of tropical fish on a coral bed.

marine species, the most specialized being the penguins; marine mammals include both carnivores such as seals, walruses, and sea lions, and also plant-eating creatures such as the sea cows (dugong and manatee) which live in the coastal waters and some of the great rivers of the tropics. Interesting adaptations are exhibited by the sea snakes of the tropics. They are long and slim in shape and swim with an undulating movement like eels. They have capacious lungs that enable them to store large quantities of air for long dives and can maintain themselves at different depths by regulating the amount of air contained in their lungs. They also absorb a certain amount of the dissolved oxygen present in the water through a network of special capillary veins situated in the mucous membrane of their gums. Sea snakes are very poisonous.

The adaptations of abyssal animals

Animals that live at great depths exhibit very marked adaptations to the special conditions found in that environment, on which we have already touched. Because of the general shortage of food, many fish have developed huge mouths and dilatable stomachs to enable them to swallow other animals as large or larger than themselves. As sunlight does not penetrate to these depths, many animals have developed luminescent organs known as photophores. The lack of light has other effects: coloration is generally drab and uniform, often tending towards the blackish; eyes may be abnormally large, abnormally small, or completely absent. Abyssal fish have very fragile skeletons; if they are brought up to the surface, their swim bladders burst as a result of the change in pressure. Many species have developed an array of tactile appendages with which they explore the sea floor and recognize the objects they find there. The benthonic Crustacea living at great depths have long and delicate legs, while other benthonic animals have developed large crawling surfaces to enable them to move about on the silt.

The adaptations of animals living in brackish water

Brackish waters have a salt content less than that of the sea because of the mixture with fresh water. They are found along coasts, mainly near estuaries, in coastal pools and lagoons, in rock pools, etc. Some seas, including the Baltic, are brackish because they receive the water of many rivers and are situated in a basin with only limited communication with the oceans. Brackish waters are subject to marked variations in salinity and temperature of their upper layers, owing to the effects of tides,

wind, waves, and rain. The animals that live in these surroundings have had to adapt themselves to changing conditions and are tolerant of wide variations of salinity and temperature. It is however, only a small number of species that has succeeded in developing the tolerances required by so unstable an environment. Thanks to the lack of competition and the wealth of nutritious material brought in by streams, the number of individual animals is often very high and the total biomass consequently very large. Coastal pools and lagoons are therefore excellent places for fish farms and for the cultivation of edible mollusks such as oysters and mussels.

Rock pools are found at the upper littoral level; they vary greatly in size and are replenished at irregular intervals either with rain water or with water from the sea. They are inhabited by a special fauna that has to be able to tolerate sharp changes of temperature and salinity. In addition to marine species, it contains some from freshwater ones, including mosquito larvae.

Another special environment is found in highly saline water, where the concentration of salt may reach the point of saturation. Saline concentrations of up to 70 parts per thousand are tolerated by *Cardium edule* (Lamellibranchia) and by *Neries diversicolor* (Polychaeta). Another inhabitant of highly saline waters is the phyllopod *Artemia salina* (Crustacea).

The pollution of the seas and its effect on marine fauna

The problem of the pollution of the seas has become steadily more serious in the past few decades, as a result of the growth in the human population of the world and the spread of industrialization. The oceans, thanks to their enormous bulk and to the ability of sea water to purify itself, have a very great capacity to absorb pollution. This capacity is however often exceeded, especially in ports and in coastal regions near cities, industrial plants or estuaries. There are several different types of pollution, including domestic sewage, the often poisonous effluent of chemical factories, hydrocarbons such as petroleum, and radioactive waste. There is also thermal pollution, caused by the discharge of hot water by industry. Yet another type of pollution is caused by the dumping of materials and soil along the coasts, which changes the nature of the sea floor.

A typical modification of the local fauna takes place in port areas, where several different forms of pollution converge: the fauna is impoverished as regards the number of species, even if the number of individual creatures remains high. We may also distinguish heavily polluted from lightly

polluted regions, both of which are often marked by the presence of characteristic species, known as "pollution indicators," such as *Capitella capitata* (Polychaeta), which is found on silty bottoms. A characteristic fauna, generally known as "fouling," is found on piers, quays, and the keels of ships; similar, but not identical, creatures may be found on submerged structures outside port areas.

Pollution by petroleum is especially serious when tankers are involved in shipwreck. When oil is emitted into the sea, marine flora and fauna (especially that of the intertidal zone) is destroyed along considerable stretches of coast. Sea birds may be killed in large numbers because their feathers are stuck together by the oil and become useless for flight and for the regulation of body temperature.

The large amount of nutritive material provided by the discharge of sewage may be harmful, because it causes eutrophication with an excessive multiplication of single-celled algae that deplete the oxygen supply and lead to high mortality among the fish population. Toxic pollution of industrial origin may be taken up by animals that filter their food from the water, or may be concentrated in the tissues of fish as they pass through the food chain, at the end of which they may enter the diet of man. Filtratory animals may also pass on the germs of disease to man.

The damage caused to the marine fauna by pollution must be considered in conjunction with the damage caused by indiscriminate fishing and hunting. These activities have caused the extinction or near-extinction of many species, one conspicuously threatened group being the whales. Protective measures include limitations of fishing and hunting, and also the institution of protected zones and marine parks to serve as regions of refuge and recovery. In spite of these efforts, the environmental situation remains serious and threatens to grow worse. Increasingly far-reaching measures are necessary on an international level.

Zoogeography of the marine environment

Animal life is present in the waters of the oceans down to the greatest known depth. It should be remembered that the Pacific Ocean has an average depth of about 13,000 feet (4,000 m) but goes down to 36,000 feet (11,000 m) in the Vitjaz abyss; that the Atlantic Ocean has an average depth of 11,000 feet (3,300 m) and a maximum depth of 30,000 feet (9,200 m) in the Puerto Rico Trench; and the Indian Ocean has an average depth of 12,870 feet (3,900 m) and a maximum of 24,500 feet (7,450 m) in the Java Trench. In terms of both area and volume the oceans offer incomparably more space for living things than the continents. It is nevertheless true that no more than 10% of known animal species live in the sea. This is all the stranger if we reflect that many groups of animals are found exclusively or almost exclusively in the sea – such as the Radiolaria, the Foraminifera, the

sponges, the Cnidaria, the Nemertina, the Polychaeta, the Pogonophora, the Echinoderma, the Cephalopoda, the Tunicata, the Cetacea, etc. Mollusks and crustaceans are admittedly well represented on dry land, but they are even better represented in the seas. This is because the oceans, considered as a whole, present a much greater uniformity of environment than the dry lands; geographical barriers are also, generally speaking, of much less importance in the seas than on the land. Isolated faunas such as we find on dry land are therefore hardly ever encountered at sea. The zoogeographical regions of the ocean are consequently based more on ecological factors than on historical ones.

Zoogeographers make use of a different zoogeographical subdivision for each of the three types of marine fauna: the benthonic fauna of the continental shelf, the abyssal benthonic fauna, and the pelagic fauna at its two levels – epipelagic and bathypelagic. The area that has been most elaborately subdivided by the zoogeographers is the benthonic area of the continental shelf which is the area most influenced by the distribution of continents and islands and consequently shows the effects of historical factors of the paleogeographical and paleoecological types. The subdivision envisages three oceanic domains: Boreal, Tropi-

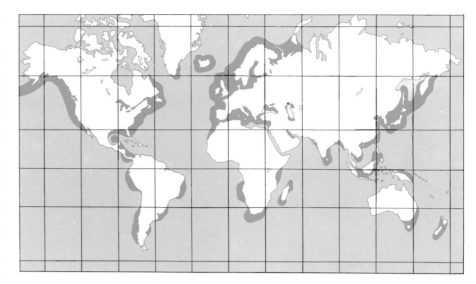

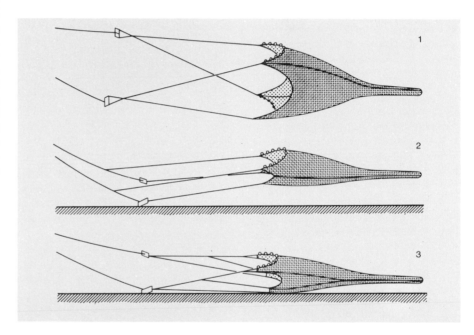

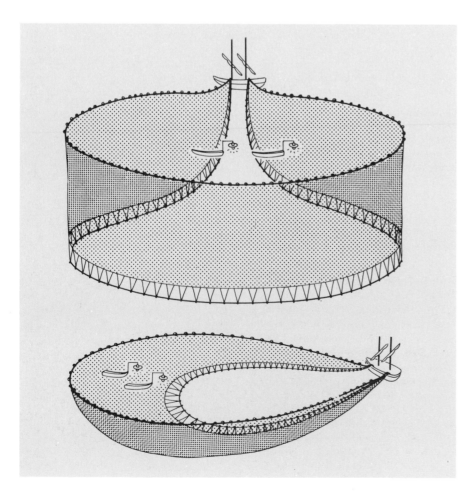

Above top: The darker color indicates the main fishing zones of the world.

Trawls or drag nets are bag-shaped nets that are pulled by one or two fishing boats, depending on the fishing method used. Above: three different types of drag net: 1) pelagic; 2) semipelagic; 3) wide aperture bottom net.

Ring nets are used to surround and catch shoals of pelagic fish. Left: operational diagram showing seining with the use of light sources.

cal, and Austral (or Antiboreal). These three domains correspond basically to three great climatic zones: the arctic, with cold waters; the intertropical zone, with warm waters; and the antarctic, with cold waters. The Boreal oceanic domain comprises six regions: Arctic, Boreoatlantic, Baltic, Mediterraneoatlantic, Sarmatic, and Boreopacific. The Tropical oceanic domain contains four regions: western Indo-Pacific,

eastern Pacific, western Atlantic, and eastern Atlantic. Finally, the Austral oceanic domain contains six regions: southern African, southern Australian, Peruvian, Kerguelen, American Antiboreal, and Antarctic.

The regions of the Tropical domain are characterized by the presence of two important animal communities: the coral reefs and the inhabitants of mangrove swamps. The coral reefs are dominated by calcium-fixing Cnidaria, which actually build the reefs, assisted by certain algae and Foraminifera. They harbor an extraordinarily rich and varied fauna. The mangrove swamps are also populated by an abundant fauna displaying many special adaptations, including some designed to give resistance to variations of salinity and the action of the tides.

In the Boreal domain the Mediterraneoatlantic region is characterized by a fauna

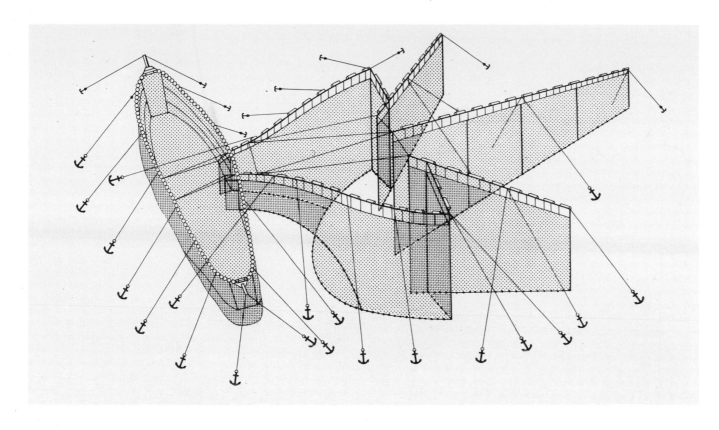

Nowadays regulations covering all fishing activities are based on strict control of the life cycles of the most commercially valuable species. With regular assessments of the extent of existing stocks, estimates can be made of how much fish can actually be caught without affecting the biological rhythms of the species. In the present climate, therefore, the survival of fish or more generally the biology determining it has become an extremely important scientific branch of the administration of the resources in the seas and rivers. A great number of other important studies have also been done into fishing techniques and yield improvement. Thanks to this vast bank of information, we are now managing our resources rather than exploiting them, with the result that the industry can remain productive without endangering the natural environment.

that is not only rich in species, but has a remarkably high percentage of endemics. Some of its members have tropical affinities that betray earlier connections with the Indian and Pacific Oceans on one side and with the West Indies on the other. These affinities probably date from the time of the Tethys Sea. This supposition is supported by another set of facts. There are certain animal species and genera of marine origin living in the subterranean waters of the West Indies that are closely similar to corresponding groups living in the subterranean waters of the coastlands of the Mediterranean; and these animals also have affinities with animals found in the Indo-Pacific area. (Most of the creatures concerned are crustaceans of the Malacostraca group.)

Another area of great interest is the Sarmatic region, which takes in the Black Sea and may be extended to include the Caspian. These two seas represent the remains of the Sarmatic Sea. This was a completely landlocked sea formed during the Miocene from the Paratethys (a branch of the Tethys) by a geological movement that cut it off from the Mediterranean. At the time of its maximum extension, the Sarmatic Sea stretched from the plains of Hungary to central Asia. It was the scene of the intensive development of a fauna specialized to live in brackish waters. The survivors of this fauna are known as the "Ponto-Caspian" species and are to be found along the coasts of the Black Sea, especially near the mouths of rivers and in the Caspian.

Above: A complex Japanese set net.

Below: "Badijini" fishermen of the Indian Ocean, fishing turtles with the aid of suckerfish.

PORIFERA

The Porifera, or sponges as they are commonly known, constitute a vast phylum of primitive animals whose organization sets them apart from the other multicellular animals. Because of this they are often placed separately in a group known as the Parazoa. The differences lie in the fact that their cells do not form well defined tissues and organs but are instead relatively independent and retain a considerable amount of mobility. In addition, they lack a nervous system, muscle cells, and sense organs. When adult, the Porifera are fixed to the substrate and they do not display any extensive body movements. As a result, they were regarded as zoophytes or plant animals until the eighteenth century.

The members of this phylum are all aquatic animals and the vast majority are marine. Most sponges have a body pierced by a network of canals in which the food-bearing water circulates. Bacteria make up a large part of their diet, but they also feed on other microorganisms suspended in the water and on organic detritus. It also appears that sponges can absorb dissolved organic matter. The water flows in through the excurrent canals. These join to form larger and larger ducts and they finally open through exhalent apertures incorrectly known as oscula. Sponges are highly efficient filter feeders, filtering several hundred pints and square feet of substrate per day and extracting almost every particle of the size of a bacterium from it.

Although the choanocytes do not form a true tissue they do form a continuous layer, the choanoderm, which lines some of the cavities inside a sponge. Another type of cell, the pinacocyte, forms a continuous layer covering the entire surface of the sponge and the canal system. On the surface of the sponge there are also specialized cells known as porocytes that enclose the ostia and control their diameter. An intermediate layer, the mesohyl, lies between the pinacoderm and the choanoderm.

With a few exceptions, all sponges possess a skeleton. This is generally composed of mineral elements, the spicules, that vary in shape and are divided into the megascleres and the microscleres. The former determine the

▲ Population of *Halichondria panicea* in a rocky, middle littoral habitat.

▶ Asconoid structure. The arrows indicate the direction of the water as it flows through the sponge, entering through the pores and leaving through the osculum.

▼ Detail of the asconoid type of structure. Note the choanocytes that line the spongocoel and the pore canal in a porocyte through which the water passes.

overall structure of the skeleton while the latter are involved in secondary roles such as protecting the surface of the sponge or binding together the megascleres, etc. The mineral skeleton may be combined with a scleroprotein known as spongin and this may form sleeves around the spicules, binding them together and giving the skeleton strength and elasticity. Alternatively, the mineral skeleton is completely replaced by horny fibers of spongin, although in the majority of the members of this order the spongin fibers are strengthened by the inclusion of grains of sand. It is only in a few species, such as *Spongia officinalis*, *Spongia zimocca*, *Spongia agaricina*, and *Hippospongia equina*, that the fibers are completely free of foreign bodies and it is this that gives their skeletons the softness, making them commercially valuable as bath sponges.

Sponges that live in deep water, particularly those belonging to the class Hexactinellida (the glass sponges), have delicate lace-like skeletons of siliceous spicules. At the base of the sponge these spicules are clustered together to form a long peduncle anchoring the sponge to the muddy sea bed. Close to the surface, on the other hand, it is the horny sponges that abound, and the elasticity of their spongin fibers protects them from the blows of the waves.

The sponges may reproduce sexually through eggs and spermatozoa, but also asexually; this latter form of reproduction is particularly well known in the freshwater Spongillidae. Several marine species, for example members of the genera *Tethya* and *Suberites*, form buds and these may be either inside or on the outside of the parent sponge.

The majority of marine sponges live on rocky bottoms in the littoral zone at depths of between 0 and 650 ft (200 m). There are, however, numerous forms occurring down to depths of 6,600 ft (2,000 m). On bathyal bottoms below this level the Porifera are represented by specialized forms that belong to the orders Tetractinellida and Monaxonida of the Demospongia and the class Hexactinellida. Some species penetrate into the abyssal and hadal zones below 20,000 ft (6,000 m) and even reach 26,000 ft (8,000 m). There are over 5,000 living species of sponges.

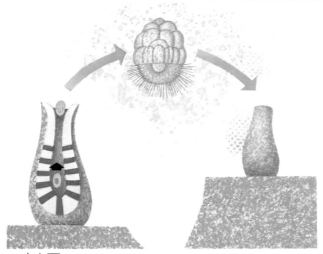

▲ | The production of amphiblastula larvae by a member of the Calcarea.

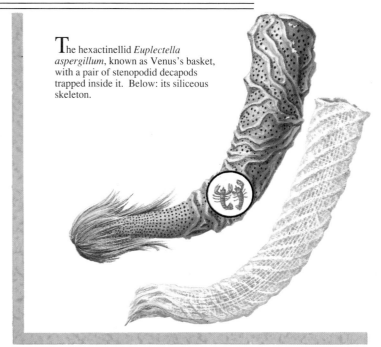

The hexactinellid *Euplectella aspergillum*, known as Venus's basket, with a pair of stenopodid decapods trapped inside it. Below: its siliceous skeleton.

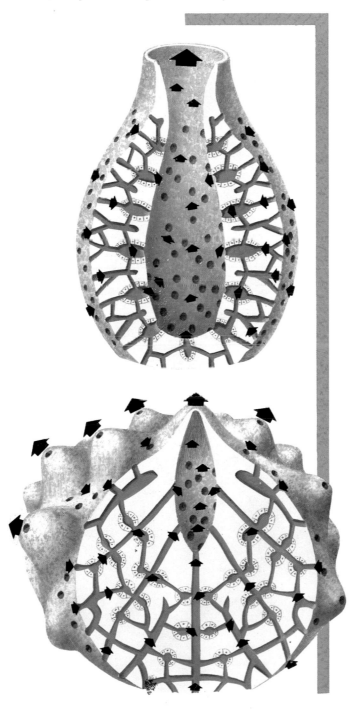

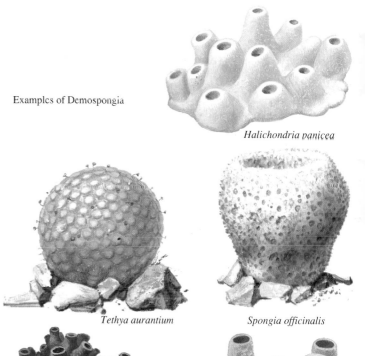

Examples of Demospongia

Halichondria panicea

Tethya aurantium

Spongia officinalis

Hymeniacidon sanguinea

Haliclona mediterranea

◄ A bove: The syconoid structure. Having entered through pores, the water passes down the canals that open into the choanocyte chambers. These, in turn, open into the spongocoel and the water leaves through the osculum.
Below: The leuconoid structure. The choanocyte chambers lie inside the body and communicate with the spongocoel by means of a system of canals. There are numerous oscula, through which the water flows out of the sponge.

CNIDARIA

The structural organization of the Cnidaria is extremely simple. The body wall is composed of two layers of epithelial tissue in between which there lies a layer of gelatinous substance (a protein gel) impregnated with water. This layer is known as the mesoglea. It is both viscous and elastic, so it is able to provide support for the body and an anchorage for the muscle cells. Water is able to enter the coelenteron (or gastrovascular cavity as it is also known) through the mouth and it is because this cavity is full of water that the turgor of the body is maintained. The outer cell layer is called the epidermis and the inner one the gastrodermis. The cells that make up these layers are only differentiated to a slight extent and the majority of them have many functions. There is only one class of highly specialized cells – the stinging cells or cnidoblasts, which are found only in the Cnidaria and which constitute both an effective means of food capture and of defense.

The members of the Cnidaria are carnivorous and predatory but they often have little or no mobility. They are not therefore able to pursue their prey and they have instead to ensnare it as it passes within reach of their tentacles. The cnidoblasts provide them with a highly effective method of doing so. These complex cells contain a chitinous capsule, the nematocyst, which is filled with a toxic liquid. Inside the nematocyst there is a hollow thread which is wound round itself. A thin process, the cnidocil, projects from the dermal surface of the cnidoblast and functions as a receptor for stimuli. When the cnidocil is struck by an animal, the nematocyst explodes, firing its thread into the prey and injecting it with the toxic fluid.

About 10,000 species of Cnidaria are known at present . Within the phylum two quite different body forms, the polyp and the medusa, occur. Each of these is adapted to a different way of life. The polyp is sessile or only slightly motile (benthic) and it is basically cylindrical in shape. The basal part, the pedal disk, is attached to the substrate whilst the mouth lies at the center of the upwards pointing apical end and is surrounded by symmetrically arranged, hollow tentacles. The medusa swims or floats freely (planktonic) and is rather

The Cnidaria are distinctive invertebrates that are found in all seas and are adapted to different ways of life. The corals, sea anemones, and jellyfish are their principal representatives. Some members of the Cnidaria spend the whole of their life cycle as polyps, others spend the whole of it as medusae, and others still alternate polypoid and medusoid stages. The medusae are usually planktonic and solitary, while the polyps are benthic and may be either solitary or colonial. However, there are benthic medusae, planktonic polyps, and, finally, planktonic colonies that are composed of both polyps and medusae.

Jellyfish (*Aurelia aurita*)

Hydromedusa (*Obelia*)

Sea anemone (*Anemonia sulcata*)

Sea anemone (*Anthopleura xanthogrammica*)

like an upside down polyp which has been flattened and broadened out sideways. In shape it resembles a mushroom or an umbrella and the body of a medusa is in fact known as the umbrella, with the convex upper surface being the exumbrella and the concave under surface being the subumbrella. Such a flattened and expanded form is well adapted to a floating way of life.

Unlike the polyp, the medusa's mouth is pointed downwards and it opens at the tip of a projection of varying length, the manubrium, which extends from the center of the subumbrella. The tentacles hang down from the margins of the umbrella and they are more distant from the mouth than they are in the polyp. To make up for this the mouth may possess four arms or lobes and these, in their turn, may be branched and extensively developed. The cnidoblasts of these oral arms are used in the capture of prey. The difference in the positions of the mouth and the tentacles in the polyp and the medusa is related to the different way in which they feed. The former lives on the bottom and catches prey which passes over it whilst the latter lives on the surface and preys on organisms which are found at lower levels. The medusa is well adapted to a planktonic life, possessing an extensive mesoglea (generally poorly developed in the polyp) as well as sense organs (absent in the polyp). The mesoglea gives the umbrella body and its low density helps the organism to float. As the medusa moves freely in all directions, it must have a means of knowing its position in space, where the light is coming from, and how strong that light is. To meet this need two types of very primitive sense organs are arranged around the margin of the umbrella. These are the statocysts, which indicate position, and the ocelli, which are photoreceptors.

Many cnidarians live symbiotically with other animals or plants. Those species living in habitats receiving a great deal of sunlight, the madrepores for example, have gastroderm cells full of unicellular algae (Zooxanthellae) belonging to the Peridinea. The algae and the animal cells actively exchange nutrients; the plant exploits the nitrogen metabolism of its host and provides oxygen, sugars, and amino acids in return. The symbiosis between some anemones (*Adamsia palliata*, *Calliactis parasitica*) and hermit crabs (Crustacea) is well known. The anemone attaches itself to the mollusk shell of a hermit

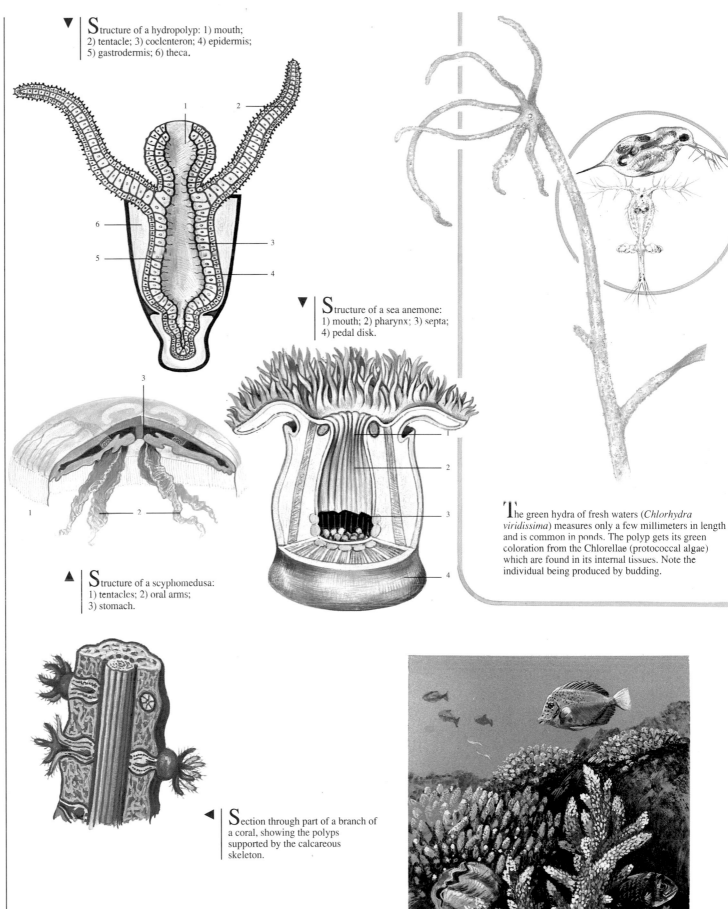

▼ Structure of a hydropolyp: 1) mouth; 2) tentacle; 3) coelenteron; 4) epidermis; 5) gastrodermis; 6) theca.

▼ Structure of a sea anemone: 1) mouth; 2) pharynx; 3) septa; 4) pedal disk.

▲ Structure of a scyphomedusa: 1) tentacles; 2) oral arms; 3) stomach.

The green hydra of fresh waters (*Chlorhydra viridissima*) measures only a few millimeters in length and is common in ponds. The polyp gets its green coloration from the Chlorellae (protococcal algae) which are found in its internal tissues. Note the individual being produced by budding.

◄ Section through part of a branch of a coral, showing the polyps supported by the calcareous skeleton.

▶ These stony branches, belonging to the members of the madrepore genus *Acropora*, abound on the reefs but they show greater development in sheltered lagoons. They offer protection to the numerous fish that dwell among them.

crab by means of its foot and in this way it is able to move about more quickly. In return the crustacean receives some of the food captured by the anemone and is protected by the latter's nematocysts.

The Cnidaria owe their success to their colonial organization and they also represent the peak of development of this way of life. The exploitation of food sources is improved in colonial forms by the fact that all the gastrovascular cavities are connected. Another advantage of colonial organization is that various functions may be divided among the individual members.

The Cnidaria phylum is divided into three classes: the Hydrozoa, the Scyphozoa, and the Anthozoa.

Hydrozoa. The Hydrozoa is the class of cnidarians displaying the greatest variety of form, way of life, and organization. It includes benthic and planktonic species, solitary and colonial ones, as well as both polypoid and medusoid forms. The majority of hydrozoans undergo alternation of generations, with both polypoid asexual and medusoid sexual phases. The order Limnomedusa contains the few freshwater members of the Cnidaria as well as some marine species with a very reduced polypoid stage. The members of the Hydroida order are the most typical representatives of the Hydrozoa. They form colonies and these are generally attached to the substrate although in some cases they may be floating. Their life cycle always involves an alternation between an independent medusoid phase and an asexual polypoid, colonial phase. The most common species in the Mediterranean, and one to be found in every other sea, is *Obelia dichotoma*. This tree-like form has delicate, flexible branches and does not exceed 3¹/₄ in (8 cm) in height. One particularly interesting group of hydroids was once included amongst the Siphonophora, the best known and most graceful of which is the purple sailor (*Velella velella*), which resembles a sailing boat. In the Trachylina the polypoid form is generally absent. They exist, therefore, exclusively as medusae and, apart from a few minor details, the structure of their medusoid form is very similar to that of the hydroids. The Milleporina are the only hydrozoans that possess a solid calcareous skeleton. This can take a variety of forms, plate-like, tabular or branched, and it is covered by the delicate tissue of the colony. The members of the genus *Millepora* are widespread in tropical seas. Siphonophores are unusual in

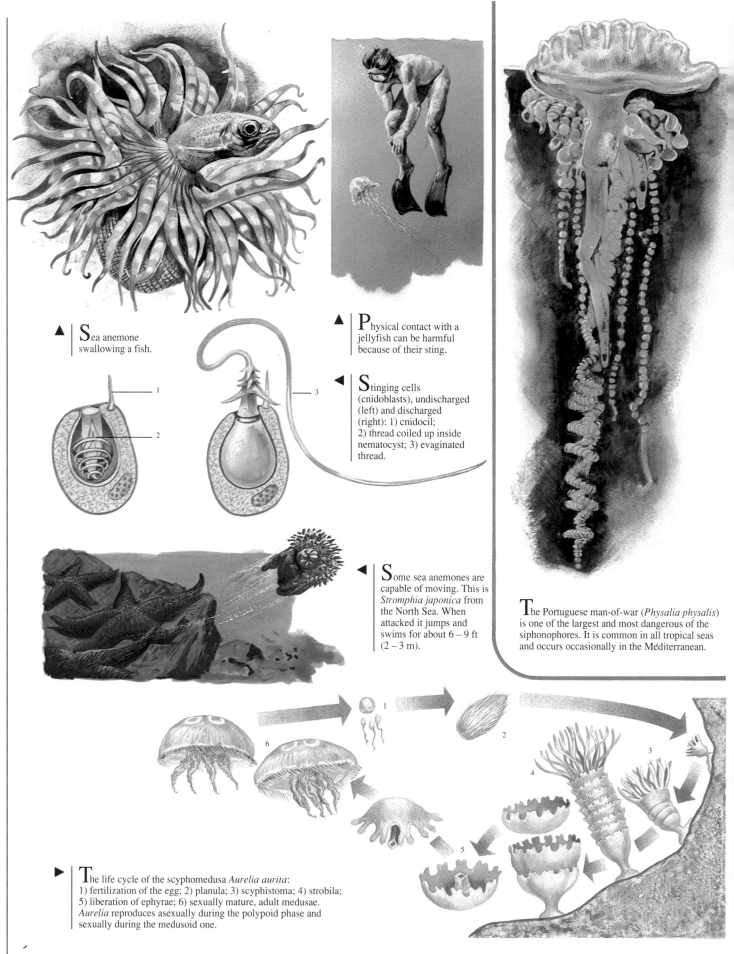

▲ Sea anemone swallowing a fish.

▲ Physical contact with a jellyfish can be harmful because of their sting.

◄ Stinging cells (cnidoblasts), undischarged (left) and discharged (right): 1) cnidocil; 2) thread coiled up inside nematocyst; 3) evaginated thread.

◄ Some sea anemones are capable of moving. This is *Stromphia japonica* from the North Sea. When attacked it jumps and swims for about 6 – 9 ft (2 – 3 m).

The Portuguese man-of-war (*Physalia physalis*) is one of the largest and most dangerous of the siphonophores. It is common in all tropical seas and occurs occasionally in the Mediterranean.

▶ The life cycle of the scyphomedusa *Aurelia aurita*: 1) fertilization of the egg; 2) planula; 3) scyphistoma; 4) strobila; 5) liberation of ephyrae; 6) sexually mature, adult medusae. *Aurelia* reproduces asexually during the polypoid phase and sexually during the medusoid one.

being both planktonic and colonial. The colonies are always very complex and they are often both elegant and striking in appearance. The best known and most striking of the siphonophores is the Portuguese man-of-war (*Physalia physalis*).

Scyphozoa. Jellyfish with large, multi-colored umbrellas are scyphomedusae and belong to the class Scyphozoa. Their polypoid stage (the scyphistoma), when it exists, is so small as to pass unobserved. Scyphozoans are found in all seas from the poles to the tropics. Some species are pelagic and do not come close to the shore, others live in deep water. The majority, however, are found in coastal waters. The order Cubomedusae includes a number of species known as sea wasps, a name owed to their painful and often fatal sting. The Coronatae jellyfish live mainly in deep waters and the abyssal zone. The order Semaeostomeae includes the largest known jellyfish: *Cyanea capillata*, which has an umbrella measuring more than 6 ft (2 m). The Rhizostomeae are the most complex and highly evolved of the jellyfish, their main feature being that they lack a true mouth. These jellyfish are voracious eaters of minute plankton.

Anthozoa. The name of this class emphasizes the similarity of these creatures with multicolored underwater flowers. The polyp is the only phase that occurs in the Anthozoa, the medusoid form is never present even in a rudimentary state, and all anthozoans are benthic. The Alcyonaria are usually colonial and possess eight tentacles and the same number of septa. The group known as gorgonians are like small trees. The well known red coral (*Corallium rubrum*) resembles the flexible gorgonians but has a stone skeleton. The strangest of the alcyonarians are undoubtedly the sea pens, which owe their name to their feather-like appearance. The Zoantharia display a greater variety of structure than do the alcyonarians, including, as they do, both solitary and colonial species and forms with or without skeletal support. The tentacles of the polyps are not pennate and they occur in multiples of six arranged in concentric circles. The sea anemones are the best known zoantharians. They never form colonies and include the largest members of the group. The madrepores are the group of zoantharians that arouse the greatest interest because of the reefs and atolls that are built from the skeletons of some tropical members of this group.

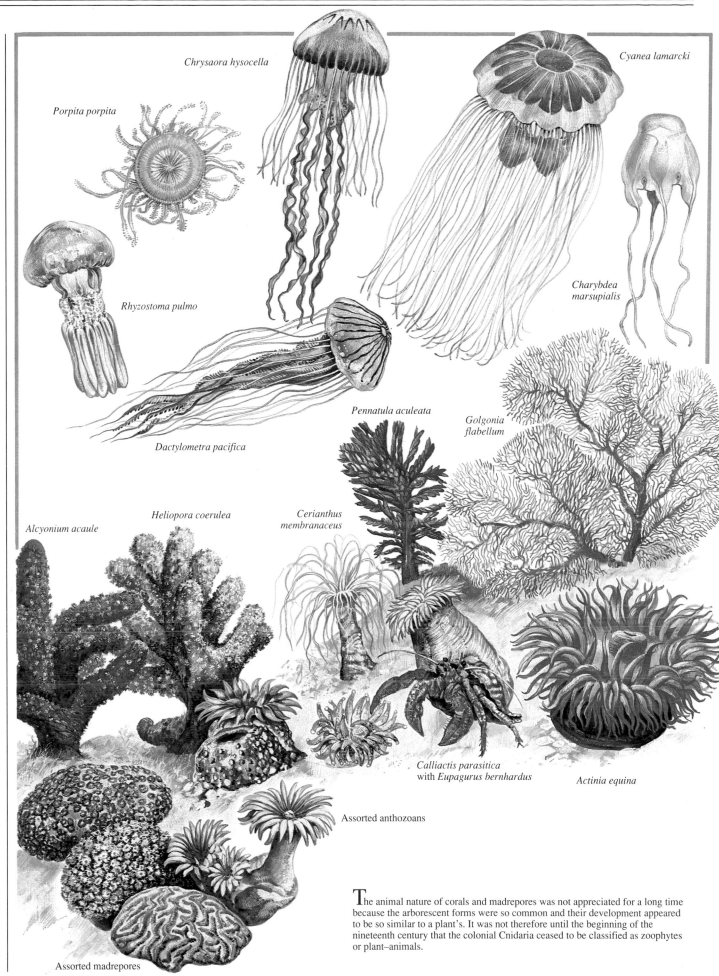

Chrysaora hysocella

Porpita porpita

Cyanea lamarcki

Rhyzostoma pulmo

Charybdea marsupialis

Dactylometra pacifica

Pennatula aculeata

Golgonia flabellum

Alcyonium acaule

Heliopora coerulea

Cerianthus membranaceus

Calliactis parasitica with *Eupagurus bernhardus*

Actinia equina

Assorted anthozoans

Assorted madrepores

The animal nature of corals and madrepores was not appreciated for a long time because the arborescent forms were so common and their development appeared to be so similar to a plant's. It was not therefore until the beginning of the nineteenth century that the colonial Cnidaria ceased to be classified as zoophytes or plant–animals.

CRUSTACEA

The Crustacea is one of the richest arthropod classes in terms of numbers of species. The class contains a total of some 30,000 different species each one being the end product of a tortuous process of evolution and each playing a unique role in its environment. A crustacean is a metameric animal or, in other words, composed of a series of segments, each of which bears a pair of jointed appendages and is covered by a cuticle (the exoskeleton). The appendages are forked, each consisting of a protopodite from which branches an endopodite and an exopodite. The first and last segments do not bear appendages. The first six segments are fused into a single structure, the head. The appendages of the second segment form the antennules and those of the third form the antennae, those of the fourth, the mandibles, the fifth, the first maxillae, and the sixth, the second maxillae. Frequently, a fold of the exoskeleton known as the carapace covers a part or, exceptionally, the whole of a crustacean's body.

In all probability the Crustacea originated in the sea but they are now present in every aquatic environment. When they possess a respiratory system it is, with some exceptions, a branchial one. The first larval stage, the nauplius, is highly characteristic of crustaceans. It is a tiny larva that possesses three pairs of appendages and a simple, unpaired eye.

Cephalocarida

These small crustaceans are a few millimeters in length, are completely blind and lacking in pigment. They live in muds and sands in various parts of the world. The slender, elongated form of these organisms enables them to move rapidly between grains of sand. They feed on detritus.

Branchiopoda

The Branchiopoda is another very ancient group of crustaceans and, although there are less than a thousand living species, the fossil evidence suggests that in the past there was a large number of species occurring in a wide variety of aquatic habitats. A characteristic of the entire group is the structure

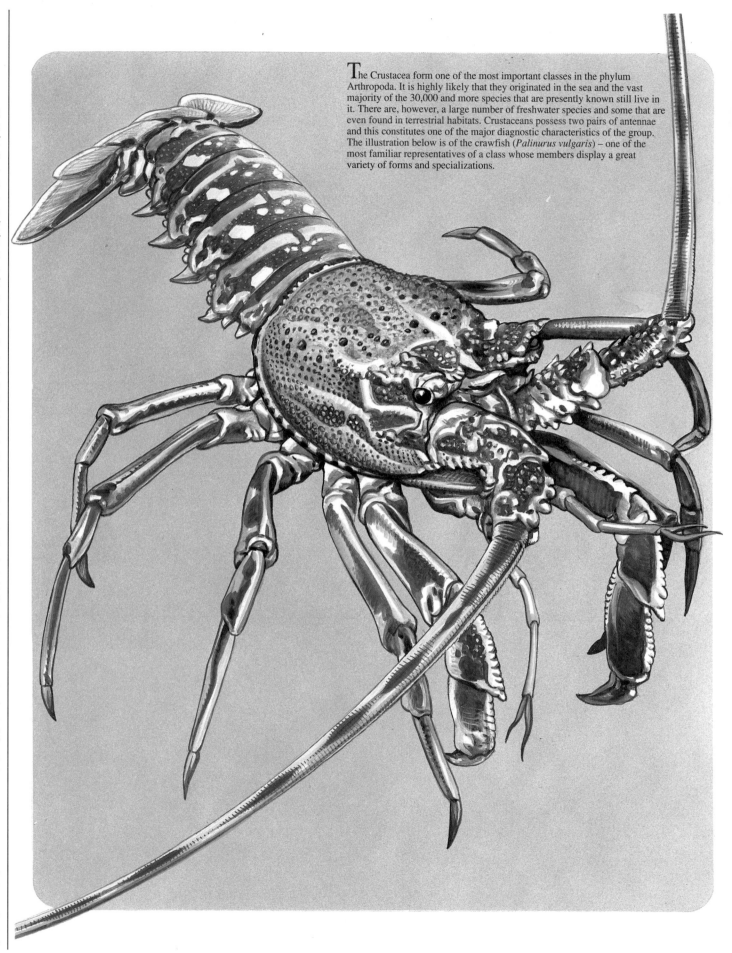

The Crustacea form one of the most important classes in the phylum Arthropoda. It is highly likely that they originated in the sea and the vast majority of the 30,000 and more species that are presently known still live in it. There are, however, a large number of freshwater species and some that are even found in terrestrial habitats. Crustaceans possess two pairs of antennae and this constitutes one of the major diagnostic characteristics of the group. The illustration below is of the crawfish (*Palinurus vulgaris*) – one of the most familiar representatives of a class whose members display a great variety of forms and specializations.

of the appendages, which are flattened and held rigid by internal fluid pressure. This differs from the situation in all other crustaceans which have "leg-like" appendages, circular in section. These appendages bear closely packed, long setae and are used for swimming, filtering out food, and for gaseous exchange.

The members of the Notostraca have a broad, flattened carapace that is only slightly convex and covers only part of the body. The Anostraca, another branchiopod order, differs from the Notostraca in being completely without a carapace. The members of the Notostraca and the Anostraca are typical components of the fauna of temporary water systems, which form after periods of heavy rain and disappear in dry weather.

The Cladocera is another interesting and important branchiopod group. Its members are the tiny and very common crustaceans known as water fleas, which are found in great numbers in any stretch of fresh water. Only a few species of Cladocera occur in the sea.

The Conchostraca is an equally characteristic branchiopod group. In these animals the carapace is in the form of two valves, rather like the shells of cockles or clams, and it completely surrounds the animal itself. Conchostracans are benthic but they too are adapted to a life in short-lived pools of water.

Mention must be made of a more unusual member of the Branchiopoda, *Artemia salina*. This is one of a number of species that live in habitats with high concentrations of salt and the mechanisms by which it has adapted to these conditions involve complex patterns of parthenogenesis.

Ostracoda

Like the members of the Conchostraca, the members of this group have a bivalved carapace enclosing the whole body, which is reduced to a small number of indistinguishable segments. The overall length of these organisms is generally a few millimeters. The majority of species are benthic and they feed off detritus on the bottom. They live both in the sea and fresh water and some species populate temporary pools of water whilst others have been found at great depths in the Pacific. Pelagic species are also known and some feed off the film of bacteria that forms on the surface of the water. An interesting feature of a number of ostracod species occurring in warm seas is their bioluminescence.

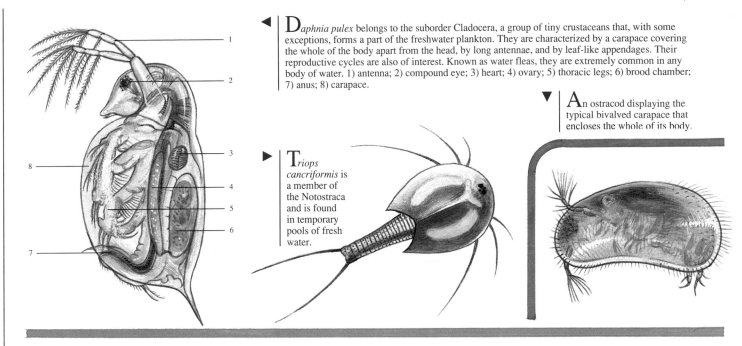

Daphnia pulex belongs to the suborder Cladocera, a group of tiny crustaceans that, with some exceptions, forms a part of the freshwater plankton. They are characterized by a carapace covering the whole of the body apart from the head, by long antennae, and by leaf-like appendages. Their reproductive cycles are also of interest. Known as water fleas, they are extremely common in any body of water. 1) antenna; 2) compound eye; 3) heart; 4) ovary; 5) thoracic legs; 6) brood chamber; 7) anus; 8) carapace.

An ostracod displaying the typical bivalved carapace that encloses the whole of its body.

Triops *cancriformis* is a member of the Notostraca and is found in temporary pools of fresh water.

A species of the genus *Balanus* that belongs to the subclass Cirripedia. These are sessile forms that are very common on the rocks in the intertidal zone. They are enclosed within a strong wall of plates and they are able to withstand the continuous and violent action of the waves as well as periods of dessication at low tide. The planktonic larva acts as a dispersal stage. 1) scutum; 2) tergum; 3) cirri; 4) wall; 5) muscle; 6) antennules; 7) ovary; 8) oviduct; 9) adductor muscle.

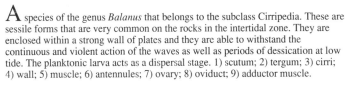

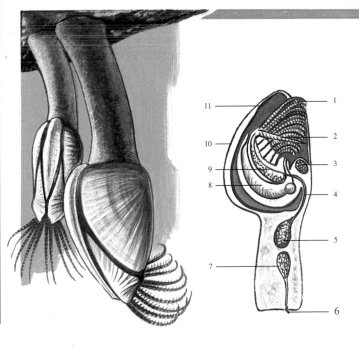

Another cirripede, belonging to the genus *Lepas*, with its distinctive fleshy peduncle. The goose barnacles are sessile hermaphrodites and, like the acorn barnacles, they pass through planktonic larval stages before attaching themselves to marine animals or floating objects. 1) cirri; 2) penis; 3) adductor muscle; 4) oviduct; 5) ovary; 6) antennule; 7) adhesive gland; 8) intestine; 9) seminal vesicle; 10) carina; 11) mantle cavity.

Copepoda

The copepods are tiny crustaceans that, apart from a few exceptions, range from less than a millimeter to a few millimeters in size. They generally form the most important component of a community, whether it be in the sea or fresh water or on the surface or the bottom, but they are particularly numerous in the plankton. Their populations can reach inconceivable levels and the entire food chain of the pelagic habitat is largely dependent upon them. The free-living marine species occupy very low levels in the food pyramid and they play much the same role in the marine plankton as the Cladocera do in the fresh water. Many copepods are especially equipped for a parasitic way of life and this has entailed complex, adaptive changes.

There are at present some 5,000 known species of copepods and only some of these are planktonic. These forms belong to the order Calanoida and many of them have assumed highly unusual shapes. All the members of the order Harpacticoida are adapted to a benthic way of life and a large number of them actually live in, rather than on, the bottom. It is possible for organisms to occupy the space between the particles on sandy or gravel bottoms, both in the sea and fresh water.

There are a number of species which are symbionts of anemones or tunicates and a brief mention should be made of the parasitic copepods, many of which are of interest to man. The various species of parasitic copepods are dependent on a wide selection of marine and freshwater organisms, ranging from polychaetes to echinoderms and from tunicates to fish.

Branchiura

The subclass Branchiura is closely related to the Copepoda. It contains less than a hundred species which are distinguished by a series of adaptations towards an ectoparasitic way of life. They are in fact ectoparasites of fish and amphibians and they attach themselves to their hosts by means of two large suckers which have evolved from the first pair of maxillae.

Mystacocarida

This is another subclass containing only a small number of species. It is closely related to the Copepoda. Its members are fairly common in coastal, interstitial habitats and they are widely distributed in different parts of the world.

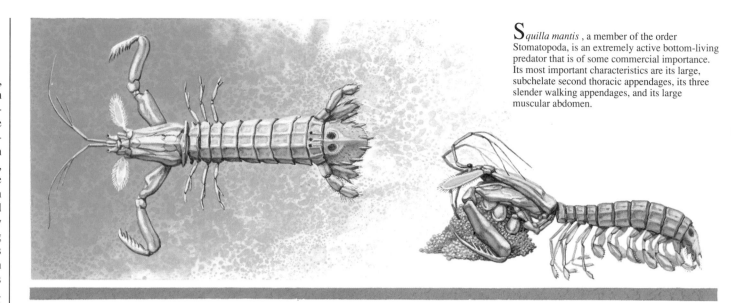

S*quilla mantis* , a member of the order Stomatopoda, is an extremely active bottom-living predator that is of some commercial importance. Its most important characteristics are its large, subchelate second thoracic appendages, its three slender walking appendages, and its large muscular abdomen.

T*he isopods, which are present both in the sea and in fresh water, are the only group of crustaceans to have a large number of terrestrial species. The illustration is of *Ligia*, an amphibious genus that has not fully adapted to life in the air. It is found in the intertidal zone on rocky coasts.

T*he sand fleas, which live along the tide line of sandy shores, have a characteristic way of moving, taking large bounds. They also display an interesting ability to orientate themselves with respect to the sun. These animals belong to the order Amphipoda, which contains a large number of small species with laterally compressed bodies. They are common both in the sea and in fresh water.

Cirripedia

It is the members of this group that, in their organization and in certain aspects of their ecology, differ most markedly from the popular image of a crustacean. The strangest feature of all is the fact that the adults are sessile, that is they live attached to the substrate, in the same way as sea anemones or sponges.

A goose barnacle possesses a large, fleshy stalk, which attaches it to the substrate. At the top of this stalk there is what appears to be a sort of bivalved mollusk with a shiny, calcareous shell. This part of the body, the capitulum, turns out to be formed from a series of five principal plates that entirely enclose the body of the animal. The cirri emerge, when the animal is alive, through an apical opening in the shell. The cirri are modified appendages and the animal possesses either four or six pairs of them. When extended through the apical opening, the cirri set up water currents that trap the food particles on which the animal feeds. Goose barnacles attach themselves to floating objects and are carried about the oceans by currents. The group includes species adapted to living on turtles, others to living on lobsters, and so on.

The acorn barnacles are a group of barnacles that occur along the low-tide mark of rocky coasts, where they form thick encrustations. They lack a peduncle and the capitulum is attached to the substrate directly. The capitulum takes the form of a wall of calcareous plates ringing a central hole which gives these barnacles the appearance of small truncated cones.

The rhizocephalan cirripedes deserve a mention as they constitute an order of exclusively parasitic species.

Malacostraca

This vast subclass contains two thirds of all crustaceans. The most important factor which suggests that this group is monophyletic, is the uniform bodily organization displayed by its members. The Malacostraca is divided into two series.

Leptostraca. The series Leptostraca contains just a single order, the Nebaliacea, and less then ten species. These, however, are of great interest because of the primitive characteristics that they display. Leptostracans occur in littoral habitats and, under certain conditions, brackish habitats. Some species, however, are bathypelagic.

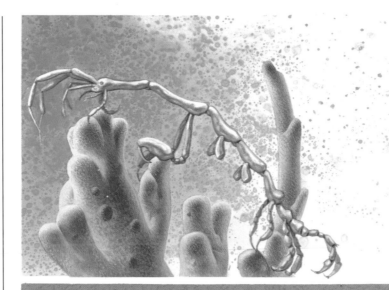

A number of very strange forms exist amongst the amphipods. The members of the family Caprellidae are small in size and are known as skeleton shrimps from the form of their thin, cylindrical bodies. They live attached to underwater vegetation by means of their posterior legs. The illustration shows *Caprella linearis* and its ventral, bladder-like gills are clearly visible.

The subclass Copepoda contains a large number of tiny species and these form a major component of the marine and freshwater plankton. Many copepods are parasitic, as is the case of *Lernaea*, pictured on the right, and they display profound modifications accordingly. The genus *Argulus*, center, belongs to the subclass Branchiura, which is related to the Copepoda and contains a number of ectoparasitic species.

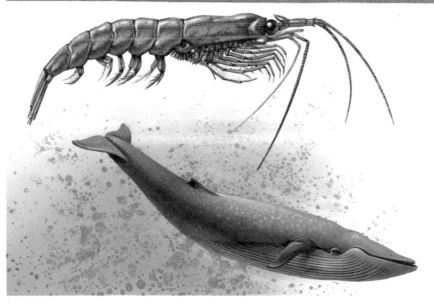

The krill, that mass of plankton on which the whales of cold seas feed, is largely composed of small, planktonic malacostracans belonging to the order Euphausiacea. The species illustrated here is *Nyctiphane couchi*. Note that the gills are not covered at the sides by the carapace, a distinguishing feature of this group.

Eumalacostraca. This series is divided into a number of superorders, which will be discussed separately, together with their constituent orders.

SYNCARIDA. The members of this group live mainly in interstitial or underground habitats. They display numerous primitive characteristics.

HOPLOCARIDA. This is a group that includes at least some familiar species. One of these is the mantis shrimp of the genus *Squilla*, a typical representative of the order Stomatopoda, the only order of living hoplocarids.

Stomatopods, as their massive bodies imply, are benthic animals. Equally, the large, stalked eyes and, in particular, the well developed raptorial legs suggest that they are predators. They spend most of their time in natural burrows or in ones which they dig themselves in the mud of the sea bed where they wait to ambush prey.

PERACARIDA. This is an extremely heterogeneous superorder and in order to understand it, it is necessary to look at each individual order.

The Mysidacea is the most primitive of the peracarid orders, containing less than 500 species. In external appearance its members resemble tiny, transparent shrimps. However there are a number of features that immediately set them apart. The members of this group are mainly marine and pelagic, occurring both on the surface as well as at great depth, and they are often an important component of the plankton.

Another order is the Cumacea, which together with the Tanaidacea and the Isopoda forms one of the two principal lines which have evolved from the archaic Mysidacea, the other being the order Amphipoda. Cumaceans are benthic marine organisms that usually live buried in the sand, from which their rostra protrude. Some species also feed off the particles of organic matter which is borne by the inhalant current. The majority, however, feed by cleaning organic matter off individual grains of sand.

The order Tanaidacea has some 250 members and it includes forms intermediate between the Cumacea and the Isopoda. Its members display considerable similarities with the Isopoda. They are benthic, partly filter feeders and partly predators. They often live buried in detritus, sometimes constructing tiny tubes for themselves.

Isopods are the only crustaceans to have evolved extensive adaptations to life on land. Others groups, such as the

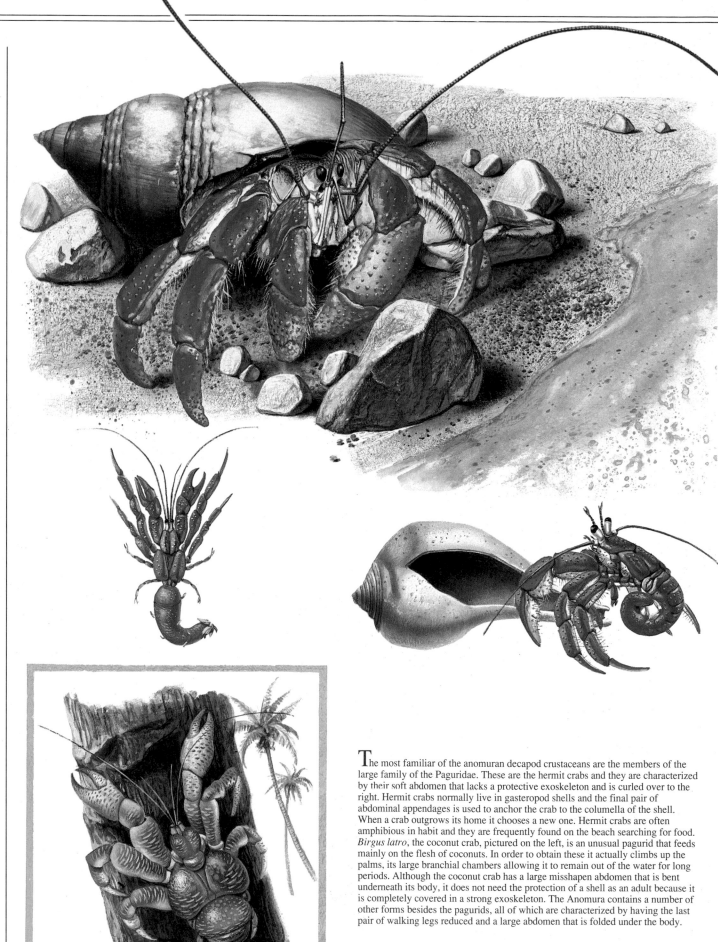

The most familiar of the anomuran decapod crustaceans are the members of the large family of the Paguridae. These are the hermit crabs and they are characterized by their soft abdomen that lacks a protective exoskeleton and is curled over to the right. Hermit crabs normally live in gasteropod shells and the final pair of abdominal appendages is used to anchor the crab to the columella of the shell. When a crab outgrows its home it chooses a new one. Hermit crabs are often amphibious in habit and they are frequently found on the beach searching for food. *Birgus latro*, the coconut crab, pictured on the left, is an unusual pagurid that feeds mainly on the flesh of coconuts. In order to obtain these it actually climbs up the palms, its large branchial chambers allowing it to remain out of the water for long periods. Although the coconut crab has a large misshapen abdomen that is bent underneath its body, it does not need the protection of a shell as an adult because it is completely covered in a strong exoskeleton. The Anomura contains a number of other forms besides the pagurids, all of which are characterized by having the last pair of walking legs reduced and a large abdomen that is folded under the body.

amphipods and the decapods have terrestrial members but these are the exceptions and are usually only partially adapted. Although the isopods have been very successful as terrestrial animals, it should not be forgotten that the group is mainly aquatic and is represented in every benthic habitat, whether it be marine or freshwater, on the surface or underground. Most isopods are detritivores but there are also predatory species, species that bore into wood, and ones that build shelters within which they set up water currents and filter out the food particles. As well as aquatic and terrestrial forms, there are also both ecto- and endoparasitic isopods. The hosts of the most specialized of these parasites are other crustaceans and, in fact, very often they are other species of isopod.

The members of the order Amphipoda resemble the Isopoda in many respects but despite this it is generally easy to tell them apart in the wild, since most amphipods are laterally compressed whilst isopods are dorsoventrally flattened. Amphipods are common in both the seas and fresh water. The members of this group have adapted to a large number of aquatic and, to some extent, to terrestrial habitats. Everyone will have seen sand fleas, genus *Talitrus*, jumping around in enormous numbers on the sea shore. These animals spend much of their time buried in the sand and it is mainly at night that they move over the surface of the beach in search of food.

The majority of amphipods are marine or freshwater and may live either on the surface or underground. There are, however, unusual species, for example those that have adapted to become ectoparasites of whales, others that are pelagic and live inside salps (tunicates), and others still that are benthic and construct tubes for themselves. EUCARIDA. With 8,500 members, this is the largest of the superorders and it is also the best known, since it contains all the large species. The Eucarida is divided into two orders: the Euphausiacea and the Decapoda.

The Euphausiacea contains the most primitive eucarids and in general appearance its members closely resemble the Mysidacea. The members of the Euphausiacea are all marine and pelagic and they occupy an important position in the ecology of the open sea, where they form immense swarms. Some of the commercially most important species of fish, such as the herring, depend on these crustaceans. These

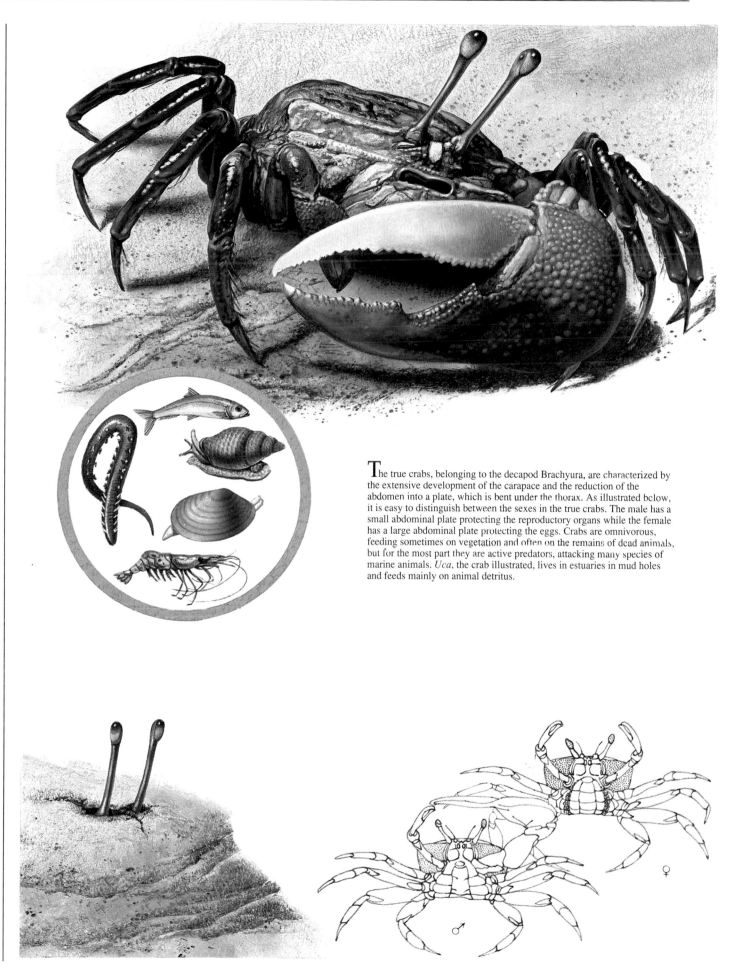

The true crabs, belonging to the decapod Brachyura, are characterized by the extensive development of the carapace and the reduction of the abdomen into a plate, which is bent under the thorax. As illustrated below, it is easy to distinguish between the sexes in the true crabs. The male has a small abdominal plate protecting the reproductive organs while the female has a large abdominal plate protecting the eggs. Crabs are omnivorous, feeding sometimes on vegetation and often on the remains of dead animals, but for the most part they are active predators, attacking many species of marine animals. *Uca*, the crab illustrated, lives in estuaries in mud holes and feeds mainly on animal detritus.

small shrimps, known as krill, also form the basis of the diet of the baleen whale and the blue whale.

Euphausiaceans themselves feed on the phyto- and zooplankton, with the individual species varying in their preferences, and they therefore occur at a very low level in the food pyramid. An interesting feature of these animals is the luminescence which almost all the known species display and which seems to play an important role in holding the swarms together.

The decapods are divided into two main groups, the Natantia and the reptants. The first group includes the more primitive forms, the true shrimps, which have retained, in part, a pelagic habit. There are about 6,000 reptant species as opposed to the 2,000 or so belonging to the Natantia and these, in their turn, are divided into a number of different sections. The first of these sections, the Macrura, contains species with large, dorsoventrally flattened abdomens. The best known representative of this section is without doubt the crawfish, a member of the genus *Palinurus*, which lives on rocky bottoms and is intensively fished. This section also contains the spiny lobster of the genus *Scyllarus*.

The Astacura are another group of decapods with a well developed, flattened abdomen and a large tail fan. The most familiar member of this group is the lobster of the genus *Homarus*. This is one of the largest of the crustaceans and it can reach weights of up to 11 1b (5 kg). It is nocturnal and a predator, spending the day hidden in a crevice in the rocks. The Dublin Bay prawn, *Nephrops norvegicus*, a species whose commercial importance in Europe can be seen by anyone who visits a fish market, is another member of this group.

The Anomura is an interesting section of reptant decapods. The mole crabs of the genus *Hippia* are a group with unusual habits living in the undertow zone along sandy shores in the tropical regions of the Atlantic and the Pacific. The best known representative of the section, however, is the hermit crab. There are a large number of hermit crab species and in all of them the abdomen lacks a hard exoskeleton. It is instead a mass of soft tissue and in order to protect it these animals have resorted to occupying the empty shells of gasteropod mollusks. Their symbiotic associations with sea anemones is the most remarkable as well as the best known feature of these animals but this is in fact something that only involves a few

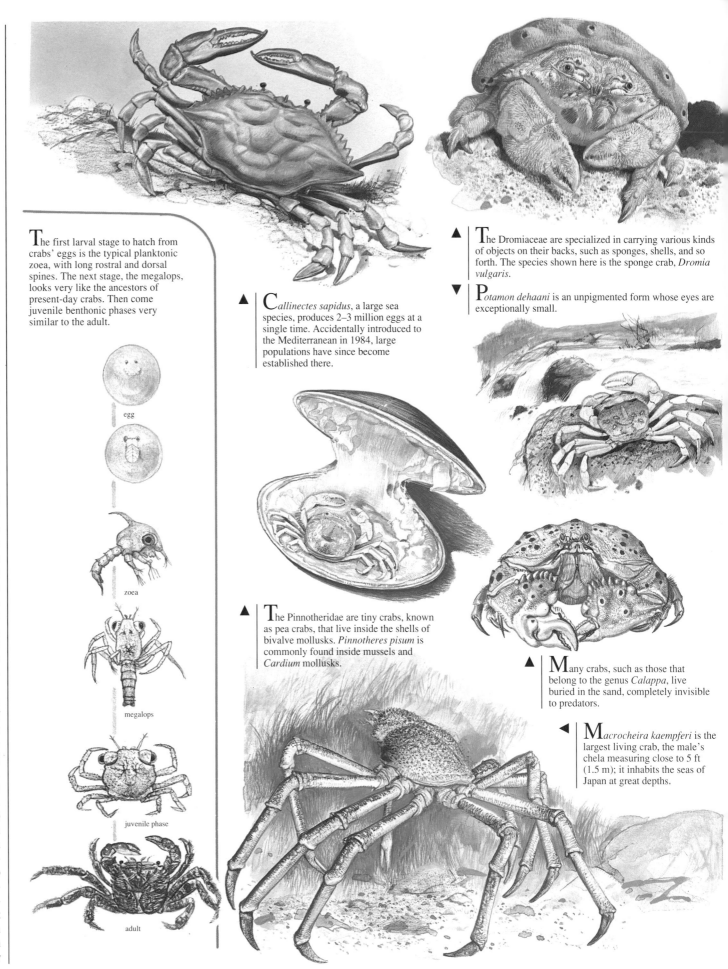

The first larval stage to hatch from crabs' eggs is the typical planktonic zoea, with long rostral and dorsal spines. The next stage, the megalops, looks very like the ancestors of present-day crabs. Then come juvenile benthonic phases very similar to the adult.

egg

zoea

megalops

juvenile phase

adult

▲ *Callinectes sapidus*, a large sea species, produces 2–3 million eggs at a single time. Accidentally introduced to the Mediterranean in 1984, large populations have since become established there.

▲ The Pinnotheridae are tiny crabs, known as pea crabs, that live inside the shells of bivalve mollusks. *Pinnotheres pisum* is commonly found inside mussels and *Cardium* mollusks.

▲ The Dromiaceae are specialized in carrying various kinds of objects on their backs, such as sponges, shells, and so forth. The species shown here is the sponge crab, *Dromia vulgaris*.

▼ *Potamon dehaani* is an unpigmented form whose eyes are exceptionally small.

▲ Many crabs, such as those that belong to the genus *Calappa*, live buried in the sand, completely invisible to predators.

◄ *Macrocheira kaempferi* is the largest living crab, the male's chela measuring close to 5 ft (1.5 m); it inhabits the seas of Japan at great depths.

species of hermit crab. A symbiotic association is one that is of benefit to both parties and the various species of sea anemones (anthozoan cnidarians) that attach themselves by means of their strong feet to the shells of hermit crab offer their hosts the protection of their stinging cells. In return they receive, in one way or another, food and a means of moving about over the bottom.

Birgus latro, the coconut crab, is another pagurid. It is a large crustacean which reaches a length of 12 in (30 cm). As in the hermit crabs, its abdomen is bent and appears deformed. Its peculiarity lies in the fact that it feeds mainly on the flesh of coconuts and it can often be seen climbing the swaying palms which fringe the beaches of coral atolls.

The section Brachyura contains all the true crabs. A large number of crabs live on beaches and of these perhaps the most unusual are the members of the Ocypodidae. Known as the ghost crabs, this is a family of swift, perfectly camouflaged predators which are found on beaches in the tropics. The numerous species of the genus *Uca,* the fiddler crabs, are another group of coastal crabs, but in this case they occur in estuarine habitats, particularly where there is rich mangrove vegetation.

The tiny commensal pinnotherids live inside various species of bivalve mollusk, tunicate or holothurian. In contrast is the high degree of camouflage displayed by the genus *Calappa.* The dorippids or sponge crabs are another group of crabs that conceal themselves, but they do so by pulling pieces of seaweed or shell over their backs and holding them in place by means of their last pair of legs, which are bent up over their backs.

Crabs can reach a considerable size and in some species belonging to the genus *Maia* the carapace can be up to 8in (20 cm) in length. The largest species, however, is *Macrocheira kaempferi,* which is a deep water, benthic form from the deep seas off Japan. It has a carapace that is 16 in (40cm) long and its appendages span a total of over 10 ft (3m), when extended.

Pachygrapsus crassipes

Hemigrapsus sanguineus

Leptodius exaratus

Helice tridens

Calappa lophos

Portunus trituberculatus

Eriocheir sinensis

Carcinoplax longimanus

Latreillia phalangium

Platylambrus validus

Atergatis subdentatus

ANNELIDA

The annelids are worm-like animals possessing a cavity between the alimentary canal and the body wall which is lined by a peritoneum. This cavity is known as a coelom and it is divided into segments or meromes, within which lie the paired excretory organs and the blood vessels. The coelom contains a fluid which acts as a hydrostatic skeleton. The common body plan of all annelids is of a vermiform animal divided into identical segments. They possess chitinous bristles, the chaetae, and these play a role in locomotion when it involves lateral undulations or peristaltic waves of the body wall. In annelids that dig the muscles contract in such a way as to produce waves of swelling which travel along the body from front to rear or vice versa.

The polychaetes are marine annelids possessing a pair of appendages known as parapodia on each segment with the exception of the first and the last. These parapodia are supported by robust chaetae known as acicula. The sexes are separate and they have a pelagic, trochophore larva. Errant polychaetes move by creeping over the sea bed and then occasionally burrowing into the sand. Some have become pelagic and others live permanently buried in a tube. They are usually predators but some feed off marine plants and the smaller species devour microorganisms which they find in the interstices between grains of sand. The sedentary polychaetes are characterized by simple parapodia that do not project far and usually lack acicula. Some of the members of this group are specialized for the gathering of detritus and small organisms which have accumulated on the sea bed. Others swallow mud or sand and digest the organic matter in it, just as earthworms do. Some pump water along the tubes in which they live in order to filter out the microplankton. Finally, there are forms which are suspension feeders, capturing organisms by means of prominent crowns of thin tentacles which are borne on their heads.

The members of the Clitellata include the Oligochaeta, the best known representatives of which are the earthworms and the Hirudinea, better known as the leeches. They colonize fresh water and the soil of dry land. The Hirudinea contains clitellates specialized as predators and ectoparasites.

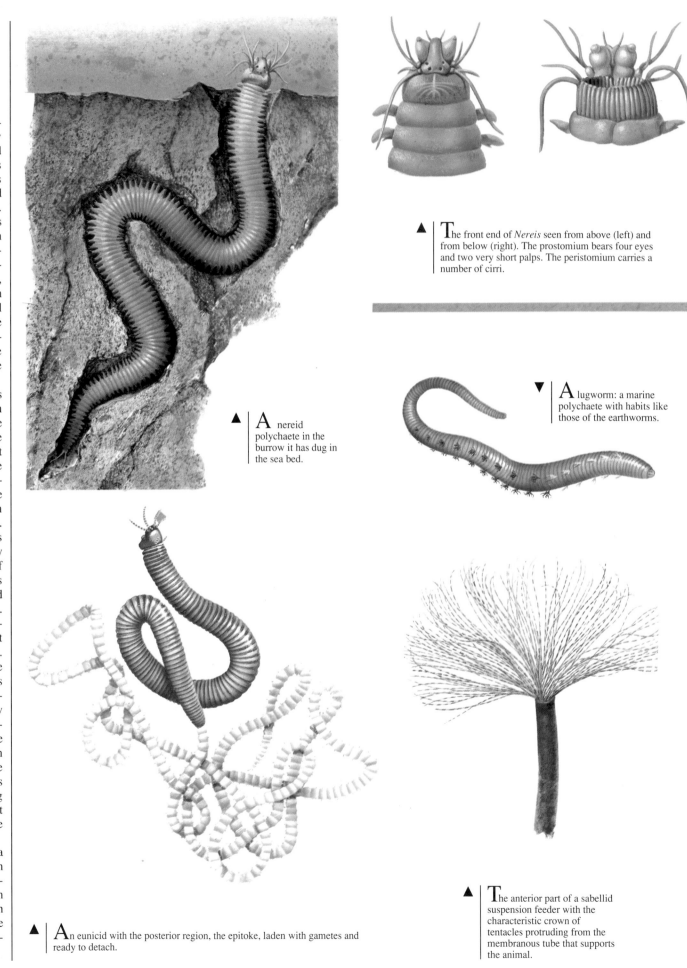

▲ A nereid polychaete in the burrow it has dug in the sea bed.

▲ The front end of *Nereis* seen from above (left) and from below (right). The prostomium bears four eyes and two very short palps. The peristomium carries a number of cirri.

▼ A lugworm: a marine polychaete with habits like those of the earthworms.

▲ An eunicid with the posterior region, the epitoke, laden with gametes and ready to detach.

▲ The anterior part of a sabellid suspension feeder with the characteristic crown of tentacles protruding from the membranous tube that supports the animal.

MOLLUSCA

The Mollusca is one of the most important as well as being one of the largest phyla in the animal kingdom and with over 100,000 species it is second only to the Arthropoda. It is also one of the most varied, since in the course of their evolution its members have diversified into an infinity of forms.

Mollusk bodies can be divided into five main parts: the foot, the head, the visceral mass, the mantle, and the shell. The foot is essentially a muscular organ used by the mollusk for locomotion. In some cases there is a head in front of the foot, often with two tentacles bearing the eyes at the base, somewhere along their length, or at the tips. Dorsal to the foot there is a sac, known as the visceral mass containing the digestive, excretory, circulatory, and genital systems. This sac is covered by a layer of epithelial cells extending around the base of the sac as a marginal fold, the mantle or pallium. This epidermal fold encloses the head and body, together with a space known as the mantle cavity or pallial cavity lying between the mantle and the rest of the body. The mantle is also responsible for producing the well known calcareous shell possessed by many members of this phylum. Respiration takes place across a pair of gills or ctenidia situated in the mantle cavity. Mollusks may be hermaphrodites or they may have separate sexes but sexual reproduction requires two individuals.

The mollusks include:
The Solenogaster and the Caudofoveata, which are primitive vermiforms, without a true shell.
The Polyplacophora, better known as chiton, which are marine mollusks mostly inhabiting rocky shores.
The Monoplacophora, a small class of limpet-like animals, discovered in the abyssal waters of Peru.
The Gastropoda, the most numerous and diverse of the mollusk classes, including both marine and freshwater forms.
The Pelecypoda or Bivalvia, sedentary or little mobile mollusks, with a shell or two articulated pieces.
The Scaphopoda, which have tooth-like, elongated conical shells and occur in sandy marine bottoms.
The Cephalopoda, the most evolved mollusks, often devoid of any shell and adapted to pelagic life in the sea.

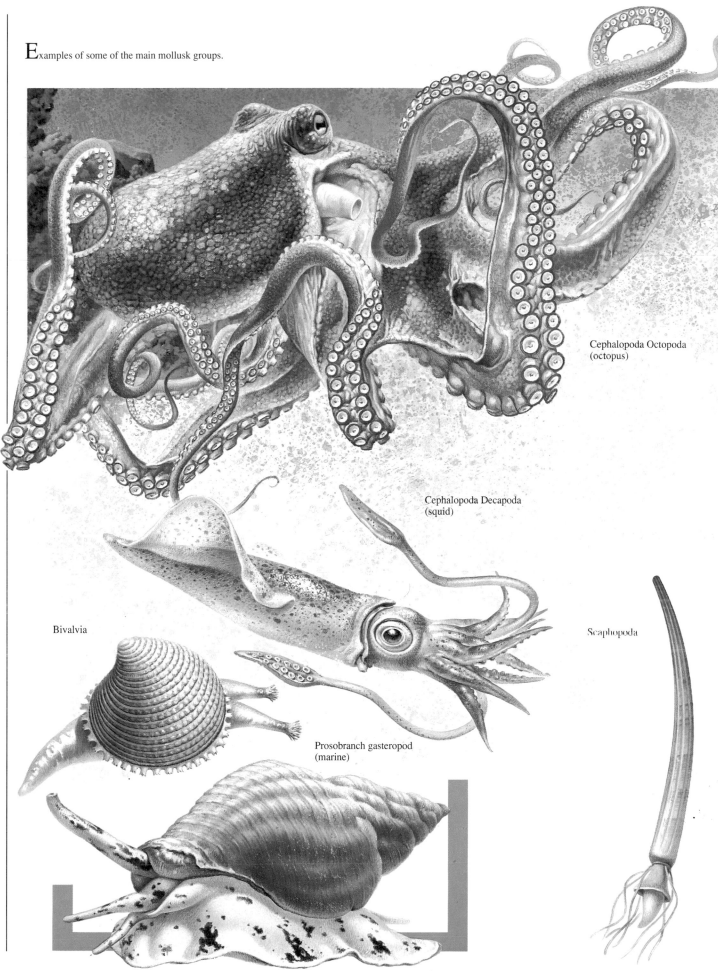

Examples of some of the main mollusk groups.

Cephalopoda Octopoda
(octopus)

Cephalopoda Decapoda
(squid)

Bivalvia

Scaphopoda

Prosobranch gasteropod
(marine)

GASTROPODA

The Gastropoda is the richest molluskan class in terms of species and the only one to have adapted to living on dry land as well as in the sea and fresh water. As its name suggests, its members usually have a ventral, sole-shaped foot which maintains contact with the substrate through a layer of mucus that it secretes. The sole is ciliated and some small gasteropods simply slide over the mucus-covered substrate by means of these cilia. However, the majority of gasteropods move by means of a series of waves produced by contractions of the foot muscles. These waves travel backwards along the foot and may extend across the whole breadth or move down the left- and right-hand sides alternately.

Dorsally, the hind part of the foot sometimes bears a horny or more rarely a calcareous structure known as the operculum. This closes the mouth of the shell once the animal has withdrawn into it. The visceral mass is coiled in a spiral and as a result the shell is helical in almost all cases.

At present the class is divided into three subclasses: the Prosobranchia, with a gill or gills pointing forwards and lying in front of the heart; the Opisthobranchia, with the heart in front of the gill and the gill pointing backwards; and the Pulmonata, with no gills and the pallial cavity transformed into a respiratory organ known as a lung. The Prosobranchia and Opisthobranchia are almost exclusively marine where as the members of the Pulmonata are virtually all freshwater or terrestrial.

The evolution of the subclass Prosobranchia has been accompanied by a gradual change from a herbivorous diet to a carnivorous one. As the diet has changed, the radula has been progressively transformed, with the teeth, particularly the marginal and lateral ones, diminishing as herbivorous forms give way to predatory, carnivorous ones.

In the Opisthobranchia we can distinguish three general morphological types, corresponding to the three different lines of evolution: forms that dig into the substrate and have an external shell; the flattened, symmetrical, benthic forms with no shell, often brightly colored; and the swimming species.

Pinctada margaritifera

Ostrea edulis

Patella vulgata

Turbo cornutus

Haliotis tuberculata

Littorina littorea

Cypraea tigris

Malleus malleus

Macoma sp.

Cypraea aurantium

Calliostoma zizyphinum

Conus marmoreus

Aplustrum amplustre

Tenagodus sp.

Mytilus edulis

Pholas dactylus

Oliva sericea

Serpulorbis arenaria

Pinna nobilis

Mya arenaria

Tonna galea

BIVALVIA SCAPHOPODA

The name Bivalvia is derived from the fact that the shell is composed of two parts or valves. However, these mollusks are also known as the Acephala, since they lack a differentiated head, or the Pelecypoda, from the axe-shaped feet which many of them have for digging in loose substrates. The mouth and anus open at opposite ends of the animal and the hindgut passes through the pericardium and the ventricle. The radula is completely absent and the gills are involved in respiration as well as playing an important role in filtering out food particles suspended in the water.

The mantle cavity surrounds the whole of the body and it is contained within two lobes of the mantle which form the valves. The margins of these lobes tend to lose tone or even fuse together so as to leave only two openings for the water circulating in the pallial cavity, a posterio-ventral inhalent opening and a posterio-dorsal exhalent one. Sometimes the mantle extends to form two siphons around these openings. The nervous systems is ganglionate and development is indirect, with a veliger. The class contains about 20,000 living species and most are marine. Bivalves generally live by digging their way into loose bottoms such as sand or mud.

The thousand or so species of scaphopods are all marine and are characterized by a tubular shell shaped like an elephant's tusk which is open at both ends. The anchor-like foot emerges through the larger of these openings. The head is reduced to a simple proboscis and this bears the mouth at its tip. Dorsal to the mouth there are several filiform, capitate processes that gather particles of food. The radula generally consists of several rows of teeth. The heart lacks auricles and there are no differentiated respiratory organs, this function being performed by the pallial cavity.

All scaphopods are marine and live buried in sand or mud, with only their posterior, thinner end projecting. It is through this opening that water enters and leaves the pallial cavity. Development is always indirect and involves a trochophore followed by a veliger, as in the bivalves.

▲ Specimen of *Meretrix lusoria*. Water with the food particles that it contains enters through the incurrent siphon and passes through the lower gill chamber and the filaments to the upper chamber, whence it is expelled through the excurrent siphon.

▶ Stages in the development of *Ostrea*. As a result of their delicate flavor, oysters, and *Ostrea edulis* in particular, and mussels (*Mytilus edulis*) are farmed throughout the world in special beds.

▼ Specimen of the genus *Lima* displaying the conspicuous red mantle with contractile tentacles along its margins.

CEPHALOPODA

The modern Cephalopoda represent the present evolutionary stage of a group of primitive mollusks in which the shell has been modified to form a floating structure. Recent theories regard the cephalopods as direct descendants of the Monoplacophora with an increased coiling of the shell. It is suggested that the apical region of the visceral mass of these primitive mollusks gradually withdrew and the mantle covering it formed a series of calcareous internal septa bounding gas-filled cavities. As a consequence of this the cephalopods became progressively lighter as they were evolving until the volume of gas was sufficient to compensate for the weight of the shell and the body of the mollusk. At this point these animals acquired neutral buoyancy and were able to rise up effortlessly from the bottom to which they had previously been confined. Another theory supposes that during their early evolutionary stages the herbivorous cephalopods became carnivores, with the head bearing structures adapted to the capture of food. Whilst these tentacular lobes were developing the foot reduced. Once cephalopods had achieved neutral buoyancy, there still remained the problem of how to move about once they had risen off the bottom. It was the foot, the simplest and most versatile of the molluskan organs, that acquired a new form and function. Since it was no longer needed for creeping over the bottom, it was reduced to a pair of mobile folds which partially overlap and can curl over to form a tube at the entrance to the mantle cavity. The rhythmical contraction of the intrinsic musculature of these folds can move the animal in a fairly coordinated fashion as well as helping to circulate water through the deep mantle cavity.

The shell, which played an essential role in the evolution of the cephalopods, has in the modern forms tended to disappear completely in the decapods and is entirely absent in the octopods. It is usually internal and considerably modified, except in the case of *Spirula spirula,* a cosmopolitan decapod whose shell was known to and described by Linnaeus.

Nearly all cephalopods are active predators and many are large in size. The digestive system has become more efficient, reducing the ciliary and mucous mechanisms of other mollusks

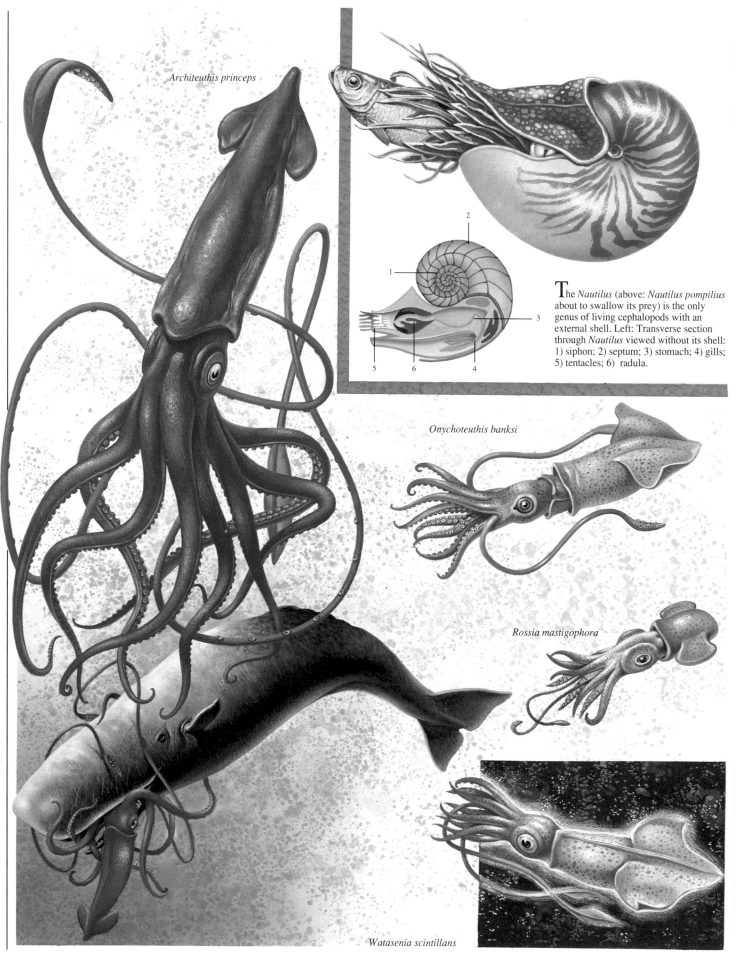

Architeuthis princeps

The *Nautilus* (above: *Nautilus pompilius* about to swallow its prey) is the only genus of living cephalopods with an external shell. Left: Transverse section through *Nautilus* viewed without its shell: 1) siphon; 2) septum; 3) stomach; 4) gills; 5) tentacles; 6) radula.

Onychoteuthis banksi

Rossia mastigophora

Watasenia scintillans

and relying mainly on smooth muscles. Food is captured in various ways. Cuttlefish, for example, hover close to the bottom in coastal waters where they catch shrimps and small fish. They use gentle jets of water from their funnels to blow prey off the sand. Then, as soon as it is within reach, the tentacular arms are shot out from pouches on either side of the mouth (the pouches themselves lie inside the ring of eight oral arms) to grasp the victim. These mechanisms of attack are innate and young cuttlefish begin by attacking small crustaceans before going on to take larger ones and fish. However, it is only with age and experience that they learn how to approach different kinds of prey. For example, after several failed attempts crabs will only be approached from behind.

Octopuses, which are also predators of crustaceans, capture their food by striking rapidly from above with their arms. The prey is grasped by the jaws and killed or paralyzed with poison secreted by the salivary glands. It is then held by the arms coiled around it whilst being injected with the digestive enzymes. After a few hours the prey, a crab for example, will be released apparently intact but in fact it has been reduced to its exoskeleton, the flesh having been completely digested and sucked out – an example of what is known as extraintestinal digestion.

Unlike octopuses, which detect their prey by sight, *Argonauta* appears unable to do so; there is no rapid response to food unless prey brushes against the membrane running between the first pair of arms, which are normally extended above the shell. When this happens, the fourth arm flies out against the membrane. Once food has been caught in this way, it is carried to the mouth and nibbled by the jaws. Before ingestion two pairs of salivary glands assist in these operations by secreting a poison to quickly paralyze the prey, a mucus, and a powerful protease.

Digestion is exclusively extracellular and food passes fairly rapidly through the digestive system. The duct of the ink sac – a gland which secretes a substance used by these cephalopods to conceal their flight from predators – opens into the final portion of the intestine.

The nervous system is both unusual and highly elaborate. The cerebral ganglia are more or less fused to form a brain enclosed within an extensively fenestrated cartilaginous capsule. This brain is connected laterally to the

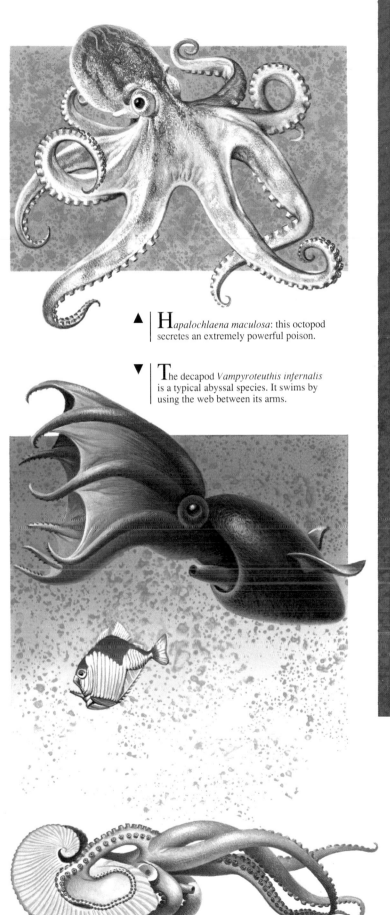

▲ H*apalochlaena maculosa*: this octopod secretes an extremely powerful poison.

▼ The decapod *Vampyroteuthis infernalis* is a typical abyssal species. It swims by using the web between its arms.

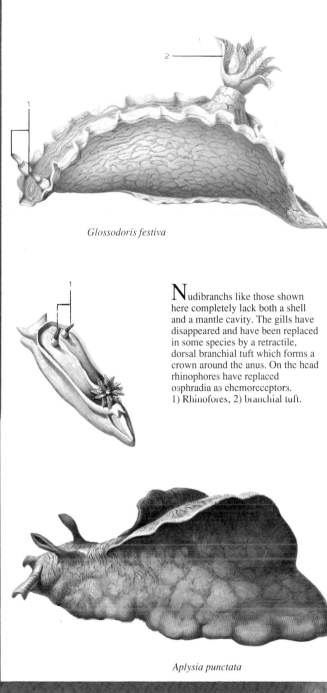

Glossodoris festiva

Nudibranchs like those shown here completely lack both a shell and a mantle cavity. The gills have disappeared and have been replaced in some species by a retractile, dorsal branchial tuft which forms a crown around the anus. On the head rhinophores have replaced osphradia as chemoreceptors. 1) Rhinofores, 2) branchial tuft.

Aplysia punctata

The cephalopod forms illustrated here offer an idea, though a limited one, of the variety found amongst the members of this class of mollusks. Besides the ancient nautiloids, there are also decapods and octopods. The former include numerous forms and some are the largest of all mollusks, whilst the latter represent the evolutionary peak of the phylum.

◄ A female of *Argonauta argo* with its nidamental shell. This shell, which contains the egg, is secreted by a pair of modified oral arms.

extremely large optic lobes where an enormous quantity of visual information is received. The cerebral mass consists of regions lying both above and beneath the esophagus, the former being the larger. The brain of *Octopus*, which will serve as an example because it has been the most intensively studied, taken as a whole may be regarded as consisting of hierarchically arranged zones, proceeding from the ventral region to the dorsal one. The subesophageal regions are occupied by the lower motor centers. These give rise to the nerves running to a pair of stellate ganglia – so called because of their appearance – in the mantle and to the arms. The stellate ganglia in turn give rise to extremely large nerve fibers of up to 0.04 in (1mm) in diameter, known as giant neurons which, amongst other things, control the chromatophores. All these centers are controlled by the supraesophageal regions. The supraesophageal cerebral mass is divided into a number of lobes which contain the higher motor centers, the centers that receive the sensory impulses, and finally the associative centers connected with learning. It is in these latter centers that the animal stores its past experiences, which can be drawn upon in order to modify subsequent activity. Dibranchiates and octopods in particular are therefore able to learn from experience since they are capable of remembering.

A characteristic of these mollusks is their ability to change color in various situations. For example, they are able to camouflage themselves on the bottom in order to escape predators thus making up for the loss of the protection offered by an external shell by means of this and other stratagems. The skin of these cephalopods possesses several types of chromatophores or small elastic sacs filled with pigment. They can be expanded by the action of radial muscles and contract again through their own elasticity. Both operations are extremely rapid and some species can completely change color in little more than half a second. In the Sepioidea there are three layers of chromatophores, a bright yellow surface one, an orange–red middle one, and a brown lower one. In addition some species can produce both blue and green as structural colors. This richness in color is characteristic of bottom-living, infralittoral forms. Pelagic cephalopods such as *Loligo* and *Argonauta* have only red and yellow chromatophores whilst *Ommastrephes* also has blue ones and its color varies from

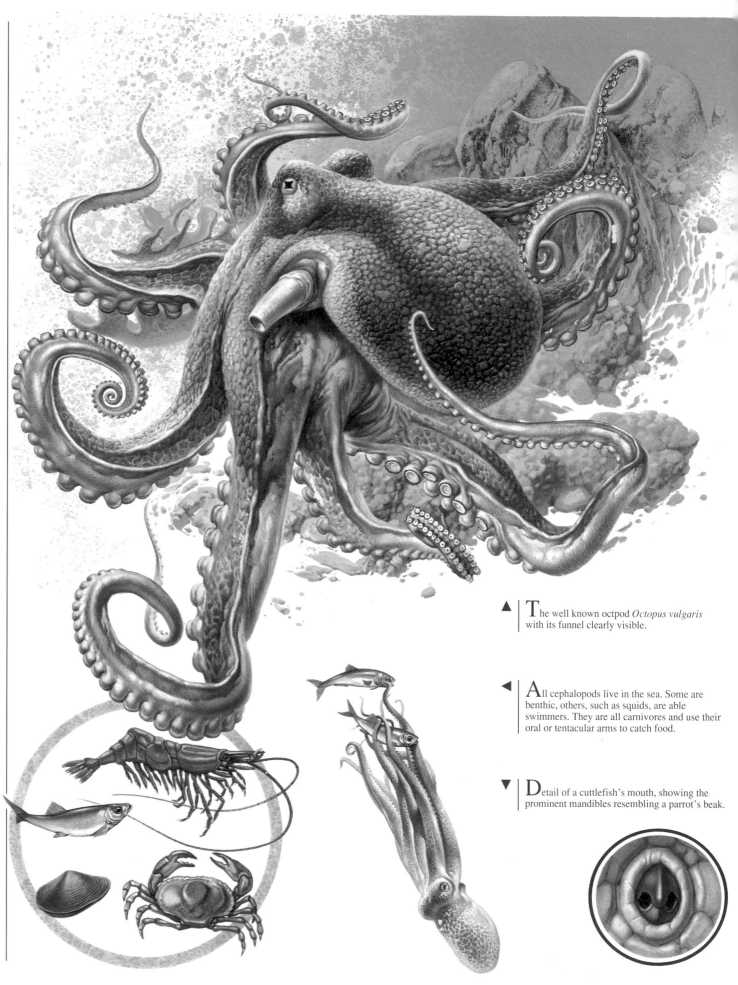

▲ The well known octpod *Octopus vulgaris* with its funnel clearly visible.

◄ All cephalopods live in the sea. Some are benthic, others, such as squids, are able swimmers. They are all carnivores and use their oral or tentacular arms to catch food.

▼ Detail of a cuttlefish's mouth, showing the prominent mandibles resembling a parrot's beak.

deep red or a uniform purple to pale almost colorless shades. Finally, deep water cephalopods may be permanently deep red or purple or even black, as in *Vampyroteuthis*, or, as in abyssal octopods, the chromatophores may be completely absent. The species with the most refined color repertoire amongst those so far studied is *Sepia officinalis*.

A number of the changes are mimetic and under experimental conditions the cuttlefish is able to reproduce a black and white checkered bottom quite well. This is due to the fact that the expansion or contraction of the pigment cells is influenced by the wave length of the light reflected from the bottom. Characteristic patterns of coloration include black and white stripes or completely white bodies in which all the chromatophores are contracted. If a cuttlefish is disturbed or angry, it can display threat colorations such as large, black, eye-like spots or the body may become completely white apart from a pair of wavy black stripes running along the back which alternate in rapid succession with black and white stripes. Males may also display patterns of coloration to attract females; as they swim alongside females, their tentacles extended, patterns of bright color appear and dark bands come and go.

The sense organs are also extremely complex and refined. The eye of coleoids is a large spherical structure, equaling the vertebrate eye in complexity. It lies inside an orbit within which it can be partially rotated. Visual accommodation is achieved by moving the lens closer to the retina or further away. Unlike nearly all other mollusks, cephalopods recognize food or enemies primarily by sight and their sense of smell is reduced.

The sexes are separate in all cephalopods. The eggs are typically deposited in clusters and are usually attached to hard substrates. In some species they are cared for in an unusual fashion. In *Octopus*, for example, the female cleans them with the tips of her arms or with jets of water. In *Argonauta* they are gathered together in a nidamental shell secreted by a pair of modified oral arms. The eggs are large, rich in yolk, undergo discoidal segmentation, and the embryos feed off a yolk sac.

▼ | Color variations in the octopus.

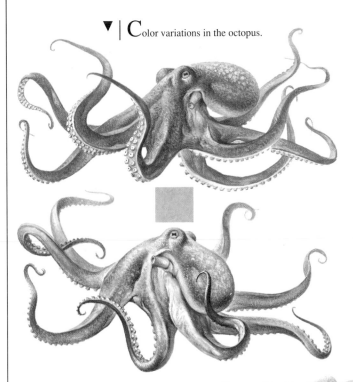

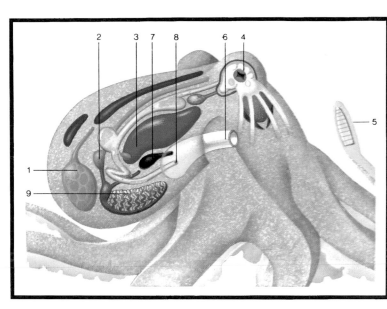

▲ | Diagram of the anatomy of the octopus: 1) gonad; 2) heart; 3) liver; 4) eye; 5) hectocotylus arm; 6) funnel; 7) ink sac; 8) anus; 9) gill.
With the exception of *Nautilus,* all cephalopods are capable of emitting a dense cloud of "ink" if disturbed. This is secreted by a special gland.

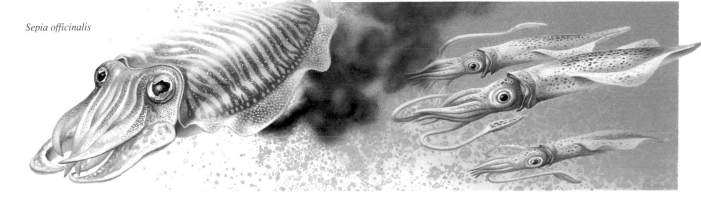

Sepia officinalis

Loligo vulgaris

Cuttlefish bone

▼ | Detail of suckers with a toothed horny ring on the oral arms of a decapod.

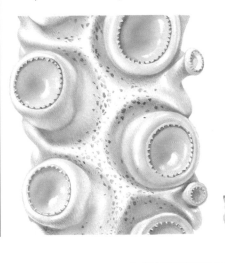

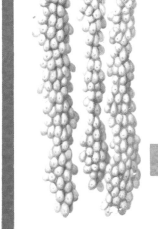

D iagram showing the stages in the development of an octopus. The eggs are attached in strings to the roof of the animal's hole. The embryos develop inside the eggs and feed off a yolk sac, which is completely absorbed by the time that the young individual hatches.

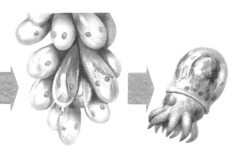

ECHINODERMATA

Starfish and sea urchins are the best known representatives of the large group of Echinodermata, invertebrates whose members are to be found throughout the world's seas from the shoreline to the deepest ocean depths. Their variety, beauty of form, and coloration make them some of the most attractive aquatic creatures.

Echinoderms are defined by three essential characteristics. Firstly, their bodies appear to have a spoked structure, the various parts being arranged around one main axis. As a result, they are radially symmetrical externally, although their internal organs are essentially bilaterally symmetrical and it is not possible to divide the body into radially arranged sections or actinomeres. Nevertheless, the majority of forms appear to display radial symmetry. The common, five-armed starfish are a particularly clear example. Their bodies can be divided into two symmetrical halves by drawing a line through any of their five arms and the opposite angle. Echinoderms are generally pentamerous since five radial and five interradial zones alternate around the central axis and this passes through the mouth.

A second notable feature of the echinoderms is their covering of calcareous plates. These are arranged in various ways and provide an armor that, while it is developed to varying degrees, is not external to the tissues of the body, since it is covered by an integument composed of an epithelium and part of the skin. The plates frequently bear granules, tubercles or spines, and these play a large part in shaping the animal's appearance.

The third feature is the presence of an internal water-vascular system consisting of fluid-filled canals. One canal circles the gut just behind the mouth and gives rise to canals that run along each radial zone. These canals are connected to numerous small and highly mobile hollow tentacles known as tube feet or podia. The tube feet often end in suckers and are arranged in two or more rows that run along each radial zone. The radial zones are in fact sometimes known as ambulacra, as opposed to the interambulacra lying between them. The circular canal of the water-vascular system also gives rise to a canal leading to the madreporite. This is a perforated plate

Echinoid

Holothuroid

▲ The starfish *Luidia ciliaris* is an intense orange color and lives down to depths of 7,350 ft (400 m) in the Mediterranean and the eastern Atlantic, preferring sandy bottoms.

◀ In the majority of starfish (Asteroidea) the body can be divided by five planes of symmetry which cross at the center, where the mouth lies.

usually situated on the body's surface and it links the water-vascular system to the sea water outside. There may sometimes be more than one madreporite.

The body cavity, the coelom, varies in extent and contains a digestive system which may be tubular and sinuous, or sac-like. In the latter case it may or may not possess diverticula. Similarly, there may or may not be an anus. There is no blood circulation but there is a system of fluid-filled cavities or lacunae. The nervous system is simple in structure, lacks ganglia, and is not associated with any well developed or definite sense organs.

Echinoderms are extremely varied in size, ranging from species measuring only a few millimeters, while the snake-like bodies of *Synapta* reach several meters in length. No echinoderms are either colonial or parasitic. All species live in the sea and are a major component of the fauna of both tropical and polar seas. Numerous echinoderms are highly adapted to an abyssal life.

They have a very varied diet. Starfish in particular are voracious predators and will even devour animals that match them in size. Their first line of defense consists of their dermal skeleton, a calcareous armor which in many cases bears a formidable array of spines.

The reproductive organs of echinoderms are very simple structures. As a rule the sexes are separate and there is no sexual dimorphism. The eggs are generally released into the water and then fertilized. They hatch into minute, bilaterally symmetrical larvae. Whereas the adults are typically benthic, the larvae are planktonic and swim about freely in the water by means of the beat of their numerous cilia. They continue to do so for a variable length of time, until, with the completion of their metamorphosis, they descend to the bottom and acquire their final adult form. It is an almost invariable rule that development is indirect, with a pelagic, bilaterally symmetrical larval phase and a benthic adult phase which usually appears to be radially symmetrical. There are, however, instances of direct development, hermaphroditism, and species that brood their young.

The five modern echinoderm classes are the Crinoidea, Holothuroidea, Asteroidea, Ophiuroidea, and Echinoidea.

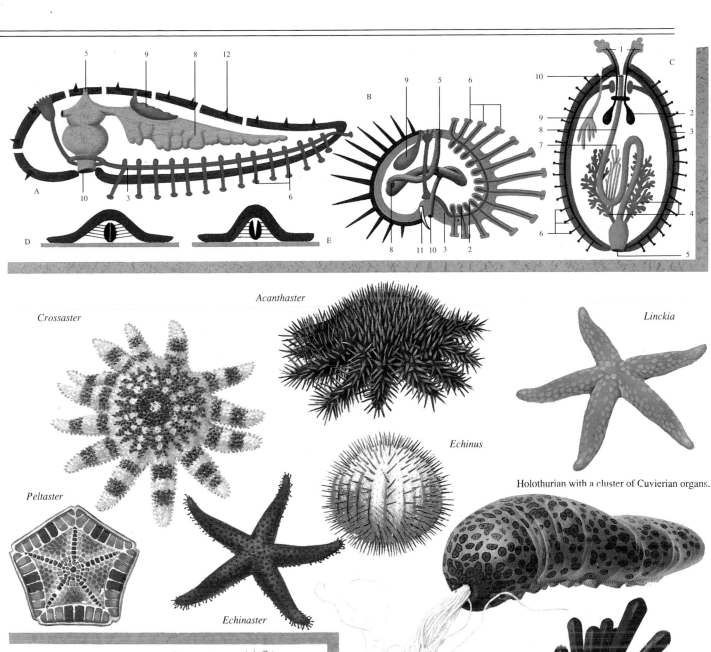

Crossaster

Acanthaster

Linckia

Peltaster

Echinus

Echinaster

Holothurian with a cluster of Cuvierian organs.

Heterocentrotus

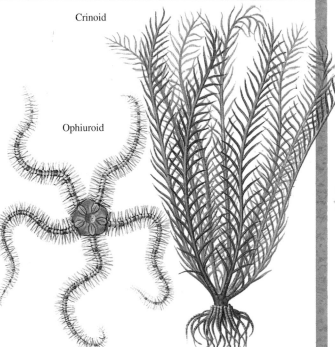

Crinoid

Ophiuroid

This plate shows some members of the large group Echinodermata, which in the variety and beauty of their forms are among the most attractive of aquatic creatures.
Top: vertical section through an asteroid (A); the anatomy of an echinoid (B); and a holothuroid (C).
For all figures: 1) oral tentacles; 2) tentacle ampullae; 3) radial canal of the water-vascular system; 4) respiratory tree; 5) anus; 6) tube feet; 7) Cuvierian organs; 8) intestine; 9) gonad; 10) mouth; 11) tooth; 12) skeletal plate with spine.
D-E) Two stages in the opening of a bivalve shell by a starfish using its tube feet.

TUNICATA
CEPHALOCHORDATA

Tunicata and Cephalochordata are two groups of marine animals closely related to vertebrates, together with which they form the phylum Chordata. This phylum includes organisms that for at least part of their lives possess a rigid and elastic chord of turgid cells enclosed in a sheath. This structure is known as the dorsal chord or notochord. It lies in the median sagittal plane beneath the neural tube and above the gut. However, this structural plan cannot easily be recognized in the various classes since, with the exception of the Cephalochordata, it may be lost in the course of development.

The Chordata is divided into three subphyla. The first is the Tunicata or Urochordata, in which the chord is only present in the tail of the larvae and in the tail of the adults, if they possess one. The second is the Acrania or Cephalochordata, in which the chord extends from one end of the animal to the other and persists throughout its life. The third is the Vertebrata or Hemicephalochordata, in which the chord is always present during embryonic development, when it extends from the mid brain to the posterior end of the animal, but in adults it is generally replaced by the vertebrae.

Tunicata are all marine animals and are characterized by the possession of a test known as the house or tunic. This is composed of a cellulose-like substance and contains a scattering of cells. Unlike other chordates, they are unsegmented. There are three classes: Ascidiacea, Thaliacea, and Larvacea.

Ascidians are all sessile with a pelagic larval phase. Some are solitary while others are colonial. Their bodies are sac-like, with two circular openings that are extended as short tubes, the oral and atrial siphons. The oral siphon leads to the sac-like pharynx or branchial chamber whose walls are perforated by numerous branchial stigmata, a fact that results in it often being referred to as the branchial basket. Posteriorly, the branchial basket opens into the esophagus, which is followed by the stomach, a looped intestine, and the rectum. This opens into the peribranchial chamber or atrium and partially surrounds it. The atrium opens to the outside through

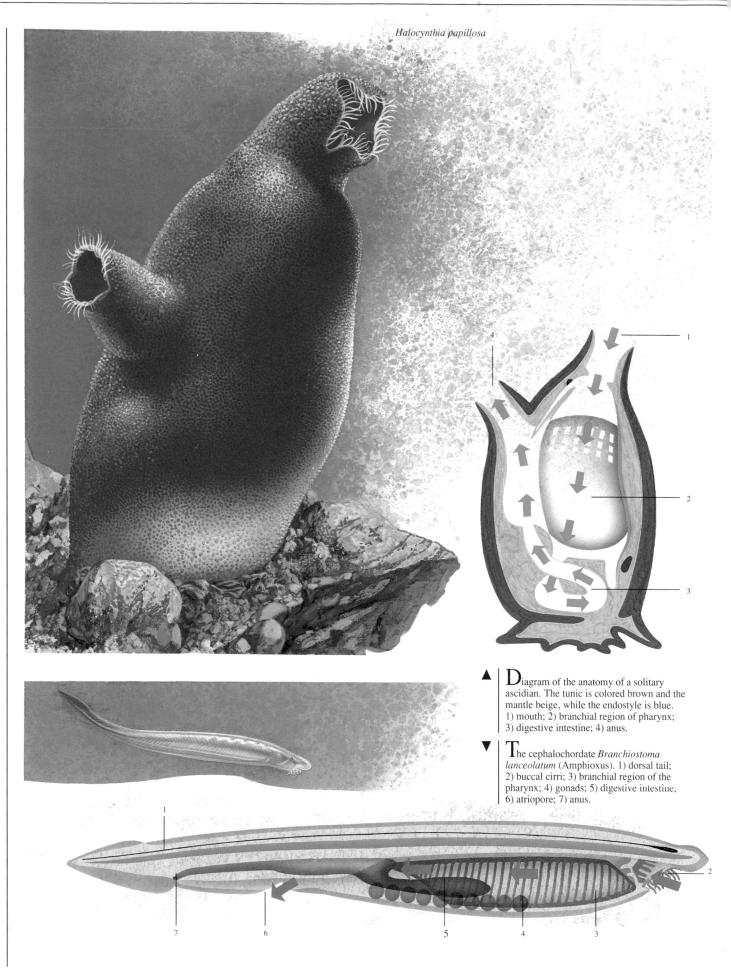

Halocynthia papillosa

▲ Diagram of the anatomy of a solitary ascidian. The tunic is colored brown and the mantle beige, while the endostyle is blue. 1) mouth; 2) branchial region of pharynx; 3) digestive intestine; 4) anus.

▼ The cephalochordate *Branchiostoma lanceolatum* (Amphioxus). 1) dorsal tail; 2) buccal cirri; 3) branchial region of the pharynx; 4) gonads; 5) digestive intestine; 6) atriopore; 7) anus.

the atrial siphon.

Ascidians are filter feeders and water flows continuously through the oral siphon, into the branchial chamber and out through the stigmata and the atrial siphon. They are hermaphrodites. The larvae lead a pelagic life for a few hours and then attach themselves to a substrate, usually a hard one, and undergo metamorphosis. The tail, together with its contents, is reabsorbed and the juvenile siphons open. Ascidians are widely distributed in the coastal waters of all the world's seas.

The class Thaliacea is composed entirely of pelagic organisms very similar in structure to the ascidians. The tunic and entire body are generally transparent, with the exception of the visceral mass and the gonads. All forms display an alternation of asexual and sexual generations. The Thaliacea is divided into three orders: the Pyrosomidea, Doliolidea, and Salpidea.

The Pyrosomidea are colonial forms, strongly luminescent, as a result of two organs lying to the sides of the branchial region immediately beneath the oral siphon. The Doliolidea are small, barrel-shaped organisms a few millimeters or, exceptionally, centimeters in length. Like other members of the Thaliacea, the Salpidea (salps) are pelagic filter feeders with transparent bodies and an intensely colored visceral mass.

Finally, Larvacea or Appendicularia is a class of small pelagic tunicates in which the typical chordate structural plan persists throughout life. Their bodies are generally transparent and consist of an ovoidal trunk and a tail. As such, they resemble ascidian larvae, hence the name Larvacea.

Larvaceans are distributed throughout the world's seas but are particularly abundant in coastal waters (the neritic zone) where the phytoplankton is richest.

Cephalochordata are small, marine organisms about 2 – 3 in (5 – 7 cm) long and fish-like in appearance. Their name derives from the fact that the chord extends from head to tail. This structure also persists in the adults. The body is nearly transparent and slightly compressed, giving it a lanceolate appearance. Only two genera are known. Cephalochordates live on soft bottoms in shallow waters. They feed by filtering small organic particles.

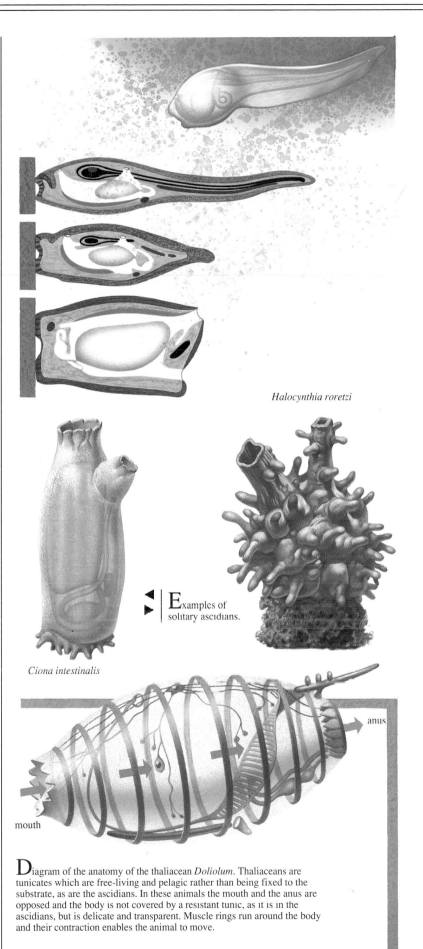

Halocynthia roretzi

Ciona intestinalis

◀
▶ Examples of solitary ascidians.

Diagram of the anatomy of the thaliacean *Doliolum*. Thaliaceans are tunicates which are free-living and pelagic rather than being fixed to the substrate, as are the ascidians. In these animals the mouth and the anus are opposed and the body is not covered by a resistant tunic, as it is in the ascidians, but is delicate and transparent. Muscle rings run around the body and their contraction enables the animal to move.

mouth

anus

◀ Stages in the metamorphosis of a larval ascidian. After it attaches itself to the substrate by its adhesive papillae, the larva, which to begin with resembles a tadpole, reabsorbs its tail. Meanwhile the developing internal organs rotate to reach their final positions.

▼ An example of a colonial ascidian, *Botryllus schlosseri*. It is common and widespread in the North Sea. The tunics of the various individuals that form the colony join together to form a gelatinous mass. In the center of the colony there is a common, shared chamber, the atrium, into which the waste is emptied.

SEA LAMPREY

Petromyzon marinus

Class Cyclostomata
Order Petromyzontiformes
Family Petromyzonidae
Length 31 – 35 in (80 – 90 cm)
Weight 3 – 5½ lb (1.5 – 2.5 kg)
Distinctive features Mouth surrounded by suctorial funnel; no fins except for the caudal and dorsal which is divided in two in the adult
Coloration Dorsal and lateral regions whitish with black spots which sometimes meet to form a dorsal lattice in the adult; the young vary in color from light gray to yellow or shades of brown
Reproductive period Migrates to rivers in spring and reproduces in the following season from May to July
Eggs 20,000 – 240,000; 1 mm in diameter
Sexual maturity 5 – 6 years of age

The sea lamprey is eel-like and the body is covered in a scaleless epidermis which is rich in mucous glands, making it highly viscous. The head terminates in an oral suctorial funnel with a series of horny teeth. The pharynx opens out in the center of the buccal funnel and the tongue also has pointed horny teeth which are used to pierce and break down the tissues of the victim. The compound eyes are well developed, for sight is perhaps the most important sense to the survival of this form which can sometimes chase and attack a fish at surprising speeds.

The respiratory system consists of gill pouches ranged along the sides of the pharynx, each coming out through its own individual gill slit. The water that carries oxygen for respiration is not conducted to the gills through the mouth but through the seven apertures by rhythmic movements of the branchial "basket."

The larvae of the sea lamprey, the ammocoetes, take three to five years to develop. The metamorphosis takes about three months to complete. The young lamprey then migrates to the sea (or the Great Lakes in America) where it generally stays in the shallow coastal depths feeding on cod, mackerel, trout or salmon, and also, at times, on sea mammals. After spending some three to five years in the sea, the lampreys reach sexual maturity and begin their migration up the rivers at about the beginning of

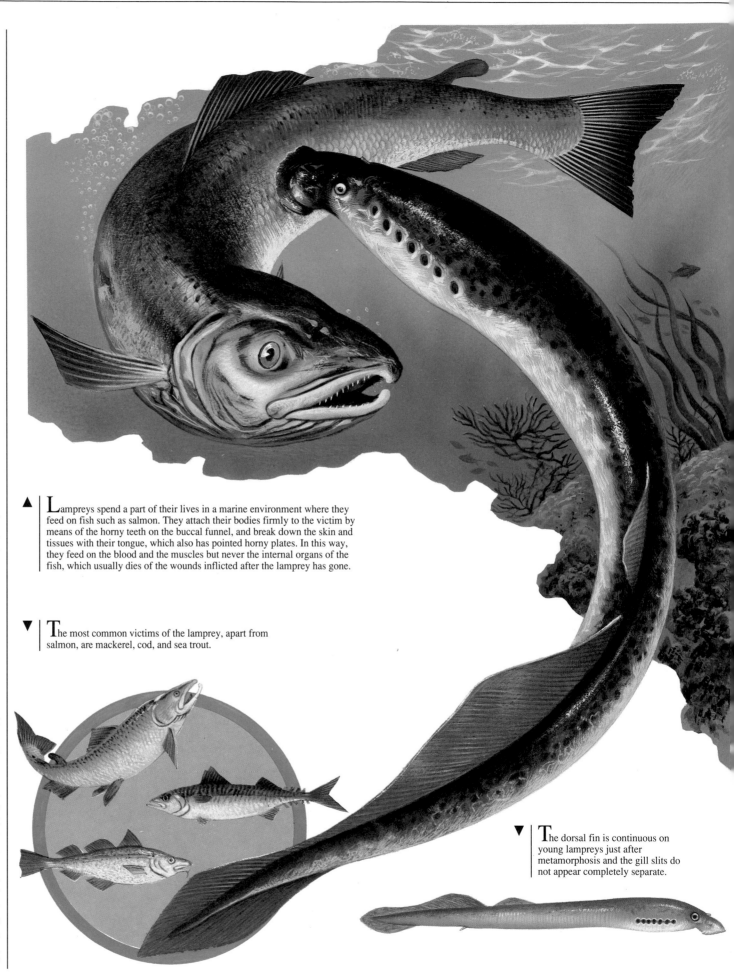

▲ Lampreys spend a part of their lives in a marine environment where they feed on fish such as salmon. They attach their bodies firmly to the victim by means of the horny teeth on the buccal funnel, and break down the skin and tissues with their tongue, which also has pointed horny plates. In this way, they feed on the blood and the muscles but never the internal organs of the fish, which usually dies of the wounds inflicted after the lamprey has gone.

▼ The most common victims of the lamprey, apart from salmon, are mackerel, cod, and sea trout.

▼ The dorsal fin is continuous on young lampreys just after metamorphosis and the gill slits do not appear completely separate.

spring. They stop feeding during this period and the horny structures in their suctorial funnels tend to regress. While climbing the rivers, the males and females undergo a series of morphological changes: the dorsal fins of the female increase in size and cutaneous swellings appear in the anal region. The second dorsal fin also increases in size on the male and the anal papilla transforms into a copulatory organ.

The lampreys also show an active interest in light just before beginning their ascent of the rivers, and so leave the shaded areas where they spent their lives at sea. This change in their habits is essential in that mating takes place in river areas that are exposed to sunlight. Once they have reached a suitable spot in which to lay their eggs, the so-called "grayling zone" where the water is not too cold but is clean and well oxygenated, the males choose a calm spot with a sandy or gravelly bottom where the water is about 30 – 48 in (80 – 120 cm) deep. There they begin to build their nest, digging a round ditch about 24 in (60 cm) in diameter, using the buccal funnel to move stones or other materials.

When the nest is complete, the female attaches to some object on the wall of the nest, such as a branch or a stone, while the male fastens to her with his buccal funnel on the branchial region and presses the abdomen of the female to aid the discharge of the eggs which are immediately fertilized before dropping into the nest. The female then moves off and mates with other males, while her partner covers the fertilized eggs as soon as they have been laid. The eggs take 10 to 20 days to develop, depending on the temperature of the water. As soon as they have emerged, the larvae absorb the yolk sac (a source of food in the earliest stages of life outside the egg) and then move to an area with a muddy bed where they dig small tunnels not much longer than their own bodies. Their anterior section projects from this tunnel with the buccal funnel pointing upstream to facilitate the entry of water containing small particles of food which are filtered by the fine branchial lamellae. The adults, which undergo a regression of the hard buccal teeth while climbing the rivers to avoid injury during mating, can no longer feed, and so die after laying the eggs.

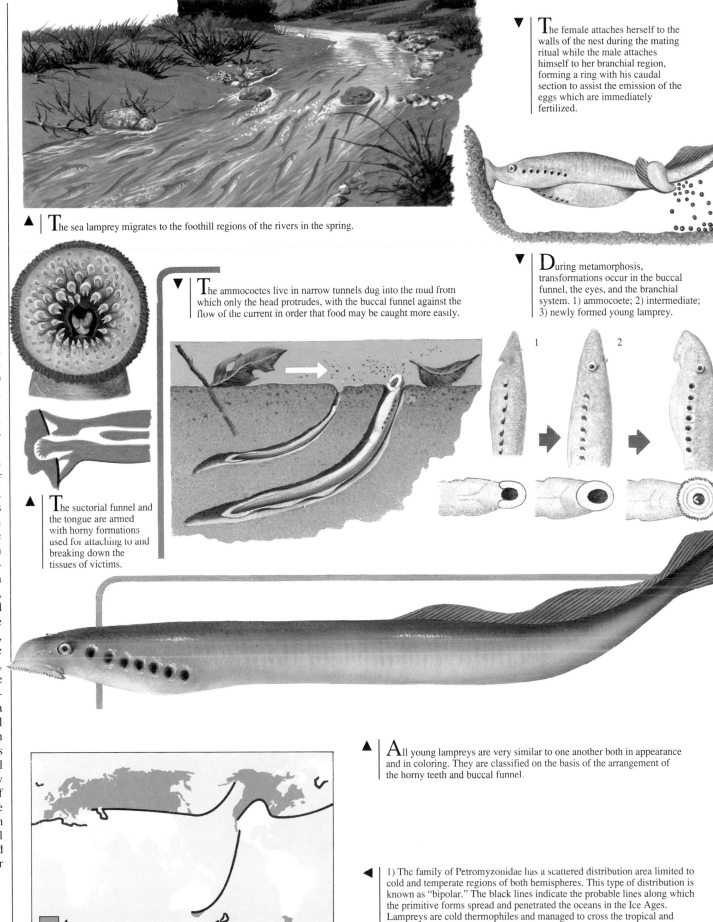

▲ | The sea lamprey migrates to the foothill regions of the rivers in the spring.

▼ | The female attaches herself to the walls of the nest during the mating ritual while the male attaches himself to her branchial region, forming a ring with his caudal section to assist the emission of the eggs which are immediately fertilized.

▼ | The ammocoetes live in narrow tunnels dug into the mud from which only the head protrudes, with the buccal funnel against the flow of the current in order that food may be caught more easily.

▼ | During metamorphosis, transformations occur in the buccal funnel, the eyes, and the branchial system. 1) ammocoete; 2) intermediate; 3) newly formed young lamprey.

▲ | The suctorial funnel and the tongue are armed with horny formations used for attaching to and breaking down the tissues of victims.

▲ | All young lampreys are very similar to one another both in appearance and in coloring. They are classified on the basis of the arrangement of the horny teeth and buccal funnel.

◄ | 1) The family of Petromyzonidae has a scattered distribution area limited to cold and temperate regions of both hemispheres. This type of distribution is known as "bipolar." The black lines indicate the probable lines along which the primitive forms spread and penetrated the oceans in the Ice Ages. Lampreys are cold thermophiles and managed to cross the tropical and equatorial zones by taking advantage of cold currents in the ocean deep.

ATLANTIC HAGFISH

Myxine glutinosa

Class Cyclostomata
Order Myxiniformes
Length 10 – 14 in (25 – 35 cm),
exceptionally 18 in (45 cm)
Weight 3 – 14 oz (80 – 400 g)
Distinctive features Gill chamber
connects with the exterior through one
single spiracle; mouth horseshoe-shaped
with one palatine tooth and two rows of
teeth on the tongue; four pairs of
tentacles (two nasal and two buccal)
Coloration Grayish brown and blue–
gray on the back, whitish on the belly
Reproductive period All year
Eggs 15 – 20, oval shaped and $1/2$ – 1 in
(1.5 – 2.5 cm) long
Sexual maturity About 2 or 3 years of
age

The hagfish is eel-like in shape and its
body is covered in a very fine and easily
removable skin. Along the lower edge
of the body there are two lines of
mucous glands which in special cases,
such as when the fish is in danger, can
secrete great quantities of mucus.
Unlike the petromyzonids, it has no lips
and the mouth is surrounded by two
pairs of marginal tentacles. There are
two cartilaginous laminae on the
tongue, one on each side. The eyes are
very small and deep-set with no crystalline lens. They do have a retina but it
does not function. There are a certain
number of photosensitive cells along the
surface of the body, concentrated
mainly at the two ends, so the animal
can move equally easily in either direction.

The hagfish, like all other members
of the family, lives entirely at sea where
it generally inhabits the bottom in small
tunnels dug into the mud. The species is
found in abundance along the north
coasts of the Atlantic Ocean on both the
European and American sides, along the
coasts of New England, in the Norwe-
gian fjords, and occasionally in the
Mediterranean.

Not much is known about the biology
of the hagfish because it is impossible to
observe in its natural habitat. They are
very difficult to rear in aquaria where
even if they are successfully kept alive
they do not reproduce, so any observations can only be purely general.

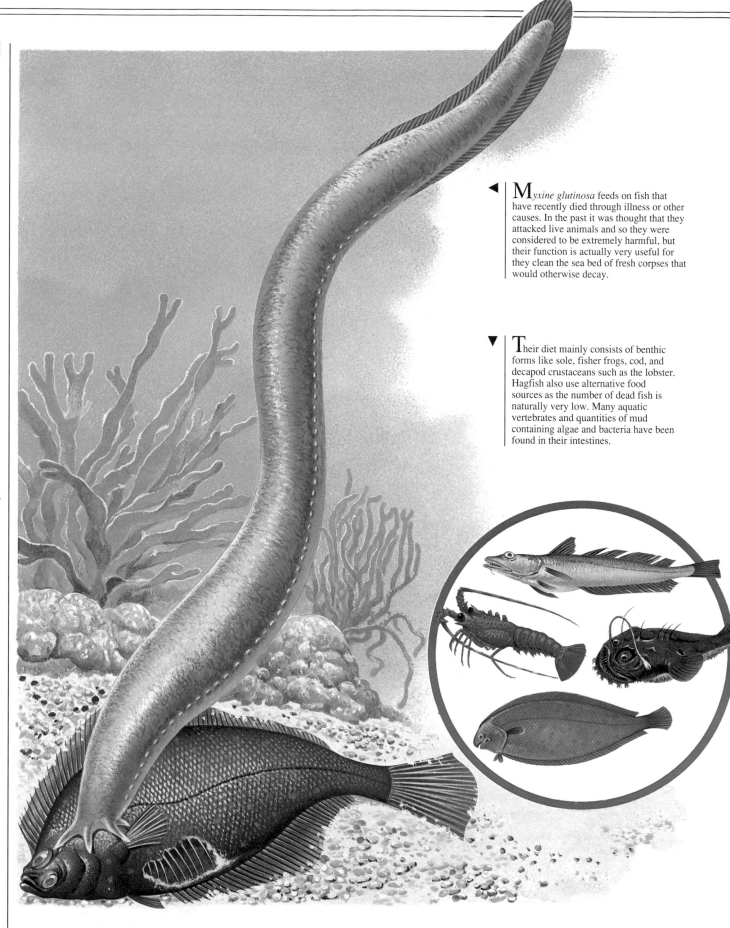

◀ M*yxine glutinosa* feeds on fish that
have recently died through illness or other
causes. In the past it was thought that they
attacked live animals and so they were
considered to be extremely harmful, but
their function is actually very useful for
they clean the sea bed of fresh corpses that
would otherwise decay.

▼ T*heir* diet mainly consists of benthic
forms like sole, fisher frogs, cod, and
decapod crustaceans such as the lobster.
Hagfish also use alternative food
sources as the number of dead fish is
naturally very low. Many aquatic
vertebrates and quantities of mud
containing algae and bacteria have been
found in their intestines.

Hagfish are gregarious and live in large communities. The areas in which they live are carpeted with a myriad of small craters making it look like a small volcanic landscape. They can also recognize and locate their own hole. Because of their elongated shape, they can dart backwards or forwards and can also form a sort of figure-of-eight knot with their bodies, winding them around to clean off mud or pull pieces of food off a victim.

Hagfish can live for long periods without food and can also live for many hours out of water if the outer temperature is not too high, which proves that their habits often take them to areas of the sea bed with little oxygen and scarse food supplies. They feed mainly off fish that have just died or which are in terrible physical condition, but can also attack fish that are trapped and immobilized in bottom nets, in which case they penetrate into the buccal cavity of the victim and agglutinate the gills with their abundant mucous secretions, causing them to die of asphyxiation. They then attack the internal organs and flesh, leaving just the skeleton and skin. Fish are not their only source of food, for examination of the stomach contents of the hagfish that have been caught has revealed the presence of all sorts of invertebrates and organic detritus from the sea bed. Consequently, the life of the hagfish is fully analogous with mud-dwelling land animals such as the earthworm.

The myxinid family has few members, all of which are marine forms, have similar habits, and no larval stage. Three genera are currently known with around twenty species. They are distinguished from each other on the basis of how many gill slits they have. The genus *Myxine* includes ten species that are commonly found throughout the temperate zones of the globe. The genus *Paramyxine* has only one species, *Paramyxine atami*, found along the coasts of Japan. The genus *Bdellostoma* includes forms distributed along the northern and southern slopes of the Atlantic and Pacific Oceans. The species *Bdellostoma okinodeanum*, which lives in the seas of Japan, grows to the largest sizes in the whole family, reaching 32 in (80 cm) in length.

The mouth of the hagfish is suctorial and there are a few rows of horny teeth on the tongue to scrape the body of the victim. Above: the mouth closed. Below: the mouth open.

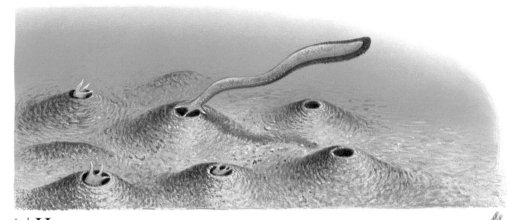

Hagfish dig small tunnels on the bottom of the sea and take refuge there when in danger. Each individual can find his own hole, even if it is some miles away.

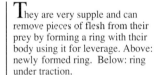

They are very supple and can remove pieces of flesh from their prey by forming a ring with their body using it for leverage. Above: newly formed ring. Below: ring under traction.

When nets and other fishing equipment are left for a long time in areas inhabited by hagfish, it is not uncommon to land fish that have been completely stripped of their flesh.

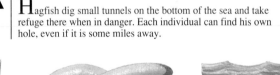

Pteraspis

Hemicyclaspis

Primitive cyclostomes, the ostracoderms spread widely from the Silurian to the Devonian periods (350 – 250 million years ago), but after the appearance of the placoderms, which were the first true fish, the former disappeared almost completely. Now modern living forms do not have the outer skeleton which was lost in the course of evolution. *Pteraspis*: modern hagfish developed from this form. *Hemicyclaspis*: ancient ostracoderms which evolved into modern petromyzonids.

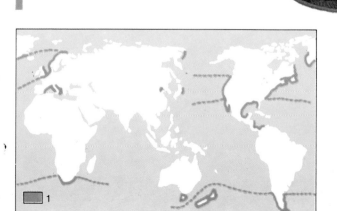

1

1) The distribution of the hagfish is similar in many ways to that of the lamprey, but the former are also found in South Africa. The numerous affinities between the species of the temperate zones of the two different hemispheres show that there is a possibility of movement between the various stocks along the ocean depths.

SHARKS
Squaliformes

Sharks are among the most interesting and particularly notorious sea creatures. The three terms "squaliforms," "sharks" and "maneaters" have to be accurately defined before any discussion, as the last two at least are commonly used and often lead to confusion. The term Squaliformes is used for all fish that, apart from having a cartilaginous skeleton, also have a body that is more or less clearly spindle-shaped, with lateral gill slits and an intestine that opens into a cloaca. Their overall appearance is highly characteristic. Shark is commonly used to replace the word "maneaters," although while all maneaters are sharks, the reverse is not true; not all sharks are maneaters. This is basically because not all sharks deserve the sinister reputation of being "killers," numbering all other living forms and even man among their prey. In fact the maneater does not even exist as a species, so it is important to remember that the name is really generic and imprecise.

The typical shark has a slender, graceful body that is slightly taller in the middle with a pointed snout, two dorsal fins, and a sickle-shaped tail. The snout is usually rather flat with ventral nostrils, each of which has one single aperture, unlike the case with nearly all bony fish. They open into a largish sac whose walls are covered with numerous parallel folds. The nasal valves are also folds of skin of various shapes located near to the nostrils which sometimes connect with the upper edge of the mouth through a naso-oral groove. Because of their carnivorous diet, their teeth are highly developed and are ranged on both jaws in many rows. They can vary in shape, often directly related to the type of food they eat, but are usually close together and have one or more points, with either smooth or serrated edges. In fact they may even differ in shape from one jaw to the other. There are usually four to six rows of teeth, of which only the first few are usually functional, with replacement teeth in the rows behind lying on the back surface of the jaw. These only straigthen up and become functional as the front teeth gradually wear and fall out.

One of the biggest, most widely distributed and most fearsome sharks is

The characteristic appearance of a large maneater such as a *Carcharodon carcharias*.

without a doubt the great white shark (*Carcharodon carcharias*). This enormous fish is found in the warm and temperate waters of all the oceans of the world, but never in great numbers. It lives in the open sea, but makes seasonal appearances near the coasts where it is unusual for it to be captured. It is a formidable predator, capable of swallowing its victims whole, even when they are quite large. It eats other sharks, tunny and other fish, tortoises, squid and octopus, and seals. There is certainly no room for doubt in its relations with man for it is truly a fearsome animal and there are many well documented records of fatal cases of aggression.

In 1884, the American ichthyologist S. Garman described a new species of shark, which he called *Chlamydoselachus anguineus*. Its overall appearance and certain structural details made this fish immediately worthy of more detailed study which brought out clear connections with the protoselachians. It is an ocean-dwelling fish that stays at the middle depths or near the sea bed.

In the whale shark (*Rhincodon typus*), particularly notable are the gill slits which are very large. Even more interesting, perhaps, are the numerous fine horny appendages on each gill arch. These make up the filtering system by which the animal traps the organisms on which it feeds. It is the largest living fish and well deserves its popular name as it can grow up to 60 ft (18 m) in length and can weigh over 10 tons. It feeds on plankton such as small crustaceans and also on small fish and mollusks.

Squaliforms include a great number of species which differ greatly from each other in appearance, way of life, and distribution. One such animal is the *Chlamydoselachus* which apart from other things has six gill slits while nearly all the other sharks have five. The *Hexanchus griseus* is found in all the oceans, where it lives at depths down to 5,900 ft (1,800 m). Its diet is made up of fish and crustaceans and it is ovoviviparous.

The first of the sharks with five pairs of gill slits is the strange *Heterodontus japonicus* which lives in the seas off China, Korea, and Japan. It lives off mollusks and sea urchins and is oviparious. *Orectolobus maculatus*, the carpet shark, is a shark with a wide, flat body that lives in the seas of Australia. It is benthic and measures about 6½ ft (2 m) in length. The sand tiger (*Odontaspis taurus*) is about 10 ft (3 m) long and is

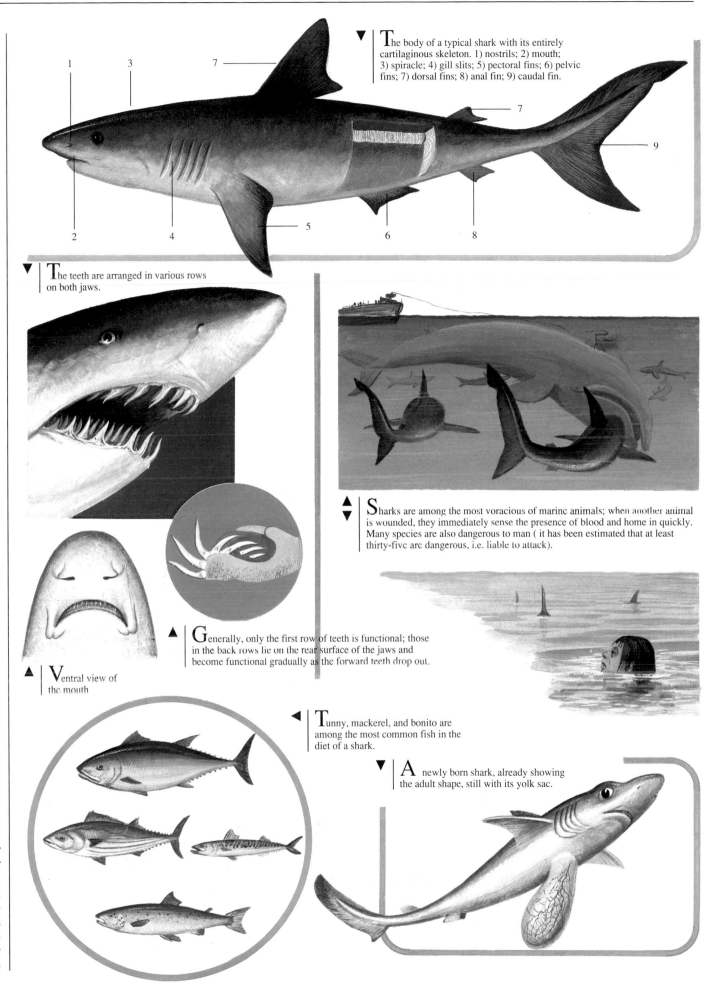

The body of a typical shark with its entirely cartilaginous skeleton. 1) nostrils; 2) mouth; 3) spiracle; 4) gill slits; 5) pectoral fins; 6) pelvic fins; 7) dorsal fins; 8) anal fin; 9) caudal fin.

The teeth are arranged in various rows on both jaws.

Sharks are among the most voracious of marine animals; when another animal is wounded, they immediately sense the presence of blood and home in quickly. Many species are also dangerous to man (it has been estimated that at least thirty-five are dangerous, i.e. liable to attack).

Ventral view of the mouth

Generally, only the first row of teeth is functional; those in the back rows lie on the rear surface of the jaws and become functional gradually as the forward teeth drop out.

Tunny, mackerel, and bonito are among the most common fish in the diet of a shark.

A newly born shark, already showing the adult shape, still with its yolk sac.

found in the Atlantic and occasionally in the Mediterranean.

The thresher shark (*Alopias vulpinus*) has an unmistakable appearance. Despite its size (up to 20 ft [6 m]), it is harmless. It is ovoviviparous and pelagic, usually staying near the surface where it feeds on fish and mollusks. The mako (*Isurus oxyrhyncus*) grows up to 13 ft (4 m) in length and is grayish blue in color. It is quite cosmopolitan as it is found in all warm and temperate seas. The porbeagle (*Lamna nasus*) is related to the mako though not found in warm seas, but in temperate and colder waters (Mediterranean and northern Atlantic). Both the mako and the porbeagle are dangerous to man.

Another of the giants of the sea that has the tail ridges is the basking shark (*Cetorhinus maximus*). It can grow up to about 43 ft (13 m) in length and weigh about 7 tons with only the whale shark being larger and heavier. Their diet consists only of planktonic organisms. It is found in the cold and temperate waters in both hemispheres of the Atlantic and Pacific Oceans.

Some of the smaller sharks are the spotted dogfish. There are two species in the Mediterranean and the eastern Atlantic: *Scyliorhinus canicula* (smaller spotted dogfish) and *Scyliorhinus stellaris* (larger spotted dogfish). The various species of the genus *Mustelus* (smooth hounds) are of considerably more value as fish products. *Mustelus mustelus*, the smooth hound, and *Mustelus asterias*, the stellate smooth hound, are common in the Mediterranean and the near Atlantic.

One of the largest groups of sharks is made up of the family of the Carcharhinidae, also classed as "maneaters." *Carcharhinus leucas* is a light or dark gray shark that grows to about 10 ft (3 m) in length. It prefers rays and other sharks for its diet; it is very aggressive and is included among the most dangerous species. It is found throughout the world in the coastal areas between the tropics, and often climbs up great stretches of rivers. Another member is *Carcharhinus plumbeus* (the gray shark) which grows up to 10 ft (3 m) in length and is commonly found in the Mediterranean and Atlantic; a related species is *Carcharhinus longimanus* which lives in all the tropical seas.

Some other sharks of the same genus are also considered dangerous to man, but the tiger shark (*Galeocerdo cuvieri*) has by far the worst reputation. It is found in all the warm seas, but even in

Various species of Squaliformes.

Isurus oxyrhynchus

Lamna nasus

Galeocerdo cuvieri

Prionace glauca

Cetorhinus maximus

Alopias vulpinus

Rhincodon typus

temperate zones, particularly in summer. This species could be said to eat anything, acting almost as an underwater dustman, as well as an insatiable predator. Another commonly found carcharhinid is the *Prionace glauca* which lives mainly in temperate seas.

The hammerhead sharks form a special family whose main feature is the shape of their heads which gives them their common name. The best known species is the *Sphyrna zygaena* which grows to about 13 ft (4 m) in length. It inhabits the warm and temperate regions of all the oceans and seems to prefer skates and stingrays as prey. The spiny dogfish (*Squalus acanthias*), which gets its common name from the sharp spine along the anterior edge of each dorsal fin, is common in the Mediterranean, the Atlantic, and the northern Pacific. Mediterranean specimens do not grow above 32 in (80 cm) but they can grow to three feet or more in other areas.

Another shark with no anal fin is the saw shark (*Pristiophorus japonicus*), particularly notable because of its similarity to the sawfish (*Pristis*). In fact its nose extends into a long flat blade-like rostrum, margined on both sides by teeth, but it has two long tentacles on the lower edge and so is not difficult to distinguish from the sawfish. It also grows to a maximum length of just 5 ft (1.5 m). This obviously shows a case of convergence, a similarity between two species that are in fact very different. The saw shark is ovoviviparous and its distribution area is limited to the seas of Japan, Korea, and China.

Another fish that is immediately recognizable because of its very special appearance is the angel shark (*Squatina squatina*) which shares its common name "angel" with other fish that are very different indeed. Its head is wide with a short nose, terminal mouth, and lateral gill slits as is normal with sharks. The pectoral fins are very wide, the dorsals very far back, and the caudal very small. Superficial examination of this fish suggests that it is more closely related to the rays than the sharks, but careful examination of its various structures clearly proves that this is not the case, and that the above characteristics are actually the result of its life on the sea bed. It is in fact benthic, preferring sandy or muddy beds where it often lies semi-interred, ready to capture fish and various invertebrates. It is ovoviviparous and can grow to more than 6½ ft (2 m). It lives in the Mediterranean and the eastern Atlantic.

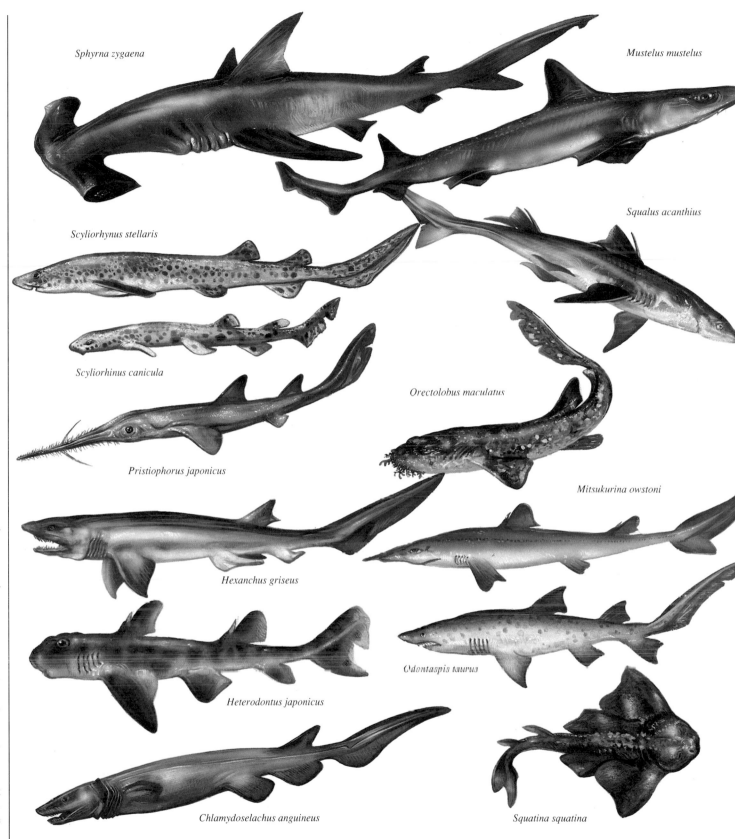

Squaliformes include numerous species that present highly varied features in the shape of the body, their customs, and distribution. Even the size and the coloring varies a lot. These fish are found in all the seas of the world and some tropical species are even found in fresh water.

RAYS
Rajiformes

There is a great number of fish with cartilaginous skeletons living on the sea beds that are no less interesting in their own way than sharks, and rays are the classic example.

The name sawfish is particularly appropriate and covers various species of the genus *Pristis*. The anterior section of the body is quite flat and the nose stretches out in a long, characteristic blade which has a series of rigid and sharp tooth-like extensions on each side; this "saw" is such a solid and powerful weapon that it could easily lead to the mistaken assumption that it is bone rather than cartilage. Several species are known to man, each with, among other things, a different number of teeth on the blade (16 – 20 per side on *Pristis pristis*, 24 – 32 on *Pristis pectinatus*).

They are all widely distributed in the hot zones of all the oceans where they stay along the coasts and often climb the rivers, sometimes for quite long stretches as they can stand great variations in salinity. They feed on various animals which they drive out of the sea bed with their saws. Sawfish are ovoviviparous and give birth to many young with each delivery. The adults can grow quite large, up to 20 ft (6 m) and weigh 3/4 ton or more.

The rhinobatids, or guitarfish (also known as violin fish) are also spindle-shaped and flat, but they have a pointed nose without the saw-like extension. This genus includes various species that are found mainly in tropical seas, although for some time two, *Rhinobatos rhinobatos* and *Rhinobatos cemiculus*, have also been known to live in the Mediterranean and the eastern Atlantic. Like members of the genus *Pristis*, they are also coastal and ovoviviparous.

With the exception of sawfish and guitarfish, all the other Rajiformes have a special characteristic appearance. Their bodies are clearly divided into two parts, the anterior end being called a "disk." The eyes are dorsal with the spiracles located behind them, although the latter may occasionally be found at the sides. The nostrils, mouth, and gill slits are ventral however, as is the cloaca aperture which is situated just before the tail.

The shape of the *Gymnura* is unmistakable for their disk is much wider than

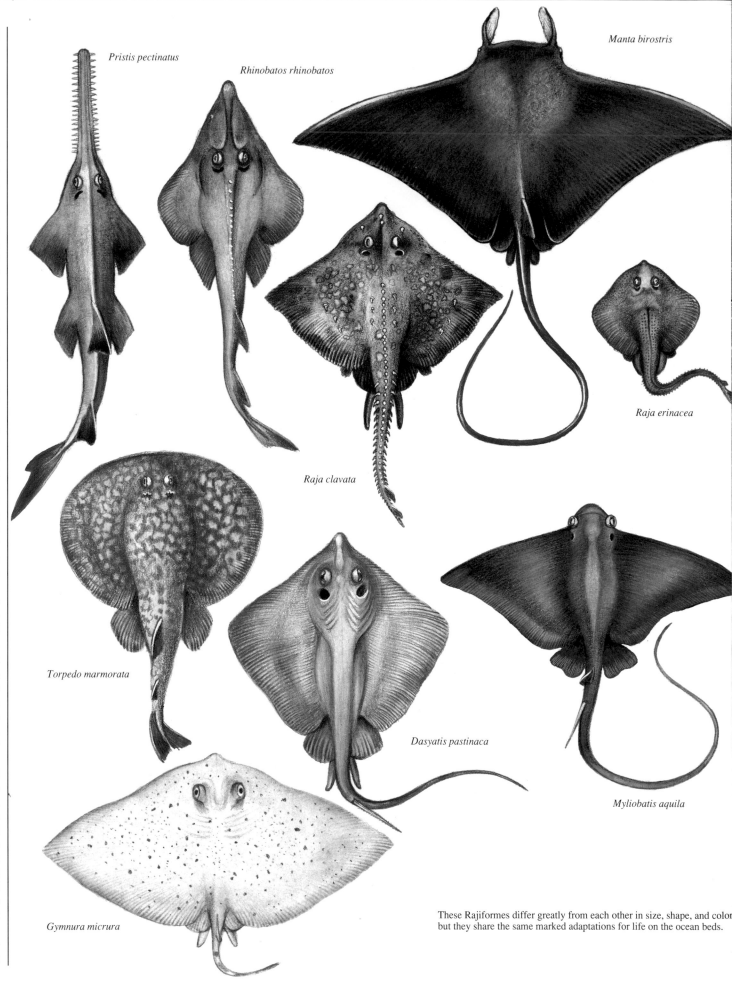

Pristis pectinatus

Rhinobatos rhinobatos

Manta birostris

Raja erinacea

Raja clavata

Torpedo marmorata

Dasyatis pastinaca

Myliobatis aquila

Gymnura micrura

These Rajiformes differ greatly from each other in size, shape, and color but they share the same marked adaptations for life on the ocean beds.

it is long. Its tail is very short and may or may not have a dorsal fin and sting. Many species are known, including the *Gymnura altavela* which is quite rare in the Mediterranean and more common in the tropical waters of the Atlantic. It grows to a maximum length of about 5 ft (1½ m) and is an olive–brown color, sometimes with darker patches. It seems to prefer mollusks in its diet and its teeth are very small with three points.

The myliobatids are generally known as eagle rays and have important features that distinguish them from the stingrays and butterfly rays. A significant distinguishing feature is the teeth, for instead of having the usual small teeth with one or more points, there are often grinding plates, one on each jaw, formed by the coalescence of flat and polygonal teeth ranged in rows. The tail is very slender, long, and almost filament-like at the end. There may be either a small dorsal fin or a poisonous caudal sting like that of the stingray. The best known species include *Myliobatis aquila* (Mediterranean and eastern Atlantic) and *Myliobatis tobijei* (China, Korea, Japan). Both of these fish can grow to over 3 ft (1 m) in length and are a uniform brown color.

They are not strictly benthic for they swim quickly, even at the surface and can be seen to leap out of the water. They are often gregarious, forming very large groups, and feed mainly on mollusks, grinding the shells easily with their dental plates which are custom-made for this purpose.

Eagle rays reproduce in the same way as the stingrays and are, in fact, ovoviviparous. They feed their embryos through the trophonemes as well as by the yolk contained in the egg, but they seem to be less prolific. The young are wrapped around themselves at birth, with the pectoral fins wrapped around their bodies, but they open out very quickly, a phenomenon which is also found in other families of Rajiformes, such as the devilfish. The young are sometimes different in color from the adults, for instead of being uniform, their back can be covered in patches or variegated with darker shades, though these patterns fade sooner or later depending on the species.

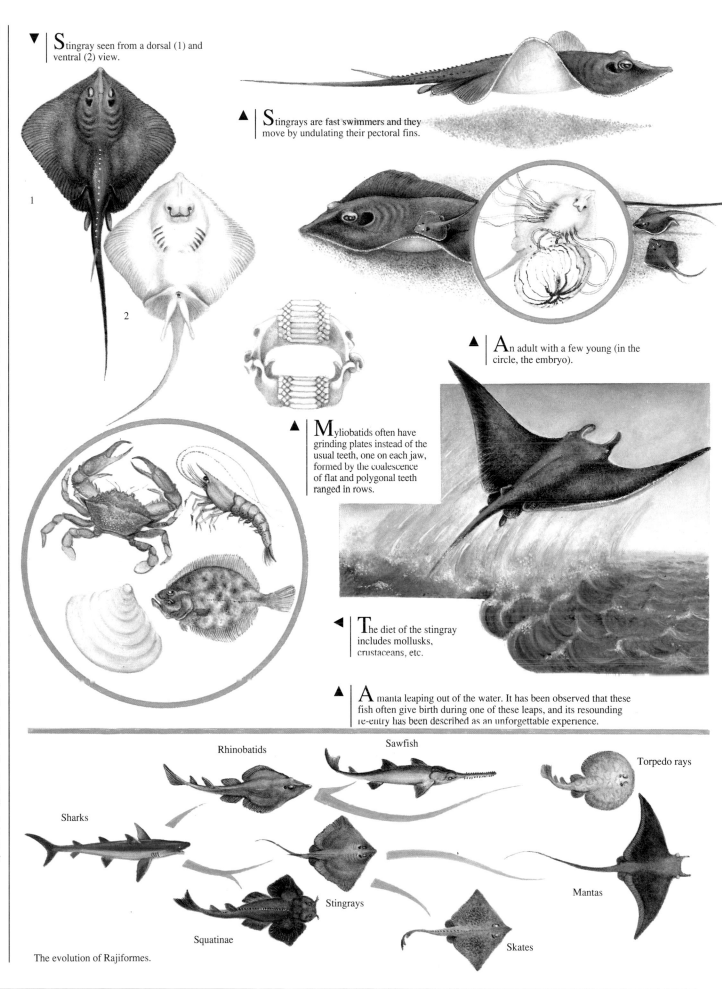

▼ Stingray seen from a dorsal (1) and ventral (2) view.

▲ Stingrays are fast swimmers and they move by undulating their pectoral fins.

▲ An adult with a few young (in the circle, the embryo).

▲ Myliobatids often have grinding plates instead of the usual teeth, one on each jaw, formed by the coalescence of flat and polygonal teeth ranged in rows.

◄ The diet of the stingray includes mollusks, crustaceans, etc.

▲ A manta leaping out of the water. It has been observed that these fish often give birth during one of these leaps, and its resounding re-entry has been described as an unforgettable experience.

Rhinobatids

Sawfish

Torpedo rays

Sharks

Squatinae

Stingrays

Skates

Mantas

The evolution of Rajiformes.

MANTAS AND STINGRAYS

The word "manta" means a blanket or cover in Spanish so the name becomes particularly appropriate for the enormous rajiform *Manta bisostris*. This species is particularly characterized by the two cephalic fins that jut out forwards like horns on either side of their wide terminal mouths. The manta can grow up to 23 ft (7 m) in width and weigh up to 1½ tons or more. This great fish with its strange appearance is found in all the tropical seas and penetrates into temperate zones in the summers. It has never been seen in the Mediterranean, however. The diet consists of small fish, crustaceans, and various types of planktonic organisms which are caught by the filtering appendages in its mouth.

Certain fish commonly found off the coasts of every sea in the world, including even quite large specimens, are especially feared because of the powerful poisonous sting in their tails. These fish are, in fact, stingrays, that is Rajiformes of the genus *Dasyatis*. They have a sharp spine sticking out of their tails with which they can inflict incredibly painful wounds because of the sting itself and also because of a powerful poison it injects. Stingrays live on different kinds of sea bed and have similar movement habits to the skates. They also feed on both fish and invertebrates. The stingray was known by the ancients who were already familiar with the Mediterranean species. We now know of the existence of many other species which are found in all the oceans of the world but particularly in the tropical regions.

Various stingrays are highly euryhaline, that is they adapt to different levels of salinity and so can penetrate inland waterways. This is the case with the great *Dasyatis sephen* (which measures up to 13 ft [4 m] in diameter), one of the most widespread stingrays in the Indian and Pacific Oceans. There are also stingrays that are exclusively river fish, but they belong to another genus: *Potamotrygon*. These can grow up to very large sizes and live only in the regions of South America east of the Andes.

Torpedo rays are among the most characteristic of sea dwellers for various reasons, but particularly because they

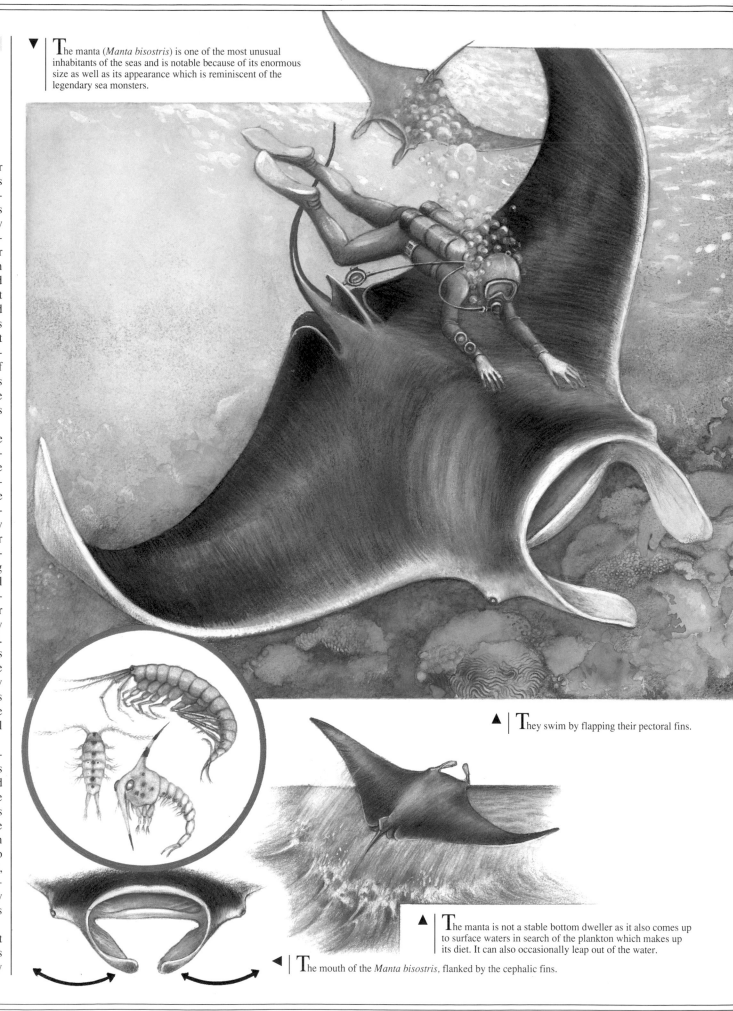

The manta (*Manta bisostris*) is one of the most unusual inhabitants of the seas and is notable because of its enormous size as well as its appearance which is reminiscent of the legendary sea monsters.

▲ | They swim by flapping their pectoral fins.

▲ | The manta is not a stable bottom dweller as it also comes up to surface waters in search of the plankton which makes up its diet. It can also occasionally leap out of the water.

◀ | The mouth of the *Manta bisostris*, flanked by the cephalic fins.

are "electric fish." They have no scales on their bodies, so their skin is bare and viscid. Their electrical power is generated by two kidney-shaped organs on the disk, one on each side between the brain and the pectoral fins. These are made up of a large number of gelatinous prisms of modified muscular tissue in a vertical arrangement similar to the plates in a battery. The electricity can be triggered for both offensive and defensive purposes. It was well known to the ancients who used it for a very basic type of early electrotherapy. Torpedoes are lazy, sedentary animals that usually settle on muddy or sandy beds. They are ovoviviparous and the young embryos look a little like sharks.

Skates are quite different from torpedoes in that their disks are more or less diamond-shaped and the nose is angular, sometimes even extending into a definite point. They are not electric fish although they do have rudimentary electric organs at the sides of the tail. They are oviparous, laying large eggs that are protected by characteristic large and rectangular horny brown shells similar to those of the smaller spotted dogfish. Skates also live on the soft sea beds where they lie for long periods, getting up now and again to swim about using their pectoral fins as wings to move quickly through the water. Their meat is edible and various species are quite commonly fished.

There are many species of skate which are often difficult to distinguish from each other, particularly when young. They are found in all the seas, but especially in cold and temperate zones. The thornback ray (*Raja clavata*) is easy to recognize because the adult has large scales, each with a sharp spine on its back and occasionally on its belly. It is gray or light brown with many black patches and can grow up to nearly 3 ft (1 m) in length, especially in the Atlantic where it is caught from the coasts of Morocco up to the most northerly coasts of Scandinavia. The starry ray (*Raja asterias*) is also very common, though in the Mediterranean only; it is smaller and decorated with light patches surrounded by a few darker points on an olive or yellowy background. Two species of giant rays found in the Mediterranean and eastern Atlantic are the *Raja alba* (the white skate) and the *Raja batis* (the flapper skate) which can grow to over 6½ ft (2 m) in length and weigh over 330 lb (150 kg) in weight. Both are found as far down as South Africa.

Dasyatis pastinaca

Stingrays are among the best known members of the Rajiformes – the cartilaginous fish that have to be classified as bottom dwellers because of their ecology. They are very reminiscent of rays in overall appearance and are distinguished mainly by the poisonous sting in their tails which are long and thin. This sting makes a formidable offensive and defensive weapon and is inserted into the dorsal section of the tail at varying distances between the base and the tip. Sometimes there are two of these stings, which are flat and covered in a fine layer of skin, with backward pointing teeth on both edges (i.e. they point towards the base of the sting). It also has small muscles, which give it a certain degree of mobility, and parallel grooves running along the whole lower surface between which lies the tissue that secretes the poison; this flows towards the far edge of the sting and is injected immediately. The serious effects were already known to the ancients and more than one writer made reference to them. These animals have a disk which is more or less quadrangular, but it can also be slightly rounded. The pectoral fins are rounded at the ends and the tail is long and thin with no terminal or dorsal fins, but often with longitudinal folds of skin. There are many small teeth.

STURGEON
Acipenseriformes

The Acipenseriformes are Chondrostei: their skeleton is mainly cartilaginous and the fins are supported by skeletal radii. The cranium remains cartilaginous all the fish's life. Ossification mainly affects the membrane bones of parts of the cranium, the jaws, and the scapular girdle.

The Acipenseriformes live both at sea and in fresh water but they all reproduce in freshwater habitats. One family of Acipenseriformes – the Chondrosteidae – is only known in the fossil state. We have known about Acipenseridae and Polyodontidae since the Upper Cretaceous period and these are the only known families at the present time.

In the Polyodontidae or paddlefish the snout is elongated in the form of a beak and considerably longer than the rest of the head. It is very flat and in some cases flexible. There are no barbels at the front of the mouth, which is set at the tip of the snout and opens forwards. The Polyodontidae live in the northeastern regions of North America (*Polyodon spathula* – the American paddlefish) and in China (*Psephurus gladius* – Chinese sturgeon).

In the Acipenseridae or true sturgeons the actual snout is slightly longer than the rest of the head. It is fairly flattened, but retains a conical shape. Beneath the snout, in front of the low-set mouth, there are four large barbels. The Acipenseridae live in temperate waters in the Northern Hemisphere. This family has four genera: *Acipenser*, which numbers 17 species; *Huso* (Adriatic sturgeon) with two species; *Scaphirhynchus* with two species; and *Pseudoscaphirhynchus*, which has three species.

The two species of the genus *Huso* are among the largest of all freshwater fish. One specimen of *Huso huso* (Adriatic sturgeon) has weighed as much as 3 tons. The genus *Huso* lives in the Adriatic basin, the Black Sea, and the Caspian Sea, and in the Amour river in Asia. The species belonging to the genus *Scaphirhynchus* are found in the Mississippi basin and the species of the genus *Pseudoscaphirhynchus* live in the Aral Sea region. The genus *Acipenser* is represented throughout the Northern Hemisphere and mainly in the Black Sea and Caspian Sea areas. The 17 species of this genus have five varieties

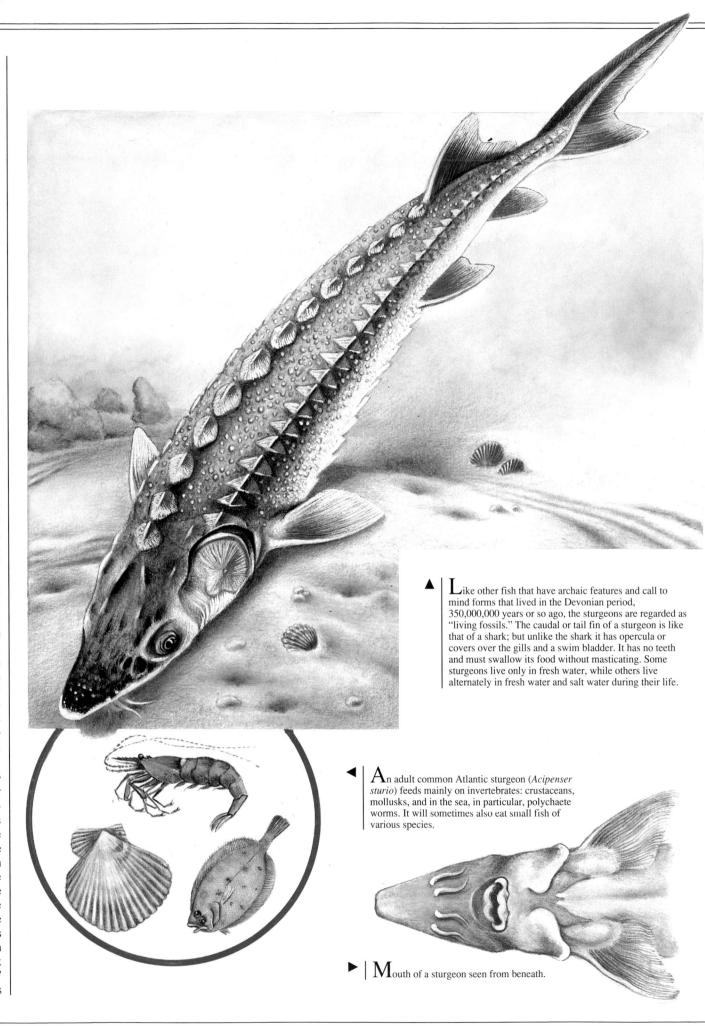

▲ Like other fish that have archaic features and call to mind forms that lived in the Devonian period, 350,000,000 years or so ago, the sturgeons are regarded as "living fossils." The caudal or tail fin of a sturgeon is like that of a shark; but unlike the shark it has opercula or covers over the gills and a swim bladder. It has no teeth and must swallow its food without masticating. Some sturgeons live only in fresh water, while others live alternately in fresh water and salt water during their life.

◄ An adult common Atlantic sturgeon (*Acipenser sturio*) feeds mainly on invertebrates: crustaceans, mollusks, and in the sea, in particular, polychaete worms. It will sometimes also eat small fish of various species.

► Mouth of a sturgeon seen from beneath.

distributed in North America, five in Europe, and seven in eastern Asia. *Acipenser sturio* can reach a length of 11 1/2 feet (3.5 m) and weigh up to 720 lb (320 kg).

In February or March sturgeons living in the Gironde estuary in France make their way up-river to breed. The males are usually more numerous than the females and also reach sexual maturity before them. The rendez-vous for egg laying is usually a gravel river bed. These breeding places are sometimes situated in the upper reaches of watercourses. When rivers had not undergone alterations to their course or banks or been effected by industrialization or pollution, sturgeons could be seen in the Garonne, as far up-river as Toulouse, in the Loire at Orléans, in the Seine in Paris, and in the Noselle at Metz. They used to be seen in the Rhône, the Saône and the Doubs, and in the Rhine there were sightings in Basle; they would swim up the Elbe right into Bohemia, the Oder as far as Breslau, and the Vistula as far as Krakow. At the present time *Acipenser sturio* has more or less vanished from the Baltic Sea and from its tributary rivers; and it has virtually disappeared from all the rivers of Britain and France, with the exception of the Gironde basin. Sturgeons also used to be fished in the Guadalquivir in Spain, but there are fewer and fewer of them. Throughout the Mediterranean basin the sturgeon has become extremely rare.

The eggs of *Acipenser sturio* are quite large – about 0.1 in (2.3 mm) in diameter on average. Once expelled from the female they cling to the bottom. Depending on the water temperature development takes 3 – 7 days (3 days at 68°F [19°C], 7 days at 57°F [14°C]). The fry grow quickly by the end of the first summer they measure 8 in (20 cm). After one year they measure 16 in (40 cm). They grow more quickly in the warm waters of the Mediterranean region than in more northerly areas. The fry gradually make their way into ever saltier waters and reach estuaries in about a year. After three more years or when they measure 24 in (60 cm) they reach the open sea. In the sea they live at various depths depending on their size: between 65 – 165 ft (20 – 50 m) individuals of 40 – 60 in (1 – 1.5 m), and at 400 ft (120 m) one can catch sturgeons measuring more than 6 1/2 ft (2m). Sturgeons have been sought after since time immemorial because of the quality of their flesh and for their eggs to make the famous caviar.

▲ To detect food the sturgeon uses its barbels round the mouth as sensory organs; there are four such "tentacles."

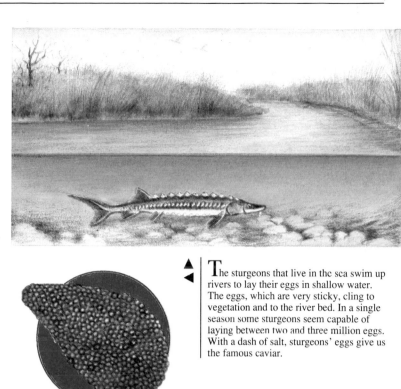

▲◀ The sturgeons that live in the sea swim up rivers to lay their eggs in shallow water. The eggs, which are very sticky, cling to vegetation and to the river bed. In a single season some sturgeons seem capable of laying between two and three million eggs. With a dash of salt, sturgeons' eggs give us the famous caviar.

▲ If the base of the tail undergoes severe strain, the fin breaks off and does not grow again.

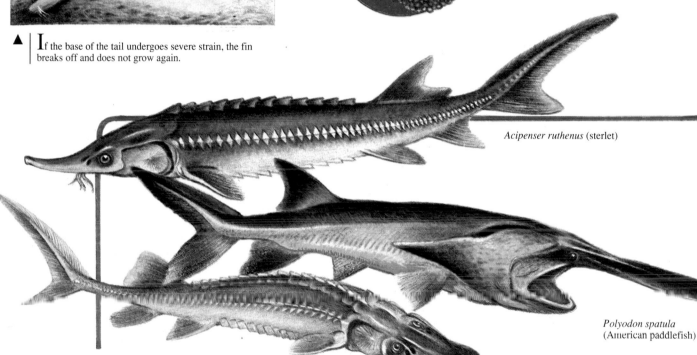

Acipenser ruthenus (sterlet)

Polyodon spatula (American paddlefish)

Scaphirhynchus platorhynchus (shovel-nosed sturgeon)

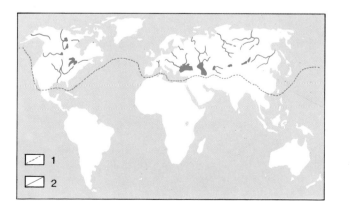

☐ 1
◫ 2

◀ 1) Lower distribution limit of the Acipenseridae. 2) The entire family of Acipenseridae, which includes four genera with about 24 species, lives in temperate waters in the Northern Hemisphere.

CHIMAERIFORMES

Chimaera monstrosa

The members of the family Chimaeridae have one median and two lateral rostral appendages instead of a cartilaginous snout. The body is stout at the front and tapers towards the back to an elongated caudal peduncle; hence the name "sea rat" by which these animals are sometimes known.

Chimaera monstrosa, known as "king of the herrings," may reach a maximum length of 3¾ ft (1.15 m), two thirds of which is accounted for by the long tail. The fish can weigh as much as 20 lb (9 kg). This species lives in the eastern Atlantic, from the Azores, Madeira, and Morocco northwards to Finland, Iceland, and the Skagerrak. It also occurs in the western Mediterranean and off South Africa.

Short-nosed chimaeras (known in Britain as rabbit fish but in other countries as sea rats or sea cats) live in fairly deep water, as far down as 650 ft (200 m), though they can occasionally be found at depths up to 3,300 ft (1,000 m). They may sometimes cross the tropical zone and swim from western Europe as far as South Africa. They feed on crustaceans, mollusks, echinoderms, and small fish. Man uses the liver which accounts for a third of the fish's whole weight and yields a valuable oil, used among other things for lubricating precision instruments. Care must be taken in catching these fish as the poisonous spine on the back can cause wounds that may prove fatal.

Chimaeras are egg-laying fish and may lay their eggs at any time of the year except in autumn. The ovaries contain up to 20 eggs.

Characteristic of the members of the family Rhinochimaeridae (long-nosed chimaeras) is an elongated snout that looks like a dagger. The species in this family live at depths from 2,000 ft (600 m) to 8,000 ft (2,600 m) and are only rarely caught.

The Callorhynchidae (plough-nosed or elephant chimaeras) have a rostrum modified to form a mobile club-shaped appendage which first projects obliquely outwards and then turns at an angle towards the mouth. The members of this family live in the temperate and cold seas of the Southern Hemisphere at depths of up to 590 ft (180 m).

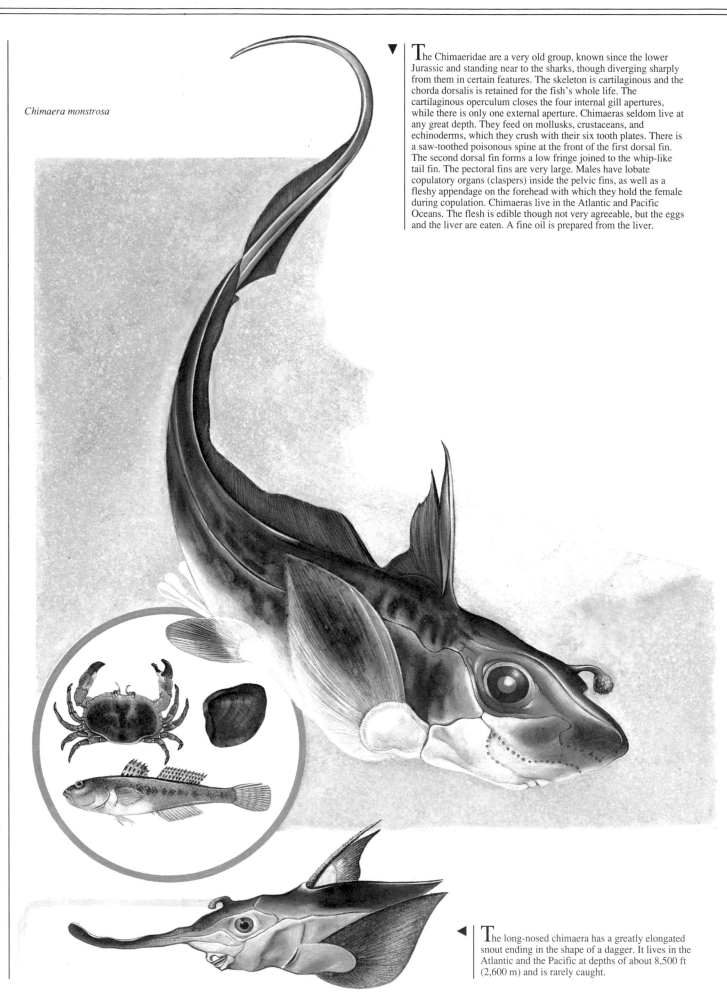

▼ The Chimaeridae are a very old group, known since the lower Jurassic and standing near to the sharks, though diverging sharply from them in certain features. The skeleton is cartilaginous and the chorda dorsalis is retained for the fish's whole life. The cartilaginous operculum closes the four internal gill apertures, while there is only one external aperture. Chimaeras seldom live at any great depth. They feed on mollusks, crustaceans, and echinoderms, which they crush with their six tooth plates. There is a saw-toothed poisonous spine at the front of the first dorsal fin. The second dorsal fin forms a low fringe joined to the whip-like tail fin. The pectoral fins are very large. Males have lobate copulatory organs (claspers) inside the pelvic fins, as well as a fleshy appendage on the forehead with which they hold the female during copulation. Chimaeras live in the Atlantic and Pacific Oceans. The flesh is edible though not very agreeable, but the eggs and the liver are eaten. A fine oil is prepared from the liver.

◄ The long-nosed chimaera has a greatly elongated snout ending in the shape of a dagger. It lives in the Atlantic and the Pacific at depths of about 8,500 ft (2,600 m) and is rarely caught.

ELOPIFORMES

From an evolutionary point of view, the order of the Elopiformes is currently considered to be one of the most archaic groups among the Teleostei. The main characteristics of the species belonging to this order are that they have a typical larval form that resembles the lepto-cephalus of the Anguilliformes. Elopi-formes are subdivided into two sub-orders: the Elopoidei with the families of elopids and megalopids, and the Albuloidei, with its family of albulids.

The family of the elopids (Elopidae) includes seven species which are all covered by one single genus. Character-istic features are the silvery coloration, the minute scales covering the body, and the large mouth. They are tropical sea species which occasionally climb into fresh water. *Elops saurus*, known as the lady fish, is the best known species, found along the western coast of the Atlantic. Young specimens live in pools and lakes, but the adults prefer to live in brackish or salty water.

The second family of the suborder of Elopoidei is that of the megalopids (Megalopidae). The family has one genus, *Megalops*, with two species, one of which, the *Megalops atlanticus*, is found in the Atlantic and the other, *Megalops cyprinoides*, lives in the Pacific and Indian Oceans. The Atlantic species is the better known of the two, particularly because of its size. It is known as the tarpon and can grow up to 8 ft (2.5 m) in length and weigh over 330 lb (150 kg). It is a silvery color and has large scales (some measuring up to 2 – 3 in [5 – 8 cm]) covering its body. Little is known about its biological cycle except that it lays a large number of eggs along the sandbanks of the west central coast of the Atlantic. They are not strictly tied to any particular envi-ronment as adults and frequently move between the coasts and brackish water to climb the rivers for short stretches.

The suborder of the Albuloidei and the family of the albulids (Albulidae) includes the marine species of the *Albula vulpes*, which is found in temperate and tropical areas. Its average weight is 2¼ – 4½ lb (1 – 2 kg) and it measures less than 3 ft (1 m) in total length. It has a pointed, conical snout which it uses to rummage around the muddy beds for the small benthic invertebrates that make up the main part of its diet.

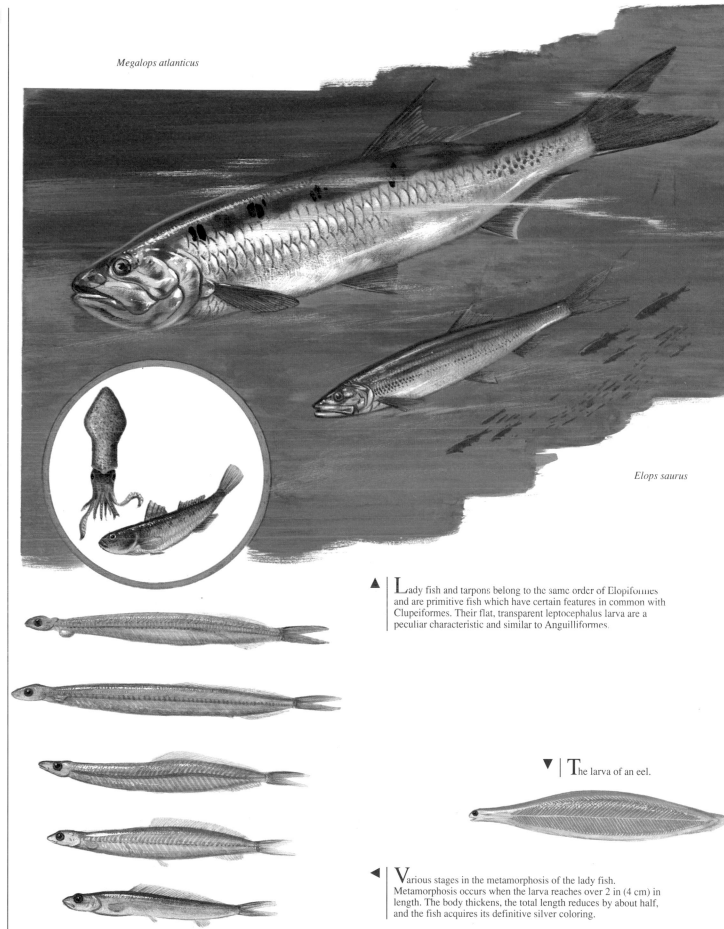

Megalops atlanticus

Elops saurus

▲ Lady fish and tarpons belong to the same order of Elopiformes and are primitive fish which have certain features in common with Clupeiformes. Their flat, transparent leptocephalus larva are a peculiar characteristic and similar to Anguilliformes.

▼ The larva of an eel.

◄ Various stages in the metamorphosis of the lady fish. Metamorphosis occurs when the larva reaches over 2 in (4 cm) in length. The body thickens, the total length reduces by about half, and the fish acquires its definitive silver coloring.

EELS
Anguilliformes

There are 16 species of eels (*Anguilla*). The best known are the following ones: the American eel, *Anguilla rostrata*, found from the northern part of South America and the Caribbean islands throughout most of the United States and Canada to southern Greenland;the European eel, *Anguilla anguilla*, widespread throughout Europe, from Iceland to North Africa, from the Canary Islands to the Black Sea; and the Japanese eel, *Anguilla japonica*, living in rivers in eastern China, Japan, and adjacent offshore islands.

The breeding behavior and the life history are among the most interesting attributes of the eel. Different species have different breeding grounds but, where known, the behavior and life histories are similar. To illustrate the general principles, the European eel will serve as an example.

For many centuries eels have been an important source of food. During those centuries countless millions of eels had been gutted for the table. Yet no eel had been found with ovaries or testes. This situation changed in 1777 when Professor Mondini of the University of Bologna identified, in a female eel, developing ovaries. The ovaries had frilled edges, immature eggs, and lay along the top of the abdominal cavity. A century later, in 1874, a Polish scientist, Syrsti, found testes in a medium-sized eel. The matter was settled in 1897 when the Italians Grassi and Calundruccio caught a sexually mature female eel in the Straits of Messina and confirmed Mondini's correct identification of the organs with the frilled edges. Six years later, in 1903, a mature male eel was caught off Norway. It was obvious that the eggs must be laid in the sea, but what happened between the eggs hatching and the larvae growing to some 6 in (15 cm) long was unknown.

Actually, the larva of the eel had already been described. In 1763 Theodore Gronovius published a description, and a figure, of a small, transparent leaf-like fish which he called Leptocephalus. Its true nature, however, was not realized. Grassi and Calundruccio in 1896 had the good fortune to catch two leptocephali alive in the Straits of Messina. They kept these alive in an aquarium and much to their aston-

All the freshwater eels belong to the genus *Anguilla*. Although born in the deep sea, they spend their adult life in fresh waters, both lakes and rivers. They can tolerate poorly oxygenated and slightly polluted waters. Eels will eat most forms of animal life of a suitable size. They are most active at night and spend the day inactive, hiding between rocks, or even buried in mud or sand with just the head exposed. All species of *Anguilla* are superficially similar and without knowledge of the locality can only be identified with difficulty.

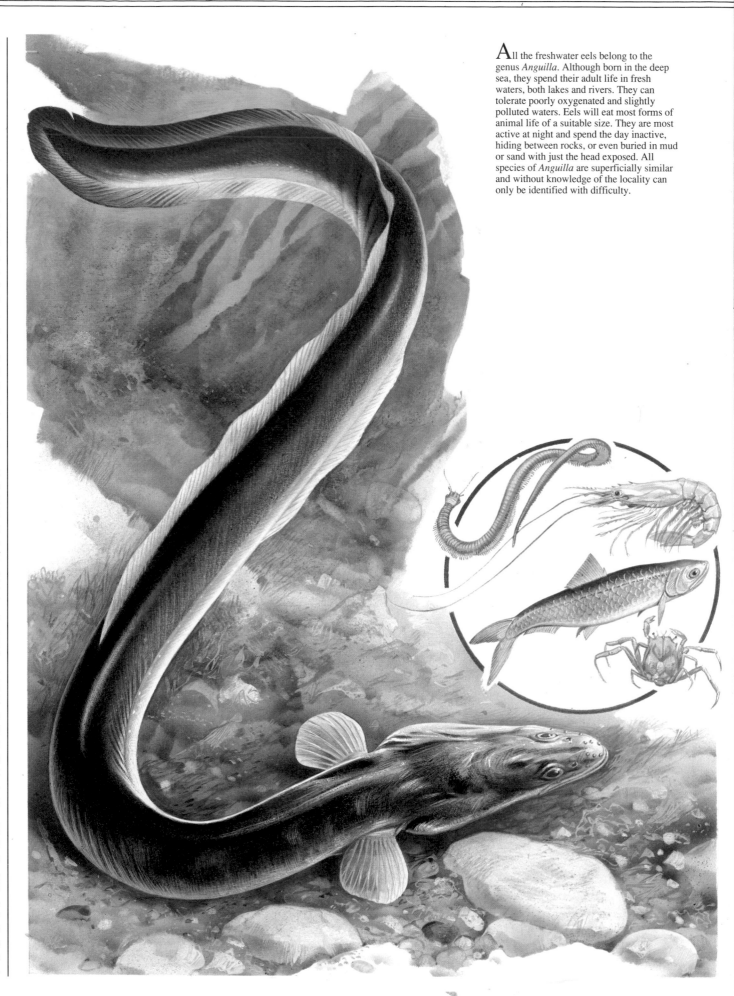

ishment the leptocephali soon changed shape and became recognizable as young eels.

A major problem remained. Where did they breed? The answer was soon found. Ships sailing across the Atlantic and Mediterranean had been taking samples of animal life at various stages. It was noticed that the smallest Mediterranean leptocephali were in the west, the largest in the east. This pointed to the Atlantic as the breeding ground. Johannes Schmidt studied the samples and found that the size of the leptocephalus diminished westward. Following this process, he gained the credit for the discovery of the breeding ground in the Sargasso Sea between 20° and 30°N, 48° and 65°W. Here, the smallest leptocephali, about 3/8 in (10 mm) long, were found near the surface.

We now know that both the European and the American eel breed in this region. However, no sexually mature adult has been caught there, nor eggs that unquestionably belong to the eel, so the depth of the spawning grounds is unknown. It is reasonable to assume, though, that this is at some depth because the eyes of adult eels enlarge as they go to sea, eels caught at sea travel at some depth, and the youngest larvae have been taken at greater depths than larger larvae.

On the basis of laboratory experiments on the sexual maturity of eels, it seems likely that eels spawn at moderate depths and at temperatures of about 68°F (20°C). The Sargasso Sea is one of the few places in the world that provides these conditions because it is nearly a basin and high temperatures extend much deeper than is usual. A look at the list of species of *Anguilla* and their distribution will show that they are absent from regions surrounding the southern Atlantic and eastern Pacific, regions in which there are no warm, deep waters.

After hatching, the leptocephali drift back along the Gulf Stream, taking about three years to reach the European shores. There, in the shallow, colder, and less saline waters, they change into elvers and move into rivers and streams where they feed and grow until they are ready to undertake the 3,750-mile (6,000-km) migration. As far as is known, adult eels die after spawning.

1) The adult eels migrate from rivers and lakes once a year into the sea to begin their journey to the Sargasso Sea.
2) In the depths of the Sargasso Sea, the eggs hatch into transparent willow leaf-like leptocephalus larvae. These larvae grow until they approach the coasts of Europe. In the shallow, less saline coastal waters they shrink and change into depigmented small imitations of the adults. These are called glass eels.
3) Glass eels move upstream and develop pigment as they do so.
4) Elvers. By now they are just like miniature versions of the adults and swim upstream in large swarms. Before rivers became so polluted, the number of elvers swimming upstream was so large and they were so densely packed that they could be easily caught and used as fertilizer on fields as well as food for humans.

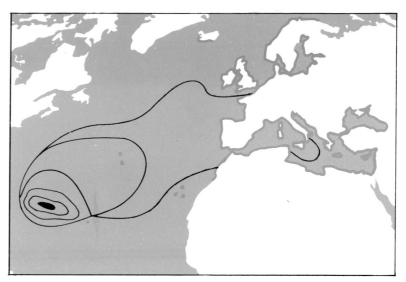

▲ | The spawning ground and diffusion of the European eel.

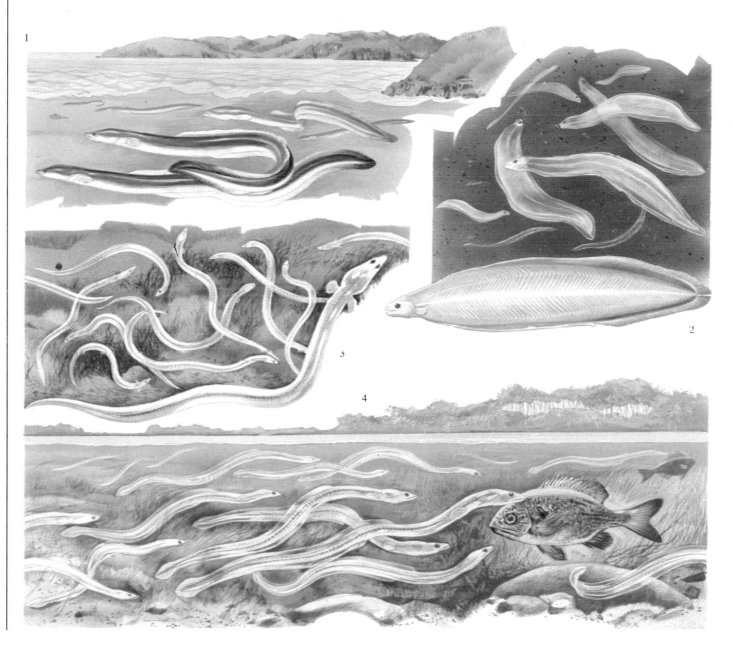

GARDEN EELS

Heterocongridae

Although seemingly dissimilar, garden eels are related to conger eels and some authorities place them in the family Congridae. They derive their common name from the fact that they live in underwater "gardens" where they are the plants – rooted in the sea bed and waving in the currents.

These colonial eels live in large colonies, usually in shallow water at many localities in the Indo-Pacific Ocean and in a few localities in the Atlantic, principally in the west Atlantic. Members of the colony stand erect, their tails buried in the sand and the top part of their bodies bent forward, like the handle of a walking stick, into the current. The first of these spectacular eel gardens was described about a century ago from off the coast of Indonesia. Since then about ten species belonging to four genera have been discovered. What little information is available suggests that the life history and daily cycle of the colonies is very similar for all species.

Colonies are occasionally found in water less than 9ft (3 m) deep and these are sparsely populated. In deeper water the colonies become denser, with an eel burrow perhaps every 1 1/2 ft (50 cm). The distance separating the eel burrows depends largely upon the size of the eel because each eel feeds in a hemisphere of water whose radius is slightly less than the body length. Eels therefore are just out of contact with each other in a well established adult colony. The burrow is a sinuous, vertical hole lined with mucus secreted by the skin. About half an hour before sunrise the eels begin to emerge from their burrows and by sunrise all are fully out and feeding.

Garden eels (including the aforementioned species) feed on plankton and other small organisms which are detected by sight. The development of gardens at over 660 ft (200 m) down would therefore seem somewhat unlikely, as there would be insufficient light for them to see their prey. Eel gardens are never found in still waters, because they rely on the current to bring a constant supply of food to them.

Garden eels (*Heterocongridae*)

▼ The garden eel's eyes are noticeably larger than those of other members of the eel family.

▲ Part of a colony of *Gorgasia maculata*. These eels, which grow to about 20 in (50 cm) long, live in colonies in warm, shallow seas. They face into the current and eat small food items carried past by the current. For this manner of feeding, they need good vision. The close-up of the head shows their large eyes. Their tails always remain in their burrows, into which the whole fish retreats when threatened, or to sleep.

MORAY EELS

Muraenidae

The generic name for the Mediterranean moray, *Muraena*, commemorates a rich Roman, Licinius Muraena, who lived before the end of the second century B.C. According to Pliny the Elder (A.D. 23-79) Licinius Muraena kept fish, including morays, alive in captivity for his aesthetic pleasure and appreciation.

Morays have the reputation of not releasing their grip once they have bitten. Furthermore, their bite is venomous. Both these often repeated statements are untrue. To deal with the last part, the bite contains no venom. It is possible that the wound may become infected, but that is chance and probably represents an absence of elementary first aid. There is, in fact, a greater danger of illness from eating moray.

Morays are normally territorial and somewhat cryptic. The day is spent with most of the body secure in a crevice, with only the head poking out to see if danger threatens or food beckons. The usual reaction to the presence of a diver is either indifference or a mild curiosity. However, if touched, or if a threat is too close, they retreat. Do not imagine, though, that morays are pet-like in their docility; they are voracious predators, though not directly antagonistic unless the provocation is severe. In the Mediterranean, morays may grow to about 3¼ ft (2 m) long and could inflict a nasty wound. Considering the large number of skin divers and the large number of morays, the relatively few incidents belie the "savagery" of the morays.

Many species of moray are mottled for camouflage in their rocky habitat. *Echidna zebra*, a moray eel from Hawaii, grows to about 3 ft (90 cm) long. Its body is dark brown with thin vertical white stripes. Unlike most other morays, it has blunt, rounded teeth. These are presumed to be more effective in crushing its main item of diet, crabs. *Rhinomuraena* is a very slender tropical genus in which the anterior nostrils are expanded into large, leaf-like structures as high as the head is deep. One species *Rhinomuraena amboinensis*, is spectacularly colored. The body is turquoise blue and the dorsal fin is bright yellow with a white margin. The head, in front of the eye and the lower jaw region, is yellow and the rest of the head is the same blue as the body.

▲ | **M**uraena helena, the moray eel of the Atlantic and Mediterranean. By day they try and hide in crevices or pipes with only their head protruding.

◀ | **T**hey feed mostly on invertebrates especially the octopus, squids, and shrimps as shown here. Crabs and carrion are also eaten.

▲ | **T**he leptocephalus larva has the shape commonly found in eels, that is many times longer than deep.

◀ | **A** large octopus can be more than a match for a moray.

DEEP SEA SPINY EELS

Notacanthiformes

Three families of these bizarre deep sea fish are known, Monognathidae, Saccopharyngidae, and Eurypharyngidae; it is, however, very likely that the monognathids may not be a distinct group of species but juveniles of the saccopharyngids.

Saccopharyngids are deep sea eels with very large mouths, distensible stomachs, long, tapering whip-like tails, and teeth on the jaws. They lack scales, swim bladders, and pelvic girdles. Individuals may grow to 6½ ft (2 m) in length, making them giants among deep sea fish, but a great proportion of their length is the tail. The development of the huge mouth has resulted in some peculiar anatomical features. The gill elements, for example, are a long way behind the skull and are not attached to it. Each half of the gill arches is separate from its fellow. There are no opercular bones and the gill chambers are only partly covered by skin. Its breathing mechanism is, therefore, quite different from that of all other fish.

There are probably four species of *Saccopharynx*. The body is jet black and the first one caught – 50 in (128 cm) long – was described as an "elongated black sausage," due to a large sized fish which was still undigested in its stomach. Although it was caught in 5,600 ft (1700 m) of water, it was still alive at the surface, largely due to the fact that it had been caught by its teeth becoming entangled in the neck of the net, so it was not crushed by the weight of the other fish.

In the upper jaw there are two rows of teeth, both curved and straight. On the lower jaw there is a single row with alternate large and small teeth. The largest tooth is about 0.1 in (2.5 mm) long.

In all saccopharyngids there is a complex, luminous tail organ. This organ, and the general arrangement of the luminous tissue, is intriguing. Starting on the top of the head are two troughs with raised edges that run back to within 20 in (50 cm) of the tail tip. Along the back they are closer together, but they separate toward the tail as the dorsal fin comes between them. Each trough is filled with a white, luminous substance

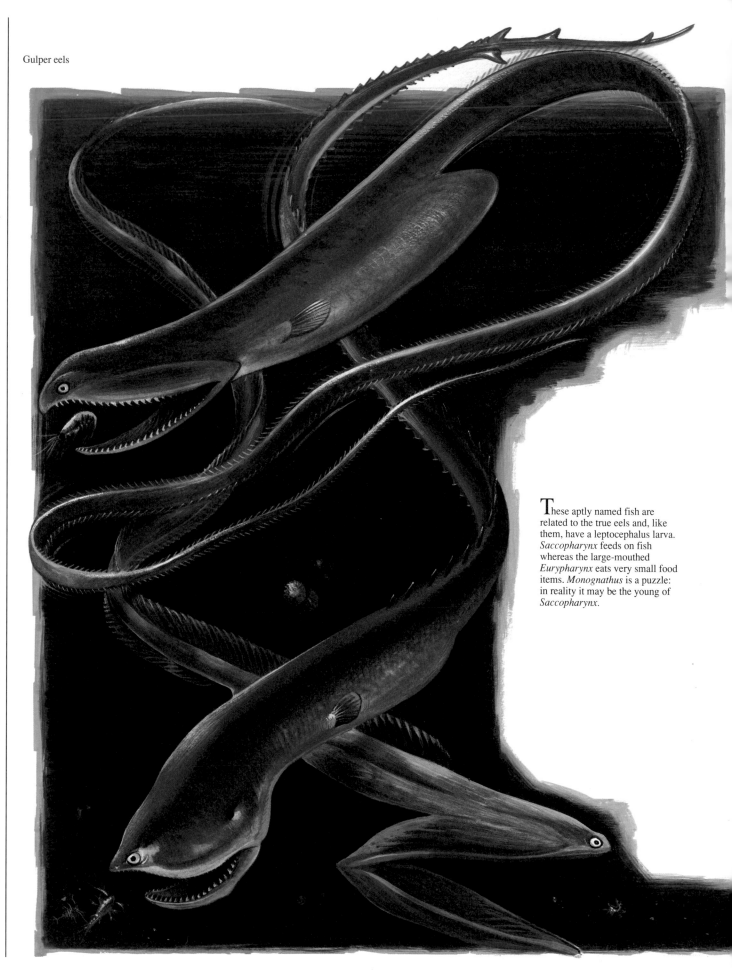

Gulper eels

These aptly named fish are related to the true eels and, like them, have a leptocephalus larva. *Saccopharynx* feeds on fish whereas the large-mouthed *Eurypharynx* eats very small food items. *Monognathus* is a puzzle: in reality it may be the young of *Saccopharynx*.

which, at least along the anterior part of the troughs, glows with a pale light. Each dorsal fin ray is associated with a pair of oblique slashes, each of which also contains a white substance.

The tail organ starts about 6 in (15 cm) before the tip of the tail. A long way behind the last fin ray is a single pink tentacle, an elongated spindle with an enlarged head arising ventrally. The fish is shallowest at this point, only about 0.1 in (2 mm) deep, because the tail is depressed here. About 2¼ in (6 cm) further back the tail becomes rounded and broader, and from its dorsal and ventral edges arise 13 scarlet papillae (six dorsal and seven ventral) on the summit of depigmented bumps. Still further back is the main luminous organ. This is a compressed, leaf-like, transparent zone with a substantial network of blood vessels.

What purpose this organ serves can only be hypothesized. *Saccopharynx* eats fairly large fish. Two specimens, each nearly 12 in (30 cm) long, were found in the stomach of *S. harrisoni*. It seems unlikely that the organ is used as a lure to catch prey. Despite the long, thin tail, the fish would need to severely contort itself, or swim round in circles, if the tail organ were used as a lure.

The family Eurypharyngidae (gulper eels) contains only one species, *Eurypharynx pelecanoides*, found in all tropical and subtropical seas at depths down to 27,000 ft (8,000 m). The largest known specimens are nearly 3 ft (1 m) long. The mouth is enormous, and the jaws are about one quarter the length of the entire body. There is an elastic membrane between each half of the lower jaw and at the back of the sides of the mouth. There are minute, irregularly arranged teeth on the jaw bones. A very small pectoral fin is present some way behind the head. The body is velvety black save for a white groove running along each side of the base of the dorsal fin for its whole length. A small caudal organ is present but it is not known if it is luminous. Very little is known about this eel's habits. It probably feeds on plankton and small fish.

A further related family is that of the giganturoids (Giganturidae). There are two genera of these midwater fish, *Bathyleptus* with three species, one in each of the tropical oceans, and *Gigantura* with two species from the tropical Atlantic.

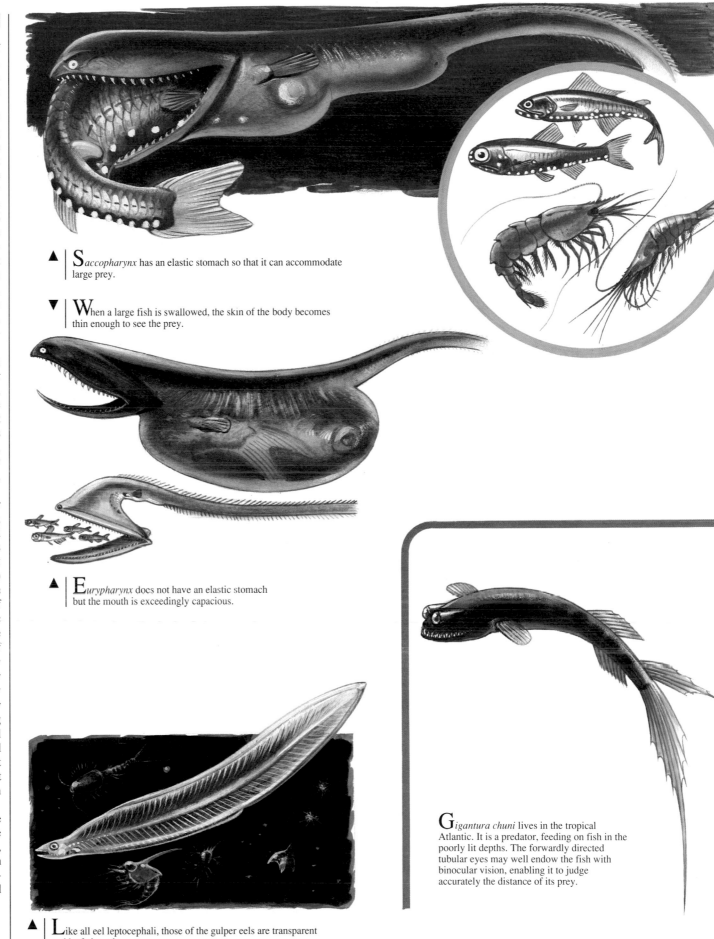

▲ | Saccopharynx has an elastic stomach so that it can accommodate large prey.

▼ | When a large fish is swallowed, the skin of the body becomes thin enough to see the prey.

▲ | Eurypharynx does not have an elastic stomach but the mouth is exceedingly capacious.

Gigantura chuni lives in the tropical Atlantic. It is a predator, feeding on fish in the poorly lit depths. The forwardly directed tubular eyes may well endow the fish with binocular vision, enabling it to judge accurately the distance of its prey.

▲ | Like all eel leptocephali, those of the gulper eels are transparent and leaf-shaped.

HERRING

Clupea harengus

Order Clupeiformes
Family Clupeidae
Length Up to 18 in (45cm)
Distinctive features An anal fin with under 25 rays and a nonstriate operculum. 45 – 50 vertebrae
Coloration Gray–silver on the belly and sides, gray–green on the back
Eggs 20 – 70,000
Sexual maturity Between 3 and 4 years
Life expectancy Over 20 years

The herring is a marine species of average size (average length 10 in [25 cm]) that lives in pelagic shoals which are often very large indeed. It is one of the most important species in the clupeid family from the point of view of the economy of world fishing. Herrings are cold and temperate water fish that are only found in the Northern Hemisphere. They are found in the Atlantic between the Arctic Sea and the English Channel, and along the eastern and western coasts of the Pacific Ocean. Numerous local races are found in these areas, subdivided into further numerous complex stocks which differ from each other on the basis of their spawning grounds and certain morphological characteristics.

There are some more major divisions that have been distinguished, namely a definable group living in the coldest waters of the Atlantic which grows to the largest size and lays its eggs along the coasts of Europe in spring, and another group in the North Sea which lives mainly on the continental shelf at not very great depths and grows to smaller sizes. These lay their eggs in autumn–winter, mainly along the eastern coasts of Great Britain. A third group is found in the coastal waters of the North Sea. Outside Europe, we would certainly find other groups of *C. harengus harengus* along the coasts of the United States and Canada and of *C. harengus pallasii* along the northern Pacific coasts.

The eggs are laid in open water and lie on the sea bed in various layers on the different substrata already present (rocks, algae, etc.), an unusual occurrence with Teleostei. Depending on the laying season and the size of the fish, the eggs can vary in size, ranging from 1 to 2 mm. The larval period lasts from four to six months and ends when the animal reaches about 1½ in (4 cm) in

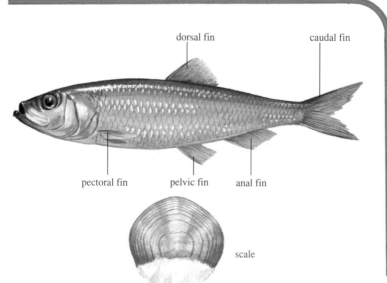

dorsal fin

caudal fin

pectoral fin

pelvic fin

anal fin

scale

▲ The herring (*Clupea harengus*) lives in the North Atlantic and the Pacific. It evolved during the period between the Mesozoic and the Jurassic and feeds on plankton which it catches by swimming with its mouth open and filtering the water that passes through. Encircled, an enlarged view of some of the typical planktonic forms on which the herring feeds.

◄ The body of the herring: the fins have no spiniform rays; the scales are cycloid and caducous; the pelvic fin is placed very far back; there is no lateral line.

length. At this point the herring enters its period of maximum growth and moves into areas with a high level of plankton. Plankton constitutes the mainstay of its diet from the larval stage to adulthood.

Apart from the migration for purposes of reproduction and the search for areas in which to raise the young and zones for feeding, the herrings also move vertically, a fact that is of great interest from the point of view of improving fishing. It has actually been observed that the herrings in the North Sea keep in close formation near the sea bed during the day and come up to the surface at night. Some researchers believe this may be connected to a reduction in their gregariousness when there is no light and, consequently, sight must have a determining role in their perception of the "school unit."

Herring fishing is without doubt a very ancient activity probably originating along the English coasts of the North Sea. There are ancient documents dating back to before the fifth century A.D. which give information on the amounts of fish landed in various periods. Little information is given on the equipment used, though the earliest methods probably involved barricading off short stretches of coast in areas where the schools most commonly came in. However, drift nets have traditionally been used for centuries for this kind of fishing as this technique gives good results with simple and economical methods.

Herring fishing increased noticeably in the period between the two wars and carried on growing even after. It was only after 1966, that for reasons still not fully understood, there were any considerable drops in the catches, especially in European waters. Herring is one of the most nutritious fish commonly landed, and the enormous quantities brought in every year allow the prices to be kept down, making this species a vital part of the food economy in many countries. Apart from the fresh product, a lot of each catch is treated and consumed locally or exported: the fish is salted, smoked or pickled and is even converted into meal for agricultural purposes.

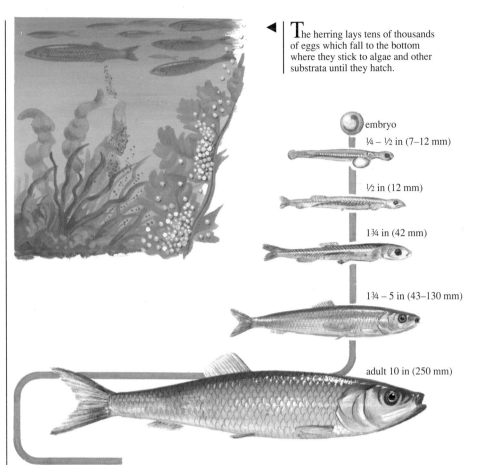

◀ The herring lays tens of thousands of eggs which fall to the bottom where they stick to algae and other substrata until they hatch.

embryo
¼ – ½ in (7–12 mm)

½ in (12 mm)

1¾ in (42 mm)

1¾ – 5 in (43–130 mm)

adult 10 in (250 mm)

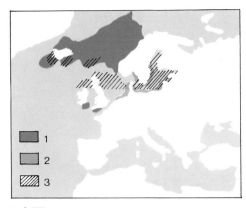

▲ The distribution area and spawning grounds of the herring of the North Atlantic:
1) Atlantic herring (*Clupea harengus*);
2) coastal herring; 3) continental shelf herring.

◀ The development and growth of the herring up to the adult stage; it reaches a maximum length of 16–18 in (40–45 cm).

▼ The movement of two stocks of herring in the North Sea: 1) the migration and distribution areas of the Dogger Bank stock; 2) movements of the Buchan Bank stock. The two stocks spend part of their lives in common areas.

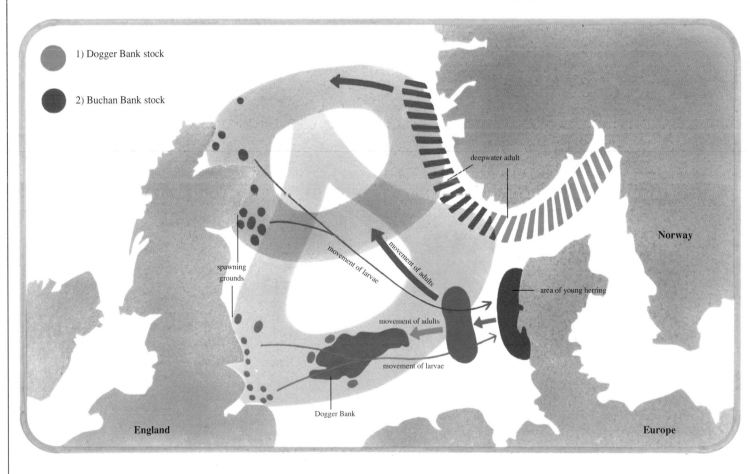

1) Dogger Bank stock

2) Buchan Bank stock

deepwater adult

Norway

spawning grounds

movement of larvae

movement of adults

area of young herring

movement of adults

movement of larvae

Dogger Bank

England

Europe

SALMON

Oncorhynchus and Salmo

Salmon can be considered to be among the best known and most important fish in the life and commerce of man, second only to herring and cod. All salmon are limited to the cold zones of the Northern Hemisphere and are divided into two genera: *Oncorhynchus* with six species found in the seas and areas of the Pacific, and *Salmo*.

The Pacific salmon (genus *Oncorhynchus*) include six species distributed over both sides of the northern Pacific, in the Beaufort Sea, and the sea of eastern Siberia. Another species that is exclusively Asian occupies an area between the river Amur in Siberia and Taiwan.

The Chinook, king or tyee salmon (*Oncorhynchus tshawytscha*) is the biggest of the Pacific salmon and can grow to 5 ft (1.5 m) in length and weigh up to 100 lb (45 kg). The reproductive adults present a dimorphism, particularly in the males who develop a characteristic deformation of the jaw, but although this is strongly marked in migratory males, it is not so with non-migratory species living in inland waters. The marine adults generally stay in the central areas of the Pacific Ocean and rarely go beyond the Bering Sea in the north and the Sea of Japan in the south, climbing the rivers of North America mainly from California to Alaska.

This species was the first to be introduced into other areas and has acclimatized to life in many countries from North America to Europe, Australia, New Zealand etc., since 1872. Many have been introduced into the Great Lakes, but it appears that in almost no case has the stock been able to keep up its numbers naturally; although the fish migrate to the river sources and mating takes place, the birth rate seems to be very low.

The pink salmon (*Oncorhynchus gorbusha*) is a species that is one of the least valued. It rarely grows above 24 – 28 in (60 – 70 cm) in length or weighs over 11 – 15 lb (5 – 7 kg). At sea, the adults are found in Arctic waters and in the Pacific and the Sea of Japan. Young and mature adults are found from about the River Lena in Siberia down to Hokkaido in northeast Asia. In North America, they are found from the

The dog salmon (*Oncorhynchus keta*) is one of the species of Pacific salmon that show the greatest homing instinct. After a period of three or four years at sea, the adults begin to make their way back to spawn and they do not eat throughout the whole journey. They also undergo great morphological and physiological changes during the migration. The jaws of the male tend to curve and elongate until they cannot close their mouths. They can overcome rapids and waterfalls obstructing their journey, leaping out of the water sometimes up to 10 ft (3 m) in the air, over 26-ft (8-m) stretches, and can travel distances of over 1,250 miles (2,000 km) at speeds of 25 – 30 miles (40 – 50 km) per day.

Mackenzie River on the Alaskan coasts down to the Sacramento River in California.

The chum or dog salmon (*Oncorhynchus keta*), like the previous species, has a somewhat modest commercial importance. The distribution of this species at sea covers an area from the Arctic seas to the Sea of Japan and the Sacramento River in California to the south.

The coho or silver salmon (*Oncorhynchus kisutch*) is the most important species from a commercial point of view. It rarely exceeds 32 in (80 cm) in length and weights of 4½ – 6½ lb (2 – 3 kg). The original distribution area of this species includes the seas and tributaries of the central Pacific area south of the Bering Straits and the southern limit goes no further than California on the North American coast and the Sea of Japan on the Asian side.

The sockeye or red salmon (*Oncorhynchus nerka*) appears under two different ecotypes: one anadromous migratory form and one living permanently in fresh water. The two types were described as two separate species, but were then classified as the same. They grow to quite modest sizes and the adults generally stay at around 24 in (60 cm) in length and 4½ – 6½ lb (2 – 3 kg) in weight when they return to fresh water. In the nonmigratory freshwater forms, the limits are even less and they do not even grow to 16 in (40 cm). Both forms are found in overlapping areas from Hope Point in Alaska down to the Klamat River in California and from Northern Hokkaido in Japan down to the Anadyr River in Siberia. Sockeye salmon were introduced into the Great Lakes and acclimatized perfectly in Lake Huron. This fish grows to a uniform size when adult so they can easily be handled by the canning industries. As a result, most of the canned salmon found on the market belongs to this species.

The masu salmon (*Oncorhynchus masou*) is generally anadromous and can adapt to permanent life in inland waters. Maximum dimensions do not exceed 28 in (70 cm) and they rarely go above 15½ – 17½ lb (7-8 kg) in weight.

The genus *Salmo* includes species that are mainly found in the Atlantic and connecting seas. The only migratory form in this area is the Atlantic salmon (*Salmo salar*). The Atlantic salmon, like the other salmon, trout, and char, has an anadromous and a nonmigratory freshwater form. Its distribution area covers the North Atlantic and connecting river mouths.

▲ The young of the dog salmon migrate immediately to the sea as soon as they leave the redds, retracing the route followed by their parents. Once they reach the sea they stay along the coasts for a few months and then move on to the open sea once they reach the smolt stage.

▼ During its life at sea, the dog salmon becomes a great predator, feeding off other fish.

▲ The lake environment becomes an alternative to the marine environment and the adults then migrate to the rivers in the same way and undergoing the same physiological changes as the marine forms.

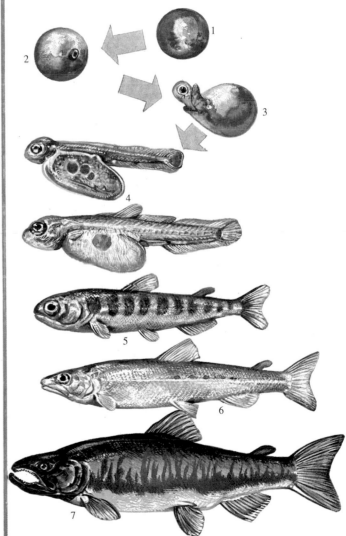

Development: 1) fertilized egg; 2) the eye appears early in the embryo and at this stage the eggs are highly resistant and can withstand movement; 3) hatching; 4) prelarval stages with the yolk sac in various stages of reabsorption; 5) "parr"; 6) "smolt"; 7) adult male in mating colors.

Salmon are born in the headwaters of the rivers, where they spend the early part of their lives before beginning their migration to the sea. After a period of growth lasting a few years that can sometimes take them hundreds of miles into the sea, they find their way back to the exact place where they were born. During this journey, they can overcome all kinds of obstacles such as rapids and waterfalls, and their physiology seems to be able to adapt both to life in fresh water and in the sea. Their greatest aid in finding their place of birth seems to be their sense of smell, for salmon can detect the "smell" of the stream where they were born and distinguish it from many others. After returning to their place of birth, whether after a long migration that began in the ocean or just from a lake, the adults choose a suitable area to lay their eggs and fertilize them.

Once they have reached a suitable spot, the females, usually accompanied by a larger dominant male and a few other smaller males, begin to build a nest (known as a redd) which is relatively simple in form. They use their tails as spades and dig a hole on the bottom large enough to fit both the male and female bodies during mating. The construction of the redd, like the choice of a suitable spot, is done exclusively by the female. The males make their contribution by keeping any possible intruders at bay, becoming territorial and aggressive during this period.

When the redd is complete, the female settles herself in the center and only then is she approached by the dominant male who settles alongside her. The fertilized eggs laid on the bottom of the redd are covered with sand and gravel by the female. Each female can repeat the nest building and mating up to three or four times and the number of eggs laid each time varies according to the species.

The newly born fish spend a dormant period in the gravel of the redds, lasting as long as it takes to completely reabsorb all the yolk sac before they begin their free lives. What happens then depends on the species to which they belong. In the pink and dog salmon the young can stay in their redds after having absorbed the yolk sac. Unlike the other species, they immediately begin their descent to the sea without spending an initial period of one, two or maybe more years in a freshwater environment. In other species of Atlantic salmon and in Pacific salmon, the journey to the sea is undertaken after a period in fresh

▶ The migration of the dog salmon to its place of birth: in April it is in Alaska, in June and July in the Bering Sea, in August in the areas around the Kamchatka Peninsula, and in September – October it arrives at the island of Hokkaido where it begins to climb the rivers. Apart from this autumn migration cycle, there is another summer cycle in which the reproductive adults appear in the Japanese river estuaries towards June – July.

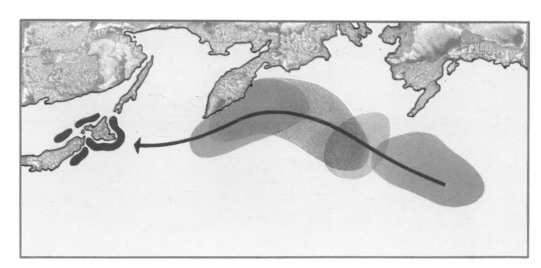

▼ Salmon can recognize the smell of their native stream and follow it to find their place of birth.

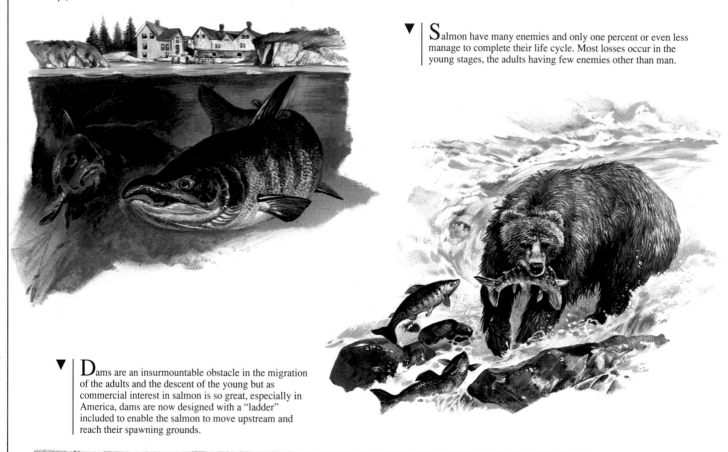

▼ Salmon have many enemies and only one percent or even less manage to complete their life cycle. Most losses occur in the young stages, the adults having few enemies other than man.

▼ Dams are an insurmountable obstacle in the migration of the adults and the descent of the young but as commercial interest in salmon is so great, especially in America, dams are now designed with a "ladder" included to enable the salmon to move upstream and reach their spawning grounds.

water. Some of the young of the silver salmon do not migrate to the sea, staying permanently in fresh water, but, although they reach the adult stage, they cannot reproduce. Unlike the silver salmon, the masu populations can also adapt to freshwater environments and reproduce successfully. The last two species of Pacific salmon, the king and the red salmon, and the Atlantic species can produce breeding stocks that stay in fresh waters. While complete acclimatization to a freshwater environment is the exception, all other species of salmon normally have to spend a period of their lives in the sea to be able to reach the adult stage and maturity.

The time spent at sea by the different species depends partly on the local conditions and partly on the length of the return journey to the birthplace where breeding will take place. Species that grow to relatively modest sizes, as in the case of the pink salmon, cannot travel too great distances during migration from the estuary to the headwaters of the rivers. Their life cycle is quite short and they generally do not stay in the sea for more than a year. Larger species like the king salmon and the silver salmon can stay at sea for a few years, sometimes up to five, and in some cases they grow to more than 3 ft (1 m) in length. The larger species, including *Salmo salar*, are able to travel as far as hundreds of miles to reach their breeding grounds.

The sea environment plays an essential role in the growth of the individuals, who can travel great distances in the oceans in search of food before migrating towards the river estuaries again to return to their place of birth. Gradually as the salmon approach the river estuaries, they stop feeding and begin to live off the reserves within their bodies. Outwardly, there is also a process of degeneration, particularly with regard to the jaws of the males which tend to grow longer and curve like a beak. The skin coloring tends to become pinkish or reddish along the sides and the back becomes darker in shade.

Salmon can distinguish the characteristic smell of their birthplace from many others and experiments have proved that the young salmon are conditioned by the smell of their own stream before they even leave it to migrate to the sea. They remember this smell throughout their growth period in the sea and can recognize it when they reach the river mouths and follow it to return to their birthplace.

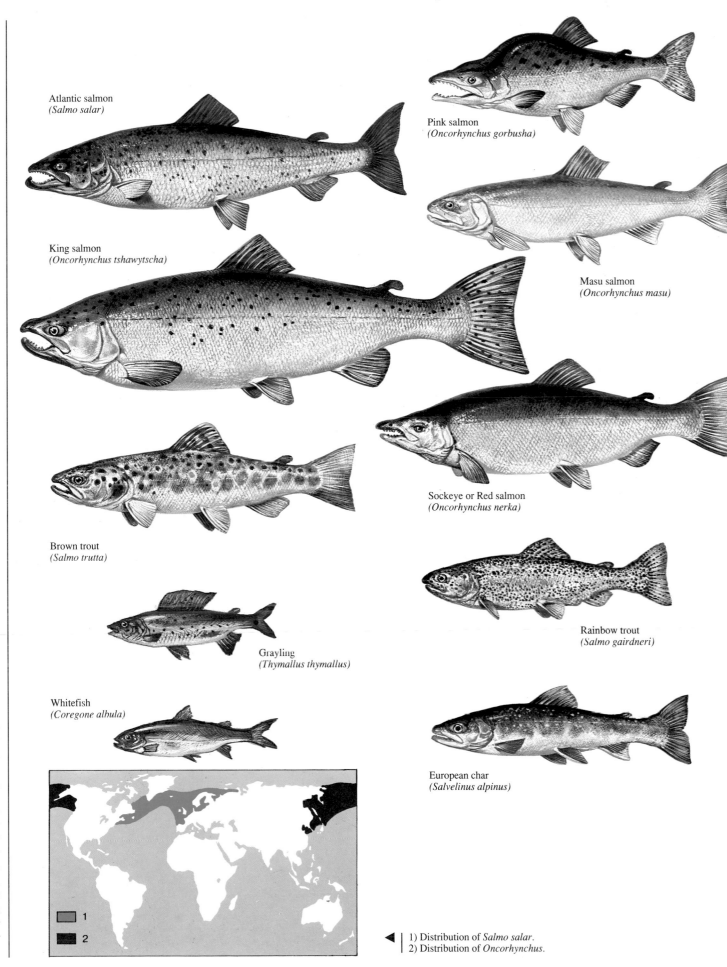

Atlantic salmon
(Salmo salar)

King salmon
(Oncorhynchus tshawytscha)

Brown trout
(Salmo trutta)

Grayling
(Thymallus thymallus)

Whitefish
(Coregone albula)

Pink salmon
(Oncorhynchus gorbusha)

Masu salmon
(Oncorhynchus masu)

Sockeye or Red salmon
(Oncorhynchus nerka)

Rainbow trout
(Salmo gairdneri)

European char
(Salvelinus alpinus)

1) Distribution of *Salmo salar*.
2) Distribution of *Oncorhynchus*.

ENGRAULIDAE

The family of the engraulids includes about a hundred species subdivided into 15 genera, the most important of which commercially is the genus *Engraulis*. This includes seven species of anchovies which are common in the Atlantic, Pacific, and Mediterranean and are found in temperate and tropical waters. The European anchovy (*Engraulis encrasicolus*) is found throughout the Mediterranean and Black Seas and in the Atlantic from Norway down to the Gulf of Guinea. It is intensively fished, especially in the Mediterranean where it is the most common catch, although it is not quite as important as other species in the same family. It is eaten either fresh or preserved and supplies a large number of canning industries.

The body of the anchovy is more slender and cylindrical than that of the clupeids; its mouth is large and extends well beyond the eyes. The snout is prominent and the eye covered by a fine membrane. It is a plankton eating species, but seems capable of selectively filtering other more suitable organisms for its diet such as the larvae of crustaceans and copepods, etc. through its gill mechanism. It also seems to feed off benthic organisms and small fish depending on the time of year and the environment in which it is living. In spring–summer, the reproductive season, it gathers in schools which move into the coasts to spawn from April to November. Each individual lays its eggs 3–5 times a season as and when they reach the right level of maturity, for studies have shown that the fish do not all mature at the same time. The number of eggs laid can vary in total from 15 – 20,000 and they have a particular cylindrical–ovoid shape; they are pelagic and are found in the top layers of water down to a maximum depth of 165 ft (50 m).

In winter the anchovy moves away from the coast and swims down to depths between 330 and 490 ft (100 and 150 m) where it probably loses its gregariousness and lives near the sea bed.

The young grow quickly and reach maturity after a year. The average life span is about three years and the maximum size is usually under 8 in (20 cm).

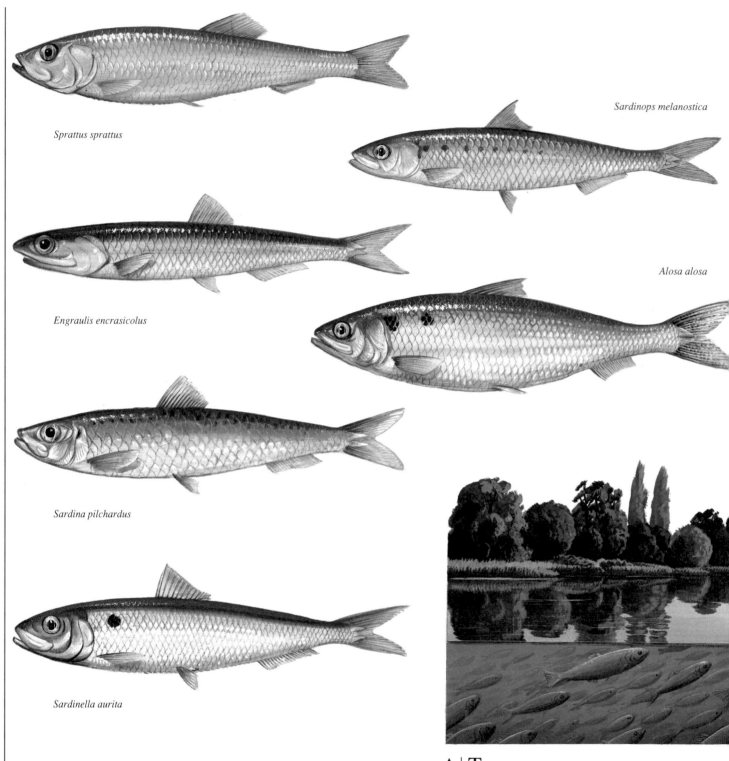

Sprattus sprattus

Sardinops melanostica

Engraulis encrasicolus

Alosa alosa

Sardina pilchardus

Sardinella aurita

▲ The shad (*Alosa alosa*) climbs the rivers upstream to reach the spawning grounds. The eggs soon hatch and the young fish begin the descent downstream after a while. Other species of shad live permanently in fresh water.

▲ The family of engraulids includes about a hundred species subdivided into 15 genera; the most important of these from the commercial point of view is the genus *Engraulis*. It includes seven species of anchovies which are common in the Atlantic, Pacific, and in the Mediterranean, spread in temperate and tropical waters. The European anchovy (*Engraulis encrasicolus*) is found in the Mediterranean and the Black Sea; it is also found in the Atlantic from Norway down to the Gulf of Guinea. Although not quite to the same extent as other species in the same family, it is intensively fished, particularly in the Mediterranean where it is the most important catch. It is eaten partly fresh and partly conserved and supplies a large number of canning industries.

LANTERN FISH
Myctophidae

Between 250 and 300 species of lantern fish are known. They are very successful fish, having colonized most mesopelagic depths of all oceans. They are not found in parts of the Arctic Ocean, and it has been written that if the lantern fish are not there, it is highly unlikely anything else is. All lantern fish are very similar in shape. They have large eyes and the body tapers evenly from the head to the forked caudal fin. There is a soft rayed dorsal fin about the mid point of the body and an adipose fin is present. The anal fin is moderately long and is situated ventrally below the space between the end of the dorsal fin and the adipose fin. The ventral fin is inserted vertically below, or in front of, the front part of the dorsal fin. The pectoral fin is long, often reaching back as far as the posterior part of the dorsal fin.

The jaws have rows of small teeth and range from small to quite large in size. Jaw size varies between species but three different groups can be distinguished depending on small, medium or large jaws. The size has some effect upon the diet. The food eaten consists of small planktonic animals in the case of the small-jawed species. Larger-jawed species will eat slightly larger prey. As lantern fish only range from 1½ – 10 in (25 – 250 mm) in length, no very large food items can be consumed.

Another feature of the lantern fish, the one that gives them their common name, is the luminous organs. The body, usually the lower half, is studded with simple organs arranged in patterns unique to each species. Larger organs may be found on the caudal peduncle (the narrow part of the body in front of the tail fin) and around the eyes, on the top of the head or on the cheek. Not all species have the larger organs, but they are present in the great majority of species. One important feature of the luminous organs, particularly the larger ones, is that they indicate the sex of the fish. This sexual dimorphism is most commonly shown by the organs on the caudal peduncle. In many species the male has one or more prominent light organs on the upper half of the peduncle. The female lacks the upper glands and those of the lower half are less conspicuous than in the male, or even absent.

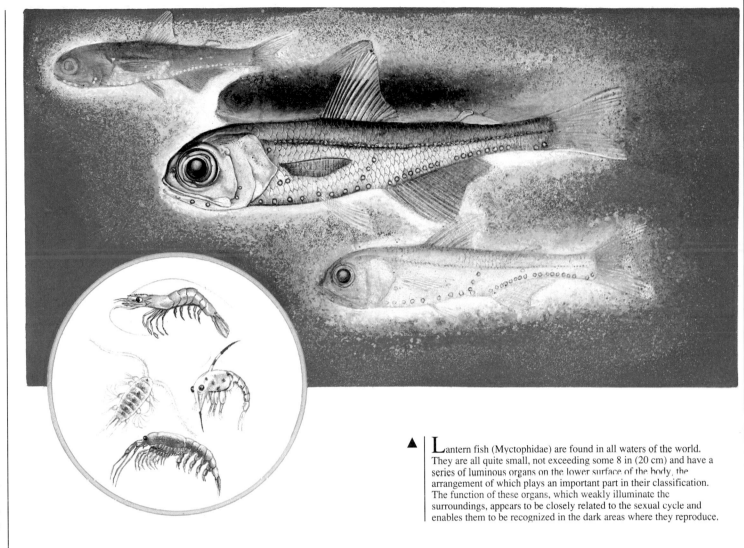

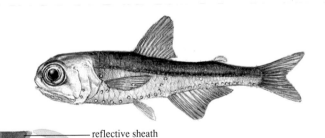

▲ | Their diet is made up of plankton.

▲ Lantern fish (Myctophidae) are found in all waters of the world. They are all quite small, not exceeding some 8 in (20 cm) and have a series of luminous organs on the lower surface of the body, the arrangement of which plays an important part in their classification. The function of these organs, which weakly illuminate the surroundings, appears to be closely related to the sexual cycle and enables them to be recognized in the dark areas where they reproduce.

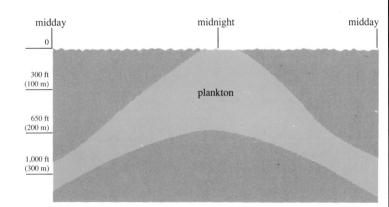

▼ Lantern fish tend to follow the movement of the plankton on which they feed and so migrate every day, moving to the surface at night and staying at depths of over 1,000 ft (300 m) during the day.

reflective sheath
luminous glands
lens

◄ The functional system of the luminous organs of the lantern fish: externally, there is a "lens" made up of a scale that thickens and is transparent; in the center, there is a "luminous bulb" that gets its light from a particular association of animal cells with luminescent bacteria; the light is projected by a "reflective sheath" at the back of the luminous organ.

midday | midnight | midday
0
300 ft (100 m)
plankton
650 ft (200 m)
1,000 ft (300 m)

VIPER FISH
Chauliodus

The genus *Chauliodus* comprises midwater (mesopelagic) predatory fish found throughout the oceans of the world between about 60°N and 40°S. The exact number of species is uncertain, but may be about half a dozen. All species of *Chauliodus*, as far as is known, migrate to much nearer the surface at night. Although many of the mesopelagic fish have swim bladders, *Chauliodus* along with some other predatory forms lacks the swim bladder. It may be that the absence of the swim bladder makes the daily vertical migration easier, because the fish will be less concerned about the substantial changes in pressure, but this could be too simple an explanation. Many of the fish living with *Chauliodus* have swim bladders and migrate the same distance, whereas others lack the swim bladder and do not migrate.

An examination of *Chauliodus* will leave one in no doubt that it is a highly specialized predator. A rather unusual feature is the regularity in the shape, position, and function of the teeth. Normally fish teeth show some variation but *Chauliodus* hardly ever does. The very size of the teeth also implies that *Chauliodus* must be able to open its mouth very wide to get the prey into the stomach. The foremost teeth on the upper jaw, which have four sharp ridges near their tips, are for stabbing. The first two teeth on the lower jaw, the largest of all, normally lie outside the upper jaw, but when they impale the prey, their particular curvature tends to push it into the roof of the mouth. At the base of both the second and third upper jaw teeth there is a small tooth sticking out laterally. These two small teeth lie either side of the large luminous organ below the eye and are thought to protect it.

A further unusual feature of *Chauliodus* is that the heart, ventral aorta, and gill filaments are all very much further forward than usual. Indeed, they lie between the lower jaws in the floor of the mouth and the gill arches extend almost to the tip of the lower jaw. The diet includes fish, squid, and deep sea shrimp. *Chauliodus* feeds throughout the day and night.

The transparent, gelatinous sheath that surrounds the body consists of a watery layer of the dermis and is

Chauliodus sloani, the deep sea viper fish, is a predator feeding on fish and crustaceans in deep waters. The front of the dorsal fin extends into a long, mobile lure, with which *Chauliodus* attracts prey close to the mouth. The large teeth prevent the escape of the prey. An indication of the success of its modifications is that this species occurs in the tropical and subtropical parts of all oceans.

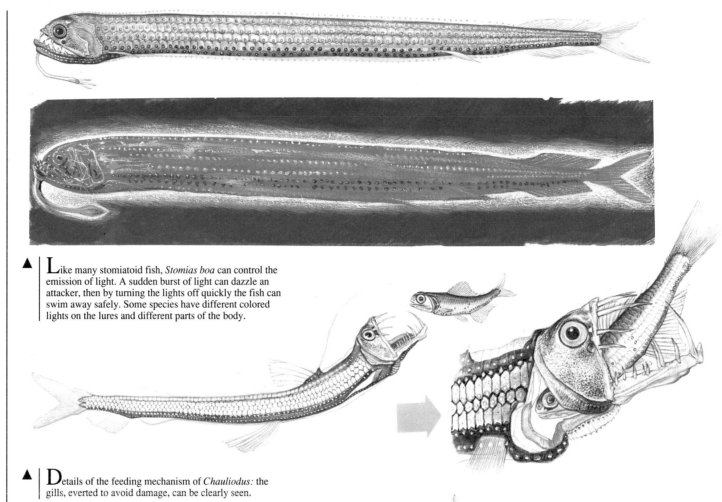

covered by a thin epidermis. It is thickest along the back and ventral region and thinnest on the sides. It contains nerves, blood vessels, a thin network of fibrous tissue and, most interestingly, a large number of small luminous organs.

Apart from the lure, there are two sorts of luminous organs in *Chauliodus*. Along the ventral part of the body and around the eyes there are complex organs composed of a pigmented sheath, a reflector, and two kinds of secretory cells. The pigment layer and the reflector direct the light ventrally from the ventral organs. The double complex light organs below the eye are protected by special teeth and transparent bones. The arrangement of the pigment layers indicates that the light from this organ shines into the eye. It is possible that their function is to make the eye more sensitive to light. A series of small light organs above and in front of the eye is thought to illuminate the prey.

Chauliodus has large and fully functional eyes so it is quite likely that sight is an important factor in detecting its food. However, the small, very simple, unpigmented light organs scattered all over the body, in the gelatinous sheath, even inside the mouth, must fulfill some function. These organs are hardly visible in preserved fish but are conspicuous and pinkish in freshly dead fish. In structure they are spherical bodies consisting of secretory cells whose bioluminous product is secreted into the hollow center of the organ. They are, unlike the ventral photophores, controlled by nerves.

What, then, is the effect of all this light-producing weaponry on *Chauliodus* in the sea? While the fish is undisturbed, the small light organs scattered all over the body, especially those in the ventral region, produce a steady bluish light. When touched, however, pulses of light illuminate its whole body. The large ventral photophores also produce a bluish light. The ventral photophores cast a downward light that, it is thought, may compensate for the faint shadow of the fish cast by the last remnants of daylight descending to these depths.

▲ Like many stomiatoid fish, *Stomias boa* can control the emission of light. A sudden burst of light can dazzle an attacker, then by turning the lights off quickly the fish can swim away safely. Some species have different colored lights on the lures and different parts of the body.

▲ Details of the feeding mechanism of *Chauliodus*: the gills, everted to avoid damage, can be clearly seen.

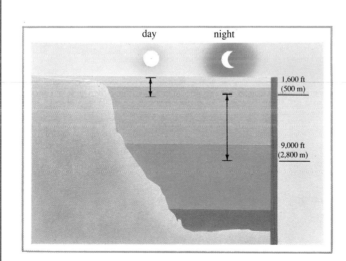

▲ Vertical migration during the night and day. Most abyssal fish are found at nighttime depths of 1,600 – 9,000 ft (500 – 2,800 m) but by means of their senses they move higher up during the daytime, following the vertical movement of plankton.

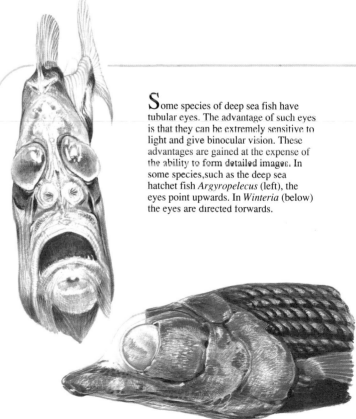

Some species of deep sea fish have tubular eyes. The advantage of such eyes is that they can be extremely sensitive to light and give binocular vision. These advantages are gained at the expense of the ability to form detailed images. In some species, such as the deep sea hatchet fish *Argyropelecus* (left), the eyes point upwards. In *Winteria* (below) the eyes are directed forwards.

STOMIATIFORMES AULOPIFORMES MYCTOPHIFORMES

These three orders include a large variety of species that often look very strange and have adapted to pelagic life in the deep stretches of the oceans; they are abyssal or bathybenthonic, but are more or less obviously related with other orders of surface fish so some experts consider them to be subgroups of Salmoniformes. It is actually very difficult to trace the evolutionary history of these fish for they have undergone great structural changes as a result of their life in areas untouched by sunlight. The lack of any constant characteristics over time combined with the fact that some of their structures are highly specialized make them very difficult to study and as a result very little is known of their biology.

Stomiatiformes are pelagic and bathypelagic fish and, according to various experts, include eight or more families. All the members of the group have more or less developed teeth on their jaws, their bodies are covered with scales that are sometimes very fine, and their organs are luminous. They often have no swim bladder or it is very small. The eyes are usually very large and often telescopic. The families in the order can be divided into two groups: the first includes two families of small species and the second has six, whose members are sometimes very large and usually predacious.

The gonostomatids are small fish that live in the middle and deep parts of all the oceans. Directly related to the gonostomatids are the sternoptychids. They are unmistakable in appearance as their bodies appear to be laterally squashed and the belly is elongated downwards resembling an axe blade. Their common name "hatchet fish" is highly suited to their shape.

The chauliodontids (viper fish) have one single genus with six or seven species, all of which are bathypelagic. The stomiatids are related to the viper fish and are morphologically similar. These are commonly known as "dragon fish" which also particularly suits their appearance. Another family related to the dragon and viper fish is that of the

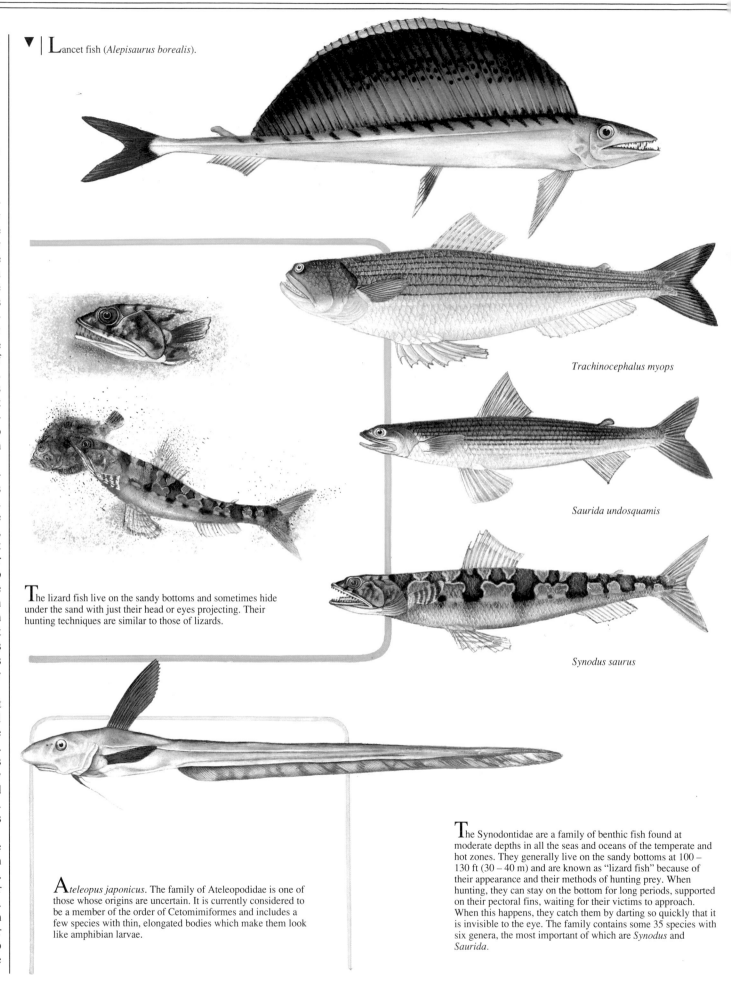

▼ | Lancet fish (*Alepisaurus borealis*).

Trachinocephalus myops

Saurida undosquamis

Synodus saurus

The lizard fish live on the sandy bottoms and sometimes hide under the sand with just their head or eyes projecting. Their hunting techniques are similar to those of lizards.

Ateleopus japonicus. The family of Ateleopodidae is one of those whose origins are uncertain. It is currently considered to be a member of the order of Cetomimiformes and includes a few species with thin, elongated bodies which make them look like amphibian larvae.

The Synodontidae are a family of benthic fish found at moderate depths in all the seas and oceans of the temperate and hot zones. They generally live on the sandy bottoms at 100 – 130 ft (30 – 40 m) and are known as "lizard fish" because of their appearance and their methods of hunting prey. When hunting, they can stay on the bottom for long periods, supported on their pectoral fins, waiting for their victims to approach. When this happens, they catch them by darting so quickly that it is invisible to the eye. The family contains some 35 species with six genera, the most important of which are *Synodus* and *Saurida*.

melanostomiatids, who differ from the previous group in that their body has no scales, so they are commonly known as naked dragon fish.

The idiacanthids have marked similarities with the stomiatids but are different in that they go through a particular larval stage during their development that ends with metamorphosis. The astronestids are commonly known as snaggletooths because of their irregular arrangement of teeth on the jaws. There are six genera with some 30 species distributed in all the ocean waters at depths from 1,300 to over 8,000 ft (400 – 2,500 m). The last family of Stomiatiformes, the malacosteids, share some features with the stomiatids and others with the astronestids. Their bodies are spindle-shaped with the median fin situated very far back.

The Aulopiformes include a vast group of mesopelagic and bathypelagic families who do not look quite as deformed as many of the previous order. The Aulopidae are the most primitive of the order and all the members of the family have a somewhat extended dorsal fin on which the front rays are elongated and often thread-like. The Chlorophthalmidae are closely related to the Aulopidae and include some 30 species of which some have adapted to abyssal life. The last of the primitive families in the group of Aulopiformes is Scopelosauridae, a small family of fish which have elongated bodies with photophores.

The Synodontidae are a family of benthic fish found at moderate depths in all the oceans and seas of the temperate and warm zones. They are known as lizard fish. The Paralepididae are a family of slender and quite fast moving fish. The Omosudidae live in the warm seas of the world, often at great depths. Among the giants of the deep are some species of Alepisauridae known as "lancet fish." These are found in all the warm seas. They are voracious creatures that feed off all kinds of organisms. The Scopelarchidae, the Evermannellidae, and the Anotopteridae are three families of abyssal forms which have small numbers of species, all of modest sizes.

The order of Myctophiformes has only two families with about 160 species, all small in size with a relatively homogenous shape. They live throughout the world below certain depths, although they do come up to the surface at night.

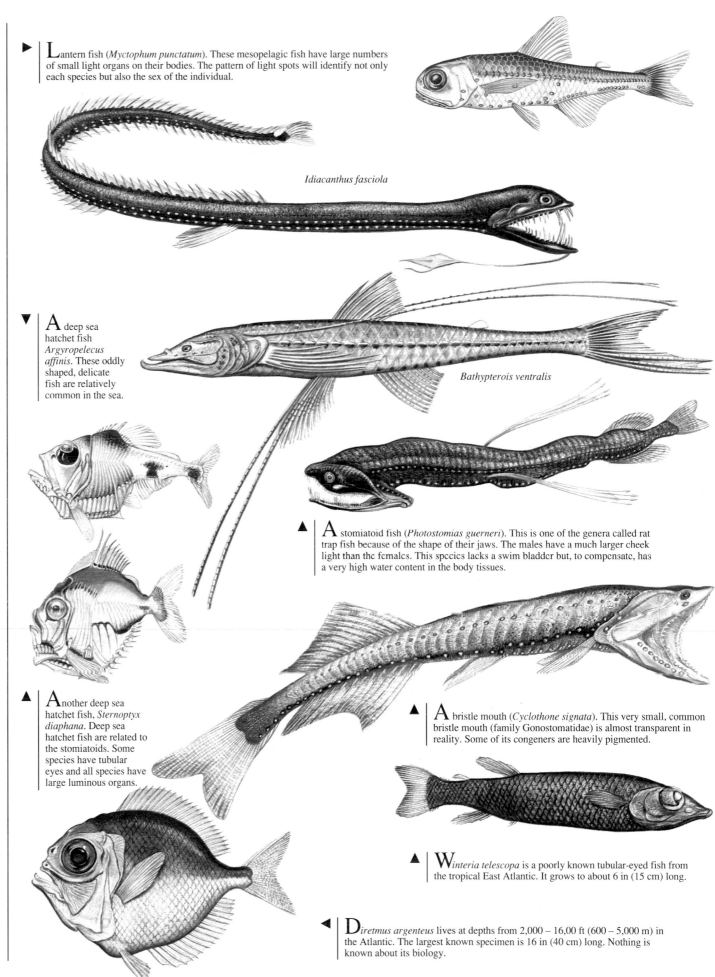

▶ Lantern fish (*Myctophum punctatum*). These mesopelagic fish have large numbers of small light organs on their bodies. The pattern of light spots will identify not only each species but also the sex of the individual.

Idiacanthus fasciola

▼ A deep sea hatchet fish *Argyropelecus affinis*. These oddly shaped, delicate fish are relatively common in the sea.

Bathypterois ventralis

▲ A stomiatoid fish (*Photostomias guerneri*). This is one of the genera called rat trap fish because of the shape of their jaws. The males have a much larger cheek light than the females. This species lacks a swim bladder but, to compensate, has a very high water content in the body tissues.

▲ Another deep sea hatchet fish, *Sternoptyx diaphana*. Deep sea hatchet fish are related to the stomiatoids. Some species have tubular eyes and all species have large luminous organs.

▲ A bristle mouth (*Cyclothone signata*). This very small, common bristle mouth (family Gonostomatidae) is almost transparent in reality. Some of its congeners are heavily pigmented.

▲ Winteria telescopa is a poorly known tubular-eyed fish from the tropical East Atlantic. It grows to about 6 in (15 cm) long.

◀ Diretmus argenteus lives at depths from 2,000 – 16,00 ft (600 – 5,000 m) in the Atlantic. The largest known specimen is 16 in (40 cm) long. Nothing is known about its biology.

TRIPOD FISH

Bathypterois

The common name of these fish derives from their habit of resting on the bottom of the sea on three "legs," that are in reality elongated and stiffened rays of each pelvic fin and the lower lobe of the caudal fin. There are currently 18 recognized species and, as a whole, the genus is distributed world-wide (although the spread is not continuous) on the bottom of the tropical and sub-tropical seas.

Tripod fish have thin, cylindrical or slightly compressed bodies. The eyes are small, even vestigial, but as far as is known, functional. The dorsal and anal fins are short based and both placed roughly in the middle of the body. A small adipose fin is also present. Perhaps the most striking feature of the living fish concerns the pectoral fins. These are curved, scythe-like and are held raised forward over the head.

How tripod fish feed is not known. Photographs of the living fish reveal that they "stand" on the bottom, facing the current and holding the pectoral fins forward over the head, so that they look rather like antlers. They are not filter feeders because they have never been seen with their mouth open. The jaws are provided with small sharp teeth and the food consists mostly of small crustaceans. The food is presumably caught off the bottom as it drifts by in the current.

The olfactory organs are small and poorly developed, as are the eyes. How tripod fish detect their prey and how they feed are also mysteries, but it is very likely that the pectoral fins are involved.

Another modification worthy of note concerns the elongated rays of the pelvic fins and lower caudal lobe. Each of these structures is tipped with a fleshy pad whose function is possibly to protect the fin ray and to provide a firmer contact with the sea bottom. It is not known how and how much tripod fish move around. It has been suggested that the elongated fin rays function like legs as organs of mobility, but such speculation has no foundation. Again, we can only guess at the advantages of developing structures to lift the fish off the bottom.

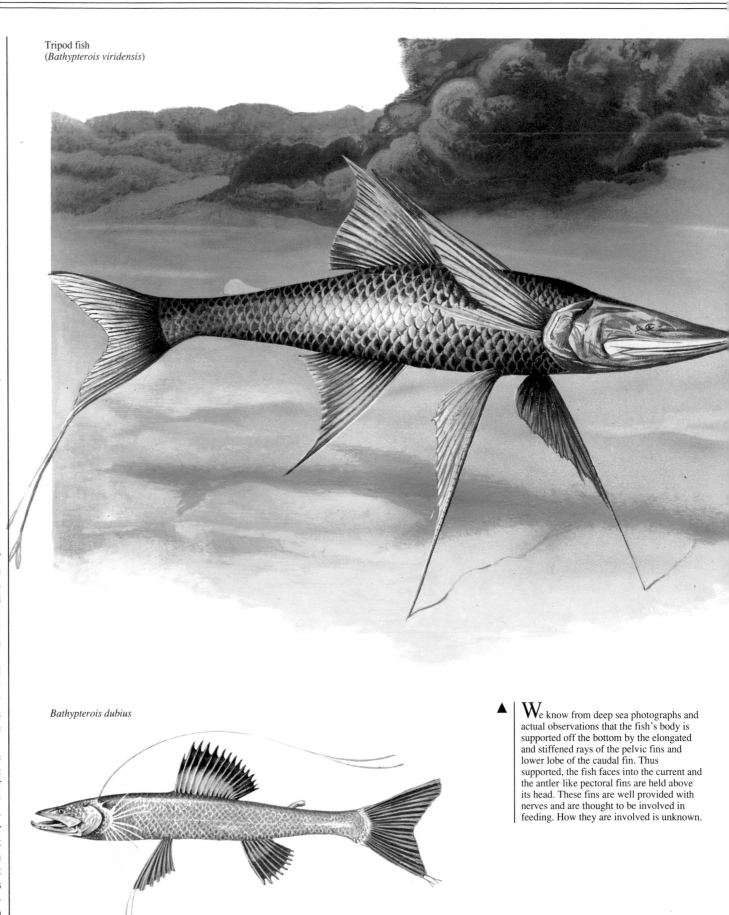

Tripod fish
(*Bathypterois viridensis*)

Bathypterois dubius

▲ We know from deep sea photographs and actual observations that the fish's body is supported off the bottom by the elongated and stiffened rays of the pelvic fins and lower lobe of the caudal fin. Thus supported, the fish faces into the current and the antler-like pectoral fins are held above its head. These fins are well provided with nerves and are thought to be involved in feeding. How they are involved is unknown.

▲ The species is distributed in the east Atlantic Ocean and lives at depths from 950 – 6,500 ft (300 – 2,000 m).

IDIACANTHIDAE
OPISTHOPROCTIDAE

The number of species belonging to the family of Idiacanthidae is uncertain; there may be only one world-wide species or as many as six localized species. In the North Atlantic *Idiacanthus fasciola* is recognized and it is remarkable for both its development and its marked sexual dimorphism. Until about 1½ in (4 cm) long, the larvae are sexually indeterminable. They are, in fact, so extraordinary that before they were shown to be the young of *Idiacanthus* they were called *Stylophthalmus*. The male never has a barbel nor teeth but develops a large luminous organ just below the eye. The female has black skin, the male pale brown. Very little is known about the diet, except that large females will eat small fish and that small crustaceans and diatoms are eaten by newly metamorphosed examples.

The opisthoproctids are deep sea fish closely related to the argentines and more distantly to the salmon and trout. They have tubular eyes which are directed anteriorly in some species, dorsally or anterodorsally in others. The deep bodied forms have eyes pointing upwards. It is difficult to focus such eyes, but their function is less to form a clear image than to detect faint light. The jaws are small, the teeth are weak, and the diet consists mostly of siphonophores.

Opisthoproctus lacks a light organ on or near the eye. Like its close relatives, it has an adipose fin indicating its affinity with the salmons. A swim bladder is present. Behind the eyes the skull is so transparent that the brain is clearly visible in live or freshly dead specimens. The body is covered with large, thin, easily shed scales. The ventral edge of the body is flattened and expanded as a sort of shallow trough, called the sole. There are probably only two species of *Opisthoproctus* and as the soles of each have a different pigmentation pattern, the sole could function as an aid to species recognition. This may well be important as at certain depths both species occur together. The pattern of illuminated pigment could be detected easily by the upwardly directed tubular eyes of a fish swimming below.

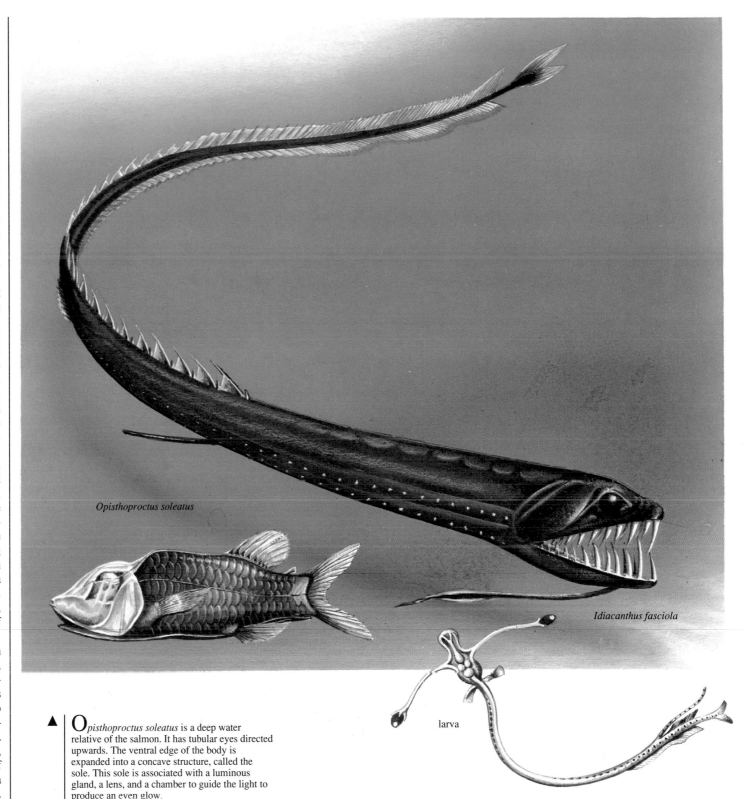

Opisthoproctus soleatus

Idiacanthus fasciola

larva

▲ O*pisthoproctus soleatus* is a deep water relative of the salmon. It has tubular eyes directed upwards. The ventral edge of the body is expanded into a concave structure, called the sole. This sole is associated with a luminous gland, a lens, and a chamber to guide the light to produce an even glow.

▲ An adult female *Idiacanthus fasciola* is much larger than the male and has well developed teeth and a luminous chin barbel. The larva has eyes supported on long stalks. At the time of metamorphosis, when the larva is 1¼ – 1½ in (3 – 4 cm) long, the eye stalks shorten and the eye takes up a more orthodox position. The male hardly grows after metamorphosis while the female can continue growing up to 12 in (30 cm).

ANGLERS
Lophiidae

The Lophiidae or anglers are fish that have adapted to a benthonic existence. Their body is flattened in a dorsoventral direction and their head is disproportionately large, very broad, with a wide mouth and a prominent lower jaw. The head may sometimes be wider than the body is long, accounting for up to two fifths of the body length; in shape it resembles a more or less circular disk. Towards the rear the body is thinner and becomes cylindrical and compressed in the caudal peduncle. The skin is not scaly and has a large number of cutaneous tree-like formations which are very jagged and form fringes along the jaws, the lateral line, and the free rays of the dorsal fin. This type of "ornament" is used for mimetic purposes and enables the fish, when crouching on the sea bed, to merge with the algae or coral surrounding it. In many species sharp spines jut out from the cranial bones and the gill cover bones, as well as the bones of the scapular girdle, providing the fish with effective means of defense; the arrangement of these spines varies from species to species.

The prefrontal protuberances are followed by only slightly ossified frontal protuberances that leave cartilaginous interfrontal zones along the central (median) line; this flat "blade" acts as a support for the "illicial base plate"; it is movable and supports the illicium and the second ray of of the first dorsal fin – a typical feature of the anglers. This structure can move about between the crests of the frontal protuberances beneath the apophyses; the synchronization between this "shift" forwards, the raising or lowering of the illicium accompanied by brisk movements of the lure, and the opening of the mouth, is perfectly organized by a complex, autonomous, and very specific muscular system, deriving from the muscles of the rays on the impar and supercarinal fins.

The family Lophiidae has two subfamilies: the Sladeiinae and the Lophiinae. The Sladeiinae, with just the one genus *Sladenia*, are a very ancient form of fish which lives deep down; there is just one ray behind the illicium. The Lophiinae have two rays behind the illicium. There are three genera in this subfamily: *Chirolophius, Lophiomus,* and *Lophius.*

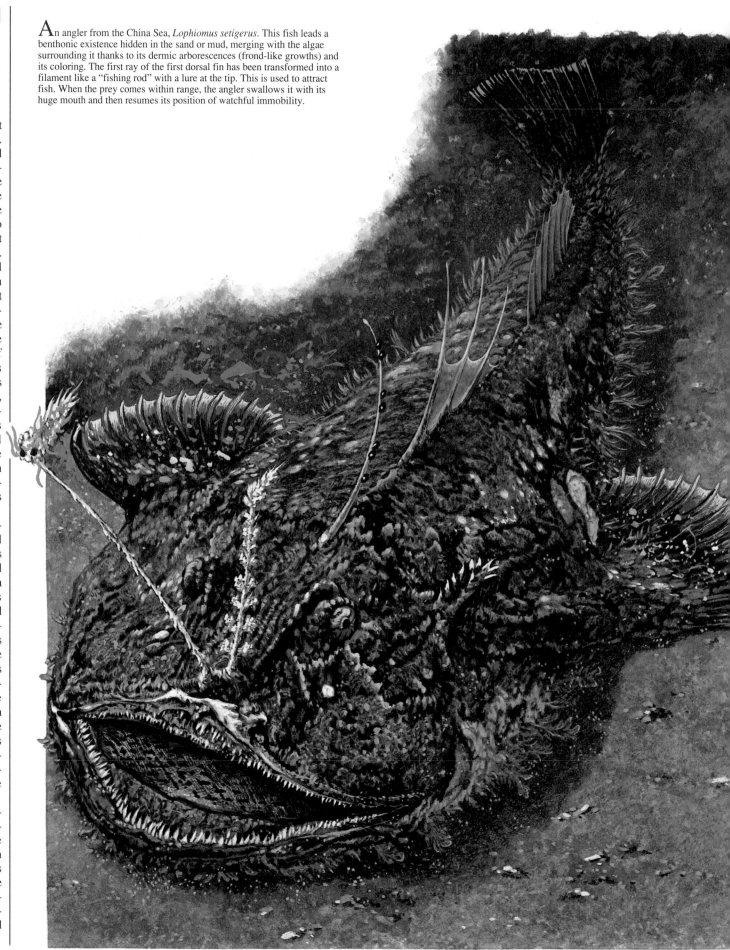

An angler from the China Sea, *Lophiomus setigerus*. This fish leads a benthonic existence hidden in the sand or mud, merging with the algae surrounding it thanks to its dermic arborescences (frond-like growths) and its coloring. The first ray of the first dorsal fin has been transformed into a filament like a "fishing rod" with a lure at the tip. This is used to attract fish. When the prey comes within range, the angler swallows it with its huge mouth and then resumes its position of watchful immobility.

The anglers (a name which aptly describes the shape and habits of the members of the family Lophiidae) are extraordinarily fertile fish, laying about 3,000,000 eggs each time. These eggs float to the surface of the sea inside a gelatinous strip called the "purple veil" that forms "streamers" about 24 – 32 in (60 – 80 cm) wide and about 33 – 40 ft (10 – 12 m) long, pinkish pale gray in color, and speckled with black dots that are, in fact, the embryos still enclosed in their eggs. During the first stages of development the embryo is more or less featureless, with a long body and narrow head. The last stages of development of *Lophius piscatorius* and *L. budegassa* involve small active fish swimming at the surface of the water. All the rays of the fins, which are large by now, have numerous dermic arborescences and extend into filaments; the illicium is still short and the head is still not very developed. The young angler swims energetically at the surface or burrows into the mud with its snout. Lastly, it lies on the sandy or muddy bed, merging with the algae. The head becomes larger and larger and the ventral fins grow smaller. The pectoral fins become pseudobrachia and the illicium develops and takes on its specific form.

The angler leads a benthonic life, lying motionless on the sea bed, well hidden among algae and stones. Its mimetic capabilities are accentuated by the arborescences of the skin and the coloring, which merges perfectly with the colors of the surrounding environment. On soft sea beds it burrows into the sand or mud, leaving just its "angling" filament or lure protruding, plus its eyes, "nostrils," and gill apertures, waiting in hiding for some passing prey to be attracted by the lure of the illicium. The thin musculature of this single (*L. budegassa, L. americanus*) or double (*L. piscatorius*) appendage enables the angler to move its lure in a way resembling small mollusks or crustaceans, on which all fish feed. When a careless fish approaches this inviting structure, the illicium bends forwards and once the prey is within reach the angler raises itself swiftly onto its pectoral "legs" with a jump which brings its huge mouth and throat to the exact spot where the illicium just was; the fish is seized, whatever its size. The movable rows of teeth on the mandible (lower jaw) fold backwards, then the prey is grabbed bodily with the vomerine and palatine teeth, the pharyngeal masticatory plates, and the ceratobranchial plates. An

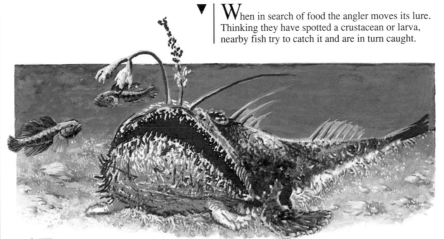

▼ When in search of food the angler moves its lure. Thinking they have spotted a crustacean or larva, nearby fish try to catch it and are in turn caught.

▼ The angler is a slow swimmer and spends most of its time on the sea bed. In order to raise up its large body and pounce on its prey, it uses its pectoral fins, which are well developed and strong, and its ventral fins, but it never walks on "all fours," as do the Antennariidae or batfish.

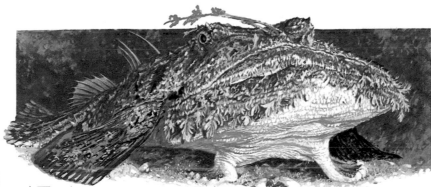

▼ The number of eggs laid is impressive. The eggs are enveloped in a gelatinous "streamer" that can be up to 40 ft (12 m) long and 20 in (50 cm) wide.

▲ The voracity of the angler is such that it will even try to devour sea birds when they dive or while they are sleeping on the surface.

▼ The metamorphosis of the angler larva: the young pass through various stages and swim about energetically before reaching the adult stage when they go to live a quiet life on the sea bed.

enormous esophagous sphincter shaped like a sleeve keeps the prey on the move towards the stomach. Because of the strength of the jaws and the power of the muscles, the angler can swallow fish as big as itself.

Its voracity is legendary and it will happily tuck into any type of prey. It would seem that its usual diet consists of rays, scorpion fish, pleuronectids, and other fish living near the bottom, but its stomach has also revealed herrings, mackerel, and conger eels, and it may well also catch small sharks or dogfish. As a result of its adaptation to life on the sea bed, the angler is a slow swimmer, but for all this the angler will sometimes go in search of prey at the surface, or in intermediate waters. People have also observed the angler attacking sea birds as they dive, or while they are sleeping quietly on the water; because they can neither ingest nor release this unusual prey, the angler ends up dying on the spot.

Anglers never seem to be present in large numbers in a given place. Small, young individuals live at a depth of some 100 ft (30 m). Large adults can live at depths in excess of 3,300 ft (1,000 m). The family Lophiidae is found in the Indian, Pacific, and Atlantic Oceans, as well as the Mediterranean, but the distribution varies according to genus. Species belonging to the genus *Chirolophius* are only found in tropical seas or subtropical waters, in coastal zones near islands or continents. They are found, in particular, around the Sunda Isles, which can undoubtedly be regarded as the cradle of this family, and along the shores of the Indian Ocean. Just two species have migrated to the tropical waters of the Atlantic Ocean. *Chirolophius* lives at a depth of 650 – 2,500 ft (200 – 800 m). The genus *Lophiomus* is found in the tropical belt and subtropical waters of the Indo-Pacific area. No species is found in the Atlantic Ocean. This genus has been fished at depths of between 100 – 2,000 ft (30 – 700 m).

The genus *Lophius,* the most evolved member of the family, is found almost exclusively in the Atlantic Ocean and the Mediterranean, with the exception of one species which lives in the Sea of Japan. These fish stand up well to low temperatures and their habitat includes cold waters: *L. piscatorius* is fished from Senegal to northern Norway. Lastly, the very ancient and very rare genus *Sladenia* is found only in deep sea habitats, 2,800 – 4,000 ft (850 – 1200 m) down, south of the Sunda archipelago or close to the Tchagos islands.

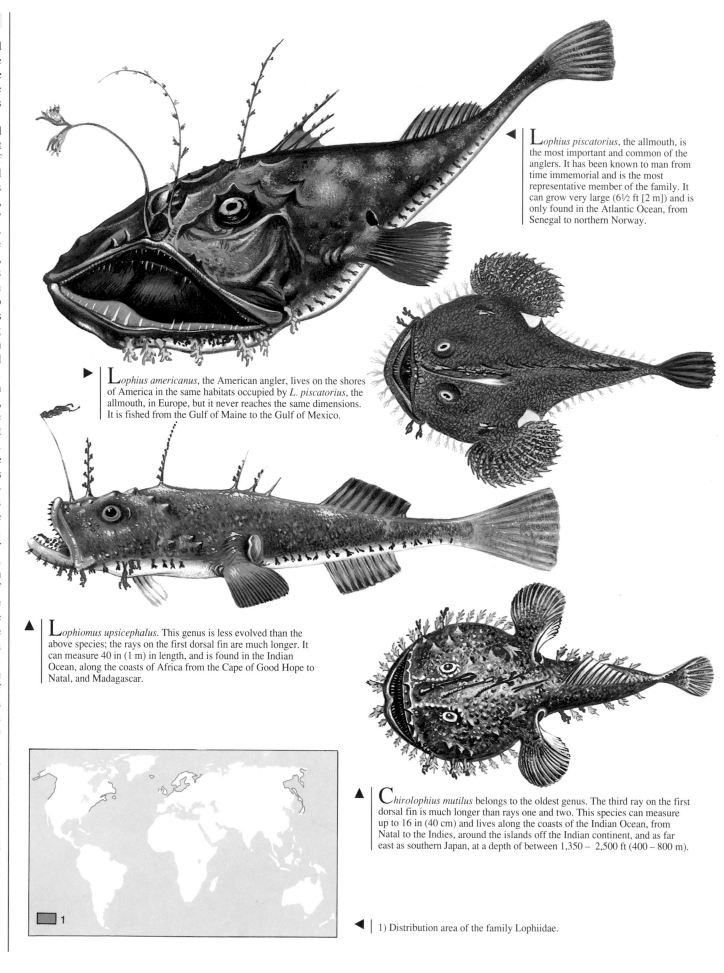

Lophius piscatorius, the allmouth, is the most important and common of the anglers. It has been known to man from time immemorial and is the most representative member of the family. It can grow very large (6½ ft [2 m]) and is only found in the Atlantic Ocean, from Senegal to northern Norway.

Lophius americanus, the American angler, lives on the shores of America in the same habitats occupied by *L. piscatorius*, the allmouth, in Europe, but it never reaches the same dimensions. It is fished from the Gulf of Maine to the Gulf of Mexico.

Lophiomus upsicephalus. This genus is less evolved than the above species; the rays on the first dorsal fin are much longer. It can measure 40 in (1 m) in length, and is found in the Indian Ocean, along the coasts of Africa from the Cape of Good Hope to Natal, and Madagascar.

Chirolophius mutilus belongs to the oldest genus. The third ray on the first dorsal fin is much longer than rays one and two. This species can measure up to 16 in (40 cm) and lives along the coasts of the Indian Ocean, from Natal to the Indies, around the islands off the Indian continent, and as far east as southern Japan, at a depth of between 1,350 – 2,500 ft (400 – 800 m).

1) Distribution area of the family Lophiidae.

BATFISH

Ogcocephalidae

The Ogcocephalidae, or batfish, seem to make up the most specialized of all the families in the order Pediculati. They are closely related to the Antennaridae (frogfish) and slightly less so to the Lophiidae (angler fish) and the Caunacidae. They are completely adapted to the benthonic life; their body, which is very flattened dorsoventrally, takes on a variety of forms, depending on the genus – diamond-shaped in *Ogcocephalus* and *Zalieutes*, triangular in *Malthopsis*, trapezoidal in *Halicmetus*, oval in *Dibranchus*, circular in *Halieutaea* and *Halieutichthys*, or truncated in *Coelophrys*.

The mouth is small, opening downwards, and is dominated by the rostrum. The teeth are small, heart-shaped, sharp, and thin, arranged in rows on the premaxillary bone; there are no teeth in the genera *Coelophrys* and *Halieutopsis*. Similarly, in most of the genera there are rows of small teeth on the palatine and vomerine bones. The tongue is rough. The eyes are large and the pupil can contract into the form of an S. The very small illicium is contained within a cavity situated directly above the mouth, at the front of the snout and beneath the rostrum. The lure resembles a single or double fleshy button, either ball-shaped or pyramidal, and each genus has its own typical shape. When resting, the illicium and its "button" are retracted inside a deep cavity situated between the nostrils beneath the rostrum, and vanish from view altogether.

The Ogcocephalidae lead a benthonic life, close to the surface or at medium depths in tropical seas. They are most commonly found in sandy–muddy environments. Their very mimetic coloring enables them to blend well with their surroundings; what is more, they are so well protected by their carapace with its spines that they are unafraid of predators. They are very poor swimmers and spend their time lying motionless on the sea bed, or dragging themselves slowly about on "all fours." They feed on small crustaceans, young fish or larvae because their small mouth does not enable them to swallow larger prey. There are about 60 species of Ogcocephalidae or batfish. They live in tropical seas, mainly in the Indo-Pacific region.

Batfish (*Ogcocephalus vespertilio*)

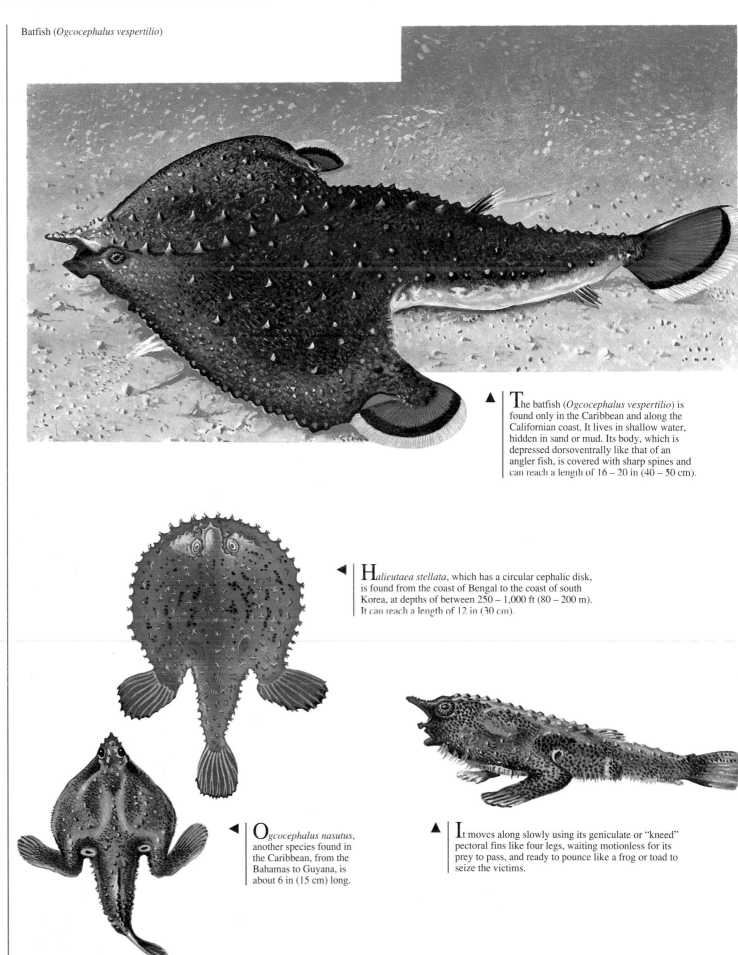

▲ The batfish (*Ogcocephalus vespertilio*) is found only in the Caribbean and along the Californian coast. It lives in shallow water, hidden in sand or mud. Its body, which is depressed dorsoventrally like that of an angler fish, is covered with sharp spines and can reach a length of 16 – 20 in (40 – 50 cm).

◀ *Halieutaea stellata*, which has a circular cephalic disk, is found from the coast of Bengal to the coast of south Korea, at depths of between 250 – 1,000 ft (80 – 200 m). It can reach a length of 12 in (30 cm).

◀ *Ogcocephalus nasutus*, another species found in the Caribbean, from the Bahamas to Guyana, is about 6 in (15 cm) long.

▲ It moves along slowly using its geniculate or "kneed" pectoral fins like four legs, waiting motionless for its prey to pass, and ready to pounce like a frog or toad to seize the victims.

FROGFISH

Antennariidae

The family Antennariidae or frogfish is made up of fish living in tropical seas in coral formations or floating gulfweed. Their remarkable camouflage of very variable and often very beautiful and bright colors enables them to blend in with their surroundings. The body is bulky, spherical, and fairly compressed; the head is broad, the mouth is diagonal in shape, and the lower jaw or mandible can project forward to seize prey. The skin is scaleless (in *Histrio* and *Histiophryne)* or covered with tiny spines that give it a rough appearance (in *Phrynelox* and *Fowlerichthys*), or velvety (in *Antennarius).* There are numerous cutaneous arborescences or branch-like growths situated along the mucous ducts, around the mouth, and on the rays of the vertex. The latero-mucous system is composed of fossettes of varying shapes and sizes; the number and arrangement of these fossettes provide very helpful taxonomic data.

The eyes are small and covered with transparent skin. The premaxillary bones have numerous rather small, heart-shaped teeth; the palatine teeth are strong and curved. The cranium is bulky, and larger than that of the Lophiidae (anglers), with no empty spaces, and additional cartilaginous formations particularly on the inner surface. The structure that supports the illicium and the second ray of the dorsal fin shifts onto the cartilaginous ethmoid bone. Its very well developed musculature derives from the motor muscles of the rays of the fin. The well developed illicium supports a lure which has a particular form in each genus. After it come two separate rays that are thick and heavy and support a membrane towards the rear. These rays are accentuated in *Antennarius* and inconspicuous in *Histiophryne*; in *Histrio* they can be erected like a rhinoceros's horn, and are sheathed with cutaneous arborescences. The second dorsal fin is much longer than the anal fin and has 11 – 18 single or ramified rays. The pseudo-branchium is well developed and has another three pterygia, the Antennariidae being more primitive than the Lophiidae; in individuals belonging to the genus *Pterophryne,* however, one of these pterygia is small in size. The hyoid bone supports eight large branchiostegal rays,

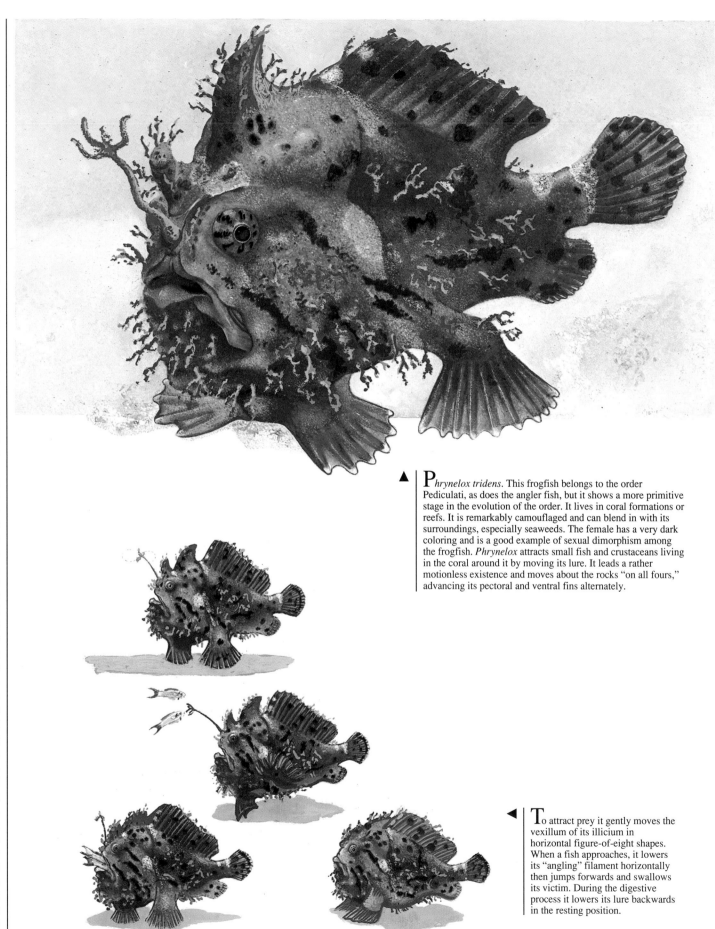

▲ Phrynelox tridens. This frogfish belongs to the order Pediculati, as does the angler fish, but it shows a more primitive stage in the evolution of the order. It lives in coral formations or reefs. It is remarkably camouflaged and can blend in with its surroundings, especially seaweeds. The female has a very dark coloring and is a good example of sexual dimorphism among the frogfish. *Phrynelox* attracts small fish and crustaceans living in the coral around it by moving its lure. It leads a rather motionless existence and moves about the rocks "on all fours," advancing its pectoral and ventral fins alternately.

◄ To attract prey it gently moves the vexillum of its illicium in horizontal figure-of-eight shapes. When a fish approaches, it lowers its "angling" filament horizontally then jumps forwards and swallows its victim. During the digestive process it lowers its lure backwards in the resting position.

with the last three spatula-shaped. The gill opening is small and situated behind the axilla of the pectoral fin; in some genera *(Abantennarius* and *Brachionichthys)* it is situated in a position towards the rear, in the center of the body. The stomach can be greatly dilated and consists of a nonmuscular pouch or pocket closed off by a cartilaginous "press-button" which opens when large prey are being swallowed. There is a swim bladder but no blind gut.

The Antennariidae can puff themselves up by means of superimposed subcutaneous muscular tunics, one with lengthwise fibers, the other with star-shaped fibers. A reinforcing band of muscle between the pectoral and pelvic fins stops the tightened tissues from tearing when large prey are being swallowed. The development of the Antennariidae is an unknown quantity. The female lays eggs in "streamers," quite like the system used by the anglers.

The Antennariidae or frogfish spend much of their time motionless, trying to attract small fish, mollusks or crustaceans with the undulating, swaying movements of the illicium. When a prey approaches, the frogfish raises itself up on the tips of its pectoral fins to help it remain balanced, and lowers the illicium horizontally forwards, guiding the prey towards its mouth. Then it suddenly lowers its pectoral fins, jumps forward, and swallows its prey. If the prey is large, the stomach opens and the whole front part of the body swells up. It takes many hours to digest its meal in a state of half-sleep, with the illicium bent backwards. After digesting it resumes its normal shape by contracting the tunics. When it moves along the sea bed, the frogfish drags itself slowly along "on all fours," alternately moving one pectoral fin with the ventral fin on the other side of the body. The frogfish can climb up rocks.

There are about 60 species and some 15 genera of Antennariidae or frogfish. The family seems to have originated close to Australia, where very ancient genera are to be found which are quite close to the fossil genus *Histionotophorus*. The family then spread out into all the tropical seas; *Antennarius* is found round offshore islands near India, in the Red Sea, in the Indian Ocean, and in the tropical regions of the Atlantic Ocean; *Uniantennatus* lives in the Pacific and Atlantic Ocean, *Abantennarius* in the Hawaiian Islands and Polynesia, *Lophiocaron* in the Red Sea, on offshore islands near India, and close to Australia.

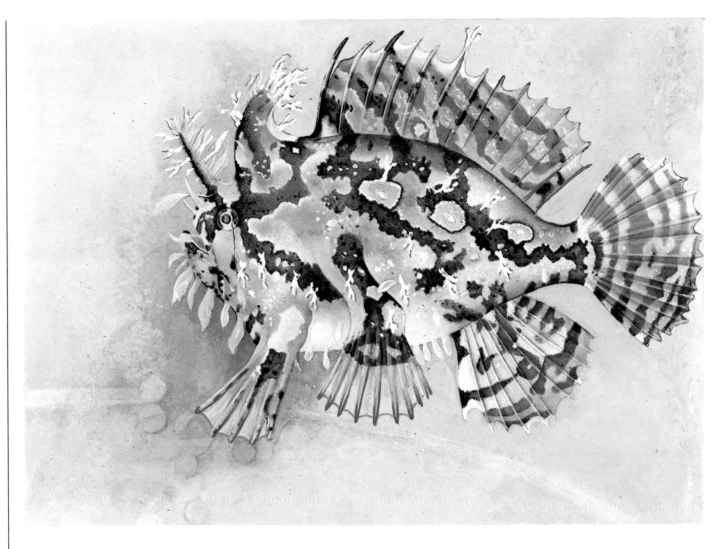

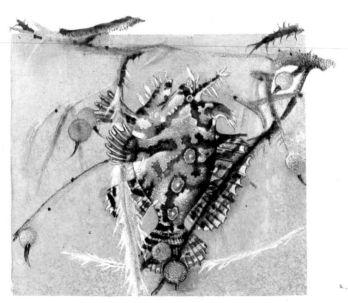

▲ The Sargasso weed fish can climb quickly up the stems of floating seaweed, using its pectoral and ventral fins.

▲ The Sargasso weed fish *(Histrio histrio)* blends perfectly with the floating seaweed in which it lives, thanks to its camouflage colors and decorative elements: in fact it looks as if it is literally encrusted with worms and parasites. It can move very swiftly and climbs around gulfweed like a water rat. It can also swim fast in the open sea; when it does so, it folds the illicium and the adjacent rays against its body, rests its ventral fins against its abdomen, and moves forwards by flapping its pectoral fins and moving its impar fins. If it wants to stop in a hurry, it brakes by splaying its paired fins and raising the cephalic rays. During its nuptial display the male does a fully fledged dance with complex figurations in front of the motionless female: it puffs up its body, parades, and erects all its cutaneous "decor." The illicium unfolds, the coloring turns brighter, and the colored ocelli become very luminous. It feeds on young fish, crustaceans, small mollusks, and insects which are typical inhabitants of gulfweed.

CERATIOID ANGLERS

Ceratioidea

Within this suborder of deep sea fish, related to the common angler fish (*Lophius* spp.) of shallow water, are to be found some of the most remarkable modifications known among vertebrates. One characteristic feature of this suborder is present in a more easily recognizable form in its shallow water relatives. The first three rays of the dorsal fin have become separated from the rest of the fin and, in the course of time, have moved forward. The first ray has become elongated and its tip elaborate and fleshy. Muscles have developed to make this first ray extremely mobile and it is used as a fishing rod. The fleshy end is moved about near the mouth in the usually optimistic assumption that some passing fish will mistake the tip for food. The bait is brought nearer the mouth and the prey is swallowed.

This fishing rod-like dorsal fin ray is called the illicium and the bait, the esca. But in the deep sea there is no light, so an esca just shaped like a tasty morsel or a small fish would not be seen and would therefore be of no use whatsoever. This apparent drawback has been overcome by making the esca luminous. Some species have, in addition, highly mobile, variously branched barbels on the chin, the tips of which, in a few species at least, are luminous. These are also thought to act as lures.

Once the prey has been lured toward the esca, the whole illicium is retracted or otherwise moved to bring the prey as close to the mouth as possible. Then there is either a sudden lunge or possibly some suction pressure and the fish is in the mouth. Large, sharply pointed teeth prevent its escape and the fish is swallowed. The stomach of ceratioid anglers, as in many deep sea fish, is extremely elastic so that fish larger than the captor can be accommodated.

Ceratioid anglers do not necessarily limit themselves to fish. Analyses of the contents of anglerfish stomachs have revealed the presence of squids, deep sea crustaceans of many sorts, arrow worms, and innumerable other forms of deep sea fish.

The deep sea anglerfish are scaleless although in a few species (e.g. *Himantolophus* and *Ceratias*) there are nodules

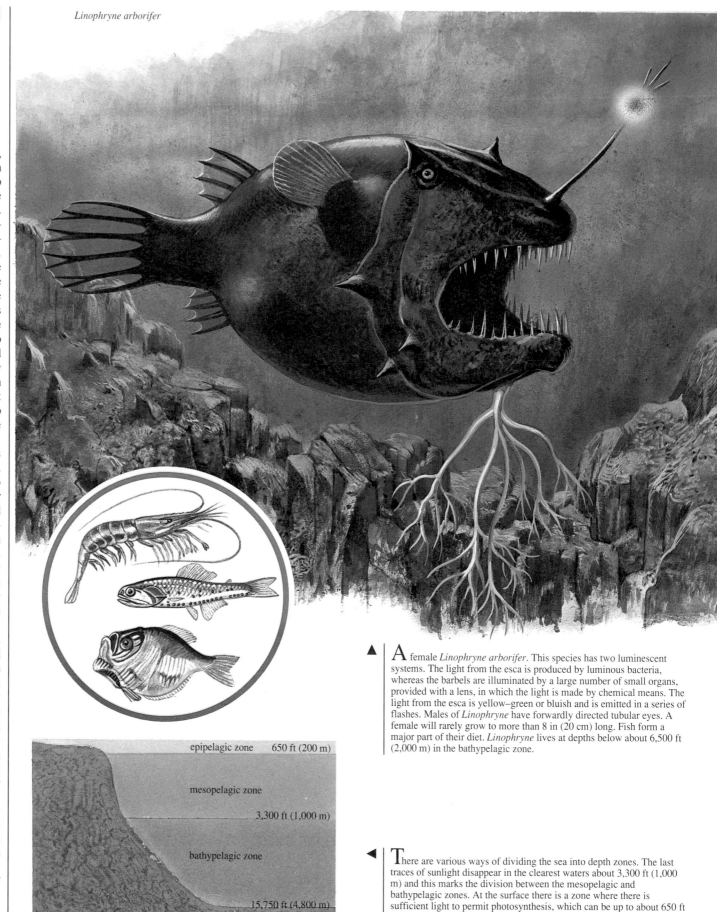

Linophryne arborifer

▲ A female *Linophryne arborifer*. This species has two luminescent systems. The light from the esca is produced by luminous bacteria, whereas the barbels are illuminated by a large number of small organs, provided with a lens, in which the light is made by chemical means. The light from the esca is yellow–green or bluish and is emitted in a series of flashes. Males of *Linophryne* have forwardly directed tubular eyes. A female will rarely grow to more than 8 in (20 cm) long. Fish form a major part of their diet. *Linophryne* lives at depths below about 6,500 ft (2,000 m) in the bathypelagic zone.

epipelagic zone   650 ft (200 m)

mesopelagic zone

3,300 ft (1,000 m)

bathypelagic zone

15,750 ft (4,800 m)

◄ There are various ways of dividing the sea into depth zones. The last traces of sunlight disappear in the clearest waters about 3,300 ft (1,000 m) and this marks the division between the mesopelagic and bathypelagic zones. At the surface there is a zone where there is sufficient light to permit photosynthesis, which can be up to about 650 ft (200 m) deep . This is called the epipelagic or euphotic zone.

in the skin. In the oneirodid genus *Spiniphryne* the skin is covered with numerous small close-set spines which even cover the bases of the fins. The dorsal and anal fins are placed opposite one another and contain very few rays. The tail fin is fan-shaped with few, widely spaced, conspicuous thick rays. The pectoral fins are variously developed but, again, contain relatively few, rather thick rays. In some species the pectoral fin is mounted on a small raised base. Pelvic fins are absent, but in some species the pelvic bones are still present beneath the skin. The eyes of the adult female are very small. In most species the adult males have relatively large, sometimes tubular eyes, but males of *Gigantactis* have small eyes. The skeleton of all species is greatly reduced. Bones are poorly calcified, much cartilage is present, and many bones are reduced in size to struts. The operculum (gill cover) in most fish is a fan-shaped bone but in oneirodid anglerfish it is reduced to a V-shape. Although the jaw bones are well developed in comparison to other skull bones, they are fragile compared to those in many other fish. Most species are deep brown or black in color.

Except for *Neoceratias*, all adult female anglerfish have an illicium with an esca at the end. Except in *Caulophryne*, this esca is luminous. The light comes from colonies of luminous bacteria living within the escal bulb.

The reproductive strategies within the ceratioid anglers vary between that generally practiced among mid water fish to the strangest among all vertebrates – the adult males becoming parasitic on the females. The female develops a functional illicium lacked by the male. It is thought that after metamorphosis the females may take several years to reach sexual maturity. It is in the subsequent fate of the males that we see the most striking differences. After metamorphosis, the males are inadequately adapted for feeding, so they must find a mate quickly. In free-living males the testes are already well developed before metamorphosis. After metamorphosis they develop pincer-like jaws thought to be for nipping the skin of the female during fertilization rather than for catching food. Often the body of the dwarf male literally fuses with the females; thereafter, the male lives as a parasite or as a simple body appendage of his partner.

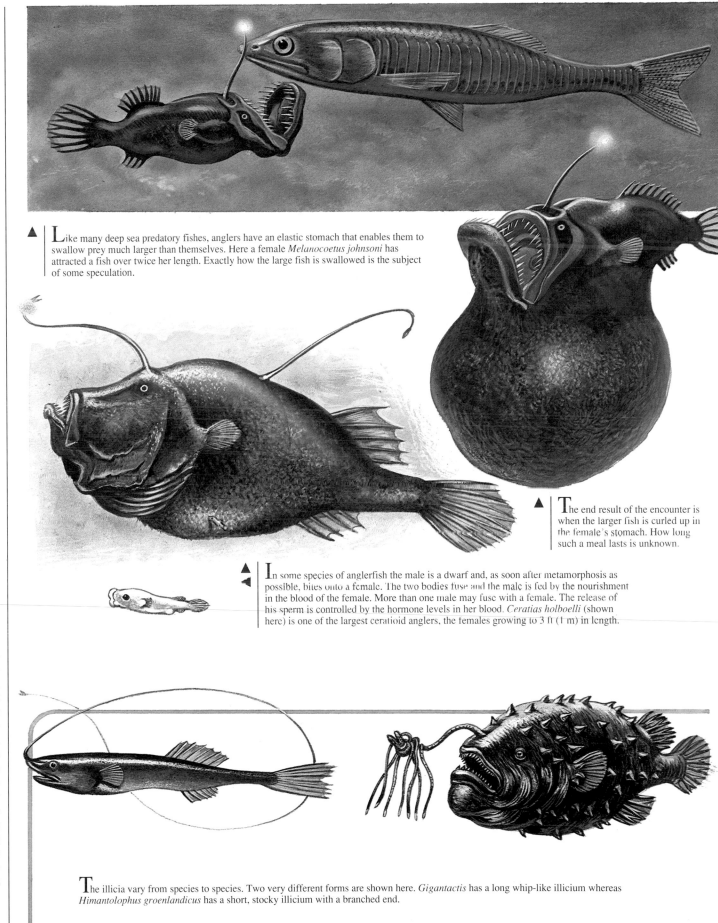

▲ Like many deep sea predatory fishes, anglers have an elastic stomach that enables them to swallow prey much larger than themselves. Here a female *Melanocoetus johnsoni* has attracted a fish over twice her length. Exactly how the large fish is swallowed is the subject of some speculation.

▲ The end result of the encounter is when the larger fish is curled up in the female's stomach. How long such a meal lasts is unknown.

▲ In some species of anglerfish the male is a dwarf and, as soon after metamorphosis as ◄ possible, bites onto a female. The two bodies fuse and the male is fed by the nourishment in the blood of the female. More than one male may fuse with a female. The release of his sperm is controlled by the hormone levels in her blood. *Ceratias holboelli* (shown here) is one of the largest ceratioid anglers, the females growing to 3 ft (1 m) in length.

The illicia vary from species to species. Two very different forms are shown here. *Gigantactis* has a long whip-like illicium whereas *Himantolophus groenlandicus* has a short, stocky illicium with a branched end.

CODFISH
Gadiformes

Codfish or Gadiformes are bony fish with a certain number of primitive features. As a result they are almost entirely without spiny rays. Their ventral fins are either thoracic or jugular ("thoracic" when they are situated on the same line as the base of the pectoral fins, "jugular" when they are situated in front of the pectoral fins, beneath the throat). The swim bladder is closed. The fairly long body and the head are covered with scales. Many species have a barbel under the chin. The Gadiformes are represented by more than 400 species, belonging to the following families: Muraenolepidae – moray eels, Moridae, Bregmacerotidae, Gadidae – the cod/haddock/pollack group, Melanodidae, Merlucciidae – hake, and Macruridae – grenadiers.

The family Gadidae is the best known of the order Gadiformes, with numerous commercially important species such as the common cod *(Gadus morhua)*, the haddock *(Melanogrammus aeglefinus)*, the whiting *(Merlangius merlangus)*, the pollacks *(Pollachius virens* and *Pollachius pollachius)*, the ling *(Molva molva)*, and so on. One fairly specific feature of the family is the fact that most of the species live on the North Atlantic continental shelf and particularly on the European slope. This is unique among fish. The Gadidae have invaded the various niches available in the temperate waters of the Atlantic Oceans.

One species, the burbot *(Lota lota)*, has even adapted to freshwater habitats, and is found throughout Europe, Asia, and North America. But most of the Gadidae live on the continental shelf, i.e. between the coastal zone and a depth of about 650 ft (200 m). Some go deeper down than the upper edge of the shelf's scarp, like the cod itself, for example, which is sometimes fished at depths of more than 2,000 ft (600 m), and certain forms of rockling *(Onogadus argentatus)*, which have been recorded at depths of 4,500 ft (1,400 m). Nearly all the Gadidae live on the sea bed or bottom, or slightly above it, such as the rocklings *(Rhinonemus cimbrius*, subspecies *Gaidrosparus* and *Ciliata)*, the haddock, and the whiting. Other species tend to live above the bed at medium depths, such as the pollacks and the ling. Others, last of all, and depending on the time of year, can live either on the sea

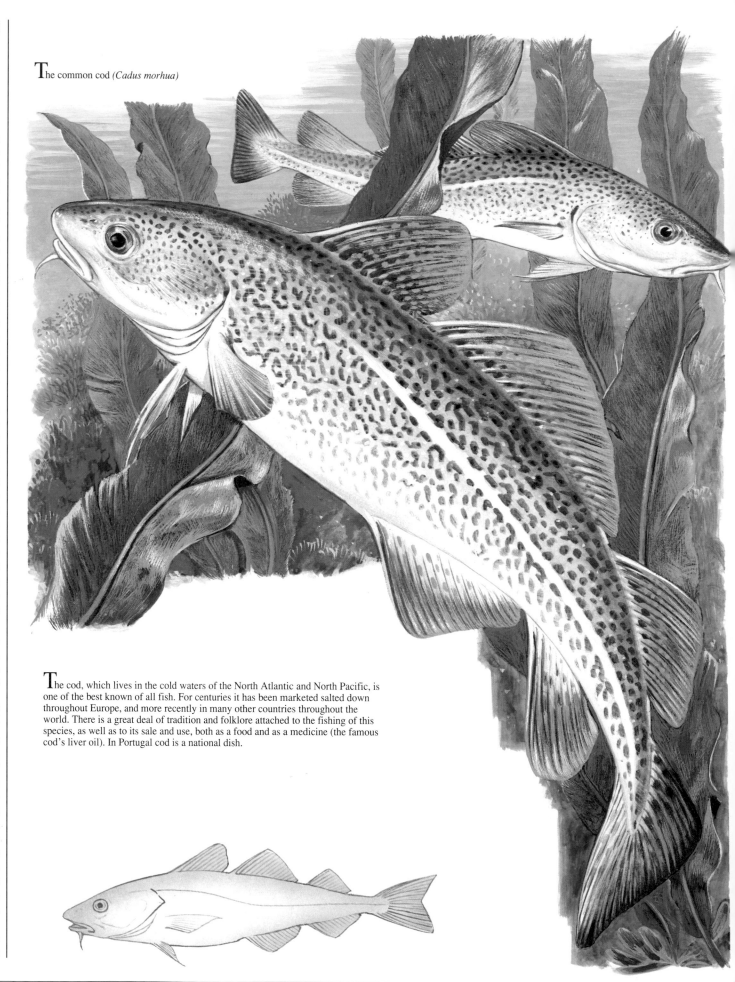

The common cod *(Cadus morhua)*

The cod, which lives in the cold waters of the North Atlantic and North Pacific, is one of the best known of all fish. For centuries it has been marketed salted down throughout Europe, and more recently in many other countries throughout the world. There is a great deal of tradition and folklore attached to the fishing of this species, as well as to its sale and use, both as a food and as a medicine (the famous cod's liver oil). In Portugal cod is a national dish.

bed, or at medium depths, such as the common cod. But the early stages of development of all the different species, even those closely associated with the sea bed, are spent initially near the surface (pelagically), sometimes for quite a long period of time.

In the order Gadiformes the Merlucciidae form the other large family of commercially important fish along with the Gadidae. The best known species of the Merlucciidae are the hakes (subspecies of *Merluccius*), with some 15 species which are very difficult to tell apart. Unlike the Gadidae which, as we have seen, are all associated with the cold waters of the North Atlantic and, to a lesser extent, with the North Pacific, the various species of hake are distributed along all the Pacific and Atlantic coasts of the American continent, the coasts of Europe, and the Atlantic seaboard of the African continent. In cold and temperate waters the hake lives on the continental shelf and on the edge of the scarp, i.e. along the coast to a depth of about 3,300 ft (1,000 m). In the warm waters of tropical regions they are only found very deep down. During the day the hake lives close to the sea bed, but as night falls it goes hunting in shallower waters. In some parts where the hake is very plentiful, as in South Africa where it accounts for 80 – 95% of all fish caught by trawling and where there are large quantities of small crustaceans *(Euphausiacea)*, it has been possible, using sounding techniques, to follow the movement of these small crustaceans towards the surface at dusk, immediately followed by a similar movement by the hake, which scatters in all directions. At dawn both the crustaceans and the hake make a similar movement in a downward direction.

The biology of the commercial species belonging to the families Gadidae and Merlucciidae has been closely studied. Recent research has shown that most of the species like the cod and the whiting have a certain number of clearly identifiable races that can be distinguished on the basis of the number of vertebrae and rays in the fins, the composition of the blood or protein of the muscles, and so on. Each one of these "races" has a clearly defined geographical distribution and specified areas where the eggs are laid. Once sexual maturity has been reached, these fish make fairly lengthy migratory journeys to reach these areas.

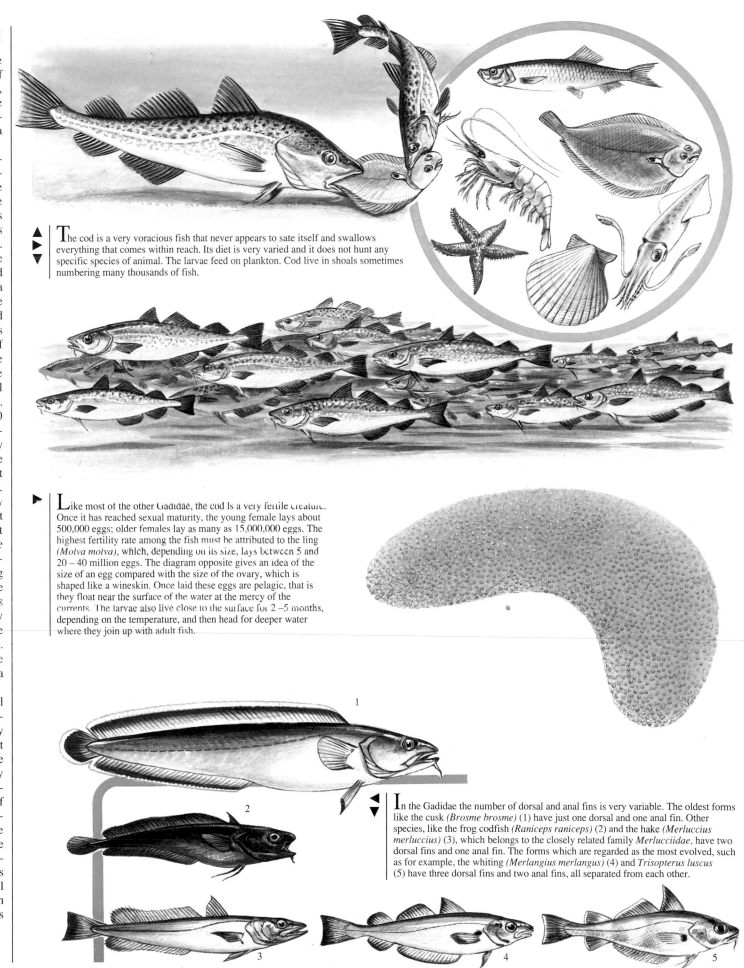

▲▶▼ The cod is a very voracious fish that never appears to sate itself and swallows everything that comes within reach. Its diet is very varied and it does not hunt any specific species of animal. The larvae feed on plankton. Cod live in shoals sometimes numbering many thousands of fish.

▶ Like most of the other Gadidae, the cod is a very fertile creature. Once it has reached sexual maturity, the young female lays about 500,000 eggs; older females lay as many as 15,000,000 eggs. The highest fertility rate among the fish must be attributed to the ling *(Molva molva)*, which, depending on its size, lays between 5 and 20 – 40 million eggs. The diagram opposite gives an idea of the size of an egg compared with the size of the ovary, which is shaped like a wineskin. Once laid these eggs are pelagic, that is they float near the surface of the water at the mercy of the currents. The larvae also live close to the surface for 2 –5 months, depending on the temperature, and then head for deeper water where they join up with adult fish.

◀▼ In the Gadidae the number of dorsal and anal fins is very variable. The oldest forms like the cusk *(Brosme brosme)* (1) have just one dorsal and one anal fin. Other species, like the frog codfish *(Raniceps raniceps)* (2) and the hake *(Merluccius merluccius)* (3), which belongs to the closely related family *Merlucciidae*, have two dorsal fins and one anal fin. The forms which are regarded as the most evolved, such as for example, the whiting *(Merlangius merlangus)* (4) and *Trisopterus luscus* (5) have three dorsal fins and two anal fins, all separated from each other.

101

CUSK EELS

Ophidiidae

The cusk eels are small or medium-sized fish, usually less than 12 in (30 cm) long, overall. Just a few forms observed along the Pacific coast of South America measure more than 24 in (60 cm), while there are a few species found off southern Africa that measure 40 in (1 m) or more. This family consists of some 40 known species, all of them benthonic or bathybenthonic. They are found in all the warm or temperate seas of the different oceans, where they live as a rule on the continental shelf and in rock formations. *Ophidium barbatum*, a Mediterranean and Atlantic species, lives on sandy or muddy sea beds at a depth of about 500 ft (150 m). During the summer months it moves closer to the shore and lives at a depth of some 65 ft (20 m).

In the Brotulidae group there are about 200 species found at all depths. They are essentially marine, abyssal fish some of which colonize the eulittoral or foreshore zones of tropical and subtropical seas. Some species are known to inhabit underground freshwater habitats, from Cuba and the Yucatan peninsula to Mexico *(Stygicola and Lucifuga)*; others are found in brackish waters in the Galapagos archipelago. Some species may be euryhaline; for example, *Dinematichthys iluocoeteoides*, which is widely distributed in all the Indo-Pacific regions, has also been recorded in freshwater environments in Borneo and in the Moluccas.

The Brotulidae are an important element in the abyssal fauna of the sea, because at least 50 species of this group are known to live at depths of more than 6,500 ft (2,000 m). These fish are found at the very lowest depths of the oceans too: one member of the group – *Bassogigas profundissimus* – is the most abyssal specimen of fish that has ever been caught, at a depth of some 26,500 ft (8,000 m). These deep sea species do not have luminous organs and only rarely show any major anatomical modifications, with the exception of the eyes. In fact the eyes can be huge, (genera *Dicrolene* and *Neobythites)* but in most cases they are small, rudimentary and covered with a thick membrane. The eyes may also be missing altogether (genus *Tauredophicium)* and blindness is more or less total in cave-dwelling species.

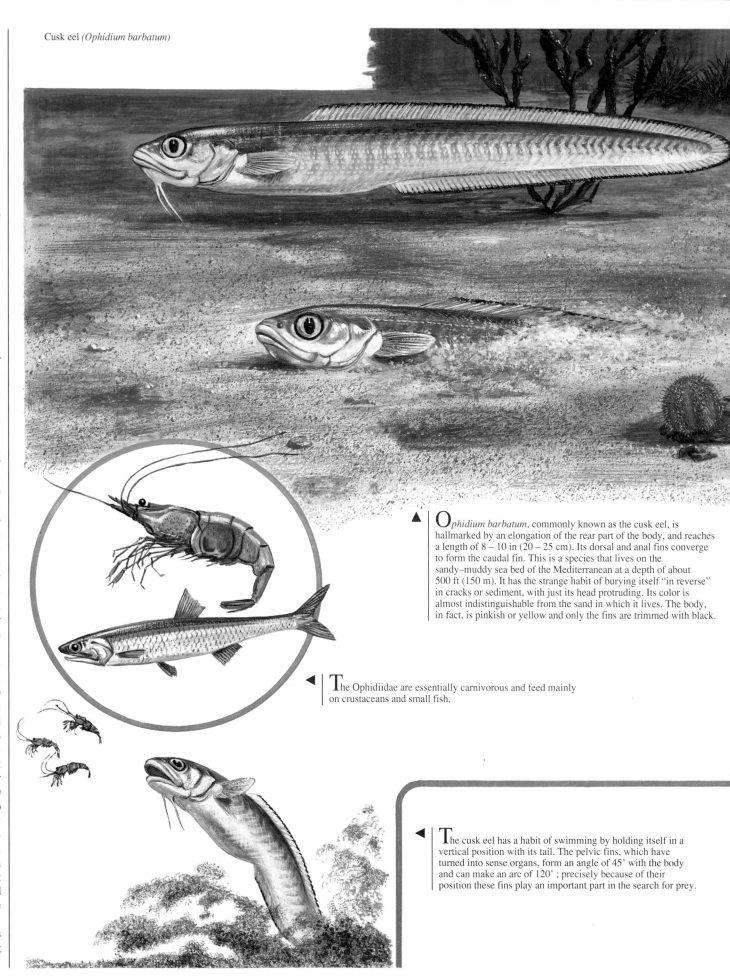

Cusk eel *(Ophidium barbatum)*

*O*phidium barbatum, commonly known as the cusk eel, is hallmarked by an elongation of the rear part of the body, and reaches a length of 8 – 10 in (20 – 25 cm). Its dorsal and anal fins converge to form the caudal fin. This is a species that lives on the sandy–muddy sea bed of the Mediterranean at a depth of about 500 ft (150 m). It has the strange habit of burying itself "in reverse" in cracks or sediment, with just its head protruding. Its color is almost indistinguishable from the sand in which it lives. The body, in fact, is pinkish or yellow and only the fins are trimmed with black.

The Ophidiidae are essentially carnivorous and feed mainly on crustaceans and small fish.

The cusk eel has a habit of swimming by holding itself in a vertical position with its tail. The pelvic fins, which have turned into sense organs, form an angle of 45° with the body and can make an arc of 120° ; precisely because of their position these fins play an important part in the search for prey.

PEARLFISH

Carapidae

Once known as Fierasferidae, pearlfish are the lowest group of the suborder Ophidioidei. They are slender in appearance, very elongated, with a relatively long head and the caudal region ending in a thin tip. There body does not have a scaly layer. The nonprotractile mouth is large and diagonal and the gill openings are quite large. In addition, the anus and the urogenital papilla are situated very far forward, immediately behind the opercula (gill covers) near the mouth, and these enable the fish to carry out its various functions without leaving the body of the holothurian or sea cucumber in which it lives as a symbiont.

Pearlfish are small marine fish, with a maximum length of 8 in (20 cm). At the present time there are about 30 known species, divided into three genera. Of these the genus *Carapus* is the most widespread in all tropical and temperate seas; *Echiodon* is found in the Atlantic and the Mediterranean; and *Encheliophis* is limited to the Philippines and Polynesia.

The morphological modifications typical of the pearlfish and their negative phototropism must be placed in context with their specific life style, because the members of this family live, for the most part, in association with other marine animals. They are quite eclectic in their choice of hosts. In fact pearlfish have been observed inside sea anemones (*Actinaria*), starfish, pyrosomes, and pearl oysters, where they sometimes die and are covered by a layer of mother-of-pearl, and thus rather clumsily inserted between the mantle and the shell itself. But pearlfish are best known for their association with the holothurians or sea cucumbers, as a result of studies which have been made about the behavior of these fish towards their hosts. The latter, which usually belong to the genera *Holothuria* and *Stichopus,* has an orifice at the caudal end of its body which opens out into a wide cloaca; from here the rectum branches off, as do two branch-like (arborescent) organs which carry out respiratory functions. The holothurian alternately sucks in and expels water with these organs, from which a flow of water enters or leaves the holothurian via the cloacal orifice.

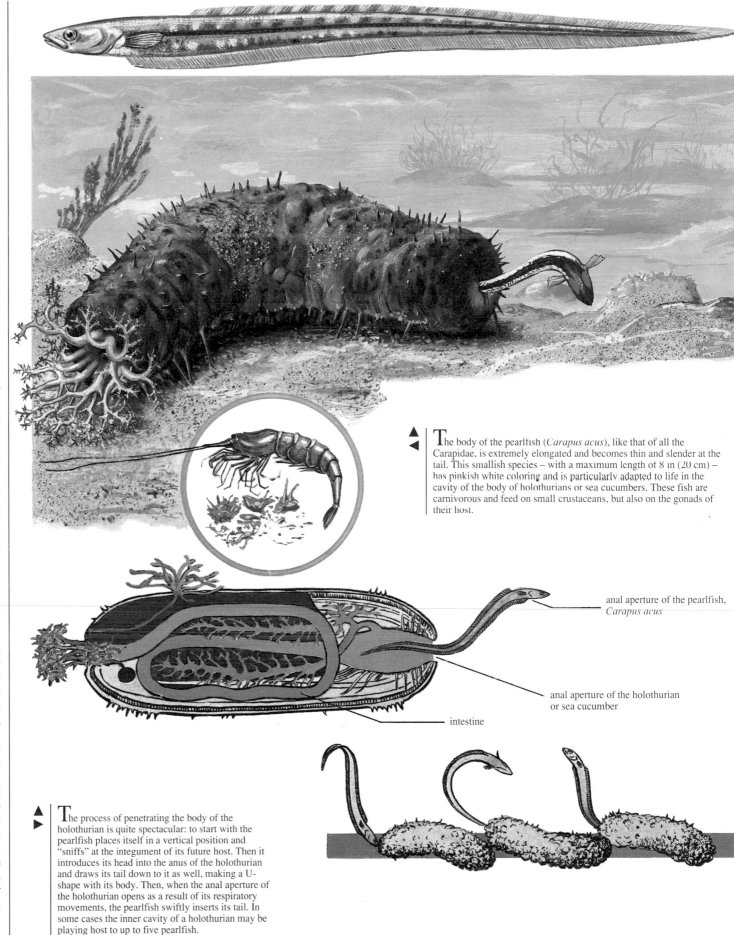

▲
◄ The body of the pearlfish (*Carapus acus*), like that of all the Carapidae, is extremely elongated and becomes thin and slender at the tail. This smallish species – with a maximum length of 8 in (20 cm) – has pinkish white coloring and is particularly adapted to life in the cavity of the body of holothurians or sea cucumbers. These fish are carnivorous and feed on small crustaceans, but also on the gonads of their host.

anal aperture of the pearlfish, *Carapus acus*

anal aperture of the holothurian or sea cucumber

intestine

▲
► The process of penetrating the body of the holothurian is quite spectacular: to start with the pearlfish places itself in a vertical position and "sniffs" at the integument of its future host. Then it introduces its head into the anus of the holothurian and draws its tail down to it as well, making a U-shape with its body. Then, when the anal aperture of the holothurian opens as a result of its respiratory movements, the pearlfish swiftly inserts its tail. In some cases the inner cavity of a holothurian may be playing host to up to five pearlfish.

FLYING FISH

Exocoetidae

Flying fish (Exocoetidae) belong to the order Atheriniformes. They are easily identifiable by the conspicuous development of certain parts of their body, which have been adapted to gliding. This development has to do above all with the pectoral fins, but also with the lower lobe of the caudal fin and the ventral fins. They have both primitive features (absence of spiny rays in the fins; pelvic fins situated distinctly to the rear of the pectoral fins; scales not equipped with small spines) and evolved features, or even specializations (lateral line situated close to the edge of the belly; dorsal and anal fins situated more or less on top of each other, and set well back from the center of the body; pectoral fins attached high up the sides of the body, and so on). In any event, they are very specialized from the anatomical and biological viewpoint, because they are the only fish capable of gliding along above the surface of the sea.

Flying fish are found in surface waters in the equatorial regions and in the tropical and subtropical regions of all the oceans. The diet consists of small crustaceans and fish larvae. At night the neritic (of shallow coastline waters) species go to feed close to the coast and return to the open sea towards dawn, where they scatter during the daylight hours. Like many other species belonging to several families (gray mullet, tunny, needlefish, balarids, etc.) they jump out of the water but instead of falling straight back into the water, as other fish do, flying fish make a gliding flight, the length of which depends on the degree of adaptation to "flying."

Flying fish can be divided into two categories: the first, known as the "monoplane" type, includes the species that have just one pair of wings, the pectoral fins. This group includes *Fodiator*, *Parexocoetus*, and *Exocoetus*. In this last genus the pectoral fins reach a length equivalent to three quarters of the fish's body length, excluding the tail, and the lower lobe of the caudal fin, the "engine," accounts for 30% of this length. The ventral fins are poorly developed: only 14%. The second category, known as the "biplane" type, includes the species that have two pairs of wings, the pectoral and the ventral fins. In the latter group, which is the

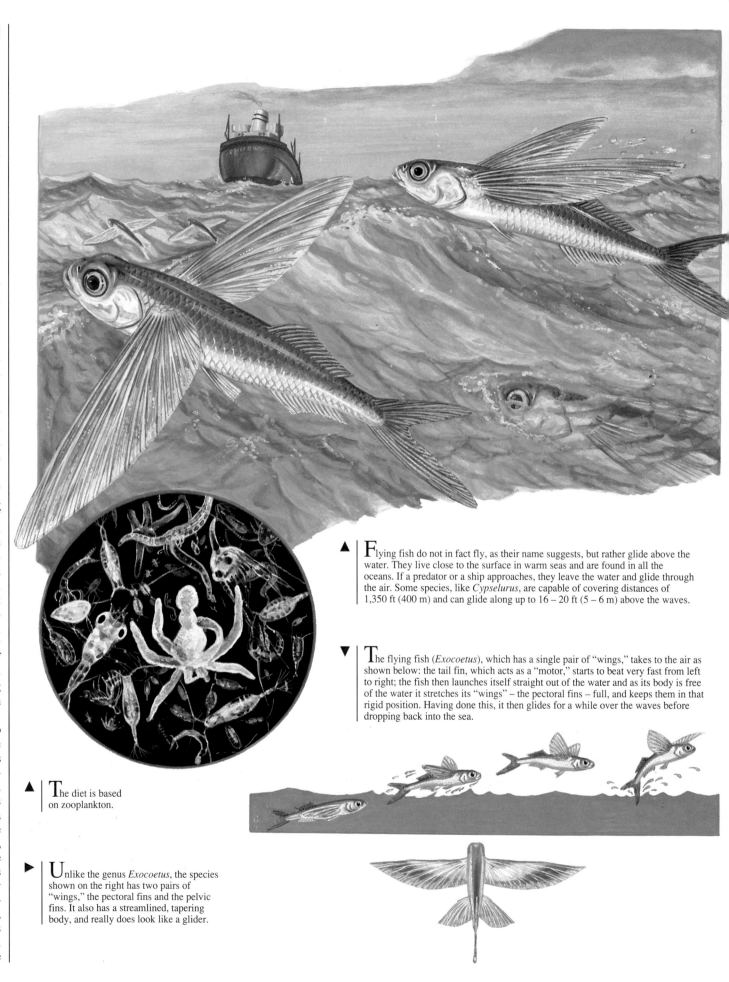

▲ The diet is based on zooplankton.

▶ Unlike the genus *Exocoetus*, the species shown on the right has two pairs of "wings," the pectoral fins and the pelvic fins. It also has a streamlined, tapering body, and really does look like a glider.

▲ Flying fish do not in fact fly, as their name suggests, but rather glide above the water. They live close to the surface in warm seas and are found in all the oceans. If a predator or a ship approaches, they leave the water and glide through the air. Some species, like *Cypselurus*, are capable of covering distances of 1,350 ft (400 m) and can glide along up to 16 – 20 ft (5 – 6 m) above the waves.

▼ The flying fish (*Exocoetus*), which has a single pair of "wings," takes to the air as shown below: the tail fin, which acts as a "motor," starts to beat very fast from left to right; the fish then launches itself straight out of the water and as its body is free of the water it stretches its "wings" – the pectoral fins – full, and keeps them in that rigid position. Having done this, it then glides for a while over the waves before dropping back into the sea.

best adapted to flying, we find *Hirundichthys*, *Prognichthys* and *Cypselurus*. In *Cypselurus* the ventral fins reach 33% of the fish's length.

We can understand the adaptations that enable the flying fish to take off by following the flight of a flying fish of the biplane type such as *Cypselurus*, in which both the pectoral fins and the ventral fins are well developed. To start with the fish swims fast with its pectoral and ventral fins folded in against its tapering body. Having reached a certain speed, the fish lifts its body out of the water, spreading out its pectoral fins and keeping them stiff. The caudal fin, and in particular the lower lobe, now beats very fast from left to right until the fish's speed – which had been 33 ft (10 m) per second in the water – increases to about 66 ft (20 m) per second. It is only possible for the fish to reach this speed because its body is now out of the water, where the density is distinctly lower than in the water. In this phase only the caudal fin is submerged in the water. The fish covers on average about 30 ft (9 m) in 0.9 seconds. The tail makes 50 – 70 complete beating movements a second, and its vibrations are felt throughout the body and even in the pectoral fins, the tips of which also vibrate. When a sufficient speed has been reached, the fish also stretches out its ventral fins, at precisely the same moment the tail leaves the water.

The fish is now completely airborne, holding itself rigid and behaving like a glider. The speed which had reached about 66 ft (20 m) per second at take off – i.e. 95 mph (72 kmh) – drops in the air until it becomes insufficient for the fish to maintain height. The fish then touches down again, and in this operation various situations may arise, according to species. The flying fish may dive into the water, but it may equally bounce back off the water surface, or just its tail may enter the water before taking off once more. A given distance may be covered in various "installments": in fact up to 12 successive "flights" have been observed. The longest observed single flight lasted 13 seconds, during a flight which lasted 28 seconds altogether.

Commercially speaking, flying fish are widely appreciated and some species are highly sought after. Their flesh is fat and they are marketed either fresh or frozen. Some species, such as *Cypselurus californicus*, are frozen and packed for use as bait for those places where people fish for sailfish and garfish.

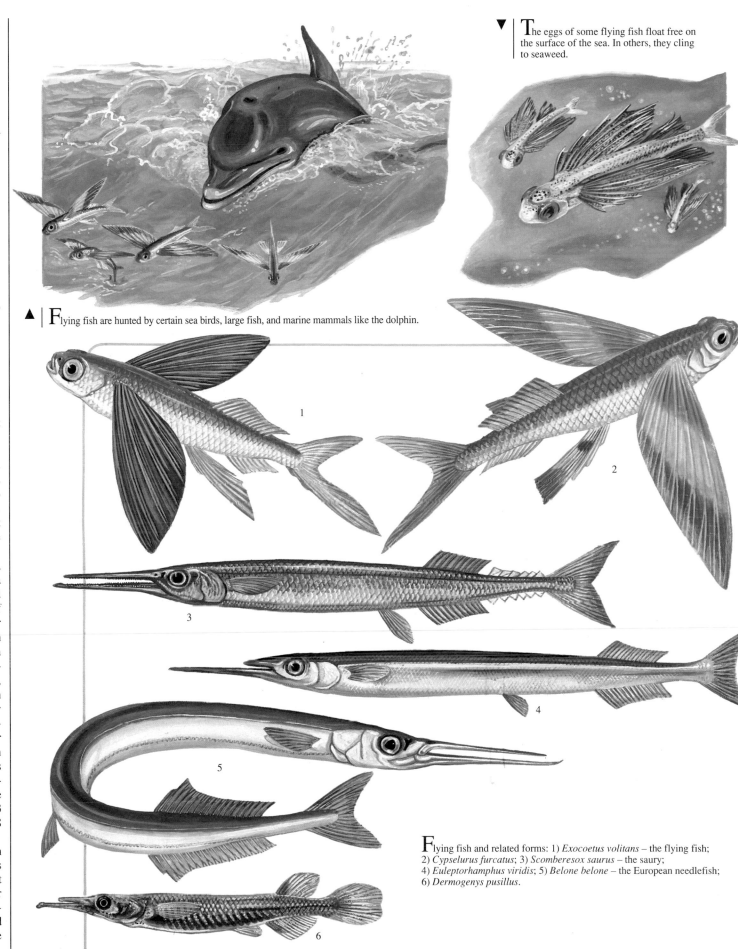

▼ The eggs of some flying fish float free on the surface of the sea. In others, they cling to seaweed.

▲ Flying fish are hunted by certain sea birds, large fish, and marine mammals like the dolphin.

Flying fish and related forms: 1) *Exocoetus volitans* – the flying fish; 2) *Cypselurus furcatus*; 3) *Scomberesox saurus* – the saury; 4) *Euleptorhamphus viridis*; 5) *Belone belone* – the European needlefish; 6) *Dermogenys pusillus*.

BERYCIFORM FISH
Beryciformes

The Beryciformes are fish with both primitive features and characteristics that relate them to more evolved bony fish. Among the primitive features, we can mention the presence of one or two supramaxillary bones and an orbitosphenoidal bone. However, they do have spines, i.e. rigid rays which are pointed and not ramified, and a swim bladder which does not connect with the digestive tube and these features draw them nearer to the more evolved fish. The order Beryciformes consists of 11 families: Polymixiidae, Berycidae, Holocentridae, Diretmidae, Anomalopidae, Monocentridae, Trachichthyidae, Anoplogasteridae (fangtooth fish), Stephanoberycidae, Melamphaeidae (deep sea big scale fish), and Gibberichthyidae (gibberfish).

The Berycidae differ from all the other families by having both two supramaxillary bones and four spiny rays in the dorsal fin. They are large fish with an oval-shaped body, laterally compressed, and a large, diagonal mouth, with rows of thin teeth on the roof of the mouth and the jaws. The family has two genera, which in turn embrace a small number of species that are all very alike. The species of the genus *Beryx* are found in the northern and southeastern Atlantic, as well as off Japan and Australia. The species of the genus *Centroberyx* are found in offshore waters round South Africa, New Zealand, Australia, and Japan.

The Anomalopidae are the only members of the Beryciformes with a subocular light organ, consisting of special cells situated side by side inside a double housing which is shiny and pigmented. The family has three genera and a small number of species. With the exception of a specimen caught near Jamaica, all the Anomalopidae known to us live in the Indian and Pacific Oceans. They are coastal fish. One might wonder why fish living in shallow waters would have a light organ: the theory is that it is used as a means of identification or to attract prey.

The Holocentridae – also known as squirrel fish – consist of seven genera with numerous species found in warm waters in all the world's oceans. The

▲ The Beryciformes have very ancient origins. In fact these fish were well represented by the end of the Secondary Era, and fossil remains dating back to the Upper Cretaceous have been found in North America, Europe, and Lebanon. The evolution of the group has involved a large variety of forms and adaptations and it is enough merely to look at the species illustrated here to realize how different they can be. As far as the various adaptations are concerned, the Beryciformes are found in offshore waters (Perycidae), in mid ocean (Melamphaeidae), and in coastal waters (squirrel fish).

▲ The Anomalopidae or lantern eye fish have a light organ beneath the eyes that, depending on the species, can be concealed by raising a sort of eyelid or tucking it away completely in a special pouch. The function of this organ is still something of a mystery: some people think it is used as a sign of identification for members of the same species; others see it as a means of attracting prey.

majority of them live in shallow environments where there are coral formations. Some species, such as *Holocentrus ascensionis*, are found at greater depths in rocky or coralled areas at 400 ft (120 m). Lastly there are the deep sea species that are found on sandy or muddy sea beds down to about 1,650 ft (500 m). Squirrel fish are nocturnal. During the day they hide in cracks or under overhanging rocks in coral reefs, emerging to feed once it is dark. Their diet consists of a wide variety of invertebrates: crabs, shrimps, and other small crustaceans (copepods, ostracods, cirripedes, sea slugs, chitons, octopus, etc.). The maximum length recorded for a squirrel fish (*H. ascensionis*) is 24 in (60 cm). They are fished with traps made of reeds or trammel nets and sold in local markets.

The Monocentridae are made up of just two very closely related genera. They are found only in the Indian and Pacific Ocean near South Africa, the American continent, and Japan. They are also coastal fish. In the Beryciformes, these fish have the most evolved defense apparatus (spines, carapace, etc.).

The Melamphaeidae are made up of five genera and numerous species, mostly living in tropical areas. They are found in all the oceans apart from the Arctic regions and the Mediterranean. They are small fish, 4 – 5 in (10 – 12 cm) long, depending on the species, and bathypelagic. As a rule each species is limited to a specific part of an ocean or sea. In fact, for each species the specific mass of water with its particular temperature, density, and salinity has been identified; these masses of water correspond to clearly defined faunal or subregions, and are associated with the distribution of the bathypelagic fish of other groups. The adults usually live deeper down than young fish. In fact warmer waters, which are more salty and richer in food and thus more suitable for young individuals, lie above the waters inhabited by adults. The young are more or less identical to mature adults.

The Gibberichthyidae, gibberfish, are the only members of this group with at least five spines, set well apart, in front of the dorsal and anal fins. On the two jaws they have a large band of small teeth. The single genus has just one species, *Gibberichthys pumilus*, a small fish which lives in the tropical regions of the central western Atlantic and southwestern Pacific.

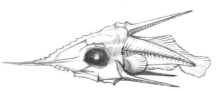

▲
◄ Squirrel fish live mainly in warm deep water in coral formations. During the day they hide in cracks and busily defend their territory, waiting for night to fall before emerging to look for food. Their larvae, called "linquicutis," have a very elongated snout and differ markedly in appearance from adults.

As soon as they have hatched, the young Berycidae float head downwards at medium depth, with their belly uppermost. This is because of the density of the vitelline sac. After three days, when this sac has been completely absorbed, they can start to swim normally. They do not rejoin the adults on the sea bed until they are a year old.

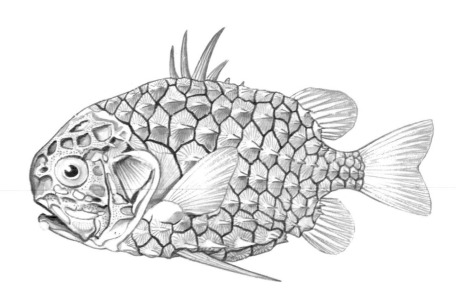

▲ The Monocentridae or pinecone fish are very distinctive, with the ventral fins reduced to a strong spine, followed by two or three small rays, and large ossified scales which cover the body like a carapace. They have two dorsal fins; the first consists of 5 – 7 strong spines which are not joined by a membrane; the second situated towards the rear of the body, has 11 or 12 soft rays. On both sides of the lower jaw there is a photophore, i.e. a phosphorescent or luminescent organ. The Monocentridae can emit sounds by moving the large spine on their belly. They live in coastal waters.

JOHN DORY
Zeus faber

The zeiforms (Zeiformes) are fish about which not very much is known. They generally live in deep water. The body is compressed, shaped like a disk, with a very high back. The mouth is situated at the extreme front. The zeids (Zeidae), one of the principal families of the zeiforms, have a very high back; they look rather like perch. They usually swim slowly, with waving motions of the dorsal and anal fins. They live near the sandy or muddy sea beds of the continental shelf and feed on squids and herrings. They may also lie hidden in the sand with the body lying flat. All are marine forms living in the Atlantic Ocean and the Indo-Pacific waters.

The John Dory (Zeus Faber) is the best known of the zeids. The dorsal fin consists of 9 – 10 spiny rays followed by 21 – 22 soft rays; the pectoral fin has 13 soft rays; the ventral fin has one spiny ray followed by 5 soft rays, and the caudal fin has 15 soft rays. The rays of the dorsal fin and ventral fin are somewhat elongated. The coloration is dark brown on the back, yellow or gray on the sides, and silvery on the underside. There is a black patch with yellow edges behind and above the pectoral fins on each side, which gives the animal the name by which it is known in some countries, St Peter's fish, from the legend that St Peter held the fish at these points and left his finger prints. The John Dory may be as much as 28 in (70 cm) long and weigh as much as 44 lb (20 kg).

Male fish, generally rather smaller than females, have a pink breeding coloration with dark red vertical stripes; that of the females is a uniform pink. John Dories live in the open sea in the eastern Atlantic as far as Mauritania and the Mediterranean. They are not found in the Indian Ocean or the Pacific, but similar species occur there. John Dories generally live in small shoals at depths of some 650 ft (200 m). Sometimes they swim with their bodies tilted sideways, or even parallel with the bottom. Although they are normally rather slow swimmers, they can move very fast when pursued by predators. They feed on small fish, mollusks, and squids. Sometimes they actually take pilchards and sardines. Their flesh has a good taste and they are eaten by man.

John Dory (*Zeus faber*)

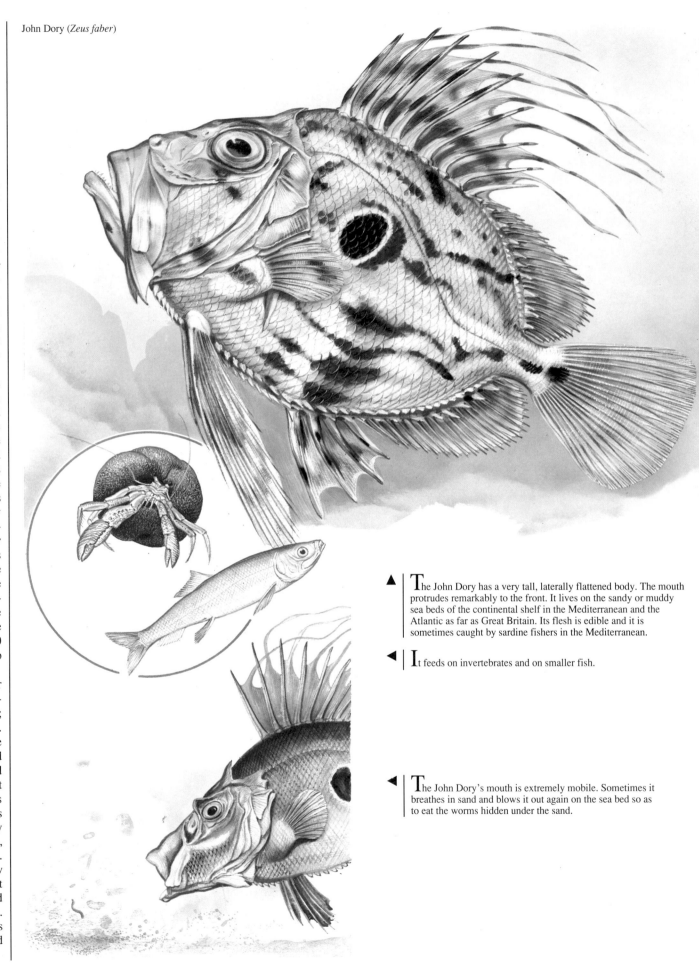

▲ The John Dory has a very tall, laterally flattened body. The mouth protrudes remarkably to the front. It lives on the sandy or muddy sea beds of the continental shelf in the Mediterranean and the Atlantic as far as Great Britain. Its flesh is edible and it is sometimes caught by sardine fishers in the Mediterranean.

◄ It feeds on invertebrates and on smaller fish.

◄ The John Dory's mouth is extremely mobile. Sometimes it breathes in sand and blows it out again on the sea bed so as to eat the worms hidden under the sand.

OPAH
Lampris regius

The Lampridoidei form a suborder that includes fish with a very deep body that is quite compressed in a lateral sense. In a word, it is shaped almost like a round disk. The fins are shaped like crescent moons. The beautiful shiny scales are small and thin and easily removed. The dorsal fin is long, with 50 – 55 rays, the anal fin has 34 – 41 rays, the pectoral fins 7, and the ventral fins 15 to 17. These fish live in the Atlantic and Pacific Oceans.

The opah (*Lampris regius*) is the only member of the suborder Lampridoidei. Its body is short and deep, with a total overall length of 60 in (1.5 m). The cranium is pointed at the front. It may weigh up to 170 lb (75 kg) in the longest specimens. The mouth is toothless. The dorsal fin has 50 – 55 rays, the anal fin 38 – 41, the pectoral fin 23 – 25, with a horizontal base. The ventral fins have 14 – 17 rays and are situated on a level with the belly. The caudal fin has 17 rays and is shorter than the cranium. There are 100 scales along the lateral line.

The coloring is dark blue on the back; the sides may be pale blue or green with silvery, purple or golden highlights. The whole body is silvery and covered with round, milk colored markings. The fins are coral red, which give this fish a magnificent combination of colors and shapes. Opahs live in the temperate waters of the North Atlantic and also in the seas around Tenerife and Madeira. They have been found as far north as Newfoundland, Iceland, northern Norway, and along the coasts of Murmansk and Oresund. The diet is made up of squid, crustaceans (*Euphausiacea*), and fish (such as herrings). Their red-colored flesh is considered quite a delicacy and is eaten like salmon. The opah is caught with hooks and harpoons or special nets set at a depth of 1,250 ft (380 m). It is nevertheless regarded as quite a rare fish.

The suborder Veliferoidei, is made up of one family, the Veliferidae, with just one genus – Velifer – and five or six species, all of which are found in the Indian and Pacific Oceans. One of the more common species is *Velifer hypselopturus* with wide dorsal and anal fins, typical of the members of this suborder.

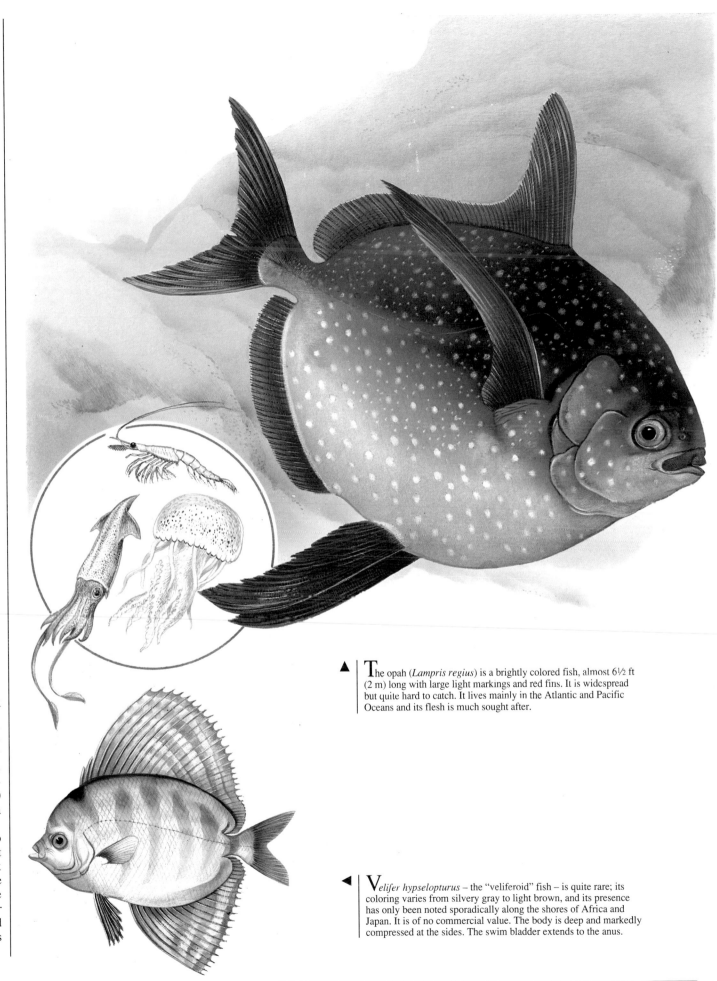

▲ The opah (*Lampris regius*) is a brightly colored fish, almost 6½ ft (2 m) long with large light markings and red fins. It is widespread but quite hard to catch. It lives mainly in the Atlantic and Pacific Oceans and its flesh is much sought after.

◀ *Velifer hypselopturus* – the "veliferoid" fish – is quite rare; its coloring varies from silvery gray to light brown, and its presence has only been noted sporadically along the shores of Africa and Japan. It is of no commercial value. The body is deep and markedly compressed at the sides. The swim bladder extends to the anus.

REGALECIDAE LOPHOTIDAE TRACHIPTERIDAE

The oarfish family (Regalecidae) includes the largest species in the suborder Trachipteroidei. These fish have a ribbon-shaped, scaleless body. The dorsal fin is as long as the body, while the anal and caudal fins are almost invariably missing. The first rays of the dorsal fin are distinctively long and erectile and look like a "crest" or "mane" (this at least is the impression one gets from the many sightings recorded).

The best known member of the family is undoubtedly the king herring (*Regalecus glesne*) which has probably provided much of the fodder for man's belief in terrible serpent-like sea monsters, living in the bowels of the ocean. The king herring can reach a length of more than 23 ft (7 m) and this is already enough to make one understand how a creature of such a size could not readily be regarded as a mere "fish" and hence the intricate legend surrounding it.

This species is a world-wide one, although the largest number of sightings has been made in the North Atlantic. Its name derives from the fact that it was frequently sighted by fishermen near large shoals of herring: it did not take long for its baptism as "king herring," and for it to be attributed with tasks such as showing the herring their way on their migrations.

The body of *Regalecus glesne* is very long and laterally compressed. The coloring is silvery with scarlet red fins. The head is relatively small with a protractile mouth that is almost vertical and completely toothless. The eyes are large and round. On the top of the head there is a brightly colored plume formed by the first rays of the dorsal fin.

This is a very rare species and most of the specimens taken have been found dead on beaches, or nearing the end of their life in shallow coastal waters. Very little is known about its biological cycle: eggs and larval stages of the species are found near the surface in the Straits of Messina between July and December.

The crestfish family (Lophotidae) belongs to the order Lampridiformes which also includes the families Trachipteridae and Regalecidae. Crestfish

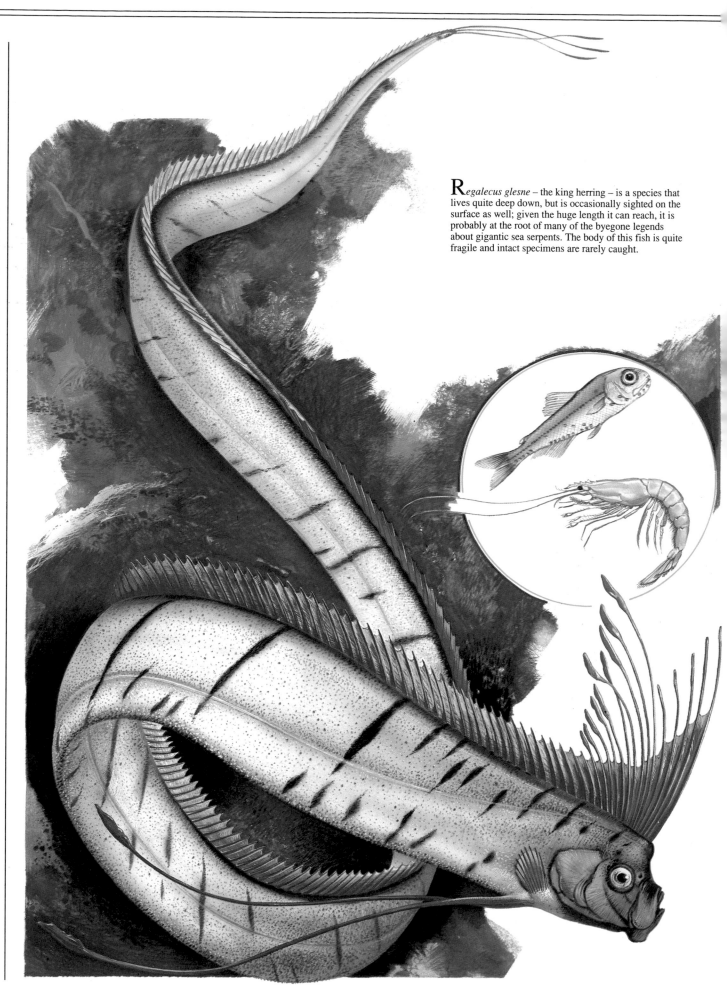

Regalecus glesne – the king herring – is a species that lives quite deep down, but is occasionally sighted on the surface as well; given the huge length it can reach, it is probably at the root of many of the byegone legends about gigantic sea serpents. The body of this fish is quite fragile and intact specimens are rarely caught.

have a laterally compressed body with a smooth skin covered with tiny scales. There are no ventral fins and the tail fin is small. A protuberance on top of the head is the site of the first ray of the dorsal fin, which is quite long when compared with the other rays. A distinctive feature of the species of this family is the ink sac that leads into a cloaca shared with the anus; this latter is situated near the rear tip of the fish.

The best known species of the family is the unicorn fish (*Lophotes cepedianus*) which is found in all the tropical regions of the Atlantic and Pacific Oceans, but it is still relatively rare; it has occasionally been seen in the Mediterranean. Its body is conspicuously compressed laterally and has small, almost invisible scales. The mouth is small with pointed, conical teeth. The coloring tends to blue on the sides of the body and the belly, when the fish is alive, but turns silvery once it is dead. The dorsal region is darker in color, while the fins are a dull red. This fish, which has been caught at depths of up to 1,650 ft (500 m), is nevertheless often sighted while swimming along the sea's surface. It is therefore a bathypelagic species that, for reasons that are still unknown to us, occasionally swims up to the surface, and sometimes stays there for long periods of time. The specimens caught can rarely be kept in good condition because this fish's body is extremely delicate and breaks up into small pieces as soon as it comes into contact with anything solid. It is a carnivorous creature with a diet made up mainly of fish, mollusks, and crustaceans.

The members of the family Trachipteridae – the ribbon- or scythefish – also have a laterally compressed body which is shaped like a sword blade. The skin is covered with bony tubercles and is sometimes entirely scaleless. There is no anal fin. The dorsal fin, which runs uniformly along the entire body, rises up at the front. The tail fin has a conventional shape, but is at the same time quite specific, being turned asymmetrically upwards. The swim bladder is either absent or quite rudimentary; there is no ink sac. *T. trachipterus* is a pelagic species, capable, apparently, of moving freely between the surface and a depth of 3,300 ft (1,000 m). It has a decidedly carnivorous diet, made up of species typical of the pelagic environment within which it lives; it is especially keen on cephalopods, crustaceans, and fish.

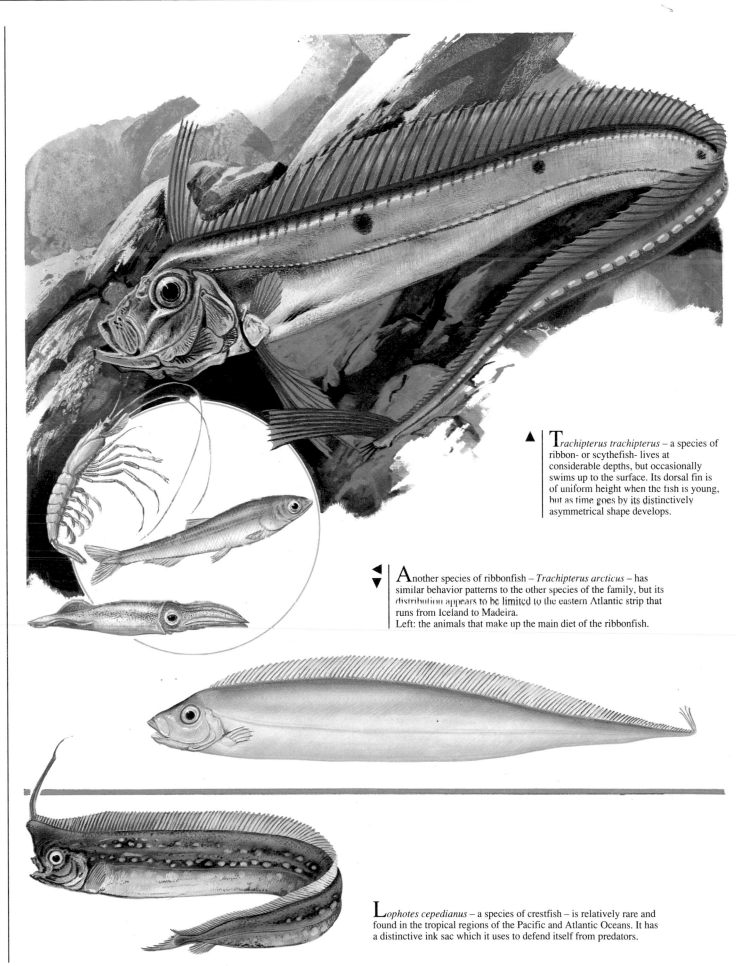

▲ *Trachipterus trachipterus* – a species of ribbon- or scythefish- lives at considerable depths, but occasionally swims up to the surface. Its dorsal fin is of uniform height when the fish is young, but as time goes by its distinctively asymmetrical shape develops.

◄ *Another species of ribbonfish – Trachipterus arcticus* – has similar behavior patterns to the other species of the family, but its distribution appears to be limited to the eastern Atlantic strip that runs from Iceland to Madeira.
Left: the animals that make up the main diet of the ribbonfish.

Lophotes cepedianus – a species of crestfish – is relatively rare and found in the tropical regions of the Pacific and Atlantic Oceans. It has a distinctive ink sac which it uses to defend itself from predators.

PIPEFISH
Syngnathidae

Pipefish live in beds of seaweed or algae near the Atlantic coasts and in the Indo-Pacific region. The end of their tail is prehensile and they can hold onto the vegetation and remain concealed and motionless. Some species stay so constantly in the same area that special geographical races or populations have been formed, distinguished by biometric features from the other races living in the surrounding waters. Other species in contrast live among floating algae, which may carry them a considerable distance from their native waters. Certain species also occur in lakes of brackish water and even in fresh water in river estuaries in the tropics. Pipefish can live in water temperatures between 40° and 85°F (6° and 30°C) and are not very sensitive to salinity, so that they can live equally well in the high salinity found in certain waters (up to 40%) and in the low salinity levels found in fresh water. Movements of the dorsal and anal fins enable these fish to travel as far as 60 miles (100 km). Their food consists mainly of small crustaceans, small young grayling, or small gobies. The hyoid arch of the long, narrow mouth tube is lowered and drawn back, the buccal cavity widened by dropping the lower jaw, and the water which this sucks in brings the prey with it into the mouth.

The brood pouch with which male pipefish are furnished has been known since 1833. Mating takes place at low tide, in shallow water; the female presses its belly against the male's brood pouch so that the eggs, mixed with a mucous secretion, are transferred from the genital papilla into the pouch. This maneuver is carried out very quickly, up to 20 eggs being transferred in 10 seconds. For the whole period during which the eggs are maturing the brood pouch is kept closed so that the embryos are completely isolated and protected from outside influences. After some three weeks the young, already over an inch long, are ready to leave the pouch. They immediately rise to the surface and swallow a little bubble of air which goes into their swim bladder.

It is interesting to note that young pipefish can catch small crustaceans as the adults do as soon as they emerge from the brood pouch.

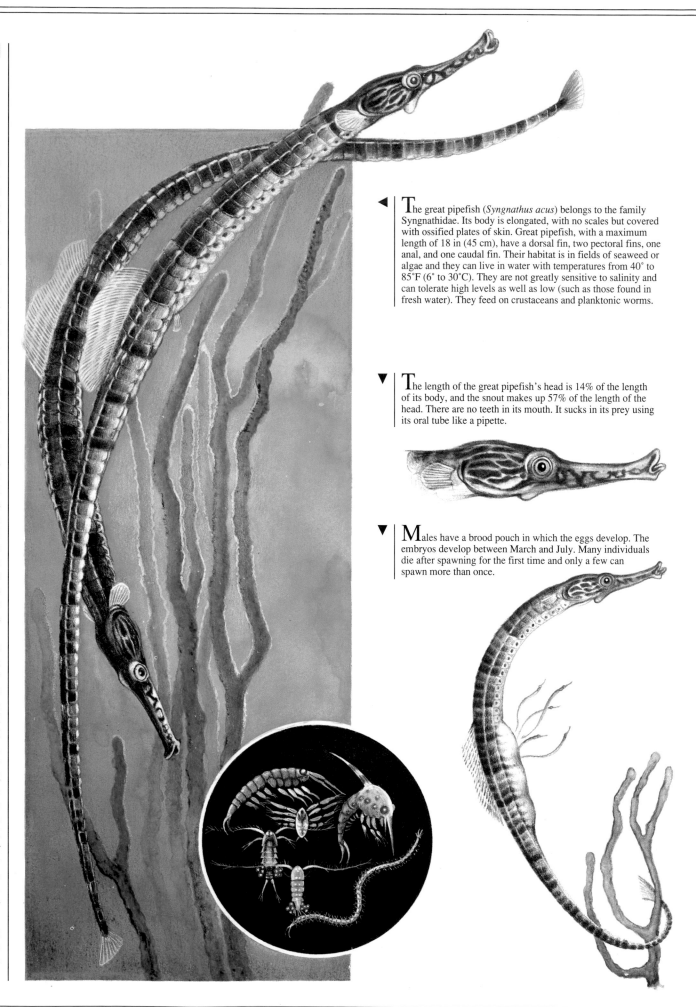

The great pipefish (*Syngnathus acus*) belongs to the family Syngnathidae. Its body is elongated, with no scales but covered with ossified plates of skin. Great pipefish, with a maximum length of 18 in (45 cm), have a dorsal fin, two pectoral fins, one anal, and one caudal fin. Their habitat is in fields of seaweed or algae and they can live in water with temperatures from 40° to 85°F (6° to 30°C). They are not greatly sensitive to salinity and can tolerate high levels as well as low (such as those found in fresh water). They feed on crustaceans and planktonic worms.

The length of the great pipefish's head is 14% of the length of its body, and the snout makes up 57% of the length of the head. There are no teeth in its mouth. It sucks in its prey using its oral tube like a pipette.

Males have a brood pouch in which the eggs develop. The embryos develop between March and July. Many individuals die after spawning for the first time and only a few can spawn more than once.

SEA HORSES

Syngnathidae

Fish belonging to the order Syngnathiformes have a tubular bony snout; they use it like a pipette, sucking in food together with water. The body is wholly or partly covered with bony plates; in the Syngnathidae (sea horses and relatives) these form a completely ossified body armor, arranged in rings around the body and tail.

The body of the sea horse (*Hippocampus hippocampus*) is covered with 11 rings, the tail with 34 – 35 rings. The dorsal fin is located on two body rings and one tail ring, and has 17 rays. The pectoral fin has 14 – 15 rays. The length of the snout makes up 40% of the length of the head; the animal may be as much as 6 in (16 cm) long overall. The body plates have sharp points which can benumb the part struck by them. The hump ("corona") is slightly oblique. The body coloration is blackish or dark brown with white patches or spots. There are no teeth in the mouth.

These fish are found off the Mediterranean and Atlantic coasts of Europe as far south as Algeria, living on beds of sand or detritus at depths of 25 – 150 ft (8 – 45 m). They prefer to live in fields of the seaweed *Posidonia* or of algae, which they cling to with their prehensile tails. The eyes can be moved to follow the movements of their prey, which they stalk very slowly. If they want to swim fast, they take up a horizontal position, with the dorsal fin pointing upward. They can also swim in a vertical position, with the head either up or down, or coiled up. The various positions are controlled by movements of the gas in the swim bladder.

Reproduction takes place between May and August. From 318 to 500 eggs are laid in the male's brood pouch, and incubation takes place from June to July. The young are hatched between August and September. Sexual maturity is reached at about one year; young fish hatched in September can copulate the following May. The majority of individuals die after spawning for the first time; only a few survive to spawn again.

Many related species live in temperate and warm waters.

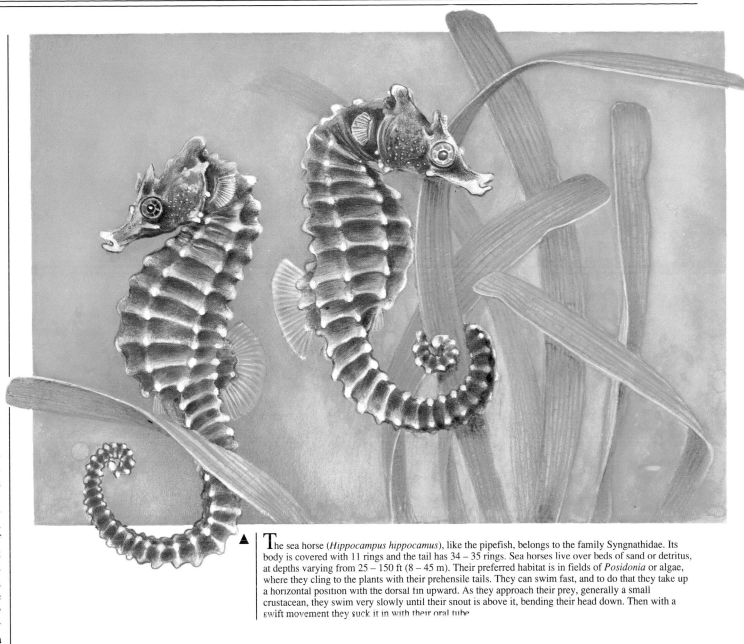

▲ The sea horse (*Hippocampus hippocamus*), like the pipefish, belongs to the family Syngnathidae. Its body is covered with 11 rings and the tail has 34 – 35 rings. Sea horses live over beds of sand or detritus, at depths varying from 25 – 150 ft (8 – 45 m). Their preferred habitat is in fields of *Posidonia* or algae, where they cling to the plants with their prehensile tails. They can swim fast, and to do that they take up a horizontal position with the dorsal fin upward. As they approach their prey, generally a small crustacean, they swim very slowly until their snout is above it, bending their head down. Then with a swift movement they suck it in with their oral tube.

◄ The sea horse's body is laterally compressed, with the head separated from the body by an area that can be described as a neck. The eyes are big and round. The branchial slits are small and so are the pectoral fins that lie behind them.

▼ Reproduction takes place between May and August. The eggs are laid in the male's brood pouch. Incubation proceeds from June to July and the young are hatched between August and September. The young are able to mate by the following May.

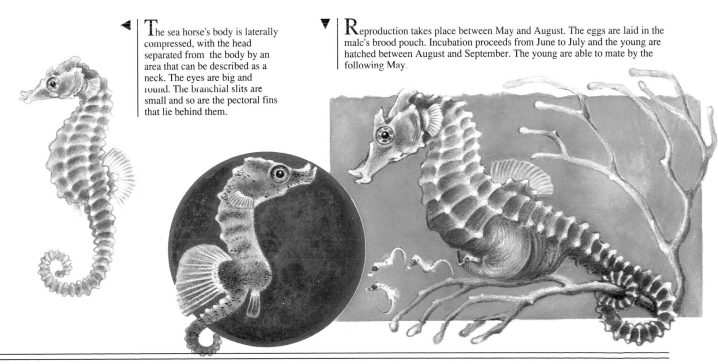

SCORPIONFISH
Scorpaena scrofa

Order Scorpaeniformes
Family Scorpaenidae
Length 20 in (50 cm)
Weight 5¼ lb (2,500 g)
Distinctive features Very marked depression on the upper part of the head; no visible scales beneath the head; the cutaneous folds (laciniae or "wattles") above the head are fleshy and flattened; the lower jaw (mandible) has numerous laciniae; the sides of the body are very scaly and rough to touch
Coloration Red or orange; the body is dotted with small dark markings
Reproductive period May to August
Eggs From 50,000 to 100,000
Sexual maturity At 3 years of age
Maximum age 15 years

The scorpionfish, *Scorpaena scrofa*, lives in the eastern Atlantic, from the Bay of Biscay south to Senegal, the Azores, Madeira, and the Canary Islands. In the Mediterranean it occurs along the Languedoc coast, in the Balearic Islands, Sardinia, and in the Adriatic. On the Atlantic shores of Morocco the various species of the Scorpaenidae are uniformly distributed on the basis of depth. The "brown" scorpionfish (*Scorpaena porcus*) is plentiful to a depth of 65 ft (20 m), living among the rocks that are uncovered at low tide, and in particular in areas rich in oarweed and similar vegetation; this (euryhaline) species can cope with considerable variations in the salinity level and lives at the mouth of coastal brackish lagoons. Beneath the layer which is directly affected by the movement of tides and waves, *Scorpaena porcus* is replaced by the small *Scorpaena notata*, bright red in color, which lives on rocky sea beds covered with brown and red seaweeds. Next, below the 65-ft (20-m) mark, we find plenty of *Scorpaena scrofa*, especially on sandy and muddy sea beds, down to a depth of about 365 ft (110 m). Deeper still, up to 660 ft (200 m), where madrepores cover the continental shelf, we find a (red) scorpionfish which is much more brightly colored. Beyond the 660-ft (200-m) mark, *Scorpaena scrofa*'s place is taken by *Scorpaena elongata* and then by *Helicolenus dactylopterus*, which lives in large numbers down to 2,700 ft (800 m). *Trachyscorpia cristulata* is even found at 6,600 ft (2,000 m).

Scorpionfish
(*Scorpaena scrofa*)

The scorpionfish belongs to the family Scorpaenidae. The habitat of these fish is either a rocky coastal zone or a coral reef. On their head they have quite long spines. The rays of their dorsal fins are poisonous. *Scorpaena scrofa* is the only species with no scales beneath the head. On the contrary, it has numerous tentacles or crests of skin called laciniae or "wattles" on the lower jaw. These fish lead a solitary existence, hidden among rocks. They have the same coloring, and in many cases the same form, as the seaweed and rocks that surround them. In this way they can easily camouflage themselves. They are very voracious creatures, feeding on crabs, shrimps, and fish which come within striking distance. The prey is swallowed in a single gulp.

To sum up, the distribution of the various species seems to be determined more by the nature of the sea bed and the prevailing ecological conditions on it than by the actual depth itself. Every individual species probably displays a clear preference either for rocky sea beds, or for sandy or muddy sea beds, or, last of all, for sea beds covered with madrepores.

The scorpionfish lays its eggs in the summer, usually between May and August. The numerous small eggs are laid in a gelatinous mass of mucus that enables them to float on the surface. When the larvae hatch they measure less than ⅛ in (3 mm) in length. The scorpionfish grows quite slowly, the growth rate varying with the age and chemical and physical conditions of the environment. The maximum length reached is 20 in (50 cm) at an age of about 15 years.

The tooth structure of the scorpionfish leaves one in no doubt about its carnivorous diet and an inventory of the contents of its stomach, together with the morphology of its digestive apparatus, confirm this hypothesis: the intestine is not particularly long; there are seven or eight pyloric appendages followed by a very muscular stomach, and huge buccal cavities furnished with teeth not only on the jaws, but also on the palatine bones, the vomer, and the gill arches.

Scorpaena scrofa only eats live prey. It lurks motionless among seaweed or in the lee of a rock until a shrimp or fish passes close by. Then, using its pectoral fins as a lever, it lunges forward towards the victim. It would seem that this scorpionfish lives permanently on the sea bed and moves very little. The thickening of the lower rays of the pectoral fins and the absence of scales on the front, lower part of the body are associated with its behavior in terms of hunting and lying-in-wait. In this fish we find a phenomenon of "molting" which is particularly visible on the surface of the pectoral fins and on the sides of the body.

One of the most noteworthy features of the scorpionfish, and of all the other members of the Scorpaenidae family, is its ability to blend well with seaweed or coral, thanks to its coloring and appearance. Numerous crests of skin embellish the head, the fin membranes, and the body scales, rendering the fish virtually invisible when it comes to rest on rocks covered with marine organisms.

▲ Like the other members of the same family, *Scorpaena scrofa* can camouflage itself easily; the result is that other fish and crustaceans swim close by it without even suspecting its presence.

▲ The ability of the scorpionfish (and of all the other members of the Scorpaenidae) to camouflage itself, thanks to its coloring and appearance, among seaweed or coral, is often the cause of serious accidents for underwater enthusiasts who carelessly brush against its poisonous spines.

▲ The scorpionfish only eats live animals. It stays motionless among seaweed or in the lee of a rock (it should be pointed out that this species never strays from the sea bed, and moves about very little) until a likely victim (a shrimp or fish) passes close by. The scorpionfish then pounces on it, in less than a split second. Its large mouth enables it to swallow prey of its own size.

▲ The kasago (*Sebasticus marmoratus*) is very akin to *Scorpaena scrofa*, but it is a viviparous species – in other words the young develop in the abdomen of the female, and are born when they have reached a length of ¼ in (4–5 mm). In Japan these creatures are highly sought after for the delicate flavor of their flesh.

◀ The oviparous scorpionfish *Scorpaena scrofa* usually lays its eggs between May and August (in exceptional cases the egg-laying period may extend into November). The numerous, small eggs are ovoidal in shape. They are enveloped in a gelatinous mass which enables them to float on the surface of the sea, as shown in the picture on the left. These eggs are frequently muddled up with those of *Scorpaena porcus*, a similar species. On hatching, the length of the larvae is less than ⅛ in (3 mm). It should be pointed out that the growth of *Scorpaena scrofa* is quite slow, and that the maximum length recorded is 20 in (50 cm) at the age of about 15 years, but the growth rate varies in accordance with the chemical and physical conditions of the environment in which the fish lives. Most of the the specimens caught rarely exceed 12 in (30 cm) in length.

CENTRISCIDS
Centriscidae

The fish of the family Centriscidae have laterally compressed bodies with a knife-like lower edge, clad in transparent bony plates which are joined together. Adult specimens have a long, robust, pointed body; the tail area is so bent down that the body does not end with the caudal fin but with the tip of the dorsal fin. The tail is short and mobile.

In the area of the head, the palatine, entopterygoid, and metapterygeal are joined with the vomero-ethmoid process of the skull. The nasal and preorbital are well developed and so is the hyoid. There are no teeth in the mouth. There are four branchial arches. The post-temporal is fused to the skull. The first five or six vertebrae are elongated and their transverse processes, except for the two ends of them, are fused to the bony plates that cover the body. There are two dorsal fins, the first having spiny rays that are joined to their interneurals. The second dorsal fin has few rays, and so does the anal fin.

Centriscids are found in the Indian and Pacific Oceans, from East Africa to Hawaii. They have never been found in the Atlantic. Underwater research has revealed that these fish swim in a vertical position with the head downwards, moving the tail along the body. The fish feed on small planktonic animals, which they can suck in through the long tubular snout.

The family Centriscidae comprises the genera *Centriscus* and *Aeoliscus*. The dorsal fin of *Centriscus,* the shrimp fish, has mobile rays at the back. The interorbital area is convex and has a groove running up to the front. This is striped. There is one single plate in the dorsal armor between the four front pairs and the fifth pair.

The dorsal fin of *Aeoliscus* does not have the mobile rays at the back. The interorbital area is convex but has no longitudinal groove. In addition to the single plate in the dorsal armor behind the first four pairs of plates in the top line there is another median plate further forward, between the back of the first pair of dorsal plates and the front of the second pair.

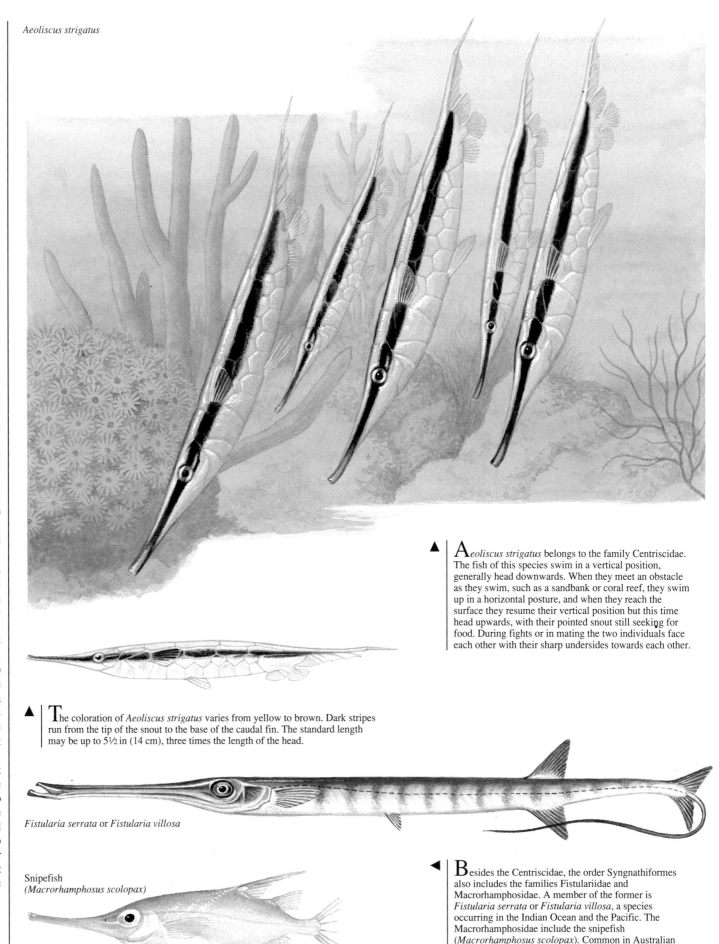

Aeoliscus strigatus

▲ The coloration of *Aeoliscus strigatus* varies from yellow to brown. Dark stripes run from the tip of the snout to the base of the caudal fin. The standard length may be up to 5½ in (14 cm), three times the length of the head.

▲ A*eoliscus strigatus* belongs to the family Centriscidae. The fish of this species swim in a vertical position, generally head downwards. When they meet an obstacle as they swim, such as a sandbank or coral reef, they swim up in a horizontal posture, and when they reach the surface they resume their vertical position but this time head upwards, with their pointed snout still seeking for food. During fights or in mating the two individuals face each other with their sharp undersides towards each other.

Fistularia serrata or *Fistularia villosa*

Snipefish
(*Macrorhamphosus scolopax*)

◄ B*esides the Centriscidae, the order Syngnathiformes also includes the families Fistulariidae and Macrorhamphosidae. A member of the former is *Fistularia serrata* or *Fistularia villosa*, a species occurring in the Indian Ocean and the Pacific. The Macrorhamphosidae include the snipefish (*Macrorhamphosus scolopax*). Common in Australian waters, this species also lives off European coasts.

REDFISH
Sebastes marinus

Order Scorpaeniformes
Family Scorpaenidae
Length 40 in (100 cm)
Weight 34 lb (15 kg)
Distinctive features Very long preoper-cular spines; the two uppermost spines are turned back and the two lower spines are turned downwards. The dorsal fin has 15 very robust spines. The pectoral fin is made up of 19–20 rays
Coloration Red
Reproductive period April to June
Sexual maturity At 11 years
Maximum age 60 years

The redfish, also called ocean perch, is a northern species which lives in the Atlantic and Arctic Oceans. It is pelagic and as a rule lives near the sea bed, at a depth of 330–1,650 ft (100–500 m).

It is a very important species of fish in commercial terms. As a result it has been closely studied to understand its general biology and in particular its behavior in terms of reproductive patterns – especially in the Barents Sea. These are in fact viviparous fish, using internal fertilization, and the eggs actually hatch out inside the oviduct. Fertilization, by mating, usually takes place in February, once the females have gathered into shoals which then migrate southwards where the water is warmer and thus more favorable to the development of the embryos.

One can liken the females to "living incubators": in fact it is a better survival technique for these fish to carry their embryos to more favorable sites than to lay their eggs in colder waters, where the growth rate would be very slow. In any event, at birth the young are very poorly developed. One female may give birth to up to 350,000 and for a long period they must survive by leading a planktonic life. The young are born between April and June, in areas off the Lofoten and Vesteralen Islands, at a depth of between 660–1,650 ft (200–500 m).

During the spring migration the red-fish feeds mainly on striped bream, whereas during autumn and winter the diet consists almost wholly of herring.

▲ The redfish is a pelagic species which usually lives near the sea bed. It often stays motionless among clumps of seaweed, in an oddly vertical position, with its head uppermost.

▲ *Sebastes marinus* is a viviparous species with internal fertilization; in fact the eggs hatch out inside the oviduct. Fertilization usually takes place in February, and the young are born in April–June.

▲ When they have reached a certain size, the fry continue to grow by catching their prey themselves, among waving clumps of seaweed. They feed mainly on planktonic crustaceans, *Sagitta* (a species of arrowworm), and the fry of various fish.

Sebastes inermis

Other species of the genus Sebastes.

Sebastes joyneri

◀ The family Scorpaenidae includes several hundred species. These species inhabit temperate waters, but are also plentiful in tropical regions. The redfish or ocean perch (*Sebastes marinus*) is a northern species living in the North Atlantic and the Arctic Ocean. It lives at depths of 330–1,650 ft (100–500 m), close to the sea bed. In some parts of the Atlantic, however, these fish can be found at depths of up to 3,300 ft (1,000 m). The genus to which the redfish belongs is very abundant: more than 80 species have been described, of which 60 or so live in the northern zones of the Pacific Ocean, off the coast of America. We should also mention *Sebastes paucispinis*, a very interesting species that occurs between Alaska and California. Its coloring is brownish on the back, red on the sides of the body, and white on the belly. 1) Redfish or ocean perch; 2) Scorpaenidae.

ZEBRAFISH
Pterois volitans

Order Scorpaeniformes
Family Scorpaenidae
Length 14 in (35 cm)
Distinctive features 13–14 elongated dorsal spines, not joined together by a membrane. All the pectoral rays are long and single. The fins have a very distinctive coloring and the caudal region has additional black markings. Beneath the eyes, on young individuals, there are ramified tentacles
Coloration In typical cases the dorsal and pelvic fins are dark red; the tail fin is light colored with black speckling. The body is striped with narrow red, brown, and light colored bands
Reproductive period March–April
Sexual maturity Uncertain
Maximum age More than 6 years

The zebrafish is considered to be one of the strangest and most spectacular members of the fauna that inhabits coral reefs. The highly developed fins, which have long rays, the slender, twisted spines that embellish the body with the brightest of colors, and the disproportionately large mouth all give this fish (*Pterois volitans*) an appearance that is at once curious, intriguing, and somewhat grotesque. The shape of the pectoral fin rays resembles feathers, hence an alternative popular name for this species – "turkey fish" (other names include the red fire fish and the lion fish).

Pterois volitans has an oblong body that is slightly compressed laterally. The bulky head has a huge mouth situated at the tip of the snout; it is slightly diagonal and protractile and has very thin teeth. The first pair of nostrils is situated at the base of a short tentacle. The eyes are large and protruding. In young individuals two long spiny and soft tentacles jut from the head slightly behind the axis of the eyeballs. These tentacles become atrophied and drop off as from a certain age (8–12 months) or when they have reached a certain size.

The upper lip also has small, flattened tentacles, and at the sides of the head, on the cheeks, and at the level of the gill covers, there is also a series of spines, which sometimes form a crest behind the eye. The first dorsal fin has 13–14 hard rays, ending in a poisonous tip; the upper part of the rays is free. The well

The zebrafish, *Pterois volitans*, is well known for its very large pectoral fins and its distinctively striped coloring. Like the scorpionfish (*Scorpaena scrofa*), the zebrafish lurks motionless behind rocks, waiting for passing prey. It has slow, elegant movements, and is regarded as one of the most beautiful of aquarium fish. Like the other members of the family it has a huge mouth that enables it to catch prey the same size as itself. Its diet includes crabs, shrimps, and fish.

developed pectoral fins have very long, single rays, joined just at the base by a membrane which is nevertheless more developed than the central rays; these latter may be longer than the caudal fin in young individuals and in more adult fish they may reach the dorsal fin.

The coloring of *Pterois volitans* is usually quite bright and reddish. The head, body, and tail have quite narrow brown bands (quite dark in color) alternating with lighter colored bands.

Like the other Scorpaenidae species, *Pterois volitans* is common throughout the Indo-Pacific region (i.e. the Indian and western Pacific Oceans), but it does not occur in the eastern Pacific. Unlike most of the scorpionfish, which have perfect camouflage, *Pterois volitans* contrasts dramatically with its habitat, in both its shape and its coloring. It is a fish that is happiest in shallow, warm waters, for example within coral reefs, where young specimens live in large numbers. The young are less gaudily colored than the adults: in fact very young individuals are more or less transparent and particularly clever at camouflaging themselves.

Pterois volitans is often found in estuaries: in fact it can tolerate considerable variations in the salinity level (from 30% to 40%), but its favorite habitat is the coral reef where it swims about rather idly with all its fins and thread-like rays fully extended, providing fortunate observers with one of nature's most beautiful spectacles.

During the daylight hours *Pterois volitans* keeps close to rocky outcrops, hiding beneath rocks or in small grottoes and recesses. At twilight it emerges from its hideout and starts hunting slightly deeper down, on the sand or coral. Towards dawn it usually returns to its hideout. Despite this apparently nocturnal behavior, an analysis of the contents of its stomach reveals the fact that its diet contains elements that are not found only at night: in fact it would seem that the "vacuity index" (i.e. the percentage of emptied stomachs) is higher at night than during the day.

During the day the prey include crabs, shrimps, and fish but at night the diet of the zebrafish consists just of shrimps and fish. *Pterois volitans* is an extremely voracious creature and feeds solely on live prey. It does not catch nonmoving prey on the sea bed, but it can remain strangely motionless, "suspended" in open water or "positioned" in front of its prey, waiting for it to make the slightest movement.

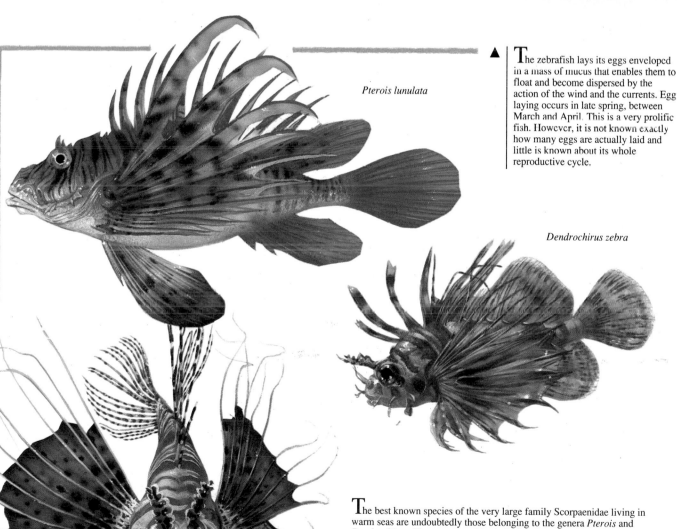

Pterois lunulata

Dendrochirus zebra

Pterois antennata

◄ Underwater swimmers tend to be lured by the magnificent appearance of the zebrafish, and some may even be tempted to try and pick it up. But this may turn out to be extremely dangerous, because this fish has poison-secreting glands in all its spines (dorsal, anal, and ventral). It should be added, however, that though powerful, this poison is not lethal.

▲ The zebrafish lays its eggs enveloped in a mass of mucus that enables them to float and become dispersed by the action of the wind and the currents. Egg laying occurs in late spring, between March and April. This is a very prolific fish. However, it is not known exactly how many eggs are actually laid and little is known about its whole reproductive cycle.

The best known species of the very large family Scorpaenidae living in warm seas are undoubtedly those belonging to the genera *Pterois* and *Dendrochirus*. These are found in the Indian Ocean and in the western Pacific. *Pterois lunulata* closely resembles the zebrafish. It is found off the Chinese coast and the coasts of Japan. Members of the genus *Dendrochirus* (and in particular *D.zebra*) are similar to the genus *Pterois*, with their bizarre form and elegant coloring.

GURNARD
Triglidae

The Triglidae are very specialized Scorpaenidae. The head and cheeks are completely protected by a carapace, formed by the particular development of the infraorbital bones. The preorbital bones form a rostrum or beak-like structure in front of the snout. Two or three rays in the pectoral fin are free and finger-shaped. The lateral line sometimes has small plates or "shields" that can also extend to the sides of the body. The fairly spindle-shaped body is covered with scales: but the small plates never actually form a real "armor" of bony plates. The mouth, which is usually situated at the end of the snout, has protactile premaxillary bones. Both the jaws and the vomer, and in many cases the palatine bones, all have small teeth on them. The anal fin is the same length as the second dorsal fin. The pectoral fins are often large and the finger-like rays have both a sense of touch and taste.

The Triglidae are predominantly coastal fish that live in warm and temperate seas. This family often embraces the Peristediae, and is sometimes included in the subfamily Peristediinae, but more recent classification has it as a separate family: the Peristediidae. This family is thinly represented in European waters but has a large number of species in the western Atlantic and western Pacific Oceans. The Triglidae family is made up as follows: 8 species in European waters, 19 in the western Atlantic, 2 in the eastern Pacific, 14 in the western Pacific, 9 south of the African continent, and 4 in the seas round Australia.

The French name, *grondin*, for this fish derives from its ability to make dull noises, almost like grunts, with its swim bladder, which is vibrated by a particular muscular structure. We still do not know the meaning of these acoustic signals.

The gurnard has neither bony plates nor small shields on the sides of its body. Instead, the lateral line has small elongated plates with a keel-shaped "fairing." In young specimens the scales in the dorsal series have spines, whereas in adults the rear edge is finely toothed. The back is usually brownish gray, speckled with markings edged with dark rings. The belly is white.

The gurnard reaches a maximum length of 18 in (45 cm) but as a rule

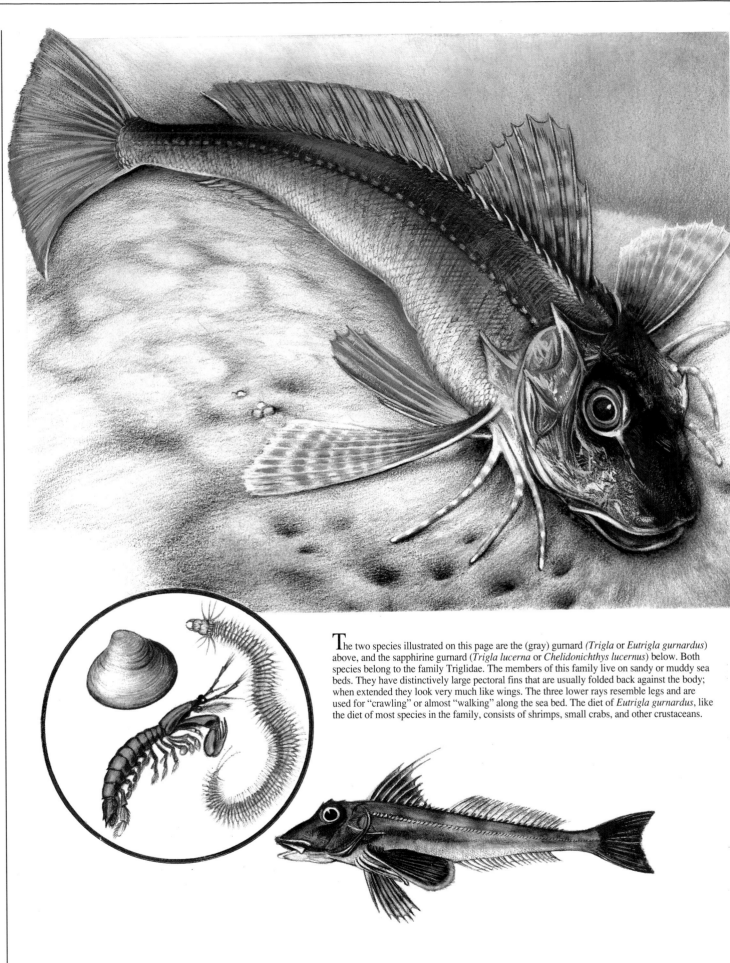

The two species illustrated on this page are the (gray) gurnard (*Trigla* or *Eutrigla gurnardus*) above, and the sapphirine gurnard (*Trigla lucerna* or *Chelidonichthys lucernus*) below. Both species belong to the family Triglidae. The members of this family live on sandy or muddy sea beds. They have distinctively large pectoral fins that are usually folded back against the body; when extended they look very much like wings. The three lower rays resemble legs and are used for "crawling" or almost "walking" along the sea bed. The diet of *Eutrigla gurnardus*, like the diet of most species in the family, consists of shrimps, small crabs, and other crustaceans.

most of those caught measure 12–14 in (30–35 cm). The females are usually larger than the males. It is a benthonic fish that is happiest living on moving sandy or muddy sea beds, or in rocky areas down to a depth of 500 ft (150 m). It is, however, a good swimmer, thanks to its large pectoral fins. When it is on the sea bed, the free rays of the pectoral fins enable it, quite literally, to "walk," and, at the same time, to single out and "sample" its food before swallowing it. In fact these "toes" have a sense of taste built into them. The pelvic fins can also help it to walk on the sea bed, by working together with the "toes" of the pectoral fins. *Eutrigla gurnardus* feeds mainly on shrimps, small crabs, and other crustaceans; every now and then it will also attack fish, mollusks, polychaete worms, and echinoderms.

Of all the Triglidae, the gurnard has the least southerly geographical distribution: in fact it lives more or less exclusively in cold, temperate waters. It is found along the shores of Europe between Portugal and the northern coast of Norway, in the Kattegat, around Iceland, and in the Mediterranean; it also occurs in the Aegean, along the coasts of Lebanon and Israel, and in the Black Sea.

In northern Europe the (gray) gurnard is not considered an economically important fish, but in southern Europe its white flesh is much appreciated. It is fished with trawl nets or lines.

The best known species in southern Europe is the sapphirine gurnard (*Trigla lucerna* or *Chelidonichthys lucernus*). This is an important commercial fish, with some 8,000 tons being fished annually (5,000 tons by the Spanish). Individuals that are still alive are easily recognizable by their color, which is usually pale red or brownish red with a white and golden belly. The pectoral fins are shiny red with blue or green markings and edges. This is undoubtedly the largest Mediterranean gurnard, sometimes exceeding 30 in (75 cm) in length and 11 lb (5 kg) in weight. It feeds mainly on fish (sprats, sardines, sand smelt, and the fry of all kinds of species), but it will also deign to eat the odd crustacean too. The biology of *Trigla lucerna* is like that of the gray gurnard, except for the fact that it can live at a slightly greater depth, down to 660 ft (200 m), on sandy, muddy or stony sea beds. Egg laying takes place between May and June and by late summer the young start to gather in shallow bays or even estuaries.

▲ The Triglidae can utter sounds by using their swim bladder, which is vibrated by means of a special muscular structure. When a large number of gurnard make these noises together, the overall effect is like the croaking of frogs. The meaning of these acoustic signals is still a mystery.

▲ When the gurnard's large pectoral fins are spread out they enable it to glide through the water. Although some species – in particular *Prionotus evolans* – have very developed pectoral fins, and therefore closely resemble certain forms of flying fish, it would be wrong to think that any species of Triglidae are capable of flying.

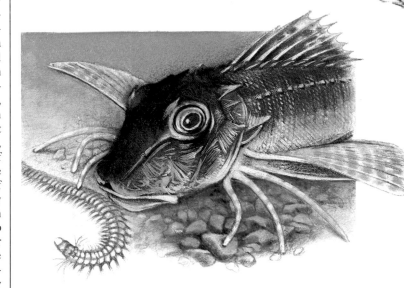

The "armed" gurnard (*Peristedion cataphractus*)

One family that is often confused with the Triglidae is the Peristediidae. *Peristedion* is one of the few genera that make up this family, and the family is in fact named after it. The "armed" gurnard (*Peristedion cataphractus*) resembles several species of the family Triglidae in appearance, but its snout is flattened, with the mouth set beneath it, and a pair of tactile barbels beneath the lower jaw. In addition its body is scaleless.

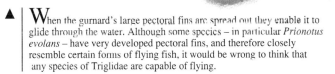

Lepidotrigla microptera

▲ One of the most interesting species found in the Pacific Ocean is *Lepidotrigla microptera*. The members of this species are found in the southern part of Hokkaido Island (Japan) and in Korea. Their flesh is edible. *Lepidotrigla microptera* measures 12 in (30 cm) overall.

◄ The lower rays of the pectoral fins can be used to pry food from the sandy sea bed and their tips have a sense of taste. In this way they enable these fish to "sample" the food before swallowing it. Among the crustaceans that make up the diet of many kinds of Triglidae we find *Crangon*, *Pandulus*, *Portunus*, *Eupagurus*, and Amphipoda.

STONEFISH
Synanceja verrucosa

Order Scorpaeniformes
Family Synancejidae
Length 12 in (30 cm)
Weight 2¼ lb (1 kg)
Distinctive features There is a bony crest running across the cheeks to the preoperculum. The body and the (broad, compressed) head are covered with spines and "wrinkles." The 13 dorsal spines are grooved and covered by a thin skin or cutis. There are also three anal spines. The pectoral fins have 18 rays
Coloration Gray, sometimes with a few scarlet markings

The stonefish, *Synanceja verrucosa*, is one of the few sea creatures that is nothing less than ugly. The shudder that this conglomeration of pustular-looking flesh provokes is aggravated by the fact that its sting is often fatal.

On its dorsal fin *Synanceja verrucosa* has 13 spines that, in the resting position, are normally folded back; but in the event of some emergency or danger they become erect, and this is when they are extremely dangerous. They are all roughly the same length and covered with a thick skin. The dorsal fin itself has 5–7 soft rays that are distally ramified. The anal fin has three spines and 5–6 soft rays. The pectoral fin has 18–19 rays. The body is more or less spherical in shape. The broad head is slightly flattened and the body is very short. The eyes are turned slightly upwards and separated by a deep hollow. The occipital area is high and has no hollow in it. Conversely, a U-shaped hollow or depression, which is smaller than the diameter of the eye, is situated below and in front of the eyes. The preorbital bone is covered with a very thick skin or cutis and has two divergent spines that pass above the maxillary bone. Most of the spines on the head are quite hard to see because they are almost hidden beneath the thick integument. The jaws have small teeth, while the vomer and the palatine bone are toothless.

Synanceja verrucosa is the most widely distributed member of the family Synancejidae. It is found throughout the Indo-Pacific region, from the Red Sea and East Africa (as far south as Zululand and Durban), to Tahiti in the Pacific, and from Australia to Japan. This species lives in shallow water, for example

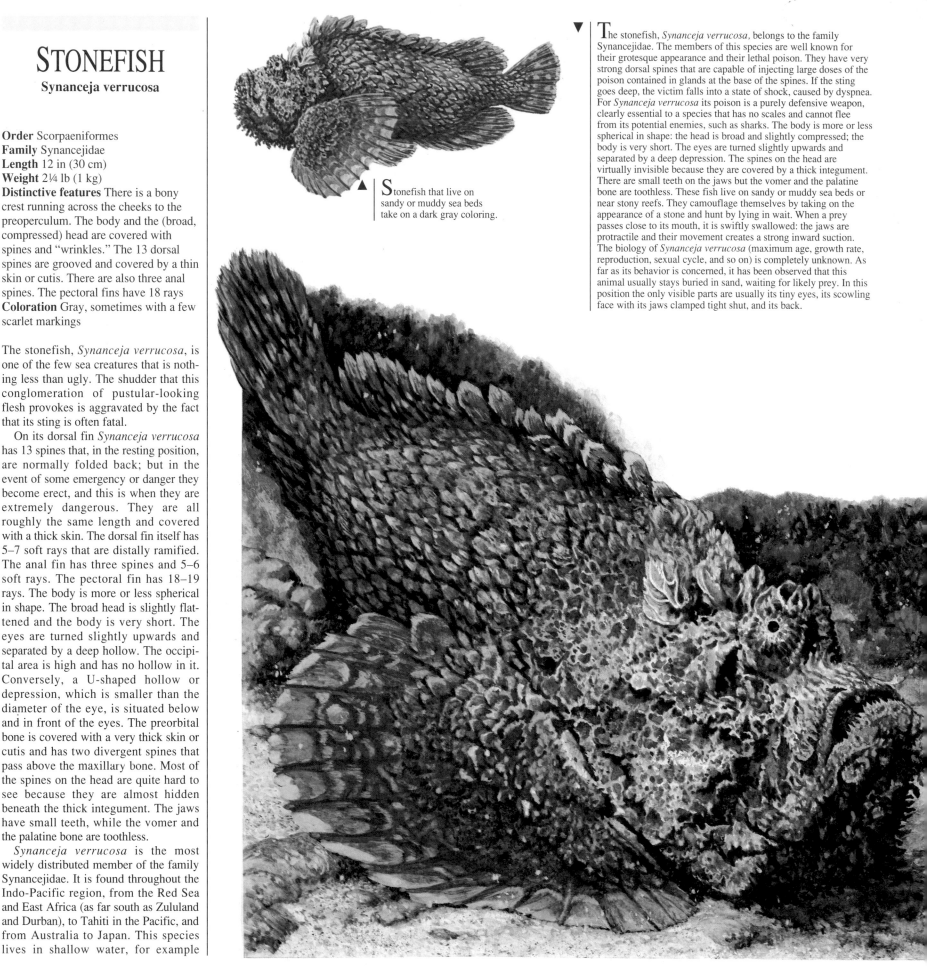

▲ **S**tonefish that live on sandy or muddy sea beds take on a dark gray coloring.

▼ **T**he stonefish, *Synanceja verrucosa*, belongs to the family Synancejidae. The members of this species are well known for their grotesque appearance and their lethal poison. They have very strong dorsal spines that are capable of injecting large doses of the poison contained in glands at the base of the spines. If the sting goes deep, the victim falls into a state of shock, caused by dyspnea. For *Synanceja verrucosa* its poison is a purely defensive weapon, clearly essential to a species that has no scales and cannot flee from its potential enemies, such as sharks. The body is more or less spherical in shape: the head is broad and slightly compressed; the body is very short. The eyes are turned slightly upwards and separated by a deep depression. The spines on the head are virtually invisible because they are covered by a thick integument. There are small teeth on the jaws but the vomer and the palatine bone are toothless. These fish live on sandy or muddy sea beds or near stony reefs. They camouflage themselves by taking on the appearance of a stone and hunt by lying in wait. When a prey passes close to its mouth, it is swiftly swallowed: the jaws are protractile and their movement creates a strong inward suction. The biology of *Synanceja verrucosa* (maximum age, growth rate, reproduction, sexual cycle, and so on) is completely unknown. As far as its behavior is concerned, it has been observed that this animal usually stays buried in sand, waiting for likely prey. In this position the only visible parts are usually its tiny eyes, its scowling face with its jaws clamped tight shut, and its back.

inside coral reefs. It generally prefers sandy or muddy sea beds, where it can blend perfectly with the surrounding environment made up of detritus, dead coral, and rocks covered with calcareous algae, the varied colors of which often occur on the stonefish. The mimetic abilities of this fish are so remarkable that it makes one think that its skin is actually covered with detritus and algae. In reality these are pigmented areas which are a carbon copy of the real thing. However, there are certain small algae that do grow on its skin, thus rounding off the camouflage to perfection.

Synanceja verrucosa is not well designed for swimming; instead it remains for the most part sunk in the sand, watching out for fish and crabs which may inadvertently, and unwisely, pass within reach. In this position the stonefish usually shows just its very small eyes (embedded in two fleshy protuberances), its sullen face, and its back. It is on its back that it has its 13 spines, all totally invisible and sheathed in a fleshy groove. When the right moment arrives, it can erect these spines to inject, under pressure, the poison that is contained in two large glands situated along each spine. These fish are considered the most poisonous of the members of the huge superorder Teleostei, both in terms of the actual toxicity of the poison and because of the high doses that the poison apparatus can inject. What is more, the mucus on the skin, which is secreted by epidermic glands in the papillae and the integumentary tubercles, is also toxic.

The stonefish's poison, which acts on the nervous system, can cause death in man within just a few hours. The poison has a dual action, neurotoxic and haemolytic. In other words, the poisoning affects the nerve, cardiac, and respiratory centers and the blood, by destroying the red corpuscles. Even if the victim does not die, the effects of the sting are often extremely serious: the pain is unbearable and after 10–15 minutes the victim starts to become delirious and in many cases even falls unconscious. After 8–12 hours the pain starts to ebb and a state of extreme debility sets in. At this stage the wound can very easily become infected and gangrene may well set in – this, of course, may mean that the affected limb has to be amputated. For the stonefish, its poison is a purely defensive weapon, vital for a species that has no scales and is incapable of fleeing from its potential enemies such as sharks and other predatory fish.

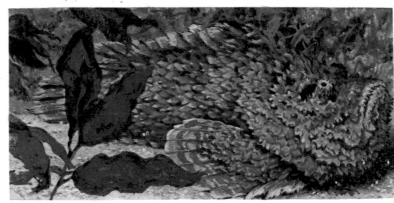

▲ The specimens that live among seaweed have a purplish red coloring. In this case the camouflage is completed by small algae that grow on the fish's skin.

▼ The surface of the body of *Synanceja verrucosa* is often covered with shreds of waving skin, resembling algae.

▲ The mimetic abilities of *Synanceja verrucosa* are truly amazing. In fact it looks precisely as if its skin is covered with the same elements that occur in the surrounding environment. As it happens, these "elements" are no more than pigmented areas which produce a carbon copy version of nature. Individuals that live deep down are reddish or yellowish.

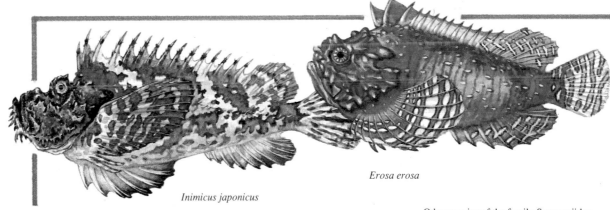

Inimicus japonicus

Erosa erosa

Other species of the family Synancejidae.

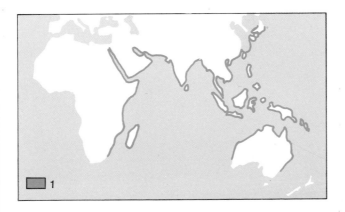

◄ 1) In the family Synancejidae, *Synanceja verrucosa* has by far and away the widest distribution. It is found throughout the Indo-Pacific region, from the Red Sea and East Africa to Tahiti in the Pacific Ocean, and from Australia to Japan. As a rule it lives in shallow waters, for example, inside coral reefs. Another species common in the Indo-Pacific region is *Synanceja horrida*, which reaches the much larger size of 24 in (60 cm). *Erosa erosa* (illustrated above) is found in Japan and Queensland. In all, the family Synancejidae (a very homogeneous group) consists of nine genera and some 20 species, all equally dangerous.

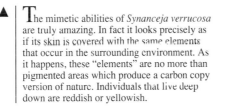

GREENLING
Hexagrammos otakii

Order Scorpaeniformes
Family Hexagrammidae
Length 12 in (30 cm)
Distinctive features The body is elongated and covered with small scales; the head is conical with a terminal mouth. The two dorsal fins are joined together. There are five lateral lines. Above the eyes there is a short, fringed fold of skin. On the back of the head there is a pair of small tentacles
Coloration Generally brown. The sides of the body are speckled with rectangular black markings; the belly is pale. The dorsal fin has black dots on it; the pectoral fin is striped with brown bands. The tips of the rays of the anal fin are white. There is a thin blue stripe running horizontally below each eye
Reproductive period June–July
Eggs 60,000 – 150,000

The Hexagrammidae, which belong to the suborder Hexagrammoidei, can be identified by their long dorsal fin which is relatively flat; the spiny part of the fin is separated from the soft part by quite a clearly defined hollow, the size of which varies from species to species. The principal feature of the family, however, is the presence of five lateral lines. The jaw bone does not extend to the level of the eye, so the mouth is quite small. The teeth on the vomer and the jaw bones are large, but irregular.

The dorsal fin has 19–20 spiny rays and 22 soft rays. The anal fin is formed by 21–23 rays. The pectoral fins, with 17 rays, are quite short and come nowhere near the anus. The body and cheeks are entirely covered with tough ctenoid scales, but the areas above and below the head are scaleless.

Hexagrammos otakii – the greenling or kelp greenling – is found mainly along the east and west coasts of Japan and as further north as the sea of Okhotsk, along the shores of Sakhalin Island and the Kurile Islands. These fish would appear to spend their lives mainly in open sea, but in spring the males take on a brighter color and head for land, slightly ahead of the females. Reproduction takes place in June or July and the females lay the eggs among seaweed or kelp, in masses that cling to any available support. The larvae move to deep waters, a long way from the coast.

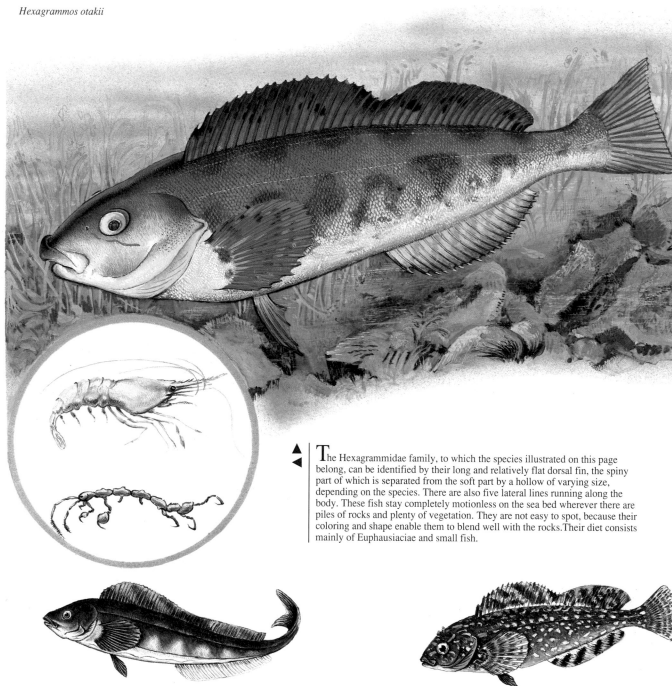

Hexagrammos otakii

The Hexagrammidae family, to which the species illustrated on this page belong, can be identified by their long and relatively flat dorsal fin, the spiny part of which is separated from the soft part by a hollow of varying size, depending on the species. There are also five lateral lines running along the body. These fish stay completely motionless on the sea bed wherever there are piles of rocks and plenty of vegetation. They are not easy to spot, because their coloring and shape enable them to blend well with the rocks.Their diet consists mainly of Euphausiaciae and small fish.

Pleurogrammus azonus

Agrammus agrammus

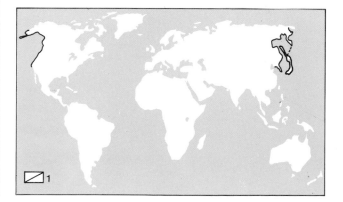

The family Hexagrammidae is distributed exclusively in the northern waters of the Pacific Ocean. *Hexagrammos otakii* – the greenling or kelp greenling – is one of the most interesting species, with a distribution area that covers the coasts of Japan, Sakhalin Island, and the Kurile Islands. Not very much is known about the ecology, biology, and behavior of these fish. They appear to spend most of their life in open sea; in the spring the males head for the coast ahead of the females. As a rule the Hexagrammidae – and in particular the larger species – are the center of a busy fishing industry. It is believed that the annual catch of *Ophidion elongatus*, which can reach a length of 60 in (1.5 m), is in excess of 30,000 tons.

FLATHEAD
Platycephalus indicus

Order Scorpaeniformes
Family Platycephalidae
Length 40 in (100 cm)
Weight 11 lb (5 kg)
Distinctive features The body is elongated, quite cylindrical, and covered with small scales. The head is large and flat, with just small, frail crests on the upper part. There are two spines on the preoperculum
Coloration Gray–brown on the back, with fine dot-like markings; the pectoral and pelvic fins are dark, speckled with brown; the dorsal and anal fins are light colored; the belly is white
Reproductive period September
Eggs 2,500,000
Sexual maturity At 2 years for males and 3 for females
Maximum age 12–15 years

The flathead, *Platycephalus indicus,* like the other species belonging to the family Platycephalidae, has the front part of the body flattened and the rear part cylindrical in shape, and entirely covered with ctenoid scales. The flattened head is quite liberally equipped with spines and crests and is covered with scales at the rear. There is a clearly visible lateral line. The mouth is large. There are thin teeth on the jaw bones and the vomer, and the palatine bones have large canine-like teeth. The caudal fin has three or four horizontal black stripes which are separated by white bands.

The flathead is very widely distributed in the warm waters of the Indo-Pacific region. It has also found its way into the Mediterranean by way of the Suez Canal and at the present time it is found along the coasts of Israel and Lebanon.

The Platycephalidae are predatory fish which live on sandy or muddy sea beds near the coast or by estuaries, at depths of up to 200 ft (60 m). They have the habit of burying themselves in sand – often in the ridges that form on the sea bed – with just their eyes protruding. This position enables them to survey the surrounding scene without being spotted, and then swiftly and accurately attack some small fish which unsuspectingly passes within range. They feed mainly by day, but do not necessarily stop being active at night.

Flathead (*Platycephalus indicus*)

The Platycephalidae are flat-bodied at the front, and cylindrical in shape at the rear, and entirely covered with ctenoid scales. *Platycephalus indicus,* one of the most interesting members of the family, is no exception to this general appearance. It is a benthonic fish that remains motionless on the sand or mud, waiting for passing prey. When it swims it also brushes the sea bed with its abdomen. It will hardly move throughout the winter months, lying covered in sand with its pectoral fins folded back against its pelvic fins and only its eyes protruding. These fish usually eat during the day, but do not necessarily stop being active at night. Their diet consists for the most part of shrimps and young fish.

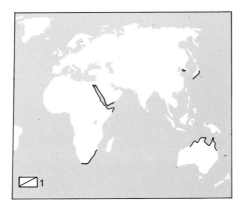

1) Almost all the species that make up the family Platycephalidae are distributed in the warm parts of the Indo-Pacific regions, and in particular in the seas lying between Japan and Australia. The most common species belong to the genera *Platycephalus, Thysanophrys, Cymbacephalus,* and *Elates.* These are all small species, rarely exceeding 14–16 in (35–40 cm) in length. *Platycephalus indicus* has a very wide geographical distribution in regions shared by other Platycephalidae: the Red Sea, the east coast of Africa, the shores of India, the coasts of Thailand, China, Japan, and western Australia, and the islands of Java and Sumatra. It is the only species that grows to a substantial size (it can reach more than 36 in [90 cm]) but its growth rate is still a mystery for the time being.

LUMPSUCKER
Cyclopterus lumpus

Order Scorpaeniformes
Family Cyclopteridae
Length Generally 16 in (40 cm),
sometimes up to 24 in (60 cm)
Weight Up to 12 lb (5.5 kg) for a length
of 24 in (60 cm)
Distinctive features There are small
teeth in the jaws but none in the palatine
and vomer
Reproductive period Spawning takes
place in the spring (April)
Eggs Laid in large strings containing as
many as 79,000 – 136,000

The Cyclopteridae are fish with a massive, swollen belly, with no scales but covered with skin that often looks warty or granular. They live in cold seas in the Northern Hemisphere, living between the rocks and the sea bed and feeding on small jellyfish, crustaceans, worms, and fish fry.

Lumpsuckers (*Cyclopterus lumpus*) are rather round-looking fish, though rather hexagonal in cross section, and covered with spiny plates. Adults have a hump on the back. The snout is broad and rounded. The adhesive disk formed by the pectoral fins enables the fish to attach itself to a submerged object so firmly that it requires a force of 80 lb (36 kg) to detach it. The coloring is bright, especially in the breeding season; males take on a reddish color on the belly and black on the head, and even their fins turn rosy. The coloration of the females varies from greenish to gray–blue, with big dark patches on the sides.

These fish live in the northern Atlantic, from the frozen Arctic Sea beyond Iceland to Chesapeake Bay on one side and to Iceland and the Bay of Biscay on the other. They also occur in the Baltic as far as Finland and Estonia. The Baltic form of the lumpsucker is smaller than that of the Atlantic. In winter the fish descend to depths of 1,200 ft (360 m) but when spring begins they can be caught off the coasts. In the winter months lumpsuckers feed mainly on crustaceans, jellyfish, worms, and the fry of sand eels. From April to November (the period of reproduction and care of the young) they feed very rarely. Flagellates and microscopic fungi also form part of their diet and play an important part in promoting digestion.

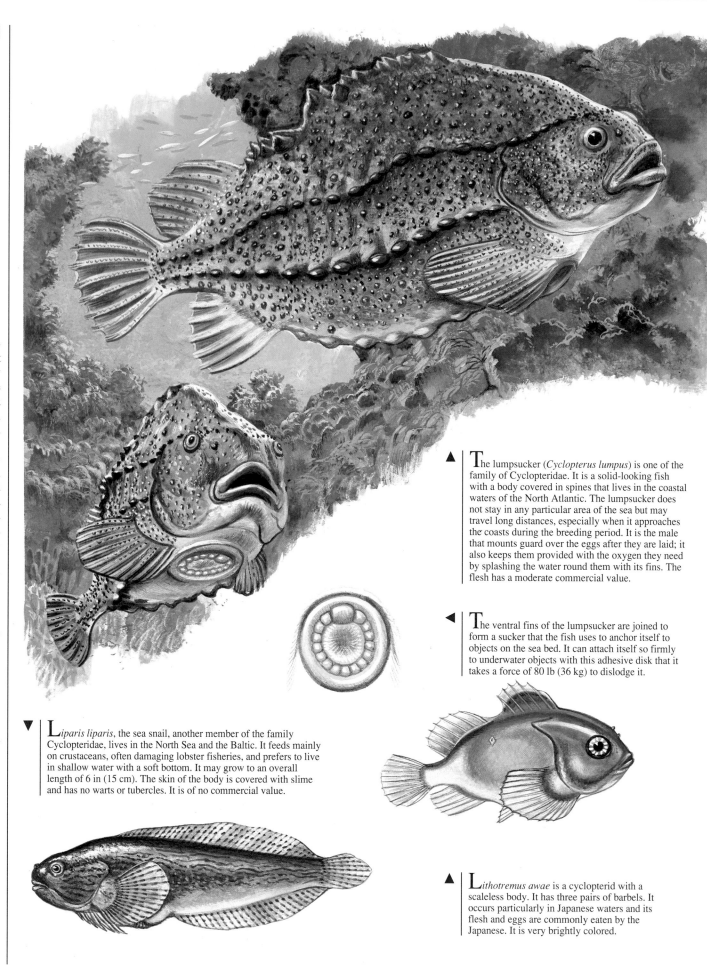

▲ The lumpsucker (*Cyclopterus lumpus*) is one of the family of Cyclopteridae. It is a solid-looking fish with a body covered in spines that lives in the coastal waters of the North Atlantic. The lumpsucker does not stay in any particular area of the sea but may travel long distances, especially when it approaches the coasts during the breeding period. It is the male that mounts guard over the eggs after they are laid; it also keeps them provided with the oxygen they need by splashing the water round them with its fins. The flesh has a moderate commercial value.

◀ The ventral fins of the lumpsucker are joined to form a sucker that the fish uses to anchor itself to objects on the sea bed. It can attach itself so firmly to underwater objects with this adhesive disk that it takes a force of 80 lb (36 kg) to dislodge it.

▼ *Liparis liparis*, the sea snail, another member of the family Cyclopteridae, lives in the North Sea and the Baltic. It feeds mainly on crustaceans, often damaging lobster fisheries, and prefers to live in shallow water with a soft bottom. It may grow to an overall length of 6 in (15 cm). The skin of the body is covered with slime and has no warts or tubercles. It is of no commercial value.

▲ *Lithotremus awae* is a cyclopterid with a scaleless body. It has three pairs of barbels. It occurs particularly in Japanese waters and its flesh and eggs are commonly eaten by the Japanese. It is very brightly colored.

FLYING GURNARD

Dactylopterus volitans

Order Dactylopteriformes
Family Dactylopteridae
Length Up to 20 in (50 cm)
Distinctive features There are blunt horny teeth in the jaws and no teeth in the palate
Coloration The upper side varies from chestnut to ruddy brown with blue patches; the sides are rufous or red; the underside is pink
Reproductive period April to August

The fish belonging to the order Dactylopteriformes are characterized by the enormous development of the pectoral fins, the hind part of which is transformed into wide expanses like wings, though the fore part is of moderate size. They are benthonic fish, which nevertheless can crawl along the sea bed using their pectoral and ventral fins and can emit sounds, soft or loud, by means of the hyomandibular. The family is distributed in the Atlantic and Indo-Pacific regions and comprises three genera, *Dactylopterus*, *Dactyloptena* and *Daicocus*.

The flying gurnard (*Dactylopterus volitans*) has a powerful head and armor and a rather small mouth. The swim bladder can be vibrated by the powerful muscles. The pectoral fins are highly developed; the upper rays are free. After a swift movement of the tail the pectoral fins are spread like wings and the fish glides across the water. It is a benthonic fish, yet it can glide for short distances above the surface.

The coloration of the upper side varies from brown to rufous, with light blue patches. The sides are rusty or light red and the underside is pink. The dorsal and caudal fins are gray or brown; the second dorsal fin has four or five dark spots or circles on the skin between the rays. The anal and ventral fins are pink or red. The pectorals are brown in front, with dark patches, and dark brown with blue patches at the back. The base of the fins is gray.

This species lives in the Atlantic, the Mediterranean, and the Red Sea. It feeds on small crustaceans, mollusks, and coelenterates.

Flying gurnard
(*Dactylopterus volitans*)

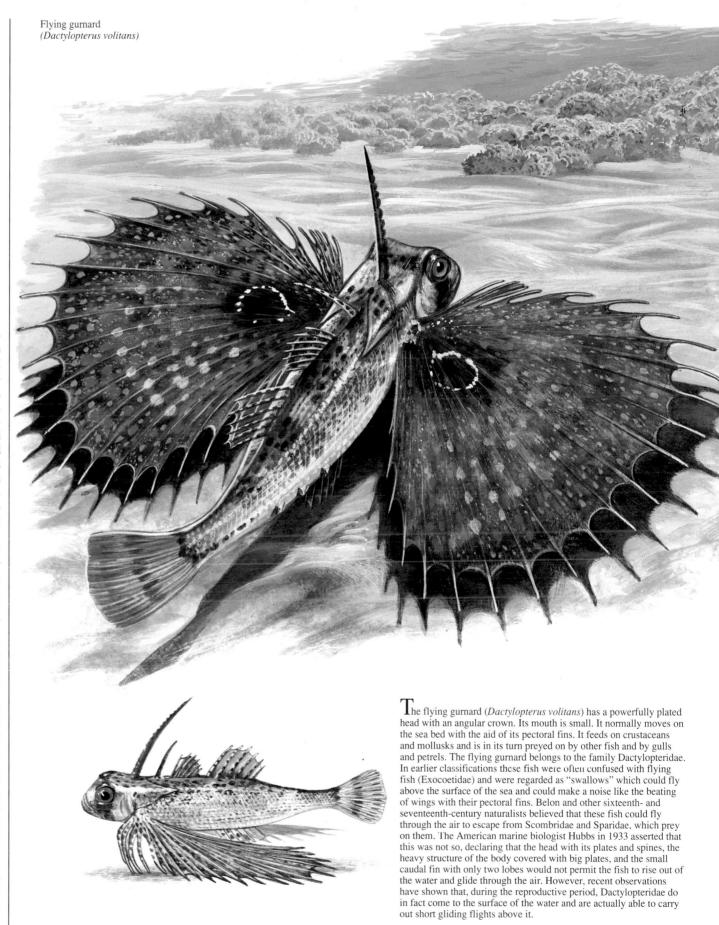

The flying gurnard (*Dactylopterus volitans*) has a powerfully plated head with an angular crown. Its mouth is small. It normally moves on the sea bed with the aid of its pectoral fins. It feeds on crustaceans and mollusks and is in its turn preyed on by other fish and by gulls and petrels. The flying gurnard belongs to the family Dactylopteridae. In earlier classifications these fish were often confused with flying fish (Exocoetidae) and were regarded as "swallows" which could fly above the surface of the sea and could make a noise like the beating of wings with their pectoral fins. Belon and other sixteenth- and seventeenth-century naturalists believed that these fish could fly through the air to escape from Scombridae and Sparidae, which prey on them. The American marine biologist Hubbs in 1933 asserted that this was not so, declaring that the head with its plates and spines, the heavy structure of the body covered with big plates, and the small caudal fin with only two lobes would not permit the fish to rise out of the water and glide through the air. However, recent observations have shown that, during the reproductive period, Dactylopteridae do in fact come to the surface of the water and are actually able to carry out short gliding flights above it.

SEA BASS
Serranidae

The family Serranidae, the sea basses, is part of the huge order Perciformes, and more specifically of the suborder Percoidei. The size of the member species ranges from a few inches to several feet. They live in most cases in saltwater habitats in the temperate and tropical belt. The body is sometimes compressed, and sometimes not, and covered usually with ctenoid scales which sometimes also cover the head. The fins, and the dorsal fin in particular, have tough spine-shaped rays. In the adult state these animals are not usually gregarious and live in many cases in close association with the sea bed. It is often hard to define the coloring of certain species because it changes at will in accordance with the conditions in which the fish is being observed.

The family is made up of more than 300 species, some of which are of considerable economic importance, and we shall discuss the most significant.

The genus *Roccus* includes species that are common in both salt and freshwater habitats: among the main species, we should mention *Roccus chrysops*, the white bass, which is found in the Great Lakes region of North America, where it spends its entire life without coming into contact with salt water. The best known species in the genus, however, is *Roccus saxatilis*, the striped bass. The coloring tends to blue–green and the body has 7–8 horizontal stripes. It is distributed along the whole length of the Atlantic seaboard of America.

The species belonging to the genus *Dicentrarchus* are morphologically similar to the previous genus: they have an elongated body, slightly compressed at the sides, clearly separated, though closely set dorsal fins, and a mouth with a prominent lower jaw. The main species is the sea bass *Dicentrarchus labrax*, which lives in brackish water, estuaries, open sea, and can also adapt to freshwater habitats. It moves quite frequently from one or other of these habitats to another and always returns to the sea to reproduce. When young it is gregarious by nature, but as an adult it usually leads a solitary life, or it may live as a pair. It likes shallow bottoms where it hides in cracks; when the sea turns rough it swims swiftly in pursuit of small fish, crustaceans, and

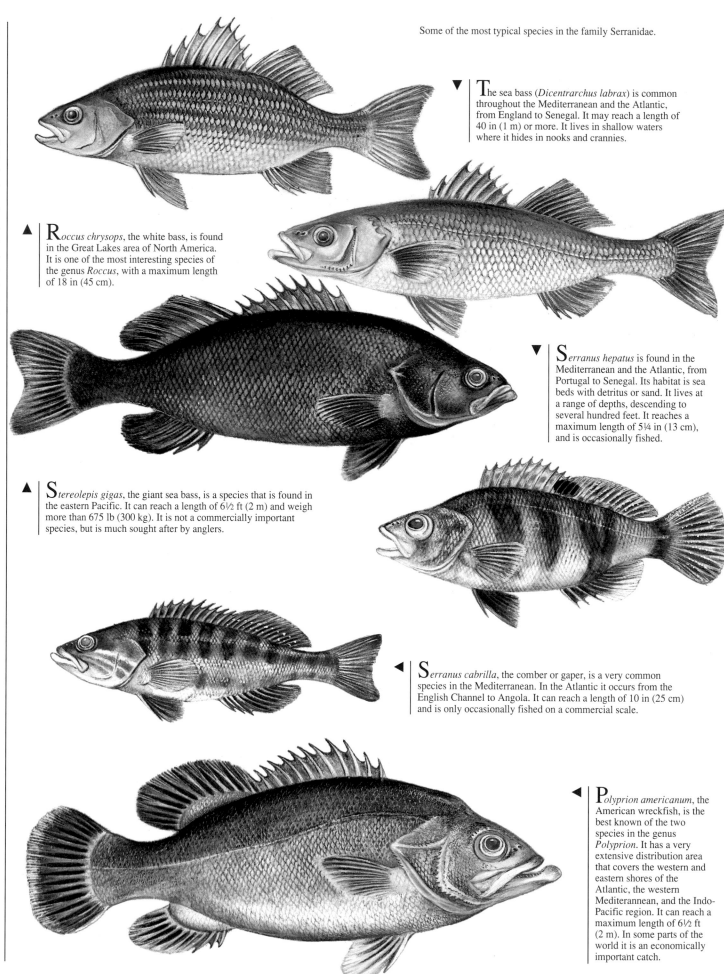

Some of the most typical species in the family Serranidae.

▼ The sea bass (*Dicentrarchus labrax*) is common throughout the Mediterranean and the Atlantic, from England to Senegal. It may reach a length of 40 in (1 m) or more. It lives in shallow waters where it hides in nooks and crannies.

▲ *Roccus chrysops*, the white bass, is found in the Great Lakes area of North America. It is one of the most interesting species of the genus *Roccus*, with a maximum length of 18 in (45 cm).

▼ *Serranus hepatus* is found in the Mediterranean and the Atlantic, from Portugal to Senegal. Its habitat is sea beds with detritus or sand. It lives at a range of depths, descending to several hundred feet. It reaches a maximum length of 5¼ in (13 cm), and is occasionally fished.

▲ *Stereolepis gigas*, the giant sea bass, is a species that is found in the eastern Pacific. It can reach a length of 6½ ft (2 m) and weigh more than 675 lb (300 kg). It is not a commercially important species, but is much sought after by anglers.

◄ *Serranus cabrilla*, the comber or gaper, is a very common species in the Mediterranean. In the Atlantic it occurs from the English Channel to Angola. It can reach a length of 10 in (25 cm) and is only occasionally fished on a commercial scale.

◄ *Polyprion americanum*, the American wreckfish, is the best known of the two species in the genus *Polyprion*. It has a very extensive distribution area that covers the western and eastern shores of the Atlantic, the western Mediterannean, and the Indo-Pacific region. It can reach a maximum length of 6½ ft (2 m). In some parts of the world it is an economically important catch.

cephalopods. It is common throughout the Mediterranean and in the Atlantic from England to Senegal.

In the wild the bass weighs more than 1 lb (500 g) in its third year and may weigh as much as 2¼ lb (1 kg) at the age of four. It may eventually measure more than 40 in (1 m) in length and weigh more than 27 lb (12 kg). In the Mediterranean egg laying usually takes place from late October to early March, with the busiest sexual activity occurring in January. Because of its biological characteristics, market demand, and the possibility of obtaining fry by artificial reproduction, the bass is a particularly suitable species for fish farming.

There are numerous smallish species (maximum length 12 in [30 cm]) in the genus *Serranus*, distributed in temperate and tropical areas, in particular in the eastern Pacific, the Atlantic, and the Mediterranean. They live in coastal waters and on rocky sea beds. Because of their voracity they are easy prey for anglers. They are hermaphroditic and because the male and female sexual products reach maturity at the same time, self-fertilization is therefore possible.

The species *Serranus cabrilla*, the comber or gaper, is very common throughout the Mediterranean and in the Atlantic, from the English Channel to Angola. It has reddish brown coloring with 7–9 darker vertical stripes, while the head has diagonal orange–yellow stripes running across it. It is commonly found in coastal waters of very varied types, such as sandy, muddy or rocky sea beds down to depths of more than 1,650 ft (500 m). It is a very inquisitive and voracious fish which dashes fearlessly towards anything that might have attracted its attention, probably in the hope of discovering that it is edible. It reproduces from April to July and when the young are barely an inch long they are already morphologically almost identical to the adult in shape. The maximum length is around 10 in (25 cm).

The genus *Variola* includes species with an elongated body and a deeply concave head. They are quite brightly colored in a range from red to yellow. They are distributed variously throughout the tropical belt. One of the best known species is *Variola louti*, common in the Red Sea and the whole Indo-Pacific region.

Members of the genus *Anthias*, the redlings, feed on invertebrates and small fish caught on the sea bed. They are themselves fished at a local level with lines, nets, and traps.

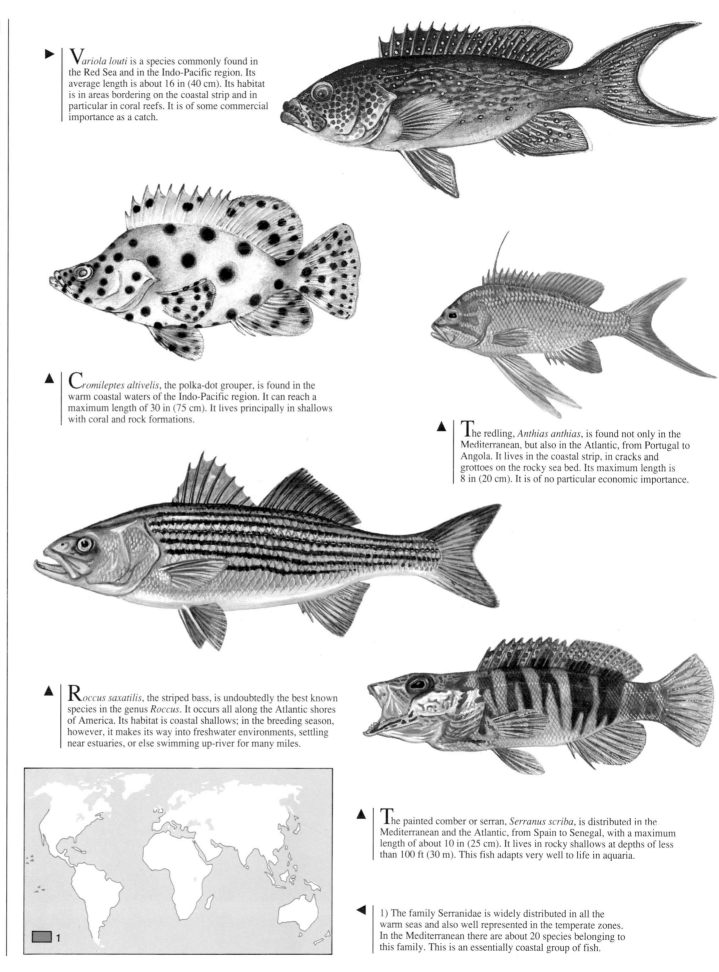

▶ *Variola louti* is a species commonly found in the Red Sea and in the Indo-Pacific region. Its average length is about 16 in (40 cm). Its habitat is in areas bordering on the coastal strip and in particular in coral reefs. It is of some commercial importance as a catch.

▲ *Cromileptes altivelis*, the polka-dot grouper, is found in the warm coastal waters of the Indo-Pacific region. It can reach a maximum length of 30 in (75 cm). It lives principally in shallows with coral and rock formations.

▲ The redling, *Anthias anthias*, is found not only in the Mediterranean, but also in the Atlantic, from Portugal to Angola. It lives in the coastal strip, in cracks and grottoes on the rocky sea bed. Its maximum length is 8 in (20 cm). It is of no particular economic importance.

▲ *Roccus saxatilis*, the striped bass, is undoubtedly the best known species in the genus *Roccus*. It occurs all along the Atlantic shores of America. Its habitat is coastal shallows; in the breeding season, however, it makes its way into freshwater environments, settling near estuaries, or else swimming up-river for many miles.

▲ The painted comber or serran, *Serranus scriba*, is distributed in the Mediterranean and the Atlantic, from Spain to Senegal, with a maximum length of about 10 in (25 cm). It lives in rocky shallows at depths of less than 100 ft (30 m). This fish adapts very well to life in aquaria.

◀ 1) The family Serranidae is widely distributed in all the warm seas and also well represented in the temperate zones. In the Mediterranean there are about 20 species belonging to this family. This is an essentially coastal group of fish.

GROUPERS
Epinephelus

The genus *Epinephelus* boasts more than a hundred species. These are the true groupers, and they are restricted in their distribution to the tropical and temperate belt. They often reach a considerable size and are well known to sporting anglers who regard them as a prize catch because of the difficulties in actually landing them.

Features of this genus include the laterally quite compressed body, which is covered with small, usually cycloid scales, the mouth with several series of small conical teeth, and the prominent lower jaw (mandible). The name of the genus derives from the Greek word *epinèfelos* which means cloudy; this is because of the markings that often cover the body of these species and that, depending on surrounding conditions, can change in brightness and coloring, just like clouds.

Possibly the best known species belonging to the genus *Epinephelus* is *Epinephelus guaza*, the grouper (also known as the "dusky perch" or "merou"), which is found throughout the Mediterranean and in the Atlantic from England to the Cape of Good Hope.

The body is bulky, the mouth large with large numbers of small teeth, the outer ones set slightly backwards, and the inner ones mobile and capable of being folded backwards if pushed from the front, but remaining firmly fixed if pushed towards the front of the mouth; this mechanism helps the fish to hang on to its prey and stops the prey slipping away. It can also easily be tested out. In fact all you need to do is slip a hand inside the mouth of a dead grouper to feel how easy it is to get your hand in and how hard it is to get it out again with just the slightest pressure on the jaws.

The fundamental coloring is dark brown with irregular yellowish white markings, varying in intensity and number, and sometimes missing in very large individuals; these markings vanish as soon as the fish dies. The maximum dimensions recorded are a length of more than 48 in (1.2 m) and a weight of 135 lb (60 kg); the average weight is between 11–34 lb (5–15 kg).

The grouper lives on rocky sea beds and is sedentary and territorial by nature: after much painstaking research,

The family Serranidae, the sea basses, which belongs to the suborder Percoidei, embraces more than 300 species, most of them exclusively marine, although some of them are capable of living in brackish or freshwater habitats as well, and a small minority are exclusively freshwater animals. Of the marine species, most are tropical. In temperate waters these fish usually lead a solitary existence, or else live in small groups; but in tropical environments they may often form large shoals. For the most part they are benthonic, mainly coastal, and generally predatory. They all share in common the fact that they select as their refuge a lair that is well concealed among rocks. Their diet consists principally of mollusks and fish. The body may or may not be compressed to varying degrees and is covered usually with ctenoid scales that sometimes extend to the head as well. The fins, and in particular the dorsal fin, have tough spine-shaped rays. They vary in size from an inch to several feet in length. The coloring is often difficult to define for some species because it is very variable and changeable, in accordance with the conditions in which the fish is being observed. Sexual maturity is reached by some species at a length of 1¼in (3 cm), and by others at 48 in (120 cm). Many of the species belonging to this family are of considerable economic importance.

carried out with great thoroughness, it selects a well sheltered cranny as its "residence," possibly with more than one entrance, often made of one or more boulders lying on the sandy sea bed. Here it leads its life with occasional sorties in search of food. The depth at which it lives ranges from a few feet up to more than 330 ft (100 m), but while it can be found for much of the year in the deeper waters, it lives in shallower waters mainly during the breeding season (spring–summer).

These fish are some of the most sought after and fiercely hunted prey of underwater fishermen; the problem of catching them resides in the swimmer's ability to reach the fish inside its lair, which is often nothing less than a labyrinth, and to drive it out before it wedges itself deep in some fissure. Once it has been wounded, in fact, it dilates its gill covers, stiffens its dorsal fin spines and the spines on its anal fins, and anchors itself in this way inside narrow crevices.

It is carnivorous and voracious, its favorite prey being cephalopod mollusks, although it will not turn up its nose at various species of fish living near the sea bed. Its hunting technique consists both in pouncing on its prey with a quick darting movement and in a sucking action, which it makes by exerting pressure on the normal respiratory flow of water by means of brusquely opening its gill covers. When it uses this second technique it remains completely motionless and concealed until a small prey passes near enough. The volume of water suddenly sucked in will drag the poor passer-by straight into the grouper's mouth.

The Alexandria grouper (*Epinephelus alexandrinus*) is quite different, both morphologically and behaviorally. The body is more slender and laterally compressed than that of the ordinary grouper; the mouth is large and the lower jaw prominent. It is common in the central and eastern Atlantic Ocean and in the eastern Mediterranean. Its maximum length is 32 in (80 cm) and it may weigh up to 18 lb (8 kg). It is by nature less territorial than the ordinary grouper and is frequent on both rocky and sandy and muddy sea beds, but invariably near the shore. It can sometimes be seen in quite numerous groups swimming fast very close to the bottom. It rarely hides in burrows and when it does it is invariably for a specific reason and only for a given period of time. Like the other species in the genus it is carnivorous and feeds mainly on mollusks and fish.

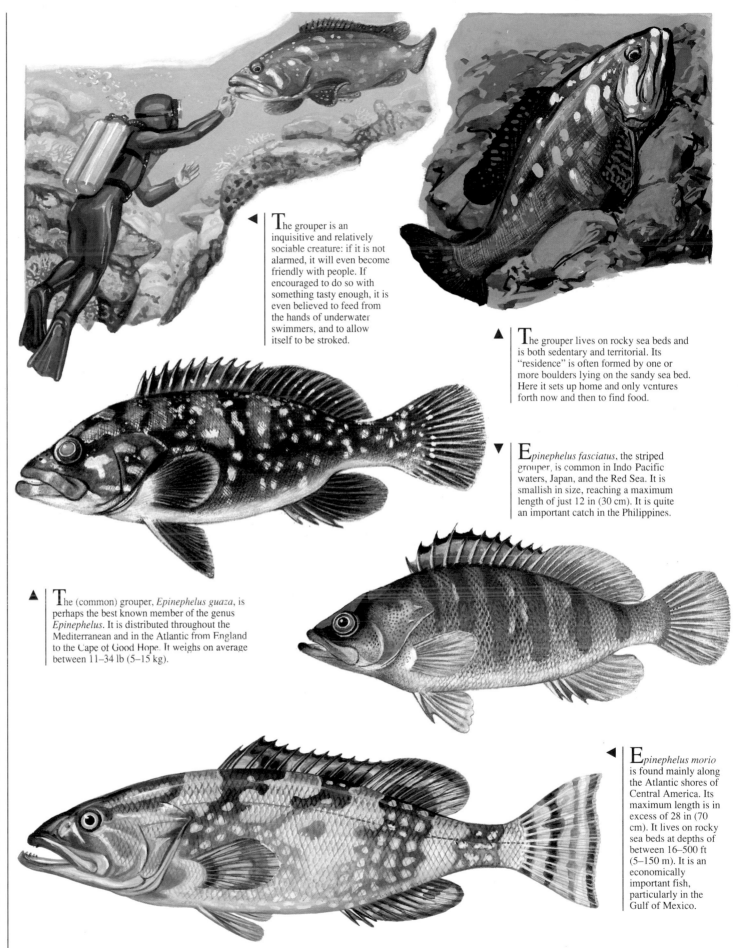

▲ The grouper is an inquisitive and relatively sociable creature: if it is not alarmed, it will even become friendly with people. If encouraged to do so with something tasty enough, it is even believed to feed from the hands of underwater swimmers, and to allow itself to be stroked.

▲ The grouper lives on rocky sea beds and is both sedentary and territorial. Its "residence" is often formed by one or more boulders lying on the sandy sea bed. Here it sets up home and only ventures forth now and then to find food.

▼ *Epinephelus fasciatus*, the striped grouper, is common in Indo Pacific waters, Japan, and the Red Sea. It is smallish in size, reaching a maximum length of just 12 in (30 cm). It is quite an important catch in the Philippines.

▲ The (common) grouper, *Epinephelus guaza*, is perhaps the best known member of the genus *Epinephelus*. It is distributed throughout the Mediterranean and in the Atlantic from England to the Cape of Good Hope. It weighs on average between 11–34 lb (5–15 kg).

◄ *Epinephelus morio* is found mainly along the Atlantic shores of Central America. Its maximum length is in excess of 28 in (70 cm). It lives on rocky sea beds at depths of between 16–500 ft (5–150 m). It is an economically important fish, particularly in the Gulf of Mexico.

UMBRA
Umbrina cirrhosa

The family Sciaenidae, the drums, includes some 30 genera of percoid fish, which, in turn, are made up of more than 150 species. The Sciaenidae are usually marine fish, but there are also species with marked euryhaline habits, some of which have adapted completely to fresh water, like, for example the freshwater drum (*Aplodinotus grunniens*) which lives on the western shores of the Atlantic, as well as other South American species.

One feature peculiar to many drums is their capacity to make sounds; this they do by means of an adaptation of the swim bladder which, when vibrated by specific muscles, is used as a resonance-producing organ. This "vocal" behavior of the drums is undoubtedly associated with the gregarious ethology of many of the species in the family, which use these sounds as summoning signals, calls of alarm, and so on. The intensity of the sounds emitted is such that they are easily picked up on recording instruments and there is many a naval joke about the alarm and confusion caused by these noises of "uncertain origin."

The umbra (or umbrine) (*Umbrina cirrhosa*) is the drum most frequently found on the sandy sea bed of the Mediterranean, where it can sometimes reach a length of 40 in (1 m) and weigh more than 22½ lb (10 kg). It lives in small shoals that tend to shed members as the fish grow larger. In coastal lakes and lagoons the umbra happily swims about in search of substrata with good food supplies. Sometimes it is even possible to catch small specimens some miles from the mouth of large rivers, which is why it is thought that this species can make its way upstream into purely freshwater habitats, just as the gray mullet (*Mugil cephalus*) does. In fact, only surface water is freshwater, and in the case of the umbra, it remains at the bottom of the watercourse, in other words where the water is the heavier salt water pushed in from the sea. The so-called saline cone can, under certain conditions, extend some miles from a river mouth. Once very common along Mediterranean shores, this fish is now rare because of over fishing, and as a result of the pollution of coastal waters.

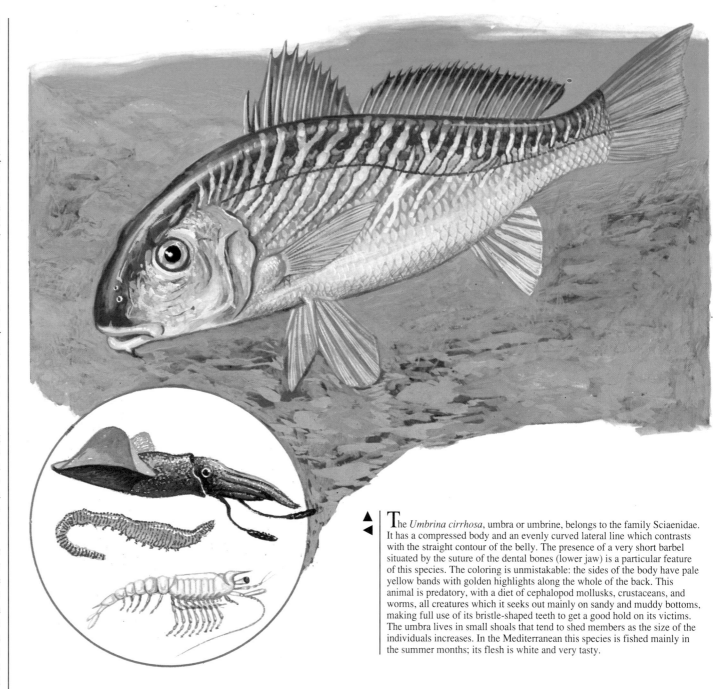

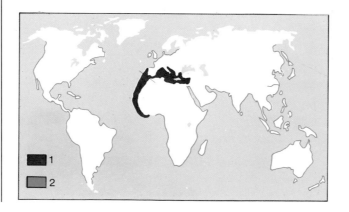

The *Umbrina cirrhosa*, umbra or umbrine, belongs to the family Sciaenidae. It has a compressed body and an evenly curved lateral line which contrasts with the straight contour of the belly. The presence of a very short barbel situated by the suture of the dental bones (lower jaw) is a particular feature of this species. The coloring is unmistakable: the sides of the body have pale yellow bands with golden highlights along the whole of the back. This animal is predatory, with a diet of cephalopod mollusks, crustaceans, and worms, all creatures which it seeks out mainly on sandy and muddy bottoms, making full use of its bristle-shaped teeth to get a good hold on its victims. The umbra lives in small shoals that tend to shed members as the size of the individuals increases. In the Mediterranean this species is fished mainly in the summer months; its flesh is white and very tasty.

The family Sciaenidae consists principally of marine fish. But there are also several markedly euryhaline species (i.e. which can tolerate varying degrees of salinity), some of which are totally adapted to freshwater life. These latter include *Aplodinotus grunniens*, the freshwater drum, which lives on the coasts of the western Atlantic. The species belonging to this family live mainly on sandy and muddy bottoms, near the mouth of large rivers. One particular feature of many is the capacity to emit sounds. This is done by means of an adaptation of the swim bladder which is vibrated by specific muscles and used like a sort of sound box. The umbra is one of the most interesting species in the family. It is found throughout the eastern Atlantic, from England to Angola, and in the Mediterranean. Here it may reach a length of 40 in (1 m) and weigh more than 22½ lb (10 kg), and it is without doubt the most frequently found type of drum. 1) Umbra (*Umbrina cirrhosa*); 2) the family Sciaenidae.

JACKKNIFE FISH
Equetus lanceolatus

Equetus lanceolatus also belongs to the family Sciaenidae and is commonly known as the jackknife fish. The chin of this fish sports "whiskers." The body is triangular in shape, with the base formed by the belly. The contour of the body rises in an abrupt vertical line from the mouth and goes on rising until the start of the dorsal fin; at this point it drops down little by little to the caudal fin. The mouth is small and terminal; on the jaws there are series of small villiform (bristle-like) teeth.

The dorsal fin is divided into a very high front section (the height in fact is one third of the total body length) with 13–14 spiny rays, and an elongated rear section (that almost reaches the caudal fin) with 49–55 soft rays. The anal fin is short; the pectoral fins have 15–16 soft rays. The abdominal pelvic fins do not reach the anus. The caudal fin is triangular and ends in a point. Individuals of this species have distinctive coloration: three brown bands, tending to black, edged with white against a gray background. The first band is vertical and situated by the eyes. The second is situated at the top of the back, crosses the gill cover, and runs over the belly and the pelvic fins. The last band starts by the first spiny rays of the dorsal fin and runs along the back; here it doubles back and runs along the terminal line, ending up at the rearmost tip of the caudal fin. This is a medium-sized fish, with a maximum length of 10 in (25 cm).

It lives in the western Atlantic, around the Bermudan and Bahaman Islands, and along the coast from the United States to Brazil. It is rare, with a habitat consisting of rocky substrata or coral reefs. It lives in quite deep water with other species of *Equetus*. These drums can be reared and are thus popular with aquarium owners.

The Sciaenidae are of some considerable economic importance and have been since earliest times, because of the quality of their flesh that can only bear comparison with that of certain species of Sparidae and Serranidae – sea bream and sea bass. They are fished in most seas, but especially along the Atlantic shores of Africa, in the Indian Ocean, and in the Pacific Ocean.

▼ The genus *Equetus* differs from all the other members of the family Sciaenidae because of the strange shape of its body and the long scythe-shaped dorsal fin.

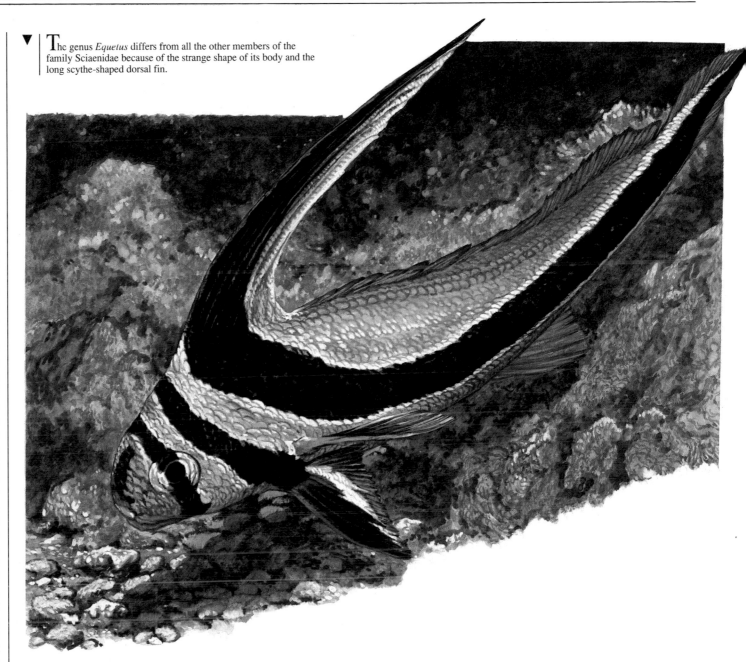

▲ *Equetus lanceolatus*, the jackknife fish, is the best known and most distinctive member of the genus *Equetus*. It is of medium size, reaching a maximum length of 10 in (25 cm). Members of this species have three brown bands – tending to black – edged with white against a gray background. The first band is vertical and situated by the eyes. The second is situated at the front of the back, runs through the gill covers, and carries on over the belly and the pelvic fins. The third band starts by the first spiny rays of the dorsal fin and runs down to the back, where it doubles back and runs along the lateral line, ending up at the rearmost tip of the caudal fin. The front part of the dorsal fin is very high; the rear section is elongated and almost reaches the caudal fin. The anal fin is short; the pectoral fins have 15–16 soft rays. The pelvic fins do not reach the anus; the caudal fin is triangular in shape and ends in a point.

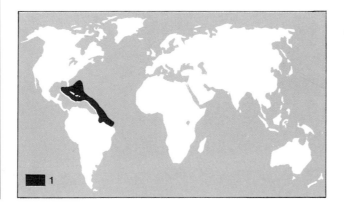

◄ 1) *Equetus lanceolatus*, the jackknife fish, is found in the western Atlantic, around the Bermudan and Bahaman Islands, and from the southern shores of the United States as far south as Brazil. Its habitat usually consists of rocky substrata and coral reefs. It lives in deep water with other members of the genus *Equetus*. Because it adapts well to life in captivity it is much sought after by aquarium owners.

WHITINGS
Sillaginidae

The Sillaginidae are percoid fish, characterized by their elongated, rather cylindrical body that is covered with small ctenoid scales. The head is conical and pointed, extending to a flattened frontal region. The opercular bone is small with a thin spine. The small, terminal, low-set mouth has two long series of villiform (bristle-like) teeth on the jaw bones and the vomer, but there are no teeth on the palatine bones. The dorsal fins are contiguous; the first has 9–12 spiny rays, the second 16–26 soft rays. The anal fin at the front has two small spiny rays, followed by 15–27 soft rays. The coloring is yellow, with conspicuous shades of brown on the back.

The Sillaginidae are a small family that embraces small coastal species which live in the Indo-Pacific region, from the eastern shores of Africa to China, Japan, and Australia, with a preference for areas near the mouths of large rivers. In Australia these fish are commonly known as whitings, a name that is also used for the European species *Gadus merlangus*, belonging to the genus *Odontogadus*, that has nothing whatsoever to do with the Sillaginidae. Of the various species, the best known are *Sillago ciliata*, *Sillago punctatus*, *Sillago japonica*, and *Sillago sihama* known locally to the natives of Port Moresby in New Guinea as the *urea*.

Sillago ciliata, the so-called sand whiting, lives on all types of sandy sea bed on the southeast coast of Australia, feeding on crustaceans and worms. This species reaches a maximum length of 16 in (40 cm) and a weight of about 2¼ lb (1 kg). Sexual maturity is reached between the second and third year. The eggs are laid in two annual reproductive cycles. The larvae have a rapid growth rate, followed by an even quicker period of growth, which usually ceases when sexual maturity has been reached – as is suggested by the small maximum size.

The species *Sillago punctatus*, the spotted whiting, is found off the southeast coast of Australia. Australian fishermen also call this fish the King George whiting, and it is one of the most sought-after fish along the southern coast; in the period from November to February at Irwin Inlet, Wilson Inlet, and Oyster, it is the main focus of attention for local anglers and professional fishermen.

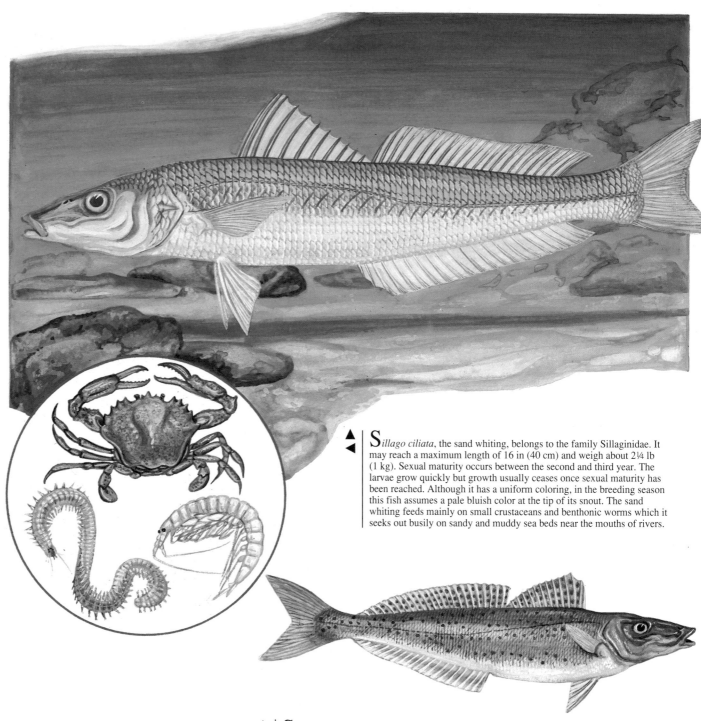

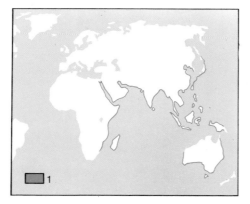

▲▼ S*illago ciliata*, the sand whiting, belongs to the family Sillaginidae. It may reach a maximum length of 16 in (40 cm) and weigh about 2¼ lb (1 kg). Sexual maturity occurs between the second and third year. The larvae grow quickly but growth usually ceases once sexual maturity has been reached. Although it has a uniform coloring, in the breeding season this fish assumes a pale bluish color at the tip of its snout. The sand whiting feeds mainly on small crustaceans and benthonic worms which it seeks out busily on sandy and muddy sea beds near the mouths of rivers.

▲ S*illago punctatus*, the spotted whiting, is one of the best known species of Sillaginidae. It is also one of the largest members of the family and can reach a maximum length of 21 in (53 cm). It has distinctive "spots" and a paler band running along the sides of its body, along the lateral line.

◄ 1) The family Sillaginidae embraces coastal species that live in the Indo-Pacific region, from the eastern shores of Africa to China, Japan, and Australia. *Sillago ciliata*, the sand whiting, lives in particular on the southeastern coast of Australia and *Sillago punctatus* is found only to the southeast of Australia. Because of the tastiness and digestibility of their flesh, the members of the Sillaginidae are much sought after. As a rule they are fished with circular nets or small drag nets.

REMORAS
Echeneidae

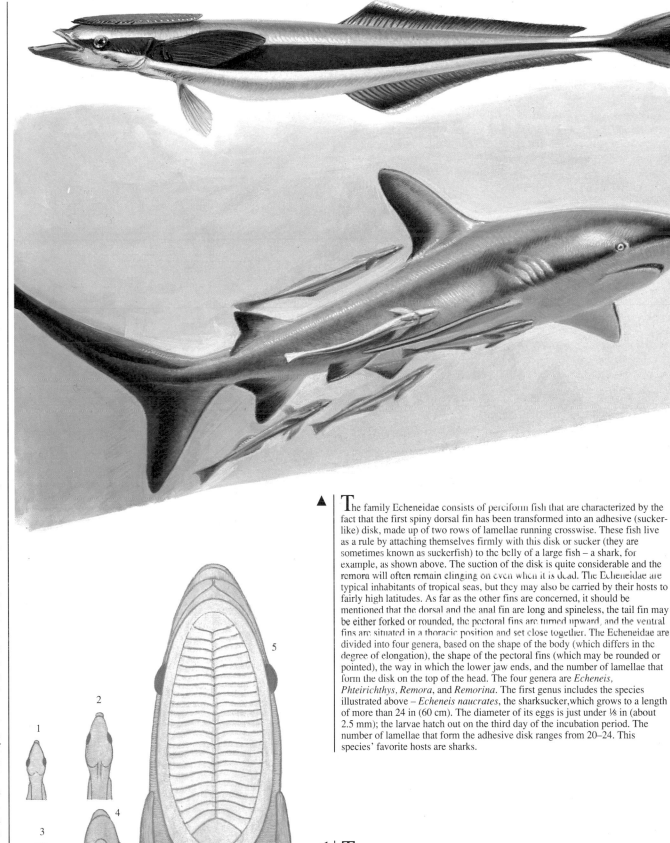

The fish belonging to this family have an elongated, spindle-shaped body. The head has a long adhesive apparatus on the top of it – a sort of long sucker formed by a double row of lamellae – by means of which these medium-sized fish attach themselves to other fish.

The Echeneidae have a distinctive coloration: the back is whitish and silvery, while the belly is colored. The most usual colors found on the belly and sides of the body are brown or blue, in quite dark shades. There are four distinct genera: *Echeneis, Phteirichthys, Remora,* and *Remorina.* These differ from one another mainly in the shape of the body, in the shape of the pectoral fins, which may be rounded or pointed, the way in which the lower jaw ends at the front, and the number of lamellae which form the cephalic disk.

The Echeneidae lay spherical, transparent eggs with a droplet of oil at the vegetative pole. The diameter of the egg is about ⅛ in (2.5 mm) in the sharksucker (*Echeneis naucrates*), the larvae of which hatch out on the third day of the incubation period.

Numerous observations confirm the role of "cleaner" carried out very efficiently by the remoras in relation to their hosts. Examination of stomach contents has revealed a large proportion of parasitic crustaceans, as well as fish, in particular pilot fish. The diet of these creatures must be quite varied because the size of the various remoras differs from species to species. In fact, while the sharksucker (*Echeneis naucrates*) may exceed 24 in (60 cm) in length, the black remora (*Remora remora*) is never more than 14 in (35 cm) long.

Somewhat surprisingly, fish belonging to the Echeneidae have been seen affixed to the palate or to the gills of large bony or cartilaginous fish. Various species have become the remoras' favorite hosts: we find the black remora (*Remora remora*) mainly on sharks; *R. brachyptera* and *R. osteochir* show a preference for the Histiophoridae (marine scombroids) and the Xiphiidae (swordfish, etc.); *Remorina albescens* tends to select large members of the genus *Manta (*the manta rays).

The family Echeneidae consists of perciform fish that are characterized by the fact that the first spiny dorsal fin has been transformed into an adhesive (suckerlike) disk, made up of two rows of lamellae running crosswise. These fish live as a rule by attaching themselves firmly with this disk or sucker (they are sometimes known as suckerfish) to the belly of a large fish – a shark, for example, as shown above. The suction of the disk is quite considerable and the remora will often remain clinging on even when it is dead. The Echeneidae are typical inhabitants of tropical seas, but they may also be carried by their hosts to fairly high latitudes. As far as the other fins are concerned, it should be mentioned that the dorsal and the anal fin are long and spineless, the tail fin may be either forked or rounded, the pectoral fins are turned upward, and the ventral fins are situated in a thoracic position and set close together. The Echeneidae are divided into four genera, based on the shape of the body (which differs in the degree of elongation), the shape of the pectoral fins (which may be rounded or pointed), the way in which the lower jaw ends, and the number of lamellae that form the disk on the top of the head. The four genera are *Echeneis, Phteirichthys, Remora,* and *Remorina.* The first genus includes the species illustrated above – *Echeneis naucrates,* the sharksucker, which grows to a length of more than 24 in (60 cm). The diameter of its eggs is just under ⅛ in (about 2.5 mm); the larvae hatch out on the third day of the incubation period. The number of lamellae that form the adhesive disk ranges from 20–24. This species' favorite hosts are sharks.

The diagram on the left shows the development of the adhesive disk in the black remora (*Remora remora*). The actual dimensions of this development are not precisely known for several of the other species in the family. 1) At a length of ¼ in (6.5 mm) there is still no sign of a sucker at all; 2) at ⅜ in (9.8 mm) an oval form appears behind the head; 3) at ½ in (12 mm) it becomes more conspicuous, but there are still no visible lamellae; 4) at ¾ in (18 mm) the development of the disk is already quite advanced; 5) at 1 in (25 mm) the adhesive disk is more or less perfectly formed.

GREATER AMBERJACK
Seriola dumerili

The genus *Seriola* is currently included in the large family Carangidae, the jacks, and is thus part of the suborder Percoidei and the order Perciformes. Along with the other genera these fish are characterized by short pectoral fins (not scythe-shaped), a bone which is supplementary to the jaw bone, and, along the lateral line, the absence of large scales transformed into plates. The group as a whole forms the subfamily Seriolinae.

They are quite large fish, pelagic, good swimmers, migratory, and living as a rule in warm and temperate seas. Their strength and fierce resistance means that for underwater fishermen and anglers alike they are difficult to hunt. Their flesh is much sought after too, so they are also fished commercially, usually with nets, and sometimes with bottom lines.

The greater amberjack (*Seriola dumerili*) is one of the best known species. The slender, tapering, slightly compressed body of this fish gives an impression of great power. The smooth-looking skin is in fact covered with very small and barely visible scales. The head is powerful, with a rounded, convex outline and a round snout. The mouth is large, with a slightly prominent lower jaw. The very small teeth are arranged in particular areas along the jaw bones, on the plate, and on the tongue. In rare cases the greater amberjack can reach a length of 6½ ft (2 m) and weigh up to 115 lb (50 kg).

The jacks are often confused with the bluefish (*Pomatomus saltator*), but differ from them by having two ribbed dorsal fins, by not having any carina on the caudal peduncle, by the shape of the tail which is much less indented, and by the teeth which are much stronger.

As they grow older the amberjacks become less sociable. They live in groups made up of just a few individuals, or often in pairs. They sometimes also lead a solitary life. They are carnivorous and feed mainly on cephalopods and fish, especially species which live in shoals. These fish are relentlessly hunted by the amberjack which will sometimes pursue its prey right into lagoons.

◄ The members of the genus *Seriola* are quite large fish. They are pelagic, strong swimmers, migratory, and usually live in warm and temperate seas. Their flesh is much sought after. The species illustrated here is *Seriola dumerili*, the greater amberjack. Its body is slender, tapering, and slightly compressed. The skin is smooth-looking, but in fact it is covered with very small and barely visible scales. These fish can reach a length of 6½ ft (2 m).

▲ The young of the greater amberjack (*Seriola dumerili*) are pelagic like their parents. They live in quite large groups and are often to be found near floating objects, where they can take refuge if necessary. Their body is thickset and differs conspicuously from the adult's body. As a result they have often been described as a different species and in some parts of the world they even have their own specific popular name.

◄ The members of the genus *Seriola* are carnivorous and feed mainly on cephalopods and fish, especially species which tend to live in shoals (tunny, sardine, and gray mullet, for example).

PILOT FISH

Naucrates ductor

Order Perciformes
Family Carangidae
Length Usually 14 in (35 cm), sometimes as long as 28 in (70 cm)
Distinctive features It has the spindle-shaped body of a strong swimmer; the first dorsal fin is formed by a series of small separate spines that are not joined together by any membrane; it has a fleshy carina which is quite long and clearly visible on either side of the caudal peduncle
Coloration The body is bluish gray, darker on the back, and very pale on the belly. There are broad dark stripes running vertically up the body; they also run across the dorsal and anal fins. The caudal lobes are dark with white edges
Reproductive period Late summer to winter

The body of the pilot fish (*Naucrates ductor*) is clearly the body of a very strong swimmer. Pilot fish are in fact tireless swimmers, with a preference for the high seas, but they are also to be found close to the coast, especially when they are still young. They swim along with ships and also with large sea creatures, in particular sharks, sometimes swimming in groups either alongside or in front of them.

This behavior has given rise to a legend. It was thought at one time that sharks had poor eyesight and that the pilot fish, with its good vision, directed them towards their prey in exchange for the "crumbs from the master's table." In fact sharks have highly tuned senses and can single out their prey quite efficiently on their own; what is more, they are not always accompanied by pilot fish. Some authors maintain that it is only its agility that saves the pilot fish from being gobbled up by sharks. But it could also be that the shark puts up with the presence of the pilot fish because it is keen to rid itself of the small crustaceans which lodge on its skin. The pilot fish, by this hypothesis, is thus a kind of "cleaner," but this is disputed by various authors. However it is generally agreed that pilot fish swim along with ships in order to scavenge the ship's waste and feed on the barnacles that grow on the hull and that they accompany sharks to pick up the leftovers from their meals.

The pilot fish (*Naucrates ductor*) belongs to the jack family – the Carangidae and thus to the suborder Percoidei. Its body is slender, spindle-shaped, and slightly compressed; it ends in a very powerful tail fin. It is obvious just from looking at it that this fish is a very strong swimmer. Pilot fish have a habit of keeping close to floating objects from their earliest days. When young, like many other jacks, they follow siphonophores, Portuguese-men-o'-war, and jellyfish. When they have reached a length of 6 in (15 cm) they start to venture closer to those fearsome creatures, the sharks. When various individuals compete with one another the skin takes on a specific coloring: it turns very pale, loses its vertical stripes, and becomes in fact almost colorless. Because it leads such an active life and is always on the move, the pilot fish cannot be kept in captivity.

▼ The amberjacks live in all the warm and temperate seas. In addition to *Seriola dumerili*, the greater amberjack, which is found along the western and eastern shores of the Atlantic, in the Mediterranean, and in the Indo-Pacific region, we should mention, among the best known species: *Seriola quinqueradiata*, the five-rayed amberjack, frequent along the coasts of Japan, and similar to *S.dumerili*; *Seriola lalandi*, found in the tropical regions of the Atlantic, and in the Pacific, and likewise very like *S.dumerili*; *Seriola rivoliana*, found in the tropical Atlantic as far as Japan, which is a uniform slate gray color; *Seriola zonata*, which lives off the Atlantic coasts of America, with a taller body and dark vertical stripes marking the body of young individuals, but also visible in adults. The species shown here, *Seriola dorsalis* is found in the Pacific Ocean and is very well known along the shores of California. The amberjack is a pelagic, tireless swimmer, and permanently on the move. Periodically it swims inshore, especially during the summer months, when it can be found near the surface, especially near promontories or small rocky islands. But it will also dive several hundred feet, and appears to live at this depth when the sea cools down.

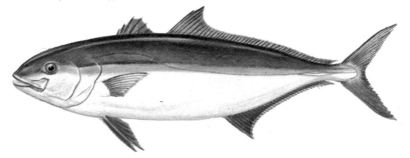

Seriola dorsalis

JACKS
Carangidae

The plentiful fossil finds of members of the Carangidae that have been unearthed in sediment deposits in many parts of the world show clearly how widespread these fish were as far back as the Cretaceous period. Nowadays they are found in tropical and temperate seas. Their slender body, which is in some cases slightly compressed laterally, is covered, either completely or partly, with small cycloid scales. In some cases, however, there are no scales at all.

The distribution area of this family is not very clearly defined because of the long migratory journeys made by many species along coasts and in the open sea, for breeding purposes, or simply in pursuit of large shoals of Clupeidae (herrings, sardines, etc.) and mackerel, which represent their favorite food. They are happiest in warm water and are thus particularly abundant in tropical and temperate waters throughout the world. Only one or two species are found in cold seas: the horse mackerel (*Trachurus trachurus*) is found quite frequently in the North Sea, along the shores of Britain and as far north as Norway and Iceland.

Other species of the same genus, such as the jack mackerel (*Trachurus symmetricus*) and *Trachurus japonicus*, are found in the Atlantic and Pacific Oceans, along the coasts of Canada, North and South America, and Japan. Many jacks lead a pelagic life and only swim close to land during certain times of the year on their migratory treks. They are often gregarious and gather together in very large shoals. It is a truly spectacular sight to see these fish hunting swift flying fish under the sea's surface, or suddenly changing direction, the entire shoal at the same precise moment.

Not all the species in this family are pelagic. Some live permanently along the coast in sandy shallows or at the edge of reefs; others venture into brackish lagoons and river estuaries in search of gray mullet and other prey. In their structure some of these coastal species differ markedly from the typical jacks. The body is often flatter and less slender than in the pelagic forms; one typical example would be *Selene vomer*, with its compressed body and extremely "tall" shape and elongated fins.

The jack family Carangidae is made up mostly of migratory fish. Their slender and very streamlined form makes them very strong swimmers. They have a mimetic form of coloring which protects them both from the eagle eyes of sea birds and from attacks from large pelagic predators such as tunny. They feed on small fish, in particular anchovies and sardines. The coloring is very similar in all the members of the family: the back is blue or green, the belly and the sides of the body are silvery or golden. The species of the genus *Trachurus* are easily identifiable by the fact that they have small bony plates or shields (scuta) along the whole length of the lateral line. This genus is made up of small fish, measuring on average 12–16 in (30–40 cm). The size of the jack family varies tremendously, for example one species, also found in the Mediterranean, the greater amberjack (*Seriola dumerili*), reaches a length of 6½ ft (2 m). But most of the species are somewhere in between these two extremes. The species illustrated here, *Trachurus japonicus*, has a maximum length of 20 in (50 cm).

The horse mackerel may reach an overall length of some 16 in (40 cm). It is an extremely greedy fish, feeding on other fish and their eggs and fry, as well as plankton. The young have the distinctive habit of herding together in small shoals among the tentacles of large jellyfish, and they seem to be immune to their poison. In this odd shelter they find refuge from large predators and they also find something to eat because they enjoy the jellyfish's gonads.

Horse mackerel
(*Trachurus trachurus*)

MORJARRAS
Gerridae

The family Gerridae is considered to be related to the Carangidae and in fact at one time was included in this family. These fish are extremely plentiful in some parts of the world and in some regions, such as the shores of India, they represent one of the most important catches.

The mojarras belong to the order Perciformes. They have an elongated, quite tall body which is laterally compressed and covered with small, caducous cycloid scales; these do not occur on the head and are sometimes also missing on the "chest," where they may be transformed into thin, transparent plates that give the fish a "naked" look. Only the species *Leiognatus elongatus* has scales on the head as well. The lateral line is usually quite visible, but in some species it can only be seen at the front end of the body.

The mouth is small, either horizontal or diagonal, and because of the particular shape of the jaw bones and the premaxillary bones it can be "evaginated," thus forming a tube that can be directed upwards or downwards. The teeth are small and set in single rows; in the genus *Gazza* there are canine-like teeth.

The coloring is usually silvery with different shading (yellow, yellow–brown, etc.) according to species. There are also dark and variegated vertical bands on the back, which are especially evident in adult fish. The fins are usually yellow.

The family Gerridae, whose members are easily identified by the particular structure of the buccal apparatus, is divided into three genera: *Leiognatus*, *Secutor*, and *Gazza*. These differ basically by the absence or presence of canine-like teeth and by the particular angle of the buccal tube when it is evaginated.

The members of this family do not occur at all in the Atlantic Ocean and the Mediterranean, but they are extremely abundant throughout the Indo-Pacific region; along the coasts of East Africa, India, China, and Japan they represent one of the most important catches. Many species often venture into brackish lagoons and estuaries, in particular in the early stages of their development. Some are even to be found in watercourses and lakes further inland.

The family Gerridae embraces species that are easily identifiable by the particular shape of the buccal apparatus (formed by the maxillary and premaxillary bones). This formation enables them to evaginate the mouth, which they wield like a tube, directing it both upwards and downwards. Some species venture into estuaries and brackish lagoons, in particular in the early stages of their development. Others are even to be found in watercourses further inland. The species illustrated here – *Leiognatus nuchalis* – is one of the most interesting.

Caranx bartholomaei

Selene vomer

▲ The species belonging to the genera *Vomer* and *Selene* are fairly distinct from the typical form of the Carangidae, especially in the juvenile stages, when the first rays of the dorsal and anal fins are very markedly developed. But one distinctive feature of the genus *Caranx* consists in the fact that the small bony shields, which in other genera cover the entire lateral line, or at least part of it, are restricted to the caudal peduncle, where they form a tough carina.

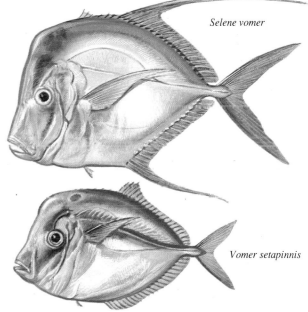

Vomer setapinnis

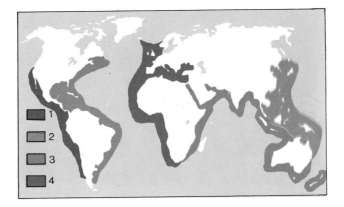

◄ The distribution area of the family Carangidae is not very clearly defined because many species make long migratory journeys both along coasts and in the high seas. These fish can be said to inhabit all the world's tropical and temperate seas and some species also venture into brackish waters. They are for the most part pelagic and very strong swimmers. The distribution area of *Trachurus symmetricus* (1) includes the western shores of the American continent. *T. japonicus* (2) is found between Japan and Australia. *Trachurus trachurus* (4), the horse mackerel, is found throughout the Atlantic Ocean, in the North Sea, in the western Baltic, in the Mediterranean, and in the Black Sea. The distribution of other species of Carangidae covers the coastal regions of the Pacific Ocean and New Zealand.

DOLPHIN FISH
Coryphaenidae

The family Coryphaenidae consists of just the one genus, *Coryphaena* with two species, the dolphin fish or dorado (*Coryphaena hippurus*) and the Pompano dolphin (*Coryphaena equisetis*). The dolphins in this group are excellent and strong swimmers; they are happiest on the high seas, well removed from land, and they live in all the world's oceans, especially in the tropical and subtropical regions.

These fish are keenly sought after by sporting anglers, because of their considerable size and the fight they put up, and by professional fishermen, because of the quality of their flesh. They are extremely voracious, with a particular liking for flying fish, although they also catch sardines and mackerel.

The family Coryphaenidae is a worldwide one; its members live in the tropical and subtropical zones of all the world's oceans. They are also to be found, though only sporadically, throughout the Mediterranean, where they were well known to the Ancient Greeks and Romans. It is presumed that this vast distribution area, which covers the whole world, applies to both species, although the exact distribution of the Pompano dolphin is not so well known, mainly because zoologists and naturalists muddled it up with the other species for a long time.

These are epipelagic fish, spending most of their time on the sea's surface. They are happiest in the high seas and usually stay well away from land. They migrate mainly in spring – probably to breed – and autumn. But when they do approach land it is always in the form of open shores, often sandy beaches, where they can sometimes be found in just a few feet of water. As a rule they do not venture into confined bays.

Dolphin fish are tireless wanderers. They swim in a normally sustained way, and can reach bursts of speed of up to 40 mph (60 kmh). They are extremely voracious and thus constantly in search of prey. They feed on crustaceans or cephalopods and a very large variety of other fish, particularly those that form shoals, like the sardine, the herring, the gray mullet or the small jack. Their favorite prey, however, is the flying fish.

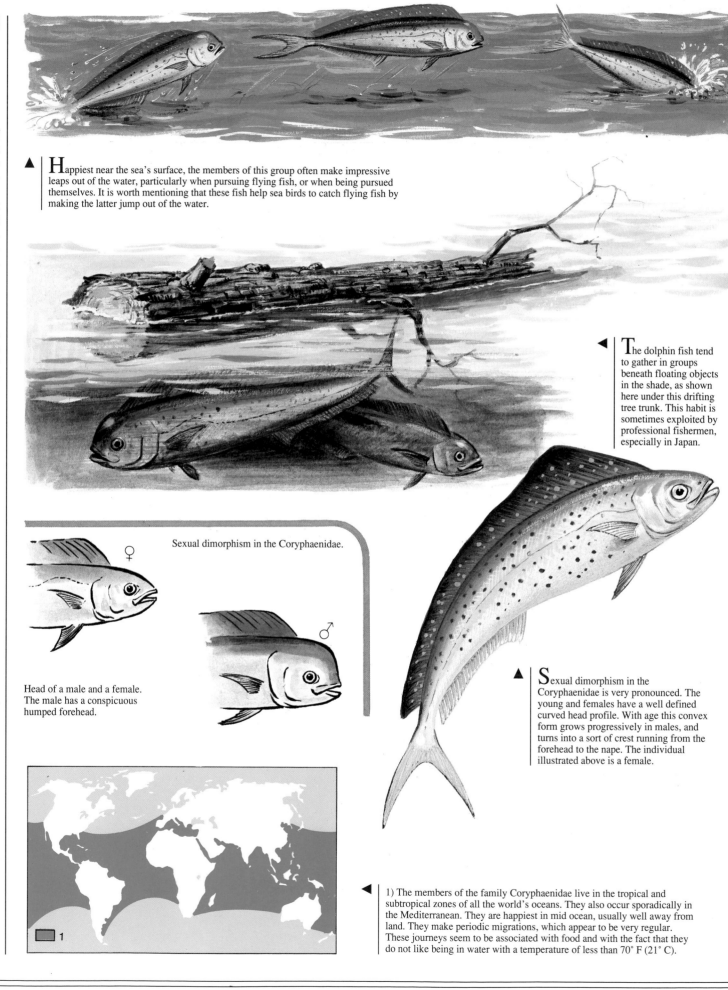

Happiest near the sea's surface, the members of this group often make impressive leaps out of the water, particularly when pursuing flying fish, or when being pursued themselves. It is worth mentioning that these fish help sea birds to catch flying fish by making the latter jump out of the water.

The dolphin fish tend to gather in groups beneath floating objects in the shade, as shown here under this drifting tree trunk. This habit is sometimes exploited by professional fishermen, especially in Japan.

Sexual dimorphism in the Coryphaenidae.

Head of a male and a female. The male has a conspicuous humped forehead.

Sexual dimorphism in the Coryphaenidae is very pronounced. The young and females have a well defined curved head profile. With age this convex form grows progressively in males, and turns into a sort of crest running from the forehead to the nape. The individual illustrated above is a female.

1) The members of the family Coryphaenidae live in the tropical and subtropical zones of all the world's oceans. They also occur sporadically in the Mediterranean. They are happiest in mid ocean, usually well away from land. They make periodic migrations, which appear to be very regular. These journeys seem to be associated with food and with the fact that they do not like being in water with a temperature of less than 70° F (21° C).

GRUNTS
Pomadasyidae

The family Pomadasyidae (or, according to some authors, Haemulidae) belongs to the order Perciformes. The body is elongated, spindle-shaped, and on the whole very tall. In most species the head has a markedly convex profile. The small or medium-sized mouth is situated low in the head; the upper jaw normally extends further forward than the lower jaw. Both jaws have thick lips. The teeth are conical, but not canine-like. They are arranged in small series on both jaws; in other words there are no teeth on the roof of the mouth. But the pharyngeal bones do have particularly well developed teeth.

The grunts have a wide variety of colors and designs based on stripes or markings that vary from species to species. The young of the genus *Haemulon* – with the exception of those belonging to the species *Haemulon plumieri* – have a dark lateral band and also a dark marking on the caudal peduncle. These markings disappear in the adult stage in almost all species. The inside of the mouth of these fish is often orange–red in color.

The grunts are found in all the world's tropical and subtropical seas; some species may live in warm temperate waters too. In the case of at least two species – *Pomadasys bennetti* and *Pomadasys stridens* – the Mediterranean is also visited, though rarely. Most of the members of this family are marine; some 30 of the 100 known species may venture into brackish water and up river mouths. Only one species – *Pomadasys bayanus* – lives in fresh water along the western shores of America. The Pomadasyidae live near the shore in the epicontinental zone. They are found at depths ranging from a few feet to more than 660 ft (200 m), but most of them live at about 330 ft (100 m). The habitat of these fish consists of fields of seaweed and coral reefs. They are also found on sandy or muddy sea beds near banks of madrepores.

One distinctive behavioral feature of the grunts is their habit of rubbing their pharyngeal teeth together, thus emitting a sound which is amplified by the swim bladder, hence the name of the family. It is possible to hear the noise produced by these fish when they swim to the surface.

▲ The family Pomadasyidae embraces fish that have a great variety of colors and designs, based on stripes or markings, which vary from species to species. They gather in shoals during the hours of daylight, in fields of seaweed in tropical and subtropical waters. During the night the shoals break up and the grunts go off alone in search of bottom-dwelling prey. They can emit sounds by rubbing their pharyngeal teeth together; this sound is then amplified by the swim bladder. The species illustrated above is *Haemulon sciurus*, which lives in the tropical western waters of the Atlantic Ocean. It is one of the most colorful of all the grunts and is common in coral reefs in this area. It is worth mentioning that the coloring is closely associated with the activities and habitat of these fish. In fact nocturnal species such as *Haemulon aurolineatum* are dull colored or grayish, thus blending in perfectly with the sandy or muddy sea bed, which is their normal habitat.

▼ When two grunts find themselves face-to-face, they push their mouths against one another, giving the impression that they are kissing. This is just another strange behavioral feature of these fish. We still do not know the significance of these "kisses." It could be that they mark a prelude to mating, or, alternatively, a mark of aggression to do with territorial defense.

▲ *Anisotremus virginicus* is a grunt that, like *Haemulon sciurus*, lives in the tropical western waters of the Atlantic Ocean. It is commonly found among madrepores, where it gathers in shoals made up of large numbers of individuals. The young feed on ectoparasites living on the bodies of other fish; the diet of adult individuals consists of a large variety of small invertebrates. The maximum length reached by these fish is 16 in (40 cm), i.e. slightly more than the average size of the various other species that make up the family, which is about 10 in (25 cm).

CARDINAL FISH

Apogonidae

The family Apogonidae belongs to the order Perciformes. The fish belonging to this family are all very uniform in appearance: the body is slender, spindle-shaped, and elongated, and sometimes compressed. The eyes are very large and the mouth, at the tip of the snout, is also large and diagonal. The teeth are small, almost like villi. In some genera there are also strong canine teeth. The body is covered with somewhat loose cycloid scales.

Some species in this group have photophores or luminous organs. These structures are found above all in species belonging to the genus *Siphamia*. The photophores form a luminous "pouch" at chin level and another "pouch" on the caudal peduncle. In *Apogon ellioti* there are three luminescent organs in the intestine, directed inwards. The role played by this "intestinal illumination" is still a mystery.

Cardinal fish are often red in color, hence their common name. Species belonging to the genus *Apogon* are orange–red, with black or white markings, while the species belonging to the genera *Astrapogon* and *Phaenoptyx* are brownish in color or else somewhat uniformly colored; members of the genus *Epigonus* are usually dark colored with silvery highlights. The cardinal fish are small in size: the average length is about 4 in (10 cm), and this is rarely exceeded. The largest species – *Apogon multitaeniatus* – reaches a length of 7 in (18 cm).

The family Apogonidae embraces about a hundred species belonging to numerous closely related genera. Cardinal fish are closely related to the sea basses (Serranidae), differing from them by having two spines in the anal fin and loose and less developed scales. They are found in shallow tropical and subtropical waters. Most of the species live in coral reefs. Some species are also found in temperate regions: *Apogon imberbis*, the king mullet, lives in the Mediterranean and along the Atlantic shores of Africa.

The large mouth attests to the fact that cardinal fish are quite voracious predators. Their diet consists of small fish – usually fry – and crustaceans. They often live in shoals and can wreak considerable damage to the young members of other coral reef-dwelling fish.

▲ The family Apogonidae, the cardinal fish, is made up of small fish: in fact most of them do not exceed 4 in (10 cm) in length. They are found in tropical and subtropical seas, in particular in coral reefs. They are, on the whole, red in color, hence their popular name. The species illustrated above – *Apogon imberbis*, the cardinal fish – is red with black markings, and the only species to be found in the Mediterranean and along the Atlantic shores of Africa. Some cardinal fish live in association with sea urchins. This is so with *Cheilodipterus novemstriatus*, *Apogon chrysotaenia*, and *Paramia bipunctata*. If some imminent danger threatens, these fish seek immediate refuge among the spines of the sea urchin, in small groups. The cardinal fish camouflage themselves in such a way that the vertical rays of their fins run parallel with the spines of the sea urchin, while the head is turned outwards. Cardinal fish leave their "hosts" at night and return to the safety of its spines at daybreak. It is therefore not easy to observe these fish in daylight. It is not known whether the sea urchin derives any benefit from this association, but it would appear that there is a certain reciprocity: in fact *Apogon chrysotaenia* has been observed busily cleaning the sea urchin's shell of various foreign bodies. The sea urchin, for its part, spreads its spines to enable the cardinal fish to find its way through them. We do not know whether all the species that live in association with sea urchins have the habit of cleaning their hosts.

▲ *Apogon semilineatus* is distributed from southern Japan to the Philippines. It can reach a maximum length of 4 in (10 cm). It is of no economic importance as food, although its flesh has quite a tasty flavor. Egg laying takes place in summer. It can be successfully reared in aquaria.

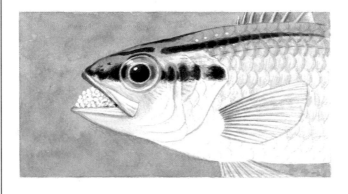

◄ The females lay their eggs in a single mass, which is immediately snapped up by the male's mouth. Oral incubation is the norm for almost all the species of cardinal fish and is crucial for the complete development of the eggs themselves. In fact if the eggs escape from the male's mouth, they will not develop fully, even though they are fertilized. After eight days the eggs hatch out, in the form of transparent planktonic larvae that need no parental care. The size and number of eggs laid vary from species to species. Some species lay many eggs that are very small in size: around 20,000 with a diameter of barely 0.5 mm. Other species, conversely, lay larger eggs in smaller quantities: 150 or so with a diameter of more than $\frac{1}{6}$ in (4 mm).

SPARIDAE

The Sparidae, porgies or sea breams, are perciform fish belonging to the suborder Percoidei. These fish are found in all the tropical and temperate seas and often form large shoals close inshore. They are particularly plentiful off South Africa, where we find, among other species, *Cymatoceps nasutus*, the musselcracker, which can reach a length of more than 40 in (1 m) and weigh more than 225 lb (100 kg).

The Sparidae lay pelagic eggs with an oily droplet attached to them, and they are known for their sexual switch overs. In fact many of these Percoidei reverse their sex at a size and an age that is known for some species but varies in others.

These are marine and coastal fish which colonize the whole coastal zone from the water's edge to a depth of 1,650 ft (500 m) and more. They are usually gregarious by nature in the juvenile phase but there are species of *Pagellus* and *Dentex* that remain gregarious as adults too, forming dense shoals, especially in the breeding season.

The diet of the porgies or sea breams varies a great deal and in describing it it is useful to analyze the dentition. For example, the white bream (*Diplodus sargus*), the two-banded bream (*Diplodus vulgaris*), and the sheepshead bream (*Diplodus puntazzo*) live normally in cracks on the rocky bottom, down to a depth of 100 ft (30 m), feeding on the fauna that lives encrusted on rocks. Their dentition is strong, made up of incisor-like, sharp teeth, with plates behind them that help the fish to grind up hard food such as bivalve mollusks, tubular worms, and sea urchins.

One specialized species living on sandy sea beds is the Mediterranean Marmor brassen or striped bream (*Lithognatus* or *Pagellus mormirus*). Although its dentition is similar to that of *Pagellus,* it has a very mobile mouth, adapted to sucking and moving sand. This is a rare feature in the Sparidae group, which is hallmarked on the whole by having a very powerful and not very mobile mouth. In fact, the Marmor brassen has a remarkable sand-burrowing ability: in a marine aquarium it is often difficult to see the young of this species as they disappear into the bottom at the least sign of alarm.

The family Sparidae (the porgies or sea breams) consists of 100 species of percoid fish, divided into 11 genera. These fish have a distinctively compressed body. A typical pattern of coloring in the Sparidae is one with dark crosswise bands on the sides of the body that gradually fade out from the back to the belly, as in the case of the Marmor brassen or striped bream (*Lithognatus mormirus*), or that end with a dark band which distinctively hallmarks the caudal peduncle, as in the case of the breams belonging to the genus *Diplodus* and the saddled bream.

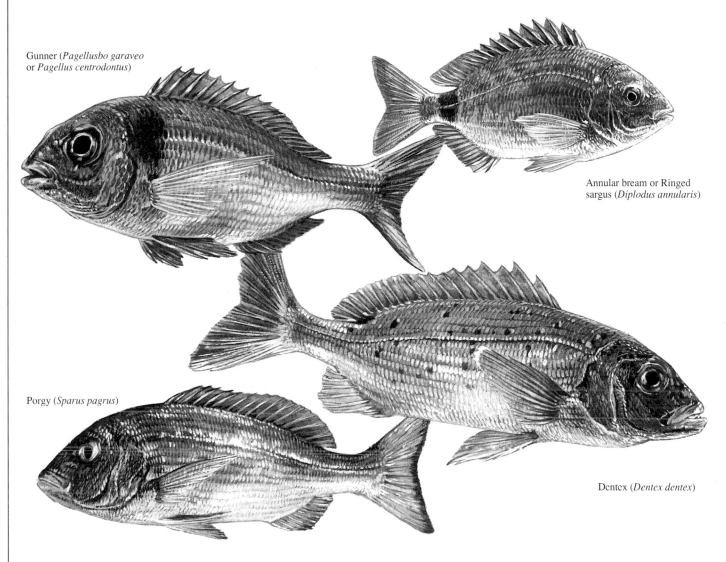

Gunner (*Pagellusbo garaveo* or *Pagellus centrodontus*)

Annular bream or Ringed sargus (*Diplodus annularis*)

Porgy (*Sparus pagrus*)

Dentex (*Dentex dentex*)

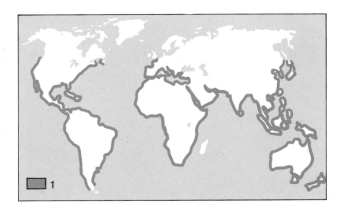

1) The Sparidae are marine and coastal fish which colonize the entire inshore zone from the water's edge to depths of 1,650 ft (500 m) and more. The diet of this group is very varied and a description of it is helped considerably by analyzing the dentition. The dentex (genus *Dentex*), which preys exclusively on fish and cephalopod mollusks, have just sharp conical teeth, designed for holding onto the prey. Members of the genus *Pagellus*, which live in deep rocky areas and have a mixed diet, have an intermediate form of dentition, with the conical teeth of a predator and plate-like teeth on the palate for grinding up food. The salpa (*Sarpa salpa*), which has an algae-based diet, has a dentition made up of very sharp-edged teeth, arranged in a single line: fishermen know only too well how effective these teeth are from the large gashes in their nylon nets.

GILTHEAD

Sparus auratus

Order Perciformes
Family Sparidae
Length Up to 28 in (70 cm)
Weight Up to 11 lb (5 kg)
Reproductive period From October to December in the Mediterranean
Eggs 1mm in diameter; floating, by means of an oily droplet
Sexual maturity This species has sexual reversal, with an initial male phase – up to the second year – followed by a female phase

The gilthead (*Sparus auratus*) is identifiable by a series of features that make it easy to tell it apart from the other Mediterranean members of the Sparidae group. The form of its body is typically compressed at the sides and the profile of the head drops almost vertically from the forehead area to the mouth. The mouth aperture, which is horizontal, is small and very powerful, with not very mobile lips. On the upper and lower jaws there are two series of strong teeth; the front series is made up of 4–6 large canine-shaped teeth with a rounded cusp; the rear series consists of plate-like teeth arranged in 3–5 rows.

The gilthead is one of the best known marine species, as far as man is concerned, and its delicate flesh has been much appreciated from earliest times. It is common throughout the Mediterranean and along the eastern coasts of the Atlantic Ocean, from England to Senegal. It is typically coastal and in fact is not really found at depths of more than 120–150 ft (35–40 m). It sometimes ventures into brackish inland coastal waters where it tends to spend the early stages of its life, in particular. When the first cold spells of autumn occur (and this happens before the breeding season starts), it returns back to the sea.

This species has an interesting ecology. It spends periods on sandy and mixed sea beds, sometimes in large shoals made up of different-sized individuals, both male and female. The formation of these shoals may be brought about by prereproductive groupings, or by brief migratory journeys made for alimentary reasons. This gregarious habit is typical of almost all the Sparidae, with the exception of old members of the genus *Dentex* which move about in small groups of 2–3 individuals.

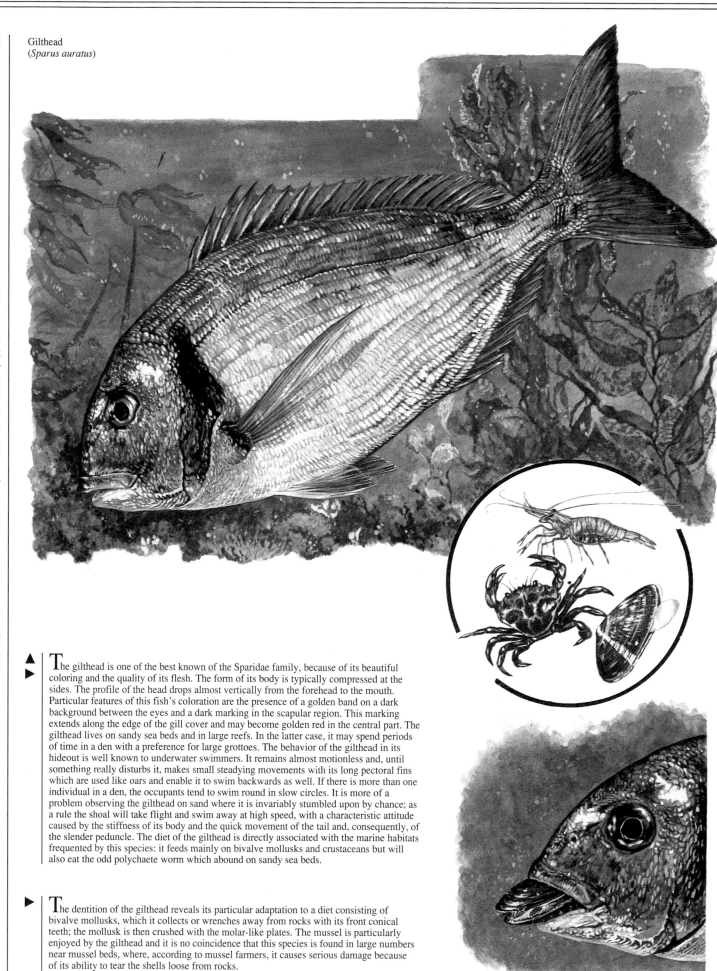

Gilthead
(*Sparus auratus*)

The gilthead is one of the best known of the Sparidae family, because of its beautiful coloring and the quality of its flesh. The form of its body is typically compressed at the sides. The profile of the head drops almost vertically from the forehead to the mouth. Particular features of this fish's coloration are the presence of a golden band on a dark background between the eyes and a dark marking in the scapular region. This marking extends along the edge of the gill cover and may become golden red in the central part. The gilthead lives on sandy sea beds and in large reefs. In the latter case, it may spend periods of time in a den with a preference for large grottoes. The behavior of the gilthead in its hideout is well known to underwater swimmers. It remains almost motionless and, until something really disturbs it, makes small steadying movements with its long pectoral fins which are used like oars and enable it to swim backwards as well. If there is more than one individual in a den, the occupants tend to swim round in slow circles. It is more of a problem observing the gilthead on sand where it is invariably stumbled upon by chance; as a rule the shoal will take flight and swim away at high speed, with a characteristic attitude caused by the stiffness of its body and the quick movement of the tail and, consequently, of the slender peduncle. The diet of the gilthead is directly associated with the marine habitats frequented by this species: it feeds mainly on bivalve mollusks and crustaceans but will also eat the odd polychaete worm which abound on sandy sea beds.

The dentition of the gilthead reveals its particular adaptation to a diet consisting of bivalve mollusks, which it collects or wrenches away from rocks with its front conical teeth; the mollusk is then crushed with the molar-like plates. The mussel is particularly enjoyed by the gilthead and it is no coincidence that this species is found in large numbers near mussel beds, where, according to mussel farmers, it causes serious damage because of its ability to tear the shells loose from rocks.

RED MULLET
Mullidae

Red mullet are small, roughly cylindrical fish that live near the sea bed off the coasts of tropical, subtropical, and temperate seas. They have a fairly stout body and straight forehead, so that some species have rather a bulldog look. Two long, pointed, fleshy barbels grow beneath the lower lip, which the fish use in searching for food in the muddy sea bed. They feed on crustaceans, mollusks, and rotting vegetable matter. Their coloring varies from pink to red. During the summer they approach the coasts in search of the deep, sandy bottoms on which they reproduce and during these movements they are pursued by great numbers of predatory fish. Man too fishes for them, for they have considerable commercial value.

There are six genera in the family – *Mullus, Mulloidichthys, Upeneus, Upeneichthys, Parupeneus,* and *Pseudupeneus* – and 55 species. *Mullus barbatus* has a shiny, light red coloring with metallic reflections. There is a row of brown scales on the back. Its weight may reach 50 oz (140 g) in specimens 9 in (23 cm) long.

Mullus barbatus lives from the Canary Islands and the Bay of Biscay to the southern coasts of Norway around Bergen and the western Baltic. It prefers muddy bottoms at a depth of about 1,000 ft (300 m). It also occurs in the Mediterranean and the Black Sea. Its food consists of various forms of invertebrates found in the mud of the sea bed. Their delicate flesh was already appreciated in the times of the Romans and the Greeks, who paid silver for them. The Romans apparently used to admire the changes of color as the fish died – they turn from deep red to pale red and finally to white.

The common red mullet, surmullet or goatfish (*Mullus surmuletus*) lives near the rocky coasts and seaweed beds of the Mediterranean. Compared with the species described above, it has a larger snout and so a more sloping profile. The yellowish longitudinal stripes are particularly evident. The French ichthyologist Fage showed that juvenile forms living among the rocks develop into *Mullus surmuletus* while those living on muddy bottoms at depths of 330–1,000 ft (100–300 m) belong to the species *Mullus barbatus*.

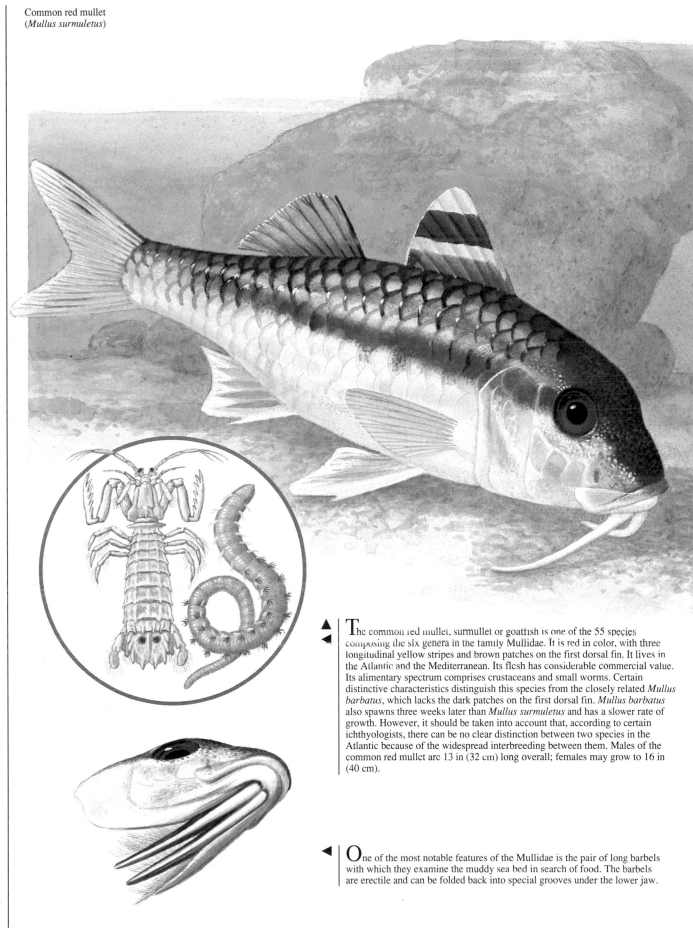

▲ The common red mullet, surmullet or goatfish is one of the 55 species composing the six genera in the family Mullidae. It is red in color, with three longitudinal yellow stripes and brown patches on the first dorsal fin. It lives in the Atlantic and the Mediterranean. Its flesh has considerable commercial value. Its alimentary spectrum comprises crustaceans and small worms. Certain distinctive characteristics distinguish this species from the closely related *Mullus barbatus*, which lacks the dark patches on the first dorsal fin. *Mullus barbatus* also spawns three weeks later than *Mullus surmuletus* and has a slower rate of growth. However, it should be taken into account that, according to certain ichthyologists, there can be no clear distinction between two species in the Atlantic because of the widespread interbreeding between them. Males of the common red mullet are 13 in (32 cm) long overall; females may grow to 16 in (40 cm).

◄ One of the most notable features of the Mullidae is the pair of long barbels with which they examine the muddy sea bed in search of food. The barbels are erectile and can be folded back into special grooves under the lower jaw.

ARCHERFISH
Toxotidae

The six species of archerfish are well known because of their extraordinary way of hunting prey, using their mouth structure like a blowgun or peashooter. They have an elongated body that is fairly compressed laterally. The eyes are well developed, situated at the sides of the head and set quite well forward.

These smallish fish, which measure 4½ – 11 in (11.5 – 27 cm) overall, live in coastal waters with low salinity, in the brackish waters of estuaries, and in rivers. They are found in eastern Asia, the Indo-Malayan archipelago, off the shores of Australia, the Philippine islands, the northern regions of Australia, the Solomon Islands, and Vanuatu.

By far the most widespread species is *Toxotes jaculator*, the archerfish or sumpit. Its favorite habitats are brackish estuaries and mangrove swamps. Apart from its hunting techniques, which will be discussed below, and about which a great deal is now known, almost nothing is known about this fish's biology. The most interesting feature of the archerfish is their ability to hunt for prey out of the water by using a powerful jet of water which is squirted from the mouth.

During the daylight hours archerfish like to stay just beneath the surface of the water from where they keep an eagle eye on the environment outside, taking on a typical "slanting" hunting posture and waiting for a likely prey – probably an insect or a spider that has had the ill-fated idea of spinning its web near the water. Once the prey has been singled out, the fish takes aim, noiselessly moving back and forth, with the tip of its snout just above the water surface; then it squirts the fatal jet of water that will inevitably strike the target and knock it into the water, where it is swiftly gobbled up.

As a rule, the archerfish never misses the bullseye; if the prey is some way off, it may fail to hit it at the first try, but the second shot never fails to strike home. However, this astonishing behavior does not occur in young individuals, which require a period of firing practice before they achieve the accuracy of adults.

The family Toxotidae – the archerfish – consists of six species, all belonging to a single genus, *Toxotes*. These fish have the extraordinary ability to catch prey outside the water by squirting jets of water by means of special modifications in the mouth structure. The species illustrated here is the most widespread and the best known, the archerfish or sumpit, *Toxotes jaculator*.

By darting swiftly out of the water, the archerfish can catch prey resting on the surface or flying close to it.

The buccal cavity of the members of the genus *Toxotes* is long and narrow. The tongue is large and fleshy at the base and not mobile. At the tip it is extremely slender.

1) The distribution of the archerfish covers a large area in the Indo-Pacific region. These fish live in coastal waters with low salinity, the brackish waters of estuaries, and in rivers. In these habitats the archerfish lies in wait just beneath the surface of the water, waiting for a likely prey to strike down with a jet of water. The mechanism that enables the archerfish to squirt these jets of water is very similar to that of a water pistol: the water collected in the mouth (the water pistol's reservoir) is subjected to pressure by means of contractions of the gill covers and the floor of the mouth (the pistol's plunger). On the roof of the mouth there is a small groove about 2 mm in diameter that channels the pressurized water (i.e. the barrel) and causes it to leave the mouth in a powerful jet through a small aperture delimited by maxillary symphyses when the mouth is shut (the pistol's muzzle). The duration and the force of the jet (equivalent to the time and pressure on the trigger) can be varied as the fish wishes.

SPADEFISH
Ephippidae

The main feature of the Ephippidae is the form of the body, which is common to all the species. It is very flat laterally, and almost as tall as it is long. The head is small and rises upwards abruptly. The small, horizontal mouth is not protractile; the small, sharp teeth are like the bristles of a brush and only occur on the jaws; in fact the palate has no teeth. The gill cover is very small. The dorsal fin is separated into two sections: the front part has 6–16 spiny rays; the rear has just soft rays, the first of which may be very long. The tail fin is broad, square or concave. The anal fin, which is situated right beneath the dorsal fin, has 3–4 short spiny rays and an adjacent soft zone. Like those in the dorsal fin, the soft rays are very long. The head and the body are covered with small or medium-sized ctenoid scales; these are particularly concentrated on the impar fins. The lateral line follows the contour of the back.

The members of this family may grow to a considerable size. Individuals belonging to the genus *Chaetodipterus* may reach 40 in (1 m) in length, but some specimens reach a truly exceptional size. The African members of the genus *Chaetodipterus* measure, on average, about 8 in (20 cm). Members of the genus *Platax* can also grow quite large, measuring a maximum of 28 in (70 cm).

Some authors include the genus *Monodactylus* in a different family – the Monodactylidae or fingerfish, which are related to the spadefish. The form of the body is almost identical to that of the Ephippidae, but they differ by the fact that only the tips of the rays of the paired fins emerge through the epidermis and the pelvic fins are rudimentary.

The Ephippidae live as a rule in tropical and subtropical seas in the Indo-Pacific region, in surface waters; they are not usually found deeper than 330 ft (100 m). Three species – *Drepane africana*, *Chaetodipterus lippei*, and *Chaetodipterus goreensis* – are found along the Atlantic coast of Africa. All the members of the family venture into river mouths and can also live in freshwater environments; the young of the genus *Platax*, for example, are often found in brackish water, in the mouths of rivers and in coastal lagoons in the Indo-Pacific region.

One of the main features of the Ephippidae is the form of the body: it is very tall, in fact almost as tall as it is long. In addition the dorsal and the anal fin are very well developed. The soft rays of these fins extend in fact well away from the body itself. Because of this abnormal development of the fins, the members of this family are commonly known as spadefish after the shape. The species illustrated on the right is *Platax pinnatus*. It lives in marine estuaries and in mangrove swamps. The young of the genus *Platax* (below, bottom) are morphologically different from the adults (below, top). The fins are very long and the coloring, which varies from individual to individual, is different in the two phases. The differences in color and the morphological variations due to age and the biotope have often caused zoologists to consider members of the genus *Platax* as belonging to different species, when in fact they are part of the same species.

BUTTERFLYFISH
Chaetodontidae

In many of the groups belonging to the suborder Percoidei it is essentially the color and in some cases the strange shapes of the fish that arouse both admiring gazes and curiosity. Less conspicuous, but no less noteworthy, are the particular features to do with the teeth and the scales. In fact in many cases the jaws carry numerous teeth that are thin and almost bristle-like, hence the scientific name *Chaetodon*, from *chèta* meaning bristle, and *odús* meaning tooth, that applies to the richest species in the genus.

Butterflyfish are particularly abundant in the Indo-Pacific region; they usually display a marked sense of territory and also an aggressive tendency towards other fish, including members of their own species.

Until very recently all the species were lumped into a single family: the Chaetodontidae. As studies have progressed, however, it was acknowledged that this was a heterogeneous grouping and that the two groups that had traditionally been lumped together – the Chaetodontidae or butterflyfish and the Pomacanthidae or angelfish – should be considered as different families.

The name "butterflyfish" is echoed in many languages, for example in Japanese with the name *Cho-chouwo-aka*. The body is short crosswise and tall, compressed, and sometimes almost disk-shaped; its profile is accentuated by the dorsal and anal fins that, with their scaly covering, appear to be almost extensions of the sides of the body. The snout is prominent and in some cases so long that it gives the head a strange configuration. The mouth is small and protractile. The dorsal fin is single and long and the anal fin is also well developed; the rear profile of the caudal fin is either straight or slightly concave.

The diet of the butterflyfish varies from species to species but it is nevertheless essentially zoophagous (carnivorous). The small and often protruding mouth is associated with this animal's method of seeking out food.

At the present time the genus *Chaetodon* includes by far the most butterflyfish: against a backdrop of coral reefs these fish really do look like brightly colored butterflies standing out amongst the numerous other creatures.

Chaetodon semilarvatus

▼ The fish belonging to the family Chaetodontidae and the family Pomacanthidae all have distinctively bright coloring and very varied patterns.

Chaetodon ephippium

Heniochus acuminatus

Chaetodon auriga

▲ Butterflyfish have been appreciated for many centuries but it is only as a result of recent studies that we have started to know something of their biology. These fish show adaptation to their environment and life style. The compressed body enables them to move with ease among coral structures: they swim mainly by means of synchronous movements made by the pectoral fins.

◀
▶ The development of the members of the family Chaetodontidae consists of a series of metamorphoses. The eggs hatch out into tiny larvae, just a fraction of an inch long, that differ quite a lot from the adult form, and as a result were once considered to be a separate genus known as *Tholichthys*. These larvae have a bony plate at the top of the back and a spine above the scapular area on each side of the body. They lead a pelagic life. In the adult state the size is smallish; only a few species reach lengths of 12 in (30 cm). The illustrations here show a side view of the larval stage (left) and a head-on view (right).

ANGELFISH
Pomacanthidae

It would seem justifiable to make a family apart for a series of fish traditionally associated with the Chaetodontidae or butterflyfish, for, like these, they are among the most magnificent of all tropical fish. This group is known as the family Pomacanthidae. The name is derived from the Greek words *pòma* meaning lid or cover and *àcanta* meaning spine, and in fact these fish have, on each side of the head, a tough spine that starts from the lower corner of the preoperculum and is turned backwards.

Angelfish (Pomacanthidae) must not be muddled up with damselfish (Pomacentridae), i.e. with a clearly distinct family that happens to have a similar scientific name.

In addition to having spines on the head, angelfish differ from butterflyfish in their generally larger size and by having a more elongated and less compressed body and a snout that does not protrude. In the larger species, and in adult individuals, the soft part of the dorsal fin often juts out like a filament.

The angelfish, like butterflyfish, are only found in warm seas, usually in coral reefs; they are solitary and display territorial tendencies. Sponges are an important feature of their diet. As they grow, conspicuous changes take place in their coloring and patterns, which is why to begin with young and adults seem to belong to different species.

Pomacanthodes imperator is a magnificent fish and as such is often chosen as the emblem of tropical fish. It reaches a length of 14 in (35 cm). It has a very extensive geographical distribution: from the Red Sea to Polynesia. The same seas also act as host to various related species with very different coloring (*P. maculosus*, for example, is greenish blue with a yellow vertical band in the middle of each side of the body), but strangely enough all young individuals are very much alike.

Like butterflyfish, angelfish are widely distributed in the warm regions of all the world's oceans but are much more numerous in the Indian and Pacific Oceans. One species worth mentioning for its contrasting chiaroscuro coloring is *Chaetodontoplus mesoleucus* which is 6½ in (16 cm) long and lives in the Indonesian archipelago.

Chaetodon xanthurus

Chaetodon collaris

Chaetodon capistratus

Chaetodontoplus mesoleucus

Chelmon rostratus

Zanclus cornutus

Heniochus acuminatus

Microcanthus strigiatus

Pomacanthodes imperator

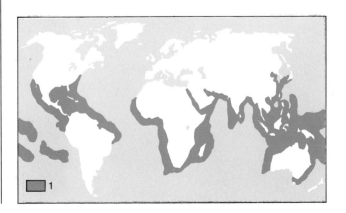

1

▲ The various behavioral patterns that have been observed in the butterflyfish are not constant in one and the same species. As a rule a particular behavior predominates in a particular place. In any event these fish are active during the day. In addition to species belonging to the butterflyfish and angelfish families, the illustration above includes two related species: *Zanclus cornutus* (belonging to the family Zanclidae) known as the Moorish Idol and *Microcanthus strigiatus* (belonging to the family Scorpidae and the suborder Percoidei).

◄ 1) Butterflyfish and angelfish are widely distributed in the warm regions of all the world's oceans. They are especially plentiful in the Indo-Pacific region. They usually show a marked sense of territory and an aggressive tendency towards other fish, even those of the same species. They are only important on a commercial basis as aquarium specimens.

SURF PERCHES

Embiotocidae

The family Embiotocidae belongs to the suborder Percoidei. The body of these fish is oval or oblong, laterally compressed, and in most cases silvery in color. The head is quite short, in proportion to the size of the body, with a terminally situated mouth which is small and has a slightly protractile upper jaw. The maxillary bones have one or two rows of small conical teeth, while the palatine bones and the vomers are completely toothless.

The members of this family are found exclusively in the Pacific Ocean. All the species of Embiotocidae are marine with the exception of *Hysterocarpus traski*, which lives in the rivers and lakes of Central California and in the Sacramento river in particular. All the other species live along the coasts of North America, from Port Wrangell in Alaska to Ensenada in Mexico (Baja California), with the exception of two species that live along the coasts of Japan, Korea, and China: *Neoditrema ransonneti* and *Ditrema temmincki*. Southern California is the main area for these fish, which – in the case of the American species – are all found between latitudes 32° – 38° North, where the water temperature ranges from 52 – 70°F (11 – 21°C). For many of these species the limiting factor seems in fact to be the water temperatures – high temperatures south of the southernmost limit, and low temperatures to the north.

These are typically coastal fish that usually live in sandy bays or, in exceptional cases, along rocky shores. They almost all live in surface waters, except for certain species that are found in deep waters. One species, *Zelembius rosaceus*, is typically found in relatively deep waters on the continental shelf, at depths of 70–330 ft (20–100 m), though it can also be found at greater depths. *Cymatogaster agaretata*, the shiner perch, has the widest geographical distribution of all the species: it is found from Ensenada in Mexico right up to Port Wrangell in Alaska.

The diet of the surf perches is an omnivorous one. In fact these fish eat algae and green marine vegetation, as well as crustaceans – mainly amphipods and isopods – mollusks, and bryozoans.

Surf perches are noteworthy for the fact that they are viviparous, which is an

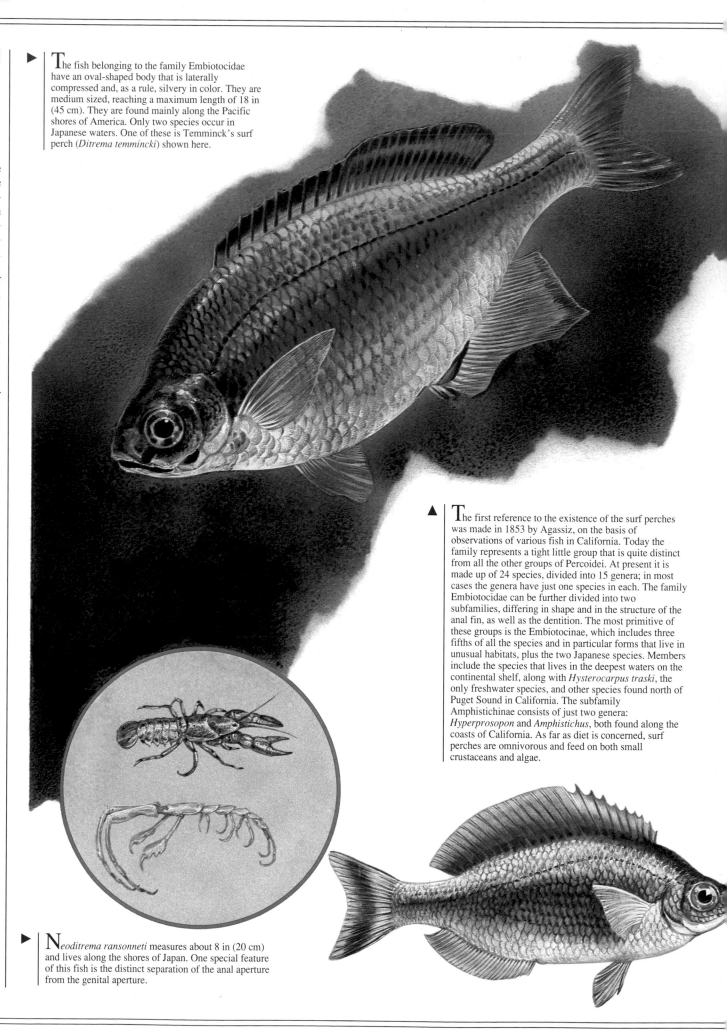

► The fish belonging to the family Embiotocidae have an oval-shaped body that is laterally compressed and, as a rule, silvery in color. They are medium sized, reaching a maximum length of 18 in (45 cm). They are found mainly along the Pacific shores of America. Only two species occur in Japanese waters. One of these is Temminck's surf perch (*Ditrema temmincki*) shown here.

▲ The first reference to the existence of the surf perches was made in 1853 by Agassiz, on the basis of observations of various fish in California. Today the family represents a tight little group that is quite distinct from all the other groups of Percoidei. At present it is made up of 24 species, divided into 15 genera; in most cases the genera have just one species in each. The family Embiotocidae can be further divided into two subfamilies, differing in shape and in the structure of the anal fin, as well as the dentition. The most primitive of these groups is the Embiotocinae, which includes three fifths of all the species and in particular forms that live in unusual habitats, plus the two Japanese species. Members include the species that lives in the deepest waters on the continental shelf, along with *Hysterocarpus traski*, the only freshwater species, and other species found north of Puget Sound in California. The subfamily Amphistichinae consists of just two genera: *Hyperprosopon* and *Amphistichus*, both found along the coasts of California. As far as diet is concerned, surf perches are omnivorous and feed on both small crustaceans and algae.

► *Neoditrema ransonneti* measures about 8 in (20 cm) and lives along the shores of Japan. One special feature of this fish is the distinct separation of the anal aperture from the genital aperture.

unusual feature among marine teleost fish. It is this feature that first attracted the attention of zoologists to this group. What is more, as part of the viviparous group of animals, the members of this family have other unique features: the sexual cycle of the males and females lasts for six months and after mating the spermatozoa remain alive in the genital apparatus of the female before fertilization takes place; in other words there is just one annual reproductive cycle.

Because of their viviparous nature these fish show sexual dimorphism; in fact all the males have a "pseudo-penis" formed from modifications of the front section of the anal fin. In some species this formation has the appearance of an oval swelling or bulge, in others there is a triangular lamina or plate, formed by transformations of the rays of the anal fin, associated with a glandular or similar type of structure. Mating takes place in the summer. The sperms remain for several months in the female's genital duct waiting for the eggs to mature, which they do by the winter.

In some species (e.g. *Cymatogaster aggregata*), at the moment of birth, the pregnant females migrate towards the shore to deliver the young in shallow water; then, when summer arrives, the males also head for the coast and mating takes place; after this, all the adults leave the coastal waters to make for deeper waters.

None of the fish in this family reach any notable size. They vary in length from 5–18 in (12–45 cm) but, while this represents the absolute maximum length, there are numerous individuals that measure less than the 5 in (12 cm). The larger species are well known to American anglers. One of the most sought after by rod fishermen is *Amphistichus argenteus*, which can grow quite large; another is *Hyperprosopon argenteum*, easily identifiable by its large eyes and the blackish color of the tips of the pelvic, anal, and tail fins. Yet another is *Phanerodon furcatus*, the tail fin of which is markedly forked and the body longer than in the other species; this species is the most commonly fished one.

Commercial fishermen also show an interest in the surf perches. The flesh of these fish is eaten, but it is not particularly tasty and has many bones.

▲ In late summer the male and the female mate after a brief nuptial ceremony. The spermatozoa remain alive in the female's ovaries for 2–3 months, for, when the two partners are locked together to mate, the eggs are still not completely mature.

▲ The embryos, ranging in number from 7–22, develop inside the ovaries, which play a similar part to that played by the uterus in mammals. The surf perch's eggs have poor vitellin reserves, so the embryos are fed additionally on ovarian secretions.

▲
▶ Before being born the young can feed themselves by absorbing food via their dorsal fin, which is expanded and extended to form spatula-like lobes. Gestation lasts for about five months and the young are delivered between May and July, complete with tails. At birth they are like the adults and measure a quarter of the overall length of their parents. A female can deliver 7–20 young.

◀ 1) Surf perches are found only in the Pacific Ocean, in two very precise areas: the coasts of North America and the waters around Japan. They are most concentrated off southern California. Fossil surf perches have been found in California which date back to the Miocene period. It is believed that these fish originated from California, that California is the only site of fossil finds, and that most of the species known to us are typical of this region; they then crossed the Pacific and reached the shores of Japan.

DAMSELFISH
Pomacentridae

The Pomacentridae, commonly known as damselfish, are small representatives of the order Perciformes. They are marine fish, almost exclusively limited to the world's tropical seas. They display striking affinities with the members of the family Cichlidae and are, phylogenetically, very close to them. The stocky body, often laterally compressed is covered with rough-edged, ctenoid scales and displays a curved, always clearly visible, lateral line. The front part of the single, undivided dorsal fin and of the anal fin is supported by spiny rays; the pectorals and ventrals are rounded. An interesting feature of the Pomacentridae, common also to the Cichlidae, is the presence of one nostril on either side of the head. The mouth is small and furnished with small conical teeth situated in three or four rows in the jaws. Damselfish are all small, seldom reaching a length of 8 in (20 cm). Many have handsome, conspicuous liveries with spots and vertical bands of contrasting colors. Such bright markings might seem unsuitable for small fish liable to be eagerly hunted by large predators, but it has been demonstrated that these very contrasts in color enable the fish to camouflage themselves perfectly against the multicolored background of the coral reef.

This family comprises numerous species that are scattered all over the world. They are found in the tropical belts of the Atlantic, the Pacific, and the Indian Oceans; only a few are adapted to life in the relatively cold waters of temperate seas. The small gregarious species *Chromis chromis* has a broad distribution through the Mediterranean, being very common along rocky coasts. The adult fish is uniformly dark brown and the young are blue. Another member of the family found in temperate waters is the Garibaldi damselfish (*Hypsypops rubicunda*), so called because of its bright red coloration, typical of the adults. The young are orange with a sprinkling of blue spots. This fish is common along the coasts of California.

All the Pomacentridae are strictly benthonic, littoral fish; only *Chromis caeruleus* leads a pelagic existence and is also fished on the high seas far from the coast. The Pomacentridae species have little commercial value as food,

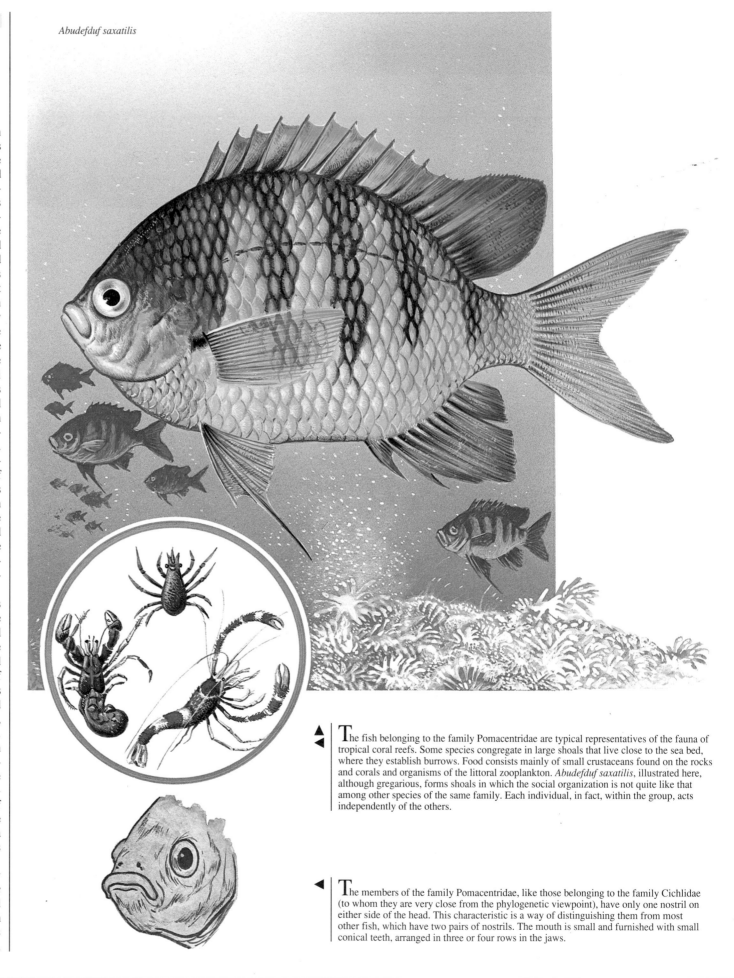

Abudefduf saxatilis

▲▲ The fish belonging to the family Pomacentridae are typical representatives of the fauna of tropical coral reefs. Some species congregate in large shoals that live close to the sea bed, where they establish burrows. Food consists mainly of small crustaceans found on the rocks and corals and organisms of the littoral zooplankton. *Abudefduf saxatilis*, illustrated here, although gregarious, forms shoals in which the social organization is not quite like that among other species of the same family. Each individual, in fact, within the group, acts independently of the others.

◄ The members of the family Pomacentridae, like those belonging to the family Cichlidae (to whom they are very close from the phylogenetic viewpoint), have only one nostril on either side of the head. This characteristic is a way of distinguishing them from most other fish, which have two pairs of nostrils. The mouth is small and furnished with small conical teeth, arranged in three or four rows in the jaws.

both because of their small size and the poor quality of their flesh. On the other hand, these small fish are of great interest to aquarists; because of their easy adaptability and decorative features, certain species are familiar inhabitants of ornamental tanks.

The social organization of this family has some highly interesting features. There are, in fact, gregarious species, strictly solitary species, and others that combine both types of behavior. *Dascyllus aruanus*, abundant along the reefs of the Red Sea, forms groups of 20 – 30 individuals, whose movements are synchronized. All leap and fall at the same time and all will flee at the merest hint of danger, as if they constituted a single large individual. *Abudefduf saxatilis*, although gregarious, forms groups in which association is looser so every individual within the group acts independently of the others. Solitary species like *Pomacentrus sulfureus* live in pairs and in well defined territories from which they chase away intruders both of their own and other species. At the center of the territory, in a rock fissure, they establish a burrow where they can hide in case of possible danger; it is rare for these fish to stray even a little distance from their zone.

Dascyllus trimaculatus exhibits a form of social organization that may be considered midway between those already described. It establishes its territory along the reefs and defends it vigorously against any invasion; when feeding, it swims away from its own territory and joins other individuals to form large shoals, in which fish of other species are often to be found. Only when it returns to its home ground does it resume its aggressive behavior. Young representatives of this species have been observed among the tentacles of sea anemones, often in association with anemone fish.

All the Pomacentridae are particularly active and lively during the daytime, whereas at night they prefer to stay in the refuge of their burrows. Along tropical reefs, where many different species of this family are to be found, distribution is fairly predicable due to the fact that each species shows a preference for a particular habitat. *Amphiprion bicinctus* inhabits the base of the reefs, while other species establish themselves on the walls; *Dascyllus aruanus* prefers to colonize the upper reef ledges; and other species, by contrast, stake out territory below the jutting formations of the coral reefs.

Abudefduf vaigiensis

Dascyllus melanurus

Microspathodon chrysurus

Dascyllus aruanus

Pomacentrus leucostictus

Chromis chromis

Amphiprion xanthurus

1

▲ As these illustrations show, the Pomacentridae are extremely varied and colorful. Shadings and contrasts of hue, plus the ease with which the fish adapt to aquarium life, make them very popular among aquarists.

◀ 1) The family Pomacentridae contains numerous species scattered all over the world, in the tropical belt of the Atlantic, Pacific, and Indian Oceans. All the fish of this family are strictly benthonic and littoral; only *Chromis caeruleus* leads a pelagic life and is also fished in the open seas.

ANEMONE FISH
Amphiprion

The small anemone fish are inhabitants of coral reefs. They are notable for the brilliance of their colors and, even more, for the strangeness of their behavior. They are always found near sea anemones, living in association with them and taking refuge inside them if danger threatens without being harmed by the sting cells of their hosts. There are various theories as to why these fish are not attacked by the anemones but the real reason for this toleration has not been wholly explained. Easy to keep in captivity, anemone fish breed freely and can also be reared on a commercial scale. This fact, in addition to their extremely decorative appearance and uncommon habits, makes them great favorites among aquarists.

The genus *Amphiprion* belongs to the family Pomacentridae, which is situated between the Cichlidae and Labridae. Like the former, anemone fish possess a single nostril on each side of the head. The Labridae resemble the Cichlidae in having fused and dentate lower pharyngeal bones; in the Pomacentridae these teeth are small and pointed, whereas in the Labridae they are shaped like molars. The protractile mouth is equipped with tiny teeth situated only in the jaws. The scales are of average size, ctenoid in form. The lateral line is interrupted along the sides. The small body is high and short, shaped like an oval and greatly compressed. There is a single dorsal fin, whose spiny part is longer than the soft part. In addition to these family characteristics, it is worth mentioning that in the genus *Amphiprion* the operculum and preoperculum are strongly dentate and the teeth are arranged in a single row along the jaws.

The coloration is conspicuous and there are usually broad vertical white stripes, edged with black, which contrast vividly with the rest of the body, normally orange. These fish are inhabitants of warm seas and coral reefs. They are to be found from the western coasts of Africa to the Pacific, but populations are especially dense, both with respect to the number of species and the number of individuals, in the zone extending from Indonesia to Australia and Micronesia.

In its natural habitat this fish does not like swimming in the open sea. It

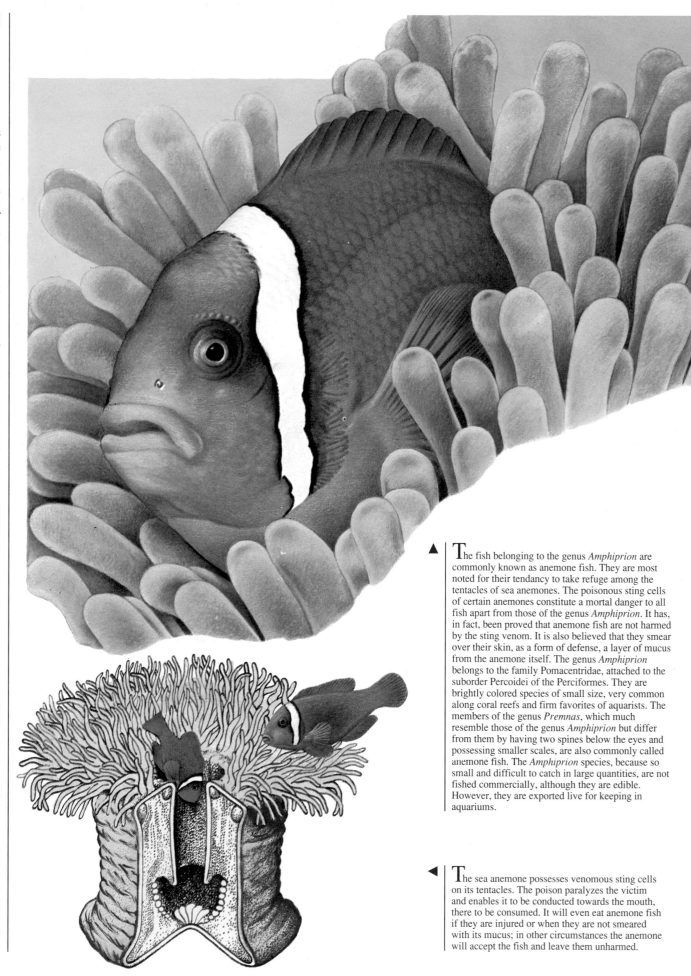

▲ The fish belonging to the genus *Amphiprion* are commonly known as anemone fish. They are most noted for their tendency to take refuge among the tentacles of sea anemones. The poisonous sting cells of certain anemones constitute a mortal danger to all fish apart from those of the genus *Amphiprion*. It has, in fact, been proved that anemone fish are not harmed by the sting venom. It is also believed that they smear over their skin, as a form of defense, a layer of mucus from the anemone itself. The genus *Amphiprion* belongs to the family Pomacentridae, attached to the suborder Percoidei of the Perciformes. They are brightly colored species of small size, very common along coral reefs and firm favorites of aquarists. The members of the genus *Premnas*, which much resemble those of the genus *Amphiprion* but differ from them by having two spines below the eyes and possessing smaller scales, are also commonly called anemone fish. The *Amphiprion* species, because so small and difficult to catch in large quantities, are not fished commercially, although they are edible. However, they are exported live for keeping in aquariums.

◄ The sea anemone possesses venomous sting cells on its tentacles. The poison paralyzes the victim and enables it to be conducted towards the mouth, there to be consumed. It will even eat anemone fish if they are injured or when they are not smeared with its mucus; in other circumstances the anemone will accept the fish and leave them unharmed.

lives permanently close to a large sea anemone and at the slightest alarm loses no time in seeking refuge among its tentacles, which close around the fish, protecting it. If the fish is sufficiently small or if the danger is considerable, it will penetrate deep into the host's body; and if the anemone's mouth is furnished with a sphincter, this retracts and encloses the fish like a bag. If the fish is large in comparison with the anemone, it will simply shelter against the latter's body. It will also regularly seek out the anemone to spend the night there.

Some species of anemone fish maintain the closest links with a particular genus of anemone (in many cases *Stoichactis*) while others can live in association with different genera. Sometimes, in the aquarium, the fish will accept species of anemones unknown in their countries of origin. In nature association would only seem necessary for the fish, who have little defense and who would undoubtedly be devoured rapidly were this protection not available. The anemones, on the other hand, are capable of living quite well without their guests.

The tentacles of an anemone attach themselves to any small organisms they happen to touch, and the sting cells (nematoblasts) with which the tentacles are equipped inject a dangerous toxin so that the organisms can be carried to the mouth for swallowing. Although numerous theories have been advanced, no satisfactory explanation has been given as to why these sting cells, normally so quick to react, tolerate the presence of anemone fish and do not attack them. Actually, the anemone fish may well be devoured if deprived of its protective mucus or if it makes too sudden a contact with its anemone. The fish is accepted by the anemone only after a certain period of familiarization, with contacts becoming ever more frequent and prolonged. More probably, as is also claimed, the fish, protected by its own mucus in the course of initial contacts, gradually covers its body with the mucus produced by the anemone, so deceiving the sensory cells of the tentacles which receive the impression of having made contact with another part of the anemone's body. This would seem to be confirmed by the fact that the fish rubs itself at regular intervals against its anemone in order to maintain the layer of mucus; and should the fish be separated for too long, it has to go through the entire procedure of gradual acceptance again.

These illustrations show some of the most typical and interesting species of the genus *Amphiprion*. *A. sandaracinus* (above, left) is distributed from the Philippines to the Solomon Islands. It measures 4½ in (11 cm). *A. ocellaris* (below, left) ranges from India to Australia and northward to Japan. It, too, measures 4½ in (11cm). *A. polymnus* (above, right) is found from Australia and Melanesia to Japan. It is 6 in (15 cm) long. *A. sebae* (center, right) inhabits the Maldive Islands and Sri Lanka, ranging eastward to Jarva. Its length is 4¾ in (12 cm). *A. bicinctus* (below, right) is found in the Red Sea. It is 6 in (15 cm) long.

COMMON GRAY MULLET

Mugil cephalus

Order Perciformes
Family Mugilidae
Length Up to 36 in (90 cm)
Weight Up to 18 – 20 lb (8 – 9 kg)
Reproductive period In Mediterranean, from July to September
Eggs Floating, like oily droplets: the diameter of each egg is less than 1 mm
Sexual maturity Up to 3 years in Mediterranean

The mullets of the family Mugilidae make up a hundred or so species, divided into about ten genera. The Mugilidae belong to the suborder Mugiloidei, of the order Perciformes, and are the sole representatives of this suborder. At one time the mullets were closely linked, by reason of a number of common features, with the Atherinidae and Sphyraenidae. Nowadays this affinity has been placed in strong doubt as a result of fresh anatomical discoveries, so that the Atherinidae have been allotted a separate order, Atheriniformes, while the Mugilidae and Sphyraenidae are regarded as fully representative Perciformes. The Mugilidae comprise coastal species that inhabit all tropical and temperate seas. Many species are notable for being able to adapt, too, to zones of brackish and fresh water; reproduction, however, is only possible in the saline conditions of sea water.

The biology of the Mugilidae has been described in much detail, particularly in respect of those species that also frequent fresh water and have from ancient times been fished and bred. Mullet feed mainly on the muddy bottom of coastal waters, using special filtrating structures and digestive adaptations. When the fish are feeding in large numbers along the coasts, they give rise to "black waters," darkening wide areas as they stir up mud from the bottom. By reason of their feeding habits, mullet play an important role in the ecosystem, probing the substratum for food not accessible to other fish. By their direct utilization of mud swarming with organic substances and of waters that are green from the high content of phytoplankton, mullet help to accelerate the decomposition and recycling of organic muds.

The mullets of the family Mugilidae have a tapering body covered with large cycloid or ctenoid scales, which are also found on the head. This family, the only one in the suborder Mugiloidei, comprises a hundred or so species, divided into about ten genera. The common gray mullet (*Mugil cephalus*) is the most typical member of the family. It is found in virtually all temperate and warm seas. It lives on sandy or muddy substrata but is also present near rocks. The diet of this mullet is highly specialized. It is made up of small organisms living in the sand and mud of the bottom, as well as species of phytoplankton. It is common to find traces of mud and sand in the stomachs of mullets; apparently they play an important part in digestion.

It is easy to observe dense shoals of mullet darting rapidly to and fro, collecting material from the sandy and muddy sea bed. When these fish are feeding offshore, they stir up so much mud from the bottom that they create "black waters"; it is this dirtying of the water that reveals their presence to fishermen of some countries.

GREAT BARRACUDA

Sphyraena barracuda

Order Perciformes
Family Sphyraenidae
Length Normally 5 ft (1.5 m); exceptionally up to 8 ft (2.5 m)
Weight 103 lb (46.7 kg) for an individual measuring 5½ ft (1.65 m); maximum weight is around 106 lb (48 kg)
Eggs Variable in number. When 3¼ ft (1 m) long, a female will lay about 600,000 eggs
Sexual maturity Males at 2 years when measuring about 18 in (46 cm); females at 3 years when measuring about 23 in (58 cm) but more often at 4 years, at about 26 in (66 cm)
Maximum age About 15 years

The fish belonging to the family Sphyraenidae have a long body, slightly compressed laterally. The head is large, with a long, pointed snout. The mouth is very wide and the lower jaw protrudes markedly beyond the upper jaw. The teeth, implanted in alveoli, are strong, conical, and pointed.

The great barracuda lives in the tropical zones of all seas, except for the eastern Pacific. In addition, there are other species, including, in the Mediterranean, the European or common barracuda (*Sphyraena sphyraena*), which may grow to 4 ft (1.2 m) in length; in the Atlantic are *S. dubia*, measuring 28 – 40 in (70 – 100 cm) and *S. picudilla*, 14 – 20 in (35 – 50 cm); and in the Indo-Pacific area, *S. forsteri*, measuring 24 in (60 cm) and *S. jello*, up to 5 ft (1.5 m).

The great barracuda is abundant in rocky coastal zones subjected to the regular ebb and flow of the tides, in normal salty water. It has no liking, in fact, for waters of low salinity and only young individuals will venture into brackish water. Sometimes it will be found near river estuaries where there is plenty of animal life (as, for example, mullet). The barracuda prefers surface waters but has been caught at depths of around 165 ft (50 m) and even up to 260 ft (80 m). The adults live as solitary predators, although two or three individuals may sometimes cruise slowly around together. In certain areas, during the winter, individual adults may form groups.

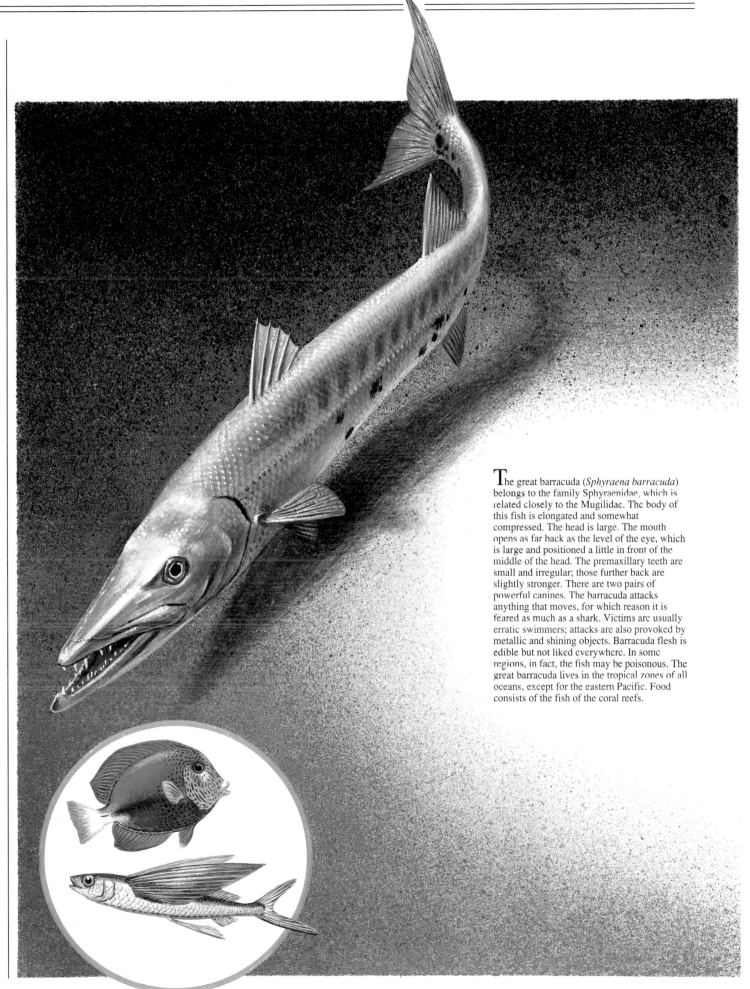

The great barracuda (*Sphyraena barracuda*) belongs to the family Sphyraenidae, which is related closely to the Mugilidae. The body of this fish is elongated and somewhat compressed. The head is large. The mouth opens as far back as the level of the eye, which is large and positioned a little in front of the middle of the head. The premaxillary teeth are small and irregular; those further back are slightly stronger. There are two pairs of powerful canines. The barracuda attacks anything that moves, for which reason it is feared as much as a shark. Victims are usually erratic swimmers; attacks are also provoked by metallic and shining objects. Barracuda flesh is edible but not liked everywhere. In some regions, in fact, the fish may be poisonous. The great barracuda lives in the tropical zones of all oceans, except for the eastern Pacific. Food consists of the fish of the coral reefs.

CUCKOO WRASSE

Labrus bimaculatus

Order Perciformes
Family Labridae
Length Male 14 in (35 cm), female 12 in (30 cm)
Weight 9 – 14 oz (250 – 400 g)
Distinctive features Protogynous hermaphrodite. Possesses 50 – 60 scales along lateral line
Reproductive period From end of spring to beginning of summer

The cuckoo wrasse (*Labrus bimaculatus*) is one of the most interesting members of the family Labridae. It is a protogynous hermaphrodite, with very accentuated sexual dimorphism. The primary livery, typical of young and females, is orange–pink, uniform on the head and back; the belly is yellow. Two or three black bands on the rear of the back may overlap a part of the dorsal fin. The secondary livery, characteristic of males, is much more showy; the head and front of the body are blue or green, while the belly and rest of the body are yellow. There are blue stripes and spots on the head, operculum, and flanks. In both sexes the fins are yellow, but they may be more or less extensively bordered with blue. Because of the phenomenon of sexual inversion, females are smaller than males. The fish can be distinguished from related species because of the higher number of scales (more than 50) along the lateral line.

The cuckoo wrasse has one of the largest distributions in the family; there are stable populations in tropical and temperate seas, but it is also abundant in the North Sea, along the coasts of England and Norway, and in many cold seas of both hemispheres. Its favorite habitats, along with the majority of Labridae, are the rocks and coral reef formations of tropical oceans. The cuckoo wrasse appears to be particularly attracted to zones of luxuriant plant growth, such as beds of *Posidonia*. It is a littoral species that prefers ocean depths down to 100 – 120 ft (30 – 35 m); in winter, however, when the water temperature goes down, it will dive much deeper where environmental conditions are more suitable. It has been caught at depths of up to 330 ft (100 m).

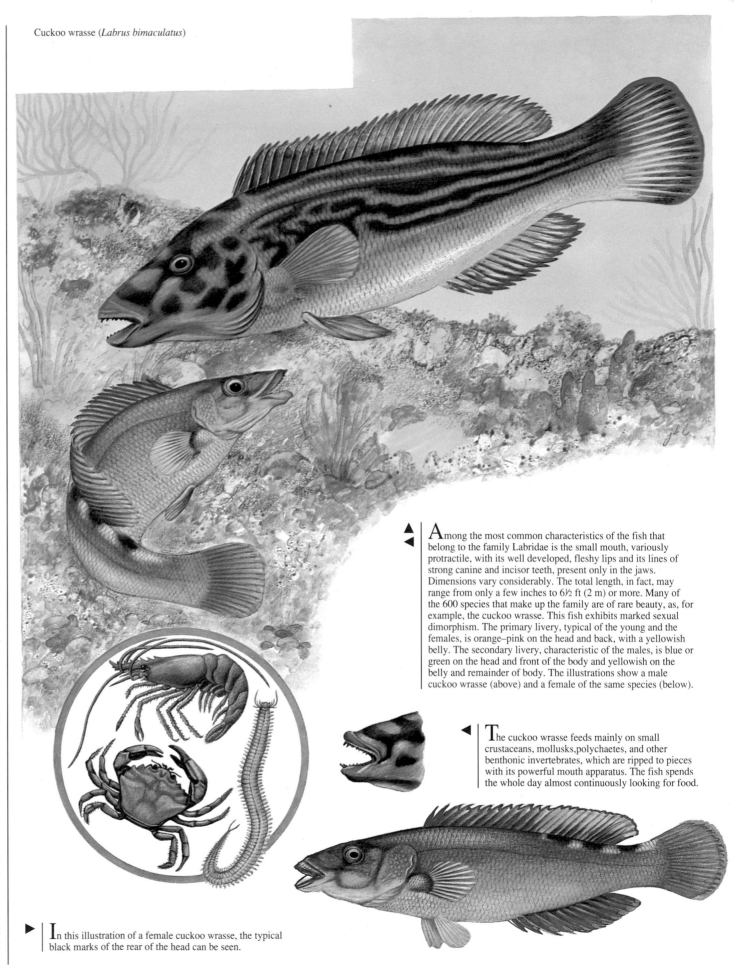

Cuckoo wrasse (*Labrus bimaculatus*)

▲
◀ Among the most common characteristics of the fish that belong to the family Labridae is the small mouth, variously protractile, with its well developed, fleshy lips and its lines of strong canine and incisor teeth, present only in the jaws. Dimensions vary considerably. The total length, in fact, may range from only a few inches to 6½ ft (2 m) or more. Many of the 600 species that make up the family are of rare beauty, as, for example, the cuckoo wrasse. This fish exhibits marked sexual dimorphism. The primary livery, typical of the young and the females, is orange–pink on the head and back, with a yellowish belly. The secondary livery, characteristic of the males, is blue or green on the head and front of the body and yellowish on the belly and remainder of body. The illustrations show a male cuckoo wrasse (above) and a female of the same species (below).

◀ The cuckoo wrasse feeds mainly on small crustaceans, mollusks, polychaetes, and other benthonic invertebrates, which are ripped to pieces with its powerful mouth apparatus. The fish spends the whole day almost continuously looking for food.

▶ In this illustration of a female cuckoo wrasse, the typical black marks of the rear of the head can be seen.

WRASSES
Labridae

A common characteristic of the Labridae (wrasses) is the small mouth, more or less protractile, with fleshy, well developed lips. Several series of strong teeth, in the form of canines or incisors, are found only in the jaws. The pharyngeal bones are modified and fused, assuming the appearance of a molar-like plate, suitable for grinding the shell and tough parts of the invertebrates which are the favorite items of diet among members of the family. Dimensions vary widely; the family includes species that are only a few inches long, like the tiny cleaner fish (*Labrus dimidiatus*), and giant species reaching or exceeding 60 – 80 in (150 – 200 cm) in length and 220 lb (100 kg) in weight.

All wrasses are marine fish and thermophilic, frequenting the warm waters of tropical seas, where they often form populations of very consistent numbers; in temperate seas there is a far smaller number of species, and only a few, such as the cuckoo wrasse (*Labrus bimaculatus*) and the ballan wrasse (*L. bergylta*), are to be found in the cold seas of both hemispheres. Certain species are adapted to salt and fresh water, finding their way into brackish lakes and, for short spells, river estuaries. The Labridae make up a characteristic element of the teeming animal life of rocks and coral reefs in tropical seas; their favorite habitats are rock clefts with abundant vegetation and zones of the sea where submerged *Posidonia* plants grow, providing safe refuge from predators.

Many of the 600 or so species constituting this family are extremely handsome in color, and therefore ideal aquarium fish. An interesting biological feature of certain species is the variation in shape and color during growth.

Wrasses are particularly lively and active during the day, spending much time looking for food, and at night they behave in a way that is most unusual for fish, for they actually go to sleep. Another fascinating aspect of behavior is the manner in which representatives of the Labridae swim: to move forward they use mainly the broad and well developed pectoral fins, while the peduncle and the caudal fin function only as a rudder. This type of swimming is especially effective in zones with all manner of cavities and obstacles, such as coral reefs.

▲
▶ Particularly active by day, when they are constantly seeking food and thus seldom engaged in any other occupation, wrasses sleep at night. To do this they hide, either in the sand, as in the case of *Coris gaymardi* (above), or like *Labrus rupestris*, among algae (right, above) or in rock clefts (right, below). This is very unusual behavior for fish, and so is their method of swimming. To move forward, they use their broad, well developed pectoral fins, while the peduncle and caudal fin serve as a rudder.

S̄ome Labridae display surprising changes of color as they grow. *Coris gaymardi* is a typical example. The illustration shows the clear difference between a young individual (above) and an adult (below).

▼ The fish belonging to the family Labridae are all marine species that favor the warm waters of tropical seas, where they often make up large, stable populations. 1) *Labrus bimaculatus*; 2) family Labridae.

Rainbow wrasse
(*Coris julis*)

Green wrasse
(*Labrus turdus*)

Ballan wrasse
(*Labrus bergylta*)

▲ B̄ecause of their varied and contrasted colors and shadings, wrasses always make an attractive display when kept in the tanks of marine aquariums. The three species illustrated here are also found in temperate seas. The rainbow wrasse, like *Coris gaymardi*, is noted for spending the night on the bottom, hidden in the sand.

159

CLEANER FISH

Labroides dimidiatus

Order Perciformes
Family Labridae
Length 3 – 4 in (8 – 10 cm)
Weight ½ oz (10 – 15 g)
Distinctive features Protogynous hermaphrodite. Possesses 52 – 53 scales along lateral line
Coloration Blue, merging to white in ventral region. The body is crossed from head to tail by a broad black band
Reproductive period Throughout year

The cleaner fish is the best known of all the fish species that perform the delicate task of keeping the bodies of other fish free of parasites. In this species, both sexes look alike; the basic color is blue, merging to white in the ventral region. The whole body, from head to tail, is crossed by a broad black band. When the female is spawning, a second, pinkish brown band appears on the head.

The cleaner fish is to be found in all the world's tropical waters, including the Atlantic and Pacific, but is especially abundant along the coasts of the Indian Ocean and the Red Sea. Its preferred habitat is constituted by the walls of coral reefs, full of fissures and natural cavities, where it can establish a burrow. It has a liking for surface waters, but it is not uncommon to find it deeper, down to 165 ft (50 m), particularly in those zones where climatic variations during the year compel it to dive to such levels to find more favorable conditions.

Often a certain number of these small fish establish private territories in neighboring zones, making up crowds of what experts describe as "cleaning stations," regularly frequented by large numbers of other species who congregate there in order to be carefully tended by the little cleaner fish.

The social organization of *Labroides dimidiatus* is centered on harems which remain stable for several years; each is made up of one male and 6 – 7 adult females. Links between individuals of the group are controlled by a precise hierarchical structure, with the bigger fish occupying higher-ranking positions. Each female possesses her own territory, inside which she performs all cleaning activities, chasing off all smaller and thus lower-ranking females. The male dominates the whole group and, apart from owning his own piece of territory,

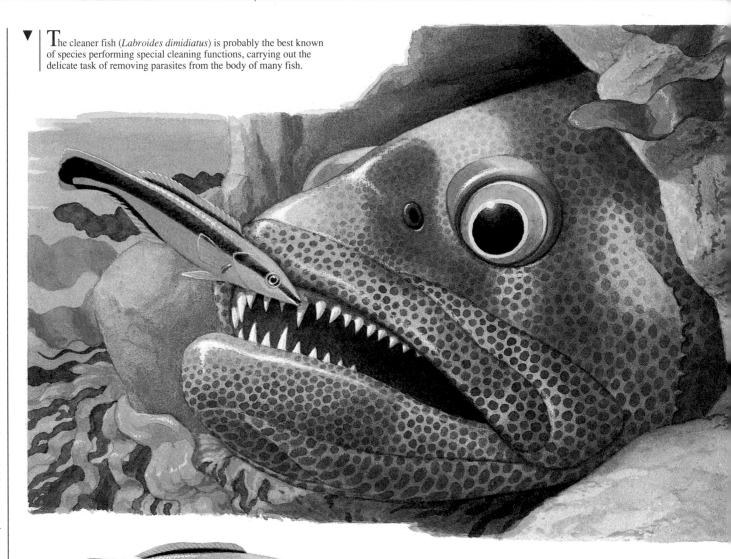

The cleaner fish (*Labroides dimidiatus*) is probably the best known of species performing special cleaning functions, carrying out the delicate task of removing parasites from the body of many fish.

Small copepods which burrow into the skin and settle in the gills of many fish are the main food items of the cleaner fish.

The small cleaner fish has a single fin on the back, a truncated, rounded caudal fin, a terminally positioned mouth and well developed lips. It seems to have no fear of approaching fish that are much larger than itself, such as stone basses and cod. The latter stay still as the little cleaner explores their entire body, searching for small parasitic crustaceans which it eats. The favorite habitat is the wall of a coral reef with plenty of clefts and natural cavities in which it can burrow.

In the mouth of *Labroides dimidiatus* are four canine-like teeth. They constitute the specialized instruments with which the cleaner fish extracts parasites from the body of its hosts.

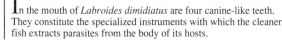

may penetrate those belonging to the females of his harem.

Like many other representatives of the family Labridae, the cleaner fish is a protogynous hermaphrodite; but in this instance sexual inversion, typical of such individuals, is regulated by the group's hierarchy. When the male dies, the largest female, occupying the highest rank, undergoes sexual inversion and assumes the leading male's role in the group.

The eggs are planktonic and the larvae that hatch from them spend their period of development in open waters.

The relationship between the cleaner fish and their hosts is defined by students of animal behavior as the process of "cleaning symbiosis"; it is one that has advantages for both individuals, the cleaner fish obtaining food and the host fish being freed of parasites. The cleaner fish attracts its customers with a series of movements which make up a so-called "cleaning dance"; the hosts, in their turn, invite the cleaner by assuming certain positions, varying according to species, some of them placing themselves in front of the smaller fish, remaining motionless and head downward, some opening their mouths wide, others exhibiting their flanks.

Cleaner fish do not only attend to the needs of those species that frequent the zones where they themselves live; many species that normally live in open waters pay regular visits to the cleaning stations, and shoals of fish can often be seen nearby, "queuing" for their turn.

Another fish, the small blenny *Aspidontus taeniatus*, is surprisingly similar in appearance to *Labroides dimidiatus* even though it belongs to a completely different family. This mimicry is so perfect that *Aspidontus taeniatus* imitates the cleaner fish, also in movement and behavior, tricking fish to allow it access; yet the blenny is not a cleaner, and will attack the fish thus approached, ripping off shreds of fin and flesh for eating.

The cleaner fish is virtually of no interest for edible purposes by reason of its small size and low-quality flesh. However, aquarists appreciate it for its liveliness and beauty as a decorative addition to the aquarium. Furthermore, thanks to its cleaning activity, it helps to keep the other aquarium fish in good condition.

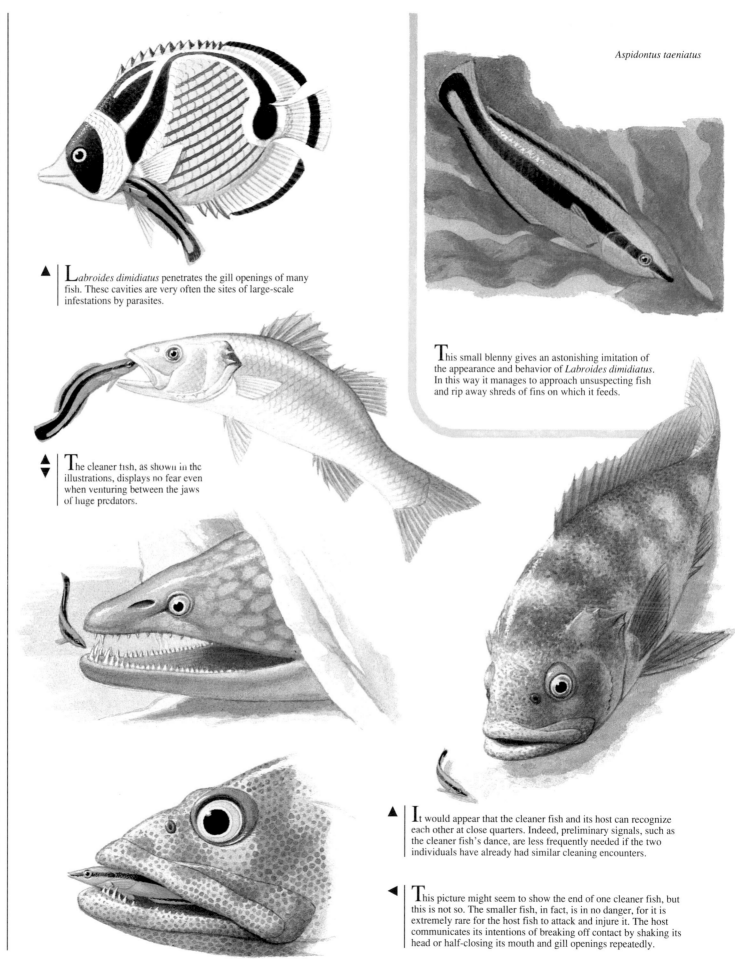

Aspidontus taeniatus

▲ *Labroides dimidiatus* penetrates the gill openings of many fish. These cavities are very often the sites of large-scale infestations by parasites.

This small blenny gives an astonishing imitation of the appearance and behavior of *Labroides dimidiatus*. In this way it manages to approach unsuspecting fish and rip away shreds of fins on which it feeds.

▲▼ The cleaner fish, as shown in the illustrations, displays no fear even when venturing between the jaws of huge predators.

▲ It would appear that the cleaner fish and its host can recognize each other at close quarters. Indeed, preliminary signals, such as the cleaner fish's dance, are less frequently needed if the two individuals have already had similar cleaning encounters.

◄ This picture might seem to show the end of one cleaner fish, but this is not so. The smaller fish, in fact, is in no danger, for it is extremely rare for the host fish to attack and injure it. The host communicates its intentions of breaking off contact by shaking its head or half-closing its mouth and gill openings repeatedly.

PARROTFISH
Scaridae

The Scaridae (or Callyodontidae) belong to the suborder Labriodei; in fact, they are similar to the Labridae in that they possess one pair of nostrils on each side of the head. The body of the Scaridae is oblong and slightly compressed. Some species exhibit sexual dimorphism: large males, in fact, have a prominence on the forehead. As a rule the front part of the head is clearly rounded. The cheeks are covered by one to four lines of scales.

The principal anatomical feature of these fish, however, is the strong "beak," formed by the fusion of certain teeth. For this reason they are commonly known as parrotfish. They have brilliant coloration. It varies, however, with age and sex.

The Scaridae have a wide geographical distribution, being found in all tropical seas. They are coastal fish that seldom descend to more than 200 ft (60 m). They swim in shoals among the coral reefs and it is not uncommon to observe them in shallow lagoon waters with their dorsal fin and part of the back showing above the surface. As a rule parrotfish live in the coral reefs; along with the Pomacentridae and Chaetodontidae, they frequent many islands of the Indo-Pacific region, such as Hawaii, Polynesia, and Samoa. They also live along Atlantic shores, in the seas around Bermuda, and off the coast of Africa.

There is only one species in the Mediterranean, the violet–blue *Sparisoma cretense*. Along the Atlantic shores of Africa are species belonging to the genera: *Cryptotomus*, small or medium in size, measuring from 4 – 8 in (10 – 20 cm); *Sparisoma*, commonly known as the gray parrotfish, which may be as long as 20 in (50 cm); and *Pseudoscarus*, notable for their marked sexual dichromatism.

Parrotfish browse on the coral reefs and they are thus mainly responsible for the erosion of such reefs, especially in those zones where surf action is weak, as in the Caribbean. In this context it is worth mentioning that the Scaridae play an important role in the formation of sand in coral reefs. Pieces of coral, after being ripped away with the "beak," are ground up by the pharyngeal mechanism and passed into the digestive tract. The nutritious substances are digested, while the inorganic material is excreted in the form of sand.

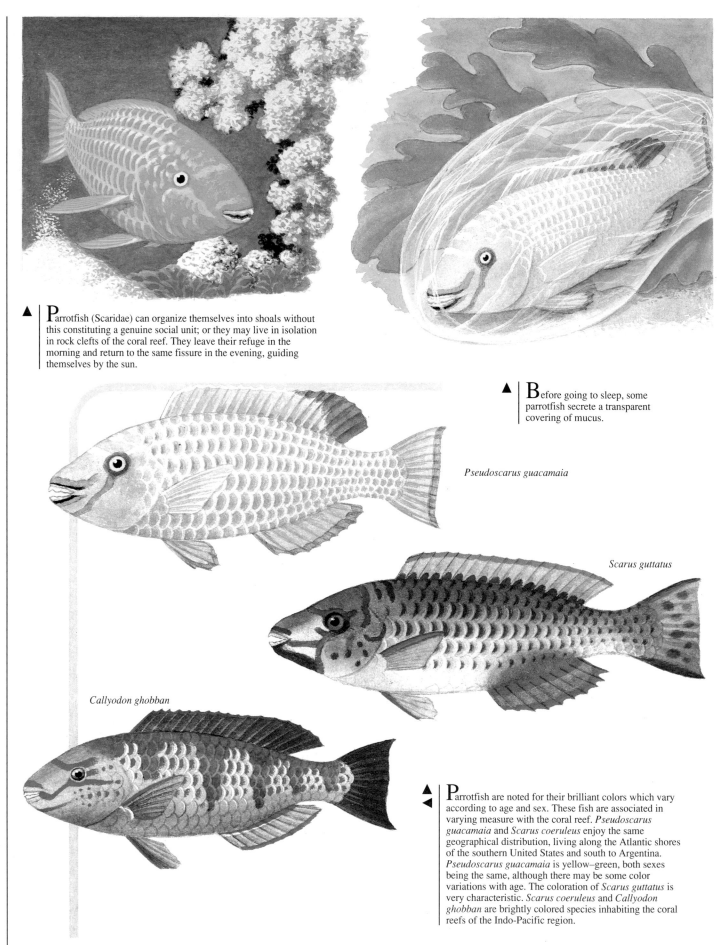

▲ Parrotfish (Scaridae) can organize themselves into shoals without this constituting a genuine social unit; or they may live in isolation in rock clefts of the coral reef. They leave their refuge in the morning and return to the same fissure in the evening, guiding themselves by the sun.

▲ Before going to sleep, some parrotfish secrete a transparent covering of mucus.

Pseudoscarus guacamaia

Scarus guttatus

Callyodon ghobban

▲
◄ Parrotfish are noted for their brilliant colors which vary according to age and sex. These fish are associated in varying measure with the coral reef. *Pseudoscarus guacamaia* and *Scarus coeruleus* enjoy the same geographical distribution, living along the Atlantic shores of the southern United States and south to Argentina. *Pseudoscarus guacamaia* is yellow–green, both sexes being the same, although there may be some color variations with age. The coloration of *Scarus guttatus* is very characteristic. *Scarus coeruleus* and *Callyodon ghobban* are brightly colored species inhabiting the coral reefs of the Indo-Pacific region.

BLUE PARROTFISH

Scarus coeruleus

Order Perciformes
Family Scaridae
Length Usually about 12 in (30 cm)
Distinctive features Teeth fused to form dentary plates. Nonprotractile mouth. Discontinuous lateral line; 22 longitudinal rows of cycloid scales
Coloration Blue, varying according to age

In the blue parrotfish, as in all Scaridae, the teeth of the upper and lower jaws are fused into two dentary plates, forming a "beak." The upper plate slightly overlaps the lower one when the mouth is closed; the latter, as in all the Scaridae, is not protractile.

The blue parrotfish is generally found along the western Atlantic shores of America, together with 20 or so related species. It also lives along the coasts of Florida and Brazil and in the coral reefs surrounding the islands of the Caribbean. It is easy to observe young individuals in the shallow waters normally inhabited by parrotfish, but adults are harder to spot because they tend to live deeper.

During the night the blue parrotfish, like others of its family, surrounds itself with a spherical capsule of secreted mucus. The fish needs about 30 minutes to construct this capsule. The cocoon probably prevents the odor of the parrotfish reaching the nostrils of predators, but its precise role is still unknown. The blue parrotfish sleeps on the sea bed or on rocks. In the morning it abandons its "nightshirt" but for a while its movements are uncoordinated: the fish collides with objects in its path and swims awkwardly. Should it be too disturbed by such interference, the fish will go to sleep again.

Members of this species live in shoals, both alone and in conjunction with closely related species such as *Scarus coelestinus* and *Pseudoscarus guacamaia*, without forming a proper social unit. Like other representatives of the family, the blue parrotfish browses on coral but also feeds on small animals such as mollusks, crustaceans, sea urchins, and also algae; so its diet is virtually omnivorous.

The blue parrotfish (*Scarus coeruleus*) is an inhabitant of the coral reefs of the western Atlantic tropical and subtropical regions. The teeth are fused into two dentary plates, with a visible central suture: this apparatus constitutes its "beak." By reason of this anatomical peculiarity and coloration, this and other related species have come to be called parrotfish. Sexual dimorphism is quite frequent: adult males, but not females, have a frontal protuberance . The Scaridae feed by nibbling pieces of coral and also the shells of sea urchins. In addition, their diet includes algae and marine plants.

NOTOTHENIOIDEI

At one time the Notothenioidei were considered to be a superfamily belonging either to the suborder Percoidei or to the suborder Blennioidei; nowadays they are regarded as a separate suborder which comprises four families: Bovichthydae, Nototheniidae (also including the family Harpagiferidae, considered by some authors to be a separate family), Bathydraconidae, and Chaenichthyidae.

These fish are distinguished by having only one nostril on either side of the head, and by the absence of the subocular plate; apart from these characteristics, there are important variations in each family.

The Notothenioidei possess a fairly long body terminating in a relatively long snout and quite a large mouth, which in some species is furnished with a barbel in the chin region. The gill cavities are large and the spines of the first dorsal fin are weak and flexible, in some cases even absent. The second dorsal fin and the anal fin, both soft, are quite long. The pectorals are large, with a broad base, and the pelvic fins are set wide apart; the caudal fin, either quadrangular or rounded, possesses only a few rays.

The body may be covered with small ctenoid or cycloid scales, which are sometimes present together, sometimes lacking. The lateral line may be simple, double or treble, and is generally adorned with tubular scales. The Nototheniidae are equipped with two dorsal fins, the first of which has 5 – 8 spines that are usually flexible. The branchiostegous membranes are linked to form a sort of bridge beneath the branchial isthmus. There are also two lateral lines, one of them high (almost at the base of the dorsal fins), the other in the center of the body in the area of the caudal peduncle.

This family is by far the largest, both with regard to the number of species and the number of individuals. It comprises, in fact, about 60 species, subdivided into five genera, and its taxonomic study is still in progress. They colonize the continental shelf to a depth of 2,000 ft (600 m) and each species has its own preferred depth. They are found on or near the sea bed, being essentially benthonic.

Notothenia hansonai

▲ The Nototheniidae have a vast geographical distribution extending to the Antarctic continent, in the case of the genera *Notothenia, Trematomus, Dissostichus*, and *Pleurogramma*, and to the temperate and temperate to warm waters of the South American coasts, for certain species of the genera *Notothenia* and *Eleginops*. These fish colonize the continental shelf to a depth of 2,000 ft (600 m) and each species has its own preferred depth. They are found on or near the sea bed, being essentially benthonic. Thus the species *Trematomus bernacchii* seldom shifts further than 12 in (30 cm) from the bottom. The Harpagiferidae, too, live along the coasts, though some individuals have been observed at depths of 450 ft (130 m). The Bathydraconidae are found at greater depths, between 1,000 ft (300 m) and 4,000 ft (1,200 m). The geographic range of the Bovichthydae is restricted to the subantarctic zone. There are some 15 known species of Chaenichthyidae, divided into two genera and limited to Antarctica, except for three species to be found in the subantarctic zone: *Champsocephalus esox* is from Patagonia, while *Chaenichthys rhinoceratus* and *Chaenichthys regosus* are found in the Kerguelen–Macquarie area, to depths of 2,000 – 2,300 ft (600 – 700 m).

▲ The environment inhabited by the Notothenioidei is characterized by two basic factors, to which the fish have to adapt, namely low temperatures and absence of light. In this context, observations have been carried out on the species *Trematomus bernacchii*: this fish has adapted to such living conditions by spending, as a rule, the whole day immobile, hidden beneath algae or rocks, and never straying more than a few feet from its refuge; in the evening, or at night, it becomes active and devotes itself to seeking food. These fish are generally sedentary or very slow-moving animals that hardly shift about at all; yet they feed on extremely agile creatures, indicating an ability to move around very rapidly. By and large, these fish enjoy a varied diet; the majority are carnivorous, eating small amphipod and isopod crustaceans, but some also feed on algae. The behavior of *Chaenichthys rhinoceratus* is exceptional, for this fish spurns almost every type of prey apart from young fish. Nevertheless, all species display seasonal variations with regard to feeding. In fact, some Nototheniidae go through a phase of fasting, to a greater or lesser extent, to coincide with the spawning period; yet the Antarctic species of this family overfeed, thus ensuring themselves of a supply of energy. Such habits have never been observed among the subantarctic species. This surplus food habit may therefore be seen as an adaptation to low temperatures. Growth is slow, particularly in the Antarctic species, and the fish are sexually mature only around the age of 7 – 10 years. At this stage certain species exhibit a color differentiation between adults and immature individuals, as, for example, in *Notothenia corriceps*, whereas in other species there is sexual color variation. Reproductive patterns vary according to species and this applies, too, to the number of eggs produced, which may range from 1,200 to 1,500. These are usually large, transparent, swelled by sea water, but also rich in yolk substance.

TRICHODONTIDAE OPISTHOGNA- THIDAE

The family Trichodontidae and the family Opisthognathidae are very close to each other; both belong to the suborder Trachinoidei, order Perciformes. The Opisthognathidae are the so-called jawfish, with a long, narrow body, similar to a cone. The head is bulbous and terminates in a high, short, and broad snout. The large mouth is a bit like that of the Blennidae, as is the rest of the head.

The family Trichodontidae, sandfish, contains only two species: *Arctoscopus japonicus*, silvery in color, measuring at most 12 in (30 cm), and *Trichodon trichodon*. Very little is known about the biology of the Trichodontidae. During the breeding season they approach the coasts and the young remain in coastal waters until the following summer, after which they seek out deeper water.

The Opisthognathidae enjoy a carnivorous diet, feeding on small invertebrates and zooplankton. They advance vertically to about 5 ft (1.5 m) from the bottom; if danger approaches, they hide inside a kind of burrow. Each fish occupies a single hole, except during the courtship parade. It has been possible to demonstrate that such fish are active by day and sleep at night; they each go into their respective burrows, close the opening of the hole, and stay there all night. The burrow is, in fact, like that of a rabbit. The fish begins by excavating vertically a hole of some 8 in (20 cm), and at this depth digs horizontally to build its chamber. Then it covers the opening of its burrow with pebbles. The whole operation takes the fish about ten hours.

The Opisthognathidae generally live in groups, each of which consists of two to ten individuals; and each fish has its own "home." The burrows are some 8 in (20 cm) apart from one another. Some species of jawfish display sexual dimorphism, the males having longer jaws than the females and also being furnished with hind extensions. This body structure may be found in other species, but will not be present in yet other species. Males of such species mouth-brood the eggs, which is a special characteristic of the family. The eggs are stuck together in a mass measuring about 6 in (15 cm) in diameter.

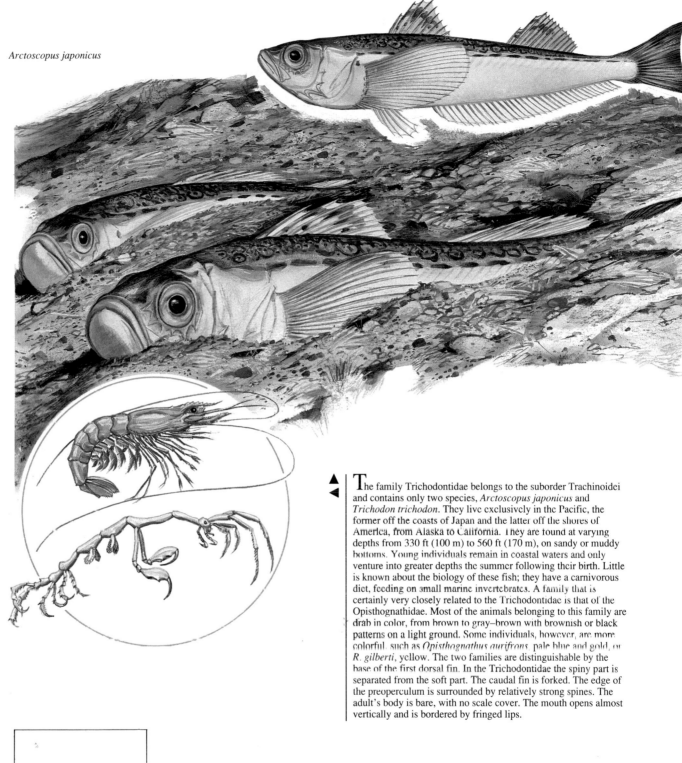

Arctoscopus japonicus

The family Trichodontidae belongs to the suborder Trachinoidei and contains only two species, *Arctoscopus japonicus* and *Trichodon trichodon*. They live exclusively in the Pacific, the former off the coasts of Japan and the latter off the shores of America, from Alaska to California. They are found at varying depths from 330 ft (100 m) to 560 ft (170 m), on sandy or muddy bottoms. Young individuals remain in coastal waters and only venture into greater depths the summer following their birth. Little is known about the biology of these fish; they have a carnivorous diet, feeding on small marine invertebrates. A family that is certainly very closely related to the Trichodontidae is that of the Opisthognathidae. Most of the animals belonging to this family are drab in color, from brown to gray–brown with brownish or black patterns on a light ground. Some individuals, however, are more colorful, such as *Opisthognathus aurifrons*, pale blue and gold, or *R. gilberti*, yellow. The two families are distinguishable by the base of the first dorsal fin. In the Trichodontidae the spiny part is separated from the soft part. The caudal fin is forked. The edge of the preoperculum is surrounded by relatively strong spines. The adult's body is bare, with no scale cover. The mouth opens almost vertically and is bordered by fringed lips.

1

Arctoscopus japonicus lives in the Pacific Ocean, especially off the shores of Japan, at depths varying from 330 – 560 ft (100 – 170 m). *Trichodon trichodon* also inhabits the Pacific, but off the American coasts, from Alaska to California. The family Opisthognathidae (close, in many respects, to the Trichodontidae) contains some two dozen species, living in the tropical and subtropical zones of all oceans. They appear to be absent from the eastern Atlantic and the central part of the Pacific. The Opisthognathidae live in surface waters, from 7 – 100 ft (2 – 30 m), on sandy beds or in the neighborhood of coral reefs. Some species go deeper, from 330 – 660 ft (100– 200 m) on muddy bottoms. 1) *Arctoscopus japonicus*.

BLENNIES
Blenniidae

The suborder Blennioidei comprises 15 families and the fish are collectively known as blennies. The various families live in all the world's oceans, some preferring warm, temperate waters, others cold waters. The principal morphological features common to the entire suborder are the ventral fins either in a jugular position or absent altogether, and the scaly covering that tends to sink deeply into the skin or even disappear completely, being replaced by an abundance of mucus.

Among the best known families are: the Blenniidae, or true blennies, described here; Anarhichadidae, or wolffish, large species, to be discussed later; Pholidae, or gunnels, including the butterfish (*Pholis gunellus*), the male of which guards the eggs by swimming around them; Tripterygiidae, furnished with a very conspicuous covering of scales and with three dorsal fins; Clinidae, or klipfish with two dorsal fins; and Stichaeidae, or pricklebacks, living in cold seas, sometimes at great depths.

The fish belonging to the family Blenniidae are littoral, generally of medium size and subdivided into many species, distributed in all seas.

The majority of blennies tolerate considerable variations of temperature and salinity: this is generally attributed to the abundant mucus that protects the skin. So it is no surprise to discover that blennies live in all the oceans of the globe, from the equatorial regions to the arctic and antarctic zones, though with a marked preference for warm and temperate seas. Blennies often make for brackish water and are to be found in ports, thus showing a tolerance for fairly polluted areas. Some species, furthermore, have even taken to freshwater zones. Although some species live at considerable depths, down to many hundred feet, the majority populate infralittoral or littoral levels of the intertidal zones, appearing quite often in pools formed at low tide.

Certain blennies can stay either temporarily or almost permanently out of the water. They are sometimes found on soft sea beds, but usually they prefer hard substrata, particularly coral formations, rocks, small islands or cliffs covered with algae.

Blennis pholis

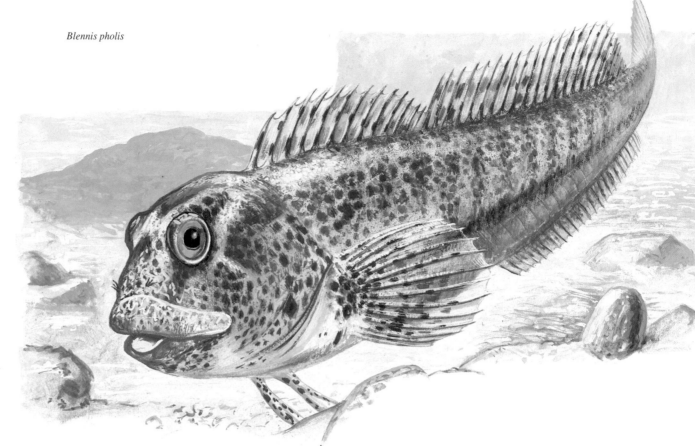

The members of the family Blenniidae are littoral species, generally of medium size, with some only measuring a few inches when adult. The body is streamlined, broad at the front, flattened in the caudal region. Blennies are found in all seas. They can also endure periods out of water, like *Atticus saliens* of the Indian Ocean, or the representatives of the genus *Andama* from the Andaman Islands, which live along rocky coasts above sea level in zones buffeted by the waves. In fact, *Andama* breathe atmospheric oxygen through the mucus of their mouth and pharynx, and move around by affixing themselves to the substratum with their lower lip, transformed into a sucker. The blennies are very voracious carnivores, feeding on small crab and squid, but some species have a vegetarian diet. The Blennidae are considered highly aggressive and this is particularly so when directed against others of their own species. The injuries are only limited to the fins but these may be torn to shreds. In the breeding period, if a number of males are compelled to occupy a restricted space, as may happen in an aquarium, one of these, the dominant male, displays a brilliant nuptial livery, while the others, inhibited, stay as normal. The species illustrated here, *Blennius pholis*, has a slender body covered with abundant mucus. This latter characteristic enables the fish to tolerate considerable variations of temperature and salinity. It is distributed in the northwest Atlantic and is often found in pools of water formed at low tide.

The drawing shows the jugular position of the ventral fins and head tentacles of many species of blenny. The snout is short and the mouth, slightly cleft and terminal, is surrounded by large, fleshy lips. The head is big and robust; the front profile is almost in a straight line. The eyes are large and very mobile, high in the head, and protruding.

Blennies are benthonic fish that are partial to biotopes affording them plenty of hiding places. Some species are fond of brightly lit zones, others prefer the shade of small coastal caves. The fish patrol their territory, swimming in their typically undulating manner, always remaining near the bottom and taking shelter at the slightest sign of danger. Those individuals who are more courageous freely expose themselves to view, whereas the more timid only leave their burrows to look for food. They often stay motionless for a long time, leaning on the rays of their ventral fins and caudal fin, so as to form a tripod.

The fertilized eggs are laid in a single mass on the side of a small refuge or in a cleft adequate for the purpose, in which the fish can perform their nuptial dance. This generally involves rocking movements of the head and front of the body. The males choose the place where fertilization is to occur and attract a succession of females who do not, as a rule, take care of the eggs. This task is undertaken by the males, who guard the eggs and violently chase off all intruders. From time to time they swim to and fro above the eggs, rubbing them with their belly; in this way the eggs are protected from the attack of microorganisms because of the antiseptic properties of the paternal mucus. After birth, the young lead a planktonic life for a while, guaranteeing in this manner that the species will be well dispersed; in due course they move towards the bottom to follow a permanent benthonic existence.

Highly resistant to pollution and tolerant of wide variations of temperature and salinity, blennies are easily raised in the aquarium. Apart from the aesthetic appeal, it is amusing and instructive to observe their behavior. They are, in fact, incredible mimics and their extremely mobile eyes give them the most expressive features, unlike the majority of fish. They are not particular about food and quickly acclimatize, accepting scraps readily from the hand. Some species reproduce regularly in captivity.

The flesh of blennies is tasty but not much liked because of the sticky mucus and rather unattractive appearance. Sometimes they are fished with line or net, but as a rule they are trawled in shallow waters. They are used together with other local fish in the preparation of various regional dishes. Certain littoral species, however, are difficult to catch by any method.

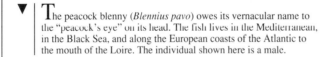

▲ The butterfly blenny (*Blennius ocellaris*) is notable for a prominent black spot on its large dorsal fin, not unlike the wing of a butterfly. It lives at depths below 100 ft (30 m).

▼ The peacock blenny (*Blennius pavo*) owes its vernacular name to the "peacock's eye" on its head. The fish lives in the Mediterranean, in the Black Sea, and along the European coasts of the Atlantic to the mouth of the Loire. The individual shown here is a male.

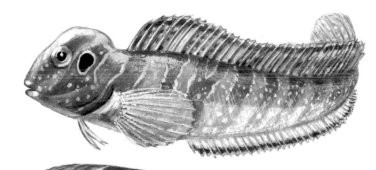

▲ *Xiphasia setifer* is undoubtedly the strangest of all the blennies. Its body is extremely long, almost eel-like. This fish from the Indo-Pacific lives at fair depths on coral reefs.

▲ The horned blenny (*Blennius tentacularis*) reaches a length of 6 in (15 cm). It is one of the species to be found in the Mediterranean. It has no practical value.

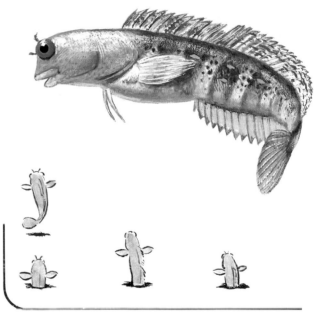

▲ *Istiblennius periophthalmus* lives, like all species belonging to the same genus, in zones affected by the tides. During the periods when the rocky sea beds that constitute its habitat are dry and exposed at low tide, this fish moves about on land by jumping, occasionally submerging itself in any available pools. This is one of the examples supporting the belief that certain blennies are capable of remaining, temporarily or permanently, out of water. On the other hand, it is true that some species live at great depths, up to many hundred feet down. Blennies are also present in ports, indicating that they can also withstand polluted waters. Sometimes they occupy soft sea beds, but they usually prefer hard substrata, particularly coral reefs, rocky zones, small islands or rocks covered with seaweed.

URANOSCOPIDAE TRACHINIDAE

The family Uranoscopidae and the family Trachinidae are very closely related and belong, according to the classification by Greenwood, to the suborder Trachinoidei, included in the order Perciformes.

The Uranoscopidae, known as stargazers, are found in the benthonic zone of warm and temperate seas. Some species, like *Uranoscopus polli*, may be encountered at fair depths, down to about 1,000 ft (300 m). *U. scaber* frequents sandy and muddy substrata or the borders of submarine prairies, as well as the Atlantic shores of Portugal and Morocco; elsewhere it is replaced by *U. albesca, U. polli,* and *U. cadenati.* Along the Atlantic coasts of America there are species belonging to the genus *Astroscopus: A. guttatus* colonizes the zone extending from New York to Cape Hatteras; *A. y-graecum* is distributed along the coasts of Brazil.

These fish are noted for their marked tendency to hide in the sand or mud, thanks to the movements of their powerful pectoral fins. Being poor swimmers, they remain submerged in the sediment, allowing only their round, highly mobile eyes and their mouth to protrude. This capacity for burying themselves in the sand has led to anatomical modifications in the genus *Astroscopus*; members of this genus in fact possess proper nostrils or choanae, which perform the same role as spiracles in rays. These openings, provided with a valve, allow water to penetrate during breathing.

The Trachinidae, known as weevers, have the same habits as the Uranoscopidae; they generally remain buried in the submarine prairies, near the coasts, swimming away during winter in search of muddy zones that are less cold.

Today some dozen species of Trachinidae are known, of which four, very similar to one another, are found in the Mediterranean and North Atlantic. Two of these have a wider distribution along European coastlines: the greater weever (*Trachinus draco*) and the lesser weever (*T. vipera*), which measure respectively 16 in (40 cm) and 6 in (15 cm). These two species differ mainly in color

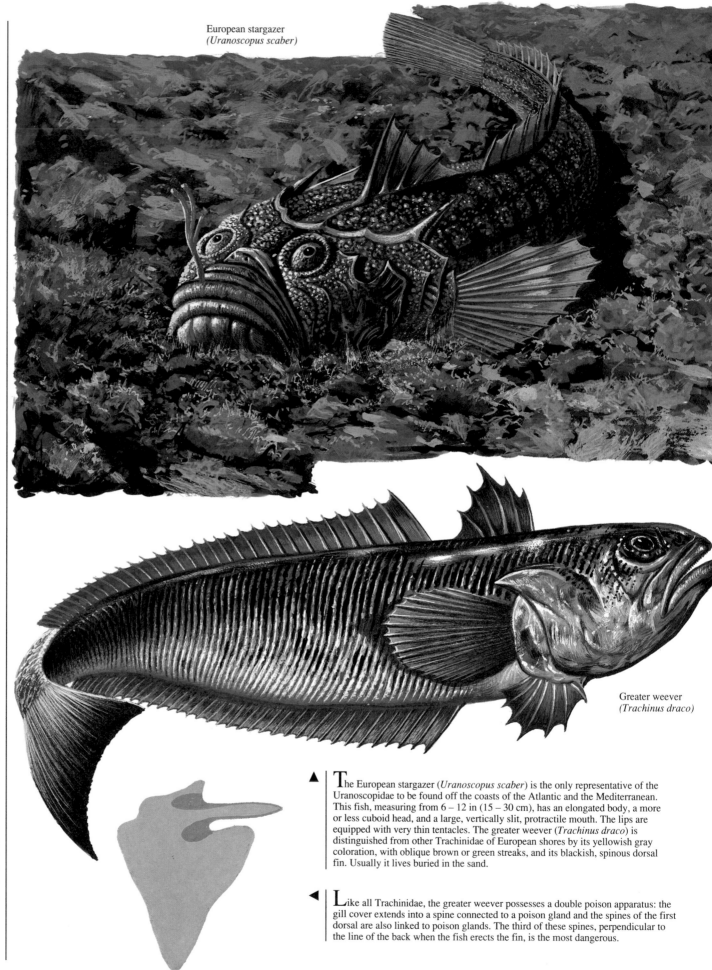

European stargazer
(Uranoscopus scaber)

Greater weever
(Trachinus draco)

▲ The European stargazer (*Uranoscopus scaber*) is the only representative of the Uranoscopidae to be found off the coasts of the Atlantic and the Mediterranean. This fish, measuring from 6 – 12 in (15 – 30 cm), has an elongated body, a more or less cuboid head, and a large, vertically slit, protractile mouth. The lips are equipped with very thin tentacles. The greater weever (*Trachinus draco*) is distinguished from other Trachinidae of European shores by its yellowish gray coloration, with oblique brown or green streaks, and its blackish, spinous dorsal fin. Usually it lives buried in the sand.

◄ Like all Trachinidae, the greater weever possesses a double poison apparatus: the gill cover extends into a spine connected to a poison gland and the spines of the first dorsal are also linked to poison glands. The third of these spines, perpendicular to the line of the back when the fish erects the fin, is the most dangerous.

WOLFFISH
Anarhichas lupus

Order Perciformes
Family Anarhichadidae
Length Up to 5 ft (150 cm) for a weight of 44 lb (20 kg) and above
Weight Up to 44 lb (20 kg) and more
Distinctive features Long, compressed body, covered with mucus, apparently without scales
Coloration Gray–brown or blue–green, with dark vertical bands
Reproductive period During cold season, from October to February
Eggs Varying in number from 3,000 to 25,000, depending on size of female
Sexual maturity At 6 – 7 years

The Anarhichadidae live in the cold waters of the Atlantic and Pacific Oceans, only in the Northern Hemisphere. They are generally divided into two subfamilies: Anarhichadinae (two genera), with a fairly long body and the dorsal and anal fins close to the caudal, but quite distinct from it; and Anarhichthyinae (only one genus), with a very long body, eel-shaped, with the dorsal and anal fins joined to the caudal fin.

The genus *Anarhichas* comprises four species: one of these, *A. orientalis*, is a characteristic resident of the coasts of Kamchatka and Alaska; the other three live off the Atlantic coasts of America and Europe. They are *A. lupus*, with conspicuous dark vertical bands and more vomerine than palatine teeth; *A. minor*, with a markedly spotted body and more rear palatine than vomerine teeth; and *A. denticulatus*, with no stripes or spots on the body and with similarly aligned rear vomerine and palatine teeth.

Anarhichas lupus feeds on benthonic invertebrates, such as mollusks, echinoderms, and crustaceans. It can grind up shells and hard or spiny carapaces with its powerful teeth, particularly since the functional teeth are replaced every year at the spawning season.

The fish of this family approach the coasts when ready to breed. Not much is known about their reproductive behavior. The very large eggs, almost ¼ in (6 mm) in diameter, are yellowish and sticky; enveloped in an oily globule, they are stuck together and deposited in round clumps in the heart of algae or underneath stones. After an incubation period of some two months they hatch.

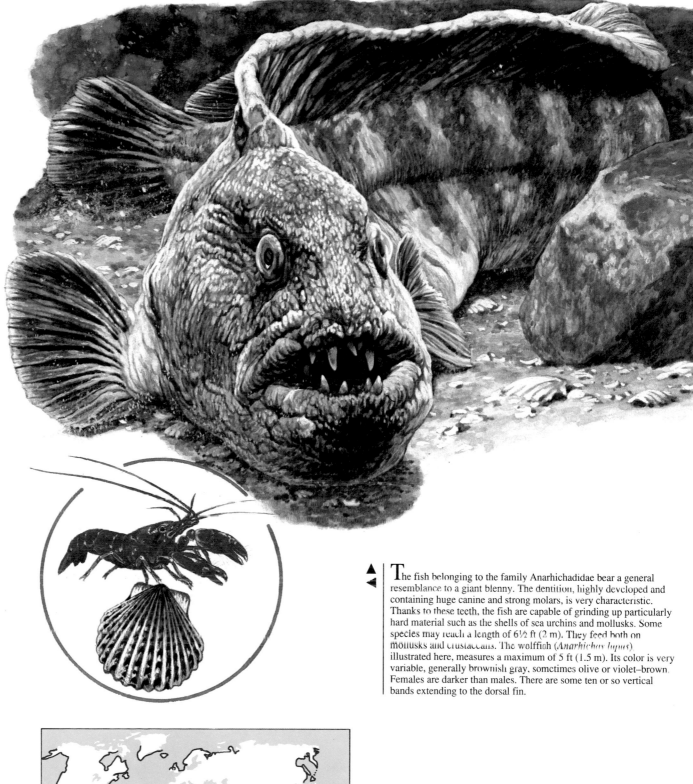

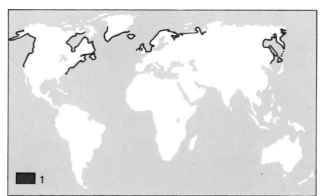

The fish belonging to the family Anarhichadidae bear a general resemblance to a giant blenny. The dentition, highly developed and containing huge canine and strong molars, is very characteristic. Thanks to these teeth, the fish are capable of grinding up particularly hard material such as the shells of sea urchins and mollusks. Some species may reach a length of 6½ ft (2 m). They feed both on mollusks and crustaceans. The wolffish (*Anarhichas lupus*) illustrated here, measures a maximum of 5 ft (1.5 m). Its color is very variable, generally brownish gray, sometimes olive or violet–brown. Females are darker than males. There are some ten or so vertical bands extending to the dorsal fin.

1) The distribution of the family Anarhichadidae is restricted to the cold and temperate seas of the Northern Hemisphere. *Anarhichas lupus* is a very common species of the North Sea and the coasts of Iceland and Norway. One individual has been observed in the Mediterranean, in the Gulf of Genoa. It is found in shallow waters but may also live at depths of more than 1,300 ft (400 m); adults, however, prefer depths of between 65 ft (20 m) and 330 ft (100 m) or more. The wolffish has a preference for very cold water, from 32° to 57°F (0° to 14°C), and for this reason in the more southerly zones of its range it lives at greater depths. It is usually present on rocky coastlines but is also to be found on soft sandy or muddy beds.

SAND EELS
Ammodytidae

The family Ammodytidae, comprising the so-called sand eels, exhibits morphological features sufficiently aberrant for it to be raised to the rank of a suborder, namely the Ammodytoidei.

The body of these fish is very elongated, low and streamlined, subcylindrical or compressed; the caudal region is narrower than the abdominal region. The anus is situated in the rear part of the body. The head is long, terminating in a point. The lower jaw is prominent, the mouth is quite large, and the premaxillary bones are markedly protractile. The jaws are devoid of teeth.

The gill openings are voluminous; the brachiostegous membranes are not joined beneath the isthmus. The dorsal fin is long and lacks spiny rays; the anal fin, similar to the dorsal, is shorter and also devoid of spiny rays. The soft rays of both these fins are short and flexible; these unpaired fins can be folded into a groove. The caudal fin is small and bilobate, separated from the anal and dorsal fins. The pectoral fins are situated low down, while the pelvic fins are in a jugular position and bear only one spiny ray and three soft rays. In some species there are no pelvic fins. The body is covered with small cycloid scales, missing in certain species. Among all sand eels, the scales never totally cover the body. In *Ammodytes tobianus* and *Hyperoplus lanceolatus* the scales are arranged in very irregular, oblique lines, separated by furrows.

The Ammodytidae inhabit the cold or temperate seas of the Northern Hemisphere. Five species are found along the European Atlantic coasts, from the White Sea to the Bay of Biscay. The sand eels are also distributed along the shores of Greenland, Canada, and the northern coasts of the United States. Representatives of the family are also to be found in the Pacific, along the coasts of Alaska and Siberia, and in the Sea of Japan; one species has also been reported along the coasts of China as far south as Taiwan.

Sand eels have a carnivorous diet. They feed principally on small crustaceans (copepods and amphipods), annelids, and small fish; some species will consume their own larvae, too.

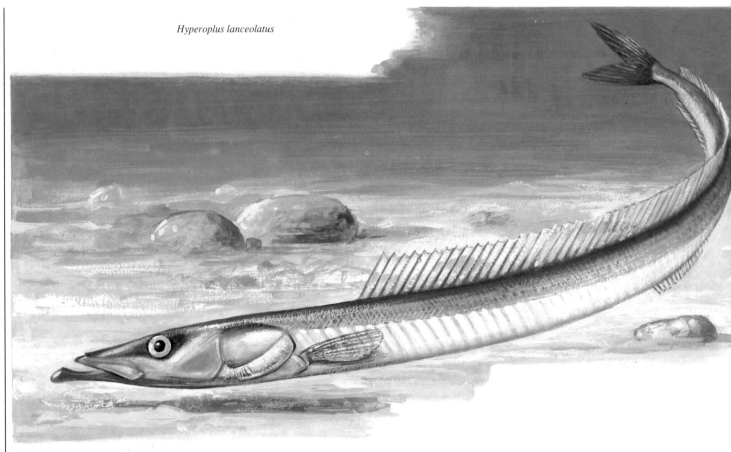

Hyperoplus lanceolatus

The fish belonging to the family Ammodytidae, only member of the suborder Ammodytoidei, have a very long, low body, streamlined and subcylindrical. For this reason they are commonly known as sand eels. The body terminates in a pointed head. The lower jaw is prominent. The mouth is rather big and, as the drawings at the foot of this page show, the premaxillary bones are markedly protractile. The sand eels are carnivores, the principal items of their diet being crustaceans (copepods and amphipods) and zooplankton. They live in the cold and temperate seas of the Northern Hemisphere. During the breeding season they come closer to shore, to the tidal zone, and dig into the sand wettened by the low tide. Here their eggs adhere to the grains of sand. *Ammodytes tobianus*, which lives along the English Channel coasts, has two spawning seasons, one in spring, the other in autumn; each individual female, however, lays eggs only in one or other period. Eggs are laid three or four days prior to full moon; afterwards the number of sand eels to be found in the sand decreases quickly, as the fish head again out to sea. The female's ovary communicates with the outside through a canal; a membrane closes the genital pore and breaks during egg laying. This membrane's function is to separate the ovarian zone from the outside environment. The diameter of the eggs ranges from 0.5 to 1 mm. Once laid, the transparent, exposed eggs affix themselves to grains of sand. After two or three weeks they hatch, giving birth to planktonic larvae measuring ⅙ – ¼ in (4 – 5 mm), furnished with float organs. The larvae grow rapidly and at the end of their first year are, on average, 4 in (10 cm) long, while in the second year the average length is 6 in (15 cm). As a rule sand eels reach sexual maturity in their second year.

DRAGONET

Callionymus lyra

Order Perciformes
Family Callionymidae
Length Males up to 12 in (30 cm); females up to 8 in (20 cm)
Coloration Yellowish brown with light and dark spots in female; yellowish with blue or violet spots in male
Reproductive period Very variable, from January to August, according to region, but usually in spring
Eggs Pelagic
Maximum age Males 5 years, females 7 years

The dragonets of the family Callionymidae live in all the world's seas, preferring warm or temperate waters. The family is generally divided into two subfamilies, given species status by some authors: Callionyminae and Draconettinae.

The common dragonet (*Callionymus lyra*) lives along the coasts of the northeastern Atlantic, from the Canaries to Norway; it may be very common in places, especially in the English Channel. It is less frequent, however, in the Mediterranean, where it sticks to the coasts, venturing as far as the Black Sea. This species prefers to live on soft substrata, in the sublittoral zone down to a depth of 165 ft (50 m), but will go as deep as 650 ft (200 m). In the breeding period it approaches the coasts; and during this season it may also be found in brackish water. The fish generally live buried in sandy or muddy sea beds, with only their eyes and breathing slits protruding. They are carnivores, feeding on small organisms such as worms, mollusks, and crustaceans.

After a phase of gonad maturation, very long in males, shorter in females, the reproductive season commences. In addition to permanent sexual features, males exhibit other seasonal sexual characteristics, determined by the action of a hormone produced by the testicles: the snout is enlarged, the color becomes brighter, the spots more conspicuous, and the eyes turn a handsome metallic green color. Each male now endeavors to attract the attention of a mature female; if he is to her liking, the two partners engage in their nuptial dance, abandoning the sea bed and performing a slow and graceful aquatic ballet.

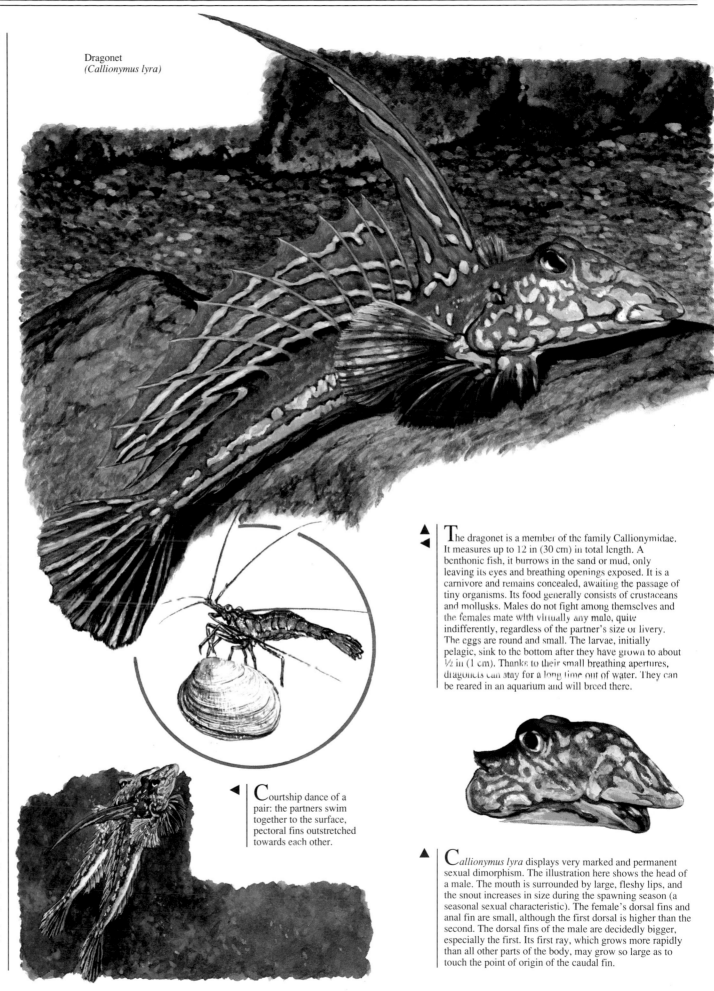

Dragonet
(*Callionymus lyra*)

The dragonet is a member of the family Callionymidae. It measures up to 12 in (30 cm) in total length. A benthonic fish, it burrows in the sand or mud, only leaving its eyes and breathing openings exposed. It is a carnivore and remains concealed, awaiting the passage of tiny organisms. Its food generally consists of crustaceans and mollusks. Males do not fight among themselves and the females mate with virtually any male, quite indifferently, regardless of the partner's size or livery. The eggs are round and small. The larvae, initially pelagic, sink to the bottom after they have grown to about ½ in (1 cm). Thanks to their small breathing apertures, dragonets can stay for a long time out of water. They can be reared in an aquarium and will breed there.

Courtship dance of a pair: the partners swim together to the surface, pectoral fins outstretched towards each other.

Callionymus lyra displays very marked and permanent sexual dimorphism. The illustration here shows the head of a male. The mouth is surrounded by large, fleshy lips, and the snout increases in size during the spawning season (a seasonal sexual characteristic). The female's dorsal fins and anal fin are small, although the first dorsal is higher than the second. The dorsal fins of the male are decidedly bigger, especially the first. Its first ray, which grows more rapidly than all other parts of the body, may grow so large as to touch the point of origin of the caudal fin.

GOBIES
Gobioidei

The representatives of the suborder Gobioidei, a large subdivision of the order Perciformes, are well distributed in all coastal waters, and are commonly known as gobies. This is an extremely polymorphous group that certainly has not fully realized its evolutionary potential; it has come to occupy all types of continental waters, salt and fresh, cold, warm, and temperate, thus adapting to many diverse biotopes, with the exclusion of deep waters and the abyss.

These fish have adapted, often in the most extreme manner, to such differing biotopes in respect of general bodily shape and structure of particular organs. The most evident of such features is the tendency, more or less wholly realized, for the ventral fins to be fused so as to form a thoracic disk that may, in the more highly evolved species, be transformed into an adhesive organ similar to a sucker.

Another characteristic, less obvious than the preceding one, is the notable development of the cutaneous sensory organs, distributed in well defined series on the head, the body, and the caudal fin; the arrangement of these sense organs, together with the absence or presence of their various components, are all diagnostic points utilized in the classifications of genera and species.

The gobies are certainly not clad in such bright and gaudy colors as those of some coral fish; yet certain of them boast extremely brilliant hues. As a rule, however, they tend to be on the drab side, light to dark gray toning to brownish; spotting is variable, tending to merge with the substratum, sandy or muddy, normally occupied. Some small species are to be found in beds of coral and these assume a mimetic coloration – reddish in keeping with their habitat. Male and female may have different liveries; in general, that of the male becomes more showy in the breeding season, often turning darker and sometimes completely black.

The gobies are normally of average size, the maximum dimensions of any representative being around 32 in (80 cm), and some species are very tiny indeed. In fact, gobies are numbered amongst the smallest of fish and even of all vertebrates. The smallest of them all, *Pandaka pygmaea*, lives off the shores

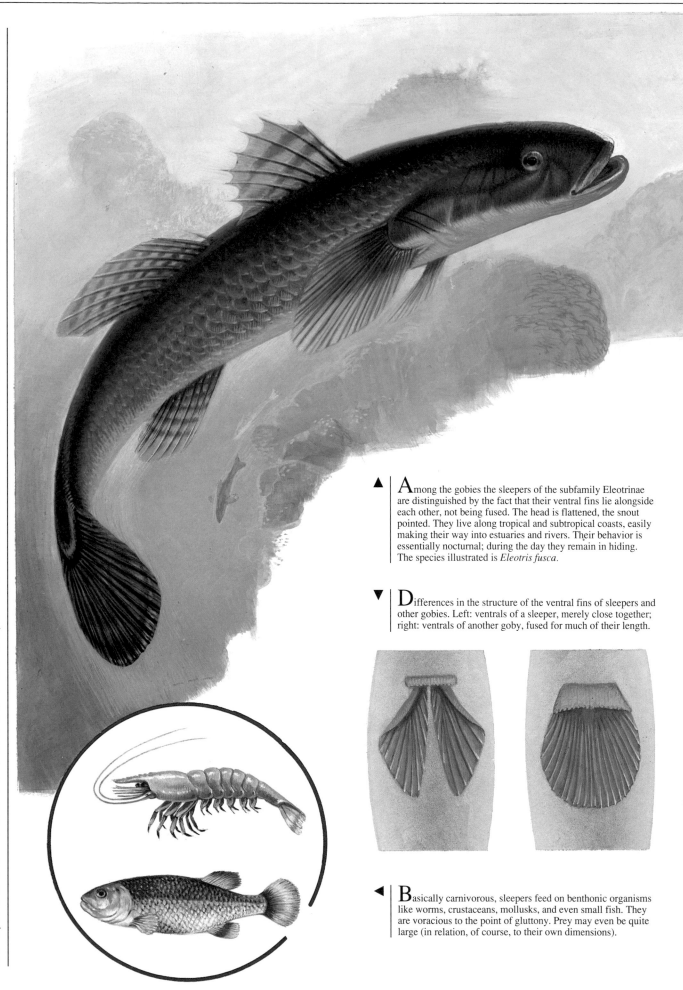

▲ Among the gobies the sleepers of the subfamily Eleotrinae are distinguished by the fact that their ventral fins lie alongside each other, not being fused. The head is flattened, the snout pointed. They live along tropical and subtropical coasts, easily making their way into estuaries and rivers. Their behavior is essentially nocturnal; during the day they remain in hiding. The species illustrated is *Eleotris fusca*.

▼ Differences in the structure of the ventral fins of sleepers and other gobies. Left: ventrals of a sleeper, merely close together; right: ventrals of another goby, fused for much of their length.

◄ Basically carnivorous, sleepers feed on benthonic organisms like worms, crustaceans, mollusks, and even small fish. They are voracious to the point of gluttony. Prey may even be quite large (in relation, of course, to their own dimensions).

of the Philippines. As an adult it reaches a length of ¼ in (6 mm). The maximum size for a male is ⅓ in (9 mm) and for a female ½ in (11 mm).

Gobies are essentially benthonic fish. Poor swimmers, generally stationary and immobile in the depths, they are supported by their ventral fins. Among most of the species, in fact, these fins are fused to form an adhesive sucker that they use to attach themselves to a rock, to the roots of a plant or to any kind of hard substratum resistant to the currents. As a rule they cannot swim very far although they can move quite fast over short distances. Thanks to their powerful pectoral fins, they can perform swift movements; in fact, they dart along in straight lines, without using their caudal fin. This style of swimming distinguishes them from the blennies, who swim with undulating body movements. Blennies, also benthonic fish, often live alongside gobies and are frequently confused with them.

Most gobies are littoral species, usually preferring soft sea beds. They may live in the open on completely sandy or muddy bottoms, but as a rule they settle on sea beds with scattered rocks or good marine plant cover, affording convenient hiding places. They are predators hunting any small creatures in their path, lying motionless in ambush. They launch themselves on their prey and do not normally pursue them if the initial attempt fails. Basically carnivorous, they feed on benthonic organisms such as worms, crustaceans, mollusks, and also small fish in the neighborhood. They are quite voracious, sometimes gluttonous, and their prey may be quite large in comparison with their own size.

Gobies are frequently found in pools of sea water and may be recognized by their rapid movements and straight, jerky manner of swimming. Most of them possess a complete, functional thoracic sucker; the upper rays of the pectoral fins, gathered into a crinoid tuft, are used as a tactile organ. Many of them exhibit sexual dimorphism, marked to a varying degree, and most of them build a nest. Some species, without venturing into the open sea, may be present a little distance above the sea bed, as, for example, on tufts of seaweed. In the littoral domain the goby's body is often large and the color very pale, usually gray or light brown among those species living on sandy bottoms; those fish that live in muddy or rocky zones tend, however, to be darker.

Without descending to the abyssal

▲ Sleepers hidden among the rocks. Predatory, they wait for their victims, hunting particularly by day. Eggs are laid in a kind of nest prepared in a rock and are guarded by the male.

Butis butis

Mogurnda obscura

Gobiomorus glehni

Hypseleotris cyprinoides

Some of the most representative species of the subfamily Eleotrinae.

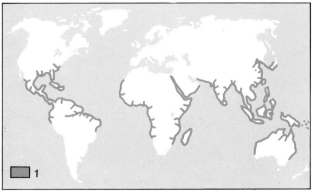

◄ 1) The subfamily Eleotrinae, belonging to the family Gobiidae, comprises species to be found in all tropical seas. It has been observed that they frequently find their way into brackish or even fresh waters. The common sleeper (*Eleotris fusca*) is one of the commonest species of the Indian Ocean and the Pacific. *Butis butis* is found in sea and brackish water in the belt extending from East Africa to Australia. *Parioglossus taeniatus* lives above the barrier reefs of the Pacific and Indian Oceans. *Hypseleotris cyprinoides* and *Mogurnda mogurnda* are two species much sought for keeping in aquariums. The former is originally from the Celebes rivers; the latter is an inhabitant of the rivers and coastal waters of northeastern Australia and New Guinea.

depths, certain species frequent the vast expanses of the continental shelf and are often fished. They have soft colors and, although a few have a markedly flattened silhouette, the majority have a cylindrically shaped body.

Gobies do not live on the high seas. Yet certain species, without straying too far from the coasts, do lead a pelagic existence, settling on the sea bed only for spawning.

Some species of gobies have penetrated freshwater zones and settled there, particularly in lakes and slow-moving rivers; they display no special adaptations. On the other hand, those species living in fast-flowing water have adapted to such habitats, and these adaptations are evident from certain anatomical changes. The mouth is situated low down, the lower lip is fringed, and the lower jaw is furnished with a horny, sharp-edged plate which is used for rasping rocks and prising loose any algae and small shells attached to them.

Many species live in underground waters or at the bottom of caves that have no light, especially in Australia, Japan, and Madagascar. Like cave-dwelling species of other groups of animals, these gobies have undergone a reduction of organs; the eyes, useless in this environment, have almost or totally disappeared. This loss is at least partially compensated by an increased number of cutaneous sensory papillae. Cave-dwelling gobies are solitary and find prey by means of touch, smell, and taste; moving victims are more easily caught.

Very many gobies live in the intertidal zone and do not abandon this habitat even when exposed as a result of low tide. In such cases many gobies seek refuge in a burrow and this enables them to remain immersed for some time; they may make use of holes dug by other animals, such as crabs. These burrows may be quite elaborate, provided with many openings at different levels. Such gobies differ from the normal type by having a ribbon-shaped body with long fins, a single dorsal and an anal, joined with the caudal. Some species, all digging tunnels, have adapted to long periods out of water, going about activities just like land animals. This peculiarity will be described more fully in the section devoted to mudskippers.

Gobies are relatively little used as food, considering the many species found off all coasts and the quality of their flesh. They are easily reared in aquariums but as a rule are not highly esteemed by aquarists.

▲ Boleophthalmus chinensis lives on Asiatic shores, from Japan, where it is very common, to the southeast of the continent. In looks and behavior it resembles the Periophthalmus mudskippers. Like the latter, it moves on dry land at low tide and digs holes in which it hides.

▼ This picture shows Boleophthalmus chinensis jumping, with all fins raised.

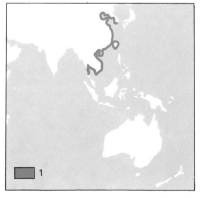

▲ Burrow of B. chinensis. This shelter is not abandoned during the winter.

◄ 1) Geographical range of Boleophthalmus chinensis. This species, like others belonging to the same genus and to the genera Scartelaos and Periophthalmus, leads a genuinely amphibious existence.

BLACK GOBY

Gobius niger

Order Perciformes
Family Gobiidae
Length 6 in (15 cm); some individuals reach 7 in (18 cm)
Coloration Brown, yellowish gray or almost black, with irregular dark markings. The front part of the dorsal fins have black spots
Reproductive period In northern regions from May to August; in Mediterranean from March to May
Eggs Vary in number from 1,000 to 6,000, according to dimensions
Maximum age 4 or 5 years

The black goby (*Gobius niger*) resembles a typical goby, but its body is relatively stocky and the caudal peduncle is high and short. Supporting a wide range of water temperatures, it lives along the coasts of the northeastern Atlantic from Cap Blanc (Mauritania) to Norway, including the North Sea and the Baltic Sea; it is also found throughout the Mediterranean, venturing into the Black Sea and the Sea of Azov, and finding its way into the Suez Canal. It is a mainly littoral species, coming close into shore but is also found at depths of up to 265 ft (80 m) or thereabouts. It shows a preference for calm waters and may venture into freshwater estuaries and coastal lagoons; it is often encountered, too, in ports, provided there is not too much pollution. The fish favors soft substrata and appears to seek refuge in zones with plenty of shelter. However, it freely inhabits littoral prairies as well. It is a very common species.

A poor swimmer, the black goby is nevertheless capable of making rapid movements thanks to its pectoral fins, which are very strong. A predator, it lies in wait for its victim, launching a direct attack, generally without any pursuit. Individuals of this species do not organize themselves into large groups, but instead live somewhat isolated, often forming pairs; this is undoubtedly attributable to a pronounced territorial instinct. The burrow and part of the surrounding territory is vigorously defended: the owner of the territory, in fact, intimidates other males who approach, assuming a menacing attitude, head raised, mouth closed, gill covers swollen, and sometimes emitting sounds audible to the human ear.

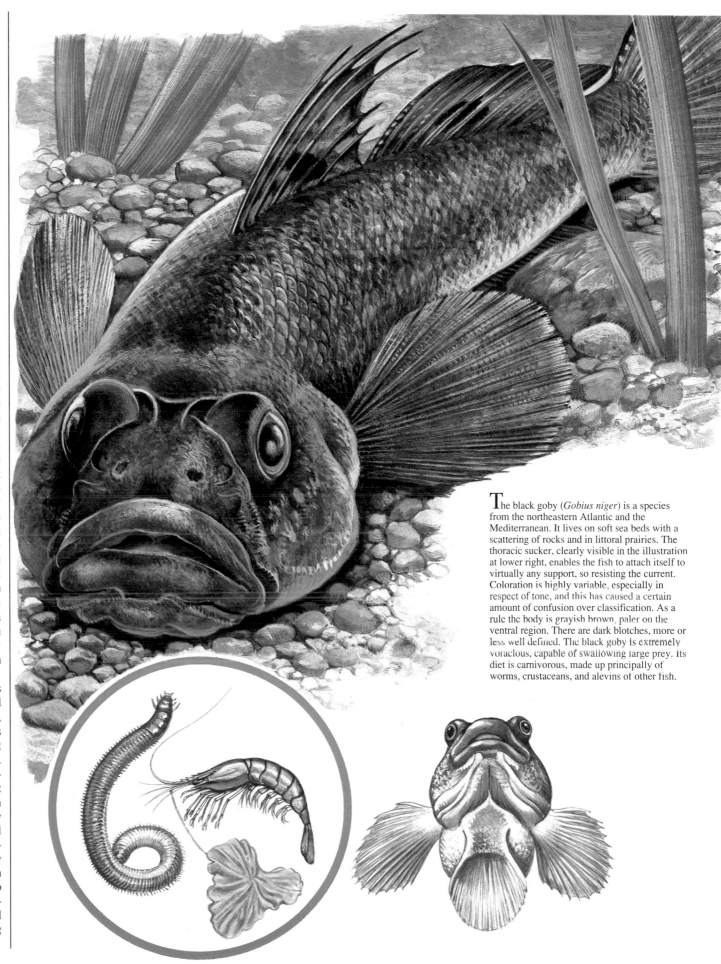

The black goby (*Gobius niger*) is a species from the northeastern Atlantic and the Mediterranean. It lives on soft sea beds with a scattering of rocks and in littoral prairies. The thoracic sucker, clearly visible in the illustration at lower right, enables the fish to attach itself to virtually any support, so resisting the current. Coloration is highly variable, especially in respect of tone, and this has caused a certain amount of confusion over classification. As a rule the body is grayish brown, paler on the ventral region. There are dark blotches, more or less well defined. The black goby is extremely voracious, capable of swallowing large prey. Its diet is carnivorous, made up principally of worms, crustaceans, and alevins of other fish.

MUDSKIPPERS
Periophthalminae

The mudskippers are fairly modest-sized fish, presenting a number of individual characteristics, due to the fact that they are specialized for life out of water. The body is elongated, very thick at the front and slightly compressed at the rear. The head is large and the facial profile is almost straight. The big snout is a little flattened at the front. As in the majority of gobies, the ventral fins are linked to form an adhesive sucker.

The habit of spending long periods out of water is associated with various modifications and adaptations in the morphology of the fins. The pectorals, which enable the fish to move about underground and support the weight of the whole body, are strong and pedunculate, formed by a kind of stump lengthened into a paddle-like fin. It operates like a small arm that terminates in a broad palmated "hand." The fin base of the mudskipper is supported by a bone structure that is stronger and more developed than that of other gobies. It is rendered more mobile and suitable for a wide variety of movements by the presence of very large, separated adductor and abductor muscles, situated on the inner and outer fin surfaces.

The subaerial habitat of mudskippers is reflected in other specific features, as, for example, the morphology of the eyes and respiratory tracts that have to perform their functions in an unaccustomed environment. The eyes are very peculiar and bear some resemblance to the eyes of amphibians. They are placed close together and bulge out; strikingly mobile, they are mounted on a kind of optical turret and can be popped out, like the eyes of flatfish, to operate as a periscope. They can, when necessary, be retracted into their sockets. In such a situation they are almost completely covered by protective folds of skin.

Mudskippers are able to breathe atmospheric oxygen for long periods thanks to the fact, that the mucus of mouth and pharynx is furnished with many blood vessels and the gill surface is relatively small. The gills must be kept moist at all times. The fish can moreover greatly expand their gill cavities, so increasing the surface for gaseous exchanges and closing the gill openings.

This system of breathing has become

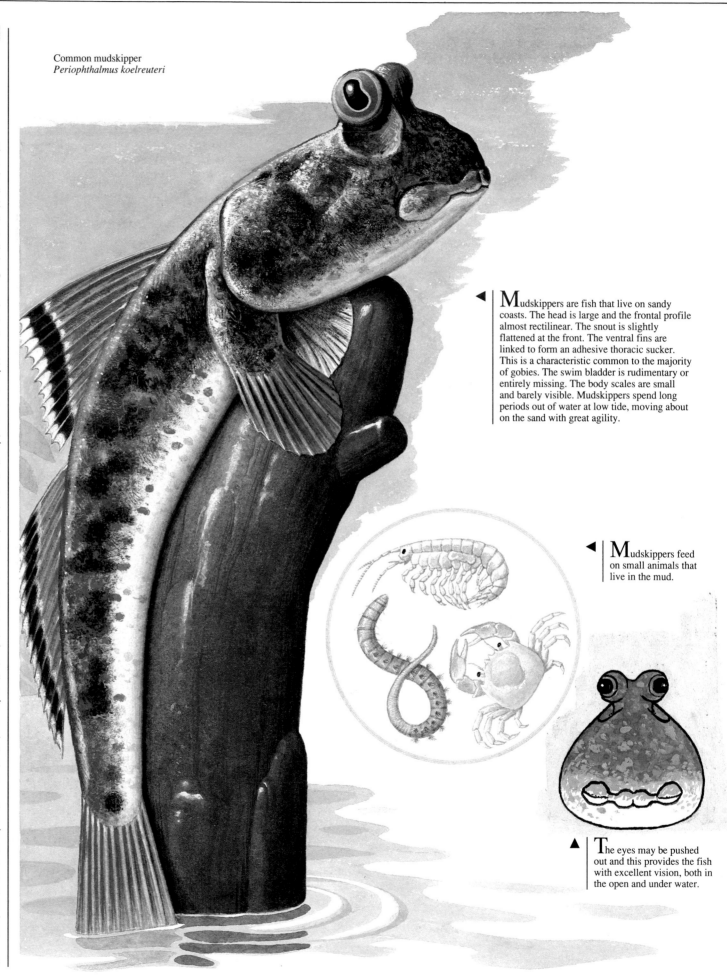

Common mudskipper
Periophthalmus koelreuteri

Mudskippers are fish that live on sandy coasts. The head is large and the frontal profile almost rectilinear. The snout is slightly flattened at the front. The ventral fins are linked to form an adhesive thoracic sucker. This is a characteristic common to the majority of gobies. The swim bladder is rudimentary or entirely missing. The body scales are small and barely visible. Mudskippers spend long periods out of water at low tide, moving about on the sand with great agility.

Mudskippers feed on small animals that live in the mud.

The eyes may be pushed out and this provides the fish with excellent vision, both in the open and under water.

so normal for these fish that it is used, at least partially, even when they are in water. In fact, when under water, mudskippers habitually assume a sloping position, with the head higher than the rest of the body; they strongly dilate the gill cavities (the rear portion of which contains water) so that water thoroughly wets the back gills, while air is stored in the front part. As a result the front gills are only moistened by a small amount of water, retained by the capillaries.

The mudskippers inhabit the equatorial and tropical zones of Africa, both west and east, including Madagascar, and the same zones in Asia, extending as far as Australia. Where suitable habitats exist, they are common and plentiful; they particularly like mangrove swamps or sandy areas left exposed at low tide and frequent beaches, the shores of lagoons and marshes, and pools of salt water that form at low tide round the mouths of rivers. These fish are, in fact, capable of withstanding considerable variations in salinity.

After digging a more or less complex burrow in soft ground, utilizing the excavated material to build a circular ledge round the opening, mudskippers retire inside. At other times, they may be found in the open, supported on the pectoral fins and the sucker, with head raised and eyes rolling comically round the sockets; this behavior undoubtedly helps to moisten the mucus and prevents it drying out.

When not resting, mudskippers move around with an agility surprising for a fish. At low tide they lead a very active life, like that of land animals, and often assemble in small groups, often quarreling and fighting among themselves. In the event of danger the fish quickly take refuge in their burrow or in a conveniently close hiding place. Alternatively, if water is not too far away, they find shelter in their natural element with a series of hops, sometimes skipping over the surface for a short distance before submerging themselves.

It has been suggested that mudskippers can even climb trees, but this is surely an exaggerated claim. However, thanks to their agility, their skipping capacity, their pectorals, and their adhesive thoracic sucker, they can find their way to a point some distance above ground, on a rock or on a tangle of mangrove roots.

Food consists of small animals living in mud, but they may also eat insects, especially spiders.

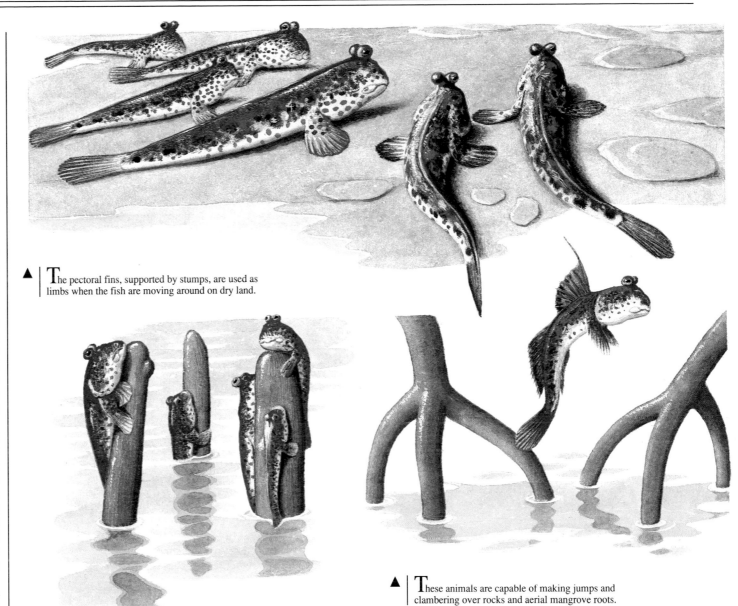

▲ The pectoral fins, supported by stumps, are used as limbs when the fish are moving around on dry land.

▲ These animals are capable of making jumps and clambering over rocks and aerial mangrove roots.

▲ Mudskippers prefer resting in an upright position, the front of the body out of the water and the caudal fin submerged.

▶ The burrow that mudskippers dig in the ground may be of varying complexity: it always has a circular mound around the opening which is constructed by the fish themselves from the excavated material.

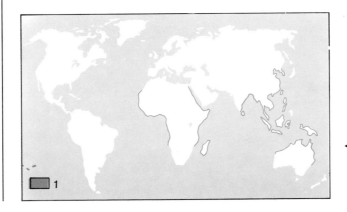

◀ 1) Mudskippers populate the equatorial and tropical zones of Africa, both east and west, and including Madagascar, as well as similar zones in Asia and as far east as Australia. They are very common and abundant in their favorite habitats, mangrove swamps or sandy soils, where they stay hidden at low tide. The fish will venture into river basins wherever the water is tidal.

ACANTHURIDAE

The suborder Acanthuroidei differs considerably from the more typical suborders of the Perciformes. Its name stems from the largest of its families (Acanthuridae) and notably from the genus *Acanthurus*; the latter includes the surgeonfish, so named because of the sharp spines lying flat on either side of the tail that can be erected so as to inflict wounds. The scientific etymology is straightforward, from the Greek, meaning "spiny tail." There are also two other families, Zanclidae and Siganidae. All three families are inhabitants of tropical and subtropical seas, especially those of the Indo-Pacific region.

Not all the Acanthuridae are surgeonfish, for this name applies only to several genera whose members possess tail spines: the most important of these is the genus *Acanthurus*, comprising many species distributed along all sea coasts. There are two spines, situated to left and right of the caudal peduncle. They are strong, sharp, and flattened. Like the blades of a penknife, they are folded into a long groove in the skin. They are fixed at the rear end but may be raised at the front to form a right angle with the body. The groove in which the spine rests and the surrounding area of skin have a particular color that often contrasts with the overall hue of the fish. Sometimes, however, the spines are not lodged in grooves; there is, for example, no groove in the species *Acanthurus sohal* and *A. lineolatus*, even though both have exceptionally long and sharp spines. It is not known how venomous these spines are, and it would seem that their action is simply mechanical. It is not far-fetched to compare them with lancets, from which feature the fish derive their vernacular name. Certainly they can cause severe wounds, but they are essentially defensive weapons, erected to the accompaniment of energetic tail movements. Some spines of the larvae belonging to certain species, like *Acanthurus triostegus*, do contain venom, but the larvae do not possess any tail spines.

Acanthurus are notable not only for the variety and beauty of their colors but also for the fact that they frequently undergo marked and rapid color changes in relation to their surroundings.

Paracanthurus hepatus

▲ The fish belonging to the Acanthuridae are characteristic inhabitants of warmer oceans, frequenting coral reefs, particularly in the Indian Ocean and Pacific. The species illustrated here is one of the most beautiful members of the family.

◀ Many Acanthuridae are known as surgeonfish, so-called because of the presence of sharp spines on either side of the tail that are erectile and capable of inflicting wounds. This is the tail spine of *Paracanthurus hepatus*.

▶ The mouth is small and situated low down. In both jaws there is a single line of teeth that are usually in the form of incisors but sometimes lobate or wavy at the edges.

▼ The Acanthuridae swim essentially with movements of the pectoral fins. This enables them to progress easily through their habitat.

SURGEONFISH

The Japanese call surgeonfish *nizadai* and some American regions know them as tang. *Acanthurus lineatus* (known to the Japanese as *nihagi*) is a very handsome fish measuring up to 11 in (28 cm). The ground color is yellow and there are contrasting longitudinal blue lines; the caudal fin is lunate, the outer rays being very long. The range of this species covers the Indian Ocean and much of the Pacific.

Acanthurus leucosternon, with elegant coloration, lives in the Indian Ocean and it congregates in large numbers in the coral beds off the coast of East Africa. This species would be a favorite ornamental aquarium fish were it not so difficult to look after. *Acanthurus triostegus*, known in Hawaii as the *manini*, has a much bigger range, which includes the Pacific. It measures up to 10 in (25 cm) and is greenish gray with five vertical black bands on either flank. The fish is gregarious and swims in formation, even in rock pools. There are far fewer Atlantic species.

One of the most beautiful members of the Acanthuridae is *Paracanthurus hepatus*. It greatly resembles the surgeonfish, but possesses only two or three instead of five soft rays on the ventral fins. The color of young individuals is exceptionally brilliant, tending to fade in the adults. Maximum length is about 10 in (25 cm). This fish is one of the most extensively distributed Indo-Pacific species, being found from the east coasts of Africa to the western Pacific (Melanesia). It is one of the most attractive and popular aquarium fish, too, though inclined to be somewhat aggressive.

Zebrasoma veliferum derives its name from its broad, sail-like fins and its conspicuous coloration. Its body is adorned with alternately light and dark brown bands, with many scattered white spots. Here, too, colors and patterns are far livelier in young fish, adults sometimes being almost black. It lives in the Indian and Pacific Oceans; in the Red Sea it is substituted by another very similar species (*Z. desjardini*). Both here and in the Indian Ocean a related species, *Z. xanthurum*, is present.

The genus *Naso* contains various Indo-Pacific fish. *Naso unicornis*, measuring up to 24 in (60 cm), is gray–brown, and is found from the Red Sea to Hawaii.

Acanthurus lineatus

Zebrasoma

Acanthurus coeruleus

Nasa unicornis

Acanthurus leucosternon

Prionurus microlepidotus

Zebrasoma veliferum

The best known of the Acanthuridae are the so-called surgeonfish, especially the numerous species of the genus *Acanthurus*. Normally fish of this family are prized for their tasty flesh, but they have their disadvantages too, for some species are capable of causing a particular type of food poisoning if eaten. The resulting illness, which may have grave consequences, has been known for over a century but is not yet fully understood.

RABBITFISH
Siganidae

The family Siganidae, belonging to the suborder Acanthuroidei, comprises the single genus *Siganus*, its members often being known as rabbitfish. The body is oblong and compressed, terminating in a rounded head. The small mouth is not protractile. The teeth, likewise small, are finely notched, similar to incisors and arranged in one row on the edges of either jaw. There are no teeth in the roof of the mouth.

The Siganidae are of small or average size, rarely exceeding 16 in (40 cm) in length. Some of them are darkly colored, whereas others are renowned for their magnificent hues and wealth of striped or spotted patterns. All rabbitfish can change color and possess spots to a varying degree.

The single genus *Siganus* is divided into two subgenera, *Siganus* and *Lo*. The latter has now been raised to the status of a genus.

The Siganidae live in the tropical waters of the Indian and Pacific Oceans. One species of the family is able to exist in colder waters, like those of the Sea of Japan, and at least four species have been sighted in the Red Sea. Two of the latter have migrated through the Suez Canal and now live along the east coasts of the Mediterranean. The majority of species form part of the coral reef fauna and some species live in brackish waters. Two species, *Siganus guttatus* and *S. vermiculatus* inhabit freshwater environments.

The diet of the Siganidae is prevalently herbivorous: the dentition and anatomy of the digestive tract show adaptations to such a diet. The small mouth enables them to browse on benthonic algae and marine plants. Certain species, nevertheless, consume small animals (amphipod and copepod crustaceans), the larvae of fish, and sponges.

The Siganidae exhibit sexual dimorphism, the males generally being smaller than the females. This characteristic is especially evident during the phase of sexual maturity. Adult males are about 6 in (15 cm) long, while females are approximately 8 in (20 cm) long. Furthermore, the abdominal region of the females is better developed than that of the males, this being even more marked when the ovules are maturing.

Siganus puellus

The Siganidae are Perciformes that live in the tropical waters of the Indian Ocean and the Pacific. Some species inhabit more temperate seas, such as the Sea of Japan and the Red Sea; others have migrated through the Suez Canal and are nowadays to be found in the Mediterranean. The principal habitat of these fish is the coral reef. There is an annual spawning cycle. This occurs from four to seven nights after the appearance of the new moon, either in May or June. The fish congregate in huge shoals, swimming in surface waters. As they swim, the females touch the abdomen of the males who respond to this "message"; when males and females expel their respective gametes, they swim about in a more agitated manner, thus facilitating the encounter of eggs and spermatozoa. There are vast numbers of fertilized eggs – from 300,000 to 500,000 – all small and transparent. The Siganidae are gregarious by instinct; they swim and seek food in shoals which vary in size according to species, and also according to the constituent individuals. But the shoal breaks up when living conditions worsen or when imminent danger threatens; at that time single individuals become aggressive and defend their territory, chasing away any potential intruders. The Siganidae are easily frightened, although the young less so than the adults.

The Siganidae have an oblong, flattened body and a rounded head. The mouth is small and the incisor-like teeth are arranged in a single row along the edges of either jaw. By reason of this morphological feature they are called rabbitfish. Such a dentition is an adaptation that permits them to browse on algae and marine plants.

TRICHIURIDAE

The Trichiuridae belong to the suborder Scombroidei. This indicates that they have a common ancestor with mackerel, tunny, swordfish, sailfish, etc. Yet with their ribbon-like body and the presence of very developed teeth in the mouth, they do not bear much resemblance to these other fish. In the course of their evolution, the Trichiuridae have adapted to a life style in deep waters close to the coasts, whereas the majority of the other fish in this group live on the surface or out in the high seas. With time they have lost their finlets – small detached fins formed of one or two rays, situated to the rear of the dorsal and anal fins. Furthermore, the caudal and pelvic fins have degenerated, the body has become flattened laterally, and the teeth have developed.

The Trichiuridae are known as cutlass fish, this name being derived from their shape. The body is, in fact, very long; indeed the length may be up to 25 times greater than the height, as in the case of *Assunger anzac*, and since it is much compressed laterally, the body is never very high. For this reason the fish are ribbon-like in form and because of their generally silvery color, the resemblance to a cutlass is genuine. From the viewpoint of etymology, the scientific name means "hair-like tail," for in some species the tail comes to a very thin tip. This is a feature of the species attached to the genera *Trichiurus, Lepturacanthus, Eupleurogrammus, Tentoriceps,* etc. In other genera (*Lepidopus, Aphanopus, Benthodesmus, Evoxymetopon,* and *Assurger*) there is a small, bifurcate, V-shaped caudal fin.

Cutlass fish are mainly found in the tropical and temperate waters of the Atlantic, Pacific and Indian Oceans. There are nevertheless exceptions. *Aphanopus carbo* is from the North Atlantic, also inhabiting the Gulf of Aden and the northwest Pacific near Japan. *Benthodesmus elongatus* has an antitropical distribution, meaning that it lives beyond the warm seas of both hemispheres.

Little is known about their reproductive habits. They are generally caught by trawling, but can also be fished on a smaller scale with various types of nets. It is interesting to note that the guanine, which is the silvery deposit found on the skin, is used for manufacturing mother-of-pearl buttons.

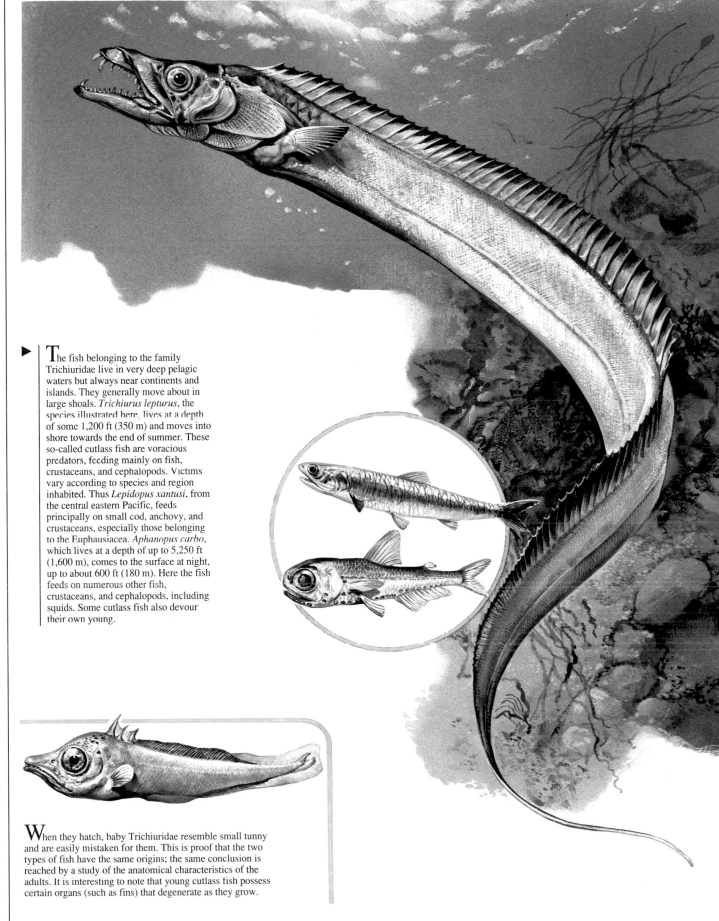

The fish belonging to the family Trichiuridae live in very deep pelagic waters but always near continents and islands. They generally move about in large shoals. *Trichiurus lepturus*, the species illustrated here, lives at a depth of some 1,200 ft (350 m) and moves into shore towards the end of summer. These so-called cutlass fish are voracious predators, feeding mainly on fish, crustaceans, and cephalopods. Victims vary according to species and region inhabited. Thus *Lepidopus xantusi*, from the central eastern Pacific, feeds principally on small cod, anchovy, and crustaceans, especially those belonging to the Euphausiacea. *Aphanopus carbo*, which lives at a depth of up to 5,250 ft (1,600 m), comes to the surface at night, up to about 600 ft (180 m). Here the fish feeds on numerous other fish, crustaceans, and cephalopods, including squids. Some cutlass fish also devour their own young.

When they hatch, baby Trichiuridae resemble small tunny and are easily mistaken for them. This is proof that the two types of fish have the same origins; the same conclusion is reached by a study of the anatomical characteristics of the adults. It is interesting to note that young cutlass fish possess certain organs (such as fins) that degenerate as they grow.

GEMPYLIDAE

The Gempylidae, like the Trichiuridae, are representatives of the Scombroidei which are adapted to life at great depths. Furthermore, like the latter family, they have small, degenerate pelvic fins and a mouth containing small, powerful tusks. Most of the Gempylidae also display little isolated fins – the finlets – behind the dorsal and anal fins. The caudal fin is almost always strong and well developed. While some of the Gempylidae have a long, laterally compressed body, like that of the cutlass fish, others are more spindle-shaped, similar to tunny. These morphological differences within the same family are associated with the biology of individual species. The forms resembling the Trichiuridae lead a life similar to the latter; whereas this is not so for those species that look more like mackerel or tunny.

Of some fifteen species belonging to this family, only four are essentially oceanic, living out at sea. The others are mainly found in waters close to continents and islands. The oceanic species are *Gempylus serpens, Diplospinus multistriatus, Paradiplospinus gracilis,* and *Nealotus tripes.*

Gempylus serpens is about 24 in (60 cm) in length but can grow to double that size. It is a pelagic species, ranging from the surface, where it settles mainly at night, down to more than 660 ft (200 m). It is widely distributed in the warm waters of the Atlantic, Pacific, and Indian Oceans. Its areas of distribution coincides roughly with the regions where, in summer, the water temperature exceeds 68°F (20°C). Like many Gempylidae, this species lives during the day at considerable depths, where it probably remains inactive. At night it goes hunting and often climbs to the surface.

Diplospinus multistriatus is also a fish of the ocean deep. It is found in the waters of the central Atlantic between latitudes 40°N and 13°N. In the Pacific it lives between latitudes 35°N and 2°N, as well as in the eastern parts around latitude 17°S and in the southern seas around Australia.

Paradiplospinus gracilis is the species most associated with cold waters. Its distribution range extends from the southern Atlantic to the Antarctic. It migrates.

▼ The fish belonging to the family Gempylidae are large predators which usually live at considerable depths. Because of their rapid swimming ability and their powerful teeth, they are fearsome animals. The species illustrated here is *Gempylus coluber.*

◀ At the start of their life, shortly after hatching, the Gempylidae feed on copepods. After reaching a certain size, their diet consists of a large variety of fish, crustaceans, and cephalopods. But although they are powerful predators, the Gempylidae are also hunted themselves. In tropical and equatorial regions tunny devour young Gempylidae that measure no more than 6 in (15 cm). Not much is known concerning the breeding habits of these species; but in equatorial zones, where they live in large numbers, they are known to spawn throughout the year. Except for the genus *Diplospinus*, the Gempylidae possess a well developed, strong, and always bifurcate caudal fin. By contrast, the pelvic fins are generally small and sometimes even degenerate. So these are reduced to a pair of spines with either a few (or no) soft rays in *Gempylus, Nealotus*, and *Prometichthys*. Considering that the Gempylidae have a spinous dorsal fin that is longer than the soft dorsal, as well as finlets and a well developed, bifurcate caudal fin, it would be true to say that on the one hand they differ from the Trichiuridae and that, on the other, they show some affinities to the Scombridae. Despite the scarce similarity between the species belonging to these two families, it is possible to argue that the fish had a common origin, with the Gempylidae as a transitional form. The coloration of the Gempylidae differs according to whether they are observed in or out of water. Thus *Prometichthys prometheus*, in its natural surroundings, is a splendid blue fish with golden tints, a blackish head, and dark brown fins. When caught and removed from the water, however, it turns slate gray or dark brown. The same happens to *Ruvettus pretiosus*, which is naturally a uniform orange–yellow, pink or brown. Out of the water it loses its bright color and becomes dark gray or even black.

SCOMBRIDAE

The family Scombridae is one of the most important from the standpoint of the food industry in as much as it contains some of the most heavily fished marine species.

Characteristic of such species is the fusiform body, slightly laterally compressed, that immediately conveys the sense of streamlining and speed. These are, in fact, pelagic fish, distributed in virtually all the world's oceans, that undertake migrations sometimes covering thousands of miles. They are speedy swimmers, with a body structure and specialized physiological attributes designed to stimulate velocity while at the same time maintaining an economic expenditure of energy.

The genus *Scomber* comprises species of average size with a slender body completely covered with small scales; the head tapers and terminates in a large mouth with equal-sized jaws provided with small teeth. The eyes are furnished with fixed adipose lids. The swim bladder is small or, in some species, totally absent. Members of this genus are the true mackerels, distributed in virtually all the world's oceans, with a preference for tropical and subtropical regions.

The most abundant species in European waters is the common mackerel (*Scomber scombrus*), found in the North Atlantic (both along the eastern and western shores) and throughout the Mediterranean, including the Black Sea. The average length is 10–14 in (25–35 cm), although specimens are often caught that measure 16 in (40 cm) and weigh more than 2¼ lb (1 kg).

Individuals of the same size form shoals which travel from deeper to shallower water as they approach the coasts. These journeys are associated as much with feeding as with spawning: in fact, these migratory movements, though they may vary seasonally from region to region, always precede the reproductive phase. In the Mediterranean they begin in spring and spawning continues to May–June.

Also members of the family Scombridae are certain fish that, related to tunny, have a very wide distribution throughout the temperate and warm oceanic belts and play an important role in commercial fisheries.

The four principal genera described

Chub mackerel
(*Scomber japonicus*)

Mackerel are distributed in almost all the world's oceans and constitute an important resource in the economy of global fisheries. They are powerful swimmers and undertake long migrations. The family Scombridae to which they belong contains pelagic fish with striking hydrodynamic features that enable them to attain considerable speeds in the water. Illustrated on this page are two of the most representative species, the chub mackerel (*Scomber japonicus*) and the common mackerel (*S. scombrus*). They feed on many planktonic organisms as well as small mollusks, crustaceans, and fish.

This illustration shows a detail of the finlets situated between the dorsal fins and the anal and caudal fins.

Common mackerel
(*Scomber scombrus*)

below are *Euthynnus*, *Katsuwonus*, *Auxis*, and *Sarda*. Here, too, there is considerable disagreement among experts concerning classification: some authors regard *Euthynnus* and *Katsuwonus* as representatives of a single genus, while *Sarda* is included by some others as belonging to the family Scomberomoridae.

Containing species of moderate dimensions, with a fusiform body that is almost circular in cross section, the genus *Euthynnus* comprises fish with quite distinct distributions: *Euthynnus alletteratus* comes from the Mediterranean and the Atlantic, *E. affinis* from the Red Sea and Indo-Pacific area, and *E. lineatus* from the tropical belt of the eastern Pacific.

The first of these, commonly known as the tunny or little tuna, has a maximum weight of around 15 lb (7 kg), with a length of under 40 in (1 m). This is a pelagic fish that often assembles in large shoals; these sometimes assume an elliptical shape and may measure 100 ft (30 m) in length. The species always inhabits a zone above the continental shelf and will only venture a considerable distance from shore when the coastline is fairly long. It is fished in many countries by a variety of methods; although it takes fixed bait quite readily, it is caught in much larger quantities with ring nets when in clearly identifiable shoals, or otherwise with drift nets. The flesh is inferior in quality to that of other species of tunny and does not fetch such a high market price.

Euthynnus affinis is found at depths between 130 ft (40 m) and 800 ft (250 m) and periodically approaches the coasts in the warm season. The maximum length is around 36 in (90 cm) and the weight about 22 lb (10 kg).

Euthynnus lineatus is a fish of modest proportions, normally not exceeding 24 in (60 cm) in length or 11 lb (5 kg) in weight. It is not of great economic value, the small quantities caught fetching low prices.

There is only one species attached to the genus *Katsuwonus*, the oceanic bonito (*K. pelamis*). It has a cosmopolitan range, being found in all warm temperate seas, including the Mediterranean. It lives in shoals that are usually quite small, though shoals tipping the scales at 130 tonnes have been netted; they consist of individuals of a similar size, either of the same or several species.

The oceanic bonito feeds on numerous species of fish, mollusks, and

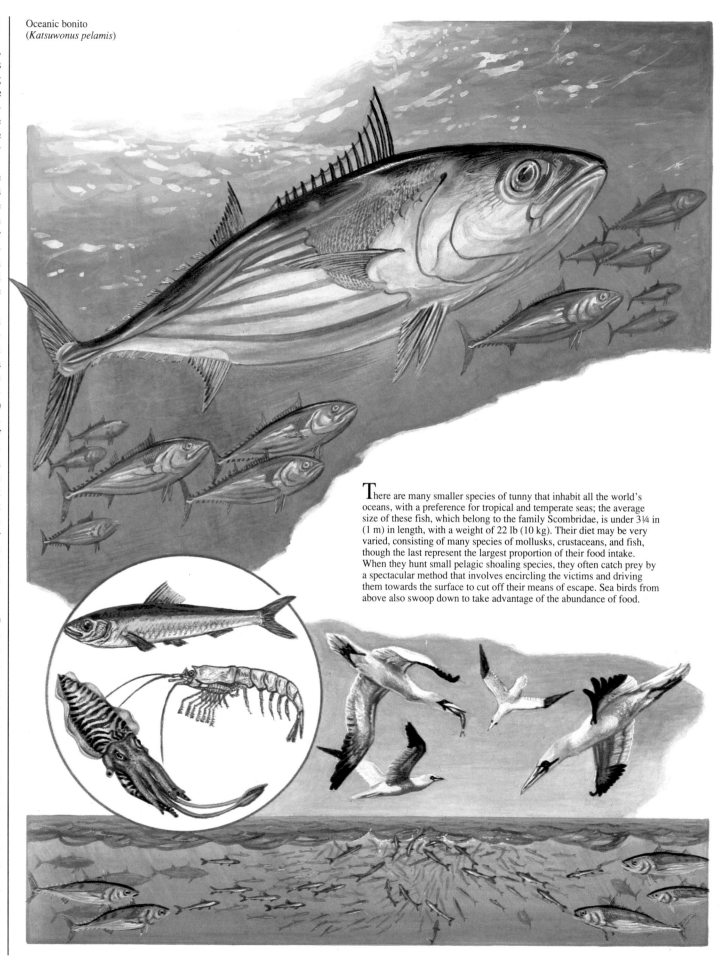

Oceanic bonito
(*Katsuwonus pelamis*)

There are many smaller species of tunny that inhabit all the world's oceans, with a preference for tropical and temperate seas; the average size of these fish, which belong to the family Scombridae, is under 3¼ in (1 m) in length, with a weight of 22 lb (10 kg). Their diet may be very varied, consisting of many species of mollusks, crustaceans, and fish, though the last represent the largest proportion of their food intake. When they hunt small pelagic shoaling species, they often catch prey by a spectacular method that involves encircling the victims and driving them towards the surface to cut off their means of escape. Sea birds from above also swoop down to take advantage of the abundance of food.

crustaceans, and prey is often captured by the coordinated hunting of all members of a shoal; as a rule the shoal will surround other groups of small pelagic fish, driving them towards the surface so as to reduce their powers of free movement, attacking the individuals on the fringes of the shoal by swimming to and fro with mouths agape. Fishing of this species is extremely widespread throughout the Pacific and especially in Japan where hundreds of thousands of tons are taken by the vessels of a large fishing fleet.

The members of the genus *Auxis* are even smaller; the genus contains only one species, the frigate mackerel (*A. thazard*), inhabiting all the world's oceans. It is about 20 in (50 cm) long and weighs about 2¼ lb (1 kg). The body is long, tapering, and almost circular in cross section. The color is dark blue on the back, with a series of irregular stripes; it fades to gray on the flanks and silvery white on the abdomen.

This a pelagic fish that lives in large shoals, often a long way from shore. Periodically, it comes closer to land; the discovery of eggs and larvae seems to indicate that eggs are laid both out at sea and nearer the coasts. Food consists of planktonic organisms and small fish. The species has no commercial value.

One of the most important species of the family is the genus *Sarda*, for it comprises fish found in seas all over the world that have high commercial value. The Atlantic bonito (*Sarda sarda*) is one of the best known fish species. Its body is long, fusiform, and slightly compressed laterally. The maximum size is about 32 in (80 cm) and 22 lb (10 kg) in weight. The bonito is an insatiable predator that hunts continuously all day long, but especially at dawn and dusk. It refuses no prey within reach, following the victim to the surface so as to restrict the latter's movements. Its most common food items are herrings, mackerels, sardines, and other small and medium-sized pelagic fish. This pelagic species is a migrant, forming huge shoals that journey far and wide in the Mediterranean. The species has, in fact, been observed at different periods in different regions. There are probably several spawning grounds, including one that has been verified in the Black Sea.

The bonito is actively fished in the Atlantic, the Mediterranean, and the Black Sea, mainly by using special fixed nets but also with ring nets and rod and line.

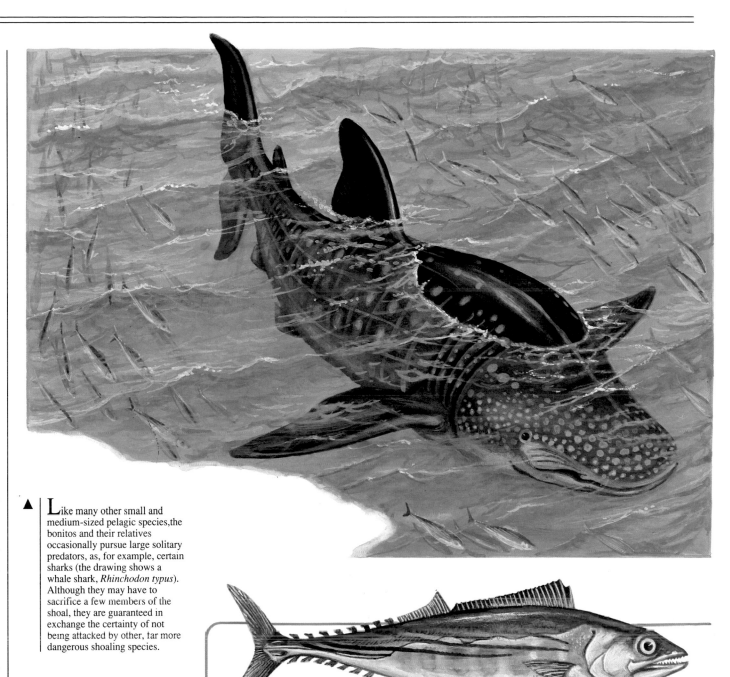

▲ Like many other small and medium-sized pelagic species, the bonitos and their relatives occasionally pursue large solitary predators, as, for example, certain sharks (the drawing shows a whale shark, *Rhinchodon typus*). Although they may have to sacrifice a few members of the shoal, they are guaranteed in exchange the certainty of not being attacked by other, far more dangerous shoaling species.

Atlantic bonito
(*Sarda sarda*)

▲ The Atlantic bonito is an extremely voracious species which reaches a maximum size of 32 in (80 cm) and a weight of 22 lb (10 kg). Its area of diffusion includes the Mediterranean, the Black Sea, and both shores of the Atlantic from latitudes 50 – 55°N to 35°S.

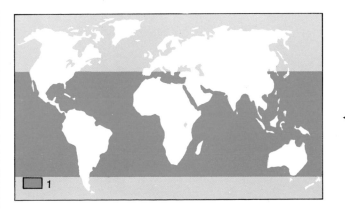

◄ 1) The oceanic bonito (*Katsuwonus pelamis*) is the only species of this genus, common to all warm and temperate seas, including the Mediterranean. The movements of this fish are very complex because there are both sedentary groups and migratory shoals; furthermore, there is evidence that, for reasons not yet clarified, migrations do not always follow an identical route. The oceanic bonito does not ever descend deeper than 650 ft (200 m). Spawning occurs throughout the year according to the region in question.

BLUEFIN TUNA

Thunnus thynnus

Order Perciformes
Family Scombridae
Length Up to 10 ft (3 m)
Weight 1,100 lb (500 kg) and over
Coloration Steel gray on back, white with irridescent reflections on abdomen
Reproductive period May – June
Eggs 10 – 18 million
Sexual maturity At 2 – 3 years

The genus *Thunnus* contains seven species of tunny or tuna, found in all the world's oceans. The bluefin tuna (*Thunnus thynnus*) is one of the most abundant species and well known fish since antiquity. Aristotle described its biology in rather fanciful terms in an attempt to interpret the periodicity of its migrations. During the time the fish came close to the shores, he happened to observe large quantities of fruits, similar to acorns, floating on the sea surface, and he deduced from this that the tuna were drawn towards the coasts by reason of the fruiting of submarine "oaks" and that they subsequently fed on them. He went on to say that the fibrous balls so common on many beaches were actually the excrement of the tuna themselves. We now know that Aristotle's "acorns" must have been the fruits of a marine grass, *Posidonia oceanica*, very plentiful in the Mediterranean; the fibrous pellets are merely the entangled residues of leaves from the same plant. They are therefore quite unconnected with the tuna, although the belief was unchallenged until the end of the nineteenth century.

The bluefin tuna has a massive, tapering body that becomes markedly narrower towards the tail. The fins are rigid and designed, like the rest of the body structure, for rapid swimming. There are two dorsals, placed close together; the first of these may, when lowered, disappear into a suitable groove, while the second is symmetrical to the anal fin. The pectorals and ventrals are likewise lodged in an apposite recess in the skin. The large, falcate tail is the animal's strong propelling organ.

A distinctive phenomenon of these fish is their blood circulation: in fact, the vascular system, particularly inside the lateral muscles, is extremely developed. This feature, together with the large size of the heart, is responsible for the

Bluefin tuna
(*Thunnus thynnus*)

The genus *Thunnus* comprises seven species of large fish that are of considerable economic importance in the context of world fisheries. They are pelagic species capable of traveling thousands of miles, and they populate the warm and temperate zones of all oceans. The bluefin tuna, illustrated here, leads a part of its life in relative isolation or in small groups: this happens particularly when seeking food and always outside the spawning season. The species is believed to have many spawning grounds. In the Atlantic the best known lie near the Azores and off Florida.

increase of body temperature, which is normally above that of the surroundings.

The tuna is one of the biggest living teleost fish: in the Atlantic it may weigh more than 1,550 lb (700 g) whereas in the Mediterranean it does not exceed 1,100 lb (500 kg).

Bluefin tuna lead part of their lives in relative isolation or in small groups (erratic phase). This occurs chiefly when looking for food and always outside the breeding period. With the arrival of spring and the maturation of the gonads, tuna start assembling in shoals of increasing size and make for the spawning grounds as rapidly as possible (gregarious phase). During these journeys the tuna regularly appear in certain coastal zones where they have been caught from time immemorial with fixed or mobile fishing equipment.

There are probably numerous tuna spawning areas; the most famous in the Mediterranean lies between Sicily, Sardinia, and the coast of North Africa. In the Atlantic there are similar zones near the Azores and off Florida. The spherical eggs are 1–1.2 mm in diameter and are planktonic; the embryonic stage lasts for about 48 hours, after which a larva of approximately ¼ in (3 mm) hatches. After a year they weigh up to 11 lb (5 kg) and measure 24 in (60 cm) in length. From then on growth continues proportionately and it would seem that the largest individuals are between 15 and 18 years old. Having reached sexual maturity, the tuna initiate their genetic migration which is then repeated periodically.

Like other species, the bluefin tuna is highly voracious, and its food is constituted of numerous types of plankton in the first juvenile phase; later it includes various fish as well as mollusks and crustaceans. It does not, however, have special food preferences and will adapt to almost anything that comes its way. During the spawning period, when the gonads reach their maximum development, suppressing that of the other organs, the tuna interrupts its feeding activities and resumes them only after spawning.

Although they are among the largest teleost fish of all oceans, tuna have various enemies; many species catch young tuna and, indeed, some of the fiercest of such foes are larger tunas. The latter, in turn, are hunted by even bigger species such as killer whales, porpoises, and sharks.

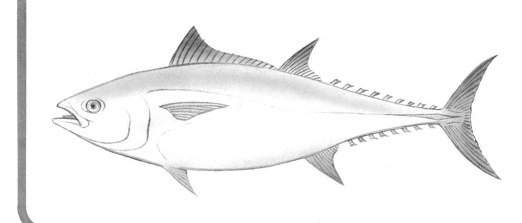

The bluefin tuna has rigid fins designed for rapid swimming. There are two dorsals, close together. The first, like the pectoral and ventral fins, slots into a small groove in the skin. The second is symmetrical with the anal fin. In front of the large falcate caudal fin are 8 – 10 upper finlets and 7 – 9 lower finlets.

► Similar in structure to other tuna, the albacore is notable for its extremely long pectoral fins.

▼ Tuna are generally omnivorous and predatory, feeding mainly on small and medium-sized pelagic fish. They reduce or completely interrupt their food intake during the spawning season.

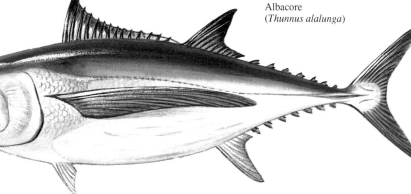

Albacore
(*Thunnus alalunga*)

▲ Although they are among the largest and most voracious teleosts of every ocean, tuna have numerous enemies, such as sharks and the killer whale (illustrated here) who often hunt them.

◄ 1) Of the various tuna the species with the most northerly distribution is undoubtedly the bluefin. In the Atlantic, in fact, it is found between latitudes 20° and 70° N on the east coasts and between latitudes 10° and 50° N on west coasts. It is also present in the Mediterranean and the Black Sea. During the spawning period it heads for warmer, less productive areas, while for the remaining time it inhabits zones where it can most easily find sufficient amounts of food.

SWORDFISH

Xiphias gladius

Order Perciformes
Family Xiphiidae
Length Over 13 ft (4 m)
Weight Up to 1,100 lb (500 kg) or more
Distinctive features Elongated upper jaw forming a flattened, sharp rostrum
Coloration Gray – black on back, white on belly
Reproductive period From spring to summer
Eggs On average 16 million

The swordfish is one of the largest existing teleosts, characterized by its flattened rostrum, which is a third of the total length of its body, with a sharp point and cutting edges. This "sword" stems from the overdevelopment of the upper jaw; the lower jaw is much shorter but is also well developed and terminates in a point. The mouth is large and the adults have no teeth. The coloration is uniform, gray–black on the back, white on the abdomen.

The swordfish is a cosmopolitan species, inhabiting virtually all the world's temperate and tropical seas: in the Atlantic, for example, it lives off all coasts and heads north at the end of summer and early fall, at which times it has been caught off the shores of Britain and in the North Sea. It is abundantly present off both coasts of the United States, but not fished commercially. It is, nevertheless, a favorite game fish. In the seas of Japan, on the other hand, it is of considerable economic importance, as it is in the Mediterranean, where it has a fairly wide distribution and where it has been fished traditionally since ancient times.

It is a pelagic, migratory fish, but it does not assemble in compact shoals even in the spawning season. At such times it often makes long journeys along fixed routes, yet still keeping a fair distance from others of its species. This behavior is derived from its solitary, aggressive nature, typical of many large predators, which prevents it making contact either with other individuals of its own kind or with other fish that could be potential competitors.

There have been many examples of whales and other big cetaceans that have been killed with fragments of a swordfish's rostrum embedded in their muscles; this seems to prove the truth of

Swordfish
(*Xiphias gladius*)

The swordfish is a large fish inhabiting the world's tropical and temperate seas. It is notable for its long, flattened, pointed snout, resulting from the overdevelopment of the upper jaw. This species may grow to a length of more than 13 ft (4 m), a third of which is represented by its "sword." Despite its size, the swordfish is an agile and speedy swimmer, and is considered, in fact, to be one of the fastest of all sea animals. The body is powerful and streamlined, almost circular in cross section. Females are generally larger than the males. The mouth is large and lacks teeth. There is a lateral line, although not clearly visible. The coloration is uniform, shaded gray–black on the back and dirty white on the abdomen. The dorsal fin is high, but its base is much shorter than is the case among the related Istiophoridae. The caudal peduncle has a single but strong keel on either side. The caudal fin is in a half-moon shape. There are no scales. The swordfish is a solitary, aggressive creature, typical of all large predators. This prevents it making contact with other members of its own or different species, the former being, in a sense, competitors. The only exception to this secluded life is during the spawning period. Partners form close links, so much so that if one is caught by fishermen the other stays circling around the vessel, as if searching for its mate.

many legends relating the deep hostility between these two giants and the violent battles that take place between them.

Undoubtedly, therefore, the terrible weapon of the swordfish is far from merely decorative and is actively employed in the daily search for food. Once it has come to grips with one or more animals, the swordfish strikes out with powerful lateral blows, killing or stunning its victim before grabbing it in the mouth. It hunts both by day and by night, showing a preference, according to circumstances, for mollusks, cephalopods, and pelagic fish such as sardines, mackerels, etc.

The only exception to this unsociability is when the time comes for spawning: then the link with a partner is very strong, and it is not uncommon to see pairs of swordfish swimming close together in surface waters. Fishermen take advantage of this behavior to harpoon two fish, knowing the couple are inseparable.

During the spawning season the swordfish regularly swims several feet below the surface with its tall dorsal fin and tail often protruding above the water, for the rest of the year it dives to depths of several hundred feet. Observations of horizontal movements have established that it reaches quite considerable speeds in the water: it can, in fact, swim at about 60 mph (100 kmh), making it one of the fastest animals in the oceans.

The spawning period of the swordfish extends from the end of spring and throughout the summer and the female ejects eggs several times. The number of eggs emitted by an adult varies according to size from 10 to 20 million; each egg is pelagic and measures 1.6 to 1.8 mm in diameter. After two and a half days from fertilization a larva, slightly over ⅙ in (4 mm) long, hatches, and when it is four days old it begins to open its mouth and soon afterward to feed.

In these early stages the general structure is entirely different from that of the adult and only later, as both jaws develop into a kind of beak, does the animal begin to take on its definitive appearance. Nevertheless, there are still many differences, such as the unified dorsal and anal fins, the presence of teeth in both jaws, and small scales on the body. As the fish grows, the scales and teeth disappear, only the upper jaw continues to develop, and the two dorsal fins and anal fins become separated.

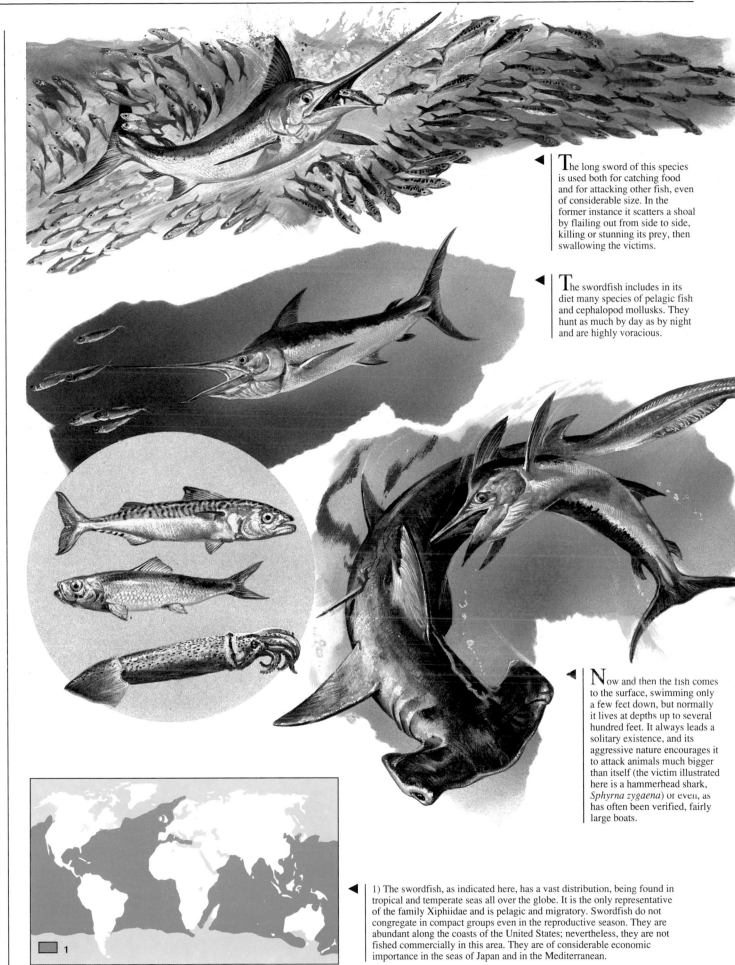

◄ The long sword of this species is used both for catching food and for attacking other fish, even of considerable size. In the former instance it scatters a shoal by flailing out from side to side, killing or stunning its prey, then swallowing the victims.

◄ The swordfish includes in its diet many species of pelagic fish and cephalopod mollusks. They hunt as much by day as by night and are highly voracious.

◄ Now and then the fish comes to the surface, swimming only a few feet down, but normally it lives at depths up to several hundred feet. It always leads a solitary existence, and its aggressive nature encourages it to attack animals much bigger than itself (the victim illustrated here is a hammerhead shark, *Sphyrna zygaena*) or even, as has often been verified, fairly large boats.

◄ 1) The swordfish, as indicated here, has a vast distribution, being found in tropical and temperate seas all over the globe. It is the only representative of the family Xiphiidae and is pelagic and migratory. Swordfish do not congregate in compact groups even in the reproductive season. They are abundant along the coasts of the United States; nevertheless, they are not fished commercially in this area. They are of considerable economic importance in the seas of Japan and in the Mediterranean.

SAILFISH
Istiophorus platypterus

The sailfish and marlins belonging to the family Istiophoridae are notable for their upper jaw, transformed into a long bony, lance-shaped snout. In this respect they resemble swordfish and are often confused with the latter, though they differ in having a circular rather than a flattened rostrum and also two ventral fins, long and narrow in form, which are absent among swordfish.

These are pelagic species, found in all the oceans and in the Mediterranean. They live in surface waters, especially on the high seas, though some species freely approach the coasts. They require warmth, and some make directly for the warmest waters of the equatorial zone; others, however, can stand or deliberately seek out somewhat more temperate waters.

The long, tapering, hydrodynamic body, allied to other morphological features, ensure that these fish are speedy and tireless swimmers. They are continually on the move, in pursuit of shoals. They can perform spectacular leaps out of the water and sometimes launch attacks, for no obvious reason, on swimmers or vessels, penetrating very deeply with their sharp snout.

Their flesh is much appreciated, and when present in large numbers they are fished on an industrial scale either with rod and line or with a harpoon. Sportsmen consider them a rare prize, valuing them according to size, weight, and combativeness.

As a group, the Istiophoridae are among the biggest of the bony fish, and also among the speediest, most powerful, and most aggressive. Some of them can swim at over 60 mph (100 kmh) and even 75 mph (120 kmh) according to some authorities, though probably this is exaggerated. They are, furthermore, capable of extraordinary spurts over short distances and can leap many feet out of the water; after crashing down on the surface they may skim along for a while, almost as if flying, supported only by their lashing tail.

The sailfish (Istiophorus platypterus) is immediately identifiable by its immense dorsal fin, from which its vernacular name is derived. This fin is formed of a small pointed lobe in front, followed by a very large rounded lobe. The body is slightly compressed, the

The sailfish (Istiophorus platypterus) is one of the most interesting members of the family Istiophoridae. Very popular among game fishermen, it is recognizable by its very high dorsal fin with a large rounded lobe that from a distance looks like a sail. These fish freely approach the coasts and move about in small groups.

snout of average size. The shape of the head is humped and the wiry ventral fins are very long. The upper part of the body is bluish gray and the belly is silver. Along the flanks is a series of light blue vertical stripes made up of tiny rows of spots. The dorsal fin is bright blue, dotted with little black spots.

The sailfish is one of the most agile members of the family and no game fish is capable of putting up a more violent struggle. It tends to be sociable, assembling in groups of up to forty individuals. When a number of fish rise to the surface, dorsal fins erect, they look like a small fleet of sailing ships. They stick to coastal zones, sometimes approaching very close to shore, diving deeper for food. Maximum size is 11½ ft (3.5 m) and maximum weight 220 lb (100 kg); in the Atlantic these figures are lower.

The young differ notably from the adults and their definitive body shape comes about very gradually. In fact they go through various phases, each with its own characteristics that subsequently disappear, so much so that the successive forms adopted by these fish have sometimes been considered and described as distinct species.

In an early stage the body is large and stocky and the strong head is furnished with bony crests and spines, including four large, backward-facing, dentate spines. The jaws are still equal in length. The very low-positioned dorsal and anal fins are still linked. The ventrals are small and the tail is not yet streamlined. In the second stage the upper jaw has grown, the dorsal is higher, and the ventrals have become sharper. In the third phase the whole body is longer, the snout begins to be visible, and the cephalic spines have regressed. The caudal fin is hollowed out and the fish starts to take on its definitive adult appearance.

Although sailfish are easily distinguished, the same is not true for the other members of the family whose outlines are often very alike and whose colors are sometimes deceptive. Actually, colors and blotches may appear and vanish, or change substantially according to the individual's mood, whether it is at rest or excited, in a moment of pain or after death.

Some authors distinguish two species: *Istiophorus platypterus*, from the Pacific and *I. albicans*, from the Atlantic. In the latter species the pectoral and anal fins are longer.

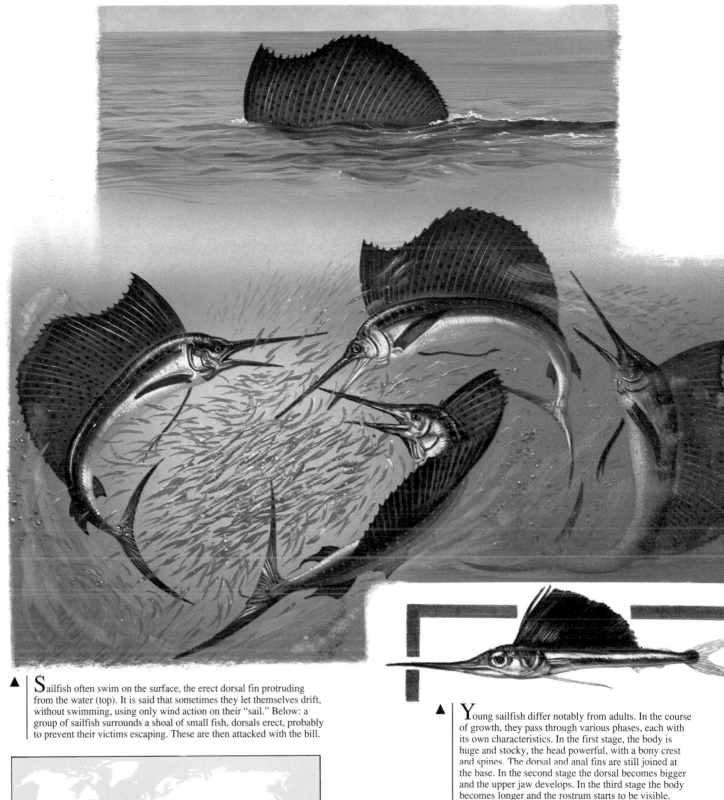

▲ Sailfish often swim on the surface, the erect dorsal fin protruding from the water (top). It is said that sometimes they let themselves drift, without swimming, using only wind action on their "sail." Below: a group of sailfish surrounds a shoal of small fish, dorsals erect, probably to prevent their victims escaping. These are then attacked with the bill.

▲ Young sailfish differ notably from adults. In the course of growth, they pass through various phases, each with its own characteristics. In the first stage, the body is huge and stocky, the head powerful, with a bony crest and spines. The dorsal and anal fins are still joined at the base. In the second stage the dorsal becomes bigger and the upper jaw develops. In the third stage the body becomes longer and the rostrum starts to be visible.

1

◄ The Istiophoridae are widely distributed through all oceans. For most of the time they keep to the surface, more or less out at sea, according to species. They undertake long and frequent migrations. The sailfish (*Istiophorus platypterus*) favors coastal zones, sometimes venturing very close to shore, hunting for food at some depth. 1) Sailfish (*Istiophorus platypterus*).

MARLINS

While the Latin name for the blue marlin – *Makaira nigricans* – suggests it is black, its vernacular name assures this species of marlin is blue. However, the blue of the back is very dark, so that blue and black marlins tend to be confused. One distinguishing feature of the former is that the pectoral fins are normally folded along the body. The blue back and silver belly are clearly divided by a line that runs along the flanks. It may often bear vertical stripes that resemble those of the striped marlin, but they are far less conspicuous and vanish rapidly after death. The body, furthermore, is stocky, the forward lobe of the dorsal fin is more pointed, and this fin becomes markedly lower in its rear portion. The snout is elongated and fairly sharp.

This is a fish of the open seas that rarely approaches the coast and feeds freely on bonitos. It is the most tropical of all marlins, having a preference for very warm waters, causing it to cross the equator to take advantage of two summer seasons, in north and south. In addition to such journeys in quest of warmth, the blue marlin migrates to spawning grounds, which appear to be well defined.

The blue marlin may grow very large, its maximum length thought to be in the region of 18½ ft (5.5 m) for a weight of 1,550 lb (700 kg), though some authors say up to 2,000 lb (900 kg).

The black marlin (*Makaira indica*) can be immediately recognized by a very strange feature that seems to be exclusive: the pectoral fins are stiff and cannot be folded along the body. This is due to a form of ankylosis (abnormal immobility of the bones), for reasons not yet explained. It is one of the most bellicose of the Istiophoridae and often launches an attack. It tolerates water temperatures of between 59° and 86°F (15° and 30°C), inhabiting the warm and temperate zones of the Indian and Pacific Oceans, from Africa to America.

The fish often congregate in small groups and although they are sometimes to be found out at sea, they much prefer to stay close to shore, particularly north of Australia, in Southeast Asia, around the Arabian peninsula, and off the coasts of Peru and Chile.

The species may reach a length of 14½ ft (4.5 m) and a weight of up to 1,550 lb (700 kg). Males are smaller than females.

The blue marlin (*Makaira nigricans*) belongs to the family Istiophoridae. It is a particularly popular game fish. The marlin much resembles the swordfish in various ways. It differs, however, in the shape of its bill, which is circular, not compressed, and also by the presence of two ventral fins.

The white marlin (*Tetrapturus albidus*) has a very long, tapering body, markedly compressed laterally. It is found in the Mediterranean together with the Mediterranean spearfish (*T. belone*) but is easily distinguished from this latter species by several features. It feeds on cephalopods, but above all on various species of herring and may reach or even exceed 8 ft (2.5 m) for a weight of 155 lb (70 kg).

This is a pelagic fish, migrating from the tropical Atlantic, and very common in some areas, especially in the region of Cuba. It sometimes ventures into the Mediterranean.

Often confused with the preceding species, the Mediterranean spearfish (*Tetrapturus belone*) is also found, as its name indicates, in the Mediterranean. Like its relatives, it seeks out warm waters and is therefore found more frequently in the southwestern zones of the Mediterranean from Spain to Sicily and Crete, and along the shores of North Africa to Libya. It normally lives on its own and, being a rapid swimmer, feeds principally on skippers (*Scomberesox*) but also on sardines and marine crustaceans. The fish is occasionally caught in nets and may grow to about 6½ ft (2 m).

The color of the striped marlin (*Tetrapturus audax*), which bears a number of vernacular names, is an unambiguous distinguishing feature. It is gray–blue on the back, fairly dark but paler on the flanks, and silver–white on the belly, the two tones being clearly separated. There are 15 narrow, regularly spaced stripes marking the back and flanks vertically, but not extending to the belly region. These zones are a fairly light gray–blue and appear pale in contrast to the back but dark compared with the abdomen. The body is elongated and not very compressed. The front lobe of the dorsal fin is slightly higher than the body.

This fish is probably one of the fastest and most agile members of the family, with a speed calculated at more than 60 mph (100 kmh). It makes spectacular leaps out of the water and sometimes skims along the surface for hundreds of yards, supporting itself only by rapid flicks of the tail. It feeds on flying fish, bonitos, carangids, and skippers.

The striped marlin may attain a length of 13 ft (4 m) and a weight of 650 lb (300 kg). It is a species of the high seas and will not deliberately approach the coasts. It inhabits the Indian and Pacific Oceans, preferring fairly cool waters, from 68° to 77°F (20° to 25°C).

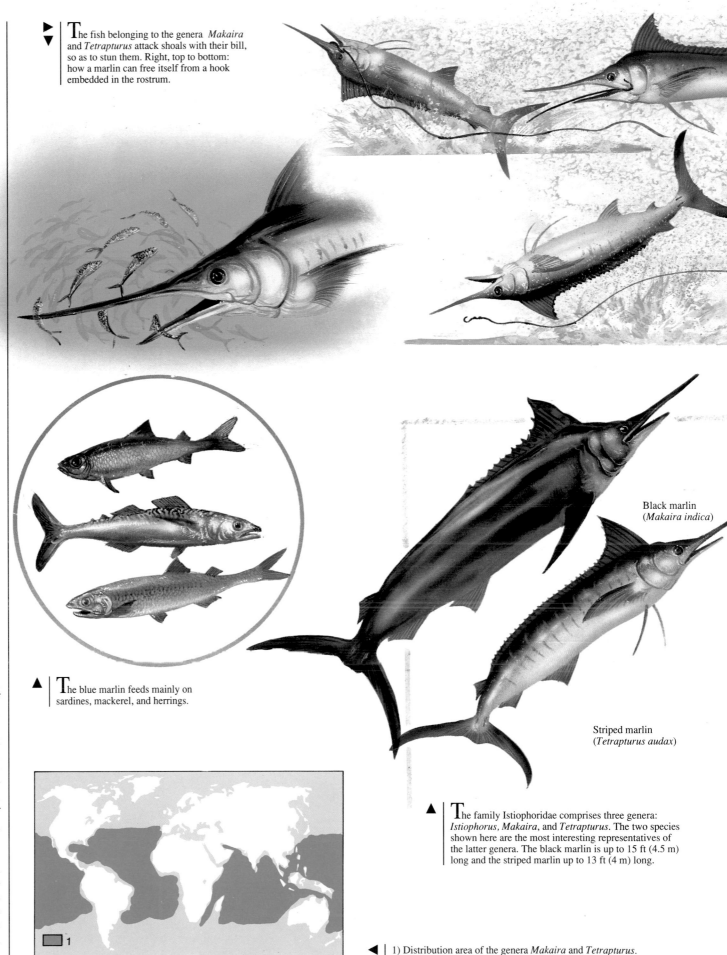

The fish belonging to the genera *Makaira* and *Tetrapturus* attack shoals with their bill, so as to stun them. Right, top to bottom: how a marlin can free itself from a hook embedded in the rostrum.

▲ The blue marlin feeds mainly on sardines, mackerel, and herrings.

Black marlin
(*Makaira indica*)

Striped marlin
(*Tetrapturus audax*)

▲ The family Istiophoridae comprises three genera: *Istiophorus*, *Makaira*, and *Tetrapturus*. The two species shown here are the most interesting representatives of the latter genera. The black marlin is up to 15 ft (4.5 m) long and the striped marlin up to 13 ft (4 m) long.

◄ 1) Distribution area of the genera *Makaira* and *Tetrapturus*.

193

FLATFISH
Pleuronectiformes

Among the bony fish, the Pleuronecti-formes, commonly known as flatfish, make up a very individual group. In fact, they are the only fish to be flattened on one side, the blind side, which is almost always colorless, and to have two eyes on the other side, usually pigmented. This somewhat peculiar arrangement cannot nevertheless be all that different from that of other fish because the larval structure is normal. The larvae, in fact, have one eye on either side and become asymmetrical only in the course of metamorphosis. In the last phase the animal shows all the characteristics of the adult and lives in the same way. The larva possesses an eye on either side and swims belly downwards. At the conclusion of the larval phase, during the post larval stage, metamorphosis commences; the main effect of this is the migration of the eye, which travels round from the side on which the fish is lying to the side turned toward the surface; this may be either the left or right side, depending on the family concerned. In the course of metamorphosis, the fish abandons the pelagic existence led during the larval stage, and becomes benthonic, living on the bottom.

The flatfish are divided into three major suborders: Psettodoidea, Pleuronectoidea, and Soleioidea. The Psettodoidea constitute the oldest of these groups. They differ from the other suborders by virtue of the dorsal fin. It starts from behind the eyes and its forward rays are spinous. There is one family, Psettodidae.

The Pleuronectoidea, like the Soleioidea, have no spinous rays on the fins and the dorsal fin originates above or in front of the eyes; they are distinguished from the latter suborder by the more or less pointed shape of the snout and by the fact that the preoperculum has a visible free edge, covered neither by skin nor scales. There are two or four families: Bothidae (sometimes subdivided into Citharidae, Bothidae, and Scophthalmidae), and Pleuronectidae.

The Soleioidea form a more specialized group. They are distinguished by the shape of the snout, more or less rounded, and by the fact that the preoperculum, completely covered by skin and sometimes by scales as well, has no free edge. There are two families:

The fish belonging to the order Pleuronectiformes, commonly called flatfish, are found in almost all the world's oceans. They are distinguished clearly from other fish by the shape of their body. They are, in fact, the only fish to be flattened on one side, the blind side, unpigmented, and to possess two eyes on the other side, the ocular side, which is pigmented. According to group, the eyes may be either on the right side (Pleuronectidae and Soleidae), or on the left side (Bothidae and Cynoglossidae), or indifferently on one or the other (Psettodidae). All these fish are carnivorous, feeding on, among other things, crayfish, squids, and marine invertebrates.

When hatched, the flatfish larva is identical in shape to the larvae of other fish and lives like them. In fact, it has an eye on both sides and swims belly downwards. Subsequently (as the drawings opposite, from top to bottom, show), it undergoes metamorphosis, the most spectacular phenomenon of which is the migration of one of the eyes to the opposite side, right or left depending on the family concerned. The flatfish, which until then has led a pelagic life, now descends to the bottom and lies on its blind side.

Soleidae and Cynoglossidae.

With regard to the world distribution of the Pleuronectiformes, they are found in all oceans, from the Arctic where the black halibut (*Reinhardtius hippoglossoides*) is found, to southern waters where *Mancopsetta maculata* is fished.

The ability to camouflage is the most notable feature of these fish. It may be found, in varying degree, among all the Pleuronectiformes. Many of them, like the turbot on its gravelly substratum, are so well concealed as they lie flat on a mottled surface that only a photograph can distinguish the animal's outline. Not only does it imitate the coloration of the sea bed, but it also faithfully reproduces the exact marks and patterns of the surrounding gravel. When a flatfish settles on a variegated bed, the sight of colors, spots, and patterns in the substratum simultaneously provokes nervous reactions and hormonal secretions that affect the concentration and dispersion of the various pigment granules.

Numerous experiments have been carried out with individuals of *Psetta maxima*, *Paralichthys*, and *Bothus podas* to clarify this mimetic capacity. The fish are placed on artificial surfaces colored black and white. Depending on the background color, the white patches on the body shrink or expand and come closer or farther apart. After half an hour the fish takes on the color of the background and is covered with white spots of a similar size, and even shape, to the artificial surface. By providing the fish with a different surface for each eye, an intermediate tonality can be obtained.

Although flatfish are able to change their color, each species has its own specific garb. Studies of a number of Pleuronectiformes have shown that the pigmentation in these fish is actually distributed in the same way. In certain other species, such as *Limanda limanda*, the pigmentation comes very close to this general pattern. Others, however, differ in varying measure by virtue of the presence or absence of certain markings, distinctive patterns, etc. It is also worth noting that not all flatfish have the same mimetic capacities. The plaice, for example, compensates for its imperfect camouflage by covering itself with a thin layer of sand, fanned over with the fins. Only the eyes peer out, attentive for a prey victim.

▲
▶ Flatfish generally live on shifting beds of sand or mud. They use their fins to cover themselves with sediment, from which only the head juts out (above). There they wait, motionless, until a prey (such as a fish, shown right) comes near. They then leap out and swallow it, immediately burying themselves once more in the sand or mud.

Imitative capacity of a flatfish.

Growth of a flatfish.

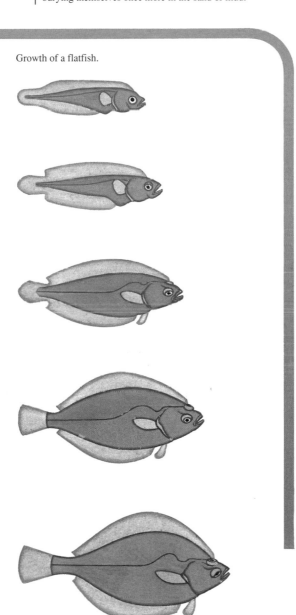

▲ The Pleuronectiformes almost all have remarkable capacities for mimicry. Indeed, the coloration of the ocular side perfectly imitates the substratum. When a flatfish lying on a sandy floor (top) leaves to settle on gravel (bottom), the light markings on the back get larger. Not only do these marks reproduce the size of the individual pieces of gravel or pebble seen by the fish, but also the shape. It has been verified, as a result of experiments carried out with certain species, that these fish, placed on artificial backgrounds colored black and white, are able to adopt similar colors and to cover themselves in white spots, the same size and shape as those chosen for the test, within about half an hour.

PLEURONECTIDAE

The fish of the family Pleuronectidae have their eyes on the right side, although there are a number of inverted individuals with eyes on the left side. The proportion of such inverted specimens varies considerably according to species and locality. The body is more or less oval and very flattened on one side. The asymmetrical mouth is furnished with small teeth that are hard to see. In the majority of species the teeth of the ocular side are far less developed than those on the blind side.

The family Pleuronectidae contains the largest flatfish. The Pacific halibut (*Hippoglossus stenolepis*) grows to a maximum length of 8¾ ft (2.6 m), although this measurement is that of a female, the male usually not exceeding 4½ ft (1.4 m). The Atlantic halibut (*Hippoglossus hippoglossus*) can be 10 ft (3 m) long and weigh 660 lb (300 kg). The other species, however, are much smaller. They are all found chiefly in the cold waters of the Atlantic and Pacific.

The plaice (*Pleuronectes platessa*) is a species of the northeastern Atlantic, easily recognizable by the presence of reddish spots on the body and 4 – 7 bony tubercles on the head, behind the eyes. It is a fish of average size, frequently exceeding 20 in (50 cm) in length but only exceptionally reaching 36 in (95 cm). It is mainly found on sandy beds, which it favors most, but not uncommonly in mud or gravel. Species of the continental shelf live from the shore to a depth of nearly 400 ft (120 m) but adults are chiefly abundant between 30 and 165 ft (10 and 50 m).

The plaice half buries itself in the sand to remain invisible because of its imperfect camouflage, leaving only its head exposed. Immobile, it watches for tiny invertebrates, which it captures with a sudden dart. Food consists of a wide variety of crustaceans, gasteropod mollusks (especially lamellibranch forms such as mussels, cockles, *Mactra, Ensis, Abra*, etc.), worms, echinoderms such as brittle stars, and small fish, including sand eels. The plaice is partial to the deep waters where such species are plentiful. It feeds more in winter than in summer and is active by day but not at night, exceptions being individuals living in the southern areas of the North Sea, which hunt brittle stars during the night.

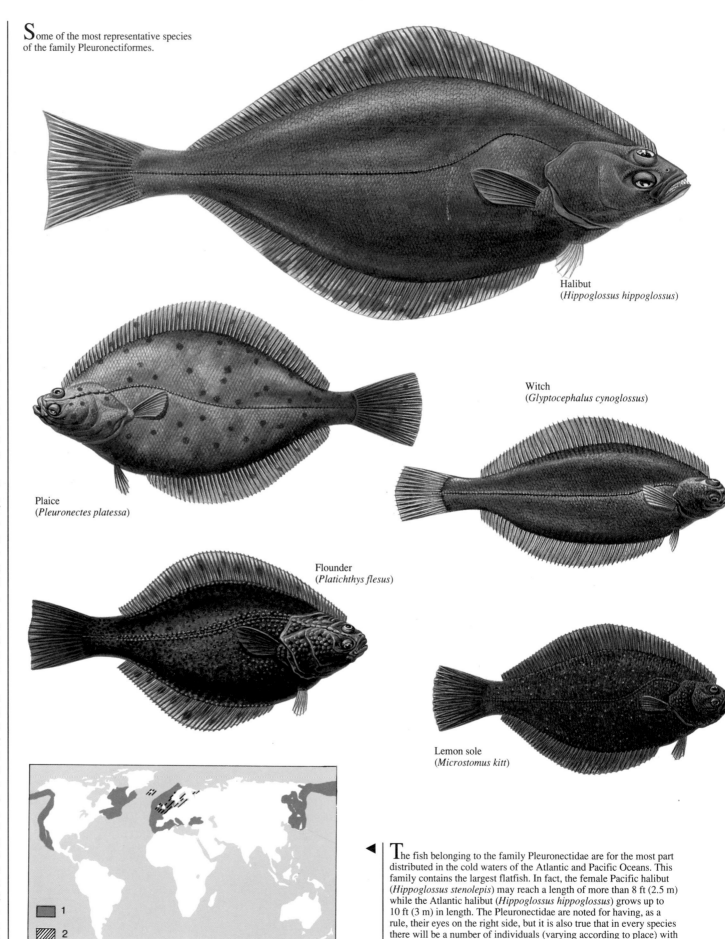

S ome of the most representative species of the family Pleuronectiformes.

Halibut
(*Hippoglossus hippoglossus*)

Witch
(*Glyptocephalus cynoglossus*)

Plaice
(*Pleuronectes platessa*)

Flounder
(*Platichthys flesus*)

Lemon sole
(*Microstomus kitt*)

◀ The fish belonging to the family Pleuronectidae are for the most part distributed in the cold waters of the Atlantic and Pacific Oceans. This family contains the largest flatfish. In fact, the female Pacific halibut (*Hippoglossus stenolepis*) may reach a length of more than 8 ft (2.5 m) while the Atlantic halibut (*Hippoglossus hippoglossus*) grows up to 10 ft (3 m) in length. The Pleuronectidae are noted for having, as a rule, their eyes on the right side, but it is also true that in every species there will be a number of individuals (varying according to place) with eyes on the left side. 1) Pleuronectidae; 2) Sole (*Limanda limanda*).

PSETTODIDAE

The Psettodidae differ from other Pleuronectiformes in a number of ways, such features being either primitive or associated with a less developed evolutionary phase. They are flat fish, more or less oval in shape, yet less flattened than the species belonging to the other flatfish families mentioned. One peculiarity of the family is that for every species the ocular side of the body may be either the left or the right.

There is still no firm explanation as to why the eyes are on the right side in the Pleuronectidae and Soleidae, on the left side in the Bothidae (generally) and Cynoglossidae, and randomly on the left or right in the Psettodidae. Some experts have put forward the theory that this may be due to the position of the swim bladder in the larvae: an interesting hypotheses, but negated by the fact that the Pleuronectidae do not have a swim bladder. It would appear that the choice of the ocular face must have a deeper cause, associated with the genetic inheritance of the larva. But in that case why are there individuals in each family whose eyes do not follow the family's normal eye position? It is clearly a complicated phenomenon, worthy of scientific investigation.

Psettodes species have a large mouth, the rear tip of which ends very far from the ventral eye. The jaws are equipped with strong teeth. The upper eye is to be found on the dorsal edge of the fish; this feature is peculiar to the Psettodidae, in whom eye migration is not, in fact, complete. Furthermore, as stated, the dorsal fin has its origin some way behind the upper eye. In other flatfish the fin originates above or in front of this eye. Finally, the front rays of the dorsal fin are spinous and the pelvic fins bear one spiny ray and five soft rays. The other Pleuronectiformes have no spinous rays.

This very individual small family comprises the single genus *Psettodes*. These fish live along the African coasts of the Atlantic and the Indian Oceans, the Asiatic coasts of the latter ocean, in Australia, and in the Pacific. Depending on species, they may grow to 20 – 24 in (50 – 60 cm) in length. They inhabit muddy or sandy beds, from the shore down to a depth of 330 ft (100 m).

Psettodes erumei

Psettodes

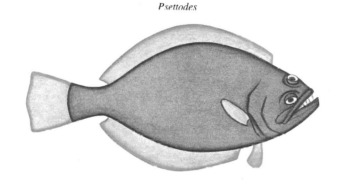

Sole
(*Limanda limanda*)

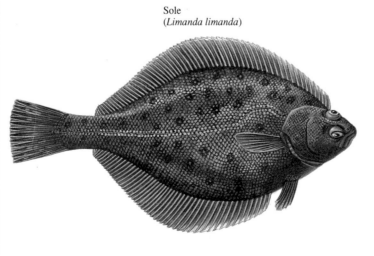

The Psettodidae are the most primitive Pleuronectiformes. They live along the coasts of warm regions in almost all oceans and exhibit a number of archaic features. This is the only family in which the eyes may appear either on the left or right side. They are also the only flatfish with spinous rays. Finally, their body is less flattened than is the case with other forms. The Psettodidae, therefore, possess characteristics of both the Perciformes and Pleuronectiformes. They are fish whose evolution seems to have begun long after that of other flatfish, assuming it was not arrested in midcourse. On the left is a sketch of *Psettodes* and a drawing of *Limanda limanda*, a member of the Pleuronectidae. The sketch does not show all the important features of the Psettodidae, such as the spinous rays, but accentuates some differences between the two types, such as the shape of the lateral line and of the caudal fin, the size of the mouth, etc. It is interesting to note that in the fish of the genus *Psettodes* the origin of the dorsal fin is a good distance behind the eyes whereas it is just behind in the sole, and sometimes above or in front in other Pleuronectiformes. The upper eye, situated on the top of the head, is sometimes halfway between the two sides (in the sole and in other flatfish it is located wholly on the side where the lower eye is situated). The large mouth, with its strong teeth, is symmetrical, because it becomes enlarged in keeping with both sides of the body, whereas in *Limanda limanda* and all other Pleuronectiformes it is asymmetrical.

TURBOT
Scophthalmus maximus

The turbot (*Scophthalmus maximus* or *Psetta maxima*) is a flatfish of the northeast Atlantic. It is a large flatfish, shaped like a rhomboid, easily recognized by the many bony turbercles on the ocular side. Greatly valued for the quality of its flesh, the turbot is a large species, usually measuring from 16 – 32 in (40 – 80 cm) and sometimes as much as 40 in (100 cm). Maximum length varies much according to region.

The turbot inhabits the European continental shelf from the coast to almost 260 ft (80 m) in depth. It is found especially on sandy beds or on harder substrata such as gravel, broken shells, pebbles, and stones. In such places the fish lies in ambush for prey. Very voracious, it feeds almost exclusively on other fish, including sand eels, sardines, sprats, cod, young whiting, gobies, dragonets, haddock, etc. Sometimes it also consumes small invertebrates such as crustaceans (crabs), lamellibranch mollusks, worms, etc.

The fish is sexually mature when between 12 and 18 in (30 and 45 cm), namely from three to five years. Spawning occurs in spring and summer, from April to August in the North Sea and Irish Sea, and from May to September on the Celtic shelf and the western English Channel; these variations are due to temperature fluctuations. The turbot spawns mainly on gravel beds between 32 and 160 ft (10 and 50 m).

Females are extremely fertile. Depending on size, each of them may lay from 5 million to 15 million eggs annually. Each egg is small, with a diameter of about 1 mm, pelagic, and floating near the surface. It hatches, depending on water temperature, from 7 – 9 days later. Larval life is of 4 – 6 months' duration and at this time the turbot feeds on copepods, euphausiaceans, the larvae of sea snails, etc. When the fish is 1⅛ – 1¼ in (13 – 16 mm) long it starts to show the first signs of metamorphosis, which terminates among individuals of 1 in (25 mm). The small turbot then sinks to the bottom in deeper coastal waters. It may also live in zones affected by the tides, following the sea's ebb and flow. The following fall the fish measures 3 – 4 in (8 – 10 cm) and will make for ever deeper waters to lead its life.

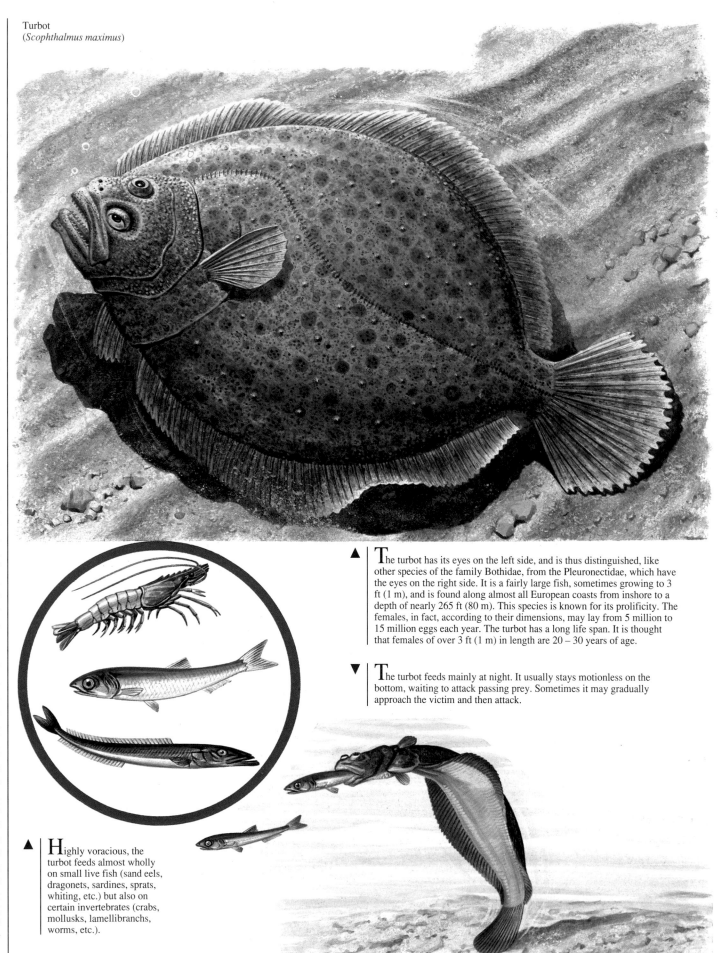

Turbot
(*Scophthalmus maximus*)

▲ The turbot has its eyes on the left side, and is thus distinguished, like other species of the family Bothidae, from the Pleuronectidae, which have the eyes on the right side. It is a fairly large fish, sometimes growing to 3 ft (1 m), and is found along almost all European coasts from inshore to a depth of nearly 265 ft (80 m). This species is known for its prolificity. The females, in fact, according to their dimensions, may lay from 5 million to 15 million eggs each year. The turbot has a long life span. It is thought that females of over 3 ft (1 m) in length are 20 – 30 years of age.

▼ The turbot feeds mainly at night. It usually stays motionless on the bottom, waiting to attack passing prey. Sometimes it may gradually approach the victim and then attack.

▲ Highly voracious, the turbot feeds almost wholly on small live fish (sand eels, dragonets, sardines, sprats, whiting, etc.) but also on certain invertebrates (crabs, mollusks, lamellibranchs, worms, etc.).

BOTHIDAE

The Bothidae in general terms, including the Citharidae and Scophthalmidae, are Pleuronectoidea. Their eyes are on the left side. The mouth is asymmetrical and protractile, capable of being projected forwards. The lower jaw, depending on species, juts out in varying measure. The jaws also carry teeth that sometimes look like canines. The dorsal fin is long, often having its origin in front of the dorsal eye, very rarely above it. The dorsal and anal fins are never joined at the tail.

In the Bothidae sexual dimorphism may occur. Thus in species of the genus *Bothus* males exhibit, in front of the ventral eye, a small spine, lacking in the female. Also the male's eyes are farther apart than those of the female. Finally, the pectoral fin of the ocular side is proportionally longer in the male.

The true Bothidae display a clearly visible lateral line, often only on the ocular side. This lateral line is sometimes subdivided behind the eyes. They are also distinguishable by their pelvic fins. The breadth of the fin on the blind side is less than that of the ocular side. Finally, the first ray of the pelvic fin of the ocular side is situated much farther forward than that of the other fin. They are, in general, small species, whose maximum dimensions range around 6 – 8 in (15 – 20 cm) in length. They inhabit all oceans.

A very common characteristic of the Bothidae is that the first rays of the dorsal fin are longer than the others, so much so that they sometimes form a small tuft, often bigger in males than in females. This can be seen in *Ancyclopsetta* species and in *Gastropsetta frontalis* of the western Atlantic, as well as in some species of *Arnoglossus* (*A. imperialis* and *A. thori*) from the eastern Atlantic.

The Citharidae have a clearly visible lateral line on both the blind and ocular sides. The bases of the pelvic fins are almost or wholly of the same breadth; but these bases are quite short, especially when compared with those of the Scophthalmidae, who also possess the first two characteristics mentioned for the Citharidae. The Scophthalmidae are larger fish. Some species, such as the megrim (*Lepidorhombus whiffiagonis*) may grow to 24 in (60 cm) in length.

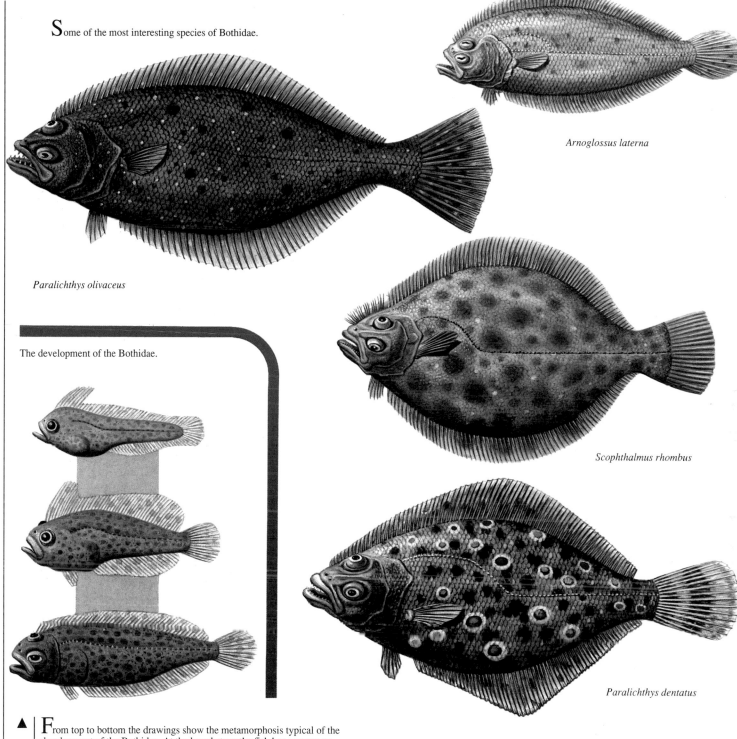

Some of the most interesting species of Bothidae.

Arnoglossus laterna

Paralichthys olivaceus

Scophthalmus rhombus

Paralichthys dentatus

The development of the Bothidae.

From top to bottom the drawings show the metamorphosis typical of the development of the Bothidae. At the larval stage the fish has one eye on either side, while at a certain length, 1 in (25 mm) in the case of the turbot, it has both eyes on the left side. It is interesting to note that in these species the first signs of metamorphosis begin to appear when the animal is 1⅛ – 1¼ in (13 –16 mm) long. Having grown, the small fish, which until then has led a pelagic existence, goes to the bottom and seeks out deeper coastal waters. It can also live in intertidal zones, following the sea's ebb and flow.

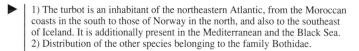

▶ 1) The turbot is an inhabitant of the northeastern Atlantic, from the Moroccan coasts in the south to those of Norway in the north, and also to the southeast of Iceland. It is additionally present in the Mediterranean and the Black Sea. 2) Distribution of the other species belonging to the family Bothidae.

SOLEIDAE

The Soleidae are flatfish that, except for inverted individuals, have their eyes on the right side. The body is therefore markedly flattened on the left side, being rounded or oval in shape and sometimes slightly elongated. The snout is more or less rounded. In some genera (*Heteromycteris, Synaptura*, etc.) the mouth has a hooked shape. The lips are fleshy and either smooth or fringed, depending on species. The teeth are small and hard to see, being larger on the blind side than on the ocular side.

In proportion to the body size, the eyes are small or very small. With respect to the fins, since the Soleidae lack spinous rays, all the rays are soft. The dorsal fin sometimes originates above the eyes but generally in front of them. In some genera, such as *Heteromycteris*, the dorsal starts almost at the level of the mouth, which opens ventrally. At the rear the dorsal and anal fins may either be separated from the caudal fin (*Pardachirus, Monochirus, Microchirus*, etc.) or connected to it by a thin membrane (*Solea, Dicologlossa, Bathysolea*, etc.) or almost completely linked to it (*Synaptura, Achiroides, Euryglossa*, etc.). The pectoral fins are sometimes absent (*Aseraggodes, Coryphillus, Pardachirus*, etc.). When present, the fins of the ocular side are always to some extent larger than those of the blind side. The pelvic fins are asymmetrical and may be free (*Zebrias, Aesopia, Solea*, etc.) or linked to the anal fin (*Phyllichthys, Heteromycteris*, etc.). The tail is more or less rounded but may sometimes be pointed. There is a single lateral line, more or less visible: it runs straight along the middle of the body, but on the head it may be ill defined, curved, wavy or bifurcate. The scales, with small spines at the rear (ctenoid), are rough.

The soles are small fish. The Dover sole (*Solea vulgris*) can measure 20 in (50 cm) and *Solea senegalensis* 24 in (60 cm). But certain species are barely 4 in (10 cm) long (*Heteromycteris proboscideus, Solea ovata, Microchirus boscanion*, etc.). The Soleidae are found in virtually all waters, warm or cold, of the oceans, except for the Arctic. They inhabit river waters (*Soleonasus finis*), the brackish waters of estuaries (*Heteromycteris*), and sea zones from the coast to the ridges of the continental

Dover sole
(*Solea vulgaris*)

The soles (Soleidae) are the most highly evolved of the flatfish. In fact they have acquired the shape that best suits their environment and way of life. The different stages of the evolution of Pleuronectiformes is shown on the opposite page. In the Psettodidae the head and tail can easily be identified. In the Bothidae the dorsal fin covers part of the head region and the caudal peduncle can still be distinguished. In the Soleidae the body is almost completely surrounded by fins. The soles, with eyes on the right side, still possess an identifiable caudal fin. This is not the case with the Cynoglossidae, in which the tail is linked to the dorsal and anal fins. The soles feed chiefly on crustaceans (amphipods, small crabs, etc.) but also include certain small fish, like gobies, in their diet. The Soleidae are found in almost all seas, warm or cold, except the Arctic zones. Most species live on the muddy or sandy beds of coastal waters. They are, as a rule, small fish. The Dover sole (*Solea vulgaris*) may grow to 20 in (50 cm).

shelf. Most species live on the muddy or sandy beds of coastal waters. Some, like *Bathysolea*, inhabit the shelf from 650 ft (200 m) to over 3,300 ft (1,000 m) down.

Because the Pleuronectiformes have adapted to a form of life on the water bottom, these fish exhibit little variety from the ecological point of view. Certain species, such as the plaice, show a preference for beds of mud or of mud and sand. Others, like *Arnoglossus laterna*, frequent a more sandy substratum. The turbot (*Psetta maxima*) is partial to sand but does not refuse a harder substratum composed of gravel or stones. One exception to this rule is the topknot (*Zeugopterus punctatus*), a small coastal species from the northeast Atlantic, from Norway to the Bay of Biscay. This fish is caught, though rarely, off the French Atlantic coasts. Underwater swimmers have seen this fish, well camouflaged with the substratum, clinging to rock walls or *Laminaria* algae.

It is interesting to note that the halibut, regarded as a benthonic species, is actually a long distance traveler that will swim far from the bottom when out at sea.

With the exception of a few individuals that can live in fresh water, like *Soleonasus* in certain American rivers, or in brackish waters, the Pleuronectiformes are essentially marine species. Most of them live in deep coastal waters. Others are found at various levels of the continental shelf. There are some deep sea species living at more than 650 ft (200 m) down. The last include Bothidae such as *Poecilopsetta*, Soleidae such as *Bathysolea*, and Cynoglossidae such as certain species of *Symphurus*. Some species also have a broad range of ocean depths. The halibut, for example, may be fished from the coast to a depth of almost 6,500 ft (2,000 m).

It has long been debated whether the Pleuronectiformes are a homogeneous or heterogeneous order. Some authors believe the Psettodoidea, Pleuronectoidea, and Soleioidea all had different origins and through adaptation to a similar life style came to have the same form. However, most specialists now believe that the flatfish had the same origin, but that the evolutionary process of each either began at different times or began simultaneously and then varied in rapidity and extent according to species. In this way there are the more primitive species of the Psettodidae, the intermediate forms of the Pleuronectidae, and the most evolved forms of the Soleidae.

► Illustrated here are some of the more representative species of the various families contained in the order Pleuronectiformes. 1) *Psettodes erumei* (Psettodidae); 2) *Arnoglossus ruepelli* (Psettodidae); 3) *Pseudorhombus cinnamoneus* (Bothidae); 4) *Platichthys stellatus* (Pleuronectidae); 5) *Heteromycteris japonicus* (Soleidae); 6) *Rhinoplagusia japonica* (Cynoglossidae).

▲ By day the sole usually stays motionless, buried in the sediment with which it covers the body using its fins. At dusk it ventures out hunting. It moves along either by swimming or by sliding; in the latter case it skims the surface of the sea bed with its fins. So strong is its adhesive capacity that it has difficulty in detaching itself from the bottom.

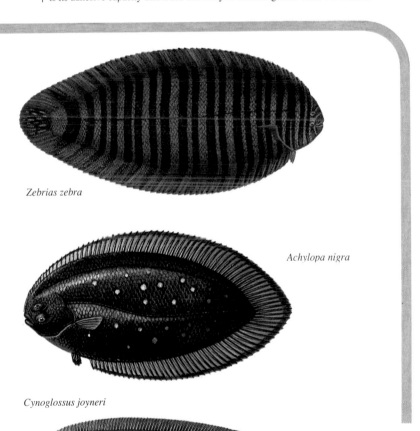

Zebrias zebra

Achylopa nigra

Cynoglossus joyneri

◄ The fish belonging to the family Soleidae are notable for the fact that, with the exception of inverted individuals, their eyes are on the right side. The body is strongly flattened on the left side, being rounded or oval, and only rarely somewhat elongated. In proportion to the size of the body, the eyes are small or even tiny.

TRIGGERFISH
Balistidae

In the fascinating fish of the family Balistidae the body is oval or oblong, covered with thick scales roughened by spines or small tubercles. The conical, incisor-like teeth are few in number and arranged in one or two rows on the jaws. The head has a characteristic appearance because of the position of the eyes, these being situated high and well removed from the small mouth. The first dorsal fin bears two or three strong spiniform rays.

The many species of Balistidae are collectively known as triggerfish. This strange name is derived from the singular functioning of the spiniform dorsal rays. The first of these can take on an erect position thanks to a mechanism at the base of the second ray; only when this mechanism is released, by being lowered behind the second ray, can the first regain its mobility or again be bent. In fact, the fish, by straightening the forward dorsal fin, manages to anchor itself firmly in crevices of rock or coral, from which it is not easily removed.

Many species of triggerfish are adorned with brilliant colors and patterns which are an aid to identification. All are marine and littoral, with various ecological characteristics. Some prefer open waters, others stay close to rocks or are associated with coral reefs. As a rule they are solitary fish, swimming slowly by flapping the second dorsal and the anal fin, but lashing the tail from side to side if speed is required. The diet is carnivorous or herbivorous. Some tropical species, like the large *Pseudobalistes flavimarginatus* – common in the Red Sea and many other Indo-Pacific regions – also consume long-spined sea urchins (*Diadema* sp.). They turn the animals over and break the abdominal shell with their strong jaws and teeth, then swallow the contents. The fish also have the remarkable ability to make sounds by contracting their swim bladder; these are audible murmurs when they are removed from the water. Equally fascinating is their habit of rolling the eyes, each independently of the other, like chameleons.

The Balistidae are usually regarded as having little commercial importance; indeed, the flesh is considered poisonous. Yet certain species are eaten and much valued as food.

▲ The family Balistidae, or triggerfish, prototype of the Balistoidea, belongs to the order Tetraodontiformes. The triggerfish has an oval, oblong body, covered with thick scales. The shape of the head is unusual, due to the position of the eyes, situated very high and well separated from the mouth. *Balistoides conspicillum*, shown here, is one of the most easily recognized members of the family, and also one of the most handsome. For this reason it changes hands in the trade at high prices, although it has difficulty in adapting to life in captivity. Its maximum length is 20 in (50 cm).

◄ *Balistoides conspicillum* is found in the Indian and Pacific Oceans. It lives close to the barrier reefs and feeds on various invertebrates, caught on the ocean bed. It is a solitary species and, like other members of the Balistidae, tends to be sedentary. With respect to food, it is interesting to note that this fish nibbles, with its powerful jaws, both coral and calcareous algae, digesting the organic part.

One of the most easily recognized triggerfish is *Balistoides conspicillum*, measuring about 20 in (50 cm) at most. It has the typical triggerfish shape and is covered with thick, rough scales similar to plates. In front of the eye is a groove, while other small bony plates are to be found behind the gill openings. Along the caudal peduncle are two and a half rows of tubercles that reinforce the animal's natural protection. The first dorsal fin consists of three spiniform rays, the third of which is not rudimentary, as in other triggerfish. The second dorsal and anal fin are not raised at the front; the tail has a straight edge. Some of these characteristics are also found in other members of the family, but the same is not true of the coloration, which is highly specific and makes this fish unmistakable. It is because of its multi-colored livery, with its unique pattern, that some have described the species as the most beautiful fish in the world, and for that reason it has often been illustrated.

B. conspicillum possesses a very particular coloration pattern that appears to separate out the various parts of the body. It is an inhabitant of coral reefs, and spends its life in close association with coral. It lives secluded and, like other triggerfish, has markedly sedentary habits. If frightened, it often squeezes into a hole from which it cannot easily be removed, so firmly does it attach itself with the mechanism of the dorsal fin already described.

This fish is essentially zoophagous, feeding on sponges, hydroids, bryozoans, and other invertebrates. It also uses its strong jaws to nibble at coral and to chew calcareous algae, consuming the organic parts and expelling the mineral contents which are deposited on the bottom, there to mingle with the fine white powder that for the same reason is ejected from the anal opening of parrotfish. The Balistidae are therefore devourers of coral who are not content to take only polyps, as other fish do, but also swallow pieces of the polypary, or supporting structure.

The area of distribution is vast, embracing a large part of the Indian Ocean and warm zones of the Pacific; from the coasts of South Africa (Natal) it extends to Japan and the Fiji Islands (Polynesia).

The fish belonging to the order Tetraodontiformes and the family Balistidae are well represented in the coastal zones of all warm seas; since they are essentially occupants of various coastal

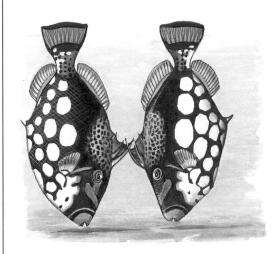

▲ | While searching for food, *Balistoides conspicillum* often assumes a vertical position.

S tructure and function of the forward dorsal fin.

I n the Balistidae, the forward dorsal fin consists of three spiniform rays. They are erectile, as the sequence of pictures shows, enabling the fish to anchor themselves in rock clefts.

▲ | If frightened, *Balistoides conspicillum* frequently hides inside a cavity, from which it is extracted only with difficulty because it attaches itself to the walls by means of its dorsal fin.

▲ | Along with other species, these fish swim close to the bottom. They move slowly, undulating the second dorsal and anal fin. If they want to go faster, they flick their tail sideways.

▲ | *Balistoides conspicillum* rests by lying down on the bottom in the spaces between clumps of coral. The coloration of the species breaks up the continuity of the various parts of the body.

zones, they are fairly well known to fishermen. Certain tropical species are also conspicuous by their vivid coloration.

Balistes carolinensis (or *B. capriscus*) is the only triggerfish in the Mediterranean and has a number of local nicknames, such as pigfish. It is found throughout the Mediterranean and also in the Adriatic and Black Sea. It has a broad distribution in the Atlantic, both along the east and west coasts. It is much rarer in northern sectors, while frequent in warmer zones, both in the Mediterranean and Atlantic. It lives mainly on rocky beds, at depths of 33 ft (10 m) to 330 ft (100 m), feeding on mollusks and crustaceans; hard-bodied prey of this nature is easily crushed with the powerful jaws

Another species, easily recognizable by its coloration, is *Balistes vetula*. In adult individuals the second dorsal fin is very high in front, so as to form a distinct lobe. It reaches lengths of up to 20 in (50 cm). *B. vetula* inhabits the tropical Atlantic both in American and African waters and it is also known in other oceans. It is a species very common in Indo-Pacific seas, from the Red Sea to Japan, Hawaii, and Polynesia. It is an inhabitant of the coral reef and consumes various types of invertebrates.

Rhinecanthus aculeatus is one of the most beautiful tirggerfish; it has a long snout and brilliant colors. The caudal spines are black and contrast with the pale ground. This fish, too, has a wide distribution in the Indian and Pacific Oceans.

The species of the genus *Melichthys*, including the black triggerfish (*M. vidua*), have no spines on the caudal peduncle. There is nothing particular about its coloration, the entire body being black or dark brown with white unpaired fins. The second dorsal and the anal have a black border. The area of distribution includes the Indian Ocean and a large part of the Pacific Ocean. Much more widespread, and thus circumtropical, is the related *M. niger*, which is uniformly dark blue–green with numerous longitudinal black lines. The unpaired fins are also dark, but there is a characteristic white line at the base of the second dorsal and anal fins. Unlike the other species, the tail has somewhat elongated upper and lower rays forming little pointed lobes.

Some species of Balistidae.

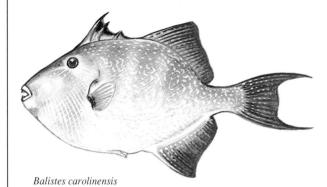

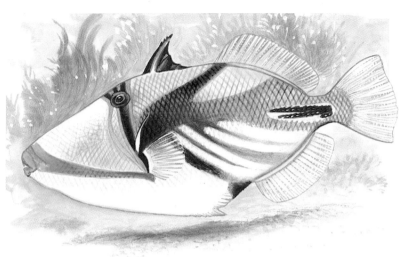

Balistes carolinensis

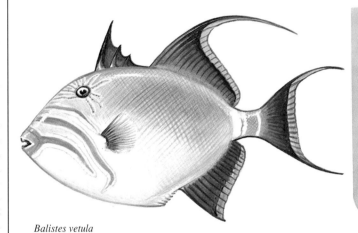

Balistes vetula

The various species of triggerfish can be recognized by the shape of their caudal fin but mainly by their distinctive coloration, often very brilliant and with striking patterns. One such easily indentifiable species is *Rhinecanthus aculeatus*, among the most beautiful members of the family Balistidae. This species, illustrated above, is widely distributed in the Indian and Pacific Oceans. In the Maldive Islands it has been sighted swimming on sandy bottoms in pairs. A characteristic feature of the genus *Rhinecanthus* is that, as in the genus *Balistapus*, the caudal peduncle is furnished on either side with short, horizontally arranged spines. In the species illustrated here they are black, standing out from the light background.

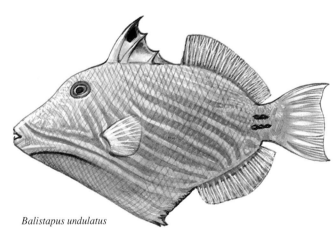

Balistapus undulatus

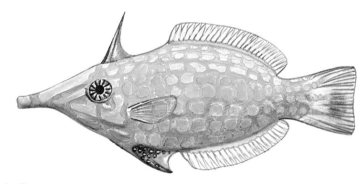

▲ *Oxymonacanthus longirostris* belongs to the family Monacanthidae, the so-called filefish, at one time classified together with the triggerfish. They do have some features in common, but there are enough distinctions to warrant their being allotted a family to themselves.

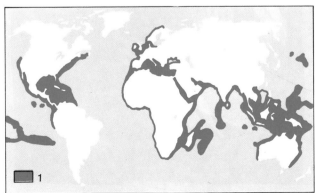

◄ 1) The suborder Balistoidea (with a wide global distribution, as shown in the adjoining map) comprises three families: Balistidae, Monacanthidae, and Ostraciontidae. The family Balistidae contains some 30 marine species from tropical and temperate waters. One of these, *Balistes carolinensis*, is also found in the Mediterranean. The Monacanthidae, mainly inhabiting tropical and subtropical seas, are likewise found in the Mediterranean, notably in the east, where the representative species is *Stephanolepis diaspros*. The family Ostraciontidae consists mainly of tropical species from the Atlantic, Indian, and Pacific Oceans.

PORCUPINE FISH
Diodontidae

As may be deduced from the name Diodontidae, the members of this family have a single dentary plate in either jaw, this beak consisting of only two pieces (hence "two teeth"). These plates are white and smooth and as broad as the mouth. The vernacular name porcupine fish is fully justified. An essential feature of the Diodontidae is the formidable armor plating which consists of strong, sharp, conical spines, distributed all over the body, except around the mouth and on the caudal peduncle.

The porcupine fish make up a small group of a few species, all living along the coasts of tropical seas. They feed mainly on hard-bodied invertebrates such as crustaceans or those furnished with shells, which they break easily with their powerful jaws. They are quite abundant among coral or on sandy bottoms; in their juvenile phase they lead a pelagic life. They are sedentary and swim slowly with flappings of the pectoral fins. When disturbed, they show a surprising habit of swelling up so as to become spherical, a complete change from their normal tapering shape. They share this behavior with the pufferfish of the family Tetraodontidae.

The ability to puff up depends on the presence of a large sac, which is an expansion of the ventral part of the stomach; it can be freely filled with water, which is kept in by the closure of powerful sphincters situated between the esophagus and stomach and between the stomach and intestine.

If the fish is removed from the water, it swells up with air and, when replaced in the water, floats there, belly upward, while the gastric diverticulum is emptied as the sphincters relax. The singular behavior of the porcupine fish is interpreted as a means of defense, which is surely correct inasmuch as the spines can be straightened much more when the fish is spherical than when it is normally shaped.

Porcupine fish are not used as food as their flesh is poisonous. However, they do have one particular use, and that is as tourist souvenirs: many specimens are swollen and dried and put on sale as marine curiosities. Large specimens may be turned into lamps by having bulbs pushed inside – a very odd form of illumination.

Diodon holacanthus

▲ ▲
▲ ▼
Like the Balistidae, the Diodontidae, or porcupine fish, belong to the Tetraodontiformes. Ancient naturalists were already aware of the strong mouth plates that replaced the teeth, one upper and one lower, hence the name *Diodon*. The skin is never covered with scales or bony plates, but usually bears sparse, isolated spines, either very small or quite big. The species illustrated, *Diodon holacanthus*, lives in varied habitats and is found in all tropical seas. It can reach a length of 16 in (40 cm). Like all members of the family, *D. holacanthus* is sedentary and swims slowly, flapping its pectoral fins. If disturbed, porcupine fish exhibit one of their oddest peculiarities: they swell up (like the individual illustrated on the left) until almost spherical. This attitude is understood to be a method of defense; in fact, the spines stick straight out when the fish assumes its circular form.

Diodon hystrix

▲
Diodon is the most representative genus of the family, containing the largest and most conspicuous species. The best known is undoubtedly *D. hystrix*, yellowish brown with many black spots. The head is large and armed with spines, like the rest of the body. Its maximum length is 36 in (90 cm). The fish is circumtropical.

BOXFISH
Ostraciontidae

The family Ostraciontidae is made up of some very curious fish. They appear to be encased in a rigid, solid wrapping, which explains why they are commonly known as boxfish or trunkfish. Their size is very small, not more than 20 in (50 cm) and usually much less.

The carapace or shell is made up of numerous polygonal plates, firmly welded together to form a mosaic. The colors are often very vivid. The carapace is polyhedral, usually triangular or quadrangular in section. The ventral side of the fish is usually flat. The forward outline of the head is oblique or almost vertical.

With regard to anatomy, there are two features associated with the rigidity of the body: the absence of axial muscles, and the presence of 14 – 16 almost wholly immobile vertebrae, forming a stiff shaft. There is also a special type of locomotion: since it has no flexibility, the fish moves by flapping the dorsal and anal fins; the swimming rhythm is slow, but can be speeded up with the aid of the tail, functioning also as a rudder.

A noteworthy characteristic is the fish's toxicity. They produce and spread through the water a poisonous substance secreted by cutaneous glands, especially those around the mouth. The action appears to be quite powerful, given that other fish placed in the same tank die, and that even when the boxfish are removed it remains effective. Yet it is strange that the boxfish can be sensitive to the poison too, and that the poison does not always protect them from predators: it has been demonstrated that sharks eat them without coming to harm.

The most widespread species is *Ostracion tuberculatus*. This fish measures up to about 12 in (30 cm) or a little more and is brown. Each plate of the carapace has a blue or white eye spot, surrounded by black spots or by a continous black ring. Young fish are almost cubical and have a very different coloration – bright yellow with scattered, irregular, round black marks. They look like living dice and make a handsome sight swimming round aquarium tanks or in rock pools among the seaweed. They also often settle in coral reefs. The species is common in the Red Sea, extending its range across the entire Indian Ocean to Hawaii and eastern Polynesia.

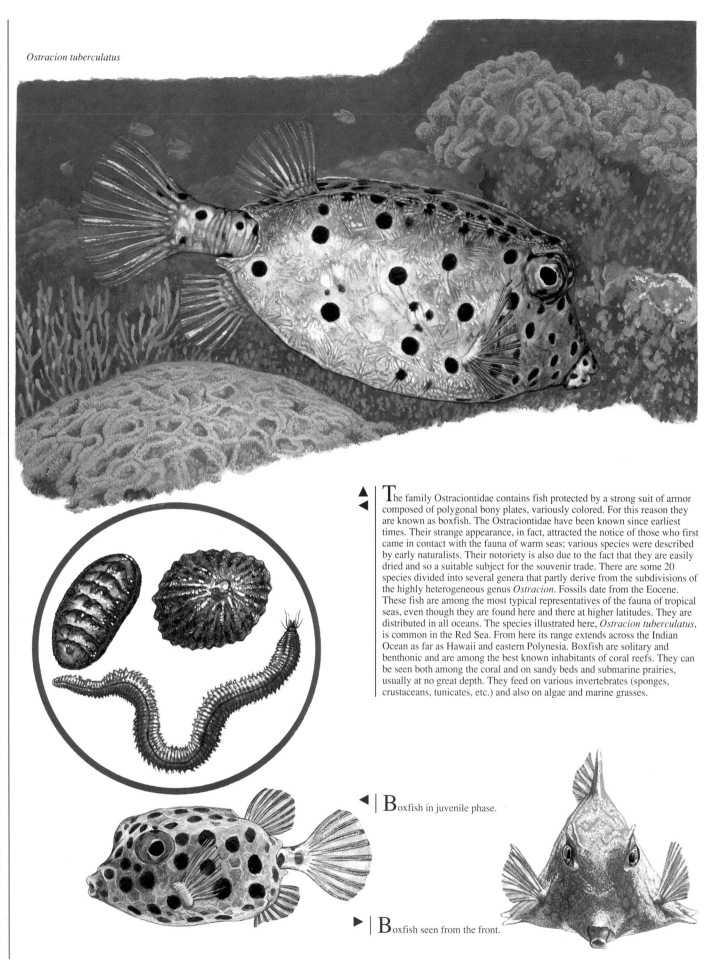

Ostracion tuberculatus

The family Ostraciontidae contains fish protected by a strong suit of armor composed of polygonal bony plates, variously colored. For this reason they are known as boxfish. The Ostraciontidae have been known since earliest times. Their strange appearance, in fact, attracted the notice of those who first came in contact with the fauna of warm seas; various species were described by early naturalists. Their notoriety is also due to the fact that they are easily dried and so a suitable subject for the souvenir trade. There are some 20 species divided into several genera that partly derive from the subdivisions of the highly heterogeneous genus *Ostracion*. Fossils date from the Eocene. These fish are among the most typical representatives of the fauna of tropical seas, even though they are found here and there at higher latitudes. They are distributed in all oceans. The species illustrated here, *Ostracion tuberculatus*, is common in the Red Sea. From here its range extends across the Indian Ocean as far as Hawaii and eastern Polynesia. Boxfish are solitary and benthonic and are among the best known inhabitants of coral reefs. They can be seen both among the coral and on sandy beds and submarine prairies, usually at no great depth. They feed on various invertebrates (sponges, crustaceans, tunicates, etc.) and also on algae and marine grasses.

◀ Boxfish in juvenile phase.

▶ Boxfish seen from the front.

The related *O. meleagris* is smaller, easily recognized by the numerous white spots that stand out from a dark brown background. It has virtually the same distribution, but is not found in the Red Sea. Here it is replaced by the endemic *O. cyanurus*, greenish on the back, with the rest of the body blue with many black spots. This latter fish exhibits marked sexual dimorphism.

The boxfish of the genus *Lactoria*, likewise quadrangular in section, also hail from the Indo-Pacific. They differ from *Ostracion* in having two frontal spines and two pelvic spines. These "horns" are especially long in *L. cornuta*, so much so that the species is sometimes known as the cowfish. These long and sharp projections give the fish a very characteristic appearance, and they extend horizontally forwards. The fish measures about 20 in (50 cm) in length, including the tail fin, which may be as big as the rest of the body. This strange fish lives along the coasts of East Africa and as far as the Pacific (Philippines, Japan, Australia, and Polynesia); it may also live in the Red Sea but is certainly rare. The appearance alters in the course of development; up to around ¾ in (20 mm) in length there are no spines and the tail is shorter than in the adults.

As for the boxfish of the Atlantic Ocean, the most important is *Acanthostracion quadricornis*, furnished with frontal and ventral spines. The body is triangular in section and markedly flattened, particularly the ventral side. The frontal horns are developed in individuals measuring 3 – 3½ in (8 – 9 cm), first appearing as stumps. The adult length may be over 16 in (40 cm). As a rule there are numerous blue or black spots and streaks scattered over a pale brown, greenish or gray background. This is the most common boxfish of the western Atlantic, found from Brazil as far as Massachusetts and Bermuda. It would seem that its range extends to southern Uruguay.

The boxfish of the genus *Lactophrys* are also triangular, but less compressed and without frontal spines; the shape of the back is markedly curved. There are three species, none of them present in the eastern Atlantic. *L. triqueter* and *L. trigonus*, both found off New England (Massachusetts) and south to Brazil, are naturally common only in warm waters, where they may be seen swimming slowly in the shallows among the seaweed. They are picturesque inhabitants of West Indian waters.

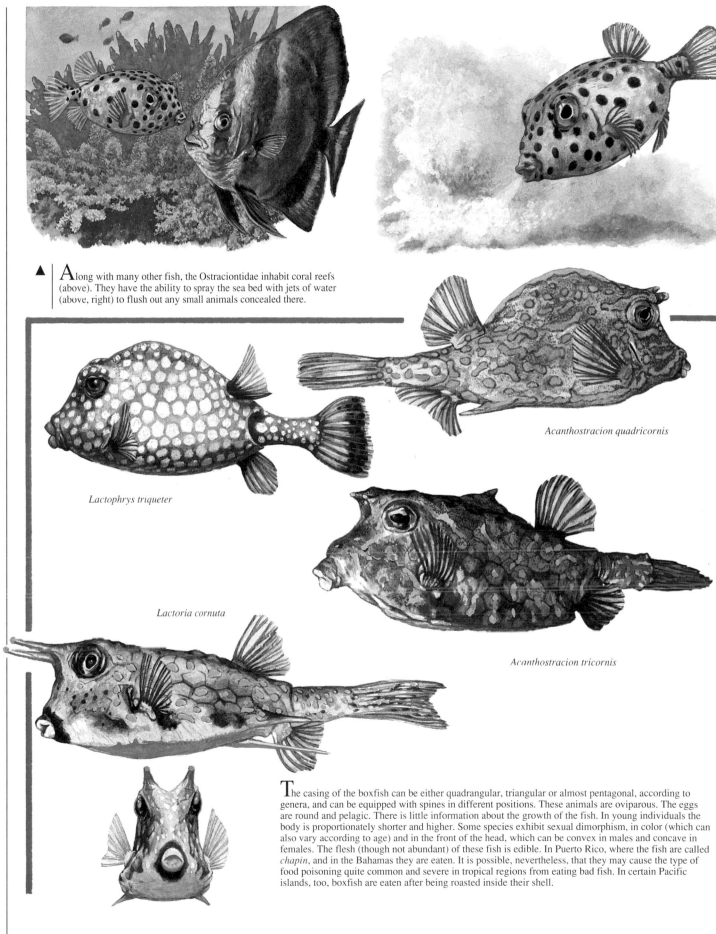

▲ Along with many other fish, the Ostraciontidae inhabit coral reefs (above). They have the ability to spray the sea bed with jets of water (above, right) to flush out any small animals concealed there.

Lactophrys triqueter

Acanthostracion quadricornis

Lactoria cornuta

Acanthostracion tricornis

The casing of the boxfish can be either quadrangular, triangular or almost pentagonal, according to genera, and can be equipped with spines in different positions. These animals are oviparous. The eggs are round and pelagic. There is little information about the growth of the fish. In young individuals the body is proportionately shorter and higher. Some species exhibit sexual dimorphism, in color (which can also vary according to age) and in the front of the head, which can be convex in males and concave in females. The flesh (though not abundant) of these fish is edible. In Puerto Rico, where the fish are called *chapin*, and in the Bahamas they are eaten. It is possible, nevertheless, that they may cause the type of food poisoning quite common and severe in tropical regions from eating bad fish. In certain Pacific islands, too, boxfish are eaten after being roasted inside their shell.

FILEFISH
Monacanthidae

The body of the Monacanthidae is very compressed and generally short and high. The snout is prominent and at the tip is a small mouth equipped with teeth fairly like incisors and arranged in small numbers in either jaw. Because of its peculiar covering, the skin has a unique appearance. It is thickly covered with small bony plates that bear spines arranged in various ways; sometimes one or more spines simply protrude from the plate, but at other times there is a projection, at the tip of which is a group of smaller spines in varying shapes and numbers. This type of skin covering makes for a velvety appearance or, when plates and spines are bigger, a much rougher aspect; this explains the name "filefish," the closest comparison being to sandpaper.

The fins, too, are noteworthy. There are two dorsal fins, the first consisting basically of a fairly long, erect spine, situated well forward, usually almost above the eyes; this spine is in many cases toothed, at least on its rear edge. The second spine is very short and thin, not easily detected, and this explains the name *Monacanthus*, "with a single spine." This second dorsal fin is placed further back, similar and opposed to the anal fin: both are formed of unbranched rays.

The Monacanthidae are of no practical interest. Some species are, however, kept in aquariums, where they are admired for their strange appearance and the ease with which they change color; such variations are common, even frequent, in these species that, like many other fish, react in relation to particular emotional states or surrounding conditions. Some species are markedly mimetic.

The genus *Monacanthus* has given its name to the whole family. One of the oldest known species is *M. ciliatus*. It is common in the warmer zones of the western Atlantic, for example in the Caribbean and near the Brazilian coasts; occasionally it may range northward to Newfoundland and south to Argentina. Like other filefish (and also species of other families), its teeth serve as sound organs: the noise is produced as the edges of the lower teeth rub against the inner sides of the upper teeth, which have parallel ridges.

Stephanolepis cirrhifer

Monacanthus ciliatus

Chaetoderma spinosissimum

The family Monacanthidae, part of the order Tetraodontiformes, comprises numerous species, somewhat different in size, color, and certain morphological features. These so-called filefish are all marine and live along coasts, particularly of tropical regions. They swim slowly, alone or in small groups, and have the curious habit of often hovering immobile, head downwards. Their diet is varied: indeed they are virtually omnivorous, because they feed on algae and on invertebrates such as sponges, hydroids, small crustaceans, etc. Like all Tetraodontiformes, the representatives of this family are oviparous. In the spawning season males show notable aggressiveness: they place themselves head to head, expanding their ventral skin flap to its maximum extent. When fully grown, many have a long, filamentous second ray to the rear dorsal fin; furthermore, there is a group of long, silky spinules on the caudal portion of each flank. It is not at all clear whether sexual dimorphism is a constant phenomenon and what are the eventual variations. The three species illustrated here are undoubtedly among the most typical. *Monacanthus ciliatus* may grow to 8 in (20 cm) and is common in the warmer zones of the western Atlantic. *Chaetoderma spinosissimum* measures at most 7 in (18 cm) and is easily recognized by the numerous appendages of skin that give it a very odd appearance and help to camouflage the fish on the sea bed. *Stephanolepis cirrhifer* grows to 10 in (25 cm) and has a very flattened body, high, and covered with very small scales, which make the surface rough and rasping.

PUFFERFISH
Tetraodontidae

The Tetraodontidae, or pufferfish, constitute one of the biggest families of their order. Apart from their strange beak, they are also clearly distinguished by other special structures. The body is generally short and rounded. The skin is naked or strewn with tiny spines over a variable surface; exceptionally there may be a few small bony plates. There is either one lateral line (as is common with other fish) or there may be two on either side.

As for anatomical features, it is worth mentioning the presence of only three gill arches, of some 20 vertebrae, of a swim bladder, and of a large diverticulum in which the ventral part of the stomach expands. Because this sac may occasionally be filled with water or air, the animal can inflate itself enormously.

This swelling capacity is evident from birth and has been interpreted as a means of defense. Something similar happens in other lower vertebrates, such as various reptiles (chameleon) and amphibians, as well as other fish, including the small shark *Cephaloscyllium*. In the pufferfish, digestion takes place mainly in the intestine, whether or not the body is distended.

The ability to swell up is related to a particular activity of the digestive apparatus. In the case of the Diodontidae, it is even more specialized. Attached to the ventral side of the stomach is a large, separate sac, with thinner walls than those of the stomach proper; once it was thought, wrongly, that this sac hung from the esophagus. The lower part of the sac is linked to the ventral wall of the body by strips of connective tissue. The abdominal muscles are more or less reduced. There is a sphincter situated in the passage between the esophagus and stomach, and another between the stomach and intestine.

To swell itself up, the fish swallows water, aided by the contractions of certain abdominal muscles; in this way the sac fills up entirely, while the passage from the stomach to the intestine, thanks to the sphincter, remains closed. The weight of water swallowed is considerable, varying from twice to four times the weight of the animal. The fish thus increases its volume enormously and, with it, changes its appearance. The inflation of the body is made possible

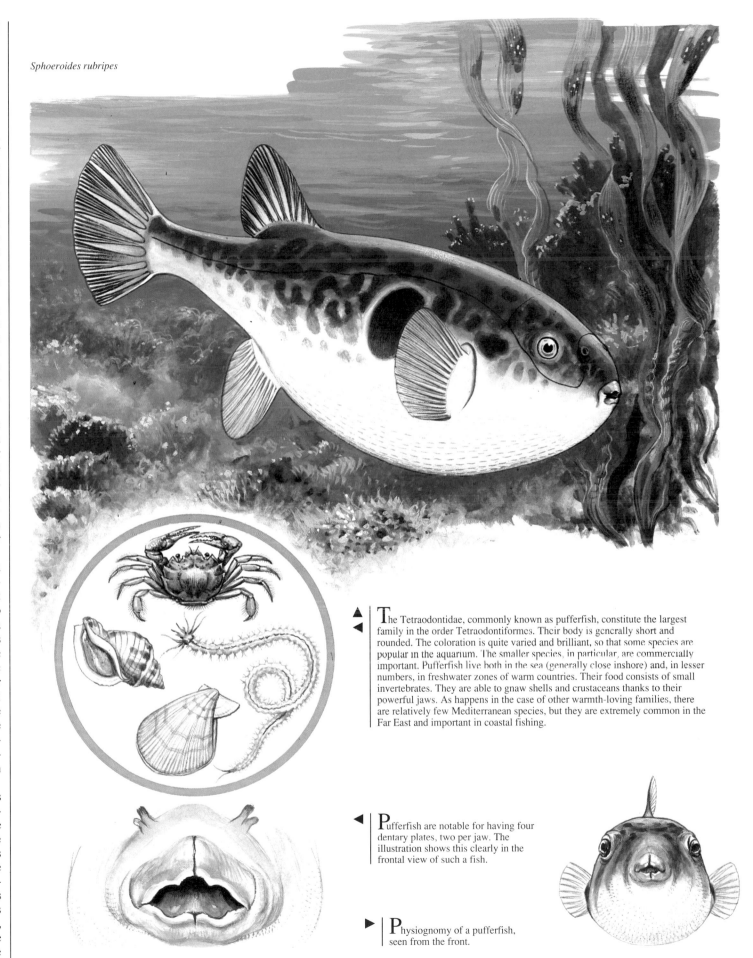

Sphoeroides rubripes

▲
◄ The Tetraodontidae, commonly known as pufferfish, constitute the largest family in the order Tetraodontiformes. Their body is generally short and rounded. The coloration is quite varied and brilliant, so that some species are popular in the aquarium. The smaller species, in particular, are commercially important. Pufferfish live both in the sea (generally close inshore) and, in lesser numbers, in freshwater zones of warm countries. Their food consists of small invertebrates. They are able to gnaw shells and crustaceans thanks to their powerful jaws. As happens in the case of other warmth-loving families, there are relatively few Mediterranean species, but they are extremely common in the Far East and important in coastal fishing.

◄ Pufferfish are notable for having four dentary plates, two per jaw. The illustration shows this clearly in the frontal view of such a fish.

► Physiognomy of a pufferfish, seen from the front.

SUNFISH
Molidae

Among the large fish that, when caught, are often considered newsworthy, are the so-called sunfish of the family Molidae. Among the most obvious features of these fish is the large size, so much so that the Molidae can claim to be among the most spectacular of all marine animals. The body is round and oblong, flattened, and oddly truncated at the rear: it seems to consist only of the head, and indeed an alternative vernacular name is headfish. The entire rear edge of the body is equipped with a fin that would appear to be the tail. However, this is a structure particular to this fish. In the course of growth the primitive tail disappears and is replaced by a pseudotail that is the fusion at the back of the dorsal and anal fins; the rays of the upper part are dorsal, and those of the lower part anal. This pseudotail is called the clavus. Naturally, there is no caudal peduncle. The skin is rough because of the presence of spinules or small plates. The mouth is small, and neither of the jaws carry teeth, but do bear very strong plates that together form a beak, similar to that of the porcupine fish, since the dentary plate of each jaw (fairly large) has no median suture; so this is a two part apparatus. The gill openings are small and the opercular processes are somewhat reduced and concealed under the skin.

The single dorsal and anal fins are especially worthy of note. Both are very tall; they are, in fact, raised and straight, similar and opposed, inserted in the rear of the body immediately in front of the clavus. There are no ventral fins and no pelvic girdle.

The skeleton is composed mainly of cartilage. The skull is fairly short and broad, with the upper part mostly occupied by the frontal bones, which extend some distance sideways. In keeping with the shortness of the body, there are few vertebrae, 16 – 20, of which eight are precaudal; in the first of these the neurospines are bifid. The muscles are clearly related to the odd methods of locomotion employed by these curious fish; the longitudinal muscles, which normally give an animal flexibility, are atrophied, but in compensation there are heavy bunches of muscle serving to raise and lower the dorsal and anal fins. There is no swim bladder. The anal and

The Molidae, or sunfish, are regarded as the most highly evolved and specialized of all the Tetraodontiformes. Their outline is unmistakable . The body appears to be cut off behind, where a pseudocaudal fin forms a clearly visible edge. The dorsal and anal fins, similar and opposed, serve for propulsion. *Mola mola*, the species illustrated here, is the best known of the few members of the family.

Ocean sunfish
(*Mola mola*)

urogenital openings are situated immediately in front of the anal fin.

Nowadays there are three genera, each represented by a single species: *Mola mola, Masturus lanceolatus*, and *Ranzania laevis*. All sunfish are pelagic and are to be found both out at sea and near the shores. It is interesting to note that all three species are widely distributed in the temperate and warm regions of the world's oceans, and may therefore be called cosmopolitan. *Mola* and *Ranzania* are also present in the Mediterranean. These fish are mainly found near the surface, although they also descend to depths of several hundred feet, probably no more. They swim slowly with sideways flaps of the dorsal and anal fins, while the body stays stiff. They feed on various organisms, especially plankton, and also plant matter.

The classic representative of the Molidae is *Mola mola*, and this species is commonly taken as the prototype of the entire family. It is one of the most enormous fish anywhere, its maximum length being almost 11 ft (3.3 m) and its weight nearly 2 tons. The body is rounded, silvery gray or olive–brown in color; in young individuals there are often circular black spots at the rear of the flanks. There are 16 – 20 rays in the dorsal fin, 14 – 18 in the anal fin. The pectoral fins are rounded. The intestine is fairly long.

This species is highly prolific; a female will carry at least 300 million immature eggs. When it hatches, the tiny larva (1.05 – 1.1 mm) looks like a pufferfish; the head is large and the rear part of the body is adorned with a continuous, primordial fin. The second larval stage is the so-called "ostracioniform" phase; the body is shorter and exhibits large, horn-like projections, together with a rear fin that gradually changes to the clavus. Finally there is a postlarval stage, corresponding to what was once assumed to be a genus called *Molacanthus*; it is still known by this name. The animal measures up to 2 in (1.5 cm); its body is shortened, high, and very compressed. The rear part is atrophied and the skin is covered with tiny bony plates, unequal in size and spaced apart, each bearing a short, conical spine. From the postlarval stage, it gradually takes on the adult appearance.

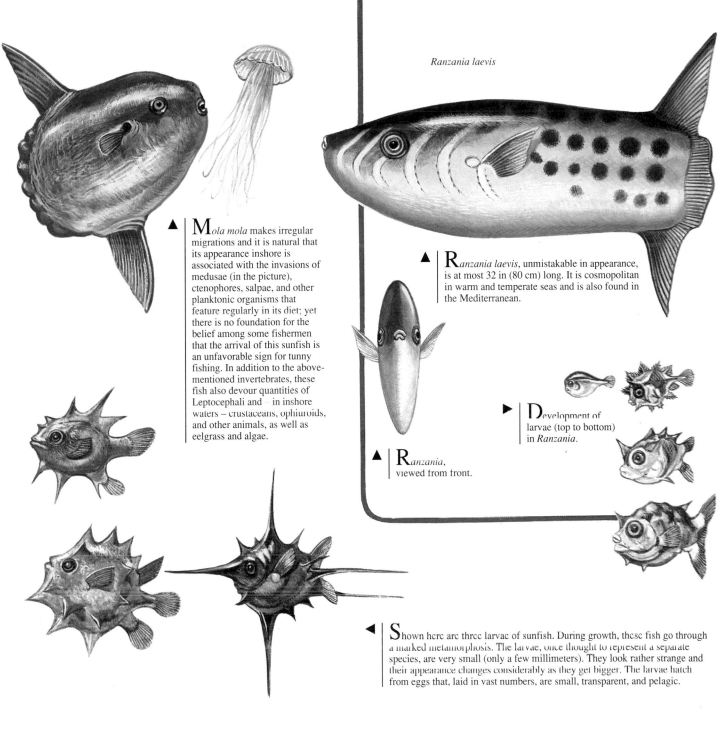

Ranzania laevis

▲ | Mola mola makes irregular migrations and it is natural that its appearance inshore is associated with the invasions of medusae (in the picture), ctenophores, salpae, and other planktonic organisms that feature regularly in its diet; yet there is no foundation for the belief among some fishermen that the arrival of this sunfish is an unfavorable sign for tunny fishing. In addition to the above-mentioned invertebrates, these fish also devour quantities of Leptocephali and – in inshore waters – crustaceans, ophiuroids, and other animals, as well as eelgrass and algae.

▲ | Ranzania laevis, unmistakable in appearance, is at most 32 in (80 cm) long. It is cosmopolitan in warm and temperate seas and is also found in the Mediterranean.

▲ | Ranzania, viewed from front.

▶ | Development of larvae (top to bottom) in *Ranzania*.

◀ | Shown here are three larvae of sunfish. During growth, these fish go through a marked metamorphosis. The larvae, once thought to represent a separate species, are very small (only a few millimeters). They look rather strange and their appearance changes considerably as they get bigger. The larvae hatch from eggs that, laid in vast numbers, are small, transparent, and pelagic.

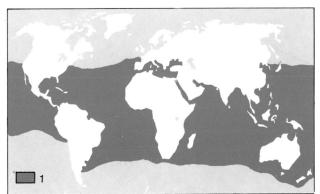

◀ | In giving *Mola* its first scientific name, Linnaeus mentioned it as inhabiting the Mediterranean, which is understandable because this fish is rare in the seas of northern Europe; occasionally it appears in the Skagerrak, off the coasts of Norway, and near Iceland. It can, however, be regarded as common in the Mediterranean. The catch consists mainly of young individuals, which are more gregarious, and often gather in large numbers inshore; but sometimes adults of considerable size are caught, which is a noteworthy occurrence. It is an indolent animal that is in the habit of staying immobile both on the surface, sometimes with its dorsal fin sticking out of the water, and deeper down near the bottom, where underwater divers are likely to see it suspended head downward. *Mola* is regarded as a surface fish but descends to a depth of at least 1,000 ft (300 m). 1) Distribution of the genus *Mola*.

CROSSOPTERYGII

During the very remote Devonian period of the Paleozoic era, the lands and seas of our globe were distributed in a very different manner from today. No less diverse were the fish. Crossopterygii are among the fish most accurately studied by paleontologists, who also assign to the same group numerous species found in more recent geological strata, namely Mesozoic. For a long time it was thought that the end of the Mesozoic era also signaled the end of this group of fish. But in 1939 it was reported that a strange fish had been caught in the sea off South Africa, and that it was certainly a crossopterygian.

In December 1938 a fishing vessel off the shores of South Africa, near the mouth of the Chalumna River around East London, caught a fish that, by reason of its unusual appearance, was dispatched to that city's museum. The museum director, Latimer, was immediately aware of its importance, and sought the advice of the ichthyologist J.L.B. Smith; the latter realized that this was a novelty, and named the animal *Latimeria chalumnae*, publishing a description in 1939.

Latimeria chalumnae or the coelacanth is a massive fish of unmistakable appearance and is truly unique among living species. The length may be up to 6 ft (1.8 m) and the weight up to 175 lb (80 kg). Females are bigger than males. While the rest of the body exhibits a normal fish-like outline, the characteristic tail immediately commands attention; the caudal fin does not appear to be preceded by a peduncle.

The color is gray–blue, varying in brightness, with irregular scattered spots on the flanks; they are lighter than the remaining body tint or even white.

The maximum height of the body is slightly less than the length of the head, which is just under one third of the whole body length. The mouth is relatively large. There are neither premaxillary nor maxillary bones (the former being replaced by a few small dentary plates) but there is a series of strong, sharp, conical teeth; smaller teeth are present in the vomer and palate. There are also some larger front teeth and some more smaller teeth, in the lower jaw. There are two nasal openings, both external, for *Latimera* lacks coanae.

Latimeria chalumnae is one of the most interesting fish in existence, being the sole representative to survive of the order Coelacanthiformes, belonging to the Crossopterygii. It was discovered off the coast of South Africa at the end of 1938, near East London. A series of studies showed that its structure is very different from that of other fish. Its length is up to 6 ft (1.8 m) and its weight 175 lb (80 kg). Females are slightly bigger than males.

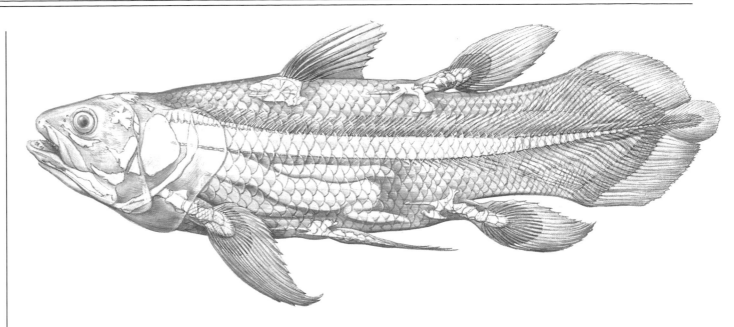

The two dorsal fins are well separated, the front one being the larger, comprising eight strong rays that bear many short spines on their surface; the rear fin is propped by a short, fleshy lobe and has softer rays. The anal fin is similar to the second dorsal, to which it is opposed. The other fins are of greater interest because it is they that provide the fish with its strange appearance.

The caudal fin displays the typical structure of Coelacanthiformes, namely the division into three parts that make the whole fin very large. The upper and lower parts, similar and opposed to each other, are the biggest; to the rear they are in contact with the median lobe, which is the portion of the fin that has a rounded edge and is supported by a prominent fleshy lobe. The latter is connected to a raised linear zone running along the back and central parts of either flank; the backbone terminates horizontally inside this lobe. At first sight the small median portion of the tail appears to represent the whole fin, although it actually forms the terminal section.

The paired fins consist mainly of a fleshy part, namely a lobe that stems from the body surface and is covered with scales that are much smaller than those of the flanks; inside it is supported by a series of cartilaginous processes. The rays are arranged inside the lobe, except for the basal part. The large pectorals are inserted low down, immediately behind the lower section of the gill aperture. The ventrals are rather smaller and their base is situated almost at the level of the tip of the pectorals. Between the two bases is the cloacal opening.

The first dorsal fin with its spinous rays, the perfectly symmetrical, three-sectioned tail, and the other pedunculate fins combine to give the fish its particular physiognomy, very different from that of better known fish.

As far as is known today, *Latimeria* is restricted to a limited area of the Indian Ocean, close to the Comoro group of islands; but it may appear occasionally outside this zone, as its original discovery in South Africa showed. Individuals have been caught mainly between 230 and 1,000 ft (70 and 300 m), but the fish has also been caught at greater depths, up to 2,000 ft (600 m). It lives a solitary existence, where the bottom is rocky, and shuns the light.

▼ Structure of the pectoral fin and its skeletal support in *Latimeria chalumnae*.

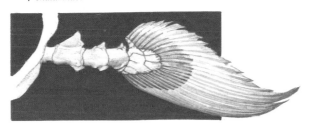

The anatomical study of *Latimeria* has revealed a series of characteristics that are not only unique among present-day fish but also enable scientists to get a better understanding of fossil forms. The skeleton is largely cartilaginous and thus shows a measure of regression compared with the coelacanthus that once lived and had more bones in their skeleton. As in all crossopterygians, the skull is divided into two parts, front and back; they are not very mobile in relation to each other, either horizontally or vertically, and they articulate by means of special muscles. The snout region is short. There are five gill arches, the last being very small. The spine is similar to a large tube with consistent, fibrous and elastic walls, it is full of liquid and is unrestricted. There is, in fact, no trace of vertebral centers, but there is a series of cartilaginous neural arches with associated neurospines. There are no ribs. The encephalus is very small (in a specimen of 90 lb [40 kg] it weighs less than 3 g!) and occupies only a small rear portion of the cranial cavity, the rest of which is filled with fat. The hypophysis is long and arranged horizontally; its glandular section contains a cavity that continues and has its outlet in the roof of the mouth. As regards the sensory organs, there is little of special mention concerning the eyes or nostrils, except to note that the latter are not accompanied by coanae, internal processes that are found in many crossopterygians but not coelacanths. The stomach is large and the intestine terminates in a cloaca, the outlet of which is situated between the ventral fins. *Latimeria*, like sharks and related fish, has a spiral valve in the intestine and a fair quantity of urea in the blood. The swim bladder is degenerate, appearing as a large mass of fat contained in the visceral cavity. The reproductive apparatus is assymetrical, especially in the female, where there is virtually only the right ovary present; also the right testicle of the male is much larger than the other. Reproduction is ovoviviparous. A large female may carry 20 eggs with a diameter of 3½ in (9 cm). Gestation lasts about 13 months and births occur usually in February. Because the length of the embryos at birth is some 13 in (32 cm), the newborn individuals may be quite large.

◀ Shown here are some of the very ancient vertebrates representing various stages in the long evolutionary history of this large zoological group. Top to bottom: a primitive shark, a coelacanthiform, *Ichthyostega*, *Eryops*. The last two are amphibians.

SEA TURTLES

The chelonians of the suborder *Cryptodira* and the superfamily *Chelonioidea* are commonly known as turtles. The family *Dermochelyidae*, consisting of a single genus, *Dermochelys*, which has only one species, is characterized by the peculiar structure of the shell. This consists of bony plates joined like a mosaic and implanted in a skin like leather.

The gigantic leatherback turtle or luth (*Dermochelys coriacea*), 3¾ – 9 ft (110 – 275 cm) long and weighing 550 – 1,900 lb (250 – 860 kg), is a cosmopolitan species mostly found in tropical and subtropical waters. It is the most widely distributed of all living reptiles, being found in the Pacific, Atlantic, and Indian Oceans, the North Sea, the Mediterranean, the Red Sea and Arabian Sea, the China Sea, the Sea of Japan, the Caribbean, and sometimes even the Baltic and seas further north and south. It normally lives in warm or temperate waters and is only found in cold waters as a stray. It is a typical high seas type that only comes into the coasts at intervals for nesting.

The leatherback turtle is a powerful and rapid swimmer, lively, and sometimes aggressive if disturbed. It feeds on fish (especially young fish), echinoderms, cephalopods, crustaceans, mollusks, coelenterates, and vegetation. The female of the leatherback lays her eggs generally late at night and usually at the beginning of the summer. The eggs, almost spherical with a soft shell, are laid in a hole as much as 39 in (1 m) deep, generally twice each season, to a total of 70 – 115 per female. This species generally reproduces every 2 – 3 years.

Migration probably takes place in isolated groups of a few individuals. The nesting sites of this species do not seem to be strictly localized. A high proportion of the young die; it is estimated that of every 1,000 born only one or two survive the first year of life. The best known nesting areas are along the coasts of Malaysia, Mexico, Costa Rica, French Guyana, South Africa, and Australia.

One member of the genus *Caretta* is the loggerhead (*Caretta caretta*) This species, 2¾ – 4¾ ft (80 – 140 cm) long and weighing 180 – 1,000 lb (80 – 450 kg), has a carapace with five pairs of lateral shields. The lateral bridge between

The green turtle is possibly the best known of the turtles. Like all turtles it lives entirely in the sea but makes it nest on land. In the water its limbs, shaped like fins, enable it to swim fast and easily, but on land it moves very clumsily. This species feeds almost exclusively on algae, while other turtles are carnivorous, feeding mainly on crustaceans, coelenterates, cephalopods, mollusks, echinoderms, and fish.

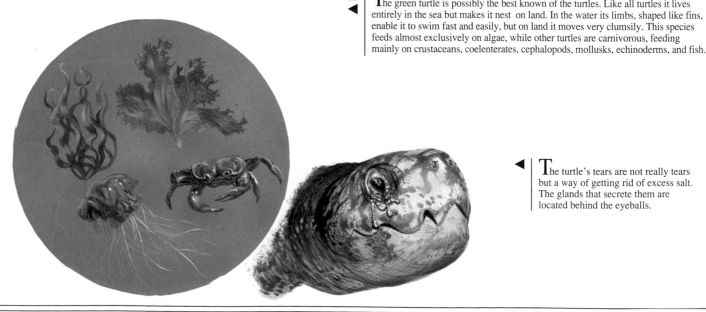

The turtle's tears are not really tears but a way of getting rid of excess salt. The glands that secrete them are located behind the eyeballs.

the carapace and the plastron has three inframarginal shields. It is another cosmopolitan species, living in the tropical and subtropical waters of the Atlantic, Pacific, and Indian Oceans, in the Black Sea and the Mediterranean, the Red Sea, the Arabian Sea, the China Sea, the Sea of Japan, and the Caribbean; also, exceptionally, in the Baltic, the Barents Sea, and the North Sea. It is mostly found in warm or temperate generally shallow waters, in bays, gulfs, inlets, river mouths, and archipelagos. It is a typical shallow water species, almost exclusively marine.

The loggerhead is a species that lives off the coasts and moves into the deep sea for the purposes of migration presumably connected with reproduction. In the Mediterranean, during the probable reproductive periods, in contrast to what is found in other seas, these turtles seem to migrate in groups, probably never more than ten strong and usually 4 – 8. Unlike the green turtle, which feeds principally on algae, the loggerhead also hunts for crustaceans, gasteropods, echinoderms, mollusks and – but only rarely – fish.

The best known of all turtles must be the green turtle (*Chelonia mydas*), 1½ – 4¾ ft (45 – 140 cm) long and 175 – 1,100 lb (80 – 500 kg) in weight. It lives in the same oceans and seas as the loggerhead, but apparently prefers deep water. The green turtle is famous for the striking migrations that groups of thousands of animals undertake from their feeding grounds to the nesting sites, as far as 1,250 miles (2,000 km) away.

The females generally lay their eggs every 2 – 3 years. The female digs 5 – 7 holes with her paddles at intervals of 10 – 15 days, and lays about 100 eggs. So many are the dangers that threaten the eggs that it has been calculated that only one in every 500 of the young reaches sexual maturity.

The hawksbill turtle (*Eretmochelys imbricata*), up to 3 ft (90 cm) long and weighing 220 – 290 lb (100 – 130 kg), has a carapace with four pairs of costal shields like the green turtle. It is found in the Atlantic and Mediterranean with the subspecies *Eretmochelys imbricata imbricata* and in the Indian and Pacific Oceans with the subspecies *E.i. bissa*.

Other marine species are the olive loggerhead (*Lepidochelys olivacea*), which may be 3¼ ft (1 m) long, and the nearly related Kemp's loggerhead (*Lepidochelys kempii*). This species mostly frequents sandy sea beds, living on plants, sea urchins, jellyfish, etc.

Stages of the turtles nesting habits.

The female turtles use their hind paddles to dig holes about 16 – 30 in (40 – 75 cm) deep in the sand several feet above the high water mark. At intervals they lay 60 – 200 eggs in them, each about as big as a mandarin. The young are born after 35 – 75 days, according to species, and immediately make for the sea.

As they try to reach the sea as quickly as possible, the young may be caught by different kinds of animals.

The Atlantic, Pacific, and Indian Oceans are also the home of the olive loggerhead, while the Kemp's loggerhead lives mainly in the Atlantic, and particularly in the Gulf of Mexico; it only enters the Mediterranean as a stray.

Of all living reptiles, turtles are those most in danger of extinction; indeed, they might be regarded as the most seriously endangered animals on earth. All turtle species are to a great extent phytophagous, so they generally concentrate in places where there are plenty of spermatophytes and algae; at certain times of the year they also assemble off certain coasts where they lay their eggs. These concentrations have made things easier for the hunters, and indeed the animals are now hunted so thoughtlessly that we may well expect turtles to become extinct in a short time.

The most interesting biological feature of the turtles is that they live in the sea but make their nest on land. They lead solitary lives for most of the year, but when the time comes for mating and nesting they assemble in small groups and migrate, always to the same places, which may sometimes be as far as 1,500 miles (2,500 km) from their usual home waters. It is still not known exactly how turtles manage to find their way across the great oceans when they migrate from their feeding grounds to the places where they reproduce or when they move from one shore to another during the nesting period. They must certainly have various marks that they follow on their journey, one of which is certainly provided by their sense of smell; the green turtle, the loggerhead, and, most evidently, the bastard turtle, seem to keep sampling the sea bed and the sand washed down from the coasts. It may be that their sense of smell tells the turtles about local changes in the water they are swimming in, so that they can follow scent trails like those that guide salmon to the spawning grounds.

It seems certain that turtles do not usually make any perceptible sounds, probably because they do not possess any echolocation technique based on the reflection of sounds from the sea bed, such as is found in some fish and certain mammals. However, turtles are exceptional navigators, and navigation requires guidance by at least an approximation of distance covered or by observation of astronomical data. The behavior of turtles in migration is too precise for us to accept that they are guided by an automatic biological mechanism or by approximate estimation.

Loggerhead (*Caretta caretta*)

Olive loggerhead (*Lepidochelys olivacea*)

Hawksbill (*Eretmochelys imbricata*)

▲ Of all living reptiles, turtles are the most seriously threatened with extinction; they may be considered among the most endangered animals in the world. Ignorance and greed, fed by industries that make fabulous profits from the international production of turtle soup, have greatly changed the early equilibrium, in which local peoples who made use of the turtles' meat, eggs, and shell were well aware that they constituted a safe source of food, so that the animals were preserved from extinction. Today, fortunately, many preservation associations, besides checking on the migration of the turtles and re-establishing the nesting colonies in the natural habitats, have undertaken the breeding of some species in properly defended, eutrophic marine farms, with the object also of reducing the catch in the natural areas.

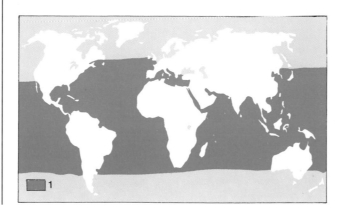

1

◄ 1) Area of distribution of the loggerhead (*Caretta caretta*). This is a cosmopolitan species, living in the tropical and subtropical waters of the Atlantic, Pacific, and Indian Oceans, the Black Sea, the Mediterranean, the Red Sea, the Arabian Sea, the China and Japanese Seas, and the Caribbean. It is generally found in warm, shallow waters, in bays, gulfs, inlets, river mouths, and archipelagos.

Some writers have therefore concluded that they possess an internal compass, whose functioning is still largely a mystery, which enables them to check their route at different times of the day by observing the position of the sun. When traveling by night, they may perhaps orient themselves by the fixed stars, as birds apparently do. We do not yet know what the turtles are able to see, but the idea that they are guided by the heavenly bodies does seem to be the simplest and most logical theory to explain how they migrate. Some support has recently emerged for the theory that the migrations are connected in some way with continental drift.

The reproduction and nesting of turtles is one of the most impressive phenomena in nature. Generally after nightfall, crawling on her belly or stretching forward with the paddles on either side alternately, the loggerhead moves up the chosen beach for 50 – 150 ft (15 – 50 m) beyond the water line and digs a hole in the sand with her hind paddles, 16 – 30 in (40 – 75 cm) deep and 8 – 12 in (20 – 30 cm) across, and there she lays her eggs, one or two at a time, 4 – 12 each minute, about 60 – 200 in an hour. The eggs are white, about the size of a mandarine orange. When she has finished, the female fills in the hole and moves off several feet, sometimes spraying the sand in different directions and actually digging false holes to disguise the whereabouts of the nest; then she returns to the sea. She lays her eggs in a number of different phases. Each female lays a very large number of eggs, no doubt an essential precaution to avoid the catastrophic possibility that some of the animal's many enemies may find the nest and destroy the contents.

Back in the sea, the females are almost immediately courted by the males. Both sexes remain near the nesting area for about two weeks. The eggs are laid from mid June to mid July, depending on the latitude of the chosen sites; it may occasionally be as late as the beginning of August.

The young are hatched after about 30 – 75 days. The eggs, incubated by the warmth of their surroundings, all hatch at more or less the same time and the young emerge from the sand, generally at night, and make for the sea, guided by the comparative luminousness of the surface of the water. During this frantic progress they may be hunted by mammals and birds and, once they are in the water, by fish; the eggs too may be taken by medium-sized and small mammals.

The leatherback turtle or luth (*Dermochelys coriacea*) is characterized by the special structure of its shell, which is composed of small bony plates joined like a mosaic and rooted in a skin like leather. It is a strong, swift swimmer, active, and sometimes aggressive. It feeds on fish, echinoderms, cephalopods, crustaceans, mollusks, coelenterates, and plants.

The shape of the snout and mouth is a singular feature.

Newly hatched leatherbacks are completely covered with scales, which later disappear.

The leatherback turtle is a typical deep sea species, visiting the coasts only intermittently, or when the time comes for laying eggs. During its long migrations it is often followed by rows of pilot fish (*Naucrates ductor*).

YELLOW-BELLIED SEA SNAKE

Pelamis platurus

Order Squamata
Suborder Ophidia
Family Hydrophiidae
Length Up to 40 in (100 cm)
Reproductive period All year round
Gestation 5 – 6 months
Number of young 2 – 6
Maximum age Unknown

The sea snakes are a family of snakes that probably returned to the sea from a terrestrial existence in the Mesozoic Era. Adaptation to life in the tropical seas has had a clearly visible effect on their bodily structure. The hinder part of the body, most of all the tail, is flattened sideways and serves these reptiles as an oar to propel them through the water. The nostrils, which can be closed by a flap of skin, lie on the top of the snout.

Peculiar to the sea snake are the salt glands in the head through which they eliminate excess salt. All sea snakes can remain under water for long periods. Most sea snakes are quite unaggressive towards man and very slow to bite. Although these animals live generally in fairly large numbers, cases of snake bite are rare.

The yellow-bellied sea snake (*Pelamis platurus*) has a flat head with a long snout, a body laterally compressed along its whole length with a vertically flattened tail like an oar, and rectangular or hexagonal scales that do not overlap. This is the most widely distributed of the sea snakes; it occurs from the Indo-Australian region eastwards across the Pacific Ocean to the west coast of Central America and westwards across the Indian Ocean to the east coast of Africa. It is exclusively marine and has been found hundreds of miles from land.

In the places where *Pelamis platurus* occurs it is generally present in fairly large numbers. It is the only sea snake that ventures into deep water. However, it usually stays on the surface, where it traps small fish, seizing them in a flash as they swim by. *Pelamis platurus* produces 2 – 6 living young after a gestation of 5 – 6 months.

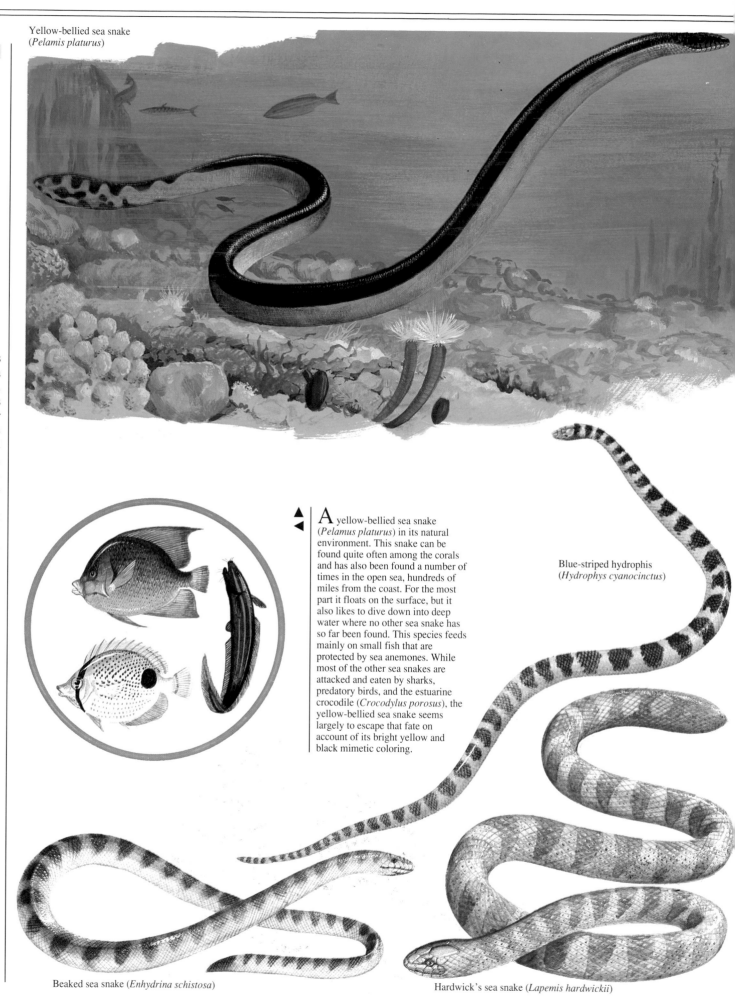

Yellow-bellied sea snake
(*Pelamis platurus*)

A yellow-bellied sea snake (*Pelamus platurus*) in its natural environment. This snake can be found quite often among the corals and has also been found a number of times in the open sea, hundreds of miles from the coast. For the most part it floats on the surface, but it also likes to dive down into deep water where no other sea snake has so far been found. This species feeds mainly on small fish that are protected by sea anemones. While most of the other sea snakes are attacked and eaten by sharks, predatory birds, and the estuarine crocodile (*Crocodylus porosus*), the yellow-bellied sea snake seems largely to escape that fate on account of its bright yellow and black mimetic coloring.

Blue-striped hydrophis
(*Hydrophys cyanocinctus*)

Beaked sea snake (*Enhydrina schistosa*)

Hardwick's sea snake (*Lapemis hardwickii*)

ESTUARINE CROCODILE

Crocodylus porosus

Order Crocodylia
Family Crocodylidae
Length Up to 29 ft (9 m), sometimes 33 ft (10 m)
Reproductive period Varies with geographical location
Egg laying October to May
Number of eggs 20 – 28
Maximum age 40 years or more

The estuarine crocodile (*Crocodylus porosus*) is the crocodile that is best adapted to life in brackish waters and sea water. It is sometimes called the "saltwater crocodile." It differs from other crocodiles in the almost complete absence of the front neck plates, though in some animals these may be slightly developed.

The estuarine crocodile has the most extensive distribution of all crocodiles, from India and Sri Lanka eastwards to all the coasts of Southeast Asia, Malaysia, and Indonesia, the Philippines, New Guinea, the northern coasts of Australia, the Solomon Islands, Vanuatu, and Fiji. It does not generally penetrate beyond the mouths of tidal reaches of rivers, though in New Guinea it is found further inland in the rivers and marshes.

Crocodylus porosus is the biggest of all the crocodiles, which makes it the biggest of all reptiles. Being normally an inhabitant of both sea coasts and the open sea, it is an excellent swimmer and diver. It feeds on shellfish, fish, turtles, smaller crocodiles, snakes, water birds, and all sorts of mammals. It attacks warm-blooded mammals from behind, drags them under water, and drowns them. Of all the crocodilians, the estuarine crocodile is the most dangerous to man.

Between October and May the female lays an average of 20, but in some cases more than 80, hard-shelled eggs in a primitive nest of mud and water plants. These crocodiles make their nests on sandbanks, generally at the mouths of rivers in areas of brackish water. The young crocodiles make a grunting sound from inside the eggs just before they hatch. They break open the egg shells from inside with the aid of the "egg tooth" on their snout.

Estuarine crocodile (*Crocodylus porosus*)

An adult estuarine crocodile (*Crocodylus porosus*) has seized a nilghai and is dragging it into the water. The prey will be dismembered before being eaten. The estuarine crocodile feeds on crustaceans, fish, turtles, small crocodiles, snakes, water birds, and all sorts of mammals. This crocodile is also the only species that can definitely be proved to be a maneater.

A monitor plundering the nest of an estuarine crocodile. During the incubation period the female defends her brood from all the animals that take crocodiles' eggs.

1) Area of distribution of the estuarine crocodile (*Crocodylus porosus*). It covers the brackish waters of the coasts of Southeast Asia, even if the species has almost disappeared today from a large part of its original distribution area. 2) Distribution of living crocodilians, except for the American and Chinese alligators.

KING PENGUIN
Aptenodytes patagonica

Order Sphenisciformes
Family Spheniscidae
Length 38 in (95 cm)
Weight 33 lb (15 kg)
Distribution Antarctic and subantarctic zones
Eggs 1
Chicks Nidicolous

Broadly speaking, penguins are marine birds that are incapable of flying and typical of the Southern Hemisphere. They are better suited to an aquatic existence than any other family of birds. The whole body is covered by a uniform, dense layer of feathers. The wings have been reduced to flippers for swimming and are stiff and solid, unbendable, and covered with scaly feathers.

The height of present day penguins ranges from 1 – 4 ft (30 – 120 cm) or more. It is interesting to note that in all species the plumage pattern is fairly uniform: the breast white and the back either black or dark brown, with no distinction between the sexes. All penguins feed on fish, mollusks, and crustaceans.

As far as distribution is concerned, the penguin family is typical of the Southern Hemisphere. They probably originated in the antarctic or subantarctic regions, for it is here that fossils dating from the Tertiary have been found.

Regarding the king penguin, it is interesting to note that, like the emperor penguin, it has difficulties in raising its larger chicks because of the harsh conditions in which these already-large animals live. The severe climate means food is scarce for eight or nine months of the year. The king penguin nests on the islands bordering the Antarctic and all over the subantarctic area free from ice. Here the weather is relatively mild and winter temperatures are of an oceanic type.

Egg laying takes place in spring and summer and the chicks are kept in the colony until the following spring. An abundance of plankton in spring means a good supply of food for the penguins. They catch fish and cephalopods in surface waters and can therefore feed their young abundantly. Adults are subject to molting and may return to lay in January – February. In three consecutive seasons couples are not able to raise three chicks but they can certainly manage two.

A group of king penguins (*Aptenodytes patagonica*) with chicks. Each pair tends a single egg which is incubated beneath an abdominal fold of skin and balanced on the feet so as to protect it from the ground below. When exchanging the eggs, the parents perform the maneuver with such dexterity that it never comes into contact with soil or snow. Nevertheless, not all the chicks manage to survive the rigors of the southern winter and the inevitable scarcity of food in the nesting colonies.

The waters of the Arctic Ocean are rich in food, especially in spring and summer, when the adult penguins find plenty for themselves and their young.

EMPEROR PENGUIN

Aptenodytes forsteri

Order Sphenisciformes
Family Spheniscidae
Length About 45 in (115 cm)
Weight About 65 lb (30 kg)
Distribution Antarctic continent
Eggs 1
Chicks Nidicolous

The coasts of the vast continent fringing the Antarctic Ocean are the home of the emperor penguin, the largest species of its order, which breeds here in enormous colonies.

In the emperor penguin, like other members of the family, the entire body is covered by dense plumage. The wings are very short in relation to the body, and the legs, completely feathered, terminate in comparatively small feet. The color of the plumage follows the general pattern found in most penguins; back, wings, and head down to the throat are shiny black while the abdomen is white with yellow tints.

The emperor penguin feeds on many kinds of marine animals, particularly the shoals of squid that often inhabit these relatively deep waters.

The penguins begin to arrive at their breeding sites in small groups, the numbers steadily increasing the closer they get to the zone where the colony regularly assembles. The journey from the coast, which is already covered by pack ice, entails a considerable expenditure of energy because the areas selected for reproduction may be a long distance from the sea. Apparently the emperor penguin returns to the same site year after year.

The single egg is incubated beneath a fold of skin between the feet. Within 6 – 12 hours of laying the egg, the female passes it over to her mate, who places it between his feet and goes off in search of food. The burden of incubation now falls exclusively on the male, who during this task will go three months without food. The females arrive back at about the time when the eggs are almost ready to hatch, so that the newborn chicks can receive fresh food from their mothers. Once they have molted and acquired proper plumage, they quit the colony for the open sea where there is now an abundance of food.

▲ The emperor penguin, largest of the living Sphenisciformes, is particularly adapted for withstanding the terrible southern winter. It, too, forms huge colonies: the one on Coulman Island brings together more than 300,000 birds.

The egg is incubated beneath a fold of abdominal skin, supported on the feet of the adult, thus ensuring that it does not come into contact with the ice.

◄ The burden of incubation falls entirely on the male. Motionless in the freezing cold winter, he carries out the task which, when complete, will have forced him to go more than three months without food.

ADÉLIE PENGUIN
Pygoscelis adeliae

Order Sphenisciformes
Family Spheniscidae
Length 28 in (70 cm)
Weight 11 lb (5 kg)
Distribution Extreme southern coasts of Antarctica and neighboring islands
Eggs Generally 2, greenish white
Chicks Nidicolous

One of the best known of many species is the Adélie penguin (*Pygoscelis adeliae*), with a widespread distribution along the southeastern shores of the Antarctic and some of the surrounding islands. This is an average-sized penguin, about 28 in (70 cm) in total length, with white plumage on throat and abdomen and black on the head and the back down to the tail, without any special distinguishing marks. The only feature differentiating it from other members of the genus *Pygoscelis* is the ring of white feathers around the eye which stand out in contrast to the black of the cheeks.

Colonies of Adélie penguins tend to be confined to rocky zones, often extending for some distance, either on the flat or on gentle slopes close to the sea. The penguins start arriving and assembling in these areas at the beginning of the southern spring, at the end of October. They emerge from the sea in small, scattered groups and are seldom seen in large numbers; in most cases the latest arrivals remain on the fringes of the zone that will subsequently be filled by the whole colony. Within a few days some thousands of birds will have appeared, seeking sites for building their rudimentary nests. Pairs of penguins return punctually every year to the same spot in the colony, apparently committing to memory the distinctive features of their little patch of stony ground, for the terrain seldom exhibits clear landmarks such as rocks. In many cases the colony seems to consist of a single huge assembly of breeding pairs, sometimes formed into individual small groups situated at various distances from one another.

It is usually the male who comes back to take possession of his territory and begins building the nest even before his mate emerges from the sea. When the

▲ Adélie penguins live in large numbers along the southeastern shores of the Antarctic and on some of the surrounding islands. They form crowded colonies near the sea in flat, rocky zones, building nests and breeding every year.

▼ There are various theories concerning the relationship of penguins to other orders of birds and the picture is far from clear. Probably these species have affinities with the Procellariiformes (albatrosses, storm petrels, shearwaters, etc.) but there are also indications that they may have derived from a specific group of Charadriiformes, as has definitely been verified in the case of the auks.

penguins

albatrosses

shearwaters

?

females arrive, they too start looking for their site and their mate but often spend several days wandering through the colony, perhaps pausing for brief periods with males who have already completed their nests.

Once they have commenced building the nest, the mates summon the females, taking up a characteristic position with beak held high and wings flapping slowly against the sides, and giving out a succession of guttural sounds, followed by a loud cry. This behavior constitutes the so-called ecstatic display. During this period territorial instinct is very pronounced and fierce fights often break out among the males, even if one of them is merely trying to make his way through the maze of occupied sites. Mating begins soon after the female reaches the colony, when the construction of the nest is still in its early stages.

The first egg is laid a few days after mating, and as a rule a second egg appears 3 – 4 days later. By the time egg laying is completed more than three weeks will have elapsed since the birds returned to the colony. At this point the females, weakened by their breeding activities, leave the nests en masse and head for the sea, there to feed on krill. When the females return to the colony after ten days or so in the sea, it is the turn of the males to quit the nests and go off to find food, having fasted for more than a month.

The eggs are incubated for 34 – 36 days. When they are almost ready to hatch they are tended by both parents, alternating at frequent intervals, so as to be ready to feed the babies the moment they are born. During the first stage of the chicks' development, both adults take turns to plunge into the sea, remaining there for some 24 hours at a time and perhaps swimming more than 62 miles (100 km) in pursuit of shoals of krill, squid, and crustaceans. When they get back to the nest, they feed the young who have no difficulty in swallowing a quantity of food equivalent to their own weight. As a rule a breeding pair manages to rear only one chick successfully.

As soon as they have acquired their complete plumage, the young Adélie penguins set off together towards the sea. The adults remain for another couple of weeks in the sea, feeding and putting on large amounts of fat that helps them to survive during the weeks or months when they are forced to remain on land to complete their molt. Afterwards they return to the ocean and lead a pelagic life from April until the following October.

▲ | Adélie penguins swim long distances, sometimes leaping like dolphins.

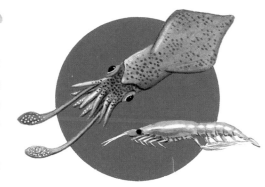

▲ | Penguins will travel for dozens of miles in pursuit of shoals of krill or cephalopods and crustaceans.

Principal stages of the breeding cycle.
1) Towards the end of October penguins emerge from the sea in small groups; 2) tobogganing, belly down, over the soft snow, they reach the sites where the colony assembles regularly year after year; 3) the nest is often rebuilt in the same place, intruders being driven away; 4) having started to make the nest, the males call and pay court to the females; 5) as a rule the male collects the stones from which the nest is constructed; 6) the male takes first turn in incubation; 7) the parents feed the chicks by regurgitating half-digested food; 8) after an initial period of attentive parental care, the chicks are left to their own devices and live together in small groups.

PROCELLARII-FORMES

The Procellariiformes are marine birds with one special and distinctive characteristic. The bill terminates in a hook and is made up of juxtaposed horny sections, the sutures being clearly defined. The tube-like nostrils, separated from the upper mandible, explain why the group used to be called Tubinares ("tube noses"). The nasal or salt glands are well developed, secreting a solution with a high saline content, which, in effect, eliminates excess salt from the blood. The tubes of the nostrils possibly serve to conduct this saline solution away from the eyes, also preventing sea spray getting into the nostrils themselves. The tubes terminate in large nasal fossae or olfactory cavities, the significance of which remains obscure. Their function may be to detect the slightest change in direction of the light winds that play over the sea's surface.

The esophagus and glandular stomach are elongated and the latter is furnished with special cells that secrete an oily substance which can be spurted out by the adult birds, and more particularly the young, when danger threatens, as a result of the contractions of the esophagus walls. This substance becomes cold on contact with the air and takes on a waxy appearance. The sharp, penetrating odor gives the plumage of the Procellariiformes a characteristic smell, a little like musk, which permeates the skin, present even on those preserved for many years in museums. The odor is apparently derived directly from this oily substance produced in the stomach and not from the uropygial gland. The chicks of certain species, namely fulmars and giant petrels, do not use this oily fluid for protection; instead, they spit out the salt solution at their enemies.

The body is very sturdy, the hind legs are short, and the three front toes are linked by a strong web. The rear toe is atrophied. The plumage is thick and its color is white, black or gray. The chicks stay in the nest for a considerable time and are initially covered in flimsy down.

The Procellariiformes contain the largest and smallest of the sea birds, albatrosses and storm petrels respectively. All, with the exception of the Pelecanoididae, are splendidly adapted to an aerial life, thanks to their highly

Black-footed albatross
(*Diomedea nigripes*)

Steller's albatross
(*Diomedea albatus*)

The diving petrels are the most untypical of the Procellariiformes. In fact, they are not good fliers but use their short wings as paddles when submerged. Their body is very similar to that of the ancient auks.

Leach's petrel
(*Oceanodroma leucorhoa*)

Fulmer
(*Fulmarus glacialis*)

Cape pigeon
(*Daption capensis*)

▲ From left: black-footed albatross, widely distributed in the North Pacific; Steller's albatross, feared to be in danger of extinction, with only about 60 nesting pairs now left on the Japanese islands of Torishima and Isa; fulmer, with two distinct races in either hemisphere; Cape pigeon, very common in the Southern Hemisphere, migrating long distances outside the breeding season; Leach's petrel, one of the most adundant species, with millions of individuals in North America alone.

◀ Distribution areas of some Procellariiformes: 1) fulmar (*Fulmarus glacialis*); 2) Steller's albatross (*Diomedea albatus*); 3) diving petrel (*Pelecanoides urinatrix*).

pneumatic bones. They can, in fact, float on the waves for long periods and it is likely that some species can sleep at the same time. The order Procellariiformes is nowadays divided into four families: Pelecanoididae, Hydrobatidae, Diomedeidae, and Procellariidae.

The Procellariiformes are found in all the world's oceans, especially those of the Southern Hemisphere. Faithful to their breeding sites, the Procellariiformes are highly gregarious, especially in the actual breeding season. The females lay a single, very large egg. Apparently there is no substitute brood in the event of the egg being lost (although little information exists concerning tropical species). Intervals between successive broods vary from two years among the large albatrosses to 8 – 9 months in the case of the tropical species. Nests may be built on the ground, in clefts, against rock walls, in underground tunnels excavated by the birds themselves or abandoned by mammals, or even in the crater of an island volcano. The young grow very slowly, perhaps because they are only fed at lengthy intervals.

Without any doubt, they are the world's best flying birds as well as the most formidable transoceanic migrants. Many investigations have shown that a large number of species follow precise and well defined flight paths, so demolishing the former theory that these birds tend to be nomadic in their migrations. The antarctic species generally migrate towards the equator and sometimes beyond it, but there are instances of species that fly in the opposite direction. Some disperse far and wide, their movements depending mainly on the amount of food to be found close to the surface and on the winds. Wilson's petrel covers 7,500 miles (12,000 km) twice a year, but this is modest compared with the distances traveled by the albatrosses, whose flights have for centuries been described in legendary terms. Assisted by the trade winds of the Southern Hemisphere, these birds can actually circumnavigate the globe twice in the interval between two breeding cycles. Two wandering albatrosses (*Diomedea exulans*) have, for example, been recovered over 6,000 miles (10,000 km) away from the place where they were ringed.

These birds also have exceptional powers of orientation. One of 700 Manx shearwaters ringed in Wales was taken by air to Boston, Mass. It made the return journey in 12 days, covering at least 3,000 miles (5,000 km).

Storm petrel
(*Hydrobates pelagicus*)

◄ The storm petrels are smaller than the shearwaters, but also possess tube-like nostrils. There are two principal forms in either hemisphere, identifiable, too, by the ways in which they capture food. Their habits are similar to those of shearwaters. The birds fly close to the surface of the sea, following ships and feeding on various types of animal plankton.

Wilson's petrel
(*Oceanites oceanicus*)

▲ The chick, like that of the shearwaters, puts on large quantities of fat until it may be one and a half times the size of the adult.

▲ The storm petrel uses its feet both for checking its flight and catching small fish. The dangling legs sometimes give the bird the appearance of walking on the water's surface and this is the reason why it was once known as St Peter's bird, petrel being a diminutive form of this name.

◄ The common storm petrel lives in the Atlantic and the western Mediterranean (1) while Wilson's petrel (2) populates the oceans in its millions, especially in the Southern Hemisphere.

WANDERING ALBATROSS

Diomedea exulans

Order Procellariiformes
Family Diomedeidae
Length 28 – 48 in (71 – 122 cm)
Weight 13 – 18 lb (6 – 8 kg)
Distribution Southern Hemisphere, North Pacific
Habits Gregarious; pelagic, transoceanic migrants
Nesting On ground
Reproductive period Autumn–winter or spring–summer
Eggs 1
Chicks Semi-inept
Sexual maturity 6 – 10 years of age
Maximum age About 40 years

The name albatross is derived from the word *alcatraz*, used by Portuguese sailors to describe all large sea birds indiscriminately. The albatrosses, members of the family Diomedeidae, are the largest known flying birds. A simple distinguishing feature is the huge bill made up of numerous horny plates. The nostrils, in the form of short tubes, are situated on either side of the central slab of the upper mandible. On both the upper and lower surfaces of the long, narrow wings there is a distinctive color pattern. The 13 recognized species are distinguished mainly by the color of the bill and the wings. The largest species are the wandering albatross (*Diomedea exulans*) and the royal albatross (*D. epomophora*).

Albatrosses are to be found in almost all of the world's oceans: nine species live in the Southern Henisphere, three in the North Pacific, and one in the tropics. Albatrosses are exceptional fliers and their migrations embrace the entire globe. The ocean is the natural habitat of these huge birds, but during the breeding season they venture onto dry land, nesting mainly on small islands and isolated parts of the continents. Their ability to find their way across the oceans and back to their original sites is astonishing.

No other bird can rival the albatross in remaining for hours on end suspended in the air, hardly ever moving its wings. It takes advantage of all the air currents playing over the water surface, gaining altitude by flying upwind (into the wind) when wind velocity

The albatrosses are the largest representatives of the order Procellariiformes. The wandering albatross (the drawing shows an adult and, on the right, an immature individual) is the largest of all marine birds. There are three species of albatross in the Northern Hemisphere and ten in the Southern Hemisphere. They are carried along by the strong sea winds, seldom flapping their wings; in flight they hold the bill downwards, repeatedly skimming the waves.

The bill of the albatross, composed of horny plates, is very stout with the nostrils situated on either side of the central plate of the upper mandible.

diminishes because of friction with the waves, soaring upward when the wind is stronger, and gliding downwind (with the wind) so as to obtain the thrust and acceleration needed to gain altitude once more when it encounters the immobile layers of air below. During flight the webbed feet are held wide on either side of the tail.

All the albatrosses feed chiefly on cephalopod mollusks (especially squid) caught on the surface either in flight or when at rest. Other important elements of diet are crustaceans (notably shrimp), fish, and tunicates. Nor do they refuse any organic refuse left floating in the sea by fishing fleets, often following the ships for days on end across an entire ocean. During the breeding season albatrosses may also hunt small penguins and other birds and it is not unusual to see them feeding on the carcasses of seals and whales.

The birds normally nest in colonies but there are some solitary species. The nests are situated in small holes scooped out with the beak or simply on the ground, and they consist of soil and mud. The wandering albatross starts paying suit to his mate by beating his wings while she takes on a submissive posture, both birds pecking each other gently. Once his overtures are accepted, both partners spread their wings, stretch the neck and give out loud, penetrating cries. This courtship ceremony is regarded as a competitive encounter between two birds that have not yet mated; both the vocal and visual signals probably help to calm the female.

Albatrosses are normally very regular in returning to the same nesting sites. The female lays one large egg, white or delicately streaked red at the bigger end, that is incubated for a period ranging from 60 to 80 days. The male is the first to incubate and is followed by the female; there after the two birds take turns with intervals of 1 – 17 days, each incubation period lasting from 7 or 10 to 21 days. The newborn chick has two successive coverings of pale gray or whitish down and is fed by both parents for the first 3 – 5 weeks on pulpy food mixed with the oily secretions of the glandular stomach.

The young are fed on regurgitated food, inserting their bill into that of the adult at right angles. Soon after birth, the young wandering albatross strays a little way from the nest and builds another, to which the parents carry food at irregular intervals.

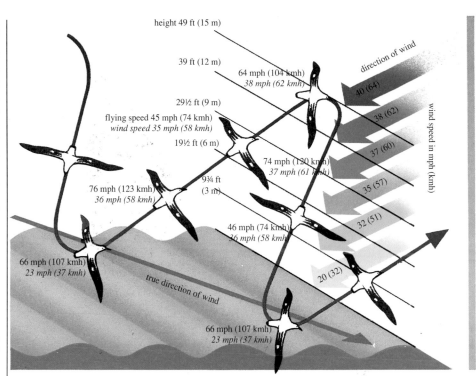

The albatross exploits the air currents at the sea's surface in the following manner: initially the bird swoops downward, picking up speed until it is almost skimming the surface; then it ricochets off the lowest, unmoving layers of air and soars up on the original air current. The strong trade winds of the Southern Hemisphere are invaluable for flying and migrating. The wings are used as rudders to change direction.

During the courtship display the male wandering albatross snaps his beak and opens his wings; then both partners spread their wings and let out loud cries.

The largest proportion of the albatross's diet consists of squid, fish, and shrimp.

The chicks demand food by repeatedly tapping the parent's beak.

Albatrosses are exceptional fliers and cover the world's oceans in the course of their migrations. They range over the Southern Hemisphere and the North Pacific, one species being tropical. 1) Distribution of family Diomedeidae; 2) Distribution of wandering albatross (Diomedea exulans).

PROCELLARIIDAE

The most distinctive characteristic of the Procellariidae is the bill, slightly curved with the nostrils opening at the end of a double tube in the upper mandible. The length of the birds varies from 10 to 35 in (25 to 90 cm), depending on species, and the weight from 3½ oz to 8¾ lb (100 g to 4 kg).

The Procellariidae are distributed all over the world. Except during the breeding season, they spend their life at sea, braving the most violent storms. They skim continuously over the waves and fly in broad circles, taking advantage of the slightest rising air currents and breaths of wind to go into glides. Evidently these birds can spend considerable periods without sleep. Their food is comprised of crustaceans, cephalopod mollusks (mainly squid), fish, and plankton, sometimes caught beneath the surface.

These birds are easily recognized by their characteristic skimming flight just above the waves. Apart from a few species that nest directly on the ground, most make use of holes or rock cavities to lay their one egg. The sites are chiefly located near the coasts, but sometimes a little way from shore or on a rocky slope. They are very large and often accommodate whole colonies.

The single egg is white and very large in proportion to the adult bird's size. Incubation lasts 40 – 60 days, according to species, and both partners take turns to guard the egg for periods of between 2 – 12 days. Both the egg and the hatched chick are capable of surviving whenever the nest is temporarily abandoned; this is probably a form of adaptation to the frequent absence of parents, which occurs initially while they change places during incubation and later when they bring food to their offspring infrequently and only at night. The chick is cared for only for the first three days and after that visited simply for feeding. The young, covered in two successive layers of brownish or grayish down, are fed on the regurgitated oily pulp of fish and other marine animals. When threatened by an enemy, they bring up their stomach oil, which in certain cases can be spat out to a distance of 3 ft (1 m). The Procellariidae are the most remarkable of all migrating birds, winging their way across the boundless oceans and always returning to their birthplace.

Manx shearwater
(*Puffinus puffinus*)

▲ The Procellariidae are medium-sized birds living at sea. They return to land only in the breeding season and are seldom observed. They fly on the ocean air currents, occasionally flapping their wings to gain a little altitude.

▼ The shearwater's bill is furnished with tubular nostrils like those of all Procellariiformes; these exude the salt filtered from the sea water drunk by the bird. The shearwater's sense of smell is so keen that it can find its mate and nest in pitch darkness.

TROPIC BIRDS
Phaethontidae

The tropic birds or bosun birds, so-called because of their habit of never straying beyond tropical seas, have a merited reputation of being tireless, exceptional fliers. Their nostrils are better developed than those of other Pelecaniformes and always distinct, while the bill is conical, laterally compressed, and slightly curved. The wings are large and the tail is made up of 12 – 16 rectrices, the central two being extremely long and wiry. The tarsi are short and the plumage is white with beautiful satin tones of yellow, gray or salmon pink. The birds are not large, from 31 – 39 in (80 – 100 cm) in length, almost two thirds of this consisting of tail; the wingspan is 35 – 43 in (90 – 110 cm) and the weight ³/₄ – 1½ lb (300 – 750 g).

The three known species, inhabiting tropical seas, are pelagic and characterized by a rapid, darting flight. They nest on cliffs, in holes close to vegetation or in rock clefts on volcanic islands. On some Pacific islands they may nest, in trees, too. Tropic birds are colonial by habit and during the courtship stage males become very excited, fighting one another to the accompaniment of sharp, strident cries.

After pairs are formed the female lays one very large egg, gray with speckles or reddish brown, this soon becoming discolored from spray. Incubation lasts 41 – 45 days, the chick being fed for the first time three days after birth and being capable of flying between the ages of 70 and 120 days. The adults never leave the nest for any reason whatsoever, reacting to intruders by flapping their wings and letting out loud cries.

Tropic birds hunt in a highly distinctive manner, using the same techniques as gannets. They dive from on high into the water, closing their wings to catch flying fish, cephalopods, and crustaceans, which are swallowed while the birds bob about on the surface. They often hunt in pairs.

Two species nesting on Ascension Island in the South Atlantic, the red-billed tropic bird (*Phaëthon aethereus*) and the white-tailed tropic bird (*P. lepturus*) have been closely studied because of their unusual rivalry. In fact, as a result of contacts between the two species, a very large number of eggs and chicks are lost.

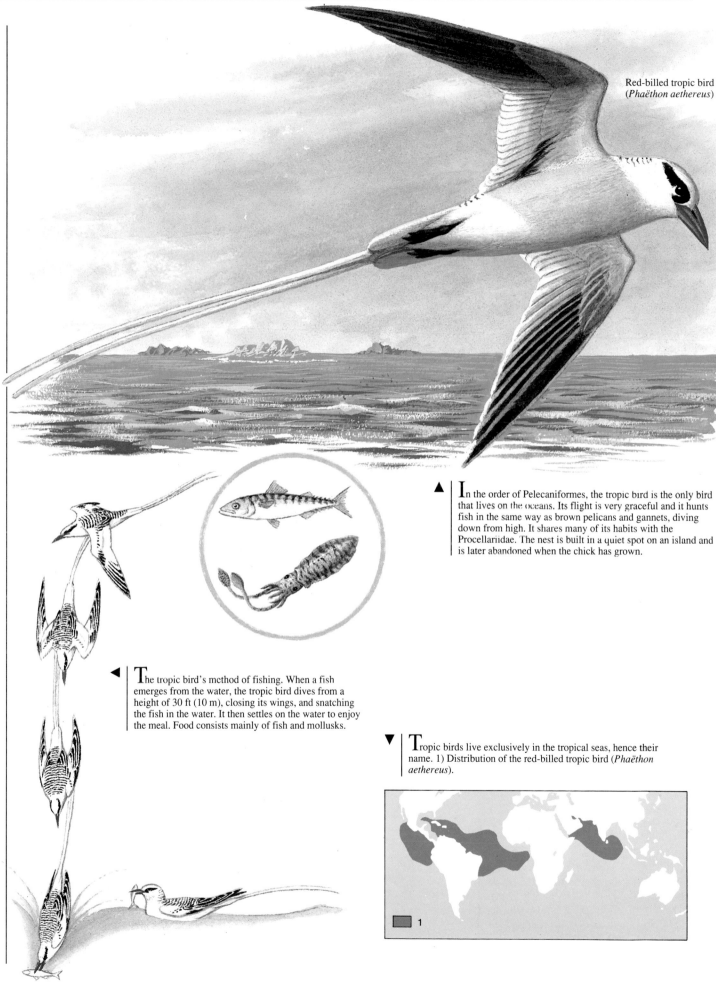

Red-billed tropic bird
(*Phaëthon aethereus*)

▲ In the order of Pelecaniformes, the tropic bird is the only bird that lives on the oceans. Its flight is very graceful and it hunts fish in the same way as brown pelicans and gannets, diving down from high. It shares many of its habits with the Procellariidae. The nest is built in a quiet spot on an island and is later abandoned when the chick has grown.

◄ The tropic bird's method of fishing. When a fish emerges from the water, the tropic bird dives from a height of 30 ft (10 m), closing its wings, and snatching the fish in the water. It then settles on the water to enjoy the meal. Food consists mainly of fish and mollusks.

▼ Tropic birds live exclusively in the tropical seas, hence their name. 1) Distribution of the red-billed tropic bird (*Phaëthon aethereus*).

COMMON CORMORANT

Phalacrocorax carbo

Order Pelecaniformes
Family Phalacrocracidae
Length 18 – 36 in (48 – 92 cm)
Weight 1½ – 7½ lb (0.7 – 3.5 kg)
Distribution Worldwide, excluding polar regions
Habits Colonial; some species migratory
Nesting In trees and rocks
Reproductive period Spring – summer or winter – spring
Incubation 27 – 30 days
Eggs 2 – 4
Chicks Inept
Sexual maturity 3 years of age

There are 29 species of cormorants: eight live only in America, eleven in Europe, Asia, and Africa, six in Australia, and the remaining four virtually all over the globe.

They have long necks, fairly small, rounded wings, and a distinctive skull structure that enables them to keep hold of prey. The plumage is generally dark, but species from the Southern Hemisphere also have white underparts. The plumage is not waterproof so although these birds can slip silently into the water, they have to expose their feathers to the air so as to dry off.

Among cormorants, the nesting site is chosen by the male who tries to attract the female with a special form of nuptial display, raising and lowering his wings repeatedly and folding the primary remiges behind the secondary and tertiary feathers.

Nest-building materials are assembled by the male but the female partner helps in the construction as soon as the eggs are laid. Both birds take it in turns to incubate, greeting each other every time they arrive or depart. Each species has its own ceremonial pattern of greeting, as does each breeding pair; in this way they manage to locate their nest among thousands of others.

Both partners take part in the rearing of the chicks. They defend the nest with threatening attitudes and raucous cries. Incubation of the 2 – 4 eggs takes 27 – 30 days.

All species feed chiefly on fish but the diet may also include cephalopod mollusks, crustaceans, and amphibians.

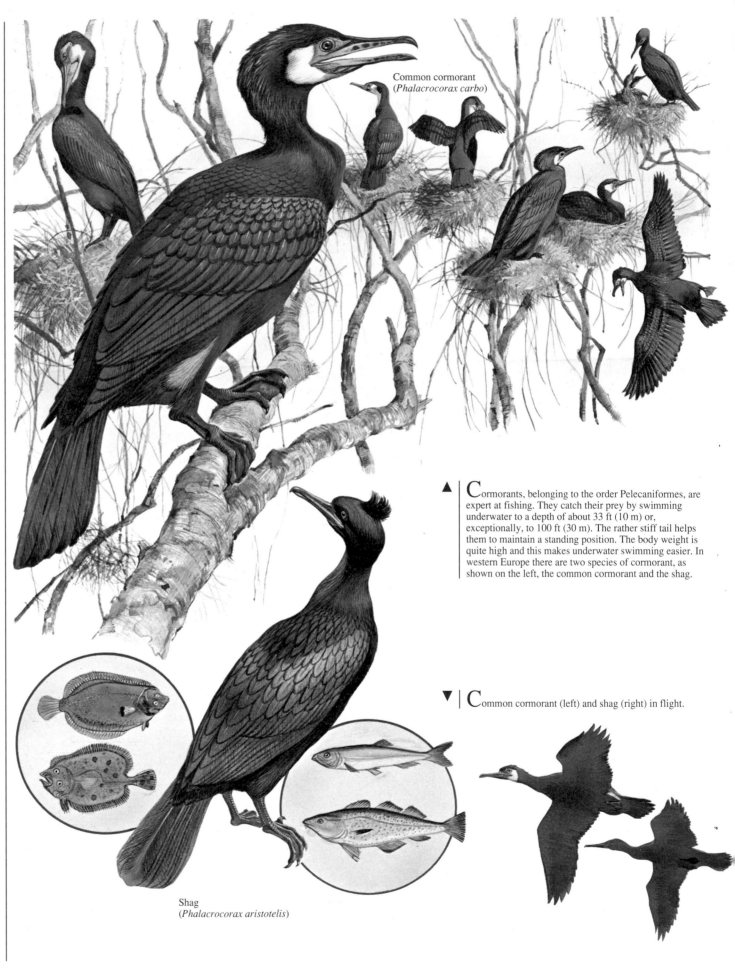

Common cormorant
(*Phalacrocorax carbo*)

▲ Cormorants, belonging to the order Pelecaniformes, are expert at fishing. They catch their prey by swimming underwater to a depth of about 33 ft (10 m) or, exceptionally, to 100 ft (30 m). The rather stiff tail helps them to maintain a standing position. The body weight is quite high and this makes underwater swimming easier. In western Europe there are two species of cormorant, as shown on the left, the common cormorant and the shag.

▼ Common cormorant (left) and shag (right) in flight.

Shag
(*Phalacrocorax aristotelis*)

BROWN BOOBY

Sula leucogaster

Order Pelecaniformes
Family Sulidae
Length 25 – 29 in (64 – 74 cm)
Distribution Atlantic, Pacific, and Indian Oceans
Habits Marine, gregarious
Eggs 1 or 2, sometimes 3
Nesting On ground
Chicks Nidicolous

Gannets and boobies are large sea birds that visit land only for breeding purposes. Their body is streamlined, the wings are long and narrow, and the strong, conical bill has sharply notched edges towards the front. The naked areas of the face and feet are often brightly colored. There are no external nostrils so that breathing is only through the mouth. The legs are short and the toes completely webbed.

These birds have a powerful, gliding flight, the grace of which is enhanced by the presence of large air sacs beneath the skin. They feed on fish and other sea animals caught under the surface after a spectacular dive from quite some height. Nests are built along the coasts and on small islands, those of tropical species often situated in zones where there is plenty of available food.

The brown booby is the most abundant species of booby in tropical and subtropical areas of the Atlantic, Pacific, and Indian Oceans. It never strays too far from rocky coasts or coral reefs where it breeds. The breeding cycle of this bird is not strictly annual but often eight-monthly, directly linked with the greater or lesser availability of food in the neighborhood of the nesting sites.

Nests are located on rocky shores, colonies being of fair size and each pair of breeding birds defending a small territory. The courtship ceremony is quite elaborate. The two partners face each other, stretching the neck upward, moving the beak rhythmically up and down, and letting out loud whistles. The brown booby has quite a varied language, with calls (different in each sex because of the structure of the vocal organs) associated with courtship, display of territorial aggression against intruders, communication with the partner while the young are being reared, and contacts between adults and chicks.

Fishing technique employed by the northern gannet: the bird dives into the water and drives the fish up to the surface. Flying fish and pelagic cephalopods are among the most frequent victims in tropical zones.

The brown booby breeds on rocky islets. The large webbed feet, with their many blood vessels, cover and warm the eggs during incubation, this method replacing the standard one because the birds have no area of naked skin on the belly.

During the courtship ritual of the red-footed booby, the two birds face each other, bill pointed high, tail spread, wings erect over the back, rocking on their feet. Special importance is attached, in the course of this ceremony, to displaying the brightly colored, naked parts of the body (beak, face, and legs).

The members of the family Sulidae live in warm and temperate seas and in the North Atlantic as far as the Polar Circle. The map shows the distribution of two species: 1) brown booby (*Sula leucogaster*); 2) red-footed booby (*S. sula*).

MAGNIFICENT FRIGATE BIRD

Fregata magnificens

Order Pelecaniformes
Family Fregatidae
Length 40 – 44 in (103 – 112 cm)
Weight 3 – 3¼ lb (1,400 – 1,500 g)
Distribution Galapagos, Antilles, and Cape Verde Islands
Habits Gregarious
Nesting In trees or on shrubs, sometimes on rocks or sloping ground
Eggs 1
Chicks Nidicolous

The magnificent frigate bird has a long gray beak that is sharp and hooked, its graceful form best visible in flight. The wings are very long and narrow with pointed tips, and the tail is forked with long outer rectrices. The male has iridescent black plumage with metallic blue tints. Under his throat is a pouch of naked skin, rough in texture and colored orange, except during the breeding season when it swells up and turns crimson. The female is slightly larger than the male and her sooty black plumage, with grayish overtones and no blue reflections, is less spectacular. She has a white patch on the breast and no red gular pouch. The legs of this species are short, orange in color, with little webbing between the toes but with long, curved claws; such feet are not conducive to swimming or walking but ideal for perching on high vantage points such as branches, outcrops of rock, and cliffs.

Half the total weight consists of the pectoral muscles and feathers. So because of their fairly low wing load, the frigate birds are among the most accomplished of all gliding birds, with great powers of endurance.

They live in tropical zones of the eastern Pacific and Atlantic Oceans. Breeding colonies are to be found on the Galapagos Islands, the Antilles, and the Cape Verde Islands. Each of these archipelagos is visited by a different subspecies, although all are much alike. The bird is strictly an inhabitant of tropical seas with a surface water temperature of about 77°F (25°C) and an abundance of flying fish. On the whole it prefers islands to mainland coastal areas and for this reason is regarded as a tropical ocean dweller even though it returns frequently to land in order to breed.

The magnificent frigate bird, like other species belonging to the same family, is an excellent flier. The plumage of the males (shown here in flight) is shiny black with blue reflection; the throat is adorned with a crimson pouch of naked skin. The female (shown perched) is duller in hue with a whitish patch on the breast. This species spends much of the time in the air, moving slowly and awkwardly on land. For this reason it usually perches or rests fairly high up, in trees or on rocks and cliffs, from which vantage points it can easily take wing.

Because the species has such markedly aerial habits, the feet have adapted by losing most of the interdigital webbing that typifies other Pelecaniformes. The birds compensate for poor swimming and walking powers by the development of prehensile claws that are ideal for gripping branches and rocks.

Food consists in the main of tiny marine creatures, especially flying fish, cuttlefish, small turtles, and jellyfish.

Nesting areas are generally near the sea, and food is normally sought on beaches and along coasts, including the neighboring waters. However, the bird is capable of flying hundreds of miles out over the open sea.

The frigate bird, or man-o'-war bird as it is also called, is both a predator and a parasite and although it seldom wanders far from the islands where it breeds, it sometimes ventures some way out over the open sea. The fact that frigate birds have been sighted hundreds of miles from the nearest land is a sure indication of the bird's flying abilities. The plumage is not impermeable and therefore it cannot come down on water, being compelled to stay on the wing during the longest journeys.

The magnificent frigate bird is noted for its parasitic habits. Because of its flying powers, it manages to obtain much of its food by pursuing other birds such as gulls, cormorants, pelicans, and, above all, boobies, harassing and tormenting them until they regurgitate the fish they have only recently swallowed. The frigate bird swoops down on the morsel, neatly catching it before it can hit the ground or water. At other times it hovers above nesting colonies of sea birds, awaiting the chance to snatch food brought by the adults for the chicks. The bird is also an active predator, renowned for its opportunism. Diving low to within a few feet of the sea surface, it snaps up flying fish by the dorsal fins and even catches ocean invertebrates furnished with membranes or expanding body parts, such as jellyfish. During the periods when turtle eggs begin to hatch, the frigate bird takes a heavy toll of newly born turtles as they make their way to the sea. It also filches eggs and chicks from the nesting colonies of boobies and other sea birds. Occasionally it will turn scavenger, feeding on refuse or pecking chunks of flesh from the carcasses of seals and whales stranded on a beach.

This species tends to nest at any time of year. Materials include sticks and dry branches, collected in the bill and for the most part taken on the wing either from the ground or from nests of other birds. The nest is situated on or near the shore, generally in trees or low bushes but also on cliffs or hillside slopes, sites where it is as easy to land as to take off. Breeding colonies are close to those of other sea birds such as boobies, cormorants, pelicans, terns, gulls, etc, all of which are regularly parasitized by the frigate bird.

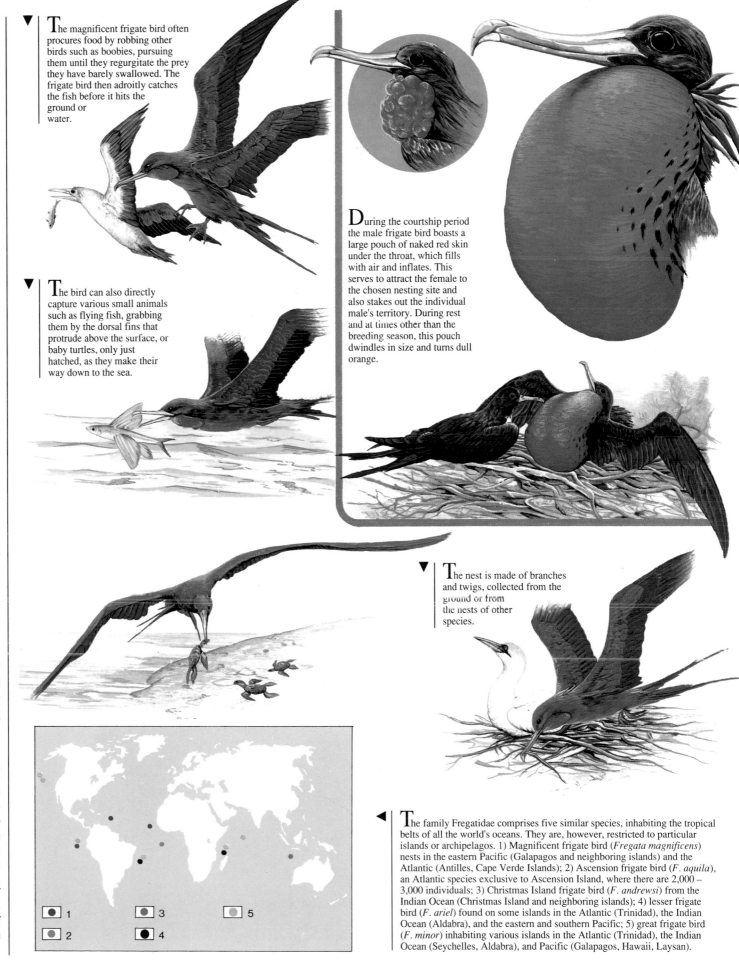

The magnificent frigate bird often procures food by robbing other birds such as boobies, pursuing them until they regurgitate the prey they have barely swallowed. The frigate bird then adroitly catches the fish before it hits the ground or water.

The bird can also directly capture various small animals such as flying fish, grabbing them by the dorsal fins that protrude above the surface, or baby turtles, only just hatched, as they make their way down to the sea.

During the courtship period the male frigate bird boasts a large pouch of naked red skin under the throat, which fills with air and inflates. This serves to attract the female to the chosen nesting site and also stakes out the individual male's territory. During rest and at times other than the breeding season, this pouch dwindles in size and turns dull orange.

The nest is made of branches and twigs, collected from the ground or from the nests of other species.

The family Fregatidae comprises five similar species, inhabiting the tropical belts of all the world's oceans. They are, however, restricted to particular islands or archipelagos. 1) Magnificent frigate bird (*Fregata magnificens*) nests in the eastern Pacific (Galapagos and neighboring islands) and the Atlantic (Antilles, Cape Verde Islands); 2) Ascension frigate bird (*F. aquila*), an Atlantic species exclusive to Ascension Island, where there are 2,000 – 3,000 individuals; 3) Christmas Island frigate bird (*F. andrewsi*) from the Indian Ocean (Christmas Island and neighboring islands); 4) lesser frigate bird (*F. ariel*) found on some islands in the Atlantic (Trinidad), the Indian Ocean (Aldabra), and the eastern and southern Pacific; 5) great frigate bird (*F. minor*) inhabiting various islands in the Atlantic (Trinidad), the Indian Ocean (Seychelles, Aldabra), and Pacific (Galapagos, Hawaii, Laysan).

1
2
3
4
5

COMMON GULL
Larus canus

Order Charadriiformes
Family Laridae
Subfamily Larinae
Distribution Central and northern Europe, central Asia, northwestern America.
Habits Gregarious
Nesting Mid May to early June. Single clutch.
Eggs Usually 3, rarely 1 – 4, varying from brown to blue with dark spots
Chicks Born with gray–yellow marbled down. Seminidifugous

Gulls are distributed all over the world but most of them come originally from the Northern Hemisphere. By reason of their cosmopolitan habits and their ready adaptation to populated surroundings, they are certainly the best known of all marine birds, even if they actually frequent the coasts rather than the open sea. Indeed, they seldom stray far from the shore and even visit inland areas provided there is some water available, such zones often being some way above sea level. Many species nest in circumpolar regions, leaving their breeding grounds at the approach of winter to seek out milder lands; others fly off on long migrations across the equator. Only kittiwakes are typically oceanic.

Gulls are equally at home on dry land, darting about and catching prey, and on water, where they come down to rest and feed. Unlike the majority of sea birds, however, they are unable to submerge entirely. They are excellent fliers, and although their normal motion through the air is slow and powerful, they can, if need be, use gusts of wind to perform acrobatic maneuvers and soar upward on thermal air currents, gliding like birds of prey. Decidedly gregarious by habit, gulls display extremely complex social behavior which has an influence on all their activities.

The common gull (*Larus canus*) is one of the most widely distributed species, for in addition to inhabiting the northern parts of the Palearctic region, it also frequents the northwest coasts of North America. Like almost all gulls, its habits are markedly gregarious and flocks of many dozens will often be seen flying over sandy beaches, river estuaries, and harbors. In winter it is likely to be encountered, more than other gulls,

Common gull (*Larus canus*)

▶ The common gull, like all gulls, is not averse to the presence of humans; it is a familiar bird of ports and harbors, perching for hours on posts and other vantage points. It feeds on fish, the eggs and young of other birds, small vertebrates, and waste of every kind.

inland around lakes, rivers, and marshes, often settling, too, on cultivated fields in its quest for food.

The common gull's body is white, the wings are gray with black, white-flecked tips, and the bill and webbed feet are yellow–green. In winter the head is streaked with brown. It greatly resembles the herring gull (*L. argentatus*) but measures barely 16 in (40 cm) in length, and is handsome in appearance because the bill is more slender and not as heavy, and the wings, when the gull is perched, extend beyond the tail, giving the body a more streamlined silhouette. The young of the first year have a gray head, gray–brown upperparts, whitish underparts, and chestnut legs and bill; in the second year, however, they look very like the adults, except for a dark band on the wing coverts. Although not very large, the common gull is not as light and agile as smaller gulls; indeed, it has a slow, sweeping flight that is more like that of even larger species.

The common gull frequently assumes the role of thief and parasite, filching food from other birds such as gulls, coots, and ducks, which learn to respect its strength and determination. When attacking a bird with a view to robbing it of its prey, the gull lets out sharp, nasal cries, but as a rule it tends to be more silent than related species. It will not turn down the chance of a dead fish or other animal carcass, and often attacks sick individuals. Broadly speaking, it includes a bit of everything in its diet, including crustaceans, small fish, vegetables such as turnips and potatoes, and in the breeding season the young and the eggs of other birds. Virtually omnivorous all gulls actively benefit from the presence of humans and often undergo such a population explosion (as in the case of the herring gull) that they become a serious threat to other birds.

The common gull nests on islets and along coasts with plenty of vegetation, but also on the banks of lakes and swamps close to the sea, streams, rivers, and heaths. The breeding season commences in mid May. Returning to their nesting sites, the gulls perform courtship parades, both sexes walking in circles, head thrust back, and making guttural sounds. The nest, as for almost all gulls, is a mass of vegetation, varying in bulk; it is assembled by both birds but prepared chiefly by the female, either on the bare ground or in the bushes. Sometimes it is no more than a simple hollow lined with scraps of grass and occasionally it is situated in a tree.

▼ The common gull is always eager to pounce on fish and refuse thrown from ships.

▼ The black-legged kittiwake nests on the narrowest rock ledges.

▲ It skims the water surface, killing prey with its beak.

Ivory gull
(*Pagophila eburnea*)

Little gull
(*Larus minutus*)

Lesser black-backed gull
(*Larus fuscus*)

Herring gull
(*Larus argentatus*)

Black-headed gull
(*Larus ridibundus*)

Black-legged kittiwake
(*Rissa tridactyla*)

▲ Other species of gulls.

Great skua
(*Stercorarius skua*)

Black skimmer
(*Rynchops nigra*)

Crested auklet
(*Aethia cristatella*)

Inca tern
(*Larosterna inca*)

◄ Relatives of the gulls are the skuas, the terns, and the auks. All are members of the order Charadriiformes.

GREAT SKUA

Stercorarius skua

Order Charadriiformes
Family Stercorariidae
Length 24 in (58 cm)
Distribution In the Northern
Hemisphere, from the Scottish isles to
Iceland; in the Southern Hemisphere, in
the circumpolar regions of Antarctica.
In winter, over the Atlantic to the
Tropic of Cancer
Nesting End May to early June. Single
clutch
Eggs Usually 2, rarely 1, olive–brown
or grayish yellow with brown spots
Chicks Born with yellowish brown
down, paler on underparts.
Seminidifugous

The family Stercorariidae contains four
species: the great skua (*Stercorarius
skua*), the pomarine skua (*S. pomari-
nus*), the parasitic skua (*S. parasiticus*),
and the long-tailed skua (*S. longicaudus*).
The great skua, measuring 24 in (58 cm)
long, is the biggest species. Its plumage
is completely brown, except at the base
of the primary flight feathers where
white patches are visible on both sides of
the wings, these areas being smaller in
the juveniles during their first two years.

The skuas are noticeably aggressive
towards other sea birds, pursuing them
relentlessly until they drop or even
regurgitate their prey, this often being
snatched up before it hits the water. The
great skua, although less prone to this
type of activity than its relatives, will
even take on the much larger gannets.
While living principally by plunder,
they also feed on fish, rodents, insects,
birds, carrion, and all kinds of refuse,
and sometimes even berries. All skuas
are highly skilled at capturing adult
birds in the air, striking out so powerfully with feet and wings that the prey
falls to the ground, where it is promptly
finished off.

Skuas live for most of the year at sea
and settle on dry land only for breeding.
The great skua usually nests close to the
sea, on moors at varying altitudes, on
bare ground or planted terrain, and in
river estuaries. They normally nest in
small colonies or isolated pairs. Each
nest, generally in an exposed spot, is
surrounded by territory, varying in size,
belonging to the breeding pair. During
their early years the young make long
journeys across the entire Atlantic.

Like all its relatives, the great skua is a
kleptoparasite, feeding on the fish it steals from other
sea birds. This aggressive habit partly explains their
family name of Stercorariidae; it used to be believed
that they ate the excrement emitted by the terrified
birds they were pursuing, but skuas actually feed on
birds, carrion, eggs and chicks, lemmings, and, of
course, fish.

The bill of skuas (below) is fairly similar to that of
gulls (above) but more prominently hooked at the tip,
in keeping with its predatory habits.

GUILLEMOT
Uria aalge

Order Charadriiformes
Family Alcidae
Length 16 in (41 cm)
Distribution Northern coasts of the Atlantic and Pacific Oceans (North America, northern Europe, Greenland, Iceland)
Habits Marine, gregarious
Nesting In colonies on rocky islets and cliffs
Eggs 1, large and pear-shaped
Chicks Seminidicolous, venturing into the sea before being able to fly

The common guillemot looks much like a penguin, with its tapered body, long neck, conical and pointed bill, and feet positioned far back under the abdomen. The plumage is white on the belly, black or chocolate brown on the back, head, and neck. The weight range is 25 to 39 oz (700 to 1,100 g).

The guillemot is a sea bird that ventures onto dry land only for nesting; much of its life is spent on the high seas. It moves about awkwardly on land and is forced to rest sitting upright on its tarsi. Nor is it notably versatile in the air; the short, narrow wings have to be kept fluttering rapidly to support the heavy body, the short tail precludes sudden changes of direction, and the webbed feet stick out widely from the sides of the body. In the sea, however, the bird comes into its own, displaying its perfect adaptation to the elements; the soft, thick plumage is covered by a layer of oil which is secreted by the uropygial gland and smeared over the feathers with the bill, protecting the body from the water and the cold.

The guillemot can dive to a depth of about 33 ft (10 m) and can go without breathing for more than a minute as it chases the fish that constitute its diet. These are mainly herring, sardines, and anchovies, supplemented to a much lesser degree by crustaceans, mollusks, and worms.

Towards the end of December the guillemots head for the shore, returning regularly to the sites used for breeding in previous years. Both sexes share incubation which lasts 32 – 34 days. Once the breeding season is over, the guillemots all head back for the open sea, swimming away in different directions.

▼ Guillemots nest on cliffs, crowding together on narrow rock ledges overlooking the sea. The clouds of birds wheeling over the cliffs as they return from fishing, the sharp, penetrating smell, the white excrement staining the rocks, and the raucous cries emitted incessantly by adults and young, provide a spectacle of great beauty and animation.

▶ Food consists of fish and, to a lesser extent, crustaceans, mollusks, and worms.

LITTLE AUK
Plautus alle

Order Charadriiformes
Family Alcidae
Length 8 in (20 cm)
Distribution North Atlantic and neighboring Arctic seas
Habits Gregarious
Nesting In colonies on small islands and cliffs
Eggs 1, sometimes 2
Chicks Seminidicolous, venturing into sea before being able to fly

In the seas that are its home the little auk cannot be mistaken for any other bird. A little bigger than a starling, it has a plump, stocky body and a short bill. The bird does not weigh more than 5½ oz (160 g). This is the most northerly species of the family, breeding in high arctic latitudes on cliffs and rocky islands. Outside the breeding season the little auks scatter over the oceans, often remaining near pack ice. During the short nesting period this small bird is to be found on cliffs and stony seashores.

The smallest of the Atlantic auks, it feeds principally on plankton (crustaceans, mollusks, and cephalopods) as well as worms and medium-sized fish. Because such prey abounds in surface waters, it does not need to stay submerged for more than 25 – 30 seconds and need only dive to about 8 ft (2.5 m). However, in the event of danger the bird can go without breathing for more than a minute. After swooping low over the sea, skimming the surface with its fluttering wings, the little auk snatches up its prey and flies back to the cliffs and the nest where its hungry chick is waiting.

Nests are built in colonies containing thousands of breeding pairs on pebbly and rocky beaches or sometimes on mountain slopes 3 – 5 miles (5 – 8 km) inland. The single egg, blue–green with brown markings, is laid around mid June in a hole among the stones or in a rock cleft, and it is incubated by both adults for 24 days. The chick, covered in thick brown down, is tended by the parents for 3 – 4 weeks and then ventures into the sea with them, incapable of flying but already able to dive expertly.

In winter little auks spend much of the time on the high seas and approach the coasts only if driven there by strong winds. Some of the Eurasian populations migrate as far as Greenland.

▶ In returning to its nest on the cliffs the little auk skims over the surface of the sea, fluttering its wings rapidly.

▲ This bird obtains food (crustaceans, small fish, and mollusks) by diving underwater and pursuing its prey, beating the wings in a paddle-like manner.

▶ At times other than the breeding season, little auks spend most of the day out at sea, often close to pack ice where there is plenty of food.

Rhinoceros auklet
(*Cerorhinca monocerata*)

Parakeet auklet
(*Cyclorrhynchus psittacula*)

Whiskered auklet
(*Aethia pygmaea*)

▼ The little auk and the Adélie penguin, although far apart in classification and size, are equally well adapted to life in the water.

COMMON PUFFIN

Fratercula arctica

Order Charadriiformes
Family Alcidae
Length 12 in (30 cm)
Distribution North Atlantic
Habits Marine, gregarious
Nesting In colonies on rocky islets and grassy slopes near seashore
Eggs 1
Chicks Seminidicolous

The puffin weighs 10 – 16 oz (300 – 450 g). The body is stocky with broad webbed feet and the massive rounded head is furnished with a high, flattened bill, more conspicuous in the breeding season when it is adorned with horny plates of vivid hues (blue, red, and yellow) which disappear in winter. The back is black, the abdomen and cheeks are white, and the legs are orange. The blackish bill of the young is more pointed and the legs are pink.

The various puffin subspecies range widely along the northern coasts of the Atlantic Ocean. They nest on cliffs with grassy slopes and seldom stray far from the shore, although in winter they swim out to sea, dispersing in various directions and following routes (not yet fully traced) that carry them into the central Atlantic and even the Mediterranean.

Around the middle of March puffins return to the breeding grounds of former years, assembling at sea in huge flocks, within sight of the coasts where nesting is to take place. The number of birds in the sea steadily grows and eventually a few individuals approach the land and start surveying the terrain, coming down to settle in suitable spots. Although some breeding pairs choose rock fissures and hollows for egg laying, most prefer to rear their chick in a grassy burrow in the soil.

Incubation, shared by both birds, lasts 40 – 43 days. The chick, in its gray cover of down, is warmed and fed by the parents, who plunge into the sea and return to the nest with a mouthful of 15 – 20 fish, firmly clutched between the tongue and lower bill. Food, now and later, consists of small fish (sardines, sand eels, etc.) caught by diving down several feet. By the beginning of August, with the departure of the last young puffins, the colony is once again silent and deserted. All the birds are now out in the open sea.

The common puffin grasps fish between its tongue and lower mandible; in this way it can continue fishing without having to return to the nest after each kill. This bird, like all other alcids, is seriously threatened by ocean pollution. When the oil tanker *Torrey Canyon* was wrecked in the English Channel, the puffin colony on Canada's Sept-Iles dwindled abruptly from 2,500 to 400 nesting pairs.

Other puffin species living in the Pacific include the tufted puffin (*Lunda cirrhata*), above, and the horned puffin (*Fratercula corniculata*), below.

The birds nest in large colonies on the grassy slopes of islands, which are often riddled with burrows excavated by the birds with bill and feet.

Like all other alcids, the puffins are typically found in northern waters of the Northern Hemisphere. 1) Common puffin (*Fratercula arctica*); 2) horned puffin (*Fratercula corniculata*), which is the Pacific counterpart of the Atlantic species, the two being very much alike. To protect the nesting sites of alcids, many natural reserves have been set apart on cliffs; but in addition to this it is essential that the sea and its resources be sensibly exploited, prohibiting the indiscriminate discharging of hydrocarbons and toxic substances, and rigidly controlling oil tanker traffic to reduce the risk of accidents.

CETACEANS

The order Cetacea make up what is perhaps the most specialized group of mammals, having broken all links with terra firma and adapted to the needs of a marine life that involves survival at extraordinary depths.

Cetaceans are the only mammals to spend their whole lives in the water. Adaptation to such an existence has brought about a series of profound transformations that have had a striking effect on their whole morphology and skeletal anatomy. In particular, this transformation has had a substantial, although not very visible, effect on the animal's physiology, especially in relation to its respiration, blood circulation, and general ability to survive extended periods of deep submersion. With the exception of a certain very small number of species that move at low speeds, such as whales, the external morphology of cetaceans reveals a perfectly hydrodynamic shape, with a fusiform body that is designed to have the least possible number of appendages, except for the fins, which are specifically developed as an aid to swimming.

In all cetaceans the mouth has a very broad opening, with a long *rima*, but without any clearly defined lips comparable to those of other mammals. They have no proper nostrils; the nasal cavities communicate with the outside by means of a vent, which is composed of two distinct orifices in Mysticeti (Balaenidae and Balaenopteridae) and of a single one in Odontoceti (all other Cetacea). This vent is situated on the top of the head, in a "periscopic" position for swimming, since it allows the most direct contact with the air with the minimum emergence of the body from the water. The eyes are small and the ears have no outer ear.

Of the quadruped terrestrial mammal, such as the far distant ancestor of the cetaceans would have been, there remain only the front limbs, radically transformed into pectoral fins, which are almost always used solely as a directional device while swimming. The hindlimbs have disappeared, as has the pelvis, and of the latter there remain only vestigial traces, in the form of two small bones of equal size contained within the muscular mass of the abdomen.

The body, more or less fusiform,

▲ The body of cetaceans is marvelously adapted to life in the sea, where these creatures, which originated from terrestrial forms more than 60 million years ago, have achieved colossal dimensions. The largest species is the one illustrated above, the blue whale (*Balaenoptera musculus*), which can be up to 100 ft (33 m) long.

▼ There is relatively little fossil documentation on the ancestors of the Cetacea. Depicted here is a representative of the genus *Dorudon*, which was already fairly highly evolved and belonged to the extinct suborder Archaeoceti.

decreases in diameter toward the posterior extremity, which has developed a broad and extremely robust tail fin that is the basic means of propulsion: it is always arranged horizontally, and not vertically, as in fish. The tail is activated by powerful motor muscles that are inserted by means of large sinews in the posterior part of the spinal column, itself very powerful. The tail fin has no real bone structure as such, only its junction with the terminal part of the spinal column, which ends in correspondence with the interlobate sinus in the middle of the "wings" of the fin itself. The majority of species have a well developed dorsal fin, even though it is of modest size when compared to the overall size of the animal (especially in the case of Balaenopteridae), which is subtriangular in form. The dorsal fin is formed by a double layer of cutaneous tissue and rises up towards the center of the back, along the median line; it has no skeletal or muscular structure.

Cetaceans are nearly always large, very large or, on occasion, colossal; the blue whale (*Balaenoptera musculus*) is, as far as we know, the largest animal ever to have existed: it can reach 100 ft (33 m) in length and more than 130 tons in weight. The minimum length is around 3 – 4 ft (1 – 1.2 m) (genus *Cephalorhynchus*), but the majority of Cetacea measure more than 6½ ft (2 m), many of them reaching 10 – 13 ft (3 – 4 m).

The skin of cetaceans is hairless and extremely smooth. The epidermis is very thin and the deep part of the derm is made up of fat or blubber, with a network of fibers enclosing enormous adipose cells. The thickness of the fat, which is always considerable, varies according to the species, the season, and the part of the body; in Phocaenidae, for example, it measures roughly 1 in (2 cm); in the 85-ft (25-m) long blue whale it varies between 4½ – 5 in (11 – 13 cm), being broader in the female, while in Balaenidae it is much thicker still – maximum 20 – 28 in (50 – 70 cm).

Cetaceans have only a very few hairs in limited parts of the body, notably on the anterior part of the head in Mysticeti. None of the Cetacea have epidermal glands or nails. The animals are rarely of uniform color, being black or grayish or, in a few isolated cases, white. In the vast majority of species the coloring consists of mixed shades of brown and dark slate gray with white, variously distributed: normally the upper parts of the body are darker and

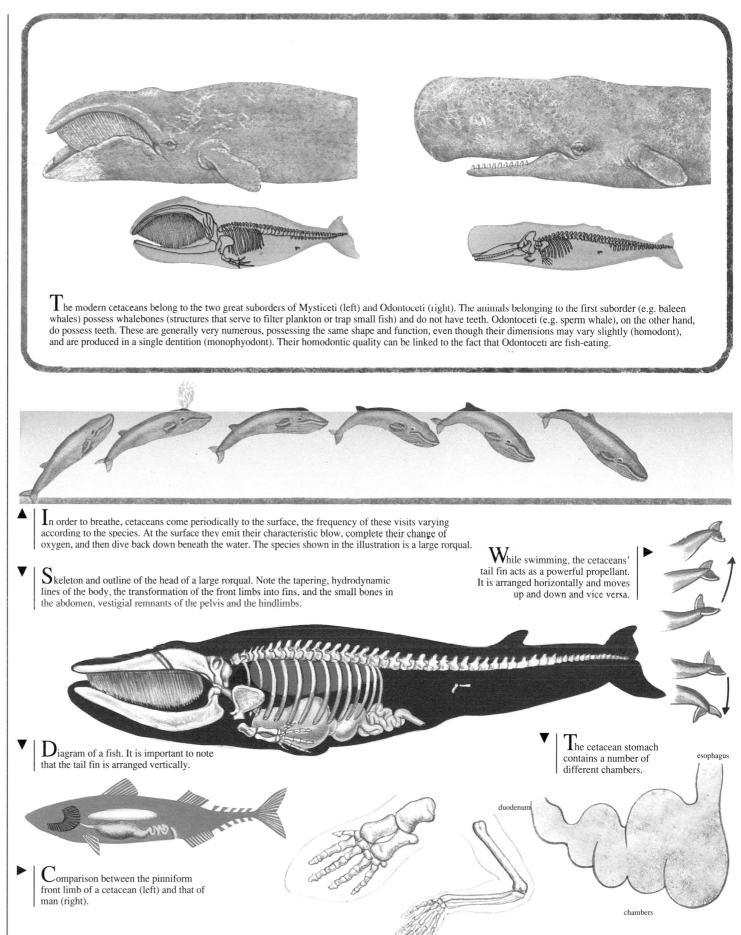

The modern cetaceans belong to the two great suborders of Mysticeti (left) and Odontoceti (right). The animals belonging to the first suborder (e.g. baleen whales) possess whalebones (structures that serve to filter plankton or trap small fish) and do not have teeth. Odontoceti (e.g. sperm whale), on the other hand, do possess teeth. These are generally very numerous, possessing the same shape and function, even though their dimensions may vary slightly (homodont), and are produced in a single dentition (monophyodont). Their homodontic quality can be linked to the fact that Odontoceti are fish-eating.

▲ In order to breathe, cetaceans come periodically to the surface, the frequency of these visits varying according to the species. At the surface they emit their characteristic blow, complete their change of oxygen, and then dive back down beneath the water. The species shown in the illustration is a large rorqual.

▼ Skeleton and outline of the head of a large rorqual. Note the tapering, hydrodynamic lines of the body, the transformation of the front limbs into fins, and the small bones in the abdomen, vestigial remnants of the pelvis and the hindlimbs.

While swimming, the cetaceans' tail fin acts as a powerful propellant. It is arranged horizontally and moves up and down and vice versa. ▶

▼ Diagram of a fish. It is important to note that the tail fin is arranged vertically.

▼ The cetacean stomach contains a number of different chambers.

esophagus

duodenum

chambers

▶ Comparison between the pinniform front limb of a cetacean (left) and that of man (right).

the lower parts either pale or white. Broken or even very striking colors are not uncommon either (as in *Orca*, for example).

In order to breathe, cetaceans come periodically to the surface, the frequency of these visits varying according to the species. At the surface they emit their characteristic blow, complete their change of oxygen, and then dive back down beneath the water.

Unlike terrestrial mammals, cetaceans need to be able to remain in a state of apnea (suspended respiration), sometimes for considerable periods. Their respiratory and circulatory apparatus has undergone modifications that allow for sufficient oxygenation of the various parts of the body during periods of immersion: it is particularly necessary that the supply of oxygen to the nervous system and the principal metabolic organs be maintained at a constant level. The apneal capacity of terrestrial mammals varies from species to species, but it is always less than in cetaceans.

There is no uniformity as to the maximum period of immersion: the common dolphin's maximum is eight minutes, whereas that of the sperm whale is more than an hour. There are numerous factors that affect their different capabilities, but among those animals that search for their food nearest the surface, such as dolphins, there is basically no need for them to remain underwater for long periods, whereas the bottle-nosed whales and the sperm whale, which feed on cephalopod mollusks from the depths, need more time in which to dive down, hunt, and then return to the surface. There are, of course, various intermediate stages within the different cetacean species that are related to the nature of the animal's diet and the depths at which the food is obtained. However, there are also exceptions: Mysticeti, which are basically plank-ton-eating, stay submerged for long intervals at great depths, even though the microcrustaceans on which they feed occur only a few feet below the surface.

Macroscopic modifications to the anatomical structure also occur in the thoracic cage, which is not rigid. The hearts of marine mammals do not differ greatly from those of terrestrial mammals. In the composition of the arteries there is a great deal of elastic tissue in the walls, which may serve the purpose of alleviating internal pressure during immersion by allowing a certain degree

Pygmy whale
(*Caperea marginata*)

Biscayan or North Atlantic right whale
(*Eubalaena glacialis*)

Bowhead whale
(*Balaena mysticetus*)

Byrde's whale
(*Balaenoptera edeni*)

Common rorqual or fin whale
(*Balaenoptera physalus*)

California gray whale
(*Eschrichtius robustus*)

Humpback whale
(*Megaptera novaeangliae*)

Sei whale or Rudolphi's rorqual
(*Balaenoptera borealis*)

Minke whale or lesser rorqual
(*Balaenoptera acutorostrata*)

of dilation. What is definite is that cetaceans have the capacity to achieve an impressive, peripheral vascular constriction during the course of immersion, which brings about a diminution in the quantity of blood in the external parts of the circulatory system.

Cetaceans swallow their prey whole, without taking the precaution of reducing it to small pieces in the oral cavity, as happens with terrestrial mammals. This is partly so as to allow for rapid ingestion of the food, whether it be plankton, cephalopods or fish, without at the same time taking in quantities of water. Naturally the digestive apparatus has consequently undergone certain modifications, and all cetaceans possess three gastric compartments, their capacity varying according to the species: the anterior stomach, the middle stomach, glandular or true stomach, and the pyloric or posterior stomach. In Ziphiidae, which eat "soft" food in the form of cephalopod mollusks, the first stomach is not very highly developed, since their food does not need to be rendered assimilable by the gastric juices of the true stomach; by way of compensation, the third stomach is unusually complex, possessing even 12 compartments.

The principal food of most Mysticeti consists of planktonic crustaceans, no bigger than a matchstick. A conspicuous number of Odontoceti eat, apart from fish, a considerable amount of cephalopod mollusks. The sperm whale is typical in this respect.

The central nervous system of cetaceans has always attracted the attention of researchers because of its anatomical peculiarities. The brain is among the most developed in all mammals, both for its size in relation to that of the body and also in absolute terms. In Odontoceti, the ratio between the weight of the brain and the weight of the body is very near that achieved by man and is at the same level as the most advanced primates. Nevertheless, this does not mean that cetaceans are as intelligent as humans.

The young of Cetacea are born at the rate of one every two years, after a pregnancy that lasts in all species regardless of their body size, between 10 – 12 months (except for the sperm whale, whose pregnancy lasts approximately 18 months).

Sperm whale
(*Physeter macrocephalus*)

Common dolphin
(*Delphinus delphis*)

Pygmy sperm whale
(*Kogia breviceps*)

Pilot whale
(*Globicephala melaena*)

Inia
(*Inia geoffrensis*)

Bottle-nosed whale
(*Hyperöodon ampullatus*)

Killer whale
(*Orcinus orca*)

Grampus
(*Grampus griseus*)

Porpoise
(*Phocaena phocaena*)

Narwhal
(*Monodon monoceros*)

Beluga or white whale
(*Delphinapterus leucas*)

Cetaceans swallow their prey whole, without taking the precaution of first breaking it down in their mouth, as terrestrial mammals do. This allows for rapid ingestion of food, without also taking in a certain amount of water. The principal food of most Mysticeti consists of planktonic crustaceans, no bigger than a matchstick. A conspicuous number of Odontoceti eat, apart from fish, a considerable amount of cephalopod mollusks. The sperm whale is typical in this respect.

HUMPBACK WHALE

Megaptera novaengliae

Order Cetacea
Family Balaenopteridae
Length 48 – 54 ft (15 – 17 m)
Weight 30 tons
Whalebones 270 – 400 on each side
Reproductive period Cold season
Gestation 1 year
Number of young 1 every 2 – 3 years
Length at birth 14 – 16 ft (4.5 – 5 m)
Sexual maturity When a length of 35 –
38 ft (11 – 12 m) has been reached

The humpback whale is, of all the Bal-aenopteridae, the one with the most massive and least slender frame, whose prime characteristic is the conspicuous length of the pectoral fins. From afar, it could be mistaken for a member of the Balaenopteridae family. Important distinguishing features are its habit of raising a large part of its body out of the water, thereby displaying its physionomical peculiarities (primarily the long pectoral fin), and the way in which it raises its tail vertically before immersing, showing off the black and white coloring of that organ.

The geographical distribution of the humpback is extremely wide ranging and involves almost all the seas of the world, with populations at both poles. They all, in fact, follow the same pattern of seasonal migration: the cold season is spent in tropical waters, where both mating and birth take place; during the hot season the humpbacks move to the cold waters of the polar regions, undertaking migrations of many thousands of miles.

When they are in colder waters it appears their main occupation is feeding. In this respect, the humpback, of all Mysticeti, is the species that shows the greatest variety of feeding techniques. One of these consists of swimming open-mouthed into a mass of potential prey. A more selective method of capturing fish and other animals if they are scattered over a wider area involves swimming in full circles underwater. During this operation, a cloud of bubbles is emitted from the blow hole and the small prey evidently feel trapped inside these bubbles, greatly increasing the humpback's haul. The humpback's diet, however, is very varied and includes a variety of shoal fish and planktonic crustaceans.

▲ The humpback whale (*Megaptera novaeangliae*) is, of all Balaenopteridae, the one with the most massive and least slender body. One of its distinguishing features is the conspicuous length of its pectoral fins, which can measure up to the equivalent of a third of the total body length. These fins are fringed along their rear edge and have prominent protuberances and excrescences, along their front edge at least. The humpback is black along the top and on the upper parts of its sides, whilst its nether regions are often white. Because of its body shape, which is not particularly hydrodynamic, this creature is perhaps the slowest of the Balaenopteridae. For this reason, and also because it is frequently found not far from the coast for part of the year, this species has been subjected to intensive hunting by the whaling industry: so much so, that despite its hunting having been banned in 1966, it must unfortunately be said, on the basis of data gathered in the northern Pacific, that the humpback is an endangered species.

▲ The humpback's diet is based on plankton, predominantly crustacean Euphausidae, but with a high intake also of shoal fish (anchovies, sardines, herrings, cod, and even salmon).

▶ The humpback's skin plays host to a large number of parasites, including balanid crustaceans. On the front of the head and on the pectoral fins it also has prominent, lumpy excrescences.

HYPEROÖDONTIDAE

The genus *Ziphius* consists of the single species *Ziphius cavirostris*, Cuvier's whale. This whale is found in almost all parts of the world, with the exception of the Polar region; it also frequents the Mediterranean, where it is relatively common and along whose coastline it sometimes beaches itself. It normally lives in small groups that seldom number more than half a dozen individuals; lone examples are rarely encountered. It feeds on squid and deep water fish.

The genus *Hyperoödon* comprises two species capable of long and deep immersion; their heads contain the spermaceti organ, situated in a cavity at the front of the head, which gives their forehead its bulging outline. The best known species is the common bottlenosed whale (*Hyperoödon ampullatus*), found in northern seas, particularly the Arctic Sea and the North Atlantic. *Hyperoödon planifrons*, on the other hand, lives in the waters of the Southern Hemisphere, particularly in the area between the South Atlantic and Australia. It is very similar to the preceding species, but with a more bulging forehead and with the dorsal fin situated further towards the tail. *Hyperoödons* dive to great depths in search of food, mainly squid, but also eat herrings and other fish and occasionally even starfish.

The genus *Berardius* includes two very similar species, but ones that have very different areas of distribution. The length of these cetaceans normally varies between 28 – 38 ft (9 – 12 m), with a skull of up to 5 ft (1.5 m) long, which makes them the giants of the family and places them amongst the largest living Odontocetae. They feed mainly on deep sea fish but also on cephalopod mollusks and echinoderm Holothuria.

The genus *Mesoplodon* is the most important genus, containing some dozen species that are spread through all the oceans of the world. Their length varies from 10 ft (3 m) to a maximum of 22 ft (7 m). One unusual feature is the particular density and heaviness of the bones of the rostrum. However, the mesoplodons are little known and fairly rare, being one of the least known genera of Cetacea. They are creatures of the open sea, living normally in small groups or by themselves. They feed mainly on squid that they capture in the deep.

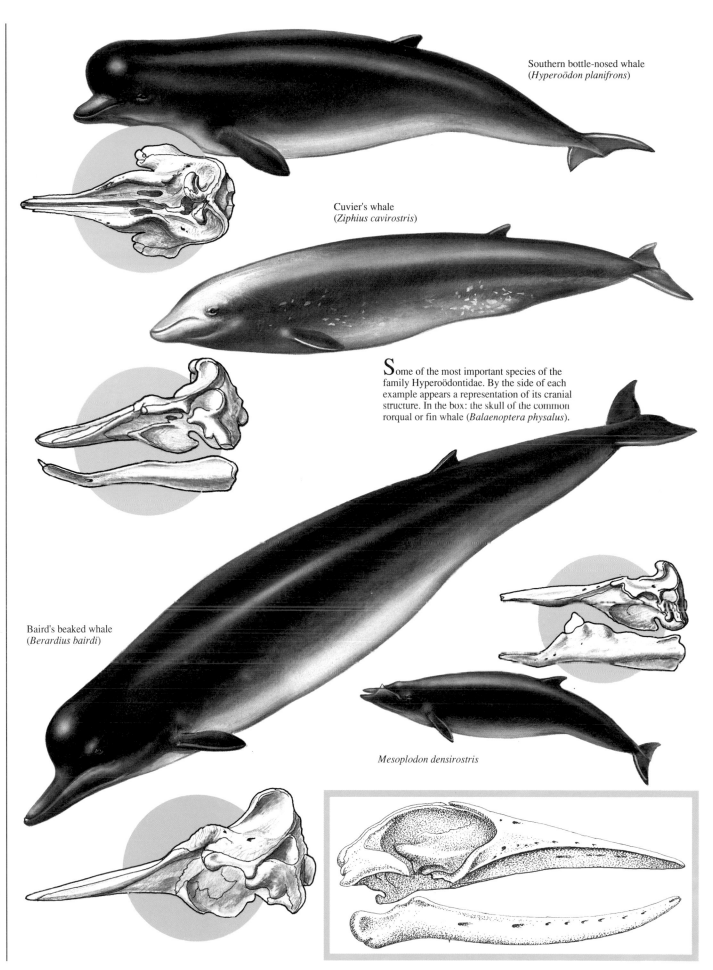

Southern bottle-nosed whale
(*Hyperoödon planifrons*)

Cuvier's whale
(*Ziphius cavirostris*)

Some of the most important species of the family Hyperoödontidae. By the side of each example appears a representation of its cranial structure. In the box: the skull of the common rorqual or fin whale (*Balaenoptera physalus*).

Baird's beaked whale
(*Berardius bairdi*)

Mesoplodon densirostris

COMMON DOLPHIN

Delphinus delphis

Order Cetacea
Family Delphinidae
Length Up to 7¾ ft (2.6 m); normally 3 – 6½ ft (1.8 – 2.2 m)
Weight 175 – 250 lb (80 – 110 kg)
Reproductive period In tropical zones, virtually throughout the year; in temperate zones, mainly during the warm months
Gestation 10 – 11 months
Number of young 1
Length at birth 32 in (80 cm)

The common dolphin is one of the most elegant and streamlined Cetacea, with a well defined rostrum. The lines of its body are fairly similar on the whole to those of other dolphins, but its coloration and markings are very distinctive and make it easy to recognize from the side. It occurs in all the seas of the world's tropical and temperate zones. It is common in the Mediterranean, where it was once sacred to Apollo. There, as in the Black sea and the Gulf of California, for example, forms have been distinguished that differ slightly in shape and color as a result of the geographical isolation of respective populations and that certain authors regard as distinct subspecies.

This is a pelagic cetacean that shuns shallows and prefers areas where there are steep underwater escarpments, such as on the edges of the continental shelf. Sometimes, however, it also ventures into gulfs and bays. It is one of the most sociable cetaceans, usually congregating in groups that range from a minimum of one dozen to several thousand head. It normally never lives in isolation. It is capable of immersion to at least 900 ft (280 m), with periods of apnea lasting 5 minutes and is a very acrobatic species that loves performing surprising jumps out of the water. Its diet is essentially based on small fish and squid.

There is no definable mating season. In tropical waters it is possible to see newly born young more or less throughout the year. There is reason to believe that pregnant females and those with young live partially segregated from the rest of the group. The common dolphin is able to produce a remarkable variety of sounds for social communication and echolocation.

Common dolphin
(*Delphinus delphis*)

Common dolphin
(*Delphinus delphis*)

▲
▼ Dolphins are amongst the most famous of cetaceans and some of their species are outstandingly lively and agile, habitually executing great leaps out of the water. They are some of the most adept cetaceans at surface antics. The bottle-nosed dolphin is undoubtedly the best known, both amongst scientists, who have been studying its behavior for a long time, especially in captivity (since 1914), and amongst the general public, who for fifty years have been able to admire its acrobatic skills in the cinema, on television, and in the large aquariums that first appeared in the United States and are now to be found in many different countries. Studies of their brain and their behavior have led to speculation, often very arbitrary and lacking any real proof, concerning the intelligence of cetaceans; there have also been rather far-fetched theories concerning the possible existence of a complex system of linguistic communication between the different species. Despite the many exaggerations, the bottle-nosed dolphin has undoubtedly revealed a surprising capacity for learning and for adapting to new situations that scientists would not expect to find in cetaceans.

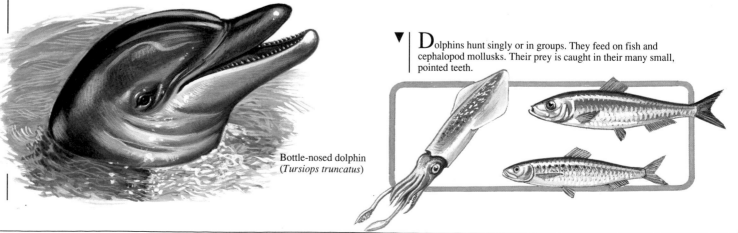

Bottle-nosed dolphin
(*Tursiops truncatus*)

▼ Dolphins hunt singly or in groups. They feed on fish and cephalopod mollusks. Their prey is caught in their many small, pointed teeth.

KILLER WHALE
Orcinus orca

Order Cetacea
Family Delphinidae
Length Males, up to 31 ft (9.5 m); females, up to 23 ft (7 m)
Weight Males, 8 tons; females, 4 tons
Reproductive period Predominantly winter – spring
Gestation 13 months or more
Number of young 1 every 2 years
Length at birth 7 – 8 ft (2.1 – 2.5 m)
Weight at birth 400 lb (180 kg)

The killer whale is the biggest and best known cetacean. It is also the most formidable predator of the seas. Its appearance is very distinctive, thereby making it almost impossible to confuse it with other species. It has a roundish head, with a blunt snout and no distinct rostrum; the trunk of its body is very powerfully built and surmounted by a high dorsal fin. Its black and white markings are also highly distinctive. The animal possesses 40 – 56 very strong conical teeth, which are up to 4 in (10 cm) in length and 1 – 2 in (2.5 – 5 cm) in diameter at the level of the gums.

Killer whales occur in all the seas of the world, most frequently in the waters of the Arctic and Antarctica. They do not normally migrate to any noticeable degree, remaining in fairly definite areas, except in high latitudes, where their seasonal movements can sometimes cover vast distances, following changes in the ice cap. They are also found in tropical and equatorial waters and sometimes, albeit very infrequently, in the Mediterranean as well. They habitually congregate in groups of 10 – 15, which are presumably composed of family units: a large male, females with young, and juveniles and sexually immature individuals of both sexes.

The killer whale is capable of achieving some speeds of up to 30 mph (45 kmh) and beyond, and of diving to depths of more than 3,300 ft (1,000 m) for periods of even longer than 20 minutes. Besides a wide variety of marine animals, the killer whale is a selective predator of Pinnipedia and Cetacea, even some of the largest ones, such as whales and rorquals, which it attacks in groups, often trying to tear out their tongues.

Orcinus orca is a great predator that practices different hunting techniques according to its prey. The reputation for fierceness ascribed to these creatures derives from eye-witness accounts of attacks by them on large Cetacea and Pinnipedia, but it has certainly been greatly exaggerated, not without an element of anthropomorphization, in their being listed as "killer whales." Their voracity has also been exaggerated, and the number of seals, dolphins, and other large creatures discovered in their stomach contents after dissection has not been related to the length of time over which they were captured. Attacks on whales and rorquals are carried out in groups and are relatively rare. The parts of the body that are the aim of such attacks are mainly the tongue, the fins, and the blubber. On one occasion a killer whale was seen to jump clean out of the water with an adult sea lion in its mouth, a technique often adopted when preying on Pinnipedia, which are lifted up and thrown violently into the air in order to stun them, as though the creature wanted to play with its food before swallowing it.

The variety of the killer whale's prey is impressive and very eclectic, and bears witness to the high calorific needs of this large and very active cetacean. Its diet includes seals and sea lions, small and large cetaceans, penguins, turtles, fish of varying size and species, ranging from herring to salmon and sharks, and also octopus and squid. Killer whales, with their highly developed methods of hunting, occupy a high place in the food-gathering hierarchy, the evolution and survival of which demonstrates the way in which the species and its habits fit harmoniously into the much wider context of the marine ecosystem. Apart from man, the species has no enemies in the sea, but it is, however, subject to parasitical infestations, mainly of an internal nature.

NARWHAL
Monodon monoceros

Order Cetacea
Family Monodontidae
Length 13 – 16 ft (4 – 5 m), excluding the tusk, which is 6 – 8 ft (1.8 – 2.5 m); maximum 20 ft (6 m)
Weight Maximum 1 ton
Reproductive period Mainly spring
Gestation About 14 months
Number of young 1, rarely 2
Size at birth 5 ft (1.5 m)
Sexual maturity 8 – 9 years old in the male; 4 – 7 in the female

This typical Arctic cetacean is unmistakable. It is 13 – 16 ft (4 – 5 m) long, and has a small head with a very short, blunt rostrum and a small, narrow mouth. There are only two teeth at the edge of the upper jaw: in the female they rarely protrude beyond the gum, whereas in the male they develop disproportionately. The one on the left forms a long, straight "tusk" of spiral shape, a characteristic feature of the species, which sticks out of the upper lip and can measure up to 8 ft (2.5 m) long in the largest males, and weigh as much as 22 lb (10 kg). The narwhal lives in Arctic waters, usually between latitudes 70°N and 80°N and rarely below latitudes 65°N or above 85°N. It frequents mainly deep waters, which is in keeping with its diet.

The narwhal is a gregarious cetacean, living habitually in groups of some 20 individuals, but sometimes they assemble in much larger congregations (up to 1,000) in order to migrate. The groups may be made up of females with young, adult males, or members of both sexes. A slow swimmer, the narwhal keeps mainly to the southern limit of the ice floes, especially in winter, whereas in summer it moves nearer the coasts and swims into gulfs and bays. It often lifts its head above the water and, in the case of the males, displays its long tusk, which is also visible when the animal breaks surface in order to breathe. Its diet is composed mainly of Arctic fish, squid, and benthonic crustaceans.

Similar to the narwhal is the beluga (*Delphinapterus leucas*), which is itself found only in Arctic waters, where it favors shallow coastal areas. Up to 18 ft (5.5 m) in length, it has a very short rostrum and a roundish, bulging head. It feeds mainly on fish such as the Arctic cod.

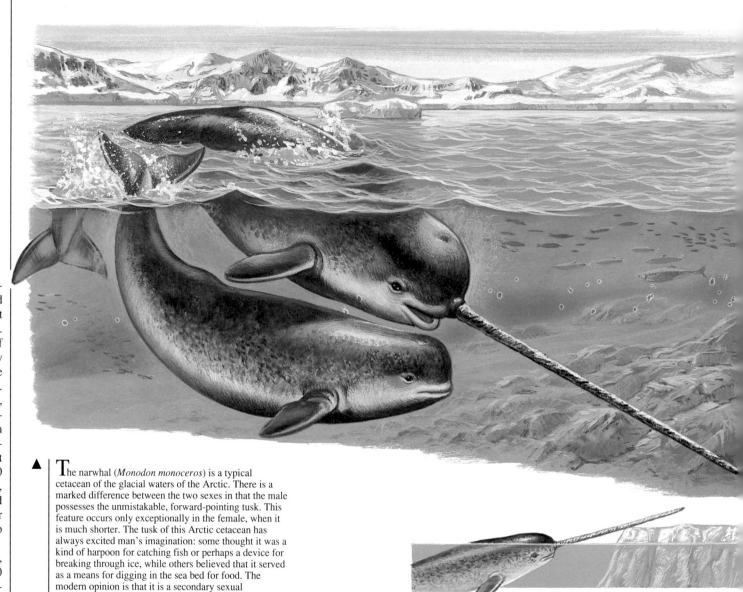

▲ The narwhal (*Monodon monoceros*) is a typical cetacean of the glacial waters of the Arctic. There is a marked difference between the two sexes in that the male possesses the unmistakable, forward-pointing tusk. This feature occurs only exceptionally in the female, when it is much shorter. The tusk of this Arctic cetacean has always excited man's imagination: some thought it was a kind of harpoon for catching fish or perhaps a device for breaking through ice, while others believed that it served as a means for digging in the sea bed for food. The modern opinion is that it is a secondary sexual characteristic that may play a part in fights between males during the mating season, as shown by the scars that can be seen on the bodies of male narwhals.

▲ According to some observations, narwhals may be able to rest at the edge of the ice, supported by their long tusk, as Eskimo traditions maintain.

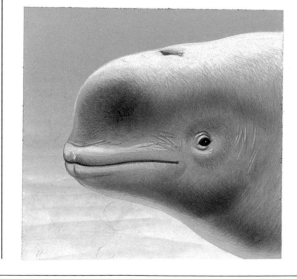

◄ The beluga (*Delphinapterus leucas*) is another Arctic species, similar to the narwhal, which is of particular interest because of its extraordinary vocalizing abilities. The protuberance at the front of its head (the so-called "melon," that also occurs in other cetaceans) alters in shape and size in accordance with the different sounds emitted by the creature. This would lend weight to the theory that the "melon" is an organ that also possesses acoustic qualities, serving to concentrate sounds like an acoustic lens and also to regulate their direction by means of a special system of muscular fibers. A slow swimmer, capable of remarkable feats of diving, *Delphinapterus leucas* is especially adapted for moving among ice floes. It is preyed upon by killer whales, polar bears, and the Eskimos. Its deep-seated fear of killer whales has been exploited by the salmon fishermen of Alaska, who, in order to safeguard their catch from its depredations, transmit underwater recordings of the killer whale's calls.

SPERM WHALE
Physeter macrocephalus

Order Cetacea
Family Physeteridae
Length Males, 50 ft (18 m); females, 38 ft (12 m)
Weight Males, up to 50 tons; females, 15 tons
Reproductive period Unclear. Mating is more frequent between June and July in the Northern Hemisphere
Gestation 16 months
Number of young 1
Size at birth 11 – 16 ft (3.5 – 5 m)
Sexual maturity 2 years old in the male; at 18 months in the female

The sperm whale is the largest of the cetacean odontocetes, with a massive, subcylindrical trunk and a bulky head of gigantic size, equivalent in length to approximately a third of the whole body. The mouth is long and broad. The tongue is very large and fleshy. The upper jaw is normally bereft of functional teeth, whereas the lower jaw generally has 48, with individual variations and frequent assymmetry. These teeth, which have no enamel, can each be 6 – 8 in (16 – 20 cm) high and weigh 1 lb (500 g). The eyes are small.

The sperm whale frequents all the seas of the world, but prefers hot and temperate waters, normally remaining far out at sea and only rarely coming in close to land. It is one of the deepest diving cetaceans and is predominantly cephalopod-eating, with a large intake of fish.

The sperm whale has an extremely long gestation period, lasting approximately 16 months. Its maximum life span is unknown, but on the basis of tagged specimens it has been ascertained that males can live for at least 32 years and females for more than 20. Other distinctive features of the species are its remarkable cerebral development, its spermaceti organ, and its secretions of ambergris. The spermaceti organ, situated in the front part of the head, within the large basin formed by the skull, consists of a lower part containing a mass of spongy and oleaginous fibers, above which is a large reservoir containing the spermaceti proper; this oily substance, which is colorless and odorless, was once believed to be sperm, whence the name "sperm whale."

▼ The mouth of cephalopods acts as a very efficient means of capture.

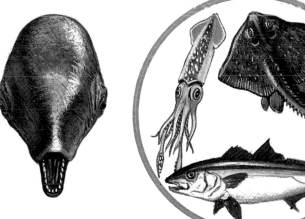

▼ Apart from cephalopods, the sperm whale also feeds on large fish, such as tunny fish, Carangidae, small sharks, skate, etc.

▲ The biology of the sperm whale (*Physeter macrocephalus*) is to a great extent determined by its habit of executing long and deep immersions, primarily in order to obtain food. It feeds especially on squid, some of which can be many feet in length and live at considerable depths (e.g. genus *Architeuthis*). Sometimes large circular scars can be seen on the creature's skin, caused by the suckers on the tentacles of these cephalopods: they are reminders of silent struggles that have been carried out in the deep. In its search for cephalopods, the sperm whale "trawls" the slimy depths, making use of the peculiar shape of its mouth. In the darkness far below the surface it certainly makes use of an efficient system of echolocation in order to pinpoint its prey, as well as using its sense of touch. Recent studies have also revealed that sperm whales emit a vast range of sounds that play a fundamental part in communications between the different members of a school.

► Spread through all the seas of the world, the sperm whale stays in hot waters during the winter and then migrates to temperate ones in the following spring. For part of the year the areas of distribution of the two sexes do not coincide. The one frequented by the females does not normally stretch beyond the tropical and subtropical zone. It would appear that this results mainly from the needs of the young to stay in warm or hot waters, since they do not as yet have a sufficient layer of fat. The males, however, migrate into the cold waters of the Southern and Northern Hemispheres during the summer. The majority of sperm whales live between 40°N and 40°S, within which there occur greater quantities of the cephalopods that form the basis of the species' diet. 1) Males; 2) females.

PINNIPEDIA

Although many scientists consider the Pinnipedia – seals, sea lions, and walruses – a separate order from the Carnivora, the classification of this group is still a matter of controversy. Pinnipeds had a dual origin that is presumed to have happened at the same time in the North Pacific and North Atlantic. In the North Pacific it was a dog-like carnivore that entered the marine environment to take advantage of a new food supply, while in the North Atlantic it was an otter-like land carnivore.

The Atlantic and Pacific types of pinnipeds form the basic subdivisions of the pinniped group. Atlantic derived pinnipeds have rear legs that are permanently extended behind them and useless for land travel. The primary propulsive organs in water are used much like the tail of a fish. These seals, which lack external ear pinnae, are called "true seals" and comprise the family Phocidae. Pacific pinnipeds are sea lions and walruses.

All pinnipeds give birth on land or ice and some species spend a great deal of time resting out of the water. Adaptations to an aquatic existence include a streamlined body to reduce drag, external ears that are reduced or absent, genitalia and mammary teats that are internal, limbs and extremities that are flattened, and eyes that are large and located well forward. Subcutaneous fat forms a substantial part of all pinniped bodies and provides reserve energy during fasts and lactation, thermal insulation, and buoyancy. Pinniped eyes are larger than land carnivores and they function at low light levels. Vision is excellent in both air and water.

Crabeater seals feed on krill which they strain from sea water through multicusped cheek teeth. The walrus feeds primarily on three bivalve mollusk genera which inhabit shallow coastal waters. Most pinnipeds feed daily except at certain times of the year (breeding, molting seasons) when segments of the population fast for prolonged periods of time. Females of all pinniped species give birth to a single pup, generally once a year. Copulation takes place within a few days of weeks of parturition; gestation including delayed implantation, which synchronizes births from year to year, generally lasts one year.

▲ The Pinnipedia can be traced back to the miacis, a primitive carnivore that is also ancestor of the modern cats, dogs, and bears.

▼ The three families of Pinnipedia: seals (top), sea lions (middle), and walruses (bottom).

▲ A young walrus (*Odobenus rosmarus*). The projecting moustaches, formed of stiff bristles that cover the upper lip, are tactile organs that help the animal to discover crustaceans and mollusks on the sea bed.

▼ Lengthening of the body is one of the most important ways in which an animal can adapt to an aquatic life. Evolution has produced a streamlined shape in both fish and seal, reducing drag to a minimum.

ANTARCTIC SEALS

The true seals of the Antarctic are represented by four closely related species, all circumpolar in distribution. The most abundant and widespread Antarctic phocid is the crabeater seal (*Lobodon carcinophagus*) that primarily inhabits the unconsolidated pack ice zone, but is also found on the coasts of both the north and south islands of New Zealand, on Tasmania, the southeast coast of Australia, and along the Atlantic coast of South America. The principal food of the crabeater seal is krill; the seal's cheek teeth have remarkably elaborate cusps for straining and filtering euphausiids from sea water. The body of this seal is long and slim and is covered with a pelage that changes color during the months following the molt. The crabeater is not migratory but moves with the pack ice in the winter to remain near its food source.

The Weddell seal (*Leptonychotes weddelli*) is the second most abundant Antarctic seal and inhabits the fast ice areas of the Antarctic continent although the major population components are associated with some subantarctic islands, such as the Falkland Islands and dependencies. Adult seals are dark dorsally and mottled laterally and ventrally with irregular white to gray spots. Females are larger than males. The Weddell seal is predominantly a fish eater but is also known to feed opportunistically on benthonic animals and squid. Weddell seals can dive to a maximum depth of almost 200 ft (60 m) and stay under for a maximum of 45 minutes. They live solitary lives and groups of this species are to be found only in the breeding season.

The leopard seal (*Hydrurga leptonyx*) is dispersed over the range of the Antarctic pack ice and the coasts of Australia, New Zealand, and South America. The wider range of this species reflects its varied feeding habits including krill, fish, penguins, and other seals. Leopard seals are not usually gregarious.

The Ross seal (*Ommatophoca rossi*) is rare in comparison to the other Antarctic species; it appears principally to inhabit the consolidated ice pack and records suggest that it is solitary.

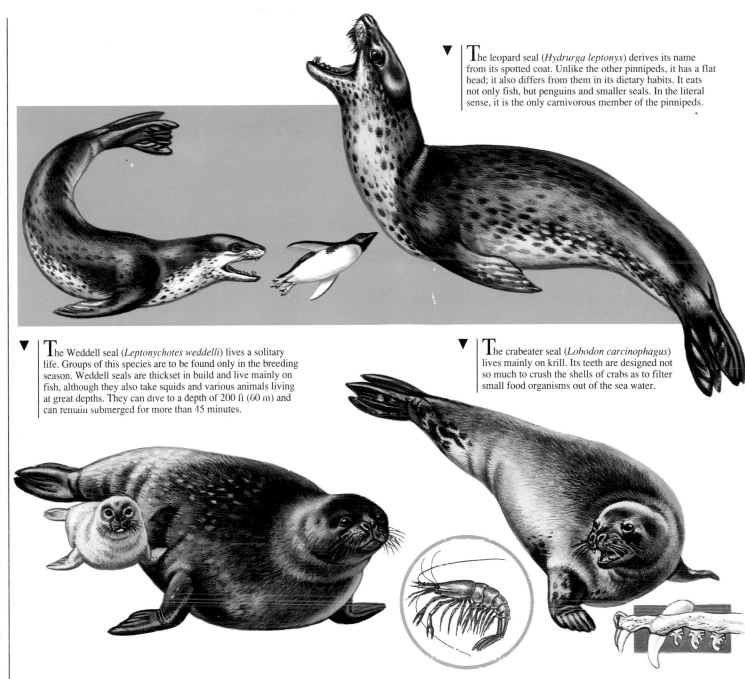

▼ The leopard seal (*Hydrurga leptonyx*) derives its name from its spotted coat. Unlike the other pinnipeds, it has a flat head; it also differs from them in its dietary habits. It eats not only fish, but penguins and smaller seals. In the literal sense, it is the only carnivorous member of the pinnipeds.

▼ The Weddell seal (*Leptonychotes weddelli*) lives a solitary life. Groups of this species are to be found only in the breeding season. Weddell seals are thickset in build and live mainly on fish, although they also take squids and various animals living at great depths. They can dive to a depth of 200 ft (60 m) and can remain submerged for more than 45 minutes.

▼ The crabeater seal (*Lobodon carcinophagus*) lives mainly on krill. Its teeth are designed not so much to crush the shells of crabs as to filter small food organisms out of the sea water.

▼ Geographical distribution of:
1) gray seal (*Halichoerus grypus*);
2) ribbon seal (*Phoca fasciata*);
3) monk seal (*Monachus* species).

▉	1
▉	2
▉	3

► Geographical distribution of Antarctic seals:
1) leopard seal (*Hydrurga leptonyx*)
2) Weddell seal (*Leptonychotes weddelli*).

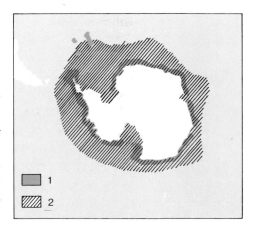

▉	1
▨	2

HARBOR SEAL
Phoca vitulina

Order Carnivora
Family Phocidae
Length Males and females, 4 – 6 ft (1.2 – 1.9 m)
Weight Males and females, 220 – 330 lb (100 – 150 kg)
Reproductive period Varies by subspecies and latitude; generally early spring to summer
Number of young 1
Sexual maturity Males, 6 years; females, 3 – 4 years
Maximum age Approximately 19 years

The harbor seal is found only in the Northern Hemisphere where it is among the most widely distributed of the Pinnipedia occurring over 40 degrees of latitude in both the North Atlantic and North Pacific Oceans. The North Pacific harbor seal is distributed in the eastern North Pacific from the Aleutian Islands southward along the west coast and islands of the United States and Canada to Baja California with the southernmost sightings being reported from Cedros, Natividad, and San Roques Islands. Throughout its range the harbor seal occupies a wide variety of habitat types. Seasonal fluctuations in numbers of seals at each site vary and are correlated with light hours. Maximum numbers of seals occur during the summer when days are longest and minimum numbers occur during the winter when days are shortest. Recent investigations have begun to suggest a semipelagic or migratory phase for harbor seals during the fall and winter periods.

Pelage in the harbor seal varies from almost completely black to entirely light gray–silver with the most commonly occuring coloration being gray with dark spots. There are regional variations in the proportions of light and dark phases. No consistent sexual differences in pelage or color patterns have been reported. Sexes are generally indistinguishable on the basis of size.

Harbor seal females give birth to single pups in the spring or summer. Variations in pupping dates have been reported in many areas with pupping generally occuring earlier as one goes southward. In the eastern North Pacific pups are born progressively later going southeast from Alaska to Puget Sound and earlier from Puget Sound to Mexico.

▲ As its alternative name of "common seal" suggests, the harbor seal is probably the most familiar and most widely distributed member of its family. It occurs mainly in the northern waters of the Atlantic and Pacific Oceans, but it is capable of penetrating a long way up rivers and into freshwater lakes at a considerable distance from the coast.

▶ It lives mainly on cod and other fish, but also takes soles, squids, and crabs.

▼ The hindlimbs of the harbor seal are useless for walking and the animal can move on dry land only by a series of grotesque contortions of its whole body.

In southern California pups are born from late February to April. Parturition is normally terrestrial with feeding and nursing lasting 3 – 6 weeks. Ovulation occurs soon after the pups are weaned. Implantation of the blastocyst is then delayed 1½ to 3 months. Harbor seals are presumed to live together during the breeding season although some competition among males for females or space has been reported in some northern areas. Seals begin molting at the end of the breeding season and each year the maximum number of animals correlates with maximum molting activity.

Harbor seals are opportunistic feeders and prey most heavily on seasonally abundant species. Small fish such as euchalon, hake, and herring, are the most common prey items, although cephalopods and flatfish are also eaten. Feeding occurs primarily at night and the greatest numbers of seals are found on the beach at midday, as they rest. Nocturnal emersion patterns have been reported around man-made quays and in areas of intense human disturbance. Where traditional resting sites occur in the littoral zone, seals tend to come out on ebbing tides and return to sea on rising or high tides.

The genus *Phoca* has become adapted to a variety of coastal habitat types and populations have differentiated and been recognized as subspecies according to geographic distribution. Local populations have also differentiated within subspecific groups in response to varying habitat type; behavior in harbor seals appears to be highly flexible and adaptable. The two North Pacific harbor seal species differ primarily in their pupping and breeding behavior. *Phoca largha* pups on pack ice in March and April and disperses northward as the ice front recedes in the spring. During the breeding season *Phoca largha* is found in widely spaced family groups consisting of one female, her pup, and one adult male. *Phoca vitulina richardsi* is associated with land during the spring breeding season, where it congregates in herds.

The harbor seal has always been of some commercial use; skins have been used for leather or fur coats. Eskimos hunt harbor seals occasionally and almost every portion of the carcass is used for clothing, food, fuel, sewing materials, and dog harnesses. Polar bears, killer whales, and sharks are natural predators on harbor seals; eagles have also been reported to kill young harbor seal pups.

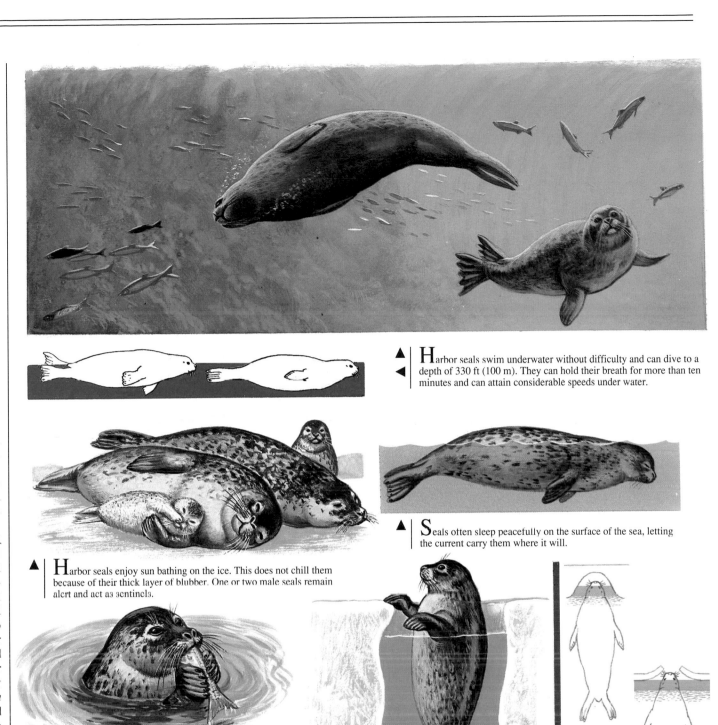

▲
◄ Harbor seals swim underwater without difficulty and can dive to a depth of 330 ft (100 m). They can hold their breath for more than ten minutes and can attain considerable speeds under water.

▲ Harbor seals enjoy sun bathing on the ice. This does not chill them because of their thick layer of blubber. One or two male seals remain alert and act as sentinels.

▲ Seals often sleep peacefully on the surface of the sea, letting the current carry them where it will.

▲
►
▼ The animals use their front flippers for walking on dry land, for scratching themselves, and to hold their prey firmly while they eat it.

► During cold winters, they spend most of their time under the ice, where temperatures are less extreme. They make holes in the ice where they can come up from time to time to fill their lungs with fresh air.

ARCTIC SEALS

The population of the harp seal (*Pagophilus groenlandicus*) is made up of three groups living in the White Sea, the east coast of Greenland, and the northern coast of Newfoundland. The species is highly migratory and the seals move north in the summer to feeding grounds as the ice retreats northward. In spring and summer months juveniles feed on mysids and euphausiids while the adult diet is composed of these planktonic crustaceans as well as polar cod, capelin, herring, and squid.

The ringed seal (*Pusa hispida*), one of the smallest seals, is circumpolar in distribution and is the commonest and most widely distributed Arctic seal. A wide variety of food items (small crustaceans, as well as fish) make up its diet.

The bearded seal (*Erignathus barbatus*) is generally solitary and has a circumpolar distribution. It maintains a year-round association with moving sea ice in the subarctic region and is restricted to relatively shallow water. In winter the bearded seal is found along the coasts of Alaska and Siberia extending into the Arctic with the center of abundance being the ice edge of the central and southern Bering Sea. It is the largest of the ice-associated pinnipeds in the Northern Hemisphere. Males are 9 ft (2.8 m) long and weigh 900 lb (410 kg); the females are 8½ ft (2.6 m) long and weigh much less than the male.

The ribbon seal (*Phoca* [*Histriophoca*] *fasciata*) is found confined to the western half of the Bering Sea and ranges into the Okhotsk as far as Sahalin Island. It inhabits open water and ice floes but is occasionally sighted on the island and mainland shores. The species is not gregarious and usually only a few animals forming small herds are seen together. It is of medium size and slender in comparison with most seals: males are 5¼ ft (1.6 m) long and weigh 210 lb (95 kg); females are 5 ft (1.5 m) long and weigh 175 lb (80 kg).

The gray seal (*Halichoerus grypus*) is a gregarious species widely distributed in temperate and subarctic waters on both sides of the North Atlantic. The species is strongly dimorphic with respect to both pelage color and size; males are much larger than females and have light spots on a darker background, while females have dark spots on a lighter background.

▼ The ringed seal (*Pusa hispida*) is the most common and most wide ranging of the Arctic seals. It lives mainly in the polar regions. It often burrows in the ice to protect itself from the cold.

Harp seal (*Pagophilus groenlandicus*). During courtship, male harp seals dance up and down in the water with their bodies held in a vertical position. ▶

▲ The ribbon seal (*Histriophoca fasciata*) lives mainly on squids.

▶ The bearded seal (*Erignathus barbatus*) has long whiskers which help it to find shells and other food on the sea floor

◀ Gray seal (*Halichoerus grypus*).

MEDITERRANEAN MONK SEAL

Monachus monachus

Order Carnivora
Family Phocidea
Length Males and females, 9 – 10 ft (2.8 – 3 m)
Weight Maximum 882 lb (400 kg)
Reproductive period May – November, peak in September
Gestation 11 months
Number of young 1 pup every 2 years
Maximum age 14 years

The main population center of the Mediterranean monk seal is the Aegean Sea; a smaller concentration within the Mediterranean Sea lies along the southern coasts of the western basin. A third major concentration exists in the eastern Mediterranean. The total monk seal population continues to decline; it has been suggested that human disturbance has driven them to areas unsuitable for reproduction.

At birth pups are approximately 3 ft (1 m) in length and weigh approximately 44 lb (20 kg). The soft, woolly natal pelage varies from dark brown to black. Female coloring is closer to that of pups than adult males. Adult male pelage varies from dark brown to black to light gray with yellowish patches along the center of the dorsal and ventral surfaces. Seals from the Black Sea are described as being gray with a brownish hue on the back and yellowish white ventrally. Monk seals are closely related to Antarctic seals and have similar structural characteristics.

Pupping is currently restricted to caves or grottoes and occurs from May to November with a peak of activity in September to October. Underwater copulation has been observed. Lactation lasts approximately six months and gestation 11 months. Young seals remain with their mothers for three years becoming sexually mature at four years and reaching a length of 83 in (210 cm).

Mediterranean monk seals appear to be opportunistic feeders on green algae, eels, carp, whiting, sardines, bonito, octopus, lobster, herring, mackerel, anchovy, flounder, and other flatfish species. Feeding has been frequently observed by day. The Mediterranean monk seal apparently does not migrate for any distance.

In the monk seal the head is rounded, the eyes are projecting and widely spaced, and the nostrils open upwards and are separated by a groove that runs along the nose. The moustache is relatively short.

▲ Unlike the other pinnipeds, monk seals live exclusively in the warm waters of the Mediterranean, the Caribbean, and the ocean around Hawaii. They live on rocky coasts and reefs. The females are heavier than the males. For various reasons, very few specimens of this species survive and it must be considered as near to extinction.

▼ The pups are about 40 in (1 m) in length at birth and the color of their fur is black.

Geographical distribution of the Phocidae.

▼ 1) Common seal (*Phoca vitulina*).
2) Harp seal (*Phoca groenlandicus*).

▼ 1) Bearded seal (*Erignathus barbatus*).
2) Ringed seal (*Phoca hispida*).

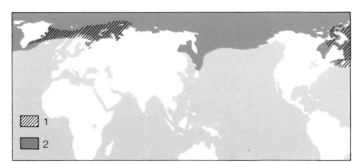

ELEPHANT SEALS

Mirounga

Order Carnivora
Family Phocidae
Length Southern elephant seal: males, 19 – 21 ft (6 – 6.5 m); females,11 – 14½ ft (3.4 – 4.4 m). Northern elephant seal: males, 15¾ – 16½ ft (4.5 – 5 m); females, 12 ft (3.6 m)
Weight Southern elephant seal: males, 8,050 lb (3,650 kg); females, 2,000 lb (910 kg). Northern elephant seal: males, 4,000 – 6,000 lb (1,800 – 2,700 kg); females, 880 lb (400 kg)
Reproductive period Northern Hemisphere, December – March; Southern Hemisphere, August – September
Gestation 11 – 12 months including 2 months delay in implantation
Number of young 1
Sexual maturity Males, 5 years; females, 2 years
Maximum age 14 – 20 years

During the Pleistocene epoch elephant seals expanded their range from the Southern Hemisphere northward across the equator. As the last glacial ice regressed, the northern, lower Californian group was isolated from the main seal population in the Southern Hemisphere by the rewarming of the oceans; these two groups have remained separate since that time and are recognized as distinct species. The current breeding range of the northern elephant seal is from central California to central Baja California, Mexico. The southern elephant seal (*Mirounga leonina*) is circumpolar in subantarctic waters and breeds as far north as 42 degrees in Argentina. The largest breeding population of the southern elephant seal is presently found on South Georgia and is estimated at 310,000 seals.

The southern elephant seal is the largest pinniped in the world. The northern elephant seal (*Mirounga angustirostris*) is somewhat smaller and less heavy. Aside from marked differences in size of the sexes, males of both species can be distinguished from females by their long noses and heavily calloused necks. Although the southern elephant seal is larger than the northern species, its nose or proboscis is generally 8 – 10 in (20 – 25 cm) shorter than

The northern elephant seal (*Mirounga angustirostris*) and the southern elephant seal (*Mirounga leonina*) are the two largest species of pinnipeds in the world. The differences between the sexes are very marked. The males are three to four times as heavy as the females and are also distinguished by their long nose and proboscis and their heavily calloused necks. In the mating season they form breeding colonies, within which each bull sets up his private harem of 10 – 20 females, or sometimes even more. The southern elephant seal is circumpolar in subantarctic waters; the northern elephant seal lives in the temperate waters of the Northern Hemisphere.

that of the northern form. There is no sexual dimorphism in coat color of either species; pelage ranges from gray in newly molted animals to beige –brown in those that are in early stages of molt. Seals are generally darker dorsally than ventrally.

Elephant seals spend most of the year at sea, hauling out on land twice a year, once to breed and once to molt. In the Northern Hemisphere the breeding season haul out begins in early December and lasts until mid March. The southern species breeds from September through November; breeding behavior in the two species is essentially the same. Adult males arrive first on traditional rookery beaches and immediately begin fighting and threatening each other. Aggressive interactions among males result in establishment of territories or dominance hierarchies, depending on beach structure. Mature individuals dominate the most preferred areas of the beaches while younger bulls are forced to occupy the beach fringes or splash zone on a temporary basis. Throughout the breeding season bulls rely primarily on vocal threats to maintain their territories, although physical encounters resulting in bloody battles do occur. The bulls emit low pitched sounds which differ in the two species. It is believed that the proboscis serves as a resonating chamber.

Pregnant cows arrive after territories and hierarchies have been established, forming dense aggregations or harems. Parturition occurs 6 – 7 days after the female arrives on the rookery; estrus begins 24 days after parturition. Pups are nursed for approximately four weeks. Females spend an average of 35 days on the rookery giving birth and suckling their pups during which time they fast. Females are bred during the last 4 – 5 days of the nursing period; copulation takes place primarily on land and is initiated and terminated by the male. A few dominant bulls do the majority of breeding during any one season and the same male may dominate a breeding area for up to three consecutive breeding seasons.

Females return to the sea soon after breeding. The young are weaned at this stage and pass another 5 – 8 weeks on the beach while they complete the postnatal molt. The departure of the whole colony takes place when the young are about three months old and is linked to the increase in the availability of food.

Toward the end of August the bulls begin to assemble at the breeding places and crawl laboriously ashore.

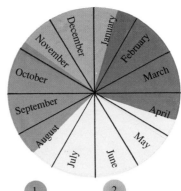

Annual cycle of the southern elephant seal: 1) breeding season; 2) fishing season; 3) molting season; 4) season of life at sea.

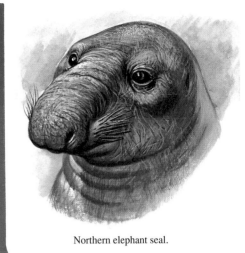
Northern elephant seal.

Having hauled out on the beaches, the bulls immediately begin a series of duels to establish dominance, accompanied by much bellowing. When the battles are over, the strongest bulls take possession of the best places on the beach.

At the end of September the females arrive.

The strongest and most aggressive males set up harems of 10–20 females each.

Females suckling their young. When the pups are old enough they leave the area of the harem.

At the end of October males and females leave the breeding grounds separately and go back to live in the sea.

They stay in the sea for at least two months, during which they eat as much as they can.

The sexes do not mingle during the molting season.

When the molt is over, all colony members go back to sea and remain there until the following spring, when the reproductive cycle begins again.

WALRUS

Odobenus rosmarus

Order Carnivora
Family Odobenidae
Length Males, 12 – 12½ ft (3.6 – 3.8 m); females, 10 ft (3 m)
Weight Males, 3,300 lb (1,500 kg); females, 1,984 lb (900 kg)
Reproductive period April – May
Gestation 1 year
Number of young 1 calf every other year at most
Sexual maturity Males, 6 – 7 years; females, 5 years
Maximum age 30 – 35 years

Walruses are circumpolar in distribution. The once abundant Atlantic walrus (*Odobenus rosmarus rosmarus*) was severely exploited and today occurs in two geographically isolated groups; one occurs confined to the east Greenland coast, Spitzbergen, Franz Josef Land, and the Barents and Kara seas, and a larger population occupies the eastern Canadian Arctic and western Greenland. The Pacific walrus (*Odobenus rosmarus divergens*) occurs in the Bering and Chukchi Seas between Russia and Alaska.

In winter, the Pacific walrus congregates in two areas; the region southwest of St Lawrence Island and from Bristol Bay to the Pribilof Island. Walruses are segregated at this time with sexually mature animals and pregnant females in one area and immature males over a large periphery. As the ice breaks up in April, walruses continue on their northward migration to summer hauling areas in the south Chukchi Sea. The return southward migration begins in October as ice begins to form. The Atlantic walrus is more sedentary, remaining within restricted areas during the year. Walruses are generally found in shallow waters around the coasts where the gravelly sea bottom supports various kinds of mollusks. Walruses in the Pacific were once abundant on the Pribilof Islands, St Matthew Island, and the Alaskan coast, but are now rare outside the Arctic Circle.

Walruses have a thick, swollen body form, a rounded head and muzzle, short neck, tough wrinkled and sparsely haired skin, and large tusks. The upper canines are the most outstanding feature of adult walruses; they grow throughout life in both sexes to lengths of 40 in

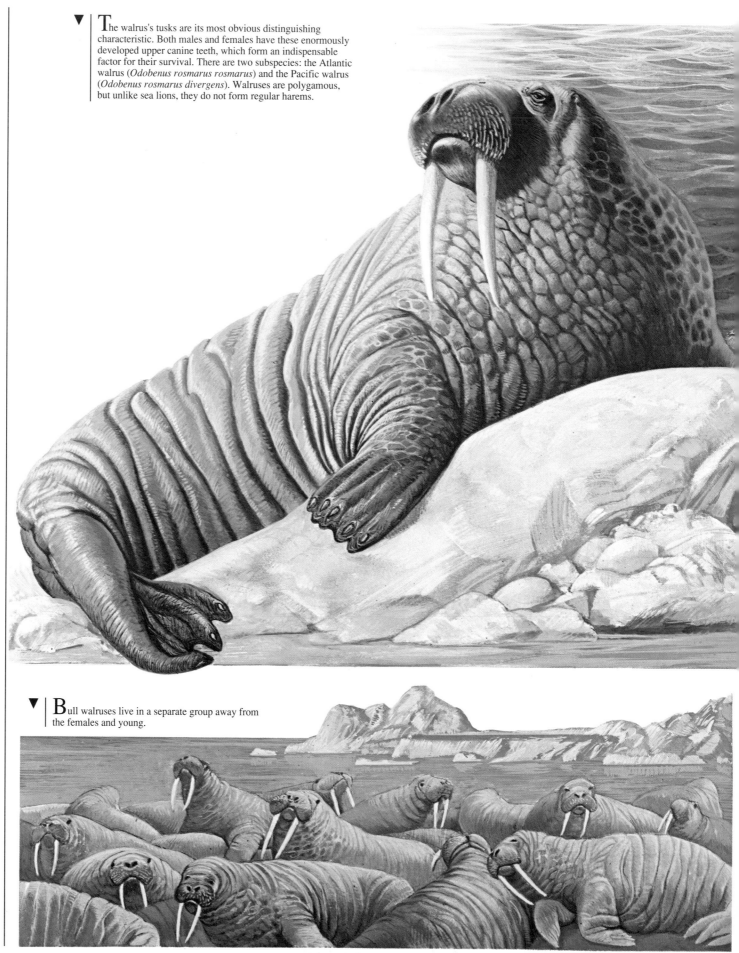

The walrus's tusks are its most obvious distinguishing characteristic. Both males and females have these enormously developed upper canine teeth, which form an indispensable factor for their survival. There are two subspecies: the Atlantic walrus (*Odobenus rosmarus rosmarus*) and the Pacific walrus (*Odobenus rosmarus divergens*). Walruses are polygamous, but unlike sea lions, they do not form regular harems.

Bull walruses live in a separate group away from the females and young.

(100 cm) in the male and 20 in (60 cm) in the female. Extremely heavy sensory vibrissae or "whiskers" are present on the muscle pads on the upper lip and are believed to act as a filter for muddy ocean bottom food organisms. Adult males may be distinguished from females by the development of fibrous tubercles on the skin of the neck and shoulders of the male. In the water the skin appears whitish in color, but when the animal hauls out to rest, blood circulation increases and the skin turns bright pink.

Walruses live in areas virtually inaccessible to man during the mating and pupping periods of their annual cycle. They are polygynous although the male does not apparently maintain harems in the sense that the northern fur seals do. Males solicit the attention of females through aquatic displays and copulation is believed to be aquatic. Gestation is approximately one year and females calve on ice floes on their northward migration in April and May. Females calve every two years at most. The young nurse for 18 – 24 months and sometimes remain with the female for another year or two. If a female's calf is attacked, she will fight and defend her pup with fierce intensity. This strong female-calf bond is partly responsible for the survival of the species in areas overhunted by man.

Although it was widely believed that tusks function most importantly in feeding by digging food from the sea bottom, recent studies of feeding ecology and functional anatomy have dispelled this idea and suggest that walrus tusks have evolved chiefly for social communication. The large tusks are used in defense against predators, for breaking through ice, in fights with other walruses, for hooking over the edge of the ice, for stability while sleeping in the water, and also in hauling out and in locomotion on ice.

Within their range, the walrus is restricted in distribution by the occurrence of suitably shallow feeding areas. The diet consists primarily of clams which it digs up from muddy bottoms with its quill-like "whiskers." The soft parts of the clams are sucked out of the shell and the shell is discarded. Where clams are not found, walruses eat a variety of invertebrates and fish. Carrion in the form of other marine mammals is sometimes eaten and walrus attacks on small seals have been reported.

The life of the walrus and how he uses his tusks.

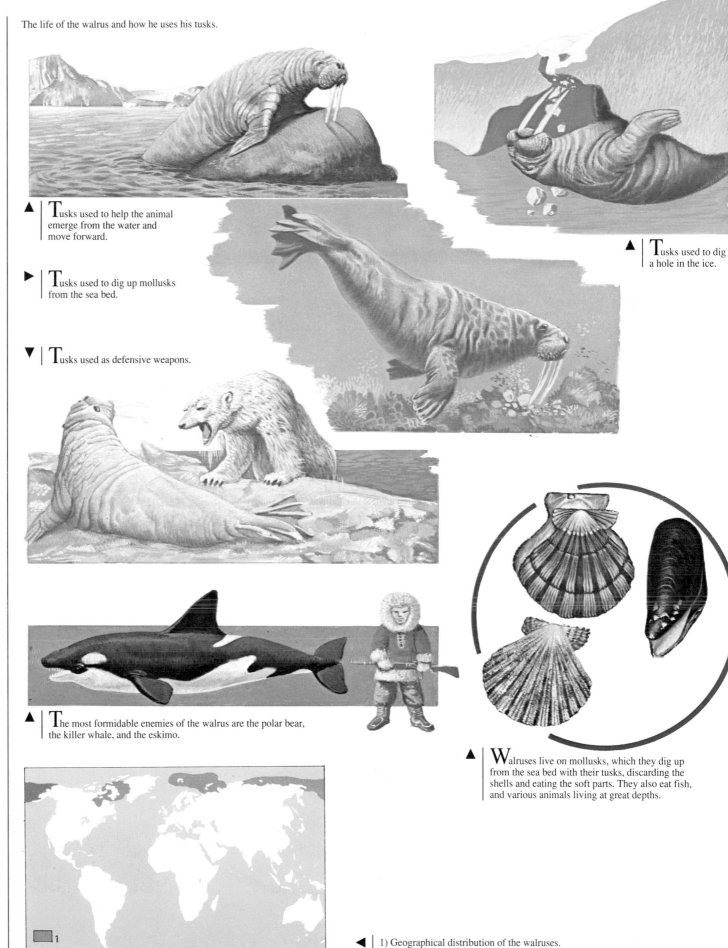

▲ | Tusks used to help the animal emerge from the water and move forward.

► | Tusks used to dig up mollusks from the sea bed.

▼ | Tusks used as defensive weapons.

▲ | Tusks used to dig a hole in the ice.

▲ | The most formidable enemies of the walrus are the polar bear, the killer whale, and the eskimo.

▲ | Walruses live on mollusks, which they dig up from the sea bed with their tusks, discarding the shells and eating the soft parts. They also eat fish, and various animals living at great depths.

◄ | 1) Geographical distribution of the walruses.

261

CALIFORNIA SEA LION

Zalophus californianus

Order Carnivora
Family Otariidae
Length Males, 8 –10 ft (2.5 – 3 m);
females, 6 – 6½ ft (1.8 – 2 m)
Weight Males, 606 – 890 lb (275 – 300
kg); females, 220 lb (100 kg)
Reproductive period May – July
Gestation 342 –365 days
Number of young 1
Sexual maturity Males, 5 years;
females, 3 years
Maximum age 15 – 20 years

The California sea lion population is presently 125, 000 in number and the breeding range extends from the southern tip of Baja California, Mexico, northward along the western coasts of North America to the Farallon Islands off San Francisco and throughout the Gulf of California. They are medium-sized "eared seals" exhibiting strong sexual dimorphism with adult males being up to three times the size of adult females. Males are dark brown with a mane of somewhat longer hair present on the neck. Females are straw colored with darker ventral surfaces and flippers; sea lion pups appear almost black at birth. A distinguishing feature is the incessant barking by males which is emphasized during the breeding season when territories are established.

The beginning of the breeding season in early June is marked by the arrival of males who establish aquatic, semi-aquatic or terrestrial territories at this time; females begin arriving on pupping grounds in early to mid June. Pups are born from June into July with the peak of activity in late June; pupping in the Galapagos population occurs from October – December. Females are bred by dominant males shortly after giving birth. While males also defend territories on dry sand on inland areas, males occupying aquatic or semiaquatic territories do the majority of the breeding.

The California sea lion is basically an opportunistic feeder; squid and octopus are preferred but herring, hake, rockfish, and ratfish are also important prey items. This is one of the best known sea lions. It occurs in almost every zoological and marine life park and is also used in circuses.

▲ The Californian sea lion (*Zalopus californianus*) belongs to the family of the Otariidae, which also includes the Australian sea lion, Steller's sea lion, the southern sea lion, and Hooker's sea lion. The flippers of sea lions are more leg-like than those of true seals and their hind flippers can be turned forward to enable them to walk and even to run (somewhat clumsily) on dry land. They have small external ear flaps and a mane of long hair on the back of the neck.

◄ Squid, octopus, herring, hake, anchovies, and reeffish are the favorite food of these animals.

▼ The difference between sea lions (left) and true seals (right) is that sea lions can twist their hindlimbs to a forward position.

OTHER SEA LIONS

Northern or Steller's sea lions (*Emetopia jubatus*) are the largest of the Otariidae; males reach lengths of between 10 – 11½ ft (3 – 3.5 m) and weigh 2,200 lb (1,000 kg), while females are no longer than 8 ft (2.5 m) and no heavier than 772 lb (350 kg). It is the most abundant sea lion in North America and breeds from San Miguel Island in the California Channel Islands northwest to the Gulf of Alaska Peninsula, throughout the Aleutian and Pribilof Islands, the Kurile Islands, Kamchatka, and on islands in the Okhotsk Sea. The Steller sea lion is a polygamous species.

The southern sea lion (*Otaria flavescens*) is found on both sides of the Atlantic and Pacific coasts of South America. It is smaller than the northern sea lion and resembles the California sea lion in appearance. Males reach lengths of 9 ft (2.7 m) and weigh 1,102 lb (500 kg), whereas females are 6½ ft (2 m) long and weigh 298 lb (135 kg). The southern sea lion is a gregarious species. They feed primarily on squid and the crustacean *Munida*; small fish are eaten as well as occasional penguins.

The Australian sea lion (*Neophoca cinerea*) occurs primarily on offshore south and western Australian islands from Kangaroo Island to Houtman Abrolhos. Adult males reach lengths of 10 – 11½ ft (3 – 3.5 m) and weigh 661 lb (300 kg). Females are between 8 and 11½ ft (2.5 and 3.5 m) long and weigh between 205 and 220 lb (93 and 100 kg). Major prey items include cephalopods, fish, and penguins.

Hooker's sea lion (*Phocarctos hookeri*) is confined to the subantarctic island of New Zealand. Whereas the Australian sea lions favor sandy beaches as hauling sites, Hooker's sea lions appear to prefer rocky habitats. Adult males reach lengths of between 8 and 10 ft (2.4 and 3 m) and weigh 882 lb (400 kg); females are between 5 and 6½ ft (1.5 and 2m) long and weigh 529 lb (240 kg). During the October to January breeding season, males establish and defend territories that have access to the surf and are bounded by natural rock formations. Major food items of Hooker's sea lions are small fish, crustaceans, and occasional sea birds and penguins. Maximum age is 12 to 15 years.

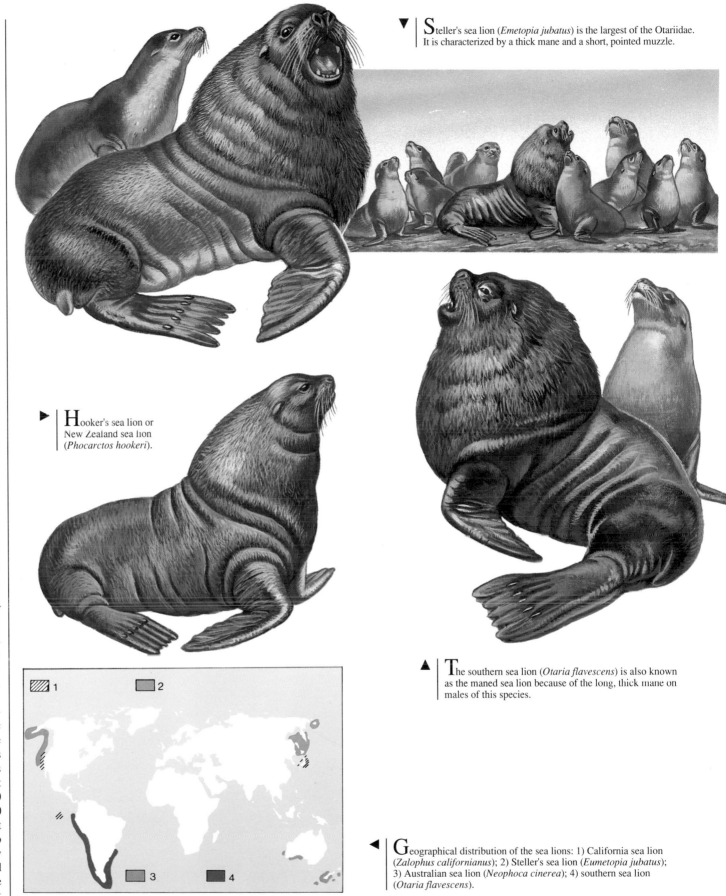

Steller's sea lion (*Emetopia jubatus*) is the largest of the Otariidae. It is characterized by a thick mane and a short, pointed muzzle.

Hooker's sea lion or New Zealand sea lion (*Phocarctos hookeri*).

The southern sea lion (*Otaria flavescens*) is also known as the maned sea lion because of the long, thick mane on males of this species.

Geographical distribution of the sea lions: 1) California sea lion (*Zalophus californianus*); 2) Steller's sea lion (*Eumetopia jubatus*); 3) Australian sea lion (*Neophoca cinerea*); 4) southern sea lion (*Otaria flavescens*).

NORTHERN FUR SEAL

Callorhinus ursinus

Order Carnivora
Family Otariidae
Length Males, 8 ft (2.5 m); females, 6 ft (1.9 m)
Weight Males, 660 lb (300 kg); females 143 – 154 lb (65 – 70 kg)
Dentition $\dfrac{2.1.5\text{–}6}{2.1.5} = 34 - 36$
Reproductive period May – July
Gestation 10 months with 2 – 4 months delay in implantation
Number of young 1
Sexual maturity Males, 5 – 6 years; females, 4 years
Maximum age 25 years

The northern fur seal or Alaskan fur seal, currently distributed in temperate subarctic North Pacific waters, is one of the most abundant, widely distributed and commercially important marine mammals. The main colony of northern fur seals is presently centered on St George and St Paul Islands in the Pribilof Islands and numbers approximately 1.5 million seals. Breeding colonies are also found on the Commander Islands and Robben Island in the Sea of Okhotsk, which account for approximately 200,000 – 500,000 seals. Some small groups have been reported on the once inhabited Kurile Islands and recolonization is believed to be underway.

The northern fur seal is a highly pelagic species and spends 300 – 330 days per year at sea. During the summer months seals congregate to pup and breed at traditional island sites. In the winter months the Pribilof population migrates south along the coasts of Canada and the United States as far south as San Diego, California. Seals from western Pacific breeding stocks also move south in winter along the Asiatic coasts as far as Japan. During their migration seals usually travel in small groups which can be made up of up to ten animals, or alone rather than in large herds.

The northern fur seal is a strongly dimorphic species, adult males generally being twice as long and weighing three to four times as much as adult females. Males also differ in color and are dark black to dark brown all over except for

The northern fur seal (*Callorhinus ursinus*) is classified among the pinnipeds and is closely related to the sea lions. Compared with the latter, however, the northern fur seal has a thicker and more luxuriant coat and a shorter and more pointed muzzle. This species exhibits pronounced sexual dimorphism. The males are darker in color than the females and are about twice as long and three to four times as heavy. The males return regularly to their island breeding grounds between the end of May and the end of June and fight hard among themselves to establish their individual territories, which are ready for the females when they arrive. A single male may collect a harem of 15 – 60 females.

Female northern fur seal.

the mane which is grayish in color. Females are slate gray above and lighter reddish gray below. The chest in both sexes bears a light patch. Seals generally darken somewhat following the annual molt. Pups are born jet black but the pelage molts to a silvery gray within a month or so of birth. The rear flippers in both sexes are greatly elongated and highly vascularized; they are waved in the air and serve to dissipate heat when the seal is under heat stress.

Most growth in females occurs during the first 4 – 5 years of life. Males begin to grow rapidly when sexual maturity is attained at 4 – 5 years of age and continue to grow until reaching sociological maturity at about 10 years; bulls generally do not achieve harem status until 10 – 12 years old. Pups leave the rookeries in September – November but migrate only relatively short distances and return to the rookeries for the following breeding season.

The males return regularly each year to their island breeding grounds between the end of May and the end of June. They fight hard among themselves to establish individual territories, which will be ready by the time the females arrive. Each male can collect a harem of 15–60 females. The young are born two to three days later and breeding occurs after one or two weeks.

While at sea during the pelagic season (August – May), seals sleep during the day by floating on the surface with the rear flippers bent forward; one of the foreflippers is raised in the air and the other is extended downward, acting as a keel or centerboard. Feeding occurs at night. In the Bering Sea, capelin is important in June; gonatid squids and walleye pollack are eaten in July; gonatid squids, capelin and walleye pollack in August; and walleye pollack and gonatid squids in September. Little is known of feeding or behavior during the pelagic phase as seals are generally solitary and very widely dispersed. The only known predators of northern fur seals are sharks, killer whales, and man.

Northern fur seals have been hunted commercially since their discovery on the Pribilof Islands in 1786 by Gerassim Pribilof, a Russian fur trader and explorer. They are migratory and have been shown to exhibit strong site fidelity; in fact early sealers used this "homing" tendency to locate rookeries by following seals on their homeward migrations to summer breeding grounds.

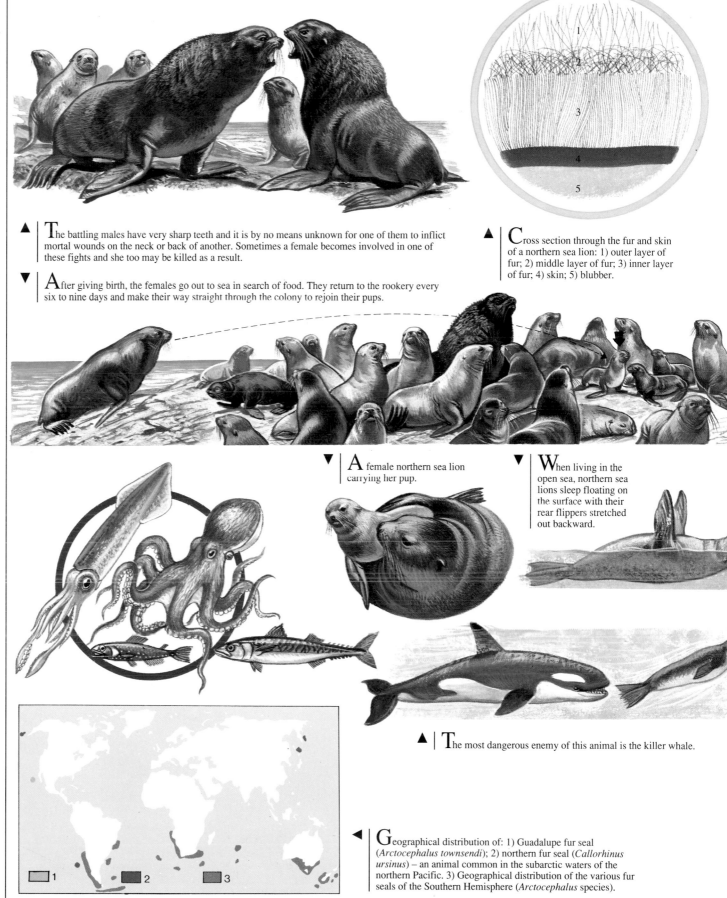

The battling males have very sharp teeth and it is by no means unknown for one of them to inflict mortal wounds on the neck or back of another. Sometimes a female becomes involved in one of these fights and she too may be killed as a result.

After giving birth, the females go out to sea in search of food. They return to the rookery every six to nine days and make their way straight through the colony to rejoin their pups.

Cross section through the fur and skin of a northern sea lion: 1) outer layer of fur; 2) middle layer of fur; 3) inner layer of fur; 4) skin; 5) blubber.

A female northern sea lion carrying her pup.

When living in the open sea, northern sea lions sleep floating on the surface with their rear flippers stretched out backward.

The most dangerous enemy of this animal is the killer whale.

Geographical distribution of: 1) Guadalupe fur seal (*Arctocephalus townsendi*); 2) northern fur seal (*Callorhinus ursinus*) – an animal common in the subarctic waters of the northern Pacific. 3) Geographical distribution of the various fur seals of the Southern Hemisphere (*Arctocephalus* species).

SEA COWS
Sirenia

The Sirenia or sea cows are more thoroughly adapted to life in the water than any other mammals except the whales. They are also the largest herbivorous animals that spend their entire life in the water. The complete absence of hindlimbs shows how thorough going this specialization has been, while the long history of the order in the geological record proves that it has been a success. The name "Sirenia" alludes to the extremely distant resemblance that can just be detected, with the aid of a powerful imagination, between these creatures and the sirens or mermaids of legend. The legend itself, however, probably arose from sightings of dugongs by the sailors of the ancient world in the Red Sea.

The sea cows are unlike any other group of mammals and are most closely related to the elephants and the hyraxes. They have absolutely no connection with the whales. The Sirenia include the only species of marine mammal which has become extinct in historic times, namely Steller's sea cow.

The species vary in length from 8 – 15 ft (2.5 – 4.5 m). The weight may exceptionally be as much as 1,300 lb (600 kg). The extinct Steller's sea cow was a much larger animal, up to 25 ft (7.5 m) in length and 5 tons in weight. The order is divided into two families – the Trichechidae or manatees and the Dugongidae or dugongs. Sea cows are to be found almost exclusively in the waters of tropical seas and certain great rivers, where they penetrate far inland. Steller's sea cow lived in the chilly waters of the Bering Sea.

The shape of the body is round and tapering, especially in the case of the dugongs. The head has a distinctive appearance, with a rounded muzzle and very thick lips. The animal has no distinct neck; the massive chest increases in diameter to a point just behind the forelimbs and then tapers progressively all the way down to the base of the tail fin, which is mounted horizontally like that of a whale. Dugongs and manatees have tails of different shapes. There is no back fin, probably because these animals are not very fast swimmers. The complete disappearance of the hind legs has left them with only two limbs, namely the fore flippers. These are

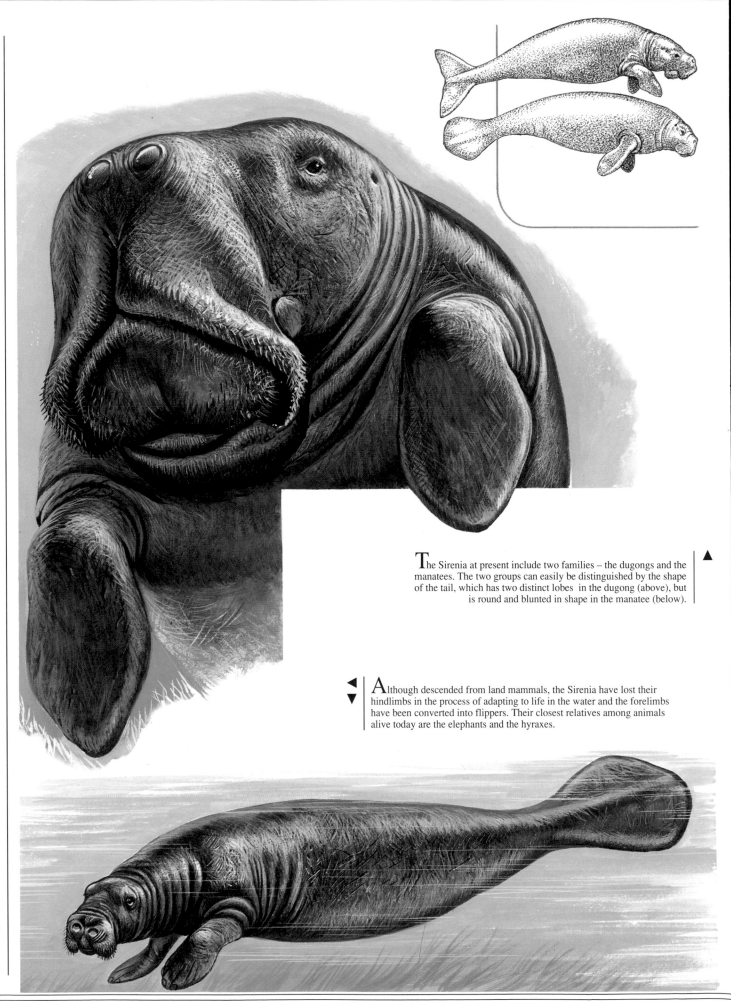

The Sirenia at present include two families – the dugongs and the manatees. The two groups can easily be distinguished by the shape of the tail, which has two distinct lobes in the dugong (above), but is round and blunted in shape in the manatee (below).

Although descended from land mammals, the Sirenia have lost their hindlimbs in the process of adapting to life in the water and the forelimbs have been converted into flippers. Their closest relatives among animals alive today are the elephants and the hyraxes.

rather small for the size of the animal, and are situated very far forward on the body. The flippers taper from front to back, with a thick, rounded leading edge and a much sharper and more flexible trailing edge. Manatees have rudimentary claws. Only the parts of the flipper corresponding to hand and forearm are externally visible; the upper arm is buried inside the body.

Sea cows are very thick-skinned, and are sometimes known as "marine pachyderms." The thickness of the hide varies from ½ – 1 in (10 – 25 mm) in different parts of the body. Most of the thickness is made up by the dermis, the epidermis being very thin. Steller's sea cow, which lived in colder water, seems to have been an exception in this respect, according to Steller himself. Its dermis was only one fifth as thick as its epidermis – an unusual formation, which is however also found in the narwhal. The growth of hair is slight in adults, though well developed in embryos. The color of the skin is brownish gray, with lighter tones on the head and sides; the belly is pale, sometimes with a pinkish tinge.

Various morphological features of the head and the sense organs illustrate the animal's extreme specialization to an aquatic life. The nostrils are situated on the upper surface of the muzzle. The eyes are mounted high up on the side of the head, like those of the hippopotamus, providing the animal with a natural periscope. The eye is small and spherical and is not flattened in front like the eye of a whale. The sclerotic is thick and the lens is crystalline, which are not features especially adapted for life in an aquatic environment.

Manatees have only six vertebrae in the neck. This is an extremely rare characteristic among the mammals. Dugongs have the normal number of seven. The brain is very small for the size of the animal, is not highly convoluted, and is generally rather primitive in structure. The heart is on the small side. The sea cow's lungs are equipped with outsize alveoli – special air sacs, more or less cylindrical in shape.

The mouth contains a number of thick, horny plates that are used for mastication and are well suited to the special vegetarian diet of these mammals. A long process of adaptive evolution has profoundly modified the dentition. The dentition of the Sirenia, in fact, has obvious analogies with that of the elephants. The teeth are roughly cylindrical in shape, have no enamel, and grow continuously throughout life.

▼ The sea cow's head shows various significant adaptations to an aquatic life. The ear channels are narrow and there are no external ear flaps; the nostrils can be closed at will and the large, mobile lips play an important role in the animal's feeding habits.

▼ The bones of the flipper. The flipper is a very versatile organ in the life of these aquatic animals, and is capable of carrying out a wide variety of movements and functions.

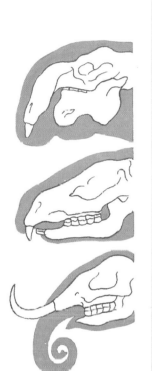

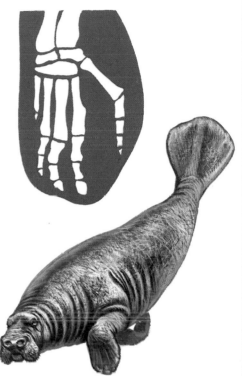

▲ The center drawing shows a hypothetical common ancestor of the elephants and sea cows.

▲ The largest member of the Sirenia was Steller's sea cow. It belonged to the Dugongidae family and was exterminated by man in the eighteenth century.

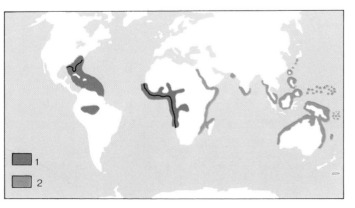

1

2

◀ Geographical distribution of the manatees (1) and the dugongs (2).

DUGONG
Dugong dugong

Order Sirenia
Family Dugongidae
Length 8 – 13 ft (2.4 – 4 m), more commonly 8 – 10 ft (2.4 – 3 m)
Weight 500 – 800 lb (230 – 400 kg)
Gestation Probably about 1 year
Number of young 1, exceptionally 2
Length at birth 43 – 55 in (1.1 – 1.4 m)
Weight at birth 44 – 55 lb (20 – 25 kg)
Sexual maturity When a length of 8 ft (2.4 m) is reached

The dugong has a round, tapered body. The skin is smooth looking, but has a thin covering of short hairs, 1 – 2 in (3 – 5 cm) apart. The hair on the muzzle is thicker and more bristly. The nostrils are situated well forward on top of the muzzle. Special muscles hold the nostrils shut when the animal is submerged. The forelimbs are shaped like paddles and have no claws. The animal uses them to steer itself while swimming, to support itself while it rests, and to grasp objects to its body. When swimming rapidly, it holds them tight against its chest. The tail fin is wide and shaped like that of the whales, with two acute-angled lobes and a strongly concave trailing edge. Adult males, and some old females, have two tusk-like upper incisors that project visibly from the mouth. Back teeth may be present to a total number of six pairs, comprising three upper and three lower molars on each side, but old specimens generally have fewer than this.

The dugong lives mainly in shallow coastal waters, only occasionally venturing a short distance upstream into the great rivers. It spends most of its time at depths of 3 – 40 ft (1 – 12 m) in the warm, often muddy, waters where it finds its food. It also makes daily journeys into deeper waters. The dugong is a sea mammal of extremely calm, cautious, and timid character, like the manatees. When it is allowed to live in peace, it shows a tendency to a gregarious way of life. It generally swims slightly below the surface, at a speed of 6 mph (10 kmh), although it can achieve double that speed over short distances when alarmed. The length of gestation is not known exactly, but is thought to be about one year. The females give birth in shallow water.

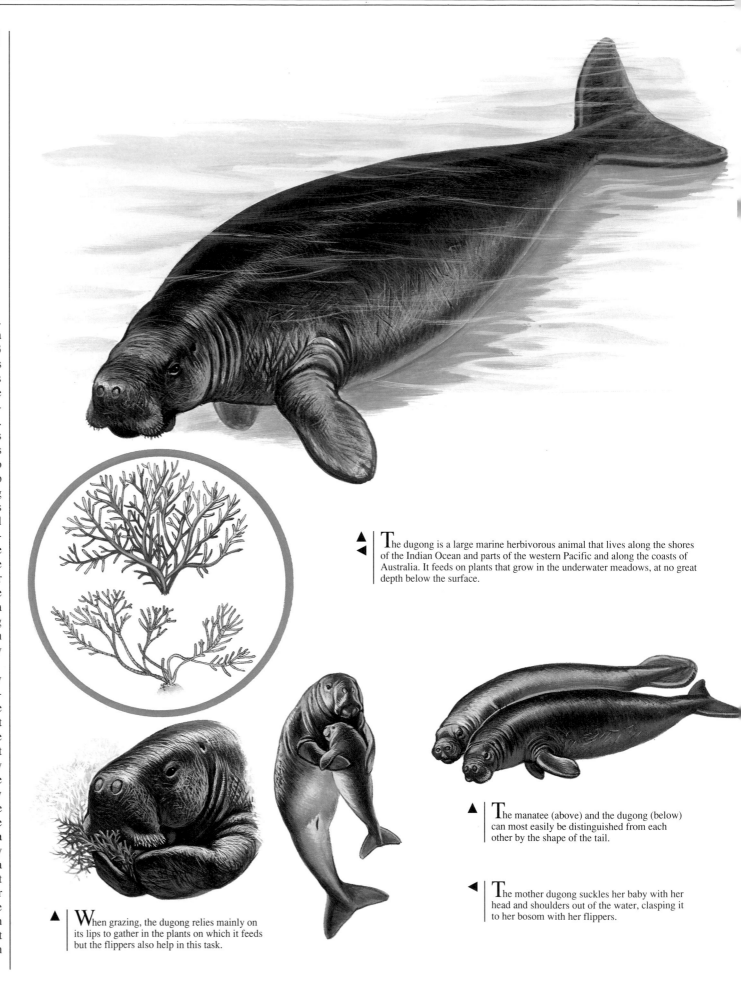

The dugong is a large marine herbivorous animal that lives along the shores of the Indian Ocean and parts of the western Pacific and along the coasts of Australia. It feeds on plants that grow in the underwater meadows, at no great depth below the surface.

The manatee (above) and the dugong (below) can most easily be distinguished from each other by the shape of the tail.

The mother dugong suckles her baby with her head and shoulders out of the water, clasping it to her bosom with her flippers.

When grazing, the dugong relies mainly on its lips to gather in the plants on which it feeds but the flippers also help in this task.

AMERICAN MANATEE

Trichechus manatus

Order Sirenia
Family Trichechidae
Length 10 – 13 ft (3.4 m)
Weight Up to 1,300 lb (600 kg)
Gestation About 13 months
Number of young 1, exceptionally 2
Length at birth Over 3 ft (1 m)
Weight at birth 33 – 44 lb (15 – 20 kg)
Sexual maturity 4 – 6 years, or when a
length of 8 ft (2.6 m) is reached

The American manatee is an aquatic mammal closely related to the dugong. The pectoral flippers are well developed and equipped with claws. The animal lives both in coastal waters and in estuaries, canals, rivers, and similar waterways throughout the tropical and subtropical regions of the western Atlantic. It is present in Florida, the Caribbean Sea, the Gulf of Mexico, and the northern coasts of South America down to the mouth of the Amazon.

The American manatee does not seem to be particularly gregarious, although large groups are sometimes found in winter in places where the water temperature is unusually high. It normally lives in couples or small groups, the most common and stable natural association in the wild state being that of mother and young. The baby is suckled under water and is not weaned before it reaches the age of one year, though it also begins to take solid food when only a few weeks old. The mother manatee often plays with her baby and shows great affection for it. Sometimes she carries it on her back.

Closely related species are the Amazon manatee (*Trichechus inunguis*) and the African manatee (*Trichechus senegalensis*). The Amazon manatee is somewhat smaller than the American manatee, with a maximum length of about 9 ft (2.8 m). Its distinctive characteristics are the absence of claws on its flippers, the smoothness of its skin, and the presence of large white patches on the underside of the body. It is a freshwater species, found only in the river basins of the Amazon and the Orinoco. The African manatee lives in the rivers and coastal waters of West Africa, from the River Senegal in the north to the River Cuanza in Angola to the south.

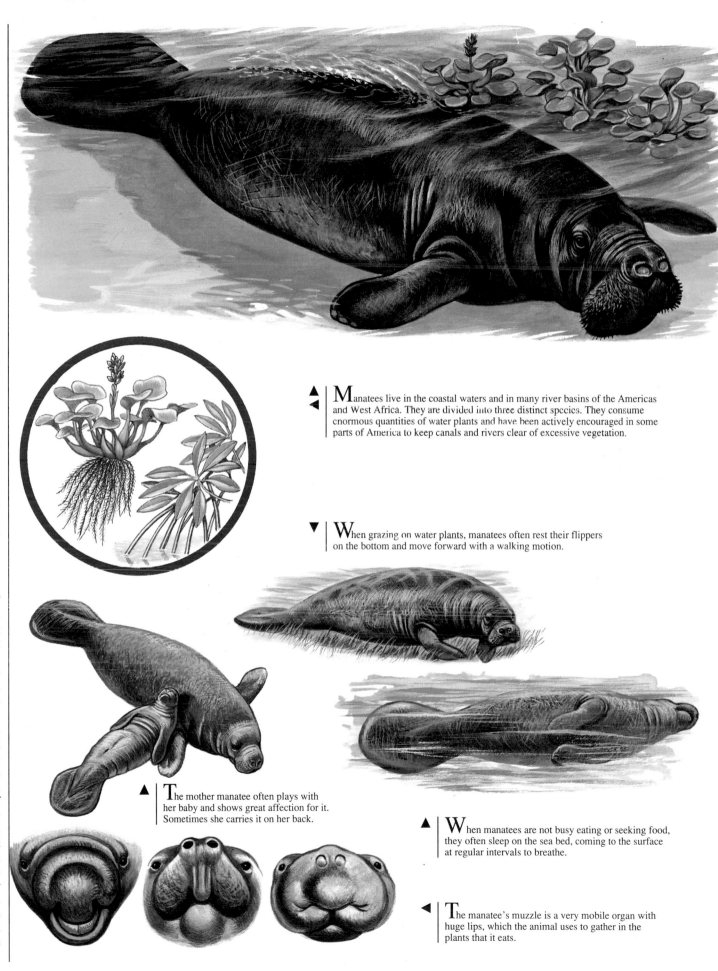

▲
◄ Manatees live in the coastal waters and in many river basins of the Americas and West Africa. They are divided into three distinct species. They consume enormous quantities of water plants and have been actively encouraged in some parts of America to keep canals and rivers clear of excessive vegetation.

▼ When grazing on water plants, manatees often rest their flippers on the bottom and move forward with a walking motion.

▲ The mother manatee often plays with her baby and shows great affection for it. Sometimes she carries it on her back.

▲ When manatees are not busy eating or seeking food, they often sleep on the sea bed, coming to the surface at regular intervals to breathe.

◄ The manatee's muzzle is a very mobile organ with huge lips, which the animal uses to gather in the plants that it eats.

INDEX